Wiley/Jossey-Ba[ss]

Hands-On Teaching Using Math Manipulatives Kit from ETA/Cuisenaire®!

SAVE OVER 30% off regular retail price on our most popular pre-service kit!

Item No. JL-1003

Hands-On Teaching Strategies for Using Math Manipulatives Kit

Includes 19 Manipulatives, a 120-page Teacher's Resource Binder by Dr. Carol Thornton and Gail Lowe-Parrino, and a convenient shoulder bag.

Plastic Manipulatives: Angle Ruler, GeoReflector™ Mirror, Fraction Tower® Cubes, PopCubes®

ManipuLite® Manipulatives: Base Ten Blocks, Color Tiles, Factor Blocks™, Two-Color Counters, Number Cubes, Pattern Blocks, Tangrams

Overhead Sets: Base Ten Blocks, Coins, Color Tiles, Fraction Circles, Geoboard with Rubber Bands, Pattern Blocks, Spinners, Tangrams

ETA® Cuisenaire

EXPANDING THE UNIVERSE OF LEARNING™

www.etacuisenaire.com

5TH
EDITION

TEACHING AND LEARNING MATHEMATICS

Pre-Kindergarten Through Middle School

LINDA JENSEN SHEFFIELD
Northern Kentucky University

DOUGLAS E. CRUIKSHANK
Linfield College

WILEY   JOHN WILEY & SONS, INC.

Acquistions Editor	Brad Hanson
Editorial Assistant	Alec Borenstein
Marketing Manager	Kate Stewart
Production Editor	Sandra Dumas
Text and Cover Designer	Madelyn Lesure
Production Management Services	Suzanne Ingrao
Photo Editor	Lisa Gee
Cover Image	©Danny Lehman/CORBIS

This book was typeset in 10/12 Meridien by Progressive Information Technologies and printed and bound by Courier(Westford). The cover was printed by Phoenix Color Company.

The paper in this book was manufactured by a mill whose forest management programs include sustained yield harvesting of its timberlands. Sustained yield harvesting principles ensure that the number of trees cut each year does not exceed the amount of new growth.

This book is printed on acid-free paper.

Photo Credits

Chapter 1 Page 1: Digital Vision/Getty Images.
Chapter 2 Page 17: PhotoDisc, Inc./Getty Images.
Chapter 3 Page 35: PhotoDisc, Inc./Getty Images.
Chapter 4 Page 77: Courtesy Doug Cruikshank.
Chapter 5 Page 103: Courtesy Bill Sheffield.
Chapter 6 Page 143: Courtesy of Doug Cruikshank.
Chapter 7 Page 187: PhotoDisc, Inc./Getty Images.
Chapter 8 Page 229: PhotoDisc, Inc./Getty Images.
Chapter 9 Page 261: Courtesy Bill Sheffield.
Chapter 10 Page 303: Courtesy Bill Sheffield. Page 316: PEANUTS reprinted by permission of United Feature Syndicate, Inc.
Chapter 11 Page 331: Courtesy Doug Cruikshank.
Chapter 12 Page 385: Courtesy Doug Cruikshank.
Chapter 13 Page 427: Digital Vision/Getty Images.

Sheffield, Linda, Jensen, Cruikshank, Douglas, E.
Teaching and Learning Mathematics: Pre-Kindergarten Through Middle School, Fifth Edition

ISBN 0–471–15160–2

Printed in the United States of America.

10 9 8 7 6 5 4 3 2 1

C O N T E N T S

C H A P T E R   4

REASONING, SOLVING, POSING, AND EXTENDING PROBLEMS   77

C H A P T E R   5

ATTACHING MEANING TO NUMBERS   103

CHAPTER 6

TEACHING AND LEARNING ADDITION AND SUBTRACTION OF WHOLE NUMBERS AND INTEGERS 143

CHAPTER 7

TEACHING AND LEARNING MULTIPLICATION AND DIVISION OF WHOLE NUMBERS AND INTEGERS 187

C H A P T E R   8

ATTACHING MEANING TO RATIONAL NUMBERS   229

C H A P T E R   9

TEACHING AND LEARNING OPERATIONS WITH RATIONAL NUMBERS   261

C H A P T E R   1 3

TEACHING AND LEARNING DATA ANALYSIS AND PROBABILITY   427

APPENDIX A
SUPPLIERS OF MANIPULATIVE MATERIALS, BOOKS, CALCULATORS, AND COMPUTER SOFTWARE   473

APPENDIX B
BLACKLINE MASTERS   475

INDEX

PREFACE

This fifth edition of *Teaching and Learning Mathematics: Pre-Kindergarten through Middle School* is designed to support you as you build mathematical understanding, strengthen students' abilities to think, help students make sense of mathematics, and assist students in attaining computational fluency. Our focus is on the future; children who acquire strong mathematical foundations from pre-kindergarten through middle school will be equipped for the world they will face in the years ahead. No one can predict all the changes that will take place as the years pass, but we do know that it will be insufficient to teach students merely to perform calculations or to solve the problems of today. The mathematical foundations are laid when children actively construct or invent mathematics, develop sound concepts and skillful applications of mathematics, exchange ideas and write about their work, question one another, and solve a variety of problems. Students must be able to think mathematically, logically, visually, and creatively. Calculators and computers are welcome tools in the learning process.

Purpose

The purpose of this text is to help you understand and carry out the teacher's role in pre-kindergarten, elementary, and middle school mathematics instruction. To this end, we have:

- used research from a variety of sources.

- reviewed and included recommendations from documents intended to guide reform in school mathematics such as those published by the National Council of Teachers of Mathematics (NCTM), including *Principles and Standards for School Mathematics* (2000).

- employed experiences gained from children and teachers. All of these have been carefully applied using, numerous activities and models to illustrate how to teach mathematics concepts and principles effectively in your classroom.

New to This Edition

We have expanded and strengthened the fifth edition of this text by

1. Revisiting the functioning of the mind as it engages in learning in general and mathematics learning in particular, and developing a theme to be used throughout the text that focuses on making sense of mathematics.

2. Integrating fully the language and intent of *Principles and Standards for School Mathematics* (NCTM, 2000).

3. Expanding the presentation of mathematical understanding and the constructivist view of learning.

4. Aligning the activities with current research on student learning and mathematics instruction and developmental practices, as well as deepening and enriching their content.

5. Including greater focus on teaching mathematics to diverse learners.

6. Developing an expanded collection of Weblinks to provide you with rich Internet resources to assist in teaching mathematics.

7. Inserting quotations from a variety of sources that explain and support sound mathematics teaching.

8. Reorganizing the chapters to more closely follow PSSM *Principles and Standards for School Mathematics.*

Text Features

The features that made the early editions of this text distinctive have been maintained:

1. The focus on the future.

2. The use of current research on how children learn specific mathematical topics.

3. The consideration of children's different learning styles and special learners, including the mathematically promising.

4. The use of introductory questions at the beginning of each chapter to guide the reader and discussion questions at the end of each chapter for further reflection.

5. The integration of computers and calculators as tools in the teaching of each content strand.

6. The focus on problem posing and problem solving, teaching children to use their own higher-level thinking processes, including mental calculation and estimation.

7. The presentation of numerous activities in each chapter using physical models for concept development and for fluency with skills.

8. The display of pages from elementary and middle school mathematics programs and the discussion of their instructional uses.

9. The inclusion of data analysis and probability, which have been emphasized recently due to the proliferation of readily available data.

10. The presentation of reference lists in each chapter that direct the reader to recent research and instructional material in each content area in print and electronic form.

11. The introduction of children's literature to enrich mathematical learning.

12. The inclusion of a series of icons to denote references to children's literature, calculators, computers, writing, Weblinks, and videos.

13. The suggestions and problems that serve as the basis for journal entries that open each chapter, with a new section focusing on reflection and refinement of ideas, encouraging teachers to think deeply about mathematics.

14. Two appendices, including an expanded selection of blackline masters for frequently used instructional materials and addresses and websites of publishers of software and commercially prepared manipulative materials.

We hope you will use many of the activities we have presented. Teachers who discover the joy of actively participating in the learning of mathematics are more enthusiastic and confident when teaching, and their interactions with children are richer and more exciting. You are encouraged to add to the collection of activities in this text, modify others for your particular students, and share activities and experiences with other teachers.

We anticipate you will be the finest teachers ever to assist children in learning. We need more skillful, knowledgeable, and compassionate teachers. If this textbook can, in any way, help prepare, direct, and encourage you in nurturing the growth of young people as they learn mathematics, then our purpose in writing this book will be fulfilled.

Acknowledgments

We would like to thank the many students we worked with as we were preparing this manuscript for their invaluable feedback on activities and the mathematics they were learning. A special thanks to students in McMinnville and Philomouth, Oregon, and Covington, Dayton, and Ft. Thomas, Kentucky, for their help and inspiration. Thanks to the pre-service and in-service teachers we have worked with over the last 30 years of college teaching, especially those at Linfield College and Northern Kentucky University. We could not have produced this book without all your feedback and suggestions.

We would like to express our sincere appreciation to the reviewers of this fifth edition. Their suggestions as well as those who reviewed the first, second, third, and fourth editions made this a much stronger textbook. Reviewers of the fifth edition were Gae Johnson, Northern Arizona University; Carol Findell, Boston University; David Slavit, Washington State University Vancouver; William Lacefield, Mercer University; Lyle Craig, University of Tennessee; Karen Higgins, Oregon State University; Michelle Smith, Cameron University; and Brad Glass, University of Delaware.

Reviewers of the first edition include Lucy Dechene, Fitchburg State College; Jon Engelhardt, Arizona State University; Boyd Holtan, West Virginia University; Charles Lamb, University of Texas at Austin; Walter Secada, University of Wisconsin–Madison; Richard Shumway, Ohio State University; and Alan Zollman, University of Kentucky. Reviewers of the second edition were Jerry Becker, Southern Illinois University at Carbondale; Joan C. Carson, University of Mississippi; Anne G. Dorsey, University of Cincinnati; Louis Fillinger, Fort Hays State University; Hiram D. Johnston, Georgia State University; William L. Merrill, Central Michigan University; and Helene J. Sherman, University of Missouri–St. Louis. Reviewers of the third edition were Lucy Dechene, Fitchburg State College; Anne G. Dorsey, University of Cincinnati; Jon Engelhardt, Arizona State University; Hiram D. Johnston, Georgia State University; Barbara Lehman, Mississippi State University; and Dorothy Spithmann, Dakota State College. Fourth edition reviewers were Betty K. Hathaway, University of Arkansas at Little Rock; Victoria Boller LaBerge, Northern Illinois University; Barbara J. Lehman, East Central University; and Kay Reinke, Oklahoma State University. Finally, our families and friends deserve much credit for their understanding and support. We are deeply grateful to Bill, Dan, Linda, Lori, and Julie.

PREPARING TO TEACH MATHEMATICS

GUIDING QUESTIONS

As you read the following pages, consider these guiding questions:

1. What is mathematics and what does it mean to know mathematics?
2. What forces shape mathematics curriculum, instruction, and assessment at the national, state, and local levels?
3. What are the common sections that can be found in each chapter in this text?
4. What can you look forward to as you start preparing to be a teacher of mathematics?

A Vision for School Mathematics

Imagine a classroom, a school, or a school district where all students have access to high-quality, engaging mathematics instruction. There are ambitious expectations for all, with accommodation for those who need it. Knowledgeable teachers have adequate resources to support their work and are continually growing as professionals. The curriculum is mathematically rich, offering students opportunities to learn important mathematical concepts and procedures with understanding. Technology is an essential component of the environment. Students confidently engage in complex mathematical tasks chosen carefully by teachers. They draw on knowledge from a wide variety of mathematical topics, sometimes approaching the same problem from different mathematical perspectives or representing the mathematics in different ways until they find methods that enable them to make progress. Teachers help students make, refine, and explore conjectures on the basis of evidence and use a variety of reasoning and proof techniques to confirm or disprove those conjectures. Students are flexible and resourceful problem solvers. Alone or in groups and with access to technology, they work productively and reflectively, with the skilled guidance of their teachers. Orally and in writing, students communicate their ideas and results effectively. They value mathematics and engage actively in learning it.

NCTM (2000), p. 3. Reprinted by permission.

Before you begin this book, we want you to think about the topic you are about to study. Take a few minutes to write down your answer to the question below. We hope you will feel free to write in the space provided or make or purchase a small notebook to use for this writing activity that will continue throughout this text. After you have read the first chapter, add other comments to your answer. Continue to add comments as the term progresses. At the end of the term, look back at your comments and see if your thoughts about mathematics have changed.

What is mathematics?

REFLECTIONS AND REFINEMENT: After you have answered the question, compare your work to that of some of your classmates. Did you respond in the same way? Did you gain any new insights? As you continue through this term, see if you can find additional information about the question. Write your thoughts here.

You are about to start on a very important journey. This journey will be an investigation of how you can be successful in your role as a pre-kindergarten, elementary, or middle school teacher of mathematics. We hope that by the end of the journey you will have gained confidence as a person and as a teacher and that you will be ready to share the joy and excitement that emerges from sound mathematics instruction. This is not a journey during which you will be asked to sit back and relax; rather, you will be challenged to develop new confidence in your own mathematical ability, to attack intriguing mathematical problems, to look inward at yourself as an individual and as a teacher, and to set personal goals for your teaching. This textbook is intended to provide assistance and offer direction on your journey. We realize, however, that the most effective test of your mathematics teaching ability will be your own teaching experiences. You will be supported by your teachers, supervisors, fellow students, and, of course, by your students, who will appreciate your methods of teaching.

How do individuals prepare to teach mathematics? At first glance, the natural question, "How will I teach mathematics?" appears to be one that will never be satisfactorily answered. The beginning of the journey to answer this question is found here in Chapter 1. Two important topics are examined to give you a foundation for your investigation of how to teach mathematics:

1. Philosophical considerations
2. Influences on the school mathematics curriculum

PHILOSOPHICAL CONSIDERATIONS

You have taken mathematics courses to prepare yourself for teaching. It is common to have taken such courses, perhaps for several years, and never have been introduced to the nature of mathematics and what it means to know mathematics. Yet knowing something about the nature of mathematics and what it means to know mathematics is considered fundamental by the Mathematical Sciences Education Board of the National Research Council (1990, p. 9). This Board has pointed out that "to realize a new vision of school mathematics will require public acceptance of a realistic philosophy of mathematics that reflects both mathematical practice and pedagogical experience."

The notion of a new vision of school mathematics comes from several sources that will be discussed in this and the next chapter. It refers to a new way to think about how children learn mathematics and how the subject may be effectively taught. You will be a part of an exciting period of new emphasis in school

mathematics. Let us turn to two questions that will serve as a philosophical basis for school mathematics in the future.

What Is Mathematics?

Mathematics is particularly well defined by the National Research Council in its publication *Everybody Counts:*

> As a practical matter, mathematics is a science of pattern and order. Its domain is not molecules or cells, but numbers, chance, form, algorithms, and change. As a science of abstract objects, mathematics relies on logic rather than on observation as its standard of truth, yet employs observation, simulation, and even experimentation as means of discovering truth. (1989, p. 31)

The idea of patterns is key to the nature of mathematics. Gardner noted "Mathematicians crave patterns in the realms of number and form; they seek to demonstrate, preserve, and explain the reasons for these patterns to all who find them of interest. Mathematicians are as compelled by the beauty of these patterns as by their truth value" (1999, p. 148). Children observe patterns long before entering school; they bring with them the ability to discover and recognize patterns. Children are introduced to patterns in counting, addition tables, geometry, fractions, and decimals. Students understand mathematics because they are able to discern patterns in physical models, pictures, and symbols (see Figure 1–1). Number and geometric patterns exhibit a regularity that is consistent and makes sense to young learners. Thinking of mathematics as the science of patterns and order helps you as a teacher when you begin to teach children mathematics. By raising awareness of patterns, you will assist children in looking for and developing patterns in their study of mathematics.

What Does It Mean to Know Mathematics?

What it means to know mathematics emerges from the nature of mathematics. Thus, to know mathematics means to know patterns and relationships among patterns. The National Research Council expands on this notion. The learner needs

> . . . to be able to discern patterns in complex and obscure contexts; to understand and transform relations among patterns; to classify, encode, and describe patterns; to read and write in the language of patterns; and to employ knowledge of patterns for various practical purposes. (1990, p. 12)

By observing patterns in our environment, we are able to construct new concepts from partial information. For example, students who have discovered that

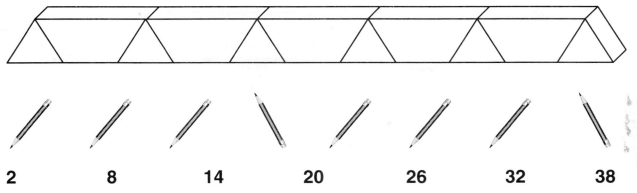

Figure 1–1 Patterns made with pattern blocks, pencil arrangement, and numbers.

small appliances on their take-apart table may be disassembled with a few simple tools "know" when a different appliance is provided that there is a way to take it apart and will begin to look for whatever holds it together. This ability to go "beyond the information given," as described by Bruner (1973), provides a powerful tool for learning and for teaching. Learning mathematics—which is a science of pattern and order— is enhanced by the ability to go beyond the information given. As students learn the structure of mathematics, they form a foundation that they can progress beyond. This is a process we would like to develop throughout this book.

Students must have the opportunity to study, discover, and invent patterns of many different types while in the process of learning and eventually knowing mathematics. The process of knowing mathematics involves active mental activity that is an outgrowth of many types of experiences. Knowing mathematics also means understanding mathematics. To understand mathematics is to grasp mathematics in such a way that it makes sense or has meaning. Understanding evolves to various levels, depending on the depth of learning and experience. As teachers, we have a responsibility to help students in their quest to know patterns and relationships among patterns and to understand mathematics.

Implications of These Philosophical Considerations

By developing a philosophical basis for mathematics education, we hope to illustrate how the new vision of school mathematics will influence the teaching of mathematics to students, pre-kindergarten through middle school. Classifying mathematics as a science suggests that mathematics is actively explored through experimentation, discovery, manipulation, and discussion, and that calculators and computers can be used as tools of mathematics. This view contrasts with the view that mathematics is only a paper-and-pencil exercise that relies on rules, formulas, and memory.

Thinking of mathematics as a search for patterns suggests that the content of a mathematics program should include patterns of many types, including those discovered in the study of numbers, geometry, measurement, and algebra, topics usually considered in contemporary mathematics programs. Problem situations, problem solving, and problem posing are provided as ways to search for patterns. This view contrasts with the view that mathematics programs should focus only on arithmetic—rules and algorithms.

Your philosophical beliefs about mathematics will serve you as you engage in teaching. You will be able to envision a broader mathematics curriculum, one that includes more than just arithmetic. You will feel comfortable about encouraging students to introduce problems from their own experiences. You will enjoy individual and group discussions that tap the thinking power of youngsters. You will see merit in the use of modern technology in teaching. You will be convincing as you discuss your beliefs with parents and colleagues. In short, you will have a strong rationale for the new vision of school mathematics.

INFLUENCES ON THE SCHOOL MATHEMATICS CURRICULUM

Many forces influence the mathematics content taught in pre-kindergarten through middle school. Some have greater influence than others, and the influence shifts as times change. Nevertheless, all of the forces interact with one another. Among the most influential forces are professional organizations; mathematics textbooks, programs, and rich learning tasks; technology; and assessment and accountability, including local and state curriculum guidelines, national and international assessments, and government bodies.

Professional Organizations

The mathematics education community in North America has strong, active membership in several professional organizations. Among those organizations are the Mathematical Association of America (MAA), National Council of Teachers of Mathematics (NCTM), School Science and Mathematics Association (SSMA), Research Council on Mathematics Learning (RCML), and Psychology of Mathematics Education (PME). In addition, individual state mathematics organizations play an important role by supporting sound programs of mathematics in their states.

The National Council of Teachers of Mathematics is perhaps best known to pre-kindergarten through middle school teachers. Its members assume leadership roles at the national, state, and local levels of mathematics education, providing a structure through which sound mathematics programs may be created. The NCTM develops position papers based on the work of its many national committees. The NCTM disseminates information to teachers and administrators through its publications. Pamphlets, yearbooks, small books, and journals provide readers with up-to-date information about teaching mathematics.

The NCTM website (Weblink 1–1) provides up-to-date information about the organization and its activities. Teachers find many teaching ideas for classroom use in *Teaching Children Mathematics,* and *Mathematics Teaching in the Middle School,* published nine times a year.

The NCTM and its affiliated state organizations hold outstanding conferences throughout the school year. Each year, there is one national meeting, and there are numerous regional conferences. These conferences are highlighted by hundreds of sessions and workshops that show teachers effective ways to present mathematics.

The leadership provided by the NCTM helps influence the direction of the school mathematics curriculum. In 2000 NCTM published its *Principles and Standards for School Mathematics* to serve as a ". . . resource and guide for all who make decisions that affect the mathematics education of students in prekindergarten through grade 12" (2000, p. ix). A discussion of *Principles and Standards* follows.

Principles and Standards for School Mathematics

This document consists of a set of principles and a set of standards for pre-kindergarten through grade 12 mathematics instruction. The principles provide direction for those who develop school mathematics programs. The standards consist of ten curriculum standards for all students. The standards suggest what students should know and what students should be able to do as a result of their mathematics education. *Principles and Standards* is a remarkable document in that it represents the thinking of a broad cross section of the mathematics community in the United States and Canada.

Accordingly, *Principles and Standards for School Mathematics* is intended to:

- set forth a comprehensive and coherent set of goals for mathematics for all students for prekindergarten through grade 12 that will orient curricular, teaching, and assessment efforts during the next decades;
- serve as a resource for teachers, education leaders, and policymakers to use in examining and improving the quality of mathematics instructional programs;
- guide the development of curriculum frameworks, assessments, and instructional materials;
- stimulate ideas and ongoing conversations at the national, provincial or state, and local levels about how best to help students gain a deep understanding of important mathematics. (NCTM, 2000, p. 6)

The NCTM is speaking to you as a pre-kindergarten through middle school teacher. Your enthusiasm for mathematics and your ability to teach mathematics effectively will depend, in part, on your thoughtful consideration of *Principles and Standards for School Mathematics.* Hopefully, you will accept the challenge put forth in this document.

PRINCIPLES FOR SCHOOL MATHEMATICS. The NCTM presents six principles for school mathematics. The principles are set forth to guide teachers and others in decisions about the content and character of school mathematics. They are briefly presented below and expanded on at appropriate places later in this text.

1. The Equity Principle: Excellence in mathematics education requires equity—high expectations and strong support for all students.
2. The Curriculum Principle: A curriculum is more than a collection of activities: it must be coherent, focused on important mathematics, and well articulated across the grades.
3. The Teaching Principle: Effective mathematics teaching requires understanding what students know and need to learn and then challenging and supporting them to learn it well.
4. The Learning Principle: Students must learn mathematics with understanding, actively building new knowledge from experience and prior knowledge.
5. The Assessment Principle: Assessment should support the learning of important mathematics and furnish useful information to both teachers and students.
6. The Technology Principle: Technology is essential in teaching and learning mathematics; it influences the mathematics that is taught and enhances students' learning. (NCTM, 2000, p. 11)

STANDARDS FOR SCHOOL MATHEMATICS. The standards are presented as content standards and process standards. They are intended to guide what is taught as students move through school from pre-kindergarten through grade 12. The standards are separated into four levels: pre-K–2, grades 3–5, grades 6–8, and grades 9–12. They are listed below. The first five are content standards and the next five are process standards.

1. Number and Operations
2. Algebra
3. Geometry
4. Measurement
5. Data Analysis and Probability
6. Problem Solving
7. Reasoning and Proof
8. Communication
9. Connections
10. Representation

In *Principles and Standards for School Mathematics,* each standard is discussed and illustrated with examples of how the standard might be realized in the classroom. You will find the standards included throughout this textbook as well as listed in Appendix C. You are encouraged to become familiar with *Principles and Standards for School Mathematics,* to use your knowledge of these standards to understand the direction taken in this document, and to establish yourself as a forward-looking teacher of mathematics. Copies of *Principles and Standards for School Mathematics* are available from the NCTM. An electronic version of the document may be found at Weblink 1–2.

Mathematical Textbooks, Programs, and Rich Learning Tasks

The mathematics textbook has been very influential in determining school mathematics curriculum. It establishes an important curricular framework. It provides a continuity from September to June and consistency from one level to another. The mathematical topics included in math texts have evolved steadily for over a hundred years of textbook publication. The textbooks change when new trends emerge and are supported by teachers, mathematics leaders, parents, and administrators. Publishers respond to their customers. Recent textbooks reflect the recommendations of the NCTM *Principles and Standards for School Mathematics.*

Well-designed textbooks in the hands of skillful teachers are powerful educational tools. With texts, teachers can diagnose and evaluate children's mathematical performance. They can assign exercises to reinforce concepts and skills already learned as well as to teach and reteach important mathematical concepts and skills that are new to the student.

Skillful teachers know that they must go beyond the pages of the textbook. Activities and projects must often replace pictures and symbols. Teaching styles that differ from the textbook presentation will be needed. Mathematical applications will require children's more active participation. The daily textbook routine should give way to other methods to allow mathematics to come alive in the minds of children.

The National Research Council expressed the challenge faced by textbook publishers in light of research findings:

> New textbooks must be designed and written to reflect the important principles of mathematics curricula: genuine problems; calculators and computers; relevant applications; reading and writing about mathematics; and active strategies for learning. (1990, pp. 49–50)

You will need to be a discerning consumer of mathematics textbooks and programs. The American Association for the Advancement of Science (AAAS) evaluated middle grades mathematics textbooks as part of its AAAS Project 2061. Its findings are found on Weblink 1–3. The Eisenhower National Clearinghouse Exemplary and Promising Mathematics Programs Report provides information about promising elementary mathematics programs (Weblink 1–4). You must decide whether textbooks serve your instructional needs and how math textbooks and programs best serve the needs of students. This is the art of teaching.

Some mathematics programs are designed for teachers to use in place of textbooks. Many of these programs guide teachers through an activity-based and problem-based curriculum. Thus, they serve as an important influence on the mathematics curriculum. Among well-known elementary math programs, including several developed with the support of the National Science Foundation, are Investigations in Number, Data, and Space® (K–5) (Weblink 1–5), Everyday Mathematics (pre-K–grade 6) (Weblink 1–6), Math Trailblazers (grades K–5) (Weblink 1–7), Bridges in Mathematics (grades K–2), and Opening Eyes to Mathematics (grades 3–4) (Weblink 1–8). At the middle school level are Connected Math, Math in Context, MathScape, MathThematics (Weblink 1–9), and Math Alive! (Weblink 1–8).

Rich learning tasks are characterized by mathematics topics that are presented in depth over the course of one or more instructional days. The approach of using rich learning tasks contrasts with a textbook curriculum that is thought by some to contain too many topics that are taught with little depth. As part of the Trends in International Mathematics and

Science Study (TIMSS, formerly known as the Third International Mathematics and Science Study), the TIMSS 1999 Video Study provides rich descriptions of mathematics teaching as it is actually experienced by eighth-grade students in seven countries. In addition to the United States, participating countries included Australia, the Czech Republic, Hong Kong SAR, Japan, The Netherlands, and Switzerland. The classroom videos of eighth-grade Japanese classrooms provide several examples of teaching using rich learning tasks (Weblink 1–10).

Technology

Access to technology influences the mathematics curriculum. Calculators and computers are powerful tools in the learning process. According to the NCTM, calculators and computers ". . . furnish visual images of mathematical ideas, they facilitate organizing and analyzing data, and they compute efficiently and accurately. They can support investigation by students in every area of mathematics, including geometry, statistics, algebra, measurement, and number" (2000, p. 24). Technology is not intended to replace understanding, reflection, and rich learning experiences. Rather, it provides an avenue to them.

As teachers continue to discover ways that technology enhances mathematics learning, mathematics teaching, and what mathematics is taught, they are influencing the curriculum. The power of calculators, from the simple to the more sophisticated graphing calculators, is available to students of all ages. Computers provide access to data, simulations, problems, and other resources on the Internet, as well as providing powerful applications such as spreadsheets, geometry software, and presentation software. Careful use of technology can greatly enrich the mathematics curriculum.

Assessment and Accountability

Assessment procedures that influence mathematics curriculum in the United States range from those that are national and international in scope to those at the state, local, and district levels. A discussion of each is presented below.

Every school district assesses its students' mathematical learning at some time during the academic year. This assessment comes from the state and local goals established to guide the districts' mathematical instruction. One purpose of assessment is for states and local schools to be accountable to the public. The form of the assessment may vary among school districts. It may take the form of nationally standardized achievement tests or district or state examinations. It may take the form of performance-based assessment procedures. It may take the form of a combination of measures. Mathematical assessment may be embedded in broad curriculum assessment. Regardless of the form of assessment, the results provide local districts and communities with a measure of the students' accomplishments in mathematics. A summary of test results is commonly published in local newspapers. Considerable importance is accorded these results. Thus, many teachers set high expectations for achievement, whether by exam or other types of performance. In this way the mathematics curriculum is heavily influenced by assessment procedures.

If the current reform efforts in mathematics education are expected to be successful, changes in the way we currently assess students' mathematical growth will have to take place. A set of assessment reforms are spelled out in *Assessment Standards for School Mathematics* (NCTM, 1995). The *Assessment Standards* is intended to be used to evaluate mathematical assessment programs. Alternative means of assessment will be expected of you as a teacher. Those who carefully design assessment procedures do not intend that the procedures be used to determine the curriculum. Assessment procedures are developed to measure growth in students' understanding of mathematical concepts as well as thinking processes commonly found in prekindergarten through middle school mathematics programs throughout the country. Assessment follows from the goals of the curriculum and determines if the instruction effectively meets those goals. As mathematics programs reflect the changes that are recommended by the NCTM *Principles and Standards for School Mathematics* and other forward-looking documents, the methods for assessment broaden to meet the expanding definition of mathematics instruction.

LOCAL AND STATE CURRICULUM GUIDELINES. Once the NCTM Standards were disseminated, state departments of education and local school districts responded by developing or revising their mathematics curriculum guidelines. These guidelines spell out in detail what the curriculum of the state or district will be. Teachers are expected to follow the curriculum guidelines in their teaching. How teachers follow the guidelines is typically spelled out by the local school district in its adoption of mathematics programs or textbooks and by its in-service training programs. The teaching materials used by a school district frequently are directly and indirectly assessed as part of annual state assessment. Local and state mathematics curriculum guidelines define how classroom instruction is conducted.

NATIONAL AND INTERNATIONAL ASSESSMENTS. Among the most influential national assessments of mathematics ability is the National Assessment of Educational Progress (NAEP). The National Center for Educational Statistics publishes the results of the NAEP examinations every four years. The NAEP has assessed mathematical progress periodically since 1969, first by age level (ages 9, 13, and 17) and later in grades 4, 8, and 12. Valuable longitudinal data have been gathered, providing useful comparative information. The mathematical perform-ance of fourth- and eighth-grade students showed steady growth from 1990 to 2000. The mathematical performance of twelfth-grade students showed growth from 1990 to 1996 but declined slightly from 1996 to 2000. Approximately 47,000 students were tested in 2000.

The results of the 2003 mathematics assessment were released in the fall of 2003, too late for publi-cation in this textbook. These results may be found on the NAEP website (Weblink 1–11). In addition, the web-site provides cross-state comparisons, a description of what the assessment measures, sample questions from the assessment, and what students should know and be able to do.

The National Center for Educational Statistics described the nature of its international assessment:

The Trends in International Mathematics and Science Study (TIMSS, formerly known as the Third International Mathe-matics and Science Study) resulted from the American education community's need for reliable and timely data on the mathematics and science achievement of our students compared to that of students in other countries. TIMSS is the most comprehensive and rigorous assessment of its kind ever undertaken. Offered in 1995, 1999, and planned for 2003, TIMSS provides trend data on students' mathematics and science achievement from an international perspective. (<http://nces.ed.gov/timss>, 2003, p. 1)

The TIMSS data were collected during the 1995 school year. Involved were more than half a million students taking mathematics and science at three grade levels in 41 countries. In the United States, about 22,000 fourth and eighth grade students were involved, as well as another 11,000 high school seniors. The TIMSS contained a variety of components: student assessments, questionnaires, curriculum analyses, per-formance assessments, videotape observations of mathe-matics instruction, and ethnographic case studies of key policy topics. The achievement data showed that U.S. fourth graders scored slightly above the international average in mathematics when compared with students from the 26 countries in the TIMSS fourth-grade assess-ment. U.S. eighth graders scored slightly below the international average in mathematics when compared with their peers in the 41 countries in their comparison group. U.S. twelfth graders scored significantly below average in mathematics when compared with their counterparts in 21 countries. The national media found these results disappointing for a country that had been

challenged to be first in the world in mathematics by the year 2000. More important, however, was the opportunity to analyze the volumes of data that were generated by the study and to find areas on which to focus attention.

For example, Burrill noted that the TIMSS video study data of eighth-grade students revealed that ". . . the goals of U.S. teachers were directed toward showing students how to do something—61 percent of the reported goals were skills oriented. In contrast, 75 percent of goals of Japanese teachers in the study were focused on helping students understand a mathe-matical concept" (1998, p. 3). Burrill then challenged U.S. teachers to consider their own approaches to teaching mathematics. TIMSS is a good example of how carefully collected assessment data may be used as a basis for a national discussion on mathematics goals, curriculum, and teaching approaches. For exam-ples of questions that were asked and more detailed discussions of the findings, see Weblink 1–12.

GOVERNMENT BODIES. Influenced by numerous national reports on education and a public concerned with the quality of education, federal and state gov-ernments have developed laws, policies, and regula-tions that have an impact on pre-kindergarten through middle school mathematics curricula. There has been concern about the overall quality of educa-tion in this country. As a result, federal, state, and local study committees have made recommendations about how to improve the quality of education. As new goals are established, curricular areas such as mathematics are being reviewed. Thus, revisions are being made to mathematics curricula, in part to align them with the NCTM Standards.

Changes in mathematics curricula in various large states result in changes in textbooks and necessitate changes in assessment procedures. There has been a greater emphasis on testing throughout North America. The forces that influence the curriculum are interrelated. These forces will affect the mathematics curriculum with which you will be working. The response you and your students have to mathematics programs and accountability will likely influence cur-ricular change in the future.

LOOKING AHEAD

Nearly all of the remaining chapters of this book (Chap-ters 4–13) include the following sections:

a. Making Sense of Concepts
b. Developing Fluency
c. The Math Program

d. Estimating, Using Benchmarks, and Mental Calculating
e. Reasoning, Solving, and Posing Problems
f. Organizing for TLC: Teaching, Learning, and Curriculum
g. Communicating
h. Connecting and Representing
i. Assessing Mathematics Learning
j. Something for Everyone

Each chapter includes a set of guiding questions for you as a reader and a section entitled For You as a Teacher: Ideas for Discussion and Your Professional Portfolio in which you are challenged to read, write, and reflect on selected content from the chapter as part of your professional portfolio. Throughout the text you will find references to children's literature as it relates to mathematics instruction, suggestions for computer software, and appropriate Internet sites, called Weblinks. Following is a brief discussion of the remaining sections.

Making Sense of Concepts

A fundamental part of teaching mathematics is doing so in such a way that it makes sense to students. As mathematical concepts or ideas are formed in the minds of children, those concepts begin to make sense and the children's understanding of them evolves. At every level of mathematics learning and with every mathematical topic, making sense of concepts is crucial. In its publication *EDThoughts,* Mid-continent Research for Education and Learning (McREL) states, "Teachers who orchestrate the integration among conceptual, procedural, and factual knowledge provide the 'sense making' that is necessary if students are to develop confidence in their ability to reason and solve problems." (2002, p. 12)

Much of Chapter 2 focuses on making sense, understanding, and conceptual thinking. Each of the following chapters emphasizes making sense of the concepts contained in those chapters. As teachers, we should strive for sense making and understanding in our teaching.

Developing Fluency

The NCTM, in *Principles and Standards for School Mathematics,* clearly defines the importance of computational fluency in learning number and operations:

> Knowing basic number combinations—the single-digit addition and multiplication pairs and their counterparts for subtraction and division—is essential. Equally essential is computational fluency—having and using efficient and accurate methods for computing. Fluency might be manifested in using a combination of mental strategies and jottings on paper or using an algorithm with paper and pencil, particularly when the numbers are large, to produce accurate results quickly. Regardless of the particular method used, students should be able to explain their method, understand that many methods exist, and see the usefulness of methods that are efficient, accurate, and general. Students also need to be able to estimate and judge the reasonableness of results. Computational fluency should develop in tandem with understanding of the role and meaning of arithmetic operations in number systems. (NCTM, 2000 p. 32)

There is an integral connection between making sense of concepts and developing computational proficiency. Developing fluency is an outgrowth of that connection. Once mathematical concepts have been introduced, skills or procedures associated with those concepts may be taught. Procedures that have not been connected with conceptual knowledge are more easily forgotten and more difficult to reconstruct. Making sense of concepts and developing fluency go hand in hand throughout this text.

The Math Program

Chapters 3 through 13 contain, in each chapter, an illustration from a mathematics program or a textbook page that corresponds to the topic emphasized in that chapter. In presenting the program examples, we recognize the important role that print materials play in the instructional program; on the other hand, we have devoted the bulk of this textbook to the presentation of activities you can use to help children learn mathematics with or without a textbook. In the math program inserts, we illustrate a variety of programs to give you an idea of those that are currently available.

Note that we use the more general sense of "math programs" with the sample pages we include in each chapter. Many of these are from textbooks. We also take the opportunity to comment on the material illustrated, to show how the author recommends that it be used, and to offer additional suggestions when we feel that they are appropriate.

Estimating, Using Benchmarks, and Mental Calculating

Estimating is an important part of the thinking process in doing mathematics. Computational fluency requires estimation and judgment to determine the reasonableness of results. Estimating helps answers make sense. Among the variety of estimation strategies is using benchmarks, that is, using 10, 50, 100, . . . as key points (benchmarks) when estimating such things as 5 + 6 (more than 10), 28 + 15 (less than 50), 45 + 42 (less than 100), and so on. It also refers to using numbers like 1 and $\frac{1}{2}$ when working with fractions, for example, $\frac{1}{3} + \frac{1}{4}$ (more than $\frac{1}{2}$ but less than 1). Benchmarks allow us to gain a sense of the size of our estimates. Mental calculation, as well as estimation, is part of the reasoning process. It is an alternative to paper-and-pencil calculation and calculator use. Employing mental calculation strategies allows us to quickly determine an answer when other means are time consuming and unnecessary. It may also be used to check work performed by other means.

Chapter 4 discusses estimating, using benchmarks, and mental calculation. In the following chapters, suggestions are made about how to employ these skills in the content presented in those chapters.

Organizing for TLC: Teaching, Learning, and Curriculum

Effective teachers organize themselves to teach. They anticipate the needs of their students, determine how mathematical topics can best be presented, decide what questions will encourage thinking and reflection, reflect on how students should be organized for instruction, and choose how learning can be assessed. Lesson planning requires insight into children's thinking, their abilities, and the mathematical topics being presented. Chapter 3 presents information about organizing for instruction. In the following chapters suggestions are made regarding organizing for teaching, learning, and curriculum for the particular topics in those chapters.

Reasoning, Solving, and Posing Problems

Throughout the study of mathematics, problem solving serves an important role. Problem situations invite students to explore their world, collect data, reflect, and make decisions. Through problem solving, new mathematical knowledge can be built. A good grasp of problem-solving skills and an analytical approach serve students as they continue to study mathematics and when they confront problems in other curriculum areas. Children's curiosity allows them to become skilled at posing problems. Children develop problem-solving dispositions when encouraged to explore, to take risks, to reason, and to learn from success and failure. Throughout the following chapters, suggestions are made to support a problem-solving approach.

Communicating

Throughout the learning process, communication is crucial. The ways that teachers and students communicate affect the quality of learning. Emphasis is given to the oral and written communication that occurs during the learning of mathematics. As students engage in problem solving and construct and invent mathematics, their discussions and writing are rich with explanations of their thinking processes. As students read and listen to the writings of those who include mathematics in their works, their imaginations and understanding are enhanced. Writing in mathematics and using literature in mathematics help students see how communication enhances understanding of their thoughts and those of others. In classrooms where communication thrives, the thought and language of mathematics is enriched. A brief description of ways that children may communicate as they learn mathematics is included in each of the content chapters.

Connecting and Representing

Connecting is showing how mathematical ideas are related to each other and how mathematics is related to daily life both in and out of the classroom. Representing is the way that mathematical ideas are seen. Representations range from physical models to drawings to graphs to symbols. By connecting mathematical ideas, we help students make sense of mathematics. The structure of mathematics is part of its beauty, and the parts that form this structure are interrelated. Teaching mathematics for understanding relies on making sure that connections are made among it parts. Because connecting and representing are so important, the NCTM has made each a Standard. Nikki's story problem (Figure 1–2) illustrates both representing and connecting. First, she used figures, symbols, and words as representations of her thinking. Second, she connected the figures and symbols and she used an example from her experience. Much of this textbook presents how mathematical ideas are connected and represented. In the Connecting and Representing section of each content chapter, we provide examples of their application.

Assessing Mathematics Learning

There are a number of reasons for assessing students' growth in understanding mathematics. Among the most important is to improve teaching and learning. Thus, teachers are able to determine where students currently are in their mathematics learning so that appropriate instruction may be planned. Currently, the most commonly used tools for assessing mathematics learning are the curriculum-embedded tests provided with basal textbook series and standardized achievement tests. The textbook tests provide diagnosis at the beginning of a chapter or section, evaluate the children's progress during and at the end of each chapter, and check their ability to recall concepts and skills

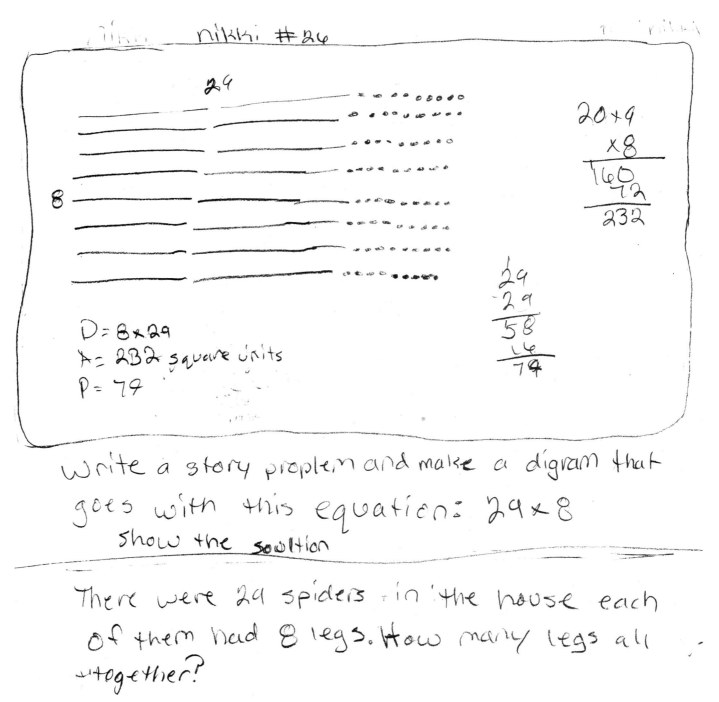

nikki #26

$20+9$
$\times 8$
$\overline{160}$
72
$\overline{232}$

24

8

$D = 8 \times 29$
$A = 232$ square units
$P = 74$

29
29
$\overline{58}$
16
$\overline{74}$

Write a story problem and make a digram that goes with this equation: 29×8 show the soultion

There were 29 spiders in the house each of them had 8 legs. How many legs all together?

Figure 1–2 Nikki's story problem using figures, symbols, and words.

from earlier chapters. Standardized tests that include sections designed to test mathematics achievement are commonly administered once per year to a group of children.

There are, however, alternative assessment techniques that overcome the shortcomings of textbook tests and standardized tests. Considerable attention has recently been focused on dynamic ways to assess growth in mathematics. These alternatives are an important part of the current mathematics reform movement. Among them are observation and questioning, performance-based assessment, diagnostic interviews, teacher-made assessment tasks, writing activities, and group problem solving. Along with the assessment techniques are procedures for collecting students' work, such as individual student portfolios. These techniques have an important role in broad-based assessment programs. A detailed description of assessment procedures is included in Chapter 3. In each chapter, assessment procedures are discussed with regard to the content emphasis of the chapter.

Something for Everyone

All schools should provide children with the most effective instruction possible. There is considerable diversity among students at all instructional levels. Some of the diversity is cultural, some is socioeconomic, some is racial and ethnic, and some is due to previous knowledge and opportunities. Providing learning opportunities for all is essential. Teachers also should consider the learning styles of their students when planning lessons. While children learn using all of their intelligences, some children depend more on a particular intelligence. Gardner's theory of multiple intelligences describes nine different forms of intelligence (see Chapter 3). Among these forms are visual/spatial, verbal/linguistic, and bodily/kinesthetic. Visual/spatial learners learn more readily by looking at pictures, graphs, and objects. Verbal/ linguistic learners learn best by reading, speaking, and listening. Bodily/kinesthetic learners learn through games, hands-on activities, and building (see Figure 1–3). The other forms of intelligence that Gardner describes suggest different ways that children should be taught. There are other students with special needs—those who have unusual difficulty learning mathematics and those who have particular talents when it comes to mathematics. Both groups require the teacher's attention. Chapter 3 further discusses the special needs of various children.

Whether the daily mathematics program is textbook-based, problem-based, project-based, or some combination of these, we must adjust our teaching to capitalize on the differences among our students. Each chapter discusses ways that we can help children with different needs and strengths master the content emphasized in the chapter.

GETTING STARTED

This textbook is for you. It is intended to provide ideas, activities, suggestions, questions, and challenges for you as a teacher of mathematics. We want you to be thoughtful, passionate teachers—teachers who are informed about how children learn and about the content of mathematics. We want you to be teachers who are curious and enthusiastic. We want you to be lifelong learners. As you are getting started, there are some thoughts that we would like to share with you. They generally are about mathematical power, ways of thinking, and inspiration. It is inspiring to read the words of Burns when she suggested that children should be ". . . taught math so that understanding is emphasized, ideas are explored, alternate methods are encouraged, and the purpose for what is being done is always evident" (1998, p. 44). This statement is one that we believe carries an important message. We want this book to follow what Burns has said. Math is not a mystery. It is a beautiful example of pattern and structure that should be made accessible to all.

The term *mathematical power* has been used for some time. The National Council of Teachers of Mathematics described its meaning by stating:

> Mathematical power includes the ability to explore, conjecture, and reason logically; to solve non-routine problems; to communicate about and through mathematics; and to connect ideas within mathematics and between mathematics and other intellectual activity. Mathematical power also involves the development of personal self-confidence and

Visual/Spatial Learner

Verbal/Linguistic Learners

Bodily/Kinesthetic Learners

Figure 1–3 Examples of three of Gardner's forms of intelligence.

a disposition to seek, evaluate, and use quantitative and spatial information in solving problems and in making decisions. Students' flexibility, perseverance, interest, curiosity, and inventiveness also affect the realization of mathematical power. (1991, p. 1)

You may need to reread the NCTM statement now and come back to it later. We believe that mathematical power should be a goal in teaching mathematics. We face that challenge in our teaching and writing and we hope that you will face it in your teaching.

Let's turn for a moment to learning. How do you learn? How do you understand? How do you raise a question? How do you think? All of these aspects of learning evolve; that is, they develop gradually from what we already know into something more complex. Knowledge and understanding are constructed in the mind, and they evolve. The processes of learning and understanding begin very early. The National Research Council noted, "[A]n infant's brain gives precedence to certain kinds of information: language, basic concepts of number, physical properties, and the movement of animate and inanimate objects. In the most general sense, the contemporary view of learning is that people construct new knowledge and understandings based on what they already know and believe" (2000, p. 10). There is a fine example of how understanding evolves in Lionni's children's book *Fish Is Fish* (1970). It is a story of a fish and a frog. The frog is able to go from the pond to land and explore other animal life. When the frog returns, he describes to the fish different animals that he has seen. Because the fish has experienced only fish in its surroundings, it sees all other animals as a kind of fish (see Figure 1–4). As we develop our understanding of mathematics, we, too, sometimes have distorted views based on limited understanding. When teachers provide additional experiences, our understanding is able to evolve to a more accurate state.

Mathematics is integral in our lives. Knowing mathematics means that we can use it in countless applications. We can count, display information, calculate simple and complex answers, determine percentage of growth and discounts, measure, appreciate shape and dimension, anticipate future events, and so on. It is sometimes said that before we can apply mathematics, we must know basic concepts and skills, which delays

"Cows," said the frog. "Cows! They have four legs, horns, eat grass, and carry pink bags of milk."

Figure 1–4   How the fish visualizes a cow in Lionni's *Fish Is Fish*. From FISH IS FISH by Leo Lionni, copyright © 1970 by Leo Lionni. Copyright renewed 1998 by Leo Lionni. Used by permission of Random House Children's Books, a division of Random House, Inc.

the application of mathematics for many. Carpenter and Lehrer tell us that this is not the case. They state: "It often has been assumed . . . that basic concepts and skills need to be learned before applications are introduced. This is a faulty assumption: children use their intuitively acquired knowledge to solve problems long before they have been taught basic skills" (1999, p. 31). This tells us that problem solving and projects belong at the earliest levels of teaching. We can excite young students to engage in mathematical thinking and learning. We can play significant roles in their mathematical development.

In this chapter we have been laying a foundation on which to base our mathematics teaching. Chapter 2 and subsequent chapters will build on this foundation, providing information and resources for you as a teacher of mathematics. We hope that you will be enriched by your experience with *Teaching and Learning Mathematics: Pre-Kindergarten Through Middle School.*

FOR YOU AS A TEACHER: IDEAS FOR DISCUSSION AND YOUR PROFESSIONAL PORTFOLIO

This section is intended to provide you the opportunity to read, write, and reflect on key elements of this chapter. We list several discussion questions. We hope that one or more of these questions will prove interesting to you and that you will choose to investigate and write about the questions. The results of your work should be considered as part of your professional portfolio. You might consider these two questions as guides for your writing: "What does the material in this chapter mean for you as a teacher?" or "How can what you are reading be translated into a teaching practice for you as a teacher?"

DISCUSSION IDEAS

1. You have written your own thoughts about the meaning of mathematics and you have read the What Is Mathematics? section in this chapter. Seek out three additional sources to answer the question. These might include a mathematics textbook, a teacher of mathematics, a dictionary, or another source. From this information construct a "new" answer to "What is mathematics?" Return to the Reflections and Refinement part of My Math Journal at the beginning of the chapter and enter it there.

2. What are your views about mathematics as an educational subject? What mathematics is important? What mathematics should students learn? How much

mathematics is enough? What role should technology (calculators and computers) and problem solving play in learning mathematics? How important is memory in learning mathematics? The responses that you make to these and other questions begin to spell out your philosophical basis for mathematics education.

3. Ask three teachers about what influences their mathematics curriculum. How broad are these influences? Compare your findings with others who have asked different teachers. Is there a pattern in the answers, perhaps by the teachers' grade levels or experience?

4. Use Weblink 1–1 to go to the home page of the National Council of Teachers of Mathematics. Explore what the NCTM can offer you as a student and as a teacher. Make a descriptive list of 10 advantages to being a member of the NCTM.

5. In this chapter, four influences on the mathematics curriculum were mentioned. Discuss how you would rank the four influences in importance based on what you read. Justify your ordering. Explain how your personal ranking may differ from the ranking you just completed.

ADDITIONAL RESOURCES

REFERENCES

Baratta-Lorton, Mary, *Mathematics Their Way: An Activity-Centered Mathematics Program for Early Childhood Education.* Menlo Park, CA: Addison-Wesley, 1995.

Bruner, Jerome S., "Going beyond the Information Given," in *Beyond the Information Given: Studies in the Psychology of Knowing,* ed. Jeremy M. Anglin. New York: Norton, 1973.

Burns, Marilyn, *The I Hate Mathematics! Book.* Boston: Little, Brown, 1975.

———, *Math for Smarty Pants.* Illustrated by Martha Weston. Boston: Little, Brown, 1982.

———, *Math: Facing an American Phobia.* Sausalito, CA: Math Solutions Publications, 1998.

Burrill, Gail, "TIMSS—What Can We Learn?" *NCTM News Bulletin.* Reston, VA: National Council of Teachers of Mathematics, March 1998.

Carpenter, Thomas P., and Richard Lehrer, "Teaching and Learning Mathematics with Understanding," in *Mathematics Classrooms That Promote Understanding,* ed. Elizabeth Fennema and Thomas A. Romberg. Mahwah, NJ: Erlbaum, 1999.

Carson, Joan C., and Ruby N. Bostick, *Math Instruction Using Media and Modality Strengths.* Springfield, IL: Thomas, 1988.

Forgione, Pascal D., Jr., "Commissioner's Statement" in U.S. Department of Education, National Center for Education Statistics, *Pursuing Excellence: A Study of U.S. Fourth-Grade Mathematics and Science Achievement in International Context* (NCES 97–255). Washington, DC: U.S. Government Printing Office, 1997.

Gardner, Howard. *Frames of Mind: The Theory of Multiple Intelligences*. New York: Basic Books, 1983.

———, *Multiple Intelligences: The Theory in Practice*. New York: Basic Books, 1993.

———, *The Disciplined Mind*. New York: Simon & Schuster, 1999.

Hiebert, James, and Patricia Lefevre, "Conceptual and Procedural Knowledge in Mathematics: An Introductory Analysis," in *Conceptual and Procedural Knowledge: The Case of Mathematics*, ed. James Hiebert, Hillsdale, NJ: Erlbaum, 1986.

National Council of Teachers of Mathematics, *Curriculum and Evaluation Standards for School Mathematics*. Reston, VA: NCTM, 1989.

———, *Professional Standards for Teaching Mathematics*. Reston, VA: NCTM, 1991.

——— *Assessment Standards for School Mathematics*. Reston, VA: NCTM, 1995.

———, *Principles and Standards for School Mathematics*: Reston, VA: NCTM, 2000.

National Research Council, *Everybody Counts: A Report to the Nation on the Future of Mathematics Education*. Washington, DC: National Academy Press, 1989.

———, *Reshaping School Mathematics: A Philosophy and Framework for Curriculum*. Washington, DC: National Academy Press, 1990.

———, *How People Learn: Brain, Mind, Experience, and School*. Edited by John D. Bransford, Ann L. Brown, and Rodney R. Cocking, Committee on Developments in the Science of Learning, Commission on Behavioral and Social Sciences and Education. Washington, DC: National Academy Press, 2000.

Ohanian, Susan, and Marilyn Burns, *Math by All Means: Division Grades 3–4*, Sausalito, CA: Math Solutions Publications, 1995.

Skemp, Richard R., *The Psychology of Learning Mathematics*. Hillsdale, NJ: Erlbaum, 1987.

Sutton, John, and Alice Krueger, eds., *EDThoughts: What We Know about Mathematics Teaching and Learning*, Aurora, CO: Mid-continent Research for Education and Learning, 2002.

U.S. Department of Education, National Center for Education Statistics, *Pursuing Excellence: A Study of U.S. Eighth-Grade Mathematics and Science Teaching, Learning, Curriculum, and Achievement in International Context* (NCES 97–198). Washington, DC: U.S. Government Printing Office, 1996.

———, *The Condition of Education 2002* (NCES 2002-025). Washington, DC: U.S. Government Printing Office, 2002.

CHILDREN'S LITERATURE

Lionni, Leo. *Fish Is Fish*, New York: Random House, 1970.

 WEBLINKS

Weblink 1–1: Home page of the National Council of Teachers of Mathematics. http://www.nctm.org

Weblink 1–2: Electronic version of *Principles and Standards for School Mathematics*. http://www.standards.nctm.org

Weblink 1–3: AAAS Project 2061 middle grades math textbook evaluations. http://www.project2061.org/tools/textbook/matheval

Weblink 1–4: Eisenhower National Clearinghouse Exemplary and Promising Mathematics Programs Report. http://www.enc.org/professional/federalresources/exemplary/promising

Weblink 1–5: Investigations in Number, Data, and Space description from TERC. http://www.terc.edu/investigations/index/html/index.html

Weblink 1–6: Everyday Mathematics (Pre-K–grade 6) website. http://everydaymath.uchicago.edu

Weblink 1–7: Math Trailblazers (Grades K–5) website. http://www.math.uic.edu/IMSE/MTB/mtb.html

Weblink 1–8: Bridges in Mathematics, Opening Eyes to Mathematics, and Math Alive! website. http://www.mlc.pdx.edu/CM.html

Weblink 1–9: Connected Mathematics, Math in Context, MathScape, and MathThematics website. http://www.showmecenter.missouri.edu//Showme/default.html

Weblink 1–10: Highlights from TIMSS video study of eighth grade mathematics teaching. http://nces.ed.gov/Timss/video.asp

Weblink 1–11: NAEP mathematics subject area section of the nation's report. http://nces.ed.gov/nationsreportcard/mathematics

Weblink 1–12: The Trends in International Mathematics and Science Study (TIMSS) website. http://nces.ed.gov/timss

Additional Weblink

Weblink 1–13: The Alternatives for Rebuilding Curricula website. The ARC Center is a collaboration between the Consortium for Mathematics and Its Applications (COMAP) and three elementary mathematics curriculum projects supported by the National Science Foundation. http://www.comap.com/elementary/projects/arc

CHILDREN AND MATHEMATICS

As you read the following pages, consider these guiding questions:

1. What factors in the child's world prepare the child for learning mathematics?

2. What is a concept? How do students form mathematical concepts and what conditions enhance that concept formation?

3. What is and what is the importance of mathematical understanding?

4. What are the characteristics of teachers with a constructivist view of learning?

5. What can we do in the classroom that is compatible with brain-functioning research?

6. How can we develop intellectual character with our students?

The Teaching Principle

Effective mathematics teaching requires understanding what students know and need to learn and then challenging and supporting them to learn it well.

NCTM (2000), pp. 16, 20. Reprinted by permission.

The Learning Principle

Students must learn mathematics with understanding, actively building new knowledge from experience and prior knowledge.

Reflect on your own mathematics experiences in prekindergarten through middle school. What do you remember as your favorite parts of learning mathematics? Describe a teacher who really made you love mathematics. Discuss a bad experience you had learning mathematics. Describe the mathematics teacher that you will be.

REFLECTIONS AND REFINEMENT: After you have completed this description, compare it to those of some of your classmates. Did you respond in the same way? As you continue through this term refine and add to your thoughts. Write your new reflections here.

Children are natural learners. Their potential and energy for learning are considerable. They are exposed to enormous amounts of information before they enter school and outside of school once they begin. They are curious. The National Research Council reported: "Young children . . . show a remarkable ability to formulate, represent, and solve simple mathematical problems and to reason and explain their mathematical activities. The desire to quantify the world around them seems to be a natural one for young children. They are positively disposed to do and understand mathematics when they first encounter it" (2001, p. 174). Mathematics touches many aspects of children's lives. For example, children play with blocks, with dollhouses, with trains on tracks that they have designed, and with cardboard houses they have built—exercises in spatial visualization. Other aspects of children's lives affected by mathematics include correspondences between family members, meal portions, routes taken to and from school, time and television programming, pricing and the ability to purchase items at the store, and baking cookies using measured ingredients. These are but a few examples. The myriad ways in which mathematics touches the experiences of children stretch the imagination.

Space, number, shape, puzzles, time, distance, and computers provide a rich milieu in which pre-kindergarten, elementary, and middle school children grow. The NCTM reminds us that "it is the responsibility of the teacher to help students see and experience the interrelation of mathematical topics, the relationships between mathematics and other subjects, and the way that mathematics is embedded in the students' world" (NCTM, 2000, p. 135). In Chapter 2, we explore two topics that influence how children learn mathematics:

1. The children's world
2. Children's thinking and learning styles

THE CHILDREN'S WORLD

As teachers, we must know and understand the world from a child's perspective, how children view the world, and how children develop knowledge. In this section, we describe the ways in which children experience the world mathematically. Their learning of mathematics, now and in the future, is built upon this foundation.

Children Have Many Number Experiences

Number experiences are a part of children's lives from the moment they begin to communicate. Communication and physical movement include intensity of sound; varying duration of activity; exploration of space;

embrace and separation; sequence of occurrences; and similarities and differences among humans, objects, places, and emotions. As youngsters record these relationships, they learn to quantify their world.

The lives of children are increasingly being affected by technology. Computers allow them to draw, design, and animate presentations; word-process ideas; organize and present data; search for and gather information; and correspond. Calculators help speed up long, routine calculations; discover patterns; and graph formulas. CDs and DVDs provide information and entertainment. Each year teachers are using these tools more skillfully.

Children begin their schooling with enthusiasm, energy, and a willingness to participate. They usually enjoy success in their early mathematical work because they have been exploring relationships for years. Mathematics is, after all, the study of patterns and relationships and how things are connected. Among the teacher's challenges will be increasing the likelihood of success by helping children see meaning and sense in their mathematics.

Children are Active in Their World

Teachers and parents rarely have to instruct children on how to be active or how to play. School is one of the first places where children are asked to be passive and quiet. Some orderliness and conformity is necessary for significant learning to take place. But, at the same time, there must be opportunities for spontaneous response and divergent thinking.

Children should be physically involved in mathematics. Materials such as stacking blocks, pattern blocks, colored cubes, attribute blocks, puzzles, Cuisenaire rods, geoboards, sand, clay, water, various containers, computers and appropriate software, and calculators should be available in the school. These and other learning aids are introduced in later chapters of this book. Children use these materials for counting, developing patterns, creating, observing, constructing, discussing, and comparing. From the manipulations and observations come the abstractions of quantitative ideas and the communication of these ideas in pictorial and, later, symbolic form.

Children Observe Relationships in Their World

Children and adults make connections among objects that seem separate at first glance. Language is often closely tied with the expression of these relationships. Relationships may be simple. For example, an infant who repeatedly hears a certain sound and then receives attention begins to learn the relationship between her name and herself. Later it becomes apparent that other individuals have names. Distinguishing between a person's name and the name of the position that person holds in the family is more difficult. That is, *Linda* and *Julie* are names, whereas *mommy* and *sister,* although used as names, state family relationships. Eventually, children discover their relationships to grandparents, uncles, aunts, and cousins.

Seventh-grade students can readily differentiate between a rectangle and other parallelograms but may be confused as to how they are related. That is, it may not be apparent to them that all rectangles are parallelograms but not all parallelograms are rectangles. Some may firmly believe that rectangles and parallelograms share no common characteristics. Experience and discussion, then, help them to understand some less obvious relationships.

As children quantify their world, they become aware of arithmetical, spatial, logical, and collective relationships through their active participation with and their discussion about their natural environment. Physical models in the school classroom provide an effective basis for mathematical learning. Some relationships are obvious. Others are not, and it becomes necessary for teachers to provide experiences to link the more subtle relationships. Eventually mathematics makes sense, because the learners understand how most of what they have been learning is connected. Learning how things relate is sharply distinguished from learning by memorizing many disconnected facts. When things are related, mathematics is presented as possessing structure; when memory is stressed, structure is generally ignored.

Relationships can be expressed in visual form. In moving from purely concrete work using physical objects to more abstract work, visual representations can be employed effectively. For example, Figure 2–1 is a visual representation of the relationships in one family drawn by a five-year-old. This representation links the physical world to the abstract idea of family relations. Teachers should be aware of relationships and are encouraged to develop experiences and representations to further the learning of how things relate.

Children Learn Mathematics in Concert with Other Subjects

By the time children enter school, they are proficient at learning interrelated skills and concepts. Walking, talking, toilet habits, rote counting, and language are learned without being isolated from other life experiences. The packaging of bits and pieces of knowledge or the separation of skills from their applications creates an artificial environment alien to the unified world of all humans. Integrated experiences in school are important in providing a more natural and balanced setting for learning.

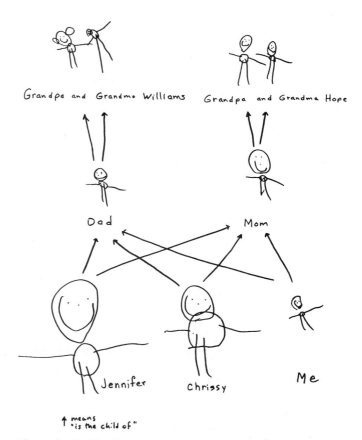

Figure 2–1 Family relationships drawn by five-year-old child.

The skillful teacher is afforded the opportunity to integrate mathematics with other subjects and the world in general. The interrelatedness of mathematics with subjects such as art, language, literature, social studies, and science illustrates the close ties of all bodies of knowledge. Just as mathematics is embedded in other subjects, other subjects are embedded in mathematics. The educative process should bring many connected experiences to children in a lifelike environment. It is crucial that children see the connections.

There are few thinking skills unique to mathematics. Rather, most thinking skills transcend specific knowledge or a specific discipline. When developed in a setting of integrated learning, thinking skills provide the opportunity for children to learn how to learn. Observing, describing, conjecturing, questioning, judging, valuing, and communicating are skills of life. They are also the foundation upon which problem solving is built.

Children's Attitudes Affect Their Ability to Learn

Children's attitudes about themselves and their ability to succeed, as well as their attitudes about others, home, school subjects, and life, affect their behavior.

Mid-continent Research for Education and Learning (McREL) reported that "students' attitudes toward mathematics have a great effect on student achievement. . . . Students who enjoy mathematics tend to perform well in their mathematics course work and are more likely to enroll in the more advanced mathematics courses" (2002, p. 86). The impact of these attitudes may vary by gender or by cultural and ethnic background. Attitudes about mathematics are only one of a number of factors that have an influence on mathematics learning.

Not all children will attack mathematics or anything else with the same energy and enthusiasm. Students should be exposed to the historical and cultural aspects of mathematics as well as its structure. Some students are interested in theoretical mathematics. Others are motivated by a historical approach. Still others are excited by the relationships between mathematics and art, mathematics and music, or mathematics and language. Applications of mathematics interest many children.

Much has been written about **math anxiety,** which can be described as reluctance to engage in, and fear of, mathematics-related activities. Individuals who exhibit such anxiety do not enjoy doing arithmetic, particularly in public. They agonize over mental arithmetic, apologize for their lack of skill, and avoid activities associated with mathematics. In short, they are dysfunctional in mathematics.

Most individuals with math anxiety are beyond elementary school age. Research shows that mathematics is liked and enjoyed by a majority of elementary students. We are unconvinced that large numbers of elementary school children suffer math anxiety.

However, we are convinced that many children have learned not to enjoy mathematics. These children have experienced considerable failure in their attempts to learn concepts and skills. They have been asked to learn certain mathematical ideas that they were not ready to learn; they have been moved through a curriculum, "learning" mathematics for which they did not have the prerequisites and struggling with new concepts that did not make any sense. They may have been pressured to memorize hundreds of unrelated basic addition and multiplication facts and subjected to timed tests in front of their peers. They believe that success in mathematics is knowing a certain "magical process" that results in correct answers. As a result, some children begin to dislike mathematics and do not want to do mathematics. Failure and humiliation are powerful forces that cause children to be reluctant to engage in mathematics. Dislike of mathematics and reluctance to participate in math activities is more prevalent in middle school, providing a challenge to teachers.

CHILDREN'S THINKING AND LEARNING STYLES

We become better teachers by developing strong backgrounds regarding how children learn and how children develop their thinking. In this section we focus on logical and psychological approaches to mathematics, ways in which children construct and make sense of mathematics, sources of information about children learning mathematics, research-based views of learning, developing mathematical fluency, children's communication of mathematical concepts, and thinking like a mathematician. As we read, we may find it interesting to compare our own thinking with that of children.

Logical and Psychological Approaches to Mathematics

Approaches to teaching mathematics have generally followed the logical structure of mathematics presented by most children's textbooks. Thus, counting is followed by adding at the pictorial and symbolic levels. Subtracting, multiplying, and dividing follow. Later or concurrently, children learn the properties of these operations. To augment learning computation, courses of study include patterns and relationships, spatial sense, probability, statistics, and simple measurement. Understanding is developed to the extent that children see meaning in what they are doing. Some children readily understand. Many others do not or cannot understand. The presentation of mathematics as an organized, logical structure does not ensure children's understanding.

To complement the logical structure of mathematics, teachers should weigh the psychological aspects of learning mathematics. Teachers who consider how children learn mathematics can provide activities that blend what is known about children and mathematics. For example, a teacher taking this approach would realize that the child's developing understanding of the concept of *number* involves classifying, relating, and ordering, along with discussion. The teacher would use objects and groups of objects to illustrate and enhance the learning of number, operation, and addition. Psychological considerations that help children learn mathematics are the focus of the next several pages.

How Children Construct and Make Sense of Mathematical Concepts

As mathematical concepts are formed, mathematics makes sense and understanding evolves. A **concept** is an idea or mental image. Words and symbols are used to describe or label concepts. For example, *potato* is a collection of sounds that brings to mind an image representing some generalized form of a garden vegetable. Exactly what image appears depends on the experiences, heritage, geographical location, and language of the listener. The symbol 5 represents a mental image of all groups containing ● ● ● ●, or five, things. Again, the precise image that appears depends on the background and experiences of the listener.

Concepts are learned. Virtually all children from the time of birth can learn concepts. Concept formation begins immediately. The language and symbols that name concepts lag behind concept formation but eventually emerge. As children grow and mature, language and symbols are introduced to name mental images already formed and are used later to teach new concepts. To learn or better understand a concept, children require a number of common experiences relating to the concept. Initially, a parent introduces potatoes to a child by spooning a white, strained substance into the child's mouth, perhaps exhorting the child to "Eat your potatoes." As this procedure continues for several months, the child begins to associate the word *potato* with the mushy substance. Obviously, the concept of *potato* is very limited at this time. Soon, mashed potatoes from the parent's plate may be introduced to the child with the same plea: "Eat your potatoes." Over time, potatoes prepared in many ways are given to the child and, finally, after two or three years, the child is informed that the vegetable the parent is washing, peeling, and cutting is a potato and can be prepared in numerous ways. The concept of *potato* begins to emerge as an accurate, generalized mental image. The various ways that potatoes are prepared makes sense.

Two aspects of this example have clear implications for teaching children. First, the concept of *potato* did not become *known* until potatoes had been seen, felt, smelled, and tasted in many ways; that is, until the child experienced potatoes in numerous guises. Each of these guises is an embodiment of potato. When several examples that appear different yet have something common about them (in this case, deriving from a single vegetable) are presented, we say that we are using the multiple embodiment principle. We are presenting the concept of *potato* in many embodiments and providing the opportunity for the child to discover the common element among them all. When the child was able to discern the common property among the various ways in which potatoes were prepared, namely, each dish originated from a certain recognized vegetable, the concept of *potato* was formed. Second, the word *potato* had to occur in concert with or had to follow the experiencing of the vegetable. The sounds that make up the word *potato* were not helpful before the experience. Hearing only the word or a definition, the child would not have understood what a potato was.

The two processes just described provide the foundation for the learning of mathematics. Children who find the common property of several seemingly disconnected examples are **abstracting.** The abstraction that is made is a **concept.** Children first learn and make sense of mathematics by abstracting concepts from experiences with physical models or pictures. The language is developed during or after concept formation, never before. Objects and events that are a part of children's lives and are easily observed are less abstract than objects and events that are not easily observed. Thus, dogs, automobiles, houses, toys, and mothers are less abstract than are color, height, number, time, and multiplication.

Skemp has stated two principles of learning mathematics that relate directly to the notion of concepts:

1. Concepts of a higher order than those which people already have cannot be communicated to them by a definition, but only by arranging for them to encounter a suitable collection of examples.
2. Since in mathematics these examples are almost invariably other concepts, it must first be ensured that these are already formed in the mind of the learner (1987, p. 18).

Children learn the meaning of number by experiencing number in many varied situations—through a suitable collection of examples. The suitable collection of examples represents the multiple embodiment principle mentioned a few paragraphs ago. Multiple embodiment is as appropriate for the concept of number as it is for the concept of *potato*. The same holds true for addition, subtraction, multiplication, division, fractions, geometry, measurement, operations on integers, variables, algebra, and so forth. Many activities presented throughout the following pages are typical examples of activities for learning mathematical concepts.

> Teachers should guide students to develop and use multiple representations effectively. (NCTM, 2000, p. 139)

In addition, developing mathematical concepts requires constantly providing experiences that build foundations on which to base further mathematical learning. Attempting to develop mathematical concepts on a foundation of previously memorized, vague notions results in frustration for both children and teacher. Skemp again notes that ". . . before we try to communicate a new concept, we have to find out what are its contributory concepts; and for each of these, we have to find out *its* contributory concepts, and so on, until we reach either primary concepts [derived from sensory and motor experiences] or experience which we can assume" (pp. 19–20).

MATHEMATICAL UNDERSTANDING. Teaching that focuses on developing understanding has been advocated for many years. The terms *developing meaning* and *developing understanding* have been used synonymously. Brownell caught the attention of mathematics educators in his meaning theory of arithmetic instruction set forth in the 1935 yearbook of the National Council of Teachers of Mathematics. According to Brownell, ". . . this theory makes meaning, the fact that children shall see sense in what they learn, the central issue in arithmetic instruction." He went on to call for an "instructional reorganization" so that arithmetic would be ". . . less a challenge to the pupil's memory and more a challenge to his intelligence" (1935, pp. 19, 31). Brownell supported his theories with his research throughout his professional career. One such study, *Meaningful vs. Mechanical Learning: A Study in Grade III Subtraction,* suggested that retention, transfer, and understanding were enhanced by teachers using a "meaning method" as opposed to a "mechanical method" of instruction (Brownell and Moser, 1949). In the ensuing years, general agreement has been reached among psychologists and educators that teaching with meaning or understanding tends to be richer and longer-lasting than other teaching. It has also been suggested that when learning is seen as a function of understanding, teaching centers on the children and their interpretations of what is being taught. Thus, teaching mathematics with understanding provides an extra incentive for the teacher to know how children learn mathematics.

> Effective mathematics teaching requires a serious commitment to the development of students' understanding of mathematics. (NCTM, 2000, p. 18)

An emphasis on understanding mathematics permeates the literature on learning. The National Research Council cautioned, "Students who have learned only procedural skills and have little understanding of mathematics will have limited access to advanced schooling, better jobs, and other opportunities. If any group of students is deprived of the opportunity to learn with understanding, they are condemned to second-class status in society, or worse" (2001, p. 144). We should be reminded that understanding is not an all-or-none proposition. As we learn, we develop increasing levels of understanding. For example, developing the meaning of number progresses from distinguishing sets of one amount from sets of another amount, to rote counting, to recognition of numerals, to counting objects, to the number property of sets of objects, and to sets of sets. This progression, in whatever order it may take, extends over a number of years and may never be complete.

What kinds of thinking processes result in mathematical understanding? Carpenter and Lehrer addressed this question. They wrote, "We propose five forms of mental activity from which mathematical understanding emerges: (a) constructing relationships, (b) extending and applying mathematical knowledge, (c) reflecting about experiences, (d) articulating what one knows, and (e) making mathematical knowledge one's own (1999, p. 20).

Let's look at each of the forms of mental activity, paraphrasing from Carpenter and Lehrer (1999, pp. 20–23). "Constructing relationships" refers to connecting new ideas or processes with already-understood ideas. For example, once children have counted objects of many different kinds and have formed sets using a variety of objects representing various numbers, the notion that number is unrelated to a particular kind of object will be better understood.

"Extending and applying mathematical knowledge" refers to developing knowledge structures that help tie together ideas or processes as they become better understood. For example, students build their understanding of integers on their understanding of whole numbers. Then, the idea of rational numbers can be better understood.

"Reflecting about experiences" refers to students examining the ideas or processes they are learning and how these ideas or processes relate to what they already know. For example, students compare the commutative property of addition in algebraic symbols with examples using Cuisenaire rods and whole numbers.

"Articulating what one knows" refers to writing, discussing, or picturing the ideas upon which students have been reflecting. For example, students discuss the various shapes they have found on their shape walk and sort them by their characteristics. Then, they draw and write about their favorite shape.

"Making mathematical knowledge one's own" refers to students constructing knowledge through their activities so that the knowledge makes sense and is their own. For example, students work to develop a division algorithm and explain why it works.

In keeping with the focus on developing understanding as a part of mathematics instruction, we will continue to emphasize understanding throughout this book.

A CONSTRUCTIVIST VIEW OF LEARNING. From the literature on teaching mathematics to young children comes an approach that is influenced by constructivism, a theory about the nature of knowledge and the nature of learning. Constructivists believe that children gain knowledge by inventing it, that they construct knowledge for themselves. According to Piaget, ". . . to understand is to discover, or reconstruct by rediscovery, and such conditions must be complied with if in the future individuals are to be formed who are capable of production and creativity and not simply repetition" (1973, p. 20). Based heavily on the work of Piaget, constructivism guides teachers to interact with children through questioning and discussion, skillfully responding to the children's ideas and allowing children to discover relationships and predict future events. Children engage in manipulating physical models, playing games, and interacting with one another. Constructivist principles are being applied to teaching at all levels of learning. Eighth-grade students who use algebra tiles to discover the meaning of factoring polynomials have the opportunity to construct that knowledge through their manipulations, questions, and discussions, as do primary students who use a geoboard to discover the meaning of $\frac{1}{2}$.

A proponent of teaching based on the principle of constructivism, Kamii noted that "Encouraging children to construct knowledge from within is the diametric opposite of trying to impose isolated skills from the outside" (1989, p. x). The approach that Kamii advocated contrasts with that of more traditional educators, who ". . . assume that the job of the teacher is to put knowledge into children's heads. They also assume that the proof of this transmission of knowledge is a high score on standardized tests. Both of these assumptions . . . are erroneous and outdated" (1989, p. 184).

Kamii's work has been based, in part, on her work with primary teachers of grades 1–3. Besides stressing the importance of children creating their own mathematical relationships, Kamii emphasizes that word problems are an important part of teaching. Children are able to construct mathematical ideas from problems arising from their personal lives; first-grade children can solve verbal problems without formal instruction. This led Kamii to note:

> If children add numerical quantities repeatedly, actively, in the context of everyday classroom occurrences, games, and problems that they understand, they will remember the results of these mental actions and will become able to read and write conventional mathematical signs. The focus of the teacher's concern should be on children's thinking rather than on their ability to write correct answers. (1985, p. 94)

Kamii suggested that the overriding aim of education is to develop moral and intellectual autonomy among learners. As a result, children should be encouraged to develop their own opinions and to judge when another opinion is better. Kamii noted:

> This is not to say that children do not learn from workbooks and transmission. They do, and they usually acquire the truth faster by being told than by constructing it themselves. But we must think of learning in a larger context

than the memorization of sums and the ability to produce high test scores. In other words, we need to see autonomy as the ultimate aim of education. . . . (1985, p. 36)

Developing autonomy among learners requires teachers to be student centered and willing to forgo the tendency to direct students' every move. This would suggest that there is a continuum on which individual teachers would find a level of comfort as they begin their teaching experience. At one end of the continuum is the student-centered teacher and at the other end, the content-centered teacher. Teaching that is consistent with a constructivist view of learning would be associated with the former. Brooks and Brooks (1993, p. 10) noted:

> . . . when the classroom environment in which students spend so much of their day is organized so that student-to-student interaction is encouraged, cooperation is valued, assignments and materials are interdisciplinary, and students' freedom to chase their own ideas is abundant, students are more likely to take risks and approach assignments with a willingness to accept challenges to their current understandings. Such teacher role models and environmental conditions honor students as emerging thinkers. (1993, p. 10)

We believe that you should consider using constructivist approaches as a teacher of elementary and middle school mathematics. Recent discussions and guidelines presented by the National Council of Teachers of Mathematics and the National Research Council are having a significant impact on school mathematics (see Chapter 1). They strongly support a shift away from a teaching model based on the transmission of knowledge and toward a model based on student-centered experiences. For example, Fennema, Sowder, and Carpenter noted:

> In the descriptions of classrooms where students are learning with understanding, instruction is not portrayed as the presentation of clear, precise explanations of procedures to be practiced by students. Instead, understanding is constructed by each student as she or he engages in the various mental activities we have found to be critical: actively constructing relationships between and among mathematical ideas by reflecting on problem solutions, extending knowledge by relating the new solutions to what has been known previously, and articulating thinking about the mathematics they have explored. (1999, p. 186)

Thus, the opportunity to employ alternative teaching approaches, including constructivist approaches, is at hand. The National Research Council cautions us, however, about always having children construct knowledge: ". . . there are times, usually after people have first grappled with issues on their own, that 'teaching by telling' can work extremely well. However, teachers still need to pay attention to students' interpretations and provide guidance when necessary"

(2000, p. 11). As you continue reading, you will find that many of the activities suggested in this textbook fit the constructivist theory of learning.

The following descriptors of constructivist behaviors were set forth by Brooks and Brooks and are presented as guidelines for those interested in using this approach (1993, pp. 103–117). Perhaps you will be one of those teachers.

1. Constructivist teachers encourage and accept student autonomy and initiative.
2. Constructivist teachers use raw data and primary sources, along with manipulative, interactive, and physical materials.
3. When framing tasks, constructivist teachers use cognitive terminology such as *classify, analyze, predict,* and *create.*
4. Constructivist teachers allow student responses to drive lessons, shift instructional strategies, and alter content.
5. Constructivist teachers inquire about students' understanding of concepts before sharing their own understanding of those concepts.
6. Constructivist teachers encourage students to engage in dialogue, both with the teacher and with one another.
7. Constructivist teachers encourage student inquiry by asking thoughtful, open-ended questions and encouraging students to ask questions of each other.
8. Constructivist teachers seek elaboration of students' initial responses.
9. Constructivist teachers engage students in experiences that might engender contradictions to their initial hypotheses and then encourage discussion.
10. Constructivist teachers allow wait time after posing questions.
11. Constructivist teachers provide time for students to construct relationships and create metaphors.
12. Constructivist teachers nurture students' natural curiosity through frequent use of the learning cycle model.

If you decide to use these descriptors, you would be well advised to read further and in more depth about their meaning. Brooks and Brooks (1993) is a good place to start. There are many other helpful resources in the literature.

You are encouraged to explore further how children learn mathematics. Only when teachers begin to understand the aspects and stages of mathematical learning will children receive the kind of instruction most appropriate to their individual learning styles. In addition, exploration will help you to understand why this textbook emphasizes manipulation of physical objects, multiple embodiments of mathematical ideas, active participation of learners, use of alternative teaching strategies, use of mathematical relationships, various kinds of communication, reflection, and formation of mathematical ideas according to the developmental characteristics of children.

Sources of Information about How Children Learn Mathematics

The study of how children learn mathematics is not new, but until relatively recently, little had been written that was directly applicable to classroom instruction. Useful works include those by Bruner (1977), Burger and Shaughnessy (1986), Copeland (1984), Ginsburg (1983), Kamii (1985, 1989, 1990), Piaget (1973), Skemp (1987), and the National Research Council (2000, 2001). These and other sources have been included in the references at the end of this chapter. Much of what appears in the following chapters rests on the foundation provided by these authors.

The work of Piaget has greatly influenced the way teachers view cognitive development. Among the most well-known ideas associated with Piaget are those dealing with the evolution of thought through a series of four stages. Children move through the stages of cognitive development as a result of the interaction between internal forces (maturation) and external forces (environment). The first stage, sensorimotor, generally occurs in the first two years of life. Here, the child begins to imitate sounds and actions and recognizes that objects still exist when they are out of sight. The second stage, preoperational, generally lasts from around age 2 to age 7. Here, the child gains an initial use of language and the ability to think in symbolic terms. The third stage, concrete operations, generally lasts from around age 7 to age 11. Here, physical objects provide the medium for learning. Children discover that objects can be changed or moved and still retain many of their characteristics and that these changes can be reversed. The fourth stage, formal operations, may begin around age 11, although many adults never operate fully at the formal level. Here, students can think logically about abstract problems. The age ranges are only approximations, but all individuals progress through these stages in the order presented here.

An important idea associated with Piaget's work and noted in the stage of concrete operations is conservation. Conservation of number means that the number of objects in a set does not change if the objects in the set are placed in different positions, as in Figure 2–2. Conservation of quantity means that the amount of liquid poured from a tall, narrow container into a short, wide container remains constant. Conservation

Figure 2-2   Child may say that there is a different number of objects in each row.

of length means that an object retains the same length if it is moved. Until children are about seven years old, they do not conserve number. Again, seven is just a benchmark; children vary in their ability to conserve number. Teachers do not, nor should they, teach conservation, for the ability to conserve results from the development of logical/mathematical knowledge — the understanding of relationships.

Two additional and complementary processes that Piaget described are assimilation and accommodation. Assimilation is the process by which an individual takes in information. The information may come from any source, such as playing with blocks, watching a bird fly, or listening to an explanation. Assimilated information may cause individuals to adjust or modify their understanding of an idea or event; in such cases, the process of accommodation takes place. The adjustment or modification of an idea resulting in a new cognitive structure is the process of equilibration. It stems from an individual's need to reach equilibrium when perceptions are in conflict with new information. Equilibration has taken place once the new information is accommodated and the conflict has dissipated. In the process of learning, assimilation and accommodation are constantly taking place, resulting in the process of equilibration. You should recognize the importance of these processes in learning mathematics. Further mention is made of assimilation and accommodation in the discussion of how children form mathematical concepts.

Piaget's work has influenced the authors, and you will find references to his work throughout the book. Perhaps Piaget's most important idea is that children can and should be involved in inventing mathematics. It is through experiences that children discover relationships

and solve problems. The theory of constructivism, discussed earlier in this chapter, emerged from the work of Piaget. That children should be guided to construct their own knowledge is a powerful notion in teaching mathematics.

Investigations on how children think mathematically have shown that young children in the preoperational stage use mental counting procedures to solve arithmetic problems. This has led to revised theories about number understanding (Resnick, 1983). Certain types of simple mathematical thinking can occur before the Piagetian stage of concrete operations. According to Carpenter (1986, p. 114), "Contrary to popular notions, young children are relatively successful at analyzing and solving simple word problems. Before receiving formal instruction in addition and subtraction, most young children invent informal modeling and counting strategies to solve basic addition and subtraction problems."

Finally, we should recall that children construct new knowledge based upon existing knowledge and beliefs. This suggests that we pay attention to what children already know and believe. The National Research Council explained that ". . . teachers need to pay attention to the incomplete understandings, the false beliefs, and the naive renditions of concepts that learners bring with them to a given subject. Teachers then need to build on these ideas in ways that help each student achieve a more mature understanding. If students' initial ideas and beliefs are ignored, the understandings that they develop can be very different from what the teacher intends" (2000, p. 10).

A Research-Based View of Learning

Learning research suggests that there are a variety of ways to introduce mathematical concepts so that virtually all students can develop a deeper understanding of more complex topics. Some of this research is related to new knowledge about how the brain functions and how different learning styles and different strengths in multiple intelligences affect this learning.

BRAIN-FUNCTIONING RESEARCH.   Recent research has shown that the structures of both the developing brain and the mature brain are changed when a student learns a new idea or grapples with a new problem. This means that the popular idea that some children are born with a mathematical mind and some are not is a risky misconception. If we as teachers believe this, we tend not to challenge students we perceive as being incapable of deep mathematical reasoning. On the other hand, it is exciting to see research that indicates that how much and how well we learn is significantly affected by the experiences we have and the problems we tackle. Children who are challenged to tackle appropriately difficult mathematical problems will develop their brain capacity and literally expand their minds. Problem solving is to the brain what exercise is to the body, a mental "neurobics." The following are some of the things that you might incorporate into your mathematics program that are supported by brain-functioning research.

1. Help students learn to plan ahead and to organize their learning. Good problem solvers use the frontal lobes of the brain, where planning and organization takes place.

2. Use investigations that actively involve students in using all the senses. This activates a variety of areas of brain that can be used to solve problems.

3. Introduce lots of problems that encourage students to look for patterns. Mathematics is the ideal subject for building on the natural tendency of the brain to learn by finding patterns. We even have a special brain wave, the P-300 wave, whose purpose in the brain is to look for patterns.

4. Use novel situations. The brain grows the most when stimulated by new problems and challenges.

5. Encourage students to construct their own knowledge and make connections between new knowledge and old. We remember things longer when we can develop our own understanding, not just memorize what someone has told us. Constructed knowledge appears to go directly into a long-term memory portion of the brain while memorized facts are stored in a different location that is more short term.

6. Select learning activities that encourage students to use a variety of learning styles. We all can get better at tasks that may not seem to fit our learning styles, such as drawing three-dimensional figures when we are better at computation. A preferred style may not be the strongest or best suited to the task. We should help children develop several skills to choose from.

7. Have fun in your mathematics classes. Use strategy games such as Tetris and chess and brainteasers to show students that learning math can be fun. Having fun sets off chemical reactions in the brain that open the neurons to learning and prevent the "fight-or-flight" fear response.

8. Believe that every child is intelligent and can be successful, and encourage parents and the students themselves to do the same. This also sets off chemical reactions in the brain that open the brain to learning.

9. Allow students time to daydream or "sleep on" difficult problems. This may allow slower brain waves, the theta and delta waves, and the preconscious mind to take over and open the way for novel and creative solutions.

10. Challenge yourself as well as your students; learn new skills, take new classes, read challenging books, and work on difficult mathematics problems. The more new skills you learn and the more difficult problems you solve, the more your brain will grow and prepare for even more learning.

Weblinks 2–1 through 2–4 provide additional brain-functioning information. You are invited to investigate these resources.

LEARNING STYLES AND MULTIPLE INTELLIGENCES.

All of us are multisensory learners who process information from a variety of stimuli in a variety of ways. Howard Gardner developed a multidimensional concept of intelligence in 1983 that has been used by teachers around the world to develop curricula that address nine forms of intelligence, including verbal/linguistic, logical/mathematical, visual/spatial, musical/rhythmic, bodily/kinesthetic, interpersonal (working with others), intrapersonal (knowing oneself), and, more recently, naturalist, and existentialist. Gardner's work as well as that of several others who look at differences in learning styles and intelligence point out how important it is to recognize that not all children will learn best in the same way we did. Two websites that provide some beginning information about multiple intelligences may be found at Weblinks 2–5 and 2–6.

Many of us who are teachers or are preparing to be teachers have entered this profession because we ourselves were good in school. We learned well, frequently in very traditional classes that emphasized memorization and practice. It is sometimes difficult for us to realize that many other students in our classes were not as successful. In mathematics, children who were not good at memorizing the information in the way the teacher or the book presented it might have become excellent mathematicians but often were stymied in their attempts to use their own strong, but unique, methods of solving problems. We now know that if we want to have powerful mathematical thinkers, we must encourage and build upon these different modes of thinking and methods of solving problems. Mathematical proficiency is a goal worth pursuing. To reach the goal means that mathematics instruction must be more than textbook instruction, more than memory, more than using physical objects. Mathematics instruction is dynamic, requiring us to focus on reasoning, thinking, reflection, and understanding. For example, in its publication *EDThoughts*, Mid-continent Research for Education and Learning told us, "Reasoning skills need to be continually developed through curricula that build on students' existing knowledge, but that present disequilibrium or discrepancies that call for resolution and continuation of the development of knowledge" (2002, p. 15). Continuing, this publication noted, "Striving to explain their thinking helps students clarify their own ideas, even when their thinking is not totally clear, or their understanding is not well formulated. Students who must explain their thinking organize their thoughts differently, analyzing the strategies they employed by engaging in self-reflection and analysis" (2002, p. 16). The NCTM added, "Researchers and experienced teachers alike have found that when children in the elementary grades are encouraged to develop, record, explain, and critique one another's strategies for solving computational problems, a number of important kinds of learning can occur" (2000, p. 35). These and other aspects of the teaching dynamic will be developed in this book.

Developing Fluency Once Concepts Are Formed

The concepts and experiences acquired by a person make up the knowledge that person possesses. As new experiences occur, they are fitted into a person's existing mental structure. This is the Piagetian process of assimilation. Depending on the familiarity of the experiences and the learning style of the learner, the experiences are received or rejected because of a person's mental structure or schema. The schema is a part of the mind used to build up the understanding of a topic. Thus, to increase or alter what is already known, the schema takes in new ideas and fits them with what is already known. Understanding a concept means an appropriate schema has accommodated that concept.

The idea of schema and how it functions provides a powerful tool for teaching mathematics. That a mental framework can be identified and developed means that mathematical relationships, patterns, and ideas can be understood rather than merely memorized; in the long run, children will have the ability to build up mathematical knowledge. When rules are memorized, children reach a point in their mathematical learning at which they are unable to remember the rules and are unable to continue learning. Understanding has long since vanished. As mathematics is introduced, its understanding is predicated on children's having already developed appropriate early schemas. As the National Research Council noted, "A critical feature of effective teaching is that it elicits from students their pre-existing understanding of the subject matter to be taught and provides opportunities to build on—or challenge—the initial understanding" (2000, p. 15). The implications are clear. Teachers should provide mathematical experiences in a form that will ensure that the mathematics is understood. Such a foundation provides a basis for all later mathematical understanding.

Developing concepts and understanding, when combined with computational proficiency, leads to fluency and the ability to apply what has been learned. The NCTM has emphasized that fluency or computational fluency, a ready command of computational processes, means that students are

. . . using a combination of mental strategies and jottings on paper or using an algorithm with paper and pencil, particularly when the numbers are large, to produce accurate results quickly. Regardless of the particular method used, students should be able to explain their method, understand that many methods exist, and see the usefulness of methods that are efficient, accurate, and general. Students also need to be able to estimate and judge the reasonableness of results. Computational fluency should develop in tandem with understanding of the role and meaning of arithmetic operations in number systems. (2000, p. 32)

Not only is it important for a seven-year-old to add two numbers such as 18 + 17; it is also important that he be able to effectively explain how he accomplished the task. Likewise, a ten-year-old student needs to effectively explain to her cooperative group members why .8 is greater than .65 when 65 is greater than 8.

Central to elementary school mathematics instruction is developing computational fluency. Central to computational fluency is making sense of numbers and operations and developing contributory concepts. Fluency will be further discussed throughout this book as we focus on various types of computation.

Children's Communication of Mathematical Concepts

"Mathematics as communication" is a common thread woven throughout all levels of the NCTM Standards. It was noted, "Communication is an essential part of mathematics and mathematics education. It is a way of sharing ideas and clarifying understanding. Through communication, ideas become objects of reflection, refinement, discussion, and amendment. The communication process also helps build meaning and permanence for ideas and makes them public" (2000, p. 60). As students mature, so does their ability to communicate. A middle school student's questions about concepts and skills or that student's writing about or discussing a problem provide the opportunity to broaden the thinking process. It is the middle school teacher's challenge to promote reading, writing, and communicating about problems to enhance mathematical understanding.

Children think quantitatively long before they engage in their first school activities. They have explored their personal space, and they begin to think about the proximity of objects; that is, they become aware that some objects are near to them while others are farther away. They notice that fingers are close to a wrist or an arm, eyes are near the nose, and grandparents live far away (even if they live down the street).

Order is another spatial relationship children observe. A child may have noticed the order of the cars on the toy train in the playpen or may be aware of the sequence of significant events. When the child cries, a parent appears, then holds and comforts the child.

Children classify objects as belonging together or not belonging together, for example, close family members versus neighbors and friends. They begin to judge objects as being few or many, big or small, tall or short, fast or slow. Obviously, they are not studying mathematics per se. The children are, however, making quantitative observations about their world.

As children experience quantitative events and develop language to express these ideas, they are able to communicate with others. They are developing the ability to classify objects and events more precisely. Although the language that emerges may not sound mathematical, it does represent the foundation on which the more exact language of mathematics is built. When children discriminate by *volume,* they may use the following words:

much	lots	some	empty
more	all	full	huge
less	little		

When discriminating by *size,* children may use the following words or phrases:

big	little	tall	bigger than
short	biggest	wide	smaller than
thin	fat	long	fatter than

When indicating *time,* children may use the following words or phrases:

before	now	spring	when the bell rings
after	later	winter	
yesterday	tomorrow	last summer	when it gets warmer

When discussing the *location* of objects, children may use the following words or phrases:

here	there	inside	on top of
up	down	outside	in the box
over	under	above	below

When describing *how many,* children may use counting strategies that they have developed through a variety of contexts. Fuson and Hall reported that children acquire a variety of number word meanings by their use in sequential, counting, cardinal, measure, ordinal, and non-numerical contexts (1983). Counting is an important part of quantitative learning.

Children develop language in concert with their experiences. The experiences are crucial for the language

to make sense. In the initial stages of mathematics learning, the quantitative experiences must be closely connected to the language that describes those experiences. Pre-kindergarten, elementary, and middle school students often benefit from using physical models before they are exposed to the language describing the concepts that are being learned. A serious mistake occurs when addition is taught before the child can bridge the gap between the intuitive notion of addition (usually involving counting and manipulating objects) and the symbolic representation of addition.

Communication is an important standard in *Principles and Standards for School Mathematics.* The NCTM emphasizes the importance of oral and written discourse and also a variety of other ways to communicate. The paraphrased communication standard, stated for all students from pre-kindergarten through grade 12, focuses on four areas: (1) organizing and consolidating mathematical thinking through communication; (2) communicating mathematical thinking coherently and clearly to peers, teachers, and others; (3) analyzing and evaluating the mathematical thinking and strategies of others; and (4) using the language of mathematics to express mathematical ideas precisely (2000, p. 60).

Providing mathematical activities and events that promote communication is an important part of our task as teachers. Another part is taking the time to encourage students to communicate in some form—with pictures, discussions, diagrams, writing, or symbols. A textbook or workbook alone cannot perform this function. Students should be physically and mentally active. Figure 2–3 illustrates the mathematical writing of a second-grade student. Cody and his fellow students were given this problem: You are going to make a macaroni necklace. The first macaroni will be plain, the next one will be colored, the next will be plain, then two will be colored, the next will be plain, then three will be colored. This pattern continues until there are five colored macaroni. Show how many of each kind of macaroni are needed for the whole necklace. The thinking process is enhanced and the mathematics makes more sense when communication becomes a regular part of the classroom culture.

To support classroom discourse effectively, teachers must build a community in which students will feel free to express their ideas. (NCTM, 2000, p. 61)

Thinking Like a Mathematician

As teachers of mathematics, we want our students to develop thinking dispositions that reflect the thinking processes of mathematicians. This is not to suggest that

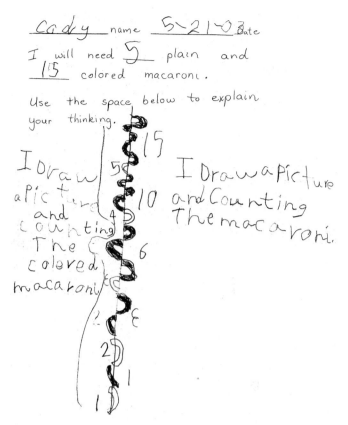

Cody _____ name 5-21-03 Date
I will need 5 plain and
15 colored macaroni.

Use the space below to explain
your thinking.

I Draw a picture and counting the colored macaroni.

I Draw a Picture and Counting The macaroni.

Figure 2–3 Cody's solution to the macaroni necklace problem.

we should attempt to make every, or even most, students mathematicians. We can, however, work toward improving thinking processes for all students.

THINKING SKILLS AND BEYOND. Thinking skills are prized in classrooms. They are prized because individuals who possess strong thinking skills such as reasoning, reflecting, and questioning are able to delve more deeply into knowledge and are able to solve challenging problems. These individuals are disposed to higher levels of thinking because theirs is a culture of deep thinking, and they are in the habit of thinking. In this section we focus on this culture of deep thinking.

Ritchhart has coined the term *intellectual character* to refer to "the overarching conglomeration of habits of mind, patterns of thought, and general dispositions toward thinking that not only direct but also motivate one's thinking-oriented pursuits" (2002, p. xxii). We suggest reading over Ritchhart's definition of intellectual character several times to help understand what he is saying. It is a powerful statement.

> We must educate students to act smart, not just to be smart. (Ritchhart, 2002, p. 34)

Developing intellectual character requires teachers who have the disposition to think and reason in depth. If we are to help students improve their thinking abilities, we must model our own abilities. We must, according to McREL:

> [P]robe for greater justification of student-generated ideas and deeper explanations of relationships and of how mathematics works using questions such as
>
> How does this operation work?
>
> What generalization can you make from this mathematical situation? Defend your ideas.
>
> What alternative strategy can you develop for this procedure?
>
> How can you justify your answer?
>
> What patterns or relationships apply to this problem? Describe the ones you found. (2002, p. 79)

The habits of mind that Ritchhart discussed are developed in classrooms where there is a culture of thinking, where norms are established for students to work toward. This begins when we as teachers set expectations for the students at the beginning of the school year followed by some sort of project or focus. There are a variety of behaviors that we may employ to encourage the development of intellectual character. A good place to begin is with guiding questions that get to the very essence of the mathematics problem being considered. The questions should center on the "why" or "how" of the problem. Children and teachers should strive to go, in the words of Bruner, "beyond the information given." (1973)

Ritchhart's words demonstrate the powerful nature of intellectual character:

> If we truly want smarter children, we need to know what smart looks like and stop confusing it with speed and knowledge. We also need to recognize that much of the substance of schooling is fleeting. After the final test has been taken, when students have long since left our doorways and the chalkboard has been erased for the last time, what will stay with our students isn't the laundry list of names, dates, computations, and procedures we have covered. What endures are the dispositions and habits of character we have been able to nurture. What stays with us, what sticks from our education, are the patterns of behavior and thinking that have been engrained and encultured over time. These are the residuals of education. These are the foundations of intellectual character. (2002, p. 229)

Reaching the ideal of intellectual character with students may be a long-term goal for us. If we believe that such a goal is a worthy one, then we can start with our personal quest for intellectual character and we can encourage our students to start as well. You are encouraged to read Ritchhart's book to see examples of intellectual character in action.

AN EXAMPLE OF MATHEMATICAL POWER. We mentioned mathematical power in Chapter 1. Recall that it refers to the ability of students to engage in challenging mathematical thought and communication. We present here an example of developing mathematical power taken from the NCTM Professional Teaching Standards. It is one of the annotated vignettes presented in the Standards. In this example primary students are working with the concept of division.

5.1 A class of primary students has been working on problems that involve separating or dividing. The teacher, Laurie Morgan, is trying to give them some early experience with multiplicative situations at the same time that she provides them with contexts for deepening their knowledge of and skill with addition and subtraction. These students can add and subtract, but their understanding of multiplication and division is still quite informal. They have begun to develop some understanding of fractions, connected to their ideas about division. They have not yet learned any conventional procedures for dividing.

The teacher has selected this problem because it is likely to elicit alternative representations and solution strategies as well as different answers. It will also help the students develop their ideas about division, fractions, and the connections between them.

Today Mrs. Morgan has given them the following problem:

If we make 49 sandwiches for our picnic, how many can each child have?

After they have worked for about twenty minutes, first alone and then in small groups, Mrs. Morgan asks if the children are ready to discuss the problem in the whole group. Most, looking up when she asks, nod. She asks who would like to begin.

The teacher allows time for the children to develop their solutions independently, with a few others, and then in the whole group. By asking who would like to share their solution, she encourages the students to take intellectual risks.

Two girls go to the overhead projector. They write:

$$
\begin{array}{r}
49 \\
-28 \\
\hline
22
\end{array}
$$

One explains, "There are twenty-eight kids in our class, and so if we pass out one sandwich to each child, we will have twenty-two sandwiches left, and that's not enough for each of us, so there'll be leftovers."

Students expect to have to justify their solutions, not just give answers.

The teacher and students are quiet for a moment, thinking about this. Then Mrs. Morgan looks over the group and asks if anyone has a comment or a question about this solution.

The teacher solicits other students' comments about the girls' solution without labeling it right or wrong. She expects the students, as members of a learning community, to decide if an idea makes sense mathematically.

One boy says that he thinks their solution makes sense, but that "nine minus eight is one, not two, so it should be twenty-one, not twenty-two." He demonstrates by pointing at the number line above the chalkboard. Starting at nine, he counts back eight using a pointer. The two girls ponder this for a moment. The class is quiet. Then one says, "We revise that. Nine minus eight is one." Mrs. Morgan is listening closely, but does not jump into the interchange.

Students respectfully question one another's ideas. The girls "revise" their solution because they have been convinced by the boy's explanation. There is no sense here that being wrong is shameful.

Another child remarks that he had the same solution as they did—one sandwich. "Frankie?" asks Mrs. Morgan, after pausing for a moment to look over the students. She remembers noticing his approach during the small-group time. Frankie announces, "I think we can give each child more than one sandwich. Look!" He proceeds to draw twenty-one rectangles on the chalkboard. "These are the leftover sandwiches," he explains. "I can cut fourteen of them in half and that will give us twenty-eight half-sandwiches, so everyone can get another half."

The students work together to solve the problem. Sometimes they build on the solutions offered by classmates. The teacher gathers insights about students through close listening and observation. At times, she takes responsibility for pushing students' thinking along.

"I agree with Frankie," says another child. "Each child can have one and a half sandwiches."

"Do you have any leftovers?" asks the teacher.

"There are still seven sandwiches left over," says Frankie.

"What do the rest of you think about that?" inquires the teacher.

The teacher expects the students to reason mathematically.

Several children give explanations in support of Frankie's solution. "I think that does make sense," says one girl, "but I had another solution. I think the answer is one plus one-half plus one-fourth."

Students seem willing to take risks by bringing up different ideas.

"I don't understand," Mrs. Morgan says. "Could you show what you mean?"

The teacher expects students to clarify and justify their ideas. (1991, pp. 58–59)

Reprinted with permission from Professional Standards for Teaching Mathematics, 1991 by the National Council of Teachers of Mathematics.

These students are gaining mathematical power as they participate in solving the sandwich problem. The teacher helps orchestrate the discussion and thinking process.

FOR YOU AS A TEACHER: IDEAS FOR DISCUSSION AND YOUR PROFESSIONAL PORTFOLIO

This section is intended to provide you the opportunity to read, write, and reflect on key elements of this chapter. We list several discussion ideas. We hope that one or more of these ideas will prove interesting to you and that you will choose to investigate and write about the ideas. The results of your work should be considered as part of your professional portfolio. You might consider these two questions as guides for your writing: "What does the material in this chapter mean for you as a teacher?" or "How can what you are reading be translated into a teaching practice for you as a teacher?"

DISCUSSION IDEAS

1. Developing understanding is a fundamental part of mathematics instruction. Read a chapter of your choice from Fennema and Romberg (1999), *Mathematics Classrooms That Promote Understanding*. Discuss the meaning of this chapter and how it might affect you as a teacher.

2. Expand your knowledge of constructivism by reading the book by Brooks and Brooks (1993), one of the books by Kamii (1985, 1989), or the article by Clements (1997). Become comfortable discussing the theory and how its application to teaching mathematics can enhance children's learning.

3. Discuss the difference between "understanding" a concept and "understanding" a skill, for example, understanding addition and understanding how to add.

4. Read Skemp's (1978) article "Relational Understanding and Instrumental Understanding." After reading it, discuss the role of the teacher in developing conceptual understanding.

5. Investigate intellectual character by reading all or parts of Ritchhart's (2002) book *Intellectual Character: What It Is, Why It Matters, and How To Get It*. Reflect on Ritchhart's message. Write about your reflections.

6. Go to The Math Forum home page on the Internet (Weblink 2–7). Investigate The Math Forum as a teacher and student resource. Describe the various parts of Forum Features. How can this site be useful to you as a teacher?

ADDITIONAL RESOURCES

REFERENCES

Allardice, Barbara S., and Herbert P. Ginsburg, "Children's Psychological Difficulties in Mathematics," in *The Development of Mathematical Thinking*, ed. Herbert P. Ginsburg. New York: Academic Press, 1983.

Baroody, Arthur J., and Herbert P. Ginsburg, "The Relationship between Initial Meaningful and Mechanical Knowledge of Arithmetic," in *Conceptual and Procedural Knowledge: The Case of Mathematics*, ed. James Hiebert. Hillsdale, NJ: Erlbaum, 1986.

Brooks, Jacqueline Grennon, "Teachers and Students: Constructivists Forging New Connections," *Educational Leadership*, 47, no. 5 (February 1990), 68–71.

Brooks, Jacqueline Grennon, and Martin G. Brooks, *The Case for Constructivist Classrooms*. Alexandria, VA: Association for Supervision and Curriculum Development, 1993.

Brownell, William A., "Psychological Considerations in the Learning and the Teaching of Arithmetic," in *The Teaching of Arithmetic* (National Council of Teachers of Mathematics, the Tenth Yearbook). New York: Bureau of Publications, Teachers College, Columbia University, 1935.

Brownell, William A., and H. E. Moser, *Meaningful vs. Mechanical Learning: A Study in Grade III Subtraction* (Duke University Research Studies in Education, No. 8). Durham, NC: Duke University Press, 1949.

Bruner, Jerome S., "Going Beyond the Information Given," in *Beyond the Information Given: Studies in the Psychology of Knowing*, ed. Jeremy M. Anglin. New York: Norton, 1973.
———, *The Process of Education*. Cambridge, MA: Harvard University Press, 1977.

Burger, William F., and J. Michael Shaughnessy, "Characterizing the Van Hiele Levels of Development in Geometry," *Journal of Research in Mathematics Education*, 17, no. 1 (January 1986), 31–48.

Carpenter, Thomas P., "Conceptual Knowledge as a Foundation for Procedural Knowledge," in *Conceptual and Procedural Knowledge: The Case of Mathematics*, ed. James Hiebert. Hillsdale, NJ: Erlbaum, 1986.

Carpenter, Thomas P., and Richard Lehrer, "Teaching and Learning Mathematics with Understanding," in *Mathematics Classrooms That Promote Understanding*, ed. Elizabeth Fennema and Thomas A. Romberg. Mahwah, NJ: Erlbaum, 1999.

Clark, Barbara. *Growing Up Gifted*. Columbus, OH: Merrill Prentice Hall, 2002.

Clements, Douglas H., "(Mis?) Constructing Constructivism," *Teaching Children Mathematics*, 4, no. 4 (December 1997), 198–200.

Copeland, Richard W., *How Children Learn Mathematics*. Englewood Cliffs, NJ: Merrill/Prentice Hall, 1984.

Fennema, Elizabeth, and Thomas A. Romberg, eds., *Mathematics Classrooms That Promote Understanding*. Mahwah, NJ: Erlbaum, 1999.

Fennema, Elizabeth, Judith Sowder, and Thomas P. Carpenter, "Creating Classrooms That Promote Understanding," in *Mathematics Classrooms That Promote Understanding*, ed. Elizabeth Fennema and Thomas A. Romberg. Mahwah, NJ: Erlbaum, 1999.

Fuson, Karen, and James W. Hall, "The Acquisition of Early Number Word Meanings: A Conceptual Analysis and Review," in *The Development of Mathematical Thinking*, ed. Herbert P. Ginsburg. New York: Academic Press, 1983.

Gardner, Howard. *Frames of Mind: The Theory of Multiple Intelligences*. New York: Basic Books, 1983.
———, *Intelligence Reframed: Multiple Intelligences for the 21st Century*. New York: Basic Books, 2000.

Geary, David C., *Children's Mathematical Development: Research and Practical Applications*. Washington, DC: American Psychological Association, 1994.

Ginsburg, Herbert P., ed., *The Development of Mathematical Thinking*. New York: Academic Press, 1983.

Ginsburg, Herbert., and Sylvia Opper, *Piaget's Theory of Intellectual Development*. Englewood Cliffs, NJ: Prentice Hall, 1969.

Jensen, Eric. *Brain-Based Learning and Teaching*. Del Mar, CA: Turning Point Publishing, 1995.

Kamii, Constance Kazoko, *Young Children Reinvent Arithmetic*. New York: Teachers College Press, 1985.

———, *Young Children Continue to Reinvent Arithmetic*. New York: Teachers College Press, 1989.

———, "Constructivism and Beginning Arithmetic (K–2)," in *Teaching and Learning in the 1990s*, ed. Thomas J. Cooney and Christian Hirsch. Reston, VA: National Council of Teachers of Mathematics, 1990.

Mid-continent Research for Education and Learning, *EDThoughts: What We Know about Mathematics Teaching and Learning*. Edited by John Sutton and Alice Krueger. Aurora, CO. Mid-continent Research for Education and Learning, 2002.

National Council of Teachers of Mathematics, *Professional Standards for Teaching Mathematics*. Reston, VA: NCTM, 1991.

———, *Principles and Standards for School Mathematics*. Reston, VA: NCTM, 2000.

National Research Council, *Reshaping School Mathematics: A Philosophy and Framework for Curriculum*. Washington, DC: National Academy Press, 1990.

———, *How People Learn: Brain, Mind, Experience, and School*. Edited by John D. Bransford, Ann L. Brown, and Rodney R. Cocking, Committee on Developments in the Science of Learning, Commission on Behavioral and Social Sciences and Education. Washington, DC: National Academy Press, 2000.

———, *Adding It Up: Helping Children Learn Mathematics*. Edited by Jeremy Kilpatrick, Jane Swafford, and Bradford Findell, Mathematics Learning Study Committee, Center for Education, Division of Behavioral and Social Sciences and Education. Washington, DC: National Academy Press, 2001.

Piaget, Jean, *The Child's Concept of Number*. New York: Norton, 1965.

———, *To Understand Is to Invent*. New York: Viking, 1973.

Resnick, Lauren B., "A Developmental Theory of Number Understanding," in *The Development of Mathematical Thinking*, ed. Herbert P. Ginsburg. New York: Academic Press, 1983.

Romberg, Thomas A., and Thomas P. Carpenter, "Research on Teaching and Learning Mathematics: Two Disciplines of Scientific Inquiry," in *Handbook of Research on Teaching*, ed. Merlin C. Wittrock. Englewood Cliffs, NJ: Merrill/Prentice Hall, 1986.

Ritchhart, Ron. *Intellectual Character: What It Is, Why It Matters, and How to Get It*. San Francisco: Jossey-Bass, 2002.

Skemp, Richard R. "Relational Understanding and Instrumental Understanding," *Arithmetic Teacher*, 26, no. 3 (November 1978), 9–15.

———, *The Psychology of Learning Mathematics*. Hillsdale, NJ: Erlbaum, 1987.

Weaver, J. Fred, "Interpretations of Number Operations and Symbolic Representations of Addition and Subtraction," in *Addition and Subtraction: A Cognitive Perspective*, ed. Thomas P. Carpenter, James M. Moser, and Thomas A. Romberg. Hillsdale, NJ: Erlbaum, 1982.

Erna Yakel, Paul Cobb, Terry Wood, Grayson Wheatley, and Graceann Merkel, "The Importance of Social Interaction in Children's Construction of Mathematical Knowledge," in *Teaching and Learning in the 1990s*, ed. Thomas J. Cooney and Christian Hirsch. Reston, VA: National Council of Teachers of Mathematics, 1990.

WEBLINKS

Weblink 2–1: New Horizons for Learning website featuring resources and articles on brain functioning. http://www.newhorizons.org/

Weblink 2–2: Center for the Neural Basis of Cognition home page with links to various resources. http://www.cnbc.cmu.edu/OtherTrain/

Weblink 2–3: Dana Alliance for Brain Initiatives gateway to brain information. http://www.dana.org/

Weblink 2–4: Neuroscience for Kids, sponsored by the National Institutes of Health's National Center for Research Resources. http://faculty.washington.edu/chudler/neurok.html

Weblink 2–5: Thirteen Ed Online and Disney Learning Partnership's Tapping into Multiple Intelligences page. http://www.thirteen.org/edonline/concept2class/month1/index.html

Weblink 2–6: Walter McKenzie's Multiple Intelligences pages. http://surfaquarium.com/MI/index.htm

Weblink 2–7: The Math Forum home page. http://mathforum.org/

ORGANIZING FOR MATHEMATICS INSTRUCTION

As you read the following pages, consider these guiding questions:

1. What are the NCTM Standards for Teaching Mathematics?

2. In what ways can teachers enhance and guide learning?

3. What considerations should teachers take into account as they plan lessons in mathematics?

4. In what ways can students' mathematical learning be assessed?

5. What responsibilities do we have in teaching our diverse population of students?

6. What are the characteristics of children with special needs?

7. How would you describe a classroom that provides a supportive, learner-centered environment?

8. What kinds of learning aids support mathematics instruction?

NCTM Principles and Standards for School Mathematics

The Equity Principle

Excellence in mathematics education requires equity–high expectations and strong support for all students.

The Curriculum Principle

A curriculum is more than a collection of activities: it must be coherent, focused on important mathematics, and well articulated across the grades.

The Teaching Principle

Effective mathematics teaching requires understanding what students know and need to learn and then challenging and supporting them to learn it well.

The Learning Principle

Students must learn mathematics with understanding, actively building new knowledge from experience and prior knowledge.

The Technology Principle

Technology is essential in teaching and learning mathematics; it influences the mathematics that is taught and enhances students' learning.

The Assessment Principle

Assessment should support the learning of important mathematics and furnish useful information to both teachers and students.

NCTM (2000), pp. 12, 14, 16, 19, 22, 24. Reprinted by permission.

In the space below, write four or five personal goals for you as a teacher of mathematics. As you write out your goals, be sure to explain each one and how you expect to accomplish it as a classroom teacher. Understand that these goals are likely to change as you gain additional insights and experience.

REFLECTIONS AND REFINEMENT: After you have written your goals, compare them to some of those of your classmates. Did you respond in the same way? Did you gain any new insights? As you continue through this term, see whether you modify existing goals or develop new ones. Write your thoughts here.

STANDARDS FOR TEACHING MATHEMATICS

The NCTM published *Professional Standards for Teaching Mathematics* in order to "give direction for moving toward excellence in teaching mathematics" (1991, p. 7). For all who wish to improve teaching, these Standards provide guidance. We hope to be counted in that group, and we hope you will consider the recommendations of the NCTM as you look ahead to teaching mathematics. Among the Professional Teaching Standards are Standards for Teaching Mathematics, of which there are six. Each is discussed below.

Worthwhile Mathematical Tasks

The first of the Standards for Teaching Mathematics is Worthwhile Mathematical Tasks. The NCTM describes tasks as ". . . the projects, questions, problems, constructions, applications, and exercises in which students engage" (1991, p. 20). The Standard, which serves as a set of criteria for determining worthwhile tasks, states:

> The teacher of mathematics should pose tasks that are based on—
>
> sound and significant mathematics;
>
> knowledge of students' understandings, interests, and experiences;
>
> knowledge of the range of ways that diverse students learn mathematics;
>
> and that
>
> engage students' intellect;
>
> develop students' mathematical understandings and skills;
>
> stimulate students to make connections and develop a coherent framework for mathematical ideas;
>
> call for problem formulation, problem solving, and mathematical reasoning;
>
> promote communication about mathematics;
>
> represent mathematics as an ongoing human activity;
>
> display sensitivity to, and draw on, students' diverse background experiences and dispositions;
>
> promote the development of all students' dispositions to do mathematics. (1991, p. 25)

The importance of worthwhile tasks is grounded in the belief that quality mathematics instruction emerges from the kind of work that we provide for and expect from our students. This work, in order to enrich the learner, should be carefully selected. There are many sources for worthwhile tasks. The resources mentioned throughout this book are a place to start. Books like those in the NCTM Navigations series, beginning in 2001, which were designed to provide ideas, activities, and materials to help implement *Principles and Standards*

for School Mathematics, are a valuable source of worthwhile tasks. The NCTM website provides the opportunity to review the entire Navigations series (Weblink 3–1). Other valuable resources, such as Awesome Math Problems for Creative Thinking, are available to suggest motivating tasks to extend mathematics instruction beyond the mathematics textbook (Weblink 3–2). Books such as Burk, Snider, and Symonds, *Math Excursions 2* (1991), one of three books for kindergarten, grade 1, and grade 2, and Burns, *A Collection of Math Lessons from Grades 6 through 8* (1990), one of three books for various grades, describe lessons based on worthwhile tasks.

Journals such as *Teaching Children Mathematics* and *Mathematics Teaching in the Middle School* are good sources for worthwhile tasks as well. The Problem Solver section of *Teaching Children Mathematics* includes a problem each month and invites teachers to present it to their students and submit their work for publication in a future journal. This is a great opportunity for budding mathematicians to share their thinking with a wide and interested audience. *Principles and Standards for School Mathematics, Professional Standards for Teaching Mathematics*, and the NCTM website, which presents the electronic Standards, are good sources of illustrative tasks and annotated vignettes on teaching. Additional resource links may be found on the Northern Kentucky Mathematics Education website (Weblink 3–3). Other teachers in your building or district or who are presenters at conferences are also sources for worthwhile tasks. As the NCTM noted:

> Teachers should choose and develop tasks that are likely to promote the development of students' understandings of concepts and procedures in a way that also fosters their ability to solve problems and to reason and communicate mathematically. Good tasks are ones that do not separate mathematical thinking from mathematical concepts or skills, that capture students' curiosity, and that invite them to speculate and to pursue their hunches. (1991, p. 25)

The Teacher's Role in Discourse

Discourse is the communication of ideas and information. It refers to conversations, discussions, written material, and representations—all ways to express mathematical reasoning, thinking, reflection, and understanding. To make it clear that discourse goes beyond discussions of solutions to mathematical problems, the National Research Council reminds us that discourse ". . . should include discussion of connections to other problems, alternative representations and solution methods, the nature of justification and argumentation, and the like" (2001, p. 426). Discourse plays a fundamental role in the dynamic of classroom instruction.

We, as teachers, are responsible for managing the discourse in our classrooms. We influence the thinking of our students by the ways in which we respond to them. We should take care to provide opportunities for all students to be heard. We should raise questions and seek questions from all students. We should give all students the chance to justify and clarify their thinking. We should encourage all students to take risks, share failures along with successes, and ask why or why not. We should also encourage students to question their answers (both right and wrong) and not to be satisfied with merely answering the questions.

Among the most important aspects of discourse is questioning. Skillfully raising questions and helping students raise questions can enrich the level of thinking in a classroom. Listed below are a series of questions that teachers may ask. These are paraphrased from the NCTM Professional Standards (1991, pp. 3–4).

Questions that help students make sense of mathematics

What would you say about what Maryann said?

Why would you agree or disagree?

Who will explain a different way to arrive at the same answer?

How can you convince the rest of us that that makes sense?

Questions that help students determine whether a solution is mathematically correct

Why do you believe that?

Why is that true?

Why does that make sense to you?

How could you make a model to show that?

Questions that help students to reason mathematically

Why do you believe that that will always work?

What counterexample can you give us?

How would you prove that?

What assumptions are you making about this case?

Questions that help students to conjecture, invent, and solve problems.

What would happen if you . . .?

What pattern do you see?

What are the possibilities here?

What decision do you believe he should make?

Questions that help students make connections

How does this relate to . . .?

What have we learned before that was useful in solving this problem?

How was mathematics used in yesterday's newspaper? What example can you provide for this situation?

Notice that there is an expectation that the student will provide information or a justification for each question that is asked. Along with the questions is the need to provide time for the student to think about his or her response. Above all, listen to the student's response and expect others to listen as well. Encourage interaction among students. Paraphrase students' responses to show students that you are listening and to make sure that you have understood them correctly. Ask students to repeat what other students have said in their own words to encourage active listening on the part of all students.

While questioning is an important part of discourse, it is not the only part. As teachers, we are responsible for orchestrating all aspects of discourse. That includes providing rich learning experiences that beg to be discussed. It includes explaining our own thinking, using examples of thinking that lead to incorrect solutions or no solution as well as more successful thinking, and modeling our own procedures. It includes returning to concepts or problems dealt with previously to reflect on new understandings and connections to new concepts. It includes being aware of how and at what level different students participate. How we communicate mathematically is fundamental to our overall understanding of mathematics. Additional examples of discourse will be provided throughout this book.

Students' Role in Discourse

The students' role in discourse and the teacher's role in discourse are intertwined. While teachers orchestrate mathematics instruction, they should promote classroom discourse that engages students in discussing, problem solving, reflecting, questioning, conjecturing, justifying, and proving. The purpose of student discourse should to be to help students make sense of mathematical ideas. Students, as well as teachers, should ask thoughtful questions. Students should be comfortable challenging one another to explain and justify solutions and conjectures. Beyond oral exchanges, student discourse includes using representations, models, computer-based presentations, written explanations, and physical materials. Figure 3–1 illustrates the writing of a fourth-grade student discussing questions about division. For student discourse to flourish in the classroom, we need to make sure that norms of discourse are established at the same time as other norms for thinking are established. The result will be very exciting mathematics learning and the growth of mathematical power in students.

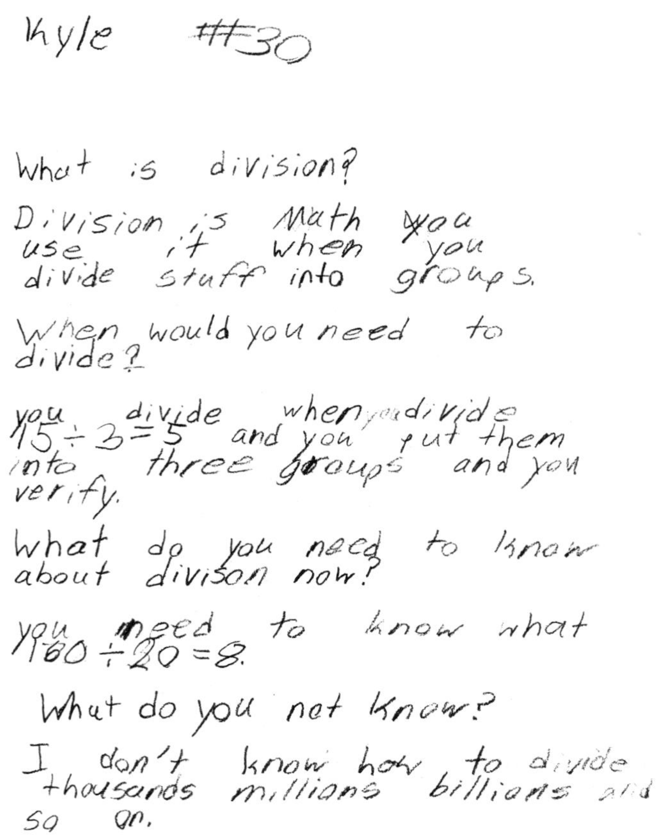

Kyle   ##30

What is division?
Division is Math you
use it when you
divide stuff into groups.

When would you need to
divide?

you divide when you divide
$15 \div 3 = 5$ and you put them
into three groups and you
verify.

What do you need to know
about division now?

you need to know what
$1760 \div 20 = 8$.

What do you not know?

I don't know how to divide
thousands millions billions and
so on.

Figure 3–1 Fourth grader Kyle answers questions about division.

Tools for Enhancing Discourse

When the NCTM encourages teachers to use tools to enhance discourse, it

encourages teachers to accept the use of—

computers, calculators, and other technology;

concrete materials used as models;

pictures, diagrams, tables, and graphs;

invented and conventional terms and symbols;

metaphors, analogies, and stories;

written hypotheses, explanations, and arguments;

oral presentations and dramatizations. (1991, p. 52)

With such varied tools available, students are able to pick the most appropriate ones for their particular discourse. The selection may relate to the mathematical problem being considered or it may relate to the learning style of an individual student. The selection may be determined by a small group of fifth-grade students working on a class presentation or by a table of kindergarten students explaining how to sort large Cuisenaire rods. The varied tools for enhancing discourse fit closely with our assessment of mathematical learning. As we discuss assessment,

we will expand on how discourse provides rich information.

Learning Environment

The learning environment encouraged in the NCTM *Professional Standards for Teaching Mathematics* refers to a type of intellectual climate ". . . in which serious mathematical thinking can take place; a genuine respect for others' ideas, a valuing of reason and sense-making, pacing and timing that allow students to puzzle and to think, and the forging of a social and intellectual community" (1991, p. 57). We mentioned earlier the need to establish norms in the classroom that lead to an environment in which "serious mathematical thinking can take place." These norms should be introduced as the school year begins and should reflect the importance of the intellectual climate at the same time that attention is given to establishing the classroom routines.

Notice in the NCTM statement above the stress on respect for others' ideas. This is a fundamental part of successful classroom interaction and one that deserves our time and patience to achieve. Likewise, when reason and sense-making are valued, time must be allocated for reflection and questioning to take place. Diverse thought processes should be respected. Finally, a social and intellectual community refers to large- and small-group interaction in which problem solving, thinking, puzzling, risk taking, and discussing can flourish and where a community of learners can thrive.

Ritchhart provides an example of a group brainstorming session that might take place in an upper elementary or middle school classroom to begin to develop the intellectual climate for the year:

In this class, I'm interested in helping you to develop your thinking, to become better thinkers. I'm working at trying to understand just what that will mean for us as a class, and I want to involve you in that process. In small groups, I'd like for you to generate a list of what you consider good thinking to be about. What does good thinking look like? What does it involve? What kinds of things do you need to be doing to be a good thinker both in this class and in the world? We'll then work from your lists to come up with a core set of thinking qualities and actions that can guide our work together in this class. (2002, p. 241)

The learning environment standard includes providing physical space and materials that support learning mathematics. We will discuss the physical environment of the classroom later in the section on Creating a Supportive, Learner-Centered Classroom Environment.

Analysis of Teaching and Learning

Analysis and reflection on teaching and learning rely on information that we gather as we teach. Much of that information comes from our ongoing, broad-based assessment program. Included in assessment procedures are observations, questions, projects, interviews, tests, writing activities, and problem-solving activities. The curriculum is another source of information. Classroom discourse also provides important information.

As we gather information, we begin the process of comparing the results of our teaching with aspects of the teaching environment. Are the curriculum goals being met? Are our personal expectations being met? How can we adjust the program so that it might better fit our expectations? Are there specific concepts or skills that need to be revisited? How might I avoid this concern next year? Are students understanding as they learn? Does the mathematics make sense to them? Do we have opportunities for higher-level thinking? Are we developing intellectual character? How could the mathematics program be enhanced?

We should continually analyze information that we gather and reflect on how we might improve our instructional program. The three major parts of the Standards for Teaching Mathematics—tasks, discourse, and environment—provide a basis for analysis. Are we meeting the criteria outlined in each of these Standards? This is an ongoing challenge for our entire teaching career.

PREPARING TO TEACH CHILDREN MATHEMATICS

Getting ready to teach mathematics is an important and sometime daunting task. What can we do to best prepare ourselves to teach mathematics? How can we assure ourselves that we are ready for success? How can we build personal confidence for teaching mathematics? In the paragraphs below, we will consider four topics intended to help answer these questions.

Teachers' Mathematical Content and Pedagogical Knowledge

The combination of a strong mathematics' background and a strong pedagogical background are considered necessary for quality mathematics teaching. The NCTM *Professional Standards for Teaching Mathematics* spoke strongly of teachers' mathematical content: "The teacher should demonstrate a deep understanding of mathematical concepts and principles, connections between concepts and procedures, connections across mathematical topics . . . and connections between mathematics and other disciplines" (1991, p. 89). The teacher should also know how students learn and the techniques that facilitate learning. Others have echoed the call for teachers with strong backgrounds in mathematics and pedagogy. The National Research Council stated, ". . . the quality of instruction is a function of teachers' knowledge and use of mathematical content, teachers' attention to and handling of students, and students' engagement in and use of mathematical tasks" (2001, p. 315).

We all wish to be effective mathematics teachers. An interesting discussion may center on the meaning of effective mathematics teachers. Among the characteristics of effective teachers are the two we mentioned above. Of course, there are the specifics of effective teaching. We have already mentioned the development of thinking skills. We have mentioned how students learn mathematics. In fact, the main purpose of this textbook is to provide suggestions about how to help children develop mathematical knowledge and thinking. We hope you accept the challenge of building a strong personal mathematics base, that you continue to learn mathematics once you have started teaching, and that you will, as the NCTM suggested, develop in students a "disposition to do mathematics" by having ". . . the teacher communicate a love of mathematics and a spirit of doing mathematics that captures the notion that mathematics is an invention of the human mind" (1991, p. 104).

Do you have the disposition to do mathematics and to appreciate its beauty and power?

Teaching Styles and the Learning Environment

Teaching means posing challenging problems, directing, channeling, providing, suggesting, expecting, and encouraging children. It also means managing a classroom of diverse individuals—some who are happy to be there and cooperative, and a few who are reluctant to be there and combative. Some people consider teaching an art; others consider it a science. It must surely be some of both. Skillful teaching is difficult and tiring, but it is rewarding, too. Although much direction is given to teachers in carefully designed guides to textbooks and workbooks, the teaching of mathematics is improved immeasurably if we do the following:

1. Establish our personal teaching style based on our beliefs about mathematics, about how children should be treated, and about how children should be taught. Teaching style refers to teaching behaviors that are based on our collection of personal traits,

beliefs, strengths, and preferences. For example, if we believe that mathematics is the study of patterns and order, we are likely to teach using an inquiry, reasoning approach. Further, Mid-continent Research for Education and Learning (McREL) noted, "Teachers who believe it is important for students to learn mathematics with understanding embrace the use of investigations, mathematical discourse, and appropriate mathematical notation and vocabulary" (2002, p. 28). Our teaching style is an outgrowth of many factors. We should be aware of and willing to alter our teaching styles as we gain further knowledge and experience.

2. Extend our teaching beyond the basal textbook. Textbooks are a primary source of mathematics curriculum and learning. Mathematics, however, is so prevalent in our lives that its breadth cannot be contained in a textbook. Look for ways to extend mathematics instruction beyond the textbook. Doing so will enrich mathematical experiences for students.

3. Commit to being lifelong learners. As we continue to learn, we bring new enthusiasm to the classroom, enthusiasm that students perceive. In order to stay current in mathematics and mathematics education, we should willingly seek out sources of knowledge. Our continued learning is a personal and professional responsibility.

4. Work to develop a classroom culture with norms that focus on extending thinking and understanding. If we value thinking and understanding, then we should develop a community of learners in our classroom. That community should be guided by norms we establish beginning on the first day of school.

Your teaching style will evolve throughout your teaching career. You will find new techniques to try, perhaps from mentor teachers, from professional conferences you attend, from reading, from reflection, or from your students. These techniques may help alter your teaching style. You will become known by your style. Cherish its importance.

There are also numerous learning environments, and within them are many teaching-learning strategies. The learning environment consists of physical settings in which teaching and learning take place. Within the context of schooling, these physical settings are generally at or near the school building. Thus, the learning environment may be the physical organization of a classroom, the confines of the playground, a nature trail, an urban neighborhood, or an auditorium. Within the learning environment, a teacher's behavior toward a particular group of children is determined by that teacher's beliefs, experiences, education, and feelings. In developing teaching-learning strategies, the teacher should be aware that many alternatives exist.

Development of a particular strategy is the function of an individual teacher. Although it is recognized that there is no one best way to teach, if you teach in only one way (that is, using one strategy continuously), you are not as likely to succeed over a period of time as you are if you use several approaches. Teachers should be aware of more than one way of teaching and learning. Variety makes teaching and learning more interesting and enjoyable and reaches a greater number of students. This is true of teaching mathematics as well as of teaching reading, science, or social studies.

Planning for Problem-Based, Inquiry Learning

Problem-based, inquiry learning means that students engage in a process of investigation that is presented as a problem and requires the student to gather information, reflect on that information, discuss with others what has crossed the student's mind about the problem, and settle on a resolution of the problem. Using inquiry as part of the mathematics program means that we must seek worthwhile problems that engage the student in deep thinking. We must also develop the thinking processes that will encourage students to use inquiry skills. These skills include problem solving, questioning, discussing, information gathering, presenting, and persisting. Each skill needs to be nurtured and practiced over time. This is part of establishing norms for thinking in our classroom that lead to problem-based inquiry learning.

In the web-based, electronic examples that accompany the grades 3–5 Standards, the NCTM presents an activity that may be used as an inquiry project. The activity is one in which students use spreadsheets and graphing software to organize, represent, and compare data. "In the first part, Collecting and Examining Weather Data, students organize and then examine data that have been collected over a period of time in a spreadsheet. In the second part, Representing and Interpreting Data, students use the graphing functions of a spreadsheet to help them interpret data" (Weblink 3–4). You are encouraged to examine this electronic example.

The problem-based inquiry here is found in the types and depth of questions that are raised as this project is initiated and carried out. Questions that require hypotheses, comparison, conjecture, and synthesis extend beyond the questions that simply report the data. For example, based on our observations of January weather, what hypotheses might we make about the past five Januarys or about next January? What common elements are found in January weather and in July weather? What role do clouds play in January weather? Describing what the data show, what the data suggest, and what questions the data raise fits nicely in this project.

For inquiry learning to be effective, the classroom should be carefully organized. In its description of such a classroom, McREL explained:

> An effective investigative mathematics classroom resembles a laboratory. Classroom experiences should promote the development of students' reasoning, justification, and mathematics content skills. Students should be encouraged to use geometric representations for numeric and algebraic concepts, make and test conjectures, and be able to construct their own proofs. (2002, p. 47)

Such a classroom should bring mathematics to life. Problem-based inquiry learning should be commonplace.

Enhancing and Guiding Learning

The primary purpose of this textbook is to provide suggestions about how to help children develop understanding of and make sense of mathematical concepts and develop computational fluency. It is inappropriate for the authors to recommend a single approach to teaching pre-kindergarten through middle school mathematics. Because of the various ways in which individuals learn and the different personalities of learners and teachers, teachers must vary their strategies and adapt them to their own specific needs and those of their students. It is appropriate at this juncture to consider a framework in which successful teaching can take place.

Duckworth remarked:

> In most classrooms, it is the quick right answer that is appreciated. Knowledge of the answer ahead of time is, on the whole, more valued than ways of figuring it out . . . If a child spends time exploring all the possibilities of a given notion, it may mean that she holds onto it longer, and moves onto the next stage less quickly; but by the time she does move on, she will have a far better foundation—the idea will serve her far better, will stand up in the face of surprises. (1987, pp. 64, 71)

We, too, want to encourage you to help all of your students understand mathematics. Based on the recommendations of the National Research Council (2000, 2001) and the National Council of Teachers of Mathematics (1991, 2000), as well as our own reading, study, and teaching experience, we have developed the following guidelines for teachers. There are 10 principles to which we adhere in designing mathematics instruction. Each is discussed briefly in the list that follows:

1. *Provide developmental instruction.* Although most of the following principles help define developmental instruction, it is appropriate to keep your attention focused on this principle. Developmental instruction suggests that teachers should attend to the cognitive growth of their students. Learning how children think and the levels of their thinking is crucial to developmental instruction. In planning your teaching, keep the children foremost in your mind. You must continually assess the understanding and progress of the students.

2. *Engage the children in active learning.* Using physical models is a cornerstone of successful mathematics instruction. One part of constructing knowledge is exploring materials freely or in problem situations. Active learning may also mean engaging in cooperative learning projects or spirited exchanges of mathematical ideas. You will find many examples of activities in this textbook that are intended to suggest ideas for your teaching. You are challenged to develop activities of your own.

> The brain learns best and retains most when the organism is actively involved in exploring physical sites and materials and asking questions to which it actually craves answers. Merely passive experiences tend to attenuate and have little lasting impact. (Gardner, 1999, p. 82)

3. *Lead discussions, question children about their thinking, and encourage children to ask questions.* Children should be encouraged to explain their thinking, offer opinions, and exchange thoughts with other students. The teacher plays an important role in this process. The types of questions you ask can lead you to discover what and how a child understands. Duckworth suggested various kinds of questions:

> What do you mean? How did you do that? Why do you say that? How does that fit with what she just said? I don't really get that; could you explain it another way? Could you give an example? How did you figure that? In every case, those questions are primarily a way for the interlocutor to try to understand what the other is understanding. Yet in every case, also, they engage the other's thoughts and take them a step further. (1987, p. 97)

The teacher seeks to discover what the students understand by carefully questioning the children and by sharing opinions with them. Students are able to share their thinking in writing as well as orally. Writing should be encouraged throughout the mathematics program.

4. *Employ calculators and computers.* Calculators provide children with a means to explore mathematics and enjoy the challenge of problem solving. Children at all levels should have calculators available as tools in the learning process as well as during examinations. Computers also serve as powerful tools in the process and provide children

with opportunities to be problem solvers. Logo programming serves as a creative outlet for children in learning aspects of geometry. With the proliferation of sites on the Internet, students have many areas of mathematics to explore. A good example of such a site is The Math Forum (see Weblink 3–5). At this location, students may link to pages with problems of the week at their learning level, to specific pages of interest for elementary and middle level students, to a page where they can ask a mathematics question of "Dr. Math, " and to several other intriguing pages.

5. *Utilize student-centered instruction.* The ideas, opinions, and interests of the children are focal points around which instruction is centered. Word problems based on the children's environment help begin the guided learning process. State and local content goals for mathematics along with textbooks are necessary for a sound mathematics program. Coupled with the interests and curiosity of children, the content of mathematics becomes fertile ground for children's intellectual growth.

6. *Develop children's mathematical power.* Children gain power in mathematics when they understand the concepts and procedures that they have constructed. Having power means that children can apply mathematics to tasks and problems because they understand what they are doing. Having power in mathematics also means that children are able to reconstruct concepts and procedures when they have been forgotten. Mathematical power provides children with the confidence to attack problems and to persist when challenges arise.

7. *Encourage higher-level thinking.* Children should be challenged with problems, puzzles, and patterns throughout their learning of mathematics. The place to start is with examples from the students' own experiences. Stories that incorporate problems can be intriguing and can stimulate considerable divergent thinking. Provide problem-based inquiry learning. Consider developing intellectual character. Warm-up activities at the beginning of a mathematics lesson can lead to creative thinking. Encouraging children to pose problems will help them think differently about problem solving.

8. *Provide opportunities for children to construct and communicate mathematics.* When children construct mathematics through their experiences and interact with teachers and peers, they develop schemas that serve them well as they continue to learn mathematics. Their understanding of mathematics is powerful in the sense mentioned above. You have the opportunity to teach in a manner that encourages students to construct mathematical concepts for at least part of the time you teach

mathematics. Be prepared for an explosion of ideas as children invent mathematics. Encourage them to share their findings both orally and in writing.

9. *Teach diagnostically.* As children learn mathematics, teachers need to constantly monitor their progress. Assessing children's work and assisting them in overcoming their misconceptions are major teaching responsibilities. The primary techniques for gathering information are observing children and discussing their thinking processes with them. You should be aware of the personal logic of students and ways to interpret their thinking. By discovering how children think, you will be a more effective teacher.

10. *Introduce new techniques.* Throughout your teaching career, you will be invited to participate in workshops and conferences at which exciting ideas for teaching mathematics will be introduced. The presenters will be successful teachers and experts. Take advantage of these opportunities and employ those techniques that you believe will enrich your classroom. Read journals such as *Teaching Children Mathematics* and *Mathematics Teaching in the Middle School* to discover the trends and new directions in mathematics education. If you wish, accept the role of change agent.

In addition to these principles, there are other considerations to be taken into account. For example, the way in which students are organized for instruction is important. Johnson and Johnson (1987), in *Learning Together and Alone: Cooperative, Competitive, and Individualistic Learning,* develop a strong argument for providing cooperative learning experiences for children. Cooperating and sharing a common goal foster personal growth and identification. When cooperation is encouraged, competitive learning and individualistic learning are decreased. In many of the activities presented in this textbook, cooperative learning is suggested. A discussion of cooperative learning is included later in this chapter, along with a presentation of other useful suggestions for teaching.

FITTING INSTRUCTION TO STUDENTS' DIFFERING NEEDS AND STYLES

Both students and teachers have distinct needs and styles of operation in the classroom. Each child's personal learning style is unique to that child. The learning style determines how and when the child discovers relationships, learns to read, and develops the concepts of mathematics.

We have mentioned that students learn in different ways. Some learn best through tactile/kinesthetic experiences, that is, through touching objects and through physical movement. Auditory learners have the ability to listen to others and understand effectively. Those who are visual learners appreciate pictorial models. Students learn in all of these modes simultaneously but tend to excel in one particular mode.

Then there are students who find learning particularly difficult; they take more time, have less interest, and seem unable to grasp concepts and skills. Likewise, some students are fast learners, enjoy intellectual challenges, and are ready to move ahead. One child may be ill at ease, self-conscious, and shy; another child may be at home in the classroom, comfortable with the surroundings and other children. As a consequence, one child may learn slowly and may be dependent on an adult, whereas another child may learn quickly, barely assisted by the teacher.

When 25 or more students are brought together for instruction, the combinations of learning styles present a formidable challenge to a teacher. Likewise, your own personal teaching style affects how you teach. Your beliefs, experiences, education, and expectations of students's behavior will cause you to be a certain kind of teacher.

Learning and teaching must be carefully planned. Granted, some of the best learning is spontaneous or incidental, but for long-term, sequential learning to occur in an enriched environment, the teacher must lay the groundwork. You may wish to include students in the planning, to share the learning objectives with the students, and even to encourage the students to lead—all are a part of the learning process.

When you are organizing for mathematics instruction based on sound principles of learning, be sure to consider a variety of different and effective-teaching learning strategies. Other strategies will emerge as thoughtful teachers reflect on how they teach and wish to teach. A particular strategy is a function of the teacher and may be successful only under the conditions experienced by that individual. Be willing to try new approaches.

Planning for Teaching

Excellent teaching occurs, in part, because it is well planned. Teachers are seldom able to spontaneously lead students day after day without pondering, reflecting, deciding, anticipating, and researching. You must be every bit the learner you would expect one of your students to be.

Planning for teaching takes numerous forms. Newcomers to teaching must carefully plan their lessons, often writing a detailed lesson plan so that the teaching situation can be controlled and later analyzed by both the teacher and the cooperating teacher or supervisor. (See Appendix B for a lesson plan outline to assist in planning lessons.) When writing a plan, the student

teacher gains skill and confidence in his or her ability to think through the teaching act. Such a plan helps teachers develop a thinking process that eventually frees them from having to write out detailed lesson plans.

Guidelines for designing a lesson plan are presented below. It is assumed the mathematical topic (concept or skill) to be taught has been selected from a math textbook, school district curriculum guide, or a project or unit guide.

The lesson plan outline that we present here provides one way to structure a lesson that focuses on problem solving or a rich learning task. It is an "open" lesson plan outline because students may make sense of the mathematics in the lesson in a variety of ways.

Designing a Lesson Plan

I. Instructional Objectives: What are the big ideas in the NCTM Content and Process Standards or your state standards that this lesson addresses?

II. Context or Prior Knowledge Needed: How does this relate to your broad goals for this unit? What prior knowledge do the students have and what would they need before this lesson begins?

III. Terms, Symbols, or Vocabulary: Which of these will need to be reviewed or introduced during the lesson?

IV. Learning Materials, Physical Models, or Other Aids: How may these be used to enhance the learning?

V. Teaching Strategy

A. Relate: Describe the introductory activity that will engage the students by relating the new knowledge to be learned to previous learning and that will set the stage for the investigation or problem.

B. Investigate: Challenge the students with an investigation or problem that will help them make sense of the mathematical concepts to be learned.

C. Evaluate: How will you and the students determine whether they have mastered your instructional objectives?

D. Communicate: How will the students communicate their learning with others—journal entries, projects, presentations, and so on?

E. Create: What new questions might the students create to build on the ideas of this lesson?

VI. Reflection and Refinement: After you have taught the lesson, reflect on what you did well and what you might need to improve. Describe your ideas for improvement.

The lesson plan orchestrates the lesson. Be sure that discussions, questions, and reflection are an integral part of teaching the lesson. A copy of the lesson plan outline may be found in Appendix B. Figure 3–2 is an illustrative lesson using the outline and based on an algebra activity from Chapter 10.

Lesson Plan

Name: Chris Robinson

Date: November 3

Grade Level: 2   **Subject/Topic:** Writing Equations   **Time:** 9:35

Instructional Objectives: Students will be able to—

1. balance an equation using a pan balance
2. write equations describing balance problems
3. invent balance equations

Context or Prior Knowledge Needed: Students are learning the concept of solving equations. They should know the meaning of "equation," be able to write equations with variables, and know how to use a pan balance.

Terms, Symbols, or Vocabulary: variable, equation, pan balance.

Learning Materials, Physical Models, or Other Aids: 8 pan balances, 16 small paper bags, 200 2-cm cubes

Teaching Strategy:

Relate: Challenge students in table group of four to take five minutes to discuss and develop a definition of *equation* with reasons for their response. Have each group spokesperson share the definition. Develop a class consensus for the meaning of *equation.*

    Discuss use of the pan balance. If the two pans balance, this is similar to the equal sign in an equation telling you that the two sides are equal to the same amount. Describe the activity, having a student from each group put a secret number of cubes in a bag. This number of cubes may be called b cubes. The bag is then placed on the left pan along with two other cubes that are visible (see Figure 10–9). Students put enough cubes on the right pan to balance the left pan, such as the 6 in the figure. Ask the students in each group to try to write an equation describing what they see. Share responses. Have students justify $b + 2 = 6$ as a response. Then, have students in each group discuss how the secret number of cubes can be determined. Let one or two groups share their reasoning, and then check the bag to determine if they are correct.

Investigate: To challenge the students, take two bags and mark them each A and mark two additional bags with a B. Tell the students that each of the bags marked with an A has the same number of cubes and each bag marked with a B has the same number of cubes. A bags and B bags may or may not have the same number of cubes. Put one of the bags with an A and one of the bags with a B on the left side of the scale and add two additional cubes on the left side so the students can see them. Show that this balances 8 cubes on the right side of the scale. Ask the students to discuss all the possible solutions for the number of cubes that are in each of the bags. Students may wish to record this in a chart such as the following:

Bag A	Bag B
0	6
1	5
2	4
3	3
4	2
5	1
6	0

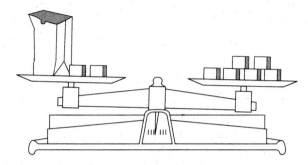

Ask the students to discuss in their groups how they might determine the number of cubes in each bag without peeking inside the bag and without just weighing one single bag. Groups might come up with a variety of suggestions. One group might suggest that you find the number of cubes that balance two of Bag A and then take half of that number. Look at the chart to determine how many cubes must be in Bag B once you determine the cubes in Bag A. Another group might suggest putting one Bag A and one Bag B on the left pan and balancing that with cubes on the right pan. Discuss whether this gives you any new information. (Note that $A + B + 2 = 8$ is the same as $A + B = 6$. You would still not know how many cubes were in each bag.)

Another group might suggest putting two Bag As on the left pan with one Bag B and balancing that with cubes on the right pan. Tell the students that this can be balanced by 10 cubes on the right pan and challenge the groups to use this information with the earlier information to determine how many cubes are in each pan.

Evaluate: Have the recorder for each group draw a representation of each of the four pan balance examples and record the equation shown.

Communicate: For this lesson, the record made by the group recorder for evaluation will serve as communication. Place the records on the bulletin board.

Create: Ask each group to see if they can make a different equation using more than one bag on the balance. If you have one or more groups who find this simple with two unknowns (Bags A and B), challenge them to add a third unknown with a Bag C and ask them to create problems for each other. Collect the results and add them to your bulletin board or a learning center so the students can continue to challenge each other.

Reflection and Refinement: To be completed following the lesson.

Figure 3–2   An illustrative lesson using the lesson plan outline from Appendix B.

By the time you begin full-time teaching, you should be able to plan a week at a time by jotting down topics and key ideas you wish to teach. You will not need to detail every activity but may write out activities that need special planning. Much of the planning, including objectives, activities, grouping, and room arrangement, can be done mentally, but it is sound practice to have the week's plans written out in global terms.

Experienced teachers also must plan. Experience has taught them what to expect, how to react, how to time a lesson, and ways to interest students. Most of the planning done by experienced teachers is done mentally and written in plan books that block out a week at a time. These block plans serve as an important guide throughout the week. Teachers must refine and prepare their teaching to fit the particular group of students with whom they are working. Experienced teachers are aware of their personal teaching styles and adjust their styles to fit the learning styles of their students. Experienced teachers can be a bit more spontaneous and less tied to a fixed lesson plan.

DEVELOPING PROBING QUESTIONS. Earlier in this chapter we discussed questioning in the section The Teacher's Role in Discourse. We listed a number of questions such as: Who will explain a different way to arrive at the same answer? What would happen if you . . .? What example can you provide for this situation? We reiterate the importance of these questions that seek thoughtful responses. They fall into the category of probing questions. As teachers, we should be ready to ask probing questions as we discuss mathematics. McREL cautioned:

Studies of questioning in typical mathematics classrooms confirm that most questions make minimal demands on student thinking. Low level questions include yes/no questions; guessing; simple recall of fact, formula, or procedure; leading or rhetorical questions; and those answered immediately by the teacher. Answers are often immediately judged right or wrong by the teacher, and the discussion moves to the next question. (2002, p. 16)

Effective teachers ask probing questions with high cognitive demand and ask clarifying questions to follow up. As a result, students learn to ask more questions as well. At another level, teaching students to ask questions as part of their problem-solving strategies provides them with a useful tool for their investigations. Questions such as these help students in their thinking process: What steps might I follow to solve this problem? Can I reverse the steps? Does a different, easier, or better way exist? We will present other examples of student questions in Chapter 4.

DESIGNING EFFECTIVE HOMEWORK. Effective homework is characterized by (1) parental involvement, (2) worthwhile tasks that are an extension of classroom work, and (3) student ownership of tasks. In the traditional classroom, students were shown a procedure or algorithm, given an assignment based on the procedure, and provided some class time to practice it. The rest of the assignment was homework. Whether it was completed or completed correctly was played out the next day in class. The general result of traditional mathematics homework was a dislike of mathematics.

Mathematics homework should be balanced with other demands for students' time and with the students' well-being in mind. Children still need time to be children, time for active play, without excessive amounts of time spent in front of a television set or a video screen. Students have classwork other than mathematics with which to contend. Teachers of younger children must carefully control the type and amount of homework. Middle school teachers should monitor the work required by other teachers to determine the cumulative amount of work expected of students. We are not suggesting that students should have homework every night.

Parents are a key to successful mathematics homework. We may need to remind parents that their negative attitudes about math may affect their child's attitude and performance. Parents should encourage their child to give the homework a try. Parents should show interest and curiosity about the assignment. Parents can model using mathematics by thinking out loud about daily activities that involve mathematics. Among these activities may be determining the amount of time it takes to get to work, figuring the amount of paint it will take to paint a room, calculating the amount of money it will take to pick up a few items at the local store, and balancing the checkbook. Parents perform many mathematics tasks each day as a regular part of life; likewise, children should be given the chance to do math around the house. Finally, there is an increasing number of children's books that have mathematical themes or that introduce puzzles and problems. Children enjoy story time and can benefit from stories that feature mathematics. In a classroom characterized by thinking, problem-solving activities and challenges prevail. Often they require computational fluency for their solutions. Just as worthwhile tasks are important in school for students to make sense of mathematics, worthwhile tasks are important as homework. Listed in the earlier section Worthwhile Mathematical Tasks were a set of criteria and a justification for worthwhile tasks. You may wish to return to that section and review its content. When homework is assigned, it should reflect the norms of the classroom. Thus, students should be expected to develop understanding and to reflect as a result of the assignment. For that to happen the assignment should, in the words of McREL, ". . . have clear criteria and/or written rubrics that describe expectations and establish student goals. The teacher must be certain that students have access to the materials and resources they will need to complete the assignment" (2002, p. 97). There will be times when development of fluency will be necessary to complete an assignment. In such cases, skill practice may be appropriate. Placing a major emphasis on basic skills practice at home is not recommended.

When students see an assignment's worthy and exciting, they develop ownership of the task. Such ownership provides motivation to complete the task, to complete it well, and to involve other members of the family. In one middle school classroom, students measured the size of their bedroom and then were challenged to design their dream bedroom using their own bedroom size and within a budget of $5000. Those with smaller bedrooms could design a two-story bedroom, provided they had a way to reach the second story. They used catalogs, newspapers, and a sheet of furniture dimensions in their designs. This project, lasting three weeks, involved entire families. Months after the completion of the project, parents commented on its positive effect on their children. Clearly, students developed ownership of the task. Such should be the case for homework assignments.

CREATING COMMUNITIES OF LEARNERS. We mentioned the dynamic of teaching earlier. In creating communities of learners, we are engaged in the dynamic of teaching. Communities of learners are found in classrooms where students work individually or together, share, and discuss mathematics with mutual respect. Communities of learners are characterized by norms of thinking and by high teacher expectations for all students. In such classrooms all subjects, including mathematics, are approached thoughtfully.

As new teachers, we are sometimes convinced that developing classroom rules and standards of behavior comes first and foremost when we begin the school year. Of course it is important to develop classroom routines that lead to productive classroom environments and interaction among students. It is equally important to lay the groundwork for mathematical understanding and thinking. Ritchhart sums it up well:

> If teachers judge success by classroom order and by students' working quietly and independently, then it makes sense for them to emphasize rules and consequences early on. However, if they judge success by intellectual character, then it may make more sense to focus on thinking-rich learning routines at the beginning of the year to establish a culture of thinking. The former procedure conveys an implicit message that school is about completing work—often nonsensical and meaningless to the student—quickly, quietly, and efficiently and that learning happens in externally structured and controlled environments. The latter position conveys to students that learning and school are about thinking and engaging with curricular content as a part of a community. (2002, p. 221)

We need to decide for ourselves what schools are about. If you agree with Ritchhart, then working toward a community of learners should become a personal teaching goal.

Cooperative Learning

Among the decisions that we make in planning for teaching is how students will be grouped. In classrooms where collaborative work is valued, cooperative learning is a common teaching approach. In the following paragraph, competition and cooperation are discussed.

COMPETITION. After visiting classrooms to observe, participate with, or teach children, you may begin to develop various concerns. Typical among comments is the following: "I saw the children playing a computation game and the boys were against the girls. The girls always seemed to win, and the teacher constantly praised the girls for being so fast. Competition is useful, isn't it? After all, life outside of school is competitive and students need to learn to compete early to survive." Typical among commercial advertisements is one telling consumers that "Being the best is not everything; it is the only thing." Seldom can one be "the best," but competition is heightened. In the classroom, emphasis on being the best, fastest, or brightest can prove destructive. For every "best" child in a group of 25, 24 feel less able, weaker, or insignificant. Diminishing the worth of children through competition can diminish the worth of the entire group. Employing competition to improve motivation or quality is often ineffective. The students who can win compete, but the others ignore the competition. A firm distinction must be maintained between *being the best* and *doing one's best.* This is not to say that all competitive situations are harmful. Friendly competition sometimes increases friendship and common appreciation among competing individuals or groups.

Cooperating and having a common cause foster personal growth and identification. Mathematics learning should be cooperative. Cooperation involves other people in constructive roles. Students who receive support from others can see the worth of working together as opposed to working against one another. More productive personal growth results through cooperation than through competition. But cooperation does not just happen; it is learned and requires a teacher who is a model of the cooperative spirit.

GROUPING. The nature of young children does not lend itself to extensive group work. Pre-kindergarten children work best in settings where other children are nearby and with some adult-led small-group activities. Six-year-olds have not fully developed the capacity to work in groups. They do enjoy games involving several other children, but these games should allow them considerable individual freedom. This is the time to introduce whole-class and small-group activities and to carefully guide children through the activities. When whole-class projects are undertaken, the teacher is the catalyst and leader. Likewise, opportunities arise to teach sharing and cooperation by developing small-group projects, such as dramatic play or mathematics activities with a short-term, definite purpose.

Eight-year-olds have developed sufficiently to work in small groups with considerable adult leadership. They are able to understand tasks and to work through them. They are able to respond to the teacher's questions and guidance. They are learning to cooperate without constantly grappling for attention. They are able to assume some leadership in small groups but can rarely lead the entire class. Take care to teach skills of democratic living and to provide time for these skills to be practiced. This is the beginning of a lifelong learning process in group interaction.

Ten-year-olds can effectively work in groups with little adult supervision. At this age, the group tasks and individual responsibilities must be well defined. Those who work well together will be pleased with the group product. Individual students can assume leadership roles and are comfortable leading the whole class.

Grouping students in cooperative learning groups as an alternative to competitive and individualistic learning has emerged in the writings of Johnson and Johnson and others. **Cooperative learning** is an organizational pattern in which students work together in small groups to accomplish academic and collaborative tasks as in Figure 3–3. The proponents of cooperative learning point to the advantages and benefits to students of working together for a common purpose. Johnson and Johnson discuss these advantages:

> Achievement will be higher when learning situations are structured cooperatively rather than competitively or individualistically. Cooperative learning experiences, furthermore, promote greater competencies in critical thinking, more positive attitudes toward the subject areas studied, greater competencies in working collaboratively with others, greater psychological health, and stronger

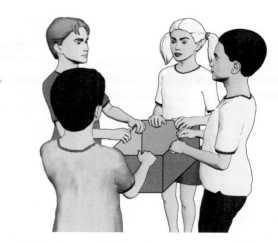

Figure 3–3 Cooperative learning group constructing a rectangular prism.

perceptions of the grading system's fairness. The implications of these results for teachers are as follows:

1. Cooperative learning procedures may be used successfully with any type of academic task, although they are most successful when conceptual learning is required.

2. Whenever possible, cooperative groups should be structured so that controversy and academic disagreements among group members are possible and are managed constructively.

3. Students should be encouraged to keep each other on task and to discuss the assigned material in ways that ensure elaborative rehearsal and the use of higher level learning strategies.

4. Students should be encouraged to support each other's efforts to achieve; to regulate each other's task-related efforts; to provide each other with feedback; and to ensure that all group members are verbally involved in the learning process.

5. As a rule, cooperative groups should contain low-, medium-, and high-ability students to help promote discussion, peer teaching, and justification of answers.

6. Positive relationships among group members should be encouraged. (1987, p. 40)

There are resources that provide detailed descriptions of cooperative learning and how to implement cooperative learning in the classroom. There are college-level and in-service courses that help teachers perfect the skills needed to use cooperative learning. But the best way for you to develop the ability to successfully use cooperative learning is to practice it in your own classroom, to evaluate your own progress, and to talk with others who are also using cooperative learning techniques. You are encouraged to use cooperative procedures as one of your options for teaching.

Multiple Intelligences

Gardner's theory of multiple intelligences speaks directly about learning styles. You will recall that, according to Gardner, there are nine forms of intelligence: verbal/linguistic, logical/mathematical, visual/spatial, musical/rhythmic, bodily/kinesthetic, interpersonal, intrapersonal, naturalist, and existentialist. All children have some association with all forms of intelligences, but they tend to favor one in particular. If there are students who are comfortable learning in a particular form, it would follow that teaching to that form would assist those students. As a result, teachers should consider different teaching approaches that match the learning styles or forms of different children. Another approach would be to use a variety of teaching approaches to provide the opportunity for students to demonstrate multiple ways of understanding. As teaching changes, assessment must also change to match the learning styles of the students.

Students who are verbal/linguistic learners respond to information that is presented through the language arts: reading, writing, speaking, and listening. Students who are logical/mathematical learners have an aptitude for problem solving, logical thought, and numbers. Students who are visual/spatial learners respond to information presented in a pictorial or graphic form. Student who are musical/rhythmic learners respond well to musical expression, patterns, and rhythms. Students who are bodily/kinesthetic learners respond to games, hands-on activities, and building. Students who are interpersonal learners are social learners and respond to group work or work with another student. Students who are intrapersonal learners are aware of their own feelings and ideas. Students who are naturalist learners enjoy the outdoors and activities like field trips. Students who are existentialist learners respond to how things fit together in their universe. While multiple intelligences is likely the most recognized aspect of Gardner's work, he believes strongly that deep understanding should be fundamental to the process of education. We support Gardner's contention and hope that you will give both his theory of multiple intelligences and his emphasis on deep understanding serious consideration in your teaching.

ASSESSING AND ACCOUNTING FOR STUDENT PROGRESS

Assessment is a multifaceted process. The NCTM defines assessment as ". . . the process of gathering evidence about a student's knowledge of, ability to use, and disposition toward mathematics and of making inferences based on that evidence for a variety of purposes" (1995, p. 3). It involves knowing the goals of the mathematics program. It requires you to know and understand students. Assessment also includes diagnosing, recording, grading, and reporting students' progress.

The Assessment Principle

The NCTM Assessment Principle states, "Assessment should support the learning of important mathematics and furnish useful information to both teachers and students" (2000, p. 22). This statement has two important parts. First, mathematics learning should be supported by assessment; second, information from assessment should be useful to students and teachers. These two parts are the basis for the next two sections.

Using Assessment to Enhance Learning

What mathematics learning is expected should be no secret to students. When goals are spelled out and when assessment follows instruction, there is a clear message to learners about what is important to learn.

Both the statement of goals and the assessment are crucial in delivering the message. The activities and thinking processes of instruction should be the activities and thinking processes of assessment. Learning is enhanced when students know what is expected of them and how it will be evaluated.

> Assessment should not merely be done to students; rather, it should also be done for students, to guide and enhance their learning. (NCTM, 2000, p. 22)

Discussions, conversations, observations, or other interactions between teachers and students help alert students to those aspects of instruction that are important. These exchanges also help students develop communication skills and new insights into the topics under discussion.

Problem-solving scoring guides contain the criteria for various levels of performance. When their problem solving has been scored, students are alerted to their strengths and to those areas needing improvement. Likewise, criteria developed for individual or group presentations serve to assess and direct mathematics learning.

That assessment enhances learning is a powerful message. We have the opportunity to strengthen teaching and learning through our discourse and activities linked to assessment.

OBSERVATION AND QUESTIONING. Teacher observing and questioning are among the most valuable methods for assessing the progress of students. Observation should focus on the individual child and the specific mathematical effort in which that child is engaged.

Many aspects of children's behavior are not assessed by tests. These behaviors include attitudes and interests, creative tendencies, and children's abilities to explain their own and other children's mathematical thinking. During discussions, work periods, play time, and instructional time, teachers observing mentally collect information about individual students. This information should then be acted on or written down in the children's mathematics folders, on an annotated class list, or wherever such information is kept. Many of the activities presented in this text are best assessed by teacher observation.

To illustrate assessment observation, we present the following description. Mr. Edwin has presented a problem to the class. There is a large maple tree on the school grounds and each fall it sheds its leaves. How could we figure out how many leaves there are on the tree and what it would cost to rake and dispose of the leaves each year? From that information is it possible to estimate the cost of leaf removal for a small city? Mr. Edwin notices that Darcy and Rob have been carrying out an animated discussion about the problem.

It is apparent that these students are discussing counting or estimating the number of leaves. Darcy is arguing that the easiest way to do that is while the leaves are still on the tree while Rob is arguing that it is better if you wait until they fall from the tree. Rob explains that you must have the leaves in hand in order to count them. Darcy says that is not necessarily so. She draws a picture of a tree and begins to explain how she might be able to estimate the number of leaves by determining the volume of the top of the tree and a sample of that volume.

Mr. Edwin is pleased with the discussion and asks a few questions about the process each student has chosen. He notes that both Darcy and Rob will have a chance to employ their own procedures in the leaf count. He believes that both are developing procedures that have merit.

The above example of observing and questioning is specific to an estimating procedure. Throughout the mathematics program, there are opportunities to question children on every aspect of mathematics. In its booklet, *Assessment Alternatives in Mathematics,* EQUALS and the California Mathematics Council suggest a number of questions that teachers may use to assess children's progress in several aspects of problem solving. For example, in questioning students about problem comprehension, these questions are suggested:

- What is the problem about? What can you tell me about it?
- How would you interpret that?
- Would you please explain that in your own words?
- What do you know about this part?
- Do you need to define or set limits for the problem?
- Is there something that can be eliminated or that is missing?
- What assumptions do you have to make? (1989, p. 24)

Many other questions are presented in this booklet, and the reader is encouraged to build a collection of good questions to use in the classroom. Clearly, the types of questions you ask must be appropriate for the age and developmental level of the children you teach.

Rowan and Robles (1998) present a series of questions and prompts to help teachers promote "the growth of mathematical power" among children. Several classroom vignettes are presented to illustrate how questions and prompts are used to assist the thinking process.

The observing and questioning teacher will gain information about all aspects of children's cognitive. growth—language and communication, social awareness, curiosity—not merely mathematical growth. This information will help guide the teacher in planning classroom experiences in a range of subjects. Because teachers make observations every day they are with students, teachers should accept this technique as providing the most consistent and abundant source of information about students.

While accepting observation and questioning as a key assessment technique, you also must accept the need to record the important observations and to collect samples of children's work to serve as written evidence of the observations. Then you will be able to track children's progress, use the information to prepare individual instruction, and accurately report the progress to children and their parents.

Finding time to make and record observations will be a challenge with your already busy schedule. Remembering your observations about a student's mathematics work from among all your daily observations will take practice and concentration, as will remembering to record the information.

PERFORMANCE-BASED ASSESSMENT AND GROUP PROBLEM SOLVING. A number of states, such as Kentucky and Oregon, have opted to substitute alternative assessment, including performance-based assessment, for standardized testing alone. In performance-based assessment, students are asked to perform tasks, either individually or in small groups, that require problem solving and higher-level thinking. The tasks are developed by teachers and are aimed at all levels of performance in elementary and middle school. Frequently, the tasks involve using a variety of concrete materials, are aimed at solving real-life problems, and cut across several different subject areas. Tasks are scored according to a scoring rubric or scoring guide that describes various aspects of the student's thinking and communication processes. Students are familiar with the rubric and know what is expected of them as they solve problems. A scoring rubric is illustrated in Chapter 4 in a discussion of problem solving.

One way to assess mathematical ability is to assess group work. We have discussed cooperative learning as an organizational procedure that encourages academic and collaborative work, typically surrounding a problem-solving task. To assess group work, you need to determine how well the assigned problem or task was dealt with. The time following a cooperative activity may be spent as a whole-class *debriefing*, that is, discussing the procedures used by each group to solve the problem. The group reporter may orally describe the work or the reporter may read the summary that was part of a writing assignment.

Another effective way to assess group work is to have the students as a class establish the criteria for an individual or a group presenting information to the rest of the class. For example, the following criteria were developed for group presentations for a sixth-grade class working on a "people in the history of mathematics" project:

1. Presenters involve the audience.
   a. Students can ask questions both during and after the presentation.
   b. Presenters answer questions directly and completely.
   c. The audience finds the people discussed interesting.
2. Presenters have practiced the presentation.
   a. Presentation is made with few pauses and few mistakes.
   b. Presenters are ready when it is their turn.
3. Presenters use pictures, overhead projector, PowerPoint, or other visuals.
   a. Visual aids are used during the presentation.
   b. Visual aids are organized and equipment works.
   c. Visual aids are carefully explained.
4. Presenters know what they are talking about.
   a. It is easy to understand what is being said.
   b. There is enough information about the historic person.
   c. Presenters tell where they found their information.
5. Presenters speak well.
   a. Presenters look at the audience when they talk.
   b. Presenters speak slowly, clearly, and loudly.
   c. Presenters are interested in their historic individual.

After the presentation, an assessment team uses the criteria to determine a score for the presentation.

The outcome of the project represents the collective work of the group. Because of the interdependence of group members in completing the project, the product is seen as the collective work of all group members. By using the techniques discussed above, the value of the project is assessed and insight into the mathematical learning is provided.

An important aspect of group assessment is to determine how well group members worked with one another to complete the task. Did each group member participate? Were ideas readily accepted and discussed? Were members praised for their contributions? Did each group member perform the role assigned to him or her? Were disagreements discussed and resolved in a constructive manner? Did group members feel good about their contribution and the group product? Did group members enjoy working with one another? You may find the answers to these questions by observing groups as they work, listening to the presentations, talking with individuals, and reading journal entries.

PORTFOLIOS, JOURNALS, AND WRITING. The mathematics portfolio is a place to collect materials that demonstrate the child's ability to think about, use, and apply mathematics. Student writing is one source of evidence for a portfolio. Writing activities help to assess students' mathematical progress. As they write, students reflect on a variety of topics and feelings and provide both themselves and the teacher with the chance to review their work and their thinking processes. The writing students do may be completed in several contexts. One opportunity for writing occurs when teachers provide questionnaires regarding recent mathematical work. For example, following several days of working with probability events, students were asked (1) to describe the activity that they thought best helped them understand how to determine the probability of an event occurring; (2) to mention one activity that surprised them; and (3) to explain to another person why some games are fair and others are not fair.

Journal writing gives students the chance to express attitudes and feelings about mathematics, as well as demonstrate problem-solving skills. Journal entries should be made on a regular basis. It is helpful for you to provide topics about which students can write. Journal "starters" might include the following: (1) Describe what you think about doing math in school. (2) If you could be a number, what number would you be and why? (3) How do you know math makes sense? (4) Draw a cartoon that shows you doing your math homework. You will gain insights about the students as they write down their thoughts about mathematics. You will be better able to serve the needs of individuals as you discover how they are thinking and what they are thinking about.

Writing activities may include describing how a particular problem was solved, how to perform a new algorithm, or how to explain an event. These writing activities focus on describing a specific skill that requires careful thinking and explanation. For example, students are asked to explain to a classmate why certain figures, such as equilateral triangles, cannot be constructed on a rectangular geoboard.

Another useful writing activity emerges from cooperative learning group work. As a group works on an assignment, problem, or project, the group recorder might be asked to describe how the group decided to complete the assignment or in what ways members of the group encouraged one another as the work progressed. The written record from group work will have been read to the group and will likely reflect some group editing.

Students appreciate it if teachers respond to their writing. As time permits, comment on a student's writing, jot down questions that arise as you read, or respond to a question raised by a student. Challenge the writer in a written dialogue.

RUBRICS AND PERFORMANCE INDICATORS. One aspect of an assessment program is likely to be performance tasks, projects, or investigations in which students engage and share with their classmates. Performance tasks may be presented orally, in a multimedia format, or in visual displays. When students engage in mathematical activities that are a part of an assessment program, it is necessary to have some type of performance criteria or indicators. These performance indicators are used to judge the quality of a mathematical task. The indicators describe the performance at one or more levels of quality. An example of a set of performance indicators was presented above in the section on Performance-Based Assessment and Group Problem Solving. The indicators were for presentations on people in the history of mathematics.

Another type of performance indicator is the rubric or scoring guide. A rubric spells out categories of a task to be assessed and indicators of quality within each category. A good example is presented in Figure 4–11 in Chapter 4. The categories to be assessed are Conceptual Understanding, Processes & Strategies, Verification, and Communication. The indicators of quality for conceptual understanding range from Level 1 ("The translation of the task uses inappropriate concepts or is minimal or not evident") to Level 6 ("The translation of the task is enhanced through connections and/or extensions to other mathematical ideas"). Similar indicators are presented for each category. Successfully using a rubric requires not only practice but the opportunity to compare scoring results with others who have scored the same problem or task. The Oregon Department of Education website (Weblink 3–6) provides practice with actual student problem-solving work. In cases where assessment focuses on national or state mathematics standards, performance indicators will be provided by those government bodies. In those cases, individuals who score student work will be specially trained. In cases where assessment may be less formal, like in your classroom, performance indicators and rubrics may be established in cooperation with the students. Then students and teachers may complete the scoring.

Using Assessment to Make Instructional Decisions

The assessment data that teachers gather can provide valuable information about the instructional program. This information may be used to make changes in the curriculum, to reallocate teaching time and focus, to determine what material needs special attention or review, and to judge progress toward instructional goals. In the following paragraphs we discuss various ways that assessment is used to make instructional decisions.

LINKING CURRICULUM AND INSTRUCTION TO ASSESSMENT. A link between curriculum and assessment should be established and maintained. Assessment is not an adjunct to the mathematics program. It is an integral part of daily instruction, for you cannot proceed without knowing how the students are performing each day. Assessment begins whenever you first come into contact with students and parents. It occurs every day throughout the school year. A curriculum intended to focus on understanding, making sense, and thinking about mathematics requires broad-based assessment procedures. Traditionally, standardized tests and textbook tests have been used as the primary means by which to assess students' mathematical progress. This procedure is limited because standardized and textbook tests provide limited information about children's thinking processes and about the mathematics that children can actually do. Children's thought processes are dynamic; they should be assessed accordingly. Thus, it is important to know about and practice a number of assessment techniques, including observation and questioning, performance-based assessment, diagnostic interviews, teacher-made assessment tasks, writing activities, group problem solving, standardized tests, and textbook tests. Information gathered from many assessment techniques can help direct how the curriculum is organized and presented. We can discover what students know and can do. We can know about individual students as well as the whole class. We can make instructional decisions about the level of understanding and the quality of thinking. We can improve our teaching.

DIAGNOSTIC INTERVIEWS. Diagnostic interviews take place when the teacher meets with individual students and asks them to perform simple tasks, to comment on tasks that are performed for them, or to discuss a mathematical concept or skill. Piaget devised many performance tasks for use with young children to determine the children's readiness to learn various mathematical topics. Baratta-Lorton's *Mathematics Their Way* (1995) provides many fine examples of diagnostic procedures. Questions devised by teachers in their daily interaction with youngsters are most helpful. Any topic that is taught in the mathematics program may form the basis for diagnostic interviews. In classrooms where there is a culture of thinking, rich diagnostic conversations can emerge. We need to determine how students are thinking. The best way to do this is to ask them.

Information from diagnostic interviews can be used to help shape future instruction for individuals as well as the class as a whole. Finding time for occasional interviews may require adjusting your teaching schedule. The effort is worth it.

STANDARDIZED VS. STANDARDS-BASED ASSESSMENT. Most of us, by experience, are familiar with standardized achievement tests. Standardized, or norm-referenced, tests are typically used for comparing the work of an individual or group with norms established for students in similar age groups or at similar grade levels.

Sometimes standardized tests help survey students' skill and knowledge in limited aspects of mathematics to provide a basis for evaluating a school district's curriculum. Standardized achievement tests measure knowledge, skills, speed and accuracy, the ability to solve one- or two-step word problems, and vocabulary. Students' scores are reported as percentiles or grade-level equivalents based on national norms.

Teachers should be cautious about relying heavily on standardized tests as a basis for assessing their students' specific mathematical abilities. Standardized achievement tests tend to be merely approximations of how well particular students in a particular section of the country perform on narrowly defined content. Such tests give little evidence of students' resourcefulness or confidence in attacking new problems.

Standards-based assessment is characterized by numerous assessment techniques, including observation and questioning, performance-based assessment, writing activities, and others already mentioned. One example may be found on the Math Program page (Figure 3–4). It illustrates an open-response question from the Massachusetts assessment program. The result of broad-based assessment is a better overall picture of an individual's mathematical performance. Thus, we can be more responsive to individual needs and classroom needs.

> Learning to use evidence from multiple sources of assessment data can yield a more accurate picture of what students know and are able to do. (McREL, 2002, p. 35)

The use of broad-based assessment does not mean that all assessment techniques are used all of the time. Rather, you have available to you alternative techniques that will provide reliable evidence of children's mathematical growth, thought processes, and abilities. You must select the most appropriate technique for the type of task being assessed.

Teachers have a major obligation once data have been gathered by any of the above means. Namely, they must decide what the data mean. The teacher's interpretations of the students' work are crucial in laying the groundwork for further instruction.

One useful function of interpretation is diagnosis. For example, students may be grouped for instruction based on concept or skill deficiencies that show up during assessment procedures. If observation reveals that three students are unable to solve word problems involving selecting the most appropriate operation, then you may wish to design instruction to assist them.

Tallying right and wrong answers is not nearly as important as determining how the child is thinking. Teachers should keep this in mind in order to provide students with the encouragement they need to maximize their potential. Most students naturally learn from failure and mistakes. All students should realize that assessment procedures represent another natural step in the learning process.

Recording, Grading, and Reporting Students' Progress

During the entire assessment process, organizing the information and work samples gathered is essential. Scores from problem solving, tasks, and tests along with other numerical data should be recorded in a gradebook, a computer database, or a similar repository for quantitative information. The work samples, including qualitative and quantitative material, may be kept in a student portfolio. It includes material that transcends the purely quantitative assessment data (test scores and worksheet or workbook scores). The portfolio will contain a profile of the student's abilities in mathematics in a variety of mediums. The portfolio will contain all work of an individual from which the student's best work may be selected.

For example, materials collected in portfolios by eighth-grade mathematics students included the following items:

- Record sheet of all assignments, exams, problem-solving activities
- All daily assignments that had been completed during a progress period
- The students' mathematics journals used throughout the year
- Problem-solving challenges that were completed each week
- Completed project materials and student assessments of the projects
- Exams and quizzes

Throughout the year, the teacher and the students reviewed the students' growth and the progress they made. The students were involved in self-assessment. At each progress period, they were guided to review the work in their portfolios and collect each of the following:

1. *Your math self-assessment guide.*
2. *Your completed math record sheet.*
3. *Your favorite work.* On a yellow half-sheet, write a paragraph explaining why this is your favorite work.
4. *Your favorite quotation.* On a sheet of paper, write your favorite quotation from your mathematics journal.
5. *Teacher's choice.* Find the assignment selected by the teacher. On a blue half-sheet, write a paragraph on your feelings about this assignment. Could the teacher have done a better job of explaining how to do it? What were the things that confused you?
6. *Showing growth in mathematical concepts.* Select two papers that show the growth you have made in mathematics this progress period. Use the green half-sheet to explain the concept and how you have improved.
7. *Your favorite problem.* Find your favorite problem that you worked on. On a pink half-sheet tell what it was about the problem that caused you to enjoy it.
8. *Quizzes and exams.* On a white half-sheet write a paragraph on your performance on your quizzes and exams. Have you gone over the problems that you missed?

The students answered several other questions that were on their math assessment guide. These questions asked about the students' class attendance, contribution, participation, and effect on the dynamics of the class, effort, honesty, and use of mathematics. At this particular school, students were given a letter grade at the end of each progress period. As part of their self-assessment they were asked to give the grade that they had earned and the reason why. Finally, the students were asked to describe how the mathematics class could be improved.

Whenever the teacher met with parents during the year, the portfolio file and self-assessment materials served as the basis for discussing the students' progress. Often, the students explained the portfolios and assessment materials to the parents as part of a joint conference.

Determining grades for students in some form has historically been a part of the education process. The further students progress through the education system, the more likely grades will be given as evidence of their academic performance. The teacher's role is to responsibly determine how to ascertain a grade that represents the ability and work of the students. Students must be aware of the grading process and, if possible, should play a role in its development. Data that support the awarding of a grade should be recorded and be available to the student at any time. Additional information about students' progress should be provided if possible.

Students, parents, and teachers should communicate about the student's growth and progress. The

Mathematics, Grade 8

Session 1, Open-Response Question

 Lionel and Tracy are playing a game using two six-sided number cubes. The faces of each cube are numbered as shown below.

| 1 | | 2 | | 3 | | 4 | | 5 | | 6 |

Lionel has a red cube and Tracy has a green cube. To play the game they both roll their cubes at the same time.
- The numbers that show face up when the cubes stop rolling are used to make a fraction.
- The number on the red cube is used for the numerator and the number on the green cube is used for the denominator.

For example, the results shown below would make the fraction $\frac{1}{2}$.

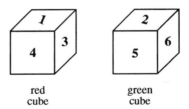

red   green
cube   cube

- Lionel wins 1 point if the fraction formed has a value less than one.
- Tracy wins 1 point if the fraction has a value greater than one.
- No one gets a point if the fraction is equal to one.

a. Make a list or a table in your Student Answer Booklet of all of the fractions possible from rolling 1 red and 1 green cube. How many total different fractions are there?

b. If Lionel (red cube) rolls a 3, what is the probability that Tracy (green cube) wins 1 point? Show your work or explain how you obtained your answer.

c. Using your table, what is the probability of each player winning a point on a given turn? Do you think this game is fair to both players? Show your work or explain how you obtained your answer.

Reporting Category for Item 22: Data Analysis, Statistics, and Probability

Figure 3–4 Grade 8 open-response question. Reprinted from material released to the public by the Massachusetts Department of Education. Publication of this page does not constitute an endorsement of this textbook by CMDE.

MATH PROGRAM

The number cube question (see Figure 3–4) is an open-response question from an eighth-grade mathematics exam that required students to provide answers and to explain how they arrived at their answers. The open-response questions were scored by professional scorers using a scoring guide.

The spring 2002 eighth-grade Massachusetts Comprehensive Assessment System (MCAS) mathematics test was based on the Massachusetts Mathematics Curriculum Framework. This particular page represented the Data Analysis, Statistics, and Probability content strand. The other strands were Number Sense and Operations; Patterns, Relations, and Algebra; Geometry; and Measurement. There were two test sessions, each one containing multiple-choice items and open-response items. The first session contained short-answer questions. Calculators were permitted in the second session.

A total of 39 questions were in the released set of the 2002 questions for the eighth grade. You may be interested in the current released, eighth-grade test items or the other released mathematics test items from grades 4, 6, and 10. You may find them on the MCAS Test Items page at Weblink 3–7.

interchange among students, parents, and teachers helps students understand the results of their efforts, helps parents determine their child's mathematical growth and progress, and helps the teacher determine the nature of the child's home environment and the child's perception of the teacher and school. The key to three-way communication is your willingness to share any information you have and any observations you have made.

You should welcome parents to school. The common interest of students, parents, and teachers in the student's growth, development, and school progress should draw them together. The student's and teacher's assessment and the parents' observations should blend together to strengthen the student-parent-teacher partnership. Edge (1998, p. 308) noted that parents have been involved in mathematics classrooms for many years and goes on to highlight two changes: "an increased demand for parental participation in the schooling of their children as well as interaction between parents and schools." So important is the role played by parents that the February 1998 issue of *Teaching Children Mathematics* focused on school-family partnerships. This is a rich resource for suggestions about how and when to involve families in the learning process.

Parents of pre-kindergarten, elementary, and middle school students are particularly interested in hearing about their children. Besides quarterly or mid-year conferences, parents should be invited to the classroom to observe the daily routine or specific activities such as mathematics.

Send notes or call parents pointing out a significant event or accomplishment of individuals or small groups of students. A note home need not have a negative connotation. A summary of the past week's activities or of events to come may be distributed to keep parents informed about classroom life. Solicit the help of parents when the parents are known to have particular skills or experiences that can enrich a class. Invite parents to participate.

When reporting the mathematical progress of students, written descriptions along with samples of the student's work are helpful. Sometimes a check sheet of concepts and skills may substitute for the written description. When students have been involved in self-assessment, their views and perceptions add to the sum of information about mathematical progress. At least twice a year, and hopefully more often, students, teachers, and parents should meet face-to-face to discuss the mathematical work and growth of the student. Above all, be open and straightforward in discussing students. Your concerns and those of the parents should be coordinated for the benefit of the children.

TEACHING MATHEMATICS TO DIVERSE LEARNERS

All classrooms are comprised of diverse learners. There are differences in learning styles, in skin color, in personal beliefs, in race, in gender, and in ability, to name a few. We teachers have a daunting task in providing the opportunity for all students to learn. Our decision to become teachers was made, in part, because we believed that we were up to the task. Mathematics is one of many avenues where we can provide quality instruction for all students.

The Equity Principle

The NCTM proclaimed equity as the first principle in *Principles and Standards for School Mathematics*. You will recall that the principles are intended to highlight characteristics of excellent mathematics education. The NCTM discussed equity by forcefully noting:

> All students, regardless of their personal characteristics, backgrounds, or physical challenges, must have opportunities to study—and support to learn—mathematics. Equity does not mean that every student should receive identical instruction; instead, it demands that reasonable and appropriate accommodations be made as needed to promote access and attainment for all students. (2000, p. 12)

Two aspects of equity form the basis for this principle—the level of expectations for students and the support provided for those students. While the principle is intended for school mathematics programs, it speaks directly to us as teachers of mathematics. The equity principle suggests that we look inward and assess our personal beliefs about our students. It suggests also that we consciously plan learning opportunities and raise our expectations for typically underserved students: ". . . students who live in poverty, students who are not native speakers of English, students with disabilities, females, and many nonwhite students . . ." (2000, p. 13).

Teachers' Attitudes about Children

Much of this book focuses on children as learners of mathematics, but it is also important just to look at the children themselves. Your beliefs about children will affect the children's performance in many academic areas, including mathematics. Children's literature abounds with rich stories and images that give glimpses into various cultures. In one such book, *A Million Fish . . . More or Less* (McKissack, 1992), exaggeration with numbers and delightful characters provide the reader with the enjoyable bayou tale of Hugh Thomas and his friends.

Teacher attitudes impact their daily choices of activities, the amount of effort expended on each, and their expectations of students' abilities to perform. (McREL, 2002, p. 28)

The beliefs we have about children, about how they should be treated, and about how they should be taught vary dramatically. Some believe that children must be left alone to grow and develop with little interference from adults, and others believe that children must be closely watched and directed. Surely the optimum treatment of children includes something in between a laissez-faire attitude and strict direction. Our overall degree of teaching success depends more on what we believe about children than on how we organize to teach them, because we interact with children in ways that reflect our beliefs about them. One example has been described in the research literature. When teachers believed certain children were low achievers, those children tended to receive marks indicating low achievement. When teachers believed comparable children were high achievers; those children tended to receive marks indicating high achievement. Teachers are often unaware that they treat children according to their personal beliefs about them. They do so through both verbal and nonverbal interaction. As beliefs about children become more positive, a greater amount of the children's potential can be realized (Rosenthal and Jacobson 1968). We need to be keenly aware of the children with whom we work. Our well-articulated set of beliefs provides the basis on which to develop a sound style of teaching. Along this line, the NCTM commented:

> Teachers communicate expectations in their interactions with students during classroom instruction, through their comments on students' papers, when assigning students to instructional groups, through the presence or absence of consistent support for students who are striving for high levels of attainment, and in their contacts with significant adults in a student's life. (2000, p. 13)

Challenges Facing All of Us

It is relatively easy to teach students who are motivated, who are interested, and who learn easily. We all wish that these would be our students and that we could show great success in developing mathematical understanding with such students. The fact of the matter is that there are many students who come to school less prepared to learn and others whose circumstances cause an impediment to learning. The National Research Council noted:

> The strong connection between economic advantage, school funding, and achievement in the United States has

meant that groups of students whose mathematics achievement is low have tended to be disproportionately African American, Hispanic, Native American, students acquiring English, or students located in urban or rural school districts. (2001, p. 143)

Following the lead of *Principles and Standards for School Mathematics,* our task is straightforward. First we must expect all students to learn mathematics, we must believe that all students can learn mathematics, and we must provide the opportunity for all students to learn mathematics. Second, we must teach in such a way that all students are supported as they learn mathematics.

Beyond the empirical evidence that teaching for understanding shows much promise for teaching children of diverse sociodemographic backgrounds, we believe that treating children as if they can and should understand what they are being taught conveys a fundamental respect for them as individuals. (Secada and Berman, 1999, p. 41)

Our responsibility to ensure equity as mathematics teachers can be enhanced by following these suggestions:

1. Believe that all students are capable of learning and doing mathematics. Expect all students to perform well. Our goal should be that all students become powerful mathematical thinkers and work both cooperatively and independently in mathematics.

2. Provide verbal and written feedback as part of the learning process. Provide time for questions and encourage discussion. Encourage a student to persist in solving a mathematical problem until the student can say "I've got it!" or "I understand."

3. Incorporate cooperative mathematics activities and limit competitive ones.

4. Monitor the composition of small groups in your classroom so that all students learn to work cooperatively and have an opportunity to make sense of the mathematics for themselves.

5. Provide students with many opportunities to see that math is a domain for all students. Convince all students that doing well in math is cool. Stress the importance and value of mathematics to all students.

6. Present a variety of role models in math and science.

7. Use physical models and hands-on activities. Begin a class activity by posing a problem for students to tackle with enough discussion to get them started, then discuss the activity with all students when it has been completed. If pupils begin working on an activity with little introduction from the teacher, everyone has access to the same experience. Discussion that follows after all students have completed an activity

encourages participation by all and gives everyone an opportunity to build his or her own mathematical understanding, competence, and confidence.

8. Work to make math a positive activity for everyone by avoiding targeting a few students for particular attention, by avoiding becoming preoccupied with those students who make the most noise, by running an orderly class, and by making sure that everyone is actively involved in making sense of the mathematics.

9. Use equitable materials, that is, materials that are free of stereotypes, that reflect different cultures, and that present the view that all students are capable of learning mathematics. Equitable materials will result in a better understanding of people, will develop more flexible attitudes, and will encourage students to imitate role behaviors contained in the materials.

Secada and Berman (1999) cautioned teachers about three concerns of equity that may arise in classrooms where teaching for understanding is a focus. The first concern arises in classrooms where students are expected to discuss their thinking aloud and in written form. As thinking is shared, peers note social and academic differences among students. Students who are English-language learners or who have been socialized to defer to others may be at a disadvantage in this setting. On the other hand, differences in thinking can be a positive part of the classroom culture when the differences are respected.

The second concern arises in classrooms where multiple solutions or strategies are encouraged in problem solving. Again, social and academic differences among students may be observed. Secada and Berman noted:

> . . . this practice, when managed with sensitivity, encourages widespread participation; expresses appreciation for diversity in thought; establishes value for these differences among students; allows the approval of the solution to come from the mathematics itself rather than from the teacher; and features the substance, content, and logic of a procedure or task rather than its performer. (1997, p. 37)

The third concern arises in classrooms where students are expected to take responsibility for learning, where students work individually and interact with other students as well as the teacher in learning mathematics. It may be challenging to maintain equity when students have diverse abilities and dispositions. Sharing the responsibility for learning, however, may give students the chance of greater equity. In some cases the classroom practices suggested above may clash with the values of the students' homes. We must be sensitive to these potential clashes and be willing to develop alternatives to deal with them. We should

embrace an equity perspective when we teach, including planning lessons that are inclusive and providing mathematical experiences to which all students can easily relate. Problems should be rich and open, allowing for multiple methods of solution on a variety of levels of complexity.

Opportunity to Learn

The meaning of *opportunity to learn* is providing access to learning for all students. We, as teachers, play an important role in the opportunity to learn because we orchestrate the curriculum intended to meet mathematics standards, we avoid bias, we provide resources to meet the standards, and we support the learning of all students. Throughout this section we have emphasized the role of the teacher and provided guidelines for teaching.

> Opportunity to learn is facilitated through student-centered classrooms that are focused on higher-order thinking skills, problem solving, substantive conversation, and real-world contexts. (McREL, 2002, p. 6)

Opportunity to learn is a necessary part of developing the highest level of mathematical literacy. We challenge you to embrace it as a personal goal in your teaching.

CHILDREN WITH SPECIAL NEEDS

In every chapter of this book, we mention children's different learning styles. We mention children who learn more slowly or more quickly than others. Your own observation of children will confirm these situations.

In addition, there may be children in your classroom with physical or mental handicaps and children qualified for assistance under federal or state guidelines. Resource rooms may be available for special instruction. Because support services are invaluable in meeting the needs of all children, use them to benefit every child in your classroom.

Adaptations for Specific Learning Disabilities

Terms such as *low achievers, emotionally disturbed*, and *culturally deprived* are labels used to describe children who are having difficulties in school. These labels often result in a child's negative performance, both socially and academically. Avoid labeling children. Consider chidren for both their strengths and weaknesses, as full members of the human family. Children who happen to learn more slowly than others deserve special attention to help them develop mathematical concepts and skills.

Slow learners may be identified by intelligence quotient, achievement, teacher observation, reading ability, readiness level, or other means. They generally fall below an average in one or more of these areas. Slow learners may have many things in common, but each child has a unique set of strengths and weaknesses. Characteristics frequently possessed by slow learners are listed below.

- *Negative self-concept.* Children may come to believe at a very young age that they are stupid. Failure is too easily learned. Many children will not even attempt a task, particularly a new task, because they are afraid of failure.

  Make an effort to ensure success and to look at failure as an acceptable route toward learning. If chidren view themselves as worthwhile, they are more apt to approach a problem with confidence and have a greater chance of success.

- *Short attention span.* Slow learners often have short attention spans. This may be because problems are too difficult, too long, or uninteresting.

  Children will work for relatively long periods on interesting problems suited to their ability levels. They will play in class much longer than they will work. Ensure that children are positively motivated toward appropriate tasks.

- *Specific mathematical disability.* Terms such as *dyscalculia, number blindness,* and *specific minimal brain damage* are used to describe children with specific problems in learning quantitative concepts. There may also be perceptual problems that affect learning spatial concepts. These include difficulties in forming concepts such as position in space (near, far, up, down, left, right), in distinguishing a figure from the surrounding background, and in eye-hand coordination.

  Children are easily distracted by extraneous stimuli. Too many problems or pictures on a workbook page, as well as too many objects or people in the classroom, can be distracting. Workbook pages and classroom environments should be relatively plain and simple for children with perceptual problems. Be alert for children with specific mathematical disabilities and seek professional help when problems demand it.

- *Poor self-control.* Some children are explosive, hyperactive, or erratic. They always seem to be in motion. They rarely sit still and often wander aimlessly about the room.

  Some research indicates that poor self-control may be triggered or aggravated by diet. Much research still needs to be done on how diet affects children. Hyperactive children require a structured environment with few extraneous distractions.

- *Language problems.* Children who have difficulty learning mathematics often have language difficulties. In addition, the language of mathematics is often abstract and complex. Children may not understand such common mathematical vocabulary as *up, down, in, out, two,* and *plus.* Even more difficult are phrases such as *divided by* and *divided into.* Children may be unable to read simple directions, equations, or mathematical symbols. They may be unable to communicate concepts they do understand.

Remember to keep conversations with children having language problems as simple as possible. Be alert for any misunderstanding of terms. Develop concepts through physical manipulation and language.

MEMORY AND APPLICATION. Studies show that slow and retarded children are capable of learning complex motor and verbal skills. Their retention may be similar to that of younger children of the same mental age. Over-learning may be required to ensure retention.

Allow for practice, drill, and repetition only after a concrete understanding of concepts has been developed. Transfer of learning is difficult for slow and retarded children but may be accomplished if it is incorporated into the lesson. Such children can retain and apply skills when they have transferred and practiced them.

Complex problem solving may be too difficult for slow and retarded children, but they can memorize simple, rote, factual material and they can learn and apply basic facts. Teaching skills such as how to use a calculator, how to be an effective consumer, and other life skills is appropriate.

GENERAL PRINCIPLES OF GOOD TEACHING. General principles of good teaching are mentioned throughout the book and pertain to all children. They are reiterated here because of their significance for children with special problems.

1. All children are ready to learn something. You must determine the level of readiness.
2. Success is important. Carefully sequence learning to ensure several levels of success. Immediate positive feedback is helpful.
3. Self-concept affects success and vice versa. Children must be worthwhile in their own eyes and in the eyes of their peers.
4. Practice is important and should follow the concrete development of concepts. It should be applied in practical situations and should contain provisions for transfer.
5. Be prepared with a variety of teaching strategies. Do not present them all at once, but if one method fails, try another. The child may be capable of mastering

the concept, but not in the context in which it was first presented. Several methods of presentation that involve the senses may be needed to meet each child's learning style.

6. Begin work on a concrete level. Move to work on an abstract level only after children understand concepts concretely.

7. Analyze children's mistakes carefully. Children periodically make careless mistakes, but there is often another reason for an error. Look for patterns in children's errors, and discuss their thinking processes to correct mistaken concepts.

8. Learning is different for each child. This book mentions several ways to diagnose and assess individual children. Lessons should be planned according to the diagnoses.

Challenging and Creating Mathematically Promising Students

Just as children having problems in mathematics need special consideration, so do children with special talents in mathematics. The regular math curriculum may be as unsuited for gifted children as it is for slow children. In 1980, the NCTM published the *Agenda for Action* that stated: "The student most neglected, in terms of realizing full potential, is the gifted student of mathematics. Outstanding mathematical ability is a precious societal resource, sorely needed to maintain leadership in a technological world" (1980, p. 18). Recognizing that the need for technological leadership is even more critical today, the NCTM, in 1994, appointed a Task Force Report on the Mathematically Promising. This Task Force attempted to broaden the traditional definition of mathematically gifted and talented by defining mathematical promise as a function of ability, motivation, belief, and experience or opportunity. None of the variables are considered to be fixed, but rather are areas that need to be developed so mathematical success might be maximized for an increased number of promising students.

This description recognizes that abilities can be enhanced and developed and acknowledges recent brain-functioning research that documents changes in the brain due to experiences. It also concedes that students are not always motivated to achieve at their highest possible levels and that the popular culture in the United States may even encourage students to disguise their mathematical abilities in order to avoid negative labels such as "nerd" or "geek." Belief in one's ability to succeed and belief in the importance of mathematical success by the students themselves, teachers, peers, and parents are also recognized as important. Lack of such beliefs, especially by females,

students of color, students from lower socioeconomic groups, and students for whom English is a second language, is acknowledged as a significant barrier to learning for several students. The importance of the fourth variable, experience or opportunity to learn, is especially evident in international comparisons of mathematics students, where research frequently finds that students in the United States are not exposed to the same high level of curriculum as students in several other countries.

Results from the *Third International Mathematics and Science Study* (TIMSS) showed that our best mathematics and science students are not achieving at the level of top students in other countries. There is widespread concern that our expectations for our students are not high enough and that our curriculum is not as challenging as that in other countries. In fourth grade, only 9 percent of the students in mathematics scored above the 90th percentile worldwide. In Singapore, 39 percent of the students scored at this level, as did over 20 percent of the fourth graders in Korea and Japan (OERI, 1997, p. 25). By eighth grade, this had dropped to 5 percent of the mathematics students in the United States, while 45 percent of students in Singapore and over 30 percent of students in Korea and Japan were scoring above the 90th percentile (OERI, 1996, p. 26). The 1999 TIMSS-R results showed that U.S. eighth graders' mathematical performance was somewhat lower relative to students in other countries (Weblink 3–8). By the end of secondary school, advanced mathematics and physics students scored significantly below advanced students in other countries.

The right of children to an education suited to their individual needs has prompted some states to legislate special programs for gifted children. Many mathematics educators in the United States are realizing that this is not enough, however. Special gifted programs generally do not focus on mathematics and rarely have teachers who are trained both in mathematics and in understanding the needs of exceptionally bright children. In addition, results from studies such as TIMSS reinforce the fact that the United States cannot afford to focus on a few students who exhibit special talents in mathematics. Teachers must develop the mathematical talents of all students to their highest levels, and these levels must be higher than those previously reached by only a few.

Whether our most promising mathematics students are in a regular classroom or a special program, there are several things to consider.

Promising mathematics students, of course, are not all alike. They are boys and girls of all races, with all types of other abilities and disabilities, from all areas of the country including the inner-city and rural areas, and with parents of all educational and economic levels. It has been popular to identify promising students by high intelligence quotients, such as a score of 130 or better. However, this is neither necessary nor a sufficient identifier of promising mathematics students; there are several other characteristics to consider. These characteristics must be nurtured and developed in all children in order to produce the greatest possible number of mathematically talented children. Some of these characteristics are listed here:

- *Creativity.* Many children, from preschool on, have special creative, mathematical talents that are obvious, and all need to have their creativity nurtured. Encourage children to explore, to manipulate, to suggest a variety of solutions to a problem, and to suggest new problems for exploration. Minimize rote memory. Stress flexible thinking.
- *Awareness.* Promising students are often sensitive to and aware of their surroundings. They perceive problems readily and can see patterns and relationships easily. They do not need to have every step of a problem spelled out for them.
- *Nonmathematical abilities.* Although some children have special talents only in mathematics, many children who are mathematically promising are also mentally and emotionally mature. Many mathematically talented children are highly verbal and can express their thought processes. Encourage students to use verbal, physical, and spatial explanations as well as numerical and algebraic ones.
- *Abstract reasoning abilities.* Talented children may be able to reason at a higher level of abstraction than their age-mates. They may work symbolically with quantitative ideas but may still benefit from manipulation of concrete materials.
- *Transfer ability.* Many promising students can transfer skills learned in one situation to novel, untaught situations. They may apply learning in social situations, when working in other subject areas, at home, and so on. Encourage children to generalize rules and principles and to test the generalizations in new settings.
- *Good memory.* Talented children often have the ability to remember and retain what they have learned. They do not need as much drill as other children do. Many are bored with repetition and may begin to "turn off" mathematically when asked to repeat things they have already mastered.
- *Curiosity.* Mathematically promising children often display intellectual curiosity. They are reluctant to believe something just because the teacher says it is true. They want to know why it works. They are interested in a wide range of ideas and often explore topics through independent reading. They ask many questions, enjoy solving puzzles, and delight in discovering winning strategies in games. Make available challenging articles, books, puzzles, and games for their use.

Challenging all students, including those performing at the top of the class, to perform at a higher level is difficult but rewarding. It is even threatening to some teachers. Such teachers are sometimes concerned that they will not be able to answer all the children's questions or that the children may be smarter than they are. This may be true but should not necessarily present a problem. Some suggested techniques that are especially appropriate for encouraging and developing mathematically promising children follow:

1. Students need challenging problems. Many of the problem-solving activities suggested in the following chapters are especially appropriate for challenging students to think more deeply about mathematics. Encourage children to create original problems for others to solve. Promising students should enjoy strategy games and complex problems.
2. Children do not need busywork. Because they often finish assignments early, bright students may be asked to do additional problems of the same type. If they can do the initial problems, it is likely that they do not need more practice. Use curriculum compacting to allow them to demonstrate their mastery of low-level work and then let them move on to more challenging tasks.
3. Encourage independent research. Promising students are often capable of independent study and research at a young age. They may even be able to set their own goals and assess their progress. This, of course, does not mean they should always be left alone.
4. Set up a buddy system. Let children work with peers of similar ability so they can challenge each other to ever-higher levels of performance. Children can often communicate with and learn from peers better than from adults.
5. Encourage creative and critical thinking. Avoid forcing children to memorize one method to the exclusion of others. Accept any correct method, and lead children to discover why some methods do not always work. Have the children assess solutions for appropriateness, ease, originality, and the like.

Perhaps you recognized the suggested approaches for teaching for the development of promising students. The same approaches might be used with all children. We mentioned them to alert you to sound practices and to remind you that extra planning is needed to encourage the growth of mathematical talents.

Educators often debate whether programs for gifted children should be enriched or accelerated. Some states have even mandated one type of program. Currently, the trend seems to be toward a third dimension of programs for the development of mathematical abilities—depth and complexity. *The Third International Mathematics and Science Study* characterized the curriculum in the United States as "an inch deep and a mile wide" (OERI, 1996). If, as this study suggests, our curriculum covers too many topics at too low a level, increasing the number of topics or covering them more rapidly will not help students develop the strong mathematical power that is necessary. Instead of racing through topics or adding additional ones, students should develop a deeper understanding of mathematics by asking more complex questions about the topics they are learning. This does not mean, however, that students should not move into traditional high school topics such as algebra and geometry in the middle grades—quite the contrary. By age 12 or 13, students in many other countries have already explored algebra and geometry on a much deeper level than many secondary students in the United States, and our middle grade students also need to move beyond repetition of elementary mathematics towards a rich exploration of these topics.

A wide range of resources is available electronically, and interesting and stimulating mathematics books, videos, and computer programs should be available either in the classroom or in the library of every school. For the teacher, a professional library, the National Council of Teachers of Mathematics, journals, and activity books are rich sources of good ideas. Students who enjoy competitions should be encouraged to explore their interests through team events such as MATHCOUNTS or through individual entries through their schools or online. The reference list has several competitions, programs, and other resources for enriching and deepening mathematics offerings to help increase the number and the mathematical understanding of promising students.

CREATING A SUPPORTIVE, LEARNER-CENTERED CLASSROOM ENVIRONMENT

We mentioned earlier the importance of an intellectual learning environment. We turn our attention in this section to the affective and physical learning environments that support the intellectual learning environment. In addition, we discuss parents and the community and the role of learning aids.

Creating an Atmosphere of Trust, Confidence, and Excitement

Effective teachers create learning environments that invite students to learn. They create these environments by their attitudes, their knowledge, their energy, their organization, and their compassion. Effective teachers encourage their students. They spend extra time providing individual instruction.

> One of the strongest predictors of students' success is the quality of their teacher. (McREL, 2002, p. 84)

A teacher's attitude toward children and toward mathematics can excite children to learn. A teacher's mathematical and practical knowledge can elicit student's confidence in their teacher and in themselves. A teacher's energy can infect the entire class. A teacher's organization can provide structure for thinking, reflection, creativity, and order. A teacher's compassion can reach out to every student every day.

Classrooms should provide the best physical environment possible for learning. It is possible to have a classroom that is too stimulating, with so many bright pictures and objects that children have difficulty finding a single object or an area in which to work that is not distracting. It is also possible to have a classroom so barren and unchanging that children have little or nothing in which to become interested. It is possible to have a classroom so informal that children do not know what to do or where to go or to have a classroom so formal that children become regimented and repressed. It is a challenge to provide a balanced, comfortable, flexible classroom, so that no matter what activity has been planned, there is space available that lends itself to the activity. Also to be considered are the different learning and teaching styles.

Several basic tenets should be kept in mind in providing the physical learning environment.

1. The physical learning environment provides a support system for the educative process. It is important that the physical environment stimulate learning to complement textbooks, teachers, games, and visual aids.

2. As learning environments improve, so does the learning. That is, there is improvement in mathematical concept and skill development as well as communication.

3. Full use of the learning environment will assist you in teaching every child more fully, so that children receive help from both you and the environment.

4. Classrooms for children should mirror the decisions and interests of the children. Children should have the opportunity to help design parts of their own learning environments. Teachers should also help design the learning space.

5. Children's behavior is affected by their learning environment. Anything that affects behavior also

affects learning. The quality of the physical environment must be maintained.

6. Be aware of the physical environment as part of the learning process. An awareness of alternative ways to use space is fundamental.

7. The utility of a classroom depends on the awareness of those who spend time in that classroom. Children and teachers do not need a new building or a new classroom to have a rich learning environment.

8. Consider the human and physical needs of children in designing learning environments. Take into account students' language and culture, their neighborhoods, and their communities.

How can the learning environment be enhanced? Provide bulletin boards that invite a response from children, like that shown in Figure 3–5. Provide bulletin boards that inform, such as one that illustrates a variety of historic mathematical tools. Construct large yarn shapes such as squares, triangles, and pentagons to decorate walls and ceilings. Let the children construct space figures by cutting and folding construction paper. Have tetrahedrons, cubes, prisms, octahedrons, dodecahedrons, icosahedrons, and so forth, hanging from the ceiling or along a wall. Build a geodesic dome that can be used by three or four children as a quiet reading place. Rearrange the student desks and learning centers every so often. Display number lines in various locations and configurations around the room. Most of all, be willing to change the decorations occasionally to provide variety and interest.

Whatever classroom you inherit, you can do much to make it a rich learning environment. Evertson and others offer sound suggestions for setting up the physical environment at the beginning of the school year (2003). A complete transformation is not expected immediately. There are limits imposed by the classroom structure, time, money, and other school personnel, but an awareness of the existing potential of each classroom and a sensitivity to the children who will spend so many hours in the classroom should serve you in developing, maintaining, and changing the learning environment.

Engaging Parental and Community Support

Involvement of parents and community considerably strengthens a school and its programs. The partnership between teachers and parents is focused on the academic success of the children in their care. School administrators and parents work together to guide the instructional program. Parents help build community support for schools. These interactions among school personnel and parents are not accidental. They are planned and nurtured.

The National Parent Teacher Association has developed a set of standards for parent/family involvement programs (Weblink 3–9). This set of standards serves as a useful guide for developing close relationships among those most concerned with children's well-being in the school setting. The six standards are listed below, with brief discussions.

Standard I: Communicating. Communication between home and school is regular, two-way, and meaningful. It is no coincidence that communication is listed first. Communication begins before a student ever enters school and continues throughout the school years. Teachers should meet parents at least twice a year to discuss their child's progress. Parents should be invited to visit classrooms and observe the instructional program. Newsletters and other written communications should flow from school to home. Activities such as Family Math and EQUALS provide students and parents with the chance to work and learn together and provide suggestions about how parents can reinforce mathematics learning. When communicating with parents, teachers should be forthcoming, sharing sincerely and directly their concerns and expectations.

Standard II: Parenting. Parenting skills are promoted and supported. Being a parent carries with it the responsibility to provide children with a safe home environment that encourages learning. Teachers can support parents by providing information about parenting and parenting programs.

Standard III: Student learning. Parents play an integral role in assisting student learning. Many parents are willing to help their children. Teachers can help by sharing suggestions on extending the thinking culture of the classroom to the home.

Standard IV: Volunteering. Parents are welcome in the school, and their support and assistance are sought.

Figure 3–5   Bulletin board that invites a response from students.

Parents are a rich source of classroom assistance and expertise. When they participate in worthwhile activities, parents come to appreciate the instructional program and provide community support for the school.

Standard V: School decision making and advocacy. Parents are full partners in the decisions that affect children and families. Community schools should seek advice from parents on decisions that affect their children. Parents should join with schools to strengthen programs for the benefit of all students.

Standard VI: Collaborating with community. Community resources are used to strengthen schools, families, and student learning. Partnerships with business, senior citizens, and families can provide support for a variety of school programs. Community members who can share their mathematical experiences with students can help enrich the mathematics program and motivate students.

Parental involvement helps increase student achievement. McREL reports "When a school or district implements a well-designed and planned parent involvement effort, all students benefit, regardless of race, ethnicity, or income. Such a program has been found to be the most accurate predictor of student achievement and success" (2002, p. 94). Plan to become involved in such a program.

CHOOSING AND CREATING APPROPRIATE LEARNING AIDS

Although some classes and school districts do not use math textbooks, the predominant learning aid in many classrooms is the math textbook. Whether a hardback book or an expendable workbook, the text will provide a curricular framework for your mathematics program, but as you strive to become a more effective teacher, you will find it necessary to move beyond textbook pages and worksheets. When concepts are to be learned, physical models are needed. When skills are to be sharpened or facts are to be memorized, repetitive games or activities are needed. When independent work is prescribed, activity cards, projects, learning centers, and computer programs are needed. Providing quality learning resources to support a sound program of mathematics instruction is basic to effective teaching.

Acquiring learning aids depends on three factors: (1) the financial resources of the school or district, (2) the energy and creativity of the teachers, and (3) the priorities established by the school or district and its intent in providing a strong mathematics program. The last factor is influenced by the other two.

Knowledgeable teachers and curriculum specialists should serve on advisory committees for developing school- or district-wide guidelines for mathematical instruction. They should make recommendations for the wise expenditure of financial resources to provide the school and classrooms with useful learning aids.

Commercial Materials

Excellent commercial materials are available for use in teaching mathematics in the elementary and middle schools. They include textbooks and workbooks, kits, games, structural materials, activity cards, and computer software. Each is briefly discussed.

TEXTBOOKS AND WORKBOOKS. For many mathematics programs from kindergarten through high school, textbooks and workbooks provide the foundation on which the program rests. These textual materials are carefully prepared by recognized authorities in mathematics education. A textbook or workbook presents a unified sequence of concepts and topics, which are reintroduced at appropriate intervals throughout the book. Textbooks and workbooks tend to be attractive, colorful, and appealing.

Selecting the mathematics textbook or workbook series is an important task, usually performed by a school district or building textbook committee. Most often, teachers have a number of series from which to choose. This list of acceptable textbooks may be compiled by the state department of education. Several general criteria for selecting textual materials should be considered. One listing of criteria is presented below. A final list of criteria is the responsibility of those who actually choose the mathematics series for a district or school. It is these individuals who have considered the goals of the mathematics program, local priorities, budgetary limitations, and teacher resources.

Here are selected general criteria for choosing mathematics textbooks or workbooks. The textbook or workbook should do the following:

1. Encourage active student involvement and investigation and discovery of mathematical ideas
2. Present task-oriented problems at the student's level of understanding and encourage higher levels of thinking
3. Suggest the use of physical models
4. Use correct vocabulary yet avoid wordiness and undue difficulty that may interfere with the student's learning
5. Provide adequate exercises to assist in introducing mathematical concepts and skills

6. Spiral the mathematical ideas so students confront an idea several times in the elementary and middle school years, each time at a slightly more advanced level, but avoiding needless rote repetition

7. Have an accompanying teacher's edition with valuable suggestions for introducing, reinforcing, diagnosing, and reintroducing mathematical concepts and skills

8. Relate mathematical concepts that have common parts, for example, ordering relations with objects (is taller than), numbers (is greater than), and measurement (is longer than)

9. Build mathematical concepts and skills on previously understood concepts and skills

10. Support the learning of basic addition, subtraction, multiplication, and division facts

11. Allow for students to progress at different rates, reflecting individual differences among children

12. Interest students because it is attractive, colorful, and motivating, page after page.

KITS.   Commercial kits for use in mathematics learning are typically of three different types. **Kits of diagnostic and learning materials** may contain physical models used to test youngsters relative to their development of prenumber and early number skills; for example, classifying, ordering, corresponding, and counting. Kits are available that provide materials useful in developing an initial understanding of classifying, relationships, number, fractions, and measurement.

Throughout this text, we introduce materials available in kits. Unifix and Cuisenaire materials are two such types of manipulatives. It is common to find structural materials in kits. *Explorations and Mathematics Their Way,* popular primary-level math programs, employ a wide variety of physical models in kits.

Kits designed to accompany textbook or workbook series provide physical models illustrated or suggested by the teacher's edition of the series. These kits may contain attribute materials, colored rods, counters, or measuring apparatus. This type of kit is a valuable resource, since it allows students to work with concrete materials as they learn mathematical ideas. Similarly, kits with physical models can be specially prepared by distributors for school districts or to meet the recommendations of state departments of education.

The third type of kit is a **skills kit.** The skills kit provides audio cassettes, cards, or games for basic skills practice. These skills may be computation with whole numbers, fractions, geometry, problem solving, or other math topics. The advantage of such materials is they they allow students to work independently or in small groups at their own level, freeing the teacher to work with other students.

The best way to find out what sorts of kits are available is to peruse catalogs from commercial distributors of educational materials. (See Appendix A for a list of suppliers of educational materials.) Exhibits of kits and other materials are found at professional meetings, such as those sponsored by the National Council of Teachers of Mathematics.

When choosing kits for classroom use, carefully review the goals of the mathematics program. The amount of time devoted to kit materials should be determined by the nature of the mathematics program and the particular kits being considered. The convenience of a kit must be weighed against the amount of interest the kit will generation and maintain. If the kit can provide a function not provided by other components of a mathematics program or by classroom materials, it should be considered for possible purchase.

GAMES.   There is a wide selection of games available to reinforce mathematical skills. Card games, race board games, tile games, target games, dice games, table games, word and picture games, and games of probability may help develop skills in recognition of characteristics, counting, recognition of number patterns, probability, matching, developing strategies, and problem solving. Children are usually motivated by commercial games.

Often, students are unaware of the mathematical value of games. At times, it may be appropriate for you to explain the relationship of a game to a particular skill the students are learning in a nongame context. For example, the popular card game Old Maid helps develop recognition and matching. Once students have played this game, you may help develop the transfer of matching playing cards to matching attribute blocks, parquetry blocks, or tessellation patterns. Be careful, however, not to destroy the students' enjoyment of the game and their motivation for the sake of the mathematics.

Games for classrooms are available from distributors of educational materials, department stores, and toy stores. Select games that fit clearly within the context of the total mathematics program. Sometimes the expense of games may prohibit their purchase. In such cases, teachers are encouraged to construct their own games using materials available in the school. A discussion of constructing games is presented below.

STRUCTURAL MATERIALS.   Structural learning aids are usually designed to help teach particular mathematical concepts and clearly illustrate the concepts for which they were developed. Examples of structural materials are Cuisenaire rods, base ten blocks, and attribute blocks. Structural materials help develop concepts of number, properties, place value, and sorting, as well as logical thinking. Sources of structural learning aids appear in Appendix A.

Although sets of structural materials tend to be expensive, they are often the most useful purchases teachers can make to support a sound mathematics program. Shop around for structural materials and purchase materials only when you know the advantages, disadvantages, and uses of the materials. Sales representatives or educational consultants sometimes offer workshops in using certain materials. Take advantage of workshops to learn the full value of materials.

ACTIVITY CARDS. Activity cards are designed to lead students through developmental sequences that provide guided discovery. Use of activity cards is often associated with classroom learning centers. Activity cards have the advantage of encouraging independent work by students, thus freeing the teacher to work with other students. There are cards for use with attribute blocks, geoboards, pattern blocks, geoblocks, color cubes, and other physical models.

Pictures and diagrams sometimes replace words to direct children to specific activities. The key in considering activity cards for students is the clarity of the instructions. A set of activity cards that children are unable to understand represents a waste of valuable funds.

When considering purchasing activity cards, consider certain general characteristics that the cards should possess. Characteristics of good activity cards are listed below:

1. The questions or activities on an activity card should tend to be open-ended; that is, they should encourage students to give a number of responses to interesting problems.
2. The objectives of an activity card should be clear to the child and the teacher.
3. The wording or directions should be concise and should be presented at the student's reading level.
4. Activity cards should provide some way for students to record their answers or responses.
5. Activity cards should allow for higher levels of thinking than just memorization.
6. Activity cards should be attractive.
7. The cards should make use of the environment— the classroom or outside.
8. The cards should encourage active exploration and manipulation of materials.

COMPUTER SOFTWARE. Computer software abounds for the educational market. It serves many functions. It provides opportunities for problem solving, direct instruction, skill practice, follow-up instruction for work with physical models such as attribute blocks and Fraction Bars, interaction between student and computer, assessment, and record keeping.

Some of the software available is of high quality in terms of both the way the mathematics is presented and the cleverness of the graphics that accompany the presentation. The future will see a greater number of software programs that are even more sophisticated and useful. New generations of computers introduced into the classroom will allow students more creative applications.

Not all software is equally useful or of the same high quality. You must be a discriminating consumer. Before you make final selections of software for your school or classroom, take the opportunity to examine the content of each program carefully. Use it on your computer. If possible, let students work with it. Test your reactions and those of your students. See if the objectives of the software match the objectives of the mathematics program. Read reviews of the software in journals devoted to computer education. Make sure the software is compatible with your computer.

Computer software is available through general educational material catalogs and software distributors and their catalogs. (See Appendix A for a list of suppliers of software.) Once on a mailing list, you will have a source for a great variety of software. Attend workshop sessions at professional meetings to find out more about computer offerings. Check with curriculum specialists to see what they recommend. And ask your colleagues in a school. Those who consistently use software will be able to suggest specific programs and sources.

Teacher-Made Learning Aids

Teachers may wish to construct their own learning aids. By doing so, they save money and at the same time tailor activities to fit their students. All that is required is an interest in such a task and the willingness to devote the time and energy needed to do a quality job. Effective teachers are renowned for these characteristics. Following are some examples of games or activities intended to assist students in practicing and remembering basic combinations associated with addition, subtraction, multiplication, division, and fractions. The significance of the games described rests in the adaptability of a single game idea to many useful games that employ the same strategy.

ADAPTING THE RULES OR THE ACTION OF AN EXISTING GAME. Most games that teachers invent are adaptations of existing games they have seen or played. The simplest way to invent games is to modify the rules or the action of one already known. For example, Addition Top It, which we introduce in Chapter 6, is an adaptation of a popular students' card game called War and may be considered merely an addition game. A little more reflection reveals many other potential practice activities. Multiplication Top It is presented in Chapter 7. Then we begin to find other uses for Top It.

1. If addition is to be stressed, the cards can be rewritten with series of three or perhaps four addends. Thus, cards may appear in the format in Figure 3–6a.

2. When students are ready for introductory multiplication work, the addition cards may have three, four, or five addends with the same value, as shown in Figure 3–6b.

3. The original instructions did not mention subtraction. Since addition and subtraction combinations may be learned in concert, Subtraction Top It is appropriate. Sample cards are shown in Figure 3–6c.

4. Cards with mixed addition and subtraction expressions can be used as practice for both operations. The cards might look like those in Figure 3–6d.

5. If younger children are involved, they can play a similar game using dot patterns instead of addition or subtraction expressions. Figure 3–6e illustrates sample cards.

6. Another way to vary the game is to use numerals, as shown in Figure 3–6f.

The essential action has been retained in each variation shown in Figure 3–6; that is, two cards are

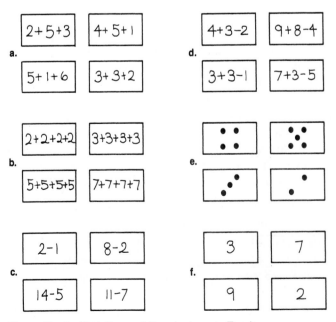

Figure 3–6   Variations of the card game Top It.

drawn, and the larger number takes the smaller. In the case of a tie, another card is picked by both of the players who tied.

The second way to modify a game is to change the rules. One general example will suffice to illustrate changing the rules. Each game discussed above could be constructed so that each numeral or figure is one of two colors, blue or orange. The rules could be altered, so that when both players draw the same color numeral or figure, the larger takes the smaller, but when the two players draw different colors, the smaller takes the larger. Thus, with one rule change, the games assume a different character, although they maintain the goal of providing practice in basic mathematical skills.

Take care to prevent boredom by spacing the uses of variations of the same game and by using only variations appropriate for the practice needed. The multitude of examples listed show how games are invented by modifying the action or the rules of existing games.

ADAPTING THE RULES AND THE ACTION.   There are times when simultaneously adapting the rules and the action of a game produces an activity quite different from the original. For example, consider three activities involving the creative use of dominoes. First, some description of the dominoes and their construction is appropriate. Although it is quite all right to use commercially produced dominoes for these activities, students are particularly attracted by larger sets, which are easily constructed from railroad board. A set that measures 10 by 20 centimeters is a good size. The complete set of 28 double-six dominoes is shown in Figure 3–7.

Domino Activity 1: Sum
Objective: to score as many points as possible in a single round by adding the numbers of dots on five dominoes.
Materials: dominoes, paper, pencil
Players: 2 to 5
Play:

1. Spread out the dominoes face down.

2. Each player picks one domino, turns it over, and adds the numbers of dots. The player with the highest total plays first.

3. Each player then chooses five of the unexposed dominoes but does not look at them.

4. The first player turns over the five dominoes one at a time. When a domino is turned over, the player adds the numbers of dots, then announces and records the total. The first player continues to turn over the dominoes, announcing and recording each sum.

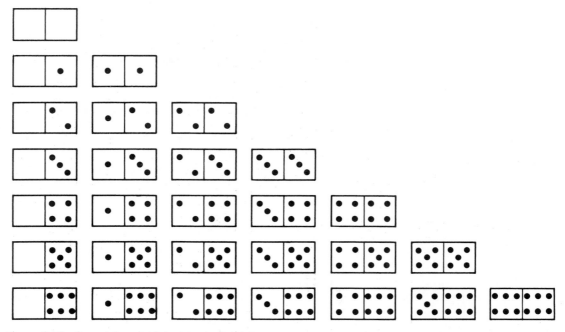

Figure 3–7 Complete set of double-six dominoes.

5. When the first player has finished with all five dominoes, he or she determines the score for the round by adding the five numbers recorded.

6. The next player continues in the same manner, hoping to find a larger total.

7. The player with the highest score wins that particular game. Play continues as before, with different students having the opportunity to win the game. Sample play for one player in one round is shown in Figure 3–8.

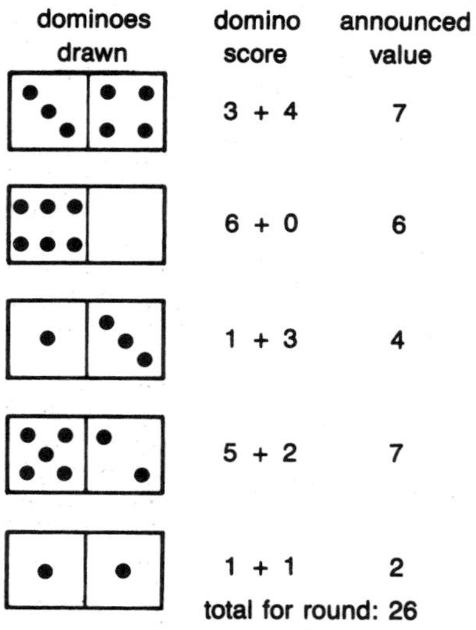

dominoes drawn	domino score	announced value
	3 + 4	7
	6 + 0	6
	1 + 3	4
	5 + 2	7
	1 + 1	2
	total for round:	26

Figure 3–8 Sample play for one player in one round of Sum.

Domino Activity 2: Going Down
Objective: to get as close as possible to zero without going below it.
Materials: dominoes, paper, pencil.
Players: 2 to 5.
Play:

1. Spread out the dominoes face down.

2. Each player picks one domino, turns it over, and finds the difference between the number of dots on the two halves. The player with the highest difference plays first. (See Figure 3–9. Player 2 would play first.)

3. Each player then chooses five of the unexposed dominoes but does not look at them. The player must use exactly four of the five dominoes during the round.

4. At the start of play, each player has 10 points.

5. The first player turns over the five dominoes one at a time. When a domino is turned over, the player finds the difference between the numbers on the two halves. The player then subtracts the difference from the starting score of 10 points and records the new

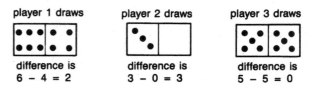

Figure 3–9 The player with the highest difference (player 2) plays first.

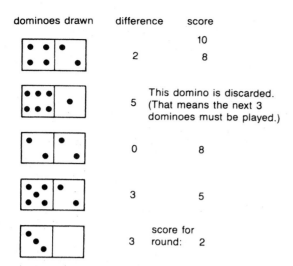

dominoes drawn	difference	score
		10
	2	8
	5	This domino is discarded. (That means the next 3 dominoes must be played.)
	0	8
	3	5
	3	score for round: 2

Figure 3–10 Sample play for one player in one round of Going Down.

score. Because the player may use only four of the five dominoes, he or she must decide which one to discard. The decision whether or not to discard a domino must be made when the difference is determined. Once a domino is used, it may not later be discarded. Likewise, once a domino has been discarded, all of the remaining dominoes must be played.

6. The first player continues until four dominoes have been used, or until the score goes below zero, in which case the player loses the round. Play continues until all players have played.

7. The player closest to zero without going below it wins the round. Sample play for one player in one round is shown in Figure 3–10.

Domino Activity 3: Match
Objective: to collect as many dominoes as possible.
Materials: dominoes
Players: 2
Play:

1. Shuffle the dominoes and stack them face down in the center of the playing area.

2. Each player picks one domino, turns it over, and adds the number of dots. The player with the highest total plays first.

3. The first player declares "Match," picks a domino from the stack, and turns it face up. The second player then picks a domino from the stack and turns it face up.

4. If there is a match, the player declaring match picks up and keeps both dominoes. If no match occurs, the second player picks up both dominoes. A match occurs when the dots on either end of one domino match the dots on either end of the other domino

or when the sum of dots on one domino matches the sum of dots on the other domino.

5. Play continues with the second player declaring match. Both players then turn over dominoes to see who will keep the dominoes.

6. Play continues with players alternately declaring match until all the dominoes have been taken.

7. The player with the greatest number of dominoes wins the game.

As you can see, these domino activities are different from the traditional games of dominoes. They do, however, represent the creative use of a common material. With additional thought, you should be able to develop some domino activities of your own. How might the dominoes be used with multiplication, fractions, or decimals?

Student-Made Learning Aids

Students are capable of developing and constructing learning aids. We have encouraged you to involve students in inventing problem-solving activities. We also encourage you to challenge students to develop fun games and activities that may be used to reinforce skills. Their first attempts to develop *new* games will most likely involve changing the rules of an existing game. Students may wish to alter games in the ways mentioned earlier for teachers.

After a little practice with games, students will be interested in trying to invent games of their own. One way we have found to generate enthusiasm for inventing games is to announce a games contest. A games contest can be effective if it is preceded by discussion and analysis of the components of various games. Kohl (1974) described six such components in detail: theme, playing board, pieces, decision devices, goals, and teaching the game. Once students know about the structure of games, they will be more effective inventors of games. Cruikshank and Martin (1981) describe how one successful games contest was organized and operated. Whether participating in a games contest, suggesting changes in how games are played, or experimenting with making games, students prove to be imaginative and creative.

Constructing Learning Aids

Once you decide on a sound, usable learning aid, begin construction. Game boards and cards should be attractive and colorful. Children enjoy bright, cheery materials with which to play. These materials can be made with brightly colored railroad board or with colorful lettering and drawings on white railroad board. Pictures cut from magazines, ready-made stickers, or students' drawings sometimes add an extra touch of color that attracts students.

Materials should be durable. Teachers willing to spend the time and effort to produce a long-lasting, durable aid will be rewarded by time saved repairing or remaking the activity. Most teacher-made materials may be protected by covering the board or cards with either plastic laminate or clear contact paper. Both protective materials are readily available at art, hardware, and variety stores. Once covered, front and back, a learning aid will last for months or even years.

The quality of an aid is improved if care is taken when lettering or attaching pictures to the material. Letters and numerals should be easy to read. They may be affixed by hand, such as rub-on letters, or stenciled. Gummed letters or numerals also may be used. Using a lettering machine such as an Ellison to cut out letters, numerals, and teaching aids such as tangrams, pentominoes, fraction pieces, attribute blocks, pattern blocks and base ten blocks can also enhance the quality of your learning aids.

Some activities should have written instructions or should be explained by the teacher. Because an activity with poorly explained rules is of little value, the instructions should be carefully worded to be clear and concise. Pictures or drawings are often useful in explaining the action of a game.

Besides motivating students, learning aids should help reinforce or teach a concept or skill. There should be no question in your mind about what concept or skill is being presented by a learning aid. As well, for nearly every learning aid, consider the potential for adapting it to make another learning aid for teaching mathematics, communication skills, social studies, science, and so on.

Concentration games are among the most versatile. Sixteen to 48 cards may reinforce shapes, number patterns, numeral-number recognition, addition, subtraction, multiplication, division, words with the same beginning sound, homonyms, names and faces, animals and habitats, and so forth. For younger children, fewer cards (8 to 16) should be used and the cards should be laid out in two rows. The simplicity of concentration games makes them practical learning aids.

When you are assigned your first classroom, take the opportunity to go into the room alone and look it over. If it is during the summer, there may be no furniture or the furniture may be in disarray. Imagine how you would like the classroom to look. Imagine children in the room and instruction taking place. Begin to sense how all of the space can be useful. When you leave, let your mind work on how that learning environment will be molded in the months to come into an exciting, alive, dynamic environment for all the children. What a wonderful place it will be in which to learn mathematics!

ONGOING PROFESSIONAL DEVELOPMENT

Your college commencement has two meanings. The first is the ceremony celebrating your completion of all degree requirements. The second is the beginning of something. That something is the beginning of a teaching career and the beginning of your professional growth. Your teaching experience will provide a springboard from which to engage in professional development. The enrichment that you will experience and the ability that you will gain will come from a variety of activities in which you participate.

The NCTM Professional Standards provides a list of professional development activities in Standard 6. Paraphrased, the list includes trying alternative teaching approaches and strategies, reflecting on learning and teaching, engaging in workshops and educational opportunities, working with others who teach mathematics, reading and discussing professional publications, discussing issues in mathematics education, helping develop professional development activities, and working for change in mathematics education (1991, p. 168).

As professionals, we thrive in situations that provide rich new ideas to consider and try. To find these ideas we must become lifelong learners.

FOR YOU AS A TEACHER: IDEAS FOR DISCUSSION AND YOUR PROFESSIONAL PORTFOLIO

This section is intended to provide you the opportunity to read, write, and reflect on key elements of this chapter. We list several discussion ideas. We hope that one or more of these ideas will prove interesting to you and that you will choose to investigate and write about the ideas. The results of your work should be considered as part of your professional portfolio. You might consider these two questions as guides for your writing: "What does the material in this chapter mean for you as a teacher?" or "How can what you are reading be translated into a teaching practice for you as a teacher?"

DISCUSSION IDEAS

1. Select a book from the NCTM Navigations series (see Weblink 3–1). Describe how that Navigation book might serve as a resource to you as a teacher of mathematics.

2. Discuss your personal learning style and your anticipated personal teaching style. How will these two factors affect you as a teacher?

3. Explain the value of developing lesson plans in detail as you begin your student teaching experiences and the value of developing block plans as you begin your teaching career. Describe a situation in which it is important to augment block plans by writing out more complete directions for yourself.

4. Investigate cooperative learning procedures by reading either Johnson and Johnson (1987), *Learning Together and Alone,* or Kagan (1992), *Cooperative Learning.* Discuss when cooperative learning groups are appropriate and when other forms of grouping are appropriate.

5. Select an issue of *Teaching Children Mathematics* or *Mathematics Teaching in the Middle School.* Find an article of interest and prepare a lesson plan to teach the topic suggested in the article. Share your lesson plan with fellow students.

6. Describe the value of various types of assessment techniques: observation and questioning, performance-based, teacher-made, writing, group problem solving, standardized tests, and textbook tests. When is one technique more or less important?

7. Develop a set of goals and a plan to meet the needs of the diverse group of children that you will have as students.

8. Sketch a classroom with which you are familiar or in which you would like to begin your teaching. Discuss the advantages of the room arrangment with respect to the mathematics teaching style that you envision for yourself and the children that you will be teaching.

ADDITIONAL RESOURCES

REFERENCES

Abruscato, Joseph, "Early Results and Tentative Implications from the Vermont Portfolio Project," *Phi Delta Kappan,* 74, no. 6 (February 1993), 474–77.

Baratta-Lorton, Mary, *Mathematics Their Way: An Activity-Centered Mathematics Program for Early Childhood Education,* Menlo Park, CA: Addison-Wesley, 1995.

Barson, Alan, "Task Cards," *Arithmetic Teacher,* 26 no. 2 (October 1978), 53–54.

Burk, Donna, Allyn Snider, and Paula Symonds, *Math Excursions 2.* Portsmouth, NH: Heinemann, 1991.

Burns, Marilyn, "Groups of Four: Solving the Management Problem," *Learning,* 10, no. 2 (September 1981), 46–51.

———, *A Collection of Math Lessons from Grades 3 through 6.* White Plains, NY: 1987.

———, *A Collection of Math Lessons from Grades 3 Through 6.* White Plains, NY: Math Solutions Publications, 1987.

Burns, Marilyn and Bonnie Tank, *A Collection of Math Lessons from Grades 1 Through 3.* White Plains, NY: Math Solutions Publications, 1988.

Burns, Marilyn and Cathy Humphreys, *A Collection of Math Lessons from Grades 6 Through 8.* White Plains, NY: Math Solutions Publications, 1990.

Charles, Randall, Frank Lester, and Phares O'Daffer, *How to Evaluate Progress in Problem Solving.* Reston, VA: National Council of Teachers of Mathematics, 1987.

Childs, Leigh, and Nancy Adams, *Math Sponges.* San Diego, CA: National Institute for Curriculum Enrichment, 1979.

Coombs, Betty, and Lalie Harcourt, *Explorations 2.* Don Mills, ON: Addison-Wesley, 1986.

Copeland, Richard W., *How Children Learn Mathematics.* Englewood Cliffs, NJ: Merrill/Prentice Hall, 1984.

Cruikshank, Douglas E., and John A. Martin, Jr. "The Mathematical Game Contest," *Arithmetic Teacher,* 28, no 5 (January 1981), 42–45.

Duckworth, Eleanor, *"The Having of Wonderful Ideas" and Other Essays in Teaching and Learning.* New York: Teachers College Press, 1987.

Edge, Dougals, "Beyond the Classroom," *Teaching Children Mathematics,* 4, no. 6 (February 1998), 308–309.

EQUALS and the California Mathematics Council Assessment Committee, *Assessment Alternatives in Mathematics: An Overview of Assessment Techniques That Promote Learning.* Berkeley, CA: EQUALS, Lawrence Hall of Science, University of California, 1989.

Evertson, Carolyn M., et al., *Classroom Management for Elementary Teachers.* Boston: Allyn & Bacon, 2003.

Harris, Holly, and Sharon Rose Jones, *Eat Your Math.* Corvallis, OR: Callan & Brooks, 1994.

Gardner, Howard. *The Disciplined Mind.* New York: Simon & Schuster, 1999.

Greenes, Carole, et al., *Navigating through Algebra in Prekindergarten–Grade 2.* Reston, VA: National Council of Teachers of Mathematics, 2001.

Johnson, David W., and Roger T. Johnson, *Learning Together and Alone: Cooperative, Competitive, and Individualistic Learning.* Englewood Cliffs, NJ: Prentice Hall, 1987.

Johnson, David W., Roger T. Johnson, and Edythe Johnson Holubec, *Circles of Learning: Cooperation in the Classroom.* Edina, MN: Interaction Book Co., 1986.

Kagan, Spencer, *Cooperative Learning.* San Juan Capistrano, CA: Resources for Teachers, Inc., 1992.

Kohl, Herbert R., *Math, Writing and Games.* New York: New York Review, 1974.

Mathematical Sciences Education Board, *Making Mathematics Work for Minorities.* Washington, DC: MSEB, 1990.

National Council of Teachers of Mathematics, *Agenda for Action.* Reston, VA: NCTM, 1980.

———, *Professional Standards for Teaching Mathematics.* Reston, VA: NCTM, 1991.

———, *Assessment Standards for School Mathematics.* Reston, VA: NCTM, 1995.

———, *Principles and Standards for School Mathematics.* Reston VA: NCTM, 2000.

National Research Council, *How People Learn: Brain, Mind, Experience, and School.* Edited by John D. Bransford, Ann L. Brown, and Rodney R. Cocking Committee on Developments in the Science of Learning, Commission on Behavioral and Social Sciences and Education. Washington, DC: National Academy Press, 2000.

———, *Adding It Up: Helping Children Learn Mathematics.* Edited by Jeremy Kilpatrick, Jane Swafford, and Bradford Findell, Mathematics Learning Study Committee, Center for Education, Division of Behavioral and Social Sciences and Education. Washington, DC: National Academy Press, 2001.

Office of Educational Research and Improvement (OERI), *Pursuing Excellence: A Study of U.S. Eighth-Grade Mathematics and Science Teaching, Learning, Curriculum, and Achievement in International Context.* Washington, DC: OERI, U.S. Department of Education, 1996.

———, *Pursuing Excellence: A Study of U.S. Fourth-Grade Mathematics and Science Achievement in International Context.* Washington, DC: OERI, U.S. Department of Education, June 1997.

Peck, Donald M., Stanley M. Jencks, and Michael L. Connell, "Improving Instruction through Brief Interviews," *Arithmetic Teacher,* 37, no. 3 (November 1989), 15–17.

Peterson, Daniel, *Functional Mathematics for the Mentally Retarded.* Englewood Cliffs, NJ: Merrill/Prentice Hall, 1973.

Reimer, Wilbert, and Luetta Reimer, *Historical Connections in Mathematics.* Fresno, CA: AIMS Educational Foundation, 1992.

Ritchhart, Ron, *Intellectual Character: What It Is, Why It Matters, and How to Get It,* San Francisco: Jossey-Bass, 2002.

Rosenshine, Barak, and Robert Stevens, "Teaching Functions," in *Handbook of Research on Teaching,* ed. Merlin C. Wittrock. Englewood Cliffs, NJ: Merrill/Prentice Hall, 1986.

Rosenthal, R., and L. Jacobson, *Pygmalion in the Classroom: Teacher Expectation and Pupils' Intellectual Development.* New York: Irvington Publishers, 1992.

Ross, Pat O'Connel, *National Excellence: A Case for Developing America's Talent.* Washington, DC: OERI, U.S. Department of Education, October 1993.

Rowan, Thomas E., and Josepha Robles, "Using Questions to Help Children Build Mathematical Power," *Teaching Children Mathematics,* 4, no. 9 (May 1998), 504–509.

Secada, Walter G., and Patricia Williams Berman, "Equity as a Value-Added Dimension in Teaching for understanding in School Mathematics," in ed. Elizabeth Fennema and Thomas A. Romberg *Mathematics Classrooms That Promote Understanding,* Mahwah, NJ: Erlbaum, 1999.

Scada, Walter G., Elizabeth Fennema, and Lisa Byrd Adajian, eds., *New Directions for Equity in Mathematics Educations.* New York: Cambridge University Press, 1995.

Schoen, Harold L., and Marilyn J. Zweng, eds., *Estimation and Mental Computation* (National Council of Teachers of Mathematics, 1986 Yearbook). Reston, VA: NCTM, 1986.

Sheffield, Linda J. ed., *Developing Mathematically Promising Students.* Reston, VA: National Council of Teachers of Mathematics, 1999.

Sheffield, Linda J., Jennie Bennett, Manuel Berriozábal, Margaret DeArmond, and Richard Wertheimer, *Report of the NCTM Task Force on the Mathematically Promising.* Reston, VA: National Council of Teachers of Mathematics, 1995.

Shroyer, Janet, and William Fitzgerald, *Mouse and Elephant: Measuring Growth.* Menlo Park, CA: Addison-Wesley, 1986.

The Slow Learner in Mathematics (National Council of Teachers of Mathematics, 35th Yearbook). Reston, VA: NCTM, 1972.

Webb, Norman L., "Assessment for the Mathematics Classroom," in *Assessment in the Mathematics Classroom* (National Council of Teachers of Mathematics, 1993 Yearbook), ed. Norman L. Webb and Arthur F. Coxford. Reston, VA: NCTM, 1993.

CHILDREN'S LITERATURE

McKissack, Patricia C., *A Million Fish . . . More or Less.* Illustrated by Dena Schutzer. New York: Knopf, 1992.

 WEBLINKS

Weblink 3–1:   Information on the NCTM Navigations series. http://www.nctm.org/standards/navigations.htm

Weblink 3–2:   Information on the Awesome Math Problems for Creative Thinking. http://www.wrightgroup.com/cgi-bin/catalog/series.cgi?series=00246

Weblink 3–3:   Northern Kentucky Mathematics Education website featuring Problems and Resources for Students. http://www.nku.edu/~mathed/p12sr.html#prob

Weblink 3–4:   NCTM electronic example featuring Collecting and Examining Weather Data. http://standards.nctm.org/document/eexamples/chap5/5.5/index.htm

Weblink 3–5:   The Math Forum home page. http://mathforum.org/

Weblink 3–6:   State of Oregon problem-solving scoring help. http://www.ode.state.or.us/asmt/mathematics/pssupport/

Weblink 3–7:   Massachusetts Comprehensive Assessment System test item page. http://www.doe.mass.edu/mcas/testitems.html

Weblink 3–8:   Updated information about the Third International Mathematics and Science Study. http://nces.ed.gov/timss/results.asp#comparison1995to1999

Weblink 3–9:   National PTA standards for parent involvement in schools. http://www.pta.org/parentinvolvement/standards/pfistand.asp

Additional Weblinks

Weblink 3–10:   National Education Association site that features 50 multicultural books every child should know. http://www.nea.org/readacross/multi/50multibooks.html

Weblink 3–11:   Comprehensive site for mathematics resources. http://equals.lhs.berkeley.edu

Weblink 3–12:   Archives of problem-solving challenges. http://www.figurethis.org

Weblink 3–13:   Trends in international mathematics and science study. http://nces.ed.gov/TIMSS

Weblink 3–14: ERIC database of documents pertaining to education. http://www.eric.ed.gov/

Weblink 3–15: Home page of the National Council of Teachers of Mathematics. http://www.nctm.org/

Weblink 3–16: Home page of the National Science Teachers Association. http://www.nsta.org

Weblink 3–17: The American Mathematics Competitions website. http://www.unl.edu/amc/

Weblink 3–18: Stanford University Education Program for Gifted Youth (EPGY). http://www-epgy.stanford.edu/

Weblink 3–19: Johns Hopkins University Center for Talented Youth talent search and testing. http://www.jhu.edu/gifted/ts/

Weblink 3–20: MATHCOUNTS, a coaching and competition program for middle school students nationwide. http://www.mathcounts.org/

Weblink 3–21: National Engineers Week Future City Competition. http://www.eweek.org/

Weblink 3–22: USA Mathematical Talent Search. http://www.nsa.gov/programs/mepp/usamts.html

REASONING, SOLVING, POSING, AND EXTENDING PROBLEMS

GUIDING QUESTIONS

As you read the following pages, consider these guiding questions:

1. What does it mean to reason mathematically and do proofs, and why is it important for students?
2. What is a problem, and what are some characteristics of good problem solvers?
3. What are your goals for students as learners of mathematics?
4. What are several heuristics and/or strategies that students might use to solve mathematical problems?
5. What are some of the influences on a child who is trying to solve and create problems?
6. What techniques might be used to assess students' knowledge and understanding of mathematics, and how might the results of the assessment be used?

Problem-Solving Standard

Instructional programs from pre-kindergarten through grade 12 should enable all students to—

- build new mathematical knowledge through problem solving;
- solve problems that arise in mathematics and in other contexts;
- apply and adapt a variety of appropriate strategies to solve problems;
- monitor and reflect on the process of mathematical problem solving.

Reasoning and Proof Standard

Instructional programs from pre-kindergarten through grade 12 should enable all students to—

- recognize reasoning and proof as fundamental aspects of mathematics;
- make and investigate mathematical conjectures;
- develop and evaluate mathematical arguments and proofs;
- select and use various types of reasoning and methods of proof.

Communication Standard

Instructional programs from pre-kindergarten through grade 12 should enable all students to—

- organize and consolidate their mathematical thinking through communication;
- communicate their mathematical thinking coherently and clearly to peers, teachers, and others;
- analyze and evaluate the mathematical thinking and strategies of others;
- use the language of mathematics to express mathematical ideas precisely.

Connections Standard

Instructional programs from pre-kindergarten through grade 12 should enable all students to—

- recognize and use connections among mathematical ideas;
- understand how mathematical ideas interconnect and build on one another to produce a coherent whole;
- recognize and apply mathematics in contexts outside of mathematics.

Representation Standard

Instructional programs from pre-kindergarten through grade 12 should enable all students to—

- create and use representations to organize, record, and communicate mathematical ideas;
- select, apply, and translate among mathematical representations to solve problems;
- use representations to model and interpret physical, social, and mathematical phenomena.

NCTM (2000), pp. 52, 56, 60, 64, 67. Reprinted by permission.

It is the first day of camp and the counselor, Mr. Martinez, has 20 campers who have never met each other. Mr. Martinez wants the campers to meet, and he suggests that they all shake hands and introduce themselves (see Figure 4–1). If each camper shakes hands with every other camper, how many handshakes will there be?

Try to find more than one way to solve this problem. We have given you a chart to help get you started, but there are several other ways to attack this problem.

Number of campers	1	2	3	4	5	6 . . .
Number of handshakes	0	1	3	6		

As you write out your work, be sure to look for patterns and explain all of your thinking.

REFLECTIONS AND REFINEMENT: After you have solved the problem, compare your work with that of some of your classmates. Did you all solve the problem in the same way? Did you get any new insights into the problem? As you read this chapter, try other strategies to solve this problem. As you continue through this semester, see if you can find other related problems that use similar strategies. Write your thoughts about those here.

Figure 4–1 Campers shaking hands.

Every day, children and adults alike are faced with the need to reason logically and to solve problems. A 10-year-old may need to construct a logical argument to convince her parents that she should be allowed to attend space camp with her classmates. A 7-year-old may be faced with the problem of saving enough money to buy a coveted baseball trading card, or a 13-year-old may have the problem of budgeting his time wisely to be sure there is enough time for homework, piano lessons, soccer games, and talking with friends. He may need to determine the most important activity if he finds there is simply not enough time in a day to do everything. In this chapter, we will look at the importance of reasoning, proof, problem solving, and problem posing as students struggle to make sense of mathematics and the world around them.

MAKING SENSE OF CONCEPTS ABOUT REASONING, PROOF, PROBLEM SOLVING, AND PROBLEM POSING

> Being able to reason is essential to understanding mathematics. . . . Reasoning mathematically is a habit of mind, and like all habits, it must be developed through consistent use in many contexts. (NCTM, 2000, p. 56)

Mathematical Reasoning and Proof

The ability to reason is increasingly important in today's world. Children attending elementary school and middle school today need an emphasis in their mathematics classrooms that is different from that of 100, 50, or even 20 years ago. As mentioned in Chapters 2 and 3, it is critical that students learn to reason, to make sense of mathematics, and to solve problems in unique ways. The rapid advances in computer technology, the proliferation of inexpensive calculators, the expanding amount of data to be dealt with every day, and the ever-increasing rate of change require that children develop new skills. It is no longer sufficient that children develop proficiency in computation and in applying that computation to their day-to-day problems. By the time these children reach adulthood, they will be faced with problems that no teacher can foresee. It is crucial, therefore, that they be taught how to think, reason, conjecture, and construct mathematical arguments and proof. Children of different ages think on different levels, but all children are capable of rational thought. Mathematics is an ideal subject through which to develop these thought processes, beginning at a very early age. The need to drastically change our usual style of mathematics teaching in order to improve the level of reasoning

ability of the average American mathematics student has been noted in three reports issued in the past 15 years. First, in a report approved by the National Science Board, *Failing Our Children: Implications of the Third International Mathematics and Science Study* (Weblink 4–1, 1998), concern over the status of mathematics and science education in the United States, especially at the secondary level, was expressed. The Third International Mathematics and Science Study (TIMSS) reported disturbing findings about the performance of U.S. secondary school students in science and mathematics, ranking them well below the international average. Together with an array of related national data, the TIMSS results raised serious concerns about the state of U.S. education.

No nation can afford to tolerate what prevails in American schooling: generally low expectations and low performance in mathematics and science, with only pockets of excellence at a world-class level of achievement. Formal education has traditionally been the path to productive careers, upward mobility, and the joy of lifelong learning. If we do not arm our children with appropriate tools, we fail them.

It is the conviction of the National Science Board that world-class achievement in science and mathematics education is of critical importance to our nation's future. In the new global context, a scientifically literate population is vital to the democratic process, a healthy economy, and our quality of life (Weblink 4–1).

The 1989 National Research Council's publication *Everybody Counts: A Report to the Nation on the Future of Mathematics Education* noted:

> More than ever before, Americans need to think for a living; more than ever before, they need to think mathematically. . . . Wake up, America! Your children are at risk. Three of every four Americans stop studying mathematics before completing career or job prerequisites. Most students leave school without sufficient preparation in mathematics to cope either with on-the-job demands for problem solving or with college requirements for mathematical literacy. (1989, pp. 1–2)

Nearly 15 years after the National Research Council report, the report from the Committee for Economic Development (CED) (Weblink 4–2), continued to sound the alarm:

> The pool of United States–educated scientists and engineers continues to shrink. Today industry cannot fill key technical positions. If we don't take dramatic steps to improve our math and science education, we could see the day when America is no longer the world center for innovation in a wide range of industrial sectors. Currently business is relying on immigration to fill slots in many technical fields, but that cannot serve as a long-term

solution. . . . If we don't increase the pool of U.S. educated scientists and technical workers by improving our math and science education, we run the risk of crippling our economy in the very near future. The need to reinvigorate technical education has never been more pressing.

All these reports point to the need to increase the rigor, depth, and complexity of the mathematics curriculum in the United States and to reduce the emphasis on the shallow, repetitive coverage of a broad range of low-level topics each year that is typical in the current U.S. curriculum. This is a pressing need for all students, not just those who will seek careers in mathematical, scientific, and technical fields. With the growing complexity of the world today, all citizens need to be scientifically literate and able to understand and produce reasoned arguments and discourse.

Problem Solving

> By learning problem solving in mathematics, students should acquire ways of thinking, habits of persistence and curiosity, and confidence in unfamiliar situations that will serve them well outside the mathematics classroom. (NCTM, 2000, p. 52)

Problem solving has long been recognized as one of the most important mathematical processes by the National Council of Teachers of Mathematics (NCTM). In 1980, the NCTM published *An Agenda for Action,* which consisted of a set of recommendations for elementary and secondary mathematics instruction in the 1980s. The first of eight recommendations was that "problem solving be the focus of school mathematics in the 1980s" (NCTM, 1980). When the NCTM published the *Curriculum and Evaluation Standards for School Mathematics* in 1989, problem solving was listed as one of the four strands that should receive increased attention at all grade levels from kindergarten through twelfth grade (NCTM, 1989). In *Principles and Standards for School Mathematics* (NCTM, 2000), problem solving is one of ten standards at all levels, pre-K–12. Frequently, students need to define or create problems on which to work. Outside of school, problems are not generally spelled out for us in advance. We need to determine the problem before we can find a solution.

This emphasis on problem solving and problem creating raises some very important questions: What is a problem? What are problem solving and problem posing? What are some characteristics of good problem solvers and good problem creators? What influences a person trying to solve or pose problems? What are some heuristics and strategies one should use when solving or posing problems? What types of grouping should be used for problem solving and problem posing? How should the processes and results of problem solving and problem posing be communicated? Answers to these questions will be explored in the remainder of this chapter and throughout this book, for it is important to make problem solving and problem creating integral parts of all the topics in a mathematics program, not separate topics to be investigated only at special times during the school year.

What Is a Problem?

A problem may be thought of as a perplexing question or situation. It should be a question or situation that does not suggest an immediate solution or even an immediate method of solution. For our purposes, a problem should involve some aspect of mathematics, but that does not mean that it must involve numbers. Some excellent mathematics problems involve spatial or logical reasoning but do not involve numbers. A good problem is one that interests the problem solver and one that the problem solver makes an attempt to work. Notice that this definition does not include many of the so-called word problems or story problems that are seen in many textbooks because the student generally has an immediate method for solving the problem and is frequently not interested in the outcome. This definition refers to those nonroutine problems for which the students do not have an immediate method of solution and those problems that arise commonly in everyday life for which there may be several methods of solution. These should be worthwhile mathematical tasks as described in Chapter 3.

Traditionally, problems that have been used in elementary and middle school classrooms have had one right answer, and often one correct method of solution. Shimada, a Japanese researcher who has studied problem solving and higher-level thinking, refers to these as "complete" or "closed" problems. He has developed what he refers to as an "open approach" where an "incomplete" problem is first presented to the students. Children are then encouraged to use many different approaches to solving the problem that may have a variety of correct responses (Becker and Shimada, 1997). Teachers are taught to use the many correct answers to help students construct new mathematical knowledge by combining students' knowledge, skills, and ways of thinking that have previously been learned. Throughout this book, you will find a variety of open-ended problems, and you should attempt to find your own unique methods of solution to as many as possible.

Solving and Posing Problems

We can think of our competencies or depth of understanding in mathematics as forming a continuum or hierarchy, as shown in Figure 4–2. At the bottom of the hierarchy is the elimination of mathematical innumeracy, the mathematical equivalent of illiteracy. In the United States, many would argue that innumeracy is far more prevalent than illiteracy. There is even a website on innumeracy (Weblink 4–3) with links to articles, commercial resources, and activities covering such topics as tips for coping with math anxiety, math in everyday life, helping your child learn mathematics, and the importance of critical thinking. Many people in the United States today seem almost proud of the fact that they do not understand or use mathematics. It is not uncommon to hear an adult say, "Oh, I always hated mathematics. I never was good at it." This attitude rubs off on students, who assume it must be all right not to be able to do mathematics. This is a very dangerous belief, however, as our world becomes ever more dependent on a mathematically and technologically literate society.

Just above innumeracy is the ability to do some computation with whole and rational numbers; students at this level are called *doers*. These students have memorized rules for addition, subtraction, multiplication, and division and generally do fairly well on tests of computation from the math text, as long as they simply have to repeat a process over and over again. Generally, however, they do not understand why they are performing an operation in a certain way.

Above the level of the doers is the student who can *compute* well with all types of rational numbers and who understands the structure of the number system and the concepts of the operations. However, we certainly cannot be satisfied with students who can merely compute, when any $5 calculator would be faster and more accurate than most of the best human calculators.

Beyond the ability to compute is the ability to apply mathematical concepts to solve everyday problems—to be a *consumer*. For our society to function, we must be able to use mathematics every day, both at work and at home. Students need to learn how to use mathematics in stores or in restaurants, when painting a house or balancing a checkbook, and in a multitude of other situations. They must use mathematics to be intelligent consumers in today's society. It is at this level that students are able to solve everyday problems that require more than one step. These problems require that students reason and plan a series of steps in order to solve routine exercises.

It is at the next level that students *solve* the problems mentioned above. These students are able to apply their knowledge of mathematics in new situations when the answer is not obvious and they have no preset rule to fall back on. They frequently use a method that they have not tried before or apply a method they have used to solve a completely different type of problem.

Beyond the ability to solve problems that someone else has suggested is the ability to create, define, or *pose* problems. This requires an ability to see important aspects of a situation and ask questions about it. Most of the mathematics known today has been discovered in the last 50 years, and new solutions would never have been found if someone had not suggested new problems on which to work. It is here that we begin to develop mathematical power. We realize that we control our ability to learn new mathematics by always questioning our results and by searching for new understanding.

At the top of the continuum is the *creation* of new mathematics. This requires first the creation of new questions upon which to work and then the discovery or invention of the mathematics to answer the questions.

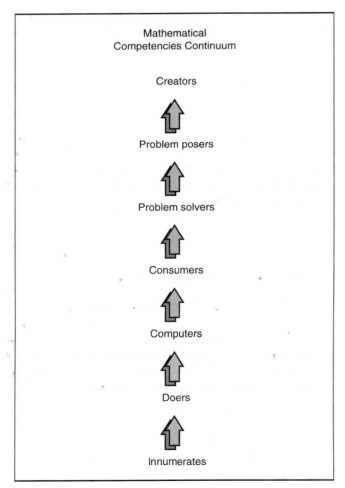

Figure 4–2 Continuum or hierarchy of depth of mathematical understanding.

Even young children can discover or create mathematics that is new to them, and they should be encouraged to do so. They will understand and remember the mathematics they have constructed for themselves much better than any of the mathematics we try to teach them.

Characteristics of Good Problem Solvers and Good Problem Creators

In *Problem Solving—A Basic Mathematics Goal: A Resource for Problem Solving*, the following are listed as traits that good problem solvers usually possess:

- Good estimation and analysis skills.
- Ability to perceive likenesses and differences.
- Reflective and creative thinking.
- Ability to visualize relationships.
- Strong understanding of concepts and terms.
- Ability to disregard irrelevant data.
- Capability to switch methods easily, but not impulsively.
- Ability to generalize on the basis of few examples.
- Ability to interpret quantitative data.
- Strong self-esteem.
- Low test anxiety. (Ohio Department of Education 1980, p. 13)

Even though this list was written around the time of the NCTM *Agenda for Action* calling for an emphasis on problem solving as critical in the 1980s, the characteristics are still considered to be important. However, today we realize the important role of discourse with peers, the teacher, and other significant adults in the development of these abilities. The ability to see relationships seems to be one of the main characteristics that separate expert problem solvers from novices. Students who are not good at solving problems tend to try to memorize rules and facts as unrelated bits of information. Good problem solvers look for the underlying structure and try to relate any new problem to information they already possess.

In creating new problems, good problem solvers use information they understand and problems they have already solved as jumping off points for new questions. They view mathematics as a topic to be explored, with rich new ideas waiting to be discovered or invented, rather than as a series of rules that they must memorize.

Good problem solvers may not be the fastest computers. They take time to think about the problem before they begin to write. They do not give up easily if a problem is difficult. They view the problem as a challenge and enjoy working on it.

It is important to realize that these characteristics of good problem solvers are not something that children are born with. These are talents that all students can

develop with the help of skilled adults. Karp (2003) noted that it is important to react mathematically to student explorations of meaningful problems. By that he meant that teachers should be able to pose and answer questions that are typical and characteristic of mathematics and should be alert and receptive to unexpected or unusual mathematical observations made by students. Students need a variety of interesting problems and probing questions to enable them to develop their problem-solving capabilities. Greenes and Mode observed that teachers of good problem solvers exhibit a number of the same characteristics as the students. "The teachers demonstrated a love of learning, task commitment, swiftness in reasoning, an appreciation for hard problems, a desire for finding more elegant solutions, and confidence in their own abilities. Furthermore, the teachers had expectations for high levels of student performance" (1999, p. 123). Thus, if we challenge all students to approach difficult problems with logic and reasoning, to use models and look for patterns, and to question their answers as well as answer the questions, all students can become much more powerful mathematical thinkers.

Influences on a Person Trying to Solve or Create Problems

> Negative attitudes about mathematics are learned, not inherited. . . . Therefore, it is important that instruction provide appropriately challenging problems so students can learn and establish the norm of perseverance for successful problem solving. (Mid-continent Research for Education and Learning [Mc REL], 2002, p. 86)

The ability to solve and create problems and to construct new mathematics is closely related to the student's attitude toward mathematics, the student's beliefs about the nature of mathematics and about his or her ability to do mathematics, the student's knowledge of mathematics, and the neurological makeup of the student's brain. All of these components may change as the student gains more experience in the construction of mathematics. The arrows in the diagram in Figure 4–3 go both ways, indicating that as the student constructs mathematical knowledge, attitudes and beliefs about mathematics and the neurology of the brain change. In addition, attitudes, beliefs, and neurology affect the ways in which the student creates mathematics.

Students with strengths in areas affecting the learning of mathematics may have different brain patterns than students with weaknesses in these areas. For example, students who process information well visually

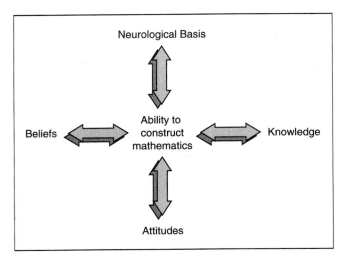

Figure 4 – 3 Factors affecting a student's ability to construct mathematics.

have different brain-processing patterns than those who do not. As students with weak visual skills practice visual tasks, their brain patterns change to more closely resemble those of strong visual processors. Attitudes toward mathematics may also be reflected in the physical makeup of the brain. Students who are afraid of mathematics may emit chemicals in the brain that inhibit the higher cognitive functions. On the other hand, a student who enjoys solving mathematical problems may emit chemicals in the brain that enhance learning. For more information about brain-compatible learning, see Weblinks 4–4, 4–5, and 4–6. Research in this area is growing and has the potential to revolutionize the learning and teaching of mathematics.

Beliefs about mathematics that affect learning include the belief that mathematics is a series of unrelated facts to be memorized as opposed to the belief that mathematics is the study of patterns and relationships. Students with one belief will approach the learning and construction of mathematics much differently than students with the other. Students' beliefs about themselves also greatly affect their learning. A student who believes that he or she cannot do math will generally work to show that this is true, while a student who is confident of success will generally be much more successful. Again, the arrow goes both ways, showing that students who succeed at constructing mathematical concepts change both their beliefs about the nature of mathematics and their beliefs about themselves.

Attitudes toward mathematics affect the construction of mathematical knowledge in much the same way as beliefs. Students who hate or fear mathematics do not do as well as students who enjoy it. Again, the arrow goes both ways, showing that students who do construct mathematics learn to enjoy it.

Background knowledge, of course, also affects a student's ability to construct new knowledge. Students need to develop fundamental concepts before they can build on that foundation to construct new information. Again, as students construct new knowledge, they naturally add to their store of knowledge. This knowledge is generally much longer lasting than anything they have tried to memorize by rote.

Heuristics or Strategies Used in Solving and Posing Problems

A *heuristic* is a general method of solving a problem. A heuristic that has proven to be useful for both the creation and the solution of problems is the model in Figure 4–4. Notice that this is not a linear model. Students can move from any point on the star to any other point.

Students may begin at the step that is represented by the point on the star labeled *Relate*. It is here that a student uses all available information that relates to the mathematical area on which he or she is working. For example, a student studying prime numbers may study the sieve of Eratosthenes, greatest common divisors or factors, least common multiples or denominators, composite numbers, even and odd numbers, and other number theory topics. After a student has investigated several related areas, he or she may create a new question on which to work. This question is then investigated, although the student may look at other relationships or create other questions to study during this process. After a thorough investigation, the solution or solutions are evaluated and promising solutions are reported to any interested individuals. These individuals may include classmates, younger students, professional mathematicians or mathematics educators (through journals, the Internet, or conferences), interested parties in industry, and teachers. Results from any investigation should then be recycled to stimulate the creation of other questions to study. The NCTM journal, *Teaching Children Mathematics*, has a section each month called Problem Solvers that introduces a

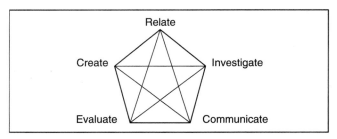

Figure 4 – 4 Heuristic for problem posing and problem solving.

rich mathematical task that can be investigated by students of all levels in a variety of ways. Teachers are encouraged to have their students explore these problems and submit their solutions to the journal for publication. These problems give teachers and students an excellent opportunity to develop their mathematical creativity.

Among the best-known general approaches to problem solving is that of Polya (1957). He outlined four steps in the problem-solving process: (1) **understand the problem,** (2) **devise a plan,** (3) **carry out the plan,** and (4) **look back.** The first step seems obvious, yet children are often frustrated because they do not understand what the problem asks. It is at this stage that students must restate the problem in their own words and reflect on the meaning of any questions in the problem. The second step suggests that reflection and planning will be rewarded later on. The third step requires children to apply one or more problem-solving skills. The fourth step calls for reviewing the process to make sure the problem is solved and there are no loose ends.

The skills that serve children as they tackle mathematical problems have been enumerated in many publications, some of which are listed at the end of the chapter. One of these publications, "Problem Solving in Mathematics" (Lane County Mathematics Project, 1983), suggests the following five skills:

1. **Guess and check.** Individuals using this skill make an educated guess and check the guess against the conditions of the problem. The result allows the problem solver to make a new, more refined guess. The process continues until a solution is reached. Here is an example.

Problem: The Ridefun Toy Store sells only wagons and bicycles. On a particular day, it sold 12 items, with a total of 32 wheels. How many wagons and how many bicycles were sold that day?

- *Understanding the problem.* Perhaps we can visualize the wagons and bicycles. The wagons each have 4 wheels; the bicycles, 2. A total of 12 items are sold on this day.

- *Devising a plan.* We can draw pictures of wagons and bicycles and count the number of wheels. This will take a while. Perhaps we can guess a number of wagons, then find the number of bicycles by subtracting. Then, we can multiply the number of wagons by 4 and the number of bicycles by 2 and add together the products to find the total number of wheels.

- *Carrying out the plan (guess and check).* We observe that 8 wagons alone have 32 wheels, so fewer than 8 wagons are purchased. Our first guess is 6 wagons and 6 bicycles. We find that those 12 items produce

24 + 12, or 36, wheels. Because the total is too many wheels, we refine our guess to 5 wagons and 7 bicycles. Now we have 20 + 14, or 34, wheels. Finally, we guess 4 wagons and 8 bicycles. Thus, we have 16 + 16, or 32, wheels, meeting the requirements of the problem.

- *Looking back.* We make sure our 4 wagons and 8 bicycles make a total of 12 items. And, because we know there are 32 wheels, we are satisfied with the results.

2. **Look for a pattern.** In some problems, we try to find patterns. These patterns may be visual, numerical, or sometimes both. Once a pattern is recognized, the problem will most likely be quickly solved.

Problem: Numbers describe the triangular dot patterns shown in Figure 4–5. below. What are the next three numbers that follow 15? As we reflect on this problem using the heuristic in Figure 4–4, we relate this to other problems that we have solved before. Since we have worked the handshake problem at the beginning of the chapter, we notice that this seems to have the same pattern. We notice that each dot pattern has one more dot in its bottom row than the previous dot pattern: 1 has one dot in the bottom row; 3, two dots in the bottom row; 6, three dots in the bottom row; 10, four dots in the bottom row; and 15, five dots in the bottom row. We also notice that as we move up each triangle, each dot row has one less dot than the previous row. Using this pattern, the next triangle would have six dots in the bottom row, for 6 + 5 + 4 + 3 + 2 + 1, or 21, total dots. Next would be a triangle with seven dots in the bottom row, for 7 + 6 + 5 + 4 + 3 + 2 + 1, or 28, total dots. The final triangle would have eight dots in the bottom row, for 8 + 7 + 6 + 5 + 4 + 3 + 2 + 1, or 36, total dots.

3. **Make a systematic list.** This skill is used when it is necessary to describe all possibilities for an event. A list is developed systematically to decrease the chance of omitting an item.

Problem: Using only quarters, dimes, nickels, and pennies, how many different ways can you pay for an item that costs $.25? Using Polya's framework for problem solving, we decide to list all the ways to

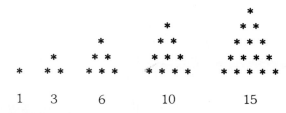

| 1 | 3 | 6 | 10 | 15 |

Figure 4–5 Triangular numbers pattern.

produce $.25 with the coins given. Here is the list that we developed:

Quarters	Dimes	Nickels	Pennies	Total
1	0	0	0	$.25
0	2	1	0	.25
0	2	0	5	.25
0	1	3	0	.25
0	1	2	5	.25
0	1	1	10	.25
0	1	0	15	.25
0	0	5	0	.25
0	0	4	5	.25
0	0	3	10	.25
0	0	2	15	.25
0	0	1	20	.25
0	0	0	25	.25

Notice that as we moved from left to right in the list, we started with the largest number of each coin we could use to produce $.25. (You may have thought of another equally effective way to make this list systematic.) As a result, we found 13 different ways to pay for an item that costs $.25.

4. **Make and use a drawing or model.** Some problems can be solved easily with a drawing or model. The drawing includes the conditions of the problem and allows the solver to see the solution.

Problem: Adams School has 11 members on its volleyball team, 6 on the court and 5 substitutes. Whenever the team scores a point, the 5 substitutes jump up and give each other a "high five" to celebrate—that is, each substitute jumps up and slaps the upheld hand of each of the other substitutes. How many high fives are given for each point scored? After understanding the problem, we decide that drawing a representation of the substitutes will be helpful. Figure 4–6 shows circles to represent the five substitutes. The line drawn between each pair of substitutes represents the hand slap between those two. When we count all the lines on the drawing, we find that there are 10 high fives for each point scored. Again, as we investigate this problem, we realize that this drawing is another way of looking at the handshake problem. Connections and relationships among seemingly different problems become even clearer as we use different representations and problem-solving strategies.

5. **Eliminate possibilities.** Using this skill allows the problem solver to reduce the number of possible responses that a problem may suggest. When possibilities are eliminated, the solution becomes more manageable.

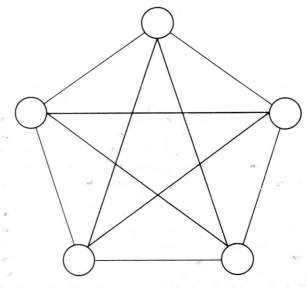

Figure 4–6 Drawing to show "high fives" of the volleyball team.

Problem: Jill threw 4 darts at a dartboard target like the one shown in Figure 4–7. Each dart hit the target and none landed on a line.

Which of the scores below could Jill have earned?

14	23	26	8	16
34	19	32	6	30

As we thought about how this problem might be solved, it occurred to us to find the largest and smallest scores possible with 4 darts. If they all landed in the region worth 8 points we would have 32 points, the largest possible score; if they all landed in the region worth 2 points, we would have 8 points, the smallest possible score given that all the darts hit the target. We can now eliminate any score below 8 or above 32.

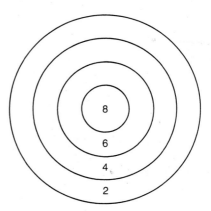

Figure 4–7 Dartboard target.

Next, we notice that all regions have even-numbered scores. Even scores mean that any combination of 4 scores will produce an even total. We can now eliminate the odd numbers. After eliminating the odd numbers, those below 8, and those above 32, we have 14, 26, 8, 16, 30, and 32. With a little checking, we find that Jill could have earned any of these scores.

The skills just discussed are but a sampling of the problem-solving skills you are likely to find as you further investigate problem solving. The skills fit well into Polya's general approach.

There are several other lists of problem-solving strategies, some of which are variations of these and some of which are a bit different. For example, you might see "make a table or chart," which would be similar to "make a systematic list," or you might see "use a simpler problem" or "use logical reasoning," which may be similar to "eliminate possibilities." Other useful problem-solving strategies include working backwards, acting out the problem, and changing your point of view.

Working backwards is useful when you know the desired outcome of a problem but are having difficulty getting started working toward it. You may be able to work to the beginning from the end more easily than working to the end from the beginning.

Problem: Hank is selling boxes of raspberries from his garden. The first person he meets buys half of his boxes. The next person buys 4 boxes of berries. When he meets a third person, he sells half of the remaining boxes. The next customer buys 7 boxes of berries. Hank now has only 1 box of berries left, and he gives this to his father for a fresh raspberry tart. How many boxes of berries did Hank have to begin with?

After understanding the problem, we may try the strategy of guess and check. It is very difficult to guess the original number of boxes, however, and this strategy may go on for quite some time before the answer is guessed. However, if we start at the end and work back to the beginning, the problem is fairly simple as shown in Figure 4–8. We know that at the end, Hank had 1 box left. If customer number 4 bought 7 boxes, he must have had 8 boxes left after the third customer. If the third customer bought half of his boxes, he must have had 16 boxes left after the second customer. The second customer bought 4 boxes, so he must have had 20 boxes left after the first customer. This was half of the original number. Therefore, Hank began with 40 boxes.

Acting out the problem is a fun strategy as well as a useful one. Children frequently need to work through the problem with their peers both to understand the problem better and to solve it.

Problem: Jack said to Andreas, "You are my father." Andreas said to Judy, "You are my mother." Judy said to Tyson, "You are my son." Tyson said to Jennifer, "You are my daughter." What is the relationship between Jack and Jennifer?

Students would probably have difficulty figuring out the relationship between Jack and Jennifer by just reading the problem. Some students may be able to figure out that the two are cousins by drawing a picture of the relationships as in Figure 4–9, but others may need to actually see children taking the roles of the people in the problem and discussing their relationships.

Changing your point of view is a useful strategy to use with some tricky problems. You might think you understand a problem when in fact you are reading into it conditions that do not exist. The following problem is a well-known example.

Problem: Connect all nine dots in the following diagram using only four line segments without lifting your pencil.

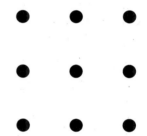

You might think that you are not allowed to break out of the restrictions of the 3-by-3 array. You have to change your point of view to realize that if you go beyond the array, you can connect the dots as follows.

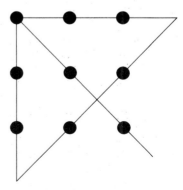

THINKING LIKE A MATHEMATICIAN. Students should learn to approach mathematics in the same manner that a mathematician does, striving to make sense of

Figure 4—8 Example of problem for working backwards strategy.

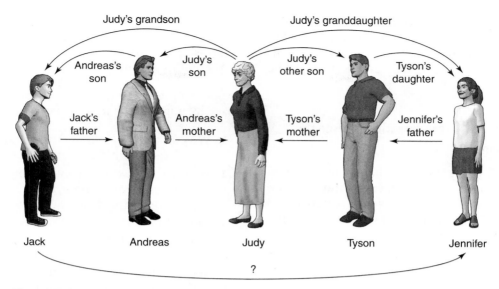

Figure 4–9 Acting out a problem to build understanding.

interesting problems that have been posed by the teacher, the book, or preferably by the students themselves. In Chapter 2 we mentioned that we should be helping student develop thinking dispositions that reflect the thinking processes of mathematicians. Students who learn mathematics in this way, constructing their own means of making sense of the world, become powerful, confident, logical problem solvers who are not dependent upon the teacher or the textbook to verify their reasoning or solutions.

Using an Open Approach to Reasoning, Problem Solving, and Problem Posing.

As noted earlier, many problems lend themselves to a variety of solutions, and children should have numerous experiences with such problems. These problems are not designed to teach any specific problem-solving strategy, but rather give the students an opportunity to use a more open-ended heuristic such as the one in Figure 4–4. In this case, they relate the question to problems they have solved earlier and then create their own strategies, thus developing higher-level thinking skills. As they investigate the problem, students might use multiple representations such as tables, drawings, symbols, physical models, and equations. Throughout the problem solving, students are asked to evaluate their solutions and to communicate their results with others.

A sample of one of these problems, with a variety of possible responses and related problems, follows. In a typical textbook problem, students might be asked to look at a series of odd numbers and determine the next numbers in the sequence. On a more difficult level, the teacher might ask the students to determine what the

100th number in the sequence would be. A more interesting way of looking at this problem would be to ask the students to do the following investigation.

Problem: Study the following diagram. Where would the number 289 appear if this sequence continues?

$$
\begin{array}{ccccccc}
 & & & 1 & & & \\
 & & 3 & & 5 & & \\
 & 7 & & 9 & & 11 & \\
13 & & 15 & & 17 & & 19 \\
21 & & 23 & & 25 & & 27 & & 29 \\
31 & & 33 & & 35 & & 37 & & 39 & & 41 \\
43 & & 45 & & 47 & & 49 & & 51 & & 53 & & 55
\end{array}
$$

Different students might attack this in different ways, such as the following:

1. One student might simply continue the pattern through the 17th row and notice that 289 is in the middle.

2. Another student might figure that 289 would be the 145th number in the sequence. Then, noting that Row One has one number, Row Two has two numbers, Row Three has three numbers, etc., and continuing this pattern, a student could discover the 145th number in the middle of Row 17.

3. Another student might notice that the numbers going down the left side of the triangle increase by 2 more each time. That is, they increase by 2, then 4, then 6, then 8, etc. Continuing this pattern, the student could find that the first number in Row 17 is 273 and the first number in Row 18 is 307.

4. A fourth student might notice that the middle number in each odd numbered row is the square of that number. Knowing that 289 is 17^2, this student might immediately notice that 289 is the middle number of Row 17.

Finding, Creating, and Extending Rich Learning Tasks and Problems

These are only a few examples of what students can do with interesting, open-ended problems. Students who have been taught to play with problems, patterns, and connections approach mathematics very differently from students who have been taught that there is one right way to solve a problem, the teachers and the textbooks know what it is, and it is the students' job to listen and find out. On the other hand, students flourish and blossom when they are asked to explore problems in depth using a variety of approaches, looking for patterns, making and verifying hypotheses and generalizations, and connecting new knowledge to earlier learning.

As students work on rich learning tasks and problems, they should be encouraged to ask themselves a number of questions designed to help them dig more deeply into the problems. In Chapter 3, we presented a number of questions that are important to discourse and probing students' thinking. It is helpful for students to approach mathematics as investigative mathematicians by using the Five Ws and an H, an adaptation of the guideline used by investigative journalists. With these, students should learn to question the answers, not just answer the questions. Questions students might ask include:

- **Who** needs high-level mathematics? – **Everyone!**
- **What or what if?**
  What patterns do I see in this data? What generalizations might I make from the patterns? What proof do I have? What are the chances? What is the best answer, the best method of solution, the best strategy to begin with . . .? What if I change one or more parts of the problem?
- **When?**
  When does this work? When does this not work?
- **Where?**
  Where did that come from? Where should I start? Where might I go for help?
- **Why or why not?**
  Why does that work? If it does not work, why not?
- **How?**
  How is this like other mathematical problems or patterns that I have seen? How does it differ? How does this relate to real-life situations or models? How

many solutions are possible? How many ways might I use to represent, simulate, model, or visualize these ideas? How many ways might I sort, organize, and present this information?

Applying this list of questions to the problem given on page 89 might result in the following investigations:

1. Why is the number in the middle of each odd-numbered row a square number?
2. Why are there not any even numbers on the triangle? Where would the even square numbers be if they were on the diagram?
3. What if I did not use odd numbers on the triangle? Would the same pattern be true for even numbers?
4. What if I added the numbers on the triangle? What patterns would I notice?
5. What generalizations might I make about the sum of all rows through any row N?
6. Why is the sum of the numbers in any row equal to the cube of the row number?
7. How are the patterns in this triangle similar to Pascal's triangle?
8. How are the patterns in this triangle different from Pascal's triangle?
9. What if I find a square number? Will it always be in the center of a row? Why?
10. What is the smallest sum of a row that is also an even number? Is there a largest sum that is an even number?
11. What is the first number in any row N? What is the last number in any row?
12. How is this problem related to finding the sum of the first N counting numbers? The sum of any consecutive numbers? The sum of any consecutive odd numbers?
13. How many other patterns do I notice on the triangle?
14. How many other interesting questions might I explore about this problem?

Open problems and rich learning tasks cannot be scored simply correct or incorrect. A variety of assessment criteria must be used. These might include:

1. Depth of understanding—the extent to which mathematical concepts are explored and developed
2. Fluency—the number of different correct answers, methods of solution, or new questions formulated
3. Flexibility—the number of different categories of answers, methods, or questions
4. Originality—solutions, methods, or questions that are unique and show insight

5. Elaboration or elegance—quality of expression of thinking, including charts, graphs, drawings, models, and words

6. Generalizations—patterns that are noted, hypothesized, and verified for larger categories

7. Extensions—related questions that are asked and explored, especially those involving why and what if.

Many teachers use scoring rubrics or guidelines to evaluate students' work on open-ended problems. One sample of these will be presented later in the chapter.

As useful as they may be, there is more to teaching problem solving than teaching about heuristics and strategies. Schroeder and Lester (1989, p. 32) distinguish between three different approaches to teaching problem solving: (1) teaching about problem solving, (2) teaching for problem solving, and (3) teaching via problem solving. In teaching about problem solving, teachers help students learn strategies and heuristics such as those discussed here, and students are encouraged to be aware of these processes as they solve problems. In teaching for problem solving, teachers help students learn to solve problems so that they may use their problem-solving abilities outside of school. In teaching via problem solving, teachers help students realize that problem solving is not only the goal of learning mathematics but also the means to learn mathematics. In this way, students begin a mathematical topic with a problem to solve and learn mathematics through the solution of the problem. They construct their own knowledge of mathematics as they work through the problem. Throughout this book, we will present problem solving as a means to learn mathematics and as a goal and a topic to be learned in its own right. The most important of these, however, is as a means of learning mathematics, for in questioning answers and solving problems students become mathematically powerful.

Problem Solving and Reasoning in Projects

Presenting individual problems for students to solve is one valuable approach. Another is to challenge students by presenting a task or a project with one or more problems imbedded in it. These tasks or projects may take several days to complete. One such project designed by preservice teachers Errin Neufeld, Tonya Peters, and Dana Reimer for middle-level students is described below. It is intended for groups of 3 to 5 students.

**Project Title: Parking at the MetroPlex Theater
Description of the Task:** The new MetroPlex Theater is being built nearby and you have been hired to design its parking lot. There will be 5 theaters in the building. Two theaters will have 175 seats each and the other

three will have 325 seats each. The theater will have only one entrance. A city ordinance states that for every 3 seats in a theater, one parking place must be provided. Also, for every 25 regular parking spaces, one handicapped space near the theater entrance must be provided. Your job is to design the most cost-efficient parking lot for the theater. Property for the parking lot sells at $12 per square foot and asphalt costs an additional $.90 per square foot. Keep in mind that your parking lot needs to be safe for vehicles and pedestrians, attractive to customers, have convenient access to the theater, and fit all of the above requirements.

Expected End Product: A drawing to scale of the entrance of the MetroPlex Theater and the entire parking lot, including a written description of how the problem was solved and a budget for the project.

Knowledge and Skills (from the NCTM Standards): *Calculation and Estimation:* Students use mathematical calculations to figure the cost per square foot of property and asphalt that they will need and how many parking spots (regular and handicapped) they will need. Further, they will calculate the units for their scale drawing. *Geometry:* Students will determine the size and shape of the most efficient parking lot. *Measurement:* Students will use measuring tools as they draw their parking lot to scale. *Mathematical Problem Solving:* Students will use pictures, models, and diagrams when making the layout of their parking lot, as well as using basic problem-solving strategies.

Scoring Criteria for the Project:
1. Attractive scale drawing
2. Carefully written description of work
3. Reasonable budget for the project
4. Appropriate number of parking spaces
5. Appropriate number and location of handicapped parking spaces
6. Safe parking lot
7. Attractive parking lot
8. Convenient access to the theater.

ORGANIZING FOR TLC: PROBLEM SOLVING, PROBLEM POSING, REASONING, AND PROOF

When organizing your classroom to emphasize student reasoning and problem solving as the means of teaching and learning, you will find that students can become more powerful mathematicians if they solve problems in a variety of ways, including individually, in pairs and small groups, and as a whole class. When first given a problem to solve, students should have time to struggle with the problem individually before working with a partner or a group. In this way, students have an opportunity to construct their own meaning and strategies before trying to discuss these with others. This helps to avoid the problem of one student telling the others what to do and the others following along without thinking. After students have developed their own understanding of a problem, discussing their thinking with one or two other students is often very effective. It gives the student a chance to discuss the problem and learn from others' mistakes and successes. Cooperative learning needs to be carefully planned, however. You cannot simply let the students work with their friends and hope for the best. If students have never worked in cooperative learning groups before, they will probably need some instruction on how best to work together. They need to learn that everyone should be actively involved in problem solving and that they cannot leave all the work to one person. Students must learn to be accepting and supportive of each other's ideas; telling one of the group members that he is stupid is counterproductive. It may help to assign roles in the group, such as an organizer, a checker, a relator, and a confidence builder, as suggested by Johnson and Johnson (1989, p. 242). Make sure that the children understand that they are each individually accountable for understanding and explaining the problem. Students then become peer coaches as they make sure that everyone in the group understands the problem. Cooperative learning was described in detail in Chapter 3.

Games and puzzles are a great way for children to solve problems and learn to enjoy mathematics at the same time. There are lots of good books that have problems and puzzles for children of all ages and several of these are listed in the references at the end of the chapter. You especially might want to look at the books by Adler, Anno, Burns, Fixx, and Gardner.

In addition to books, several videos and computer games give students a chance to enjoy challenging problem solving. Some of these are listed in the reference list and you and your students will find several others. Be sure to preview some of the videos from Learning Wave and some of the software from Sunburst and Broderbund. The Math Mystery videos are a great way for intermediate and middle-grade students to use their mathematical problem-solving and problem-posing skills in a variety of settings.

Roper (1990) has developed a series of books for exploring cooperative problem solving using a variety of manipulative materials such as unifix cubes, pattern blocks, tangrams, and attribute materials. Each problem is written on a set of four cards, which are dealt to four students. Each student keeps the card he or she was dealt and does not show it to anyone else.

Students do, however, read their clues to each other. All four cards are essential to solving the problem. The students must work cooperatively to piece all the clues together and solve the problem.

Not all problem solving goes on in small groups. There are times when the teacher will want to present a problem to the entire class at once. Be careful when using problems with a number of children at once. These problems should have lots of correct answers or methods of solution, so that when one child finds an answer, the rest of the children can continue to work on the problem to discover other correct answers or methods.

Problems that can be solved on a variety of levels are an excellent way for students of all backgrounds to be challenged appropriately. As students are working individually or in small groups on problems, be sure to observe their progress and challenge them to continue to develop new insights. Encourage students to use the questions of an investigative mathematician once they have solved the original problem posed. For example, you may have one or two students who can solve the original problem almost immediately and thus need more of a challenge. Avoid putting these children in a group of students who have not yet solved the problem and thereby risk ruining the fun for the other children as they solve the problem themselves. Challenge the students who have already solved the problem to think more deeply, asking themselves questions of why, why not, what if, how many ways, and so on.

When children work on problems individually, be sure to leave time for a discussion of the solutions. Children may need time to construct information for themselves without the distractions of others, but after a solution has been found, discussion with others opens up many other possibilities.

COMMUNICATING ABOUT REASONING AND PROBLEM SOLVING

As students work together to solve problems, they are naturally communicating. This should be encouraged whenever possible. It changes your classroom from a setting with one teacher and 25 students to a setting with 26 teachers and 26 learners. Let students take turns solving problems with a partner where one is the speaker and the other the listener. The speaker should describe what she is thinking about at each stage of the problem solving. The listener should not interrupt, but may ask questions for clarification such as, "Is this what you mean . . .?" or "Could you explain that in another way?" Do not limit yourself to oral communication, however.

Students should be encouraged to draw pictures or build models to demonstrate the solutions to problems whenever possible. Students of all ages benefit when they see how someone else has solved a problem. You might even challenge students occasionally to demonstrate their solutions without using words.

Problem solving is also an area in which students can use writing. Not only can they write out a description of how they went about solving a problem, they can write out word problems for other students to solve. These problems are very motivating for the other students. It is much more fun to solve problems written by your friends than to solve the ones in the book.

Be sure not to restrict problem solving to mathematics. The communication of mathematical learning enhances the language arts curriculum, strengthens reading skills, and is a necessary skill in science and social studies. Ask the students to be on the lookout for opportunities to express their mathematical problem-solving abilities in all of these areas. For example, students may keep a daily journal in which a discussion of the solutions of any new problems might be a prominent part. All of this should be included in a portfolio where the students keep a collection of their best work.

As students are writing in their daily journals or responding to oral questions, be sure that the questions of an investigative mathematician are included frequently. Students should discuss the patterns that they see and the reasons that they occur. They should be asked to justify the statements that they make and should try to generalize the patterns that they notice. Include in the journals a section for reflections where students go beyond the original problem, suggest additional problems, and write insights or questions that come up as they are working. Encourage them to return to their problems throughout the year and make additional connections as they learn new concepts and solve additional problems.

CONNECTING AND REPRESENTING REASONING AND PROBLEM SOLVING

Ms. Greiner's fourth-grade class is planning a party for the kindergarten to celebrate Halloween. They are trying to estimate the amount of food, drink, and supplies that they will need. They have determined that each student will have two glasses of Witches' Brew and two black-cat cookies. They have a recipe for two gallons of punch and six dozen cookies. They also need to buy napkins that come in packages of 24 and cups that come in packages of 12. There will be 42 children and 2 teachers at the party. The class is divided into three groups, one for drinks, one for cookies, and one for supplies. They have a budget of $36 to work with. Each group has surveyed at least three different grocery stores to determine the best place to shop, and they are preparing to present their reasoning to the class. They are keeping a journal on the processes that they are using.

Mr. Rodriguez's eighth-grade class is surveying the community to determine the level of support for a new recycling program. They have talked to the city council and two different waste-removal companies and have outlined three different possible recycling plans: a drop-off center, a curbside recycling program for paper and metal cans only, and a more complete curbside program that also includes glass and several types of plastic. They are organizing data for a presentation to the city council next month. They are hopeful that they will be able to implement the more complete curbside program if they have a convincing presentation. In addition, the students see that their study of mathematics has a practical application in their daily lives.

ASSESSING LEARNING OF REASONING AND PROBLEM SOLVING

The assessment of a student's ability to reason and solve problems will require methods other than the traditional paper-and-pencil test. Although paper-and-pencil tests seem to be getting better at testing skills and processes other than computation and rote memorization, there are better ways to determine if a student is competent at problem solving.

Charles, Lester, and O'Daffer (1987) discuss **holistic scoring** as one way to assess problem solving. Holistic scoring refers to assessing the solution to a problem by considering all the written evidence produced by the student in solving the problem. The focus of holistic scoring is the process the student used to reach a solution. This approach is different from the typical approach: first check the answer, then, if the answer is incorrect, try to figure out what the student did wrong. Holistic scoring helps the teacher assess the student's overall performance.

One type of holistic scoring is analytic scoring. With this approach, the teacher assigns a certain number of points to each aspect of the problem-solving process. An example of an analytic scoring guide, or rubric, to guide the teacher in an assessment is one developed for use in Oregon (see Figure 4–11). The aspects of the problem-solving process that are scored with this scoring guide are (1) conceptual understanding, (2) processes and

Some students placed points on circles.
They drew lines to join the points.
Lines that join two points are called
line segments.

1. Count the number of points on each
   circle. What pattern do you see?

2. What shapes do you see within each
   circle?

3. Copy this table.
   Count the
   connecting lines
   on each circle.
   Write the missing
   numbers.

Number of points	Number of connecting lines
3	3
4	6
5	
6	
7	

4. What number of connecting lines do
   you predict you will get for circles with:
   a. 8 points?   **b.** 9 points?

5. How did you make your prediction?

6. Do some research about
   triangular numbers.
   Then find the
   triangular numbers
   on this page.

7. Look at the Chinese
   checkers board.
   How could you use it to
   show triangular numbers?

62   Connecting points to create number patterns

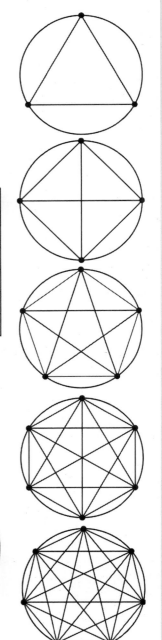

Figure 4–10   From Calvin Irons and Paul Trafton, *Growing with Mathematics,* Fourth-Grade Discussion Book, Denver, CO: Mimosa, 2000, p. 62. Reprinted with permission of The McGraw-Hill Companies.

Figure 4–10 is an activity from the Fourth-Grade Discussion Book in the program *Growing with Mathematics.* This program introduces triangular numbers on a concrete level using pegs on a pegboard in the second grade and then builds on that construction with this problem in the fourth grade. At this level, students make observations about drawings of line segments between points on a circle, record this information in a table, and look for patterns. Students are asked to reason and make predictions about the number of lines they will get for 8 and 9 points and then to discuss their reasons for making these predictions. Notice that students are encouraged to do research about triangular numbers and to relate these to other visual representations, this time on a Chinese checkers board. In this program, activities such as these are used to assess reasoning skills. Teachers use these to determine which strategies students use to solve a variety of problems. Note the emphasis on the development of reasoning from the use of pictures and charts to research, writing, and other visual representations. This use of concrete and pictorial materials as a bridge to mathematical language and symbols is one of the main features of the program from the primary level on. In addition, the program recommends that students' written work such as this be kept in individual portfolios that can be shared periodically with families to let them see the growth of children's understanding of concepts, basic skills, and problem solving. Other assessments in this program include an ongoing assessment checklist for each topic and paper-and-pencil assessment of concepts and skills.

Mathematical language and reasoning are also developed using *Mathtales* designed specifically for the program, a giant-sized *Discussion Book,* and investigations from *Mathematics from Many Cultures.* All of these encourage students to use their natural language and spatial visualization to see how mathematics relates to their everyday lives.

2000–2003 Mathematics Problem Solving Official Scoring Guide

	Conceptual Understanding — Interpreting the concepts of the task and translating them into mathematics — WHAT?	Processes & Strategies — Choosing strategies that can work, and then carrying out the strategies chosen — HOW?	Verification — In addition to solving the task, identifiable evidence of a second look at the concepts/strategies/calculations to defend a solution — DEFEND!	Communication — Using pictures, symbols, and/or vocabulary to convey the path to the identified solution — THE CONNECTING PATH!
6	The translation of the task is enhanced through connections and/or extensions to other mathematical ideas	Elegant, complex and/or enhanced mathematical processes/strategies used to solve the task are completed	The review is related to the task, and enhanced, possibly by using a different perspective as the defense	The connecting path is enhanced (e.g., graphics, examples) allowing the reader to move easily and make connections from one thought to another
5	The translation of the task into mathematical concepts is thoroughly developed	Pictures, models, diagrams, and/or symbols used to solve the task are thoroughly developed	The review is a thoroughly developed look at the concepts/strategies/calculations in relation to the task	The path connecting concepts, strategies, and/or verification to the identified solution is thoroughly developed
4	The translation of the task into adequate mathematical concepts using relevant information is completed	Pictures, models, diagrams, and/or symbols used to solve the task are complete	The review is completed (concepts/strategies/calculations), and supports a solution	The path connecting concepts, strategies and/or verification to the identified solution is complete
3	The translation of the major concepts of the task is partially completed and/or partially displayed	Pictures, models, diagrams, and/or symbols used to solve the task may be only partially useful and/or partially recorded	The review is partially completed, partially recorded, and/or partially effective	The path connecting concepts, strategies and/or verification to the solution is partially complete, and/or partially displayed with significant gaps that have to be inferred
2	The translation of the task is underdeveloped or sketchy	Pictures, models, diagrams, and/or symbols used to solve the task are underdeveloped or sketchy	The review is underdeveloped or sketchy (e.g., focusing only on its reasonableness)	The path connecting concepts, strategies and/or verification toward a solution is underdeveloped or sketchy
1	The translation of the task uses inappropriate concepts or is minimal or not evident	Pictures, models, diagrams, and/or symbols used to solve the task are ineffective, minimal, not evident, or may conflict with their solution	The review is ineffective, minimal, inappropriate and/or not evident	The path connecting concepts, strategies and/or verification toward a solution is ineffective, minimal or not evident

Accuracy:

5)	The answer given is mathematically justifiable and supported by the work	
4)	The answer given is adequate or it may contain a minor error, but no additional instruction in the key concepts appears necessary	1) The answer given is incorrect, incomplete or correct but conflicts with the work

Figure 4–11 Oregon Department of Education Mathematics Scoring Guide. Used with permission. From *http://www.ode.state.or.us/asmt/mathematics/pssuport/.*

strategies, (3) verification, and (4) communication. Each of these aspects is defined in general and also specifically in each column of the scoring guide. For each aspect of the problem, the score may range from 1 to 6 depending on the criteria spelled out in the scoring guide and in the judgment of the teacher. An additional score is given for the level of accuracy in the solution. We illustrate this scoring guide applied to a student's work on the problem in Figure 4–12.

Figure 4–13 is the solution to the problem by a fifth-grade student. The student has worked through the solution and included an explanation of the work. When the problem was assessed using the scoring guide, the student received the following score: conceptual understanding—5; processes and strategies—6; verification—5; and communication—6. The student received a 5 for accuracy. For this problem, the student met the problem-solving standard established by Oregon. You may find other examples of student work and scoring using the Oregon scoring guide at Weblink 4–7.

Holistic scoring techniques provide alternative assessment tools for teachers who wish to collect information that is helpful both in designing problem-solving instruction for students and in helping students become aware of their own thinking processes. Students may use a problem-solving guide or checksheet that corresponds to the criteria on the scoring guide to help them develop improved skill in problem solving.

If students are keeping journals, one method of assessing their work would be to ask the students to record not only the methods of solution, but also how well they are doing at understanding concepts or mastering particular skills. Even young students are often quite capable of self-assessment and can fairly accurately judge their own strengths and weaknesses. You could collect three or four journals each day and keep your own log of the students' progress. Be sure you review everyone's journal at least once every two weeks.

Students working in groups can often do a peer assessment. They know which students are strong on particular skills, and they can help each other and you pinpoint weaknesses, as well as work to help each other strengthen those areas.

There is no substitute for direct observation in assessing some problem-solving and reasoning skills. If you want to know if a student can mentally add two two-digit numbers or multiply a percent by a whole number, you need to give the student a problem and listen for a response. If you want to know if students are working well in cooperative learning groups, you need to sit in on the group and observe. Checklists

CLASS BOOTH PROBLEM

Directions:
Be sure to identify the answer.
Show the work you did to get the answer, and the review of your concepts, strategies, & calculations.

1. S/P   Four classes had a booth at a fair. One class sold hats for $3.00 each. Another class sold pepperoni sticks for $0.75 each. The third class sold popcorn for $1.00 a bag, while the last class sold pickles for $0.50 each. The chart shows the number of items each class sold.
ONE SYMBOL STANDS FOR 12 ITEMS. How much money did the four classes make?

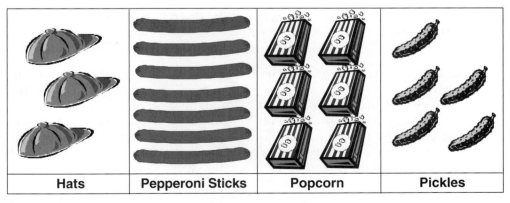

| Hats | Pepperoni Sticks | Popcorn | Pickles |

Figure 4–12   Sample problem from Oregon State Mathematics Assessment. Used with permission. From *http://www.ode.state.or.us/asmt/mathematics/pssuport/*.

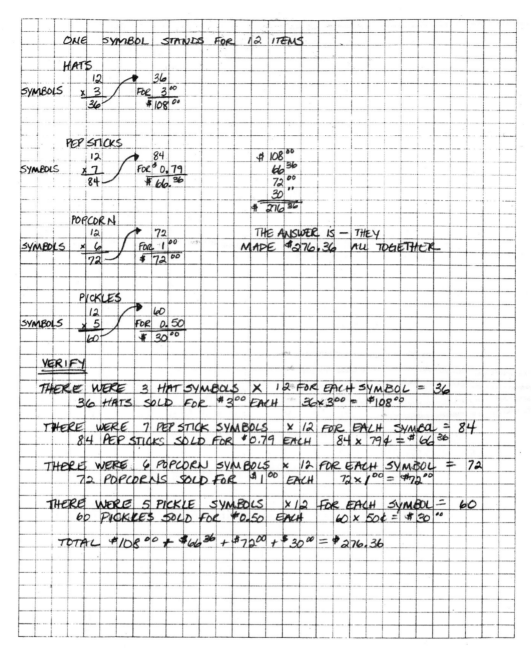

Figure 4–13 Sample solution by fifth-grade student to the class booth problem. Used with permission. From *http://www.ode.state.or.us/asmt/mathematics/pssuport/*.

and a teacher's journal help you remember what you have seen.

You might also want to enlist the aid of parents in this assessment. You could send home a note explaining that you are interested in assessing the student's ability to solve a problem involving making change or estimating volumes and ask parents to observe the students as they go to the store or cook and to question them on their understanding.

The skills you are assessing are as important as the assessment methods you use. In problem solving, you should be concerned with more than whether or not students get the correct answer. The processes they use and the strategies they attempt are also important. You should observe if students can work on problems independently or if they always seem to need help, if they give up before really trying or if they are persistent, if they will try more than one method of solution or if they quit if the first method does not work, and whether or not they check their answers.

In assessing reasoning, estimation, and mental calculation, look beyond the answer to determine if the students have a good understanding of the numeration system, if they can use a variety of techniques, if they can apply the principles and properties of operations, and whether or not they double check to determine whether answers are reasonable.

SOMETHING FOR EVERYONE

Problem solving is an excellent topic for all types of learners. Auditory learners do well in cooperative learning groups, in which they can discuss their ideas and listen to those of others. Kinesthetic learners do well using concrete materials and models to solve problems, and visual learners may draw sketches to illustrate their solutions. It helps all types of students to realize that there are lots of ways to solve problems and that they can use their areas of strength to attack a problem.

Auditory learners frequently enjoy discussing their reasoning but visual and kinesthetic learners may find it difficult. Be sure that problems are often presented visually as well as orally. Let the students use concrete materials when they are first developing the mental algorithms, for they may later manipulate these images in their heads.

Cooperative learning groups give students of all ability levels a chance to participate with others of varying abilities. Students who are good at paper-and-pencil computation, who may have been the shining stars in the classrooms of yesterday, will learn to appreciate students with other abilities in areas such as spatial reasoning or mental estimation and calculation. All students can learn to be accepting of differences and they will find there is much to be learned from those with different learning styles. Be sure to be flexible when setting up groups. There are times when you will want students of different abilities to work together, but be sure that there are also times when you have your top students together so that they may challenge each other. They need time to build on each other's strengths, to learn from each other, and to gain new and deeper insights into a variety of problems.

You should strive to use problems that can be worked on a variety of levels so that all students can be successful at some level, and talented students are challenged to perform at very high levels. Open-ended questions that ask students to solve the problem in a variety of different ways and to ask and solve related questions are very good for this purpose. Some excellent problems can be found online at a variety of sites. Several of these are listed in the references. Also, encourage students who enjoy competitions to join such competitions as MATHCOUNTS, American Mathematics Competitions, Mathematics Pentathlon, and Math Olympiads (Weblinks 4–8, 4–9, 4–10, and 4–11).

FOR YOU AS A TEACHER: IDEAS FOR DISCUSSION AND YOUR PROFESSIONAL PORTFOLIO

This section is intended to provide you the opportunity to read, write, and reflect on key elements of this chapter. We list several discussion ideas. We hope that one or more of these ideas will prove interesting to you and that you will choose to investigate and write about the ideas. The results of your work should be considered as part of your professional portfolio. You might consider these two questions as guides for your writing: "What does the material in this chapter mean for you as a teacher?" or "How can what you are reading be translated into a teaching practice for you as a teacher?"

DISCUSSION IDEAS

1. Investigate the problem on p. 89, finding the location of the number 289. Choose one of the related problems that follow it, and solve that problem. Compare your results to those of another student in your class. Did you use the same strategies to solve the problem?

2. In Chapter 3, we introduced the idea of mathematically promising students as defined by the NCTM Task Force on Mathematically Promising Students. Read the report of the task force at Weblink 4–12. How does the concept of mathematical promise as a function of ability, motivation, belief, and experience or opportunity compare to the model in Figure 4–3 of the bases for the ability to construct mathematics.

3. Choose three children to solve one "closed" and one "open" problem. You might use problems from this chapter or find good problems on the Internet or in any of the problem-solving books listed in the reference list. Observe the children as they work. What strategies did they use? Did they seem to follow Polya's four problem-solving steps? How do they compare on the criteria for evaluating open-ended problems listed on page 90? Share your results with the class.

4. Observe children using one of the problem-solving computer programs listed at the end of this chapter. How does their work on a computer compare to their work solving problems using paper and pencil?

5. Investigate whether your state has a state assessment program that includes the assessment of mathematical problem solving. If it does, what types of tests are given to the students at what grade levels? What criteria are used to judge student responses? If possible, review several of the items that are used along with their scoring rubrics (if they exist) and report your findings to the class. You might want to use the Internet to find examples from other states.

ADDITIONAL RESOURCES

REFERENCES

Becker, Jerry P., and Shigeru Shimada, eds., *The Open-Ended Approach: A New Proposal for Teaching Mathematics*. Reston, VA: National Council of Teachers of Mathematics, 1997.

Brown, Stephen I., and Marion I. Walter, *The Art of Problem Posing*. Hillsdale, NJ: Erlbaum, 1983.

Burns, Marilyn, *The I Hate Mathematics Book*. Boston: Little, Brown, 1975.

———, *The Book of Think*. Boston: Little, Brown, 1976.

———, *Math for Smarty Pants*. Boston: Little, Brown, 1982.

California State Department of Education, *A Question of Thinking: A First Look at Students' Performance on Open-Ended Questions in Mathematics*. Sacramento, CA: Bureau of Publications, California State Department of Education, 1989.

Charles, Randall, and Frank Lester, *Teaching Problem Solving: What, Why & How*. Palo Alto, CA: Dale Seymour, 1982.

Charles, Randall, Frank Lester, and Phares O'Daffer, *How to Evaluate Progress in Problem Solving*. Reston, VA: National Council of Teachers of Mathematics, 1987.

Coburn, Terence, "The Role of Computation in the Changing Mathematics Curriculum," in *New Directions for Elementary School Mathematics*. ed. Paul R. Trafton and Albert P. Shulte. Reston, VA: National Council of Teachers of Mathematics, 1989.

Davidson, Neil, *Cooperative Learning in Mathematics*. New York: Addison-Wesley, 1990.

Del Regato, John C., Mary E. Gilfeather, and Jane A. Schwarm, *Mathematics Pentathlon*. Indianapolis, IN: Pentathlon Institute, 1986. (Divisions I–IV, Grades K–7)

Fixx, James, *Solve It! A Perplexing Profusion of Puzzles*. Garden City, NY: Doubleday, 1978.

Gardner, Martin, *Aha! Insight*. San Francisco: Freeman, 1978.

———, *Aha! Gotcha*. San Francisco: Freeman, 1982.

———, *Puzzles from Other Worlds*. New York: Vintage, 1984.

Greenes, Carole, and Maggie Mode, "Empowering Teachers to Discover, Challenge, and Support Students with Mathematical Promise," in *Developing Mathematically Promising Students*, ed. Linda Jensen Sheffield. Reston, VA: National Council of Teachers of Mathematics, 1999.

Johnson, David W., and Roger T. Johnson, "Cooperative Learning in Mathematics Education," in *New Directions for Elementary School Mathematics*, ed. Paul R. Trafton and Albert P. Shulte. Reston, VA: National Council of Teachers of Mathematics, 1989.

Karp, Alexander, "What Research Has to Say about Talented Students and Their Teachers," in ed. *Activating Mathematical Talent*. Bruce R. Vogeli, and Alexander Karp. Golden, CO: National Council of Supervisors of Mathematics, 2003.

Krulik, Stephen, and Jesse A. Rudnick, *Problem Solving: A Handbook for Elementary School Teachers*. Boston: Allyn & Bacon, 1988.

Kulm, Gerald, ed., *Assessing Higher Order Thinking in Mathematics*. Washington, DC: American Association for the Advancement of Science, 1990.

Lane County Mathematics Project, *Problem Solving in Mathematics*. Palo Alto, CA: Dale Seymour, 1983.

Lenchner, G., *Creative Problem Solving in School Mathematics*. Boston: Houghton Mifflin, 1983.

Mid-continent Research for Education and Learning, *ED Thoughts: What We Know about Mathematics Teaching and Learning*. Edited by John Sutton and Alice Krueger. Aurora, CO: Mid-continent Research for Education and Learning.

Moses, Barbara, Elizabeth Bjork, and E. Paul Goldenberg, "Beyond Problem Solving: Problem Posing," in *Teaching and Learning Mathematics in the 1990s*, ed. Thomas J. Cooney and Christian R. Hirsch. Reston, VA: National Council of Teachers of Mathematics, 1990.

National Council of Teachers of Mathematics, *An Agenda for Action*. Reston, VA: NCTM, 1980.

———, *Curriculum and Evaluation Standards for School Mathematics*. Reston, VA: NCTM, 1989.

———, *Principles and Standards for School Mathematics*. Reston, VA: NCTM, 2000.

National Research Council, Everybody Counts: A Report to the Nation on the Future of Mathematics Education. Washington, DC: National Academy Press, 1989.

Ohio Department of Education, *Problem Solving—. A Basic Mathematics Goal: A Resource for Problem Solving*. Columbus, OH: Ohio Department of Education, 1980.

———, *Problem Solving—. A Basic Mathematics Goal: Becoming a Better Problem Solver*. Columbus, OH: Ohio Department of Education, 1980.

Page, David A., and Kathryn Chval, *Maneuvers with Number Patterns: Student Lab Book*. White Plains, NY: Dale Seymour, 1995.

Polya, George, *How to Solve It*. Garden City, NY: Doubleday, 1957.

Roper, A., *Cooperative Problem Solving*. Worth, IL: Creative Publications, 1990.

Rowan, Thomas E., and Josepha Robles, "Using Questions to Help Children Build Mathematical Power," *Teaching Children Mathematics*, 4, no. 9 (May 1998), 504–509.

Schroeder, Thomas L., and Frank K. Lester, Jr., "Developing Understanding in Mathematics via Problem Solving," in *New Directions for Elementary School Mathematics*, ed. Paul R. Trafton and Albert P. Shulte. Reston, VA: National Council of Teachers of Mathematics, 1989.

Sheffield, L. J., *Extending the Challenge in Mathematics: Developing Mathematical Promise in K–8 Students*. Thousand Oaks, CA: Corwin Press, 2002.

Skinner, Penny, *What's Your Problem?* Portsmouth, NH: Heinemann, 1990.

Sowder, Judith T., "Mental Computation and Number Sense," *Arithmetic Teacher*, 37, no. 7 (March 1990), 18–20.

Stenmark, Jean, Virginia Thompson Kerr, and Ruth Cossey, *Family Math*. Berkeley, CA: Regents, University of California, 1986.

Stone, Janet I., *Hands-On Math: Manipulative Math for Young Children*. Glenview, IL: Scott, Foresman, 1990.

Van Delft, Pieter, and Jack Botermans. *Creative Puzzles of the World*. Berkeley, CA: Key Curriculum, 1995.

Whitin, David J., and Sandra Wilde, *Read Any Good Math Lately?* Portsmouth, NH: Heinemann, 1992.

Whitney, Julie G., and Linda J. Sheffield, *Adventures in Science and Math: Integrated Activities for Young Children*. New Rochelle, NY: Cuisenaire, 1991.

Williams, David E., *Creative Mathematics Teaching with Calculators: Explorations and Investigations.* Sunnyvale, CA: Stokes, 1992.

Yeager, David C., *Problem Solver Projects: Collaborative Group Activities.* Mountain View, CA: Creative Publications, 1996.

CHILDREN'S LITERATURE AND PROBLEM-SOLVING BOOKS

Adler, Irving, *Magic House of Numbers.* New York: John Day, 1974.

———, *Math Puzzles.* New York: Franklin Watts, 1978.

Anno, Mitsumasa, *Anno's Math Games.* New York: Philomel, 1982.

———, *Anno's Math Games II.* New York: Philomel, 1989.

———, *Anno's Math Games III.* New York: Philomel, 1991.

Sheffield, Linda J., Carole E. Greenes, Carol R. Findell, and M. Katherine Gavin, *Awesome Math Problems for Creative Thinking.* Chicago: Creative Publications, 2000.

Silverstein, Shel, "How Many, How Much?" In *A Light in the Attic.* New York: Harper & Row, 1981.

TECHNOLOGY

Annenberg/CPB, *Teaching Math: A Video Library,* K–4. Boston: WGBH Educational Foundation, 1995.

———, *Mathematics Assessment: A Video Library,* K–12. Boston: WGBH Educational Foundation, 1995.

Broderbund, *Carmen Sandiego Math Detective.* Novato, CA: Broderbund. (Software)

———, *Logical Journey of the Zoombinis.* Novato, CA: Broderbund. (Software)

Connell, David D., and Jim Thurman, *The Case of the Unnatural, Mathnet TM Casebook No. 1.* New York: Children's Television Workshop/Freeman, 1993. (Video and guidebook)

Davidson, *Math Blaster Jr.* Torrance, CA: Davidson, 1997. (Software)

Edmark, *Mighty Math Zoo Zillions.* Orlando, FL: Harcourt Brace, 1996. (Software)

———, *Stanley's Sticker Stories Grades K–2.* Orlando, FL: Harcourt Brace, 1996. (Software)

Koetke, Walter, *Hot Dog Stand.* Pleasantville, NY: Sunburst. (Software)

Learning Company *Cluefinders' Math.* CD-ROM Cambridge, MA: The Learning Co. (Software)

Learning Wave, *Codebreakers.* Pleasantville, NY: Learning Wave. (CD-ROM and linked website)

———, *Curriculum in a Box: Math Mysteries.* Pleasantville, NY: Learning Wave. (Series of four video kits: The Pizza Perfect Caper, The Manor House Mystery, The Phantom of the Bell Tower, Mr. Marfil's Last Will and Testament)

Sunburst Communications. *The Kings Rule.* Disk. Pleasantville, NY: Sunburst Communications, 1995. (Software)

———, *The Pond.* Pleasantville, NY: Sunburst. (Software)

———, *Puzzle Tanks.* CD-ROM. Pleasantville, NY: Sunburst Communications, 1997. (Software)

———, *Ten Tricky Tiles.* CD-ROM. Pleasantville, NY: Sunburst Technology, 2001. (Software)

WEBLINKS

Weblink 4–1: Failing Our Children: Implications of the Third International Mathematics and Science Study, approved by the National Science Board, July 28, 1998. http://bohr.winthrop.edu/nsb98msreport.pdf

Weblink 4–2: Learning for the Future: Changing the Culture of Math and Science Education to Ensure a Competitive Workforce, May 2003. http://www.ced.org/

Weblink 4–3: A collection of links to articles and sites pertaining to numeracy and critical thinking. http://innumeracy.com/

Weblink 4–4: New Horizons for Learning: News from the Neurosciences. http://www.newhorizons.org/neuro/front_neuro.html

Weblink 4–5: Website for brain information. http://www.dana.org/

Weblink 4–6: Neuroscience for Kids. http://faculty.washington.edu/chudler/neurok.html

Weblink 4–7: Oregon Department of Education problem-solving support. http://www.ode.state.or.us/asmt/mathematics/pssupport/

Weblink 4–8: MATHCOUNTS (middle school math competition). http://www.mathcounts.org/

Weblink 4–9: American Mathematics Competitions (middle school and high school). http://www.unl.edu/amc/

Weblink 4–10: Mathematics Pentathlon (games competition for K–7). http://www.mathpentath.org/

Weblink 4–11: Math Olympiads (elementary and middle school competitions). http://www.moems.org/

Weblink 4–12: Report of the NCTM Task Force on Mathematically Promising Students. http://www.nku.edu/~sheffield/taskforce.html

ATTACHING MEANING TO NUMBERS

GUIDING QUESTIONS

As you read the following pages, consider these guiding questions:

1. What are the differences among cardinal, ordinal, and nominal uses of numbers? Describe activities that would help children learn each.

2. How is associating numbers with sets of discrete objects different from associating numbers with measurement? Describe events in everyday life that use numbers in both ways.

3. Why should children learn to recognize small numbers of objects by sight, without counting? How might you help children learn to do this? How can you use combinations and partitioning of sets to help children develop number concepts as you are laying the foundation for addition and subtraction?

4. How could you determine whether a child can conserve numbers and how would you adjust your teaching for a child who does not yet conserve? Describe some common errors that students make as they learn to count and to understand number concepts and place value. How will you use these errors in your lesson planning?

5. What is the difference between rote and rational counting and how should you make use of each?

6. What is the importance of place value to the Hindu-Arabic numeration system, and what is the purpose of teaching about other numeration systems and other bases?

7. Describe proportional and nonproportional materials for teaching place value in base ten and in other bases. How might you use technology (calculators and computer programs) for these same purposes?

NCTM Principles and Standards for School Mathematics

Number and Operations

Instructional programs from prekindergarten through grade 12 should enable all students to:

Understand numbers, ways of representing numbers, relationships among numbers, and number systems

Pre-K to 2

• count with understanding and recognize "how many" in sets of objects;

• use multiple models to develop initial understandings of place value and the base-ten number system;

• develop understanding of the relative position and magnitude of whole numbers and of ordinal and cardinal numbers and their connections;

• develop a sense of whole numbers and represent and use them in flexible ways, including relating, composing, and decomposing numbers;

• connect number words and numerals to the quantities they represent, using various physical models and representations.

Grades 3–5

• understand the place-value structure of the base-ten number system and be able to represent and compare whole numbers and decimals;

• recognize equivalent representations for the same number and generate them by decomposing and composing numbers;

• explore numbers less than 0 by extending the number line and through familiar applications;

• describe classes of numbers according to the characteristics such as the nature of their factors.

Grades 6–8

• develop an understanding of large numbers and recognize and appropriately use exponential, scientific, and calculator notation;

• use factors, multiples, prime factorization, and relatively prime numbers to solve problems;

• develop meaning for integers and represent and compare quantities with them.

NCTM (2000), pp. 78, 148, 214. Reprinted by permission.

Think of something you could find 1 million of in your school, home, or community. How will you prove that there are 1 million? Write your plan below for finding 1 million, carry out your plan, and describe your results. As you write out your work, be sure to explain all of your thinking.

REFLECTIONS AND REFINEMENT: After you have solved the problem, compare your work to that of some of your classmates. Did anyone else find a million of the same objects? Did you agree on what it would take to make a million? Did you get any new insights into the problem? Compare your results to those of David Schwartz in his books *If You Made a Million* (1989), *How Much Is a Million?* (1986), and *On Beyond a Million: An Amazing Math Journey* (1999).

All people possess, even within their first year of life, a well-developed intuition about numbers. (Dehaene, 1997, p. 5)

Number concepts begin early in a child's life and extend far beyond being able to count or to recognize numerals. A good foundation in number concepts is crucial in the primary years because it is the basis for much of the work in mathematics throughout the school years and indeed throughout one's life. According to Piaget, children do not acquire number concepts when these concepts are taught to them. They cannot learn arithmetic by internalizing rules or algorithms. They must acquire knowledge by constructing it themselves, not by internalizing it from the environment. Piaget distinguishes between *physical knowledge,* which is present in external objects and includes facts such as weight and color, and *logical-mathematical knowledge,* which consists of relationships that must be constructed by the individual and includes the concept of number. The concept of number takes many years to develop, and children who have mastered number concepts up to 10 may not necessarily have mastered number concepts up to 50 or 100 (Kamii, 1990).

It is almost impossible to live in today's world without encountering numbers. Being able to use and understand numbers is a basic skill that no child or adult can ignore. Using numbers intelligently is as important, if not more important, than being able to read critically and intelligently. According to the National Research Council:

> Without the ability to understand basic mathematical ideas, one cannot fully comprehend modern writing such as that which appears in the daily newspapers. Numeracy requires more than just familiarity with numbers. To cope confidently with the demands of today's society, one must be able to grasp the implications of mathematical concepts—for example, chance, logic, and graphs—that permeate daily news and routine decisions. Literacy is a moving target, increasing in level with the rising technological demands of society. . . . Mathematical literacy is essential as a foundation for democracy in a technological age. (1989, pp. 7–8)

One important component of mathematical literacy and reasoning is number sense, which the NCTM *Principles and Standards for School Mathematics* lists as a major component of the core of the elementary mathematics program, noting that "students should attain a rich understanding of numbers—what they are; how they are represented with objects, numerals, or on number lines; how they are related to one another; and how numbers are embedded in systems that have structures and properties" (NCTM, 2000,

p. 32). In this chapter, we will look at ways to help students build a solid foundation and develop this number sense as they progress through elementary and middle school.

There are three number concepts with which a child should be familiar: cardinal numbers, ordinal numbers, and the nominal use of numbers. The **cardinal number** of a set tells how many objects are in the set. The **ordinal number** of an object refers to its order in a set, such as first, second, and last; and the **nominal use of a number** is simply the use of a number to name something, such as putting a numeral on a football jersey.

Children encounter these number concepts when very young but often attach little meaning to the numbers they hear or recite. Try this experiment: Close your eyes and think of a tree. Now think of autumn. Think of good-looking. Now think of seventeen. Have you done it? When you thought of a tree did you see a picture in your mind? Did you see pictures for autumn and good-looking? Did you see a picture for "seventeen," or did you see the numeral 17? Why is it that we do not see the letters *g-o-o-d-l-o-o-k-i-n-g,* even though good-looking is a fairly abstract concept, yet we see the numerals for number concepts? Perhaps as children we never truly developed a good foundation in these concepts.

Children should be able to use numbers in their cardinal, ordinal, and nominal senses as well as understand the use of numbers for such measurement ideas as money, time, temperature, length, area, and volume. This chapter contains ideas for using numbers in their cardinal, ordinal, and nominal senses. The measurement chapter includes ideas for those uses of number.

Both parents and teachers should encourage children to use numbers informally whenever possible. You may ask the children to keep a scrapbook of the ways in which numbers are used. You can help the children separate the uses into cardinal, ordinal, nominal, and measurement, with a bulletin board to show the uses the children find.

Encourage children to find the number of objects in a set (the cardinal number). Ask the children to take attendance or the lunch count. Children can help inventory books or count the Cuisenaire rods to make sure none is missing. Parents can ask the children to count the plates, knives, spoons, and forks while setting the table, or to count out prizes for everyone at a party.

Children can use ordinal numbers to find the location of something. Julio can note that he sits in the first row in the fourth seat. This skill can be extended to finding the location of the car in a large parking lot or the location of seats at the circus. Nominal numbers may be noted on the jerseys of the players on the basketball team or used to identify anonymous drawings posted in a display.

Older children can look out for very large numbers. The newspaper reports such things as the national debt or the distance to a newly found star. *Guinness World Records* reports many interesting facts that the children can challenge each other to discover. They can interview store owners to find how numbers are used to predict future sales.

Children can think of many other interesting projects themselves. Discussion of the uses of numbers should arise naturally throughout the children's day.

As children work with numbers, give them the opportunity to recognize numbers by sight as well as to count. When there are three or four children in a group, the children should be able to look at the group and tell you the number of children in it without stopping to count each child individually. Give the children plenty of opportunities to count larger amounts. Counting can be used for real problems such as those just noted or for contrived problems such as counting the number of times a child can jump rope without missing or the number of stop signs between school and home. Let the children think of other things they would like to count.

Children often have misconceptions when they are learning to count. Here are some examples that typify a child's misunderstanding:

1. If a child sees a group of buttons in a pile and then sees the same buttons spread out, he or she may think that there were fewer buttons when they were piled up.

2. If a child is counting six buttons on the table, the child may point at each of the buttons, but may count to 10 before reaching the last button.

3. A child may miss certain items or recount them, especially when counting items placed in a circle or spread out randomly.

4. If you ask a child to give you three apples, he or she may give you only the third apple counted.

Parents and teachers should be aware of these difficulties as they help children attach meaning to numbers. Many good commercial materials exist, but parents and teachers should also take advantage of materials in the child's environment such as dried beans or peas for counting and coffee stirrers for regrouping. Useful commercial materials include Cuisenaire rods, multibase blocks, chips for trading, abaci, dot cards, interlocking cubes, counters, counting sticks, some computer programs, and calculators. The specific material is not as important as using some physical or visual material to represent the concept. We must realize that 17 is not just the numeral we visualize or just the word we say after 16.

MAKING SENSE OF NUMBER CONCEPTS

The concepts that underlie early number ideas include pattern, conservation, one-to-one correspondence, classification, comparison, and sequence. Later number concepts include place value and matching sets to numerals and number words. To understand the difficulties a young child has with number concepts, you must first understand the way a child views the world of numbers.

Very young children do not use or understand terms for number ideas the way they do terms for objects in their immediate environment, such as dog, mommy, and cup. Children under the age of two may not be able to understand the meaning of the words *one, two,* or *three,* but they can distinguish between sets of one, two, or three objects. Around the age of two, they begin to understand the number words when a parent asks whether they would like to have one cookie or two cookies. At this time, number words begin to have some meaning for the child.

It is not uncommon for a two- or three-year-old to be able to count to 3 or 4 or even to 10 and beyond and yet not understand the meaning of 6. It is up to the teacher or parent to help the child understand the cardinal usage of numbers. The concepts of numbers beyond two or three were not developed until relatively recently in history, and the concept of zero came even later. We should not expect children to learn these ideas automatically. Some children enter kindergarten with an unclear notion of what numbers really are, beyond being words to recite in order.

The following activities are designed to help young children understand early number concepts. They begin on the concrete level with the manipulation of actual objects and the oral discussion of number words. Later, numerals and other written symbols are associated with objects and pictures.

A C T I V I T I E S

Pre-Kindergarten – Kindergarten

OBJECTIVE: to develop early number concepts through observations and the use of one-to-one correspondence.

1. Go on a scavenger hunt for the number 2. Have the children hold up their hands and discuss the fact that they each have two hands. If they pick up an object in each hand, how many objects will they be holding? Let the children see how many sets of two items they can find in the classroom. Repeat the activity for other amounts.

2. Play the Alike and Different game using a set of cards such as those pictured in Figure 5–1. This is a

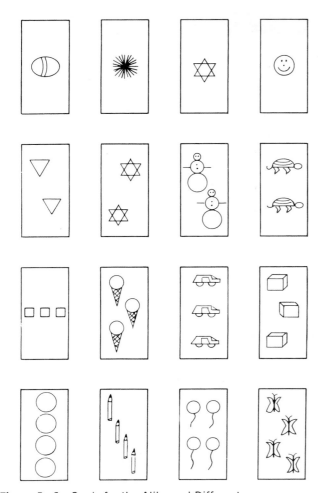

Figure 5-1 Cards for the Alike and Different game.

good game for children to play alone or in a small group. Shuffle all the cards and place them in a pile face down in the middle of the table. Give the children a target number such as 2. Children should turn the cards over one at a time and place each card in the "alike" or "different" pile. If the card shows the same number as the target number (in this case 2), the cards go in the "alike" pile. If the card has a different number of objects, it goes in the "different" pile.

3. Play the One More game using the cards from the Alike and Different game. This game can be played in groups of two to four children. To begin the game, deal all the cards out to the children. The first player to the left of the dealer with a card that has one object begins by placing that card in the middle of the table. The next child then has to play a card on top of that that shows one more object. If this child does not have a card with two objects, the child must pass. The game proceeds clockwise, with each child placing a card with one more object or passing if he or she does not have the proper card. The child who plays a card with four

objects picks up all four cards and places them face down in front of him or her. It is then the next child's turn to place a card with one object or to pass. The winner at the end of the game is the child with the most cards in front of him or her when all the cards have been played.

Another variation of this game is the One Less game. In this game, play starts with a player playing a card showing four objects and each player in turn playing a card with one fewer object.

4. Use the cards from the Alike and Different game to play several variations. Show the child a set of cards in which all of the cards but one show the same number of objects. Ask the child which card does not belong. If the child responds with a card you do not expect, ask the child the reason for his or her response; the answer may be a legitimate correct response.

Show the child a set of cards that show the same number of objects. Ask the child to give you another card that shows this number.

Ask the child to sort the cards so that cards in each pile show the same number.

OBJECTIVE: to reinforce early number concepts on a pictorial, connecting level.

5. Let the children draw pictures of all the body parts they can think of that come in sets of two. Encourage responses that we may not think of immediately, such as elbows and thumbs, as well as the more conventional responses of arms and legs.

Notice that in these activities, the numerals are not introduced. The numbers are discussed orally with the children, and counting is not used. The children learn to associate a number with a set simply by looking at the set, but they can check their answers, obtained by sight, by counting the objects in the sets. After children are comfortable with these activities, add numerals to the activities.

Conservation

For children in pre-kindergarten and kindergarten, the number concepts up to five should be stressed. Piagetian research has shown that most five-year-olds do not conserve numbers beyond 5. To see if a child can conserve, try the following experiment. Show the child two groups of seven beans each. First, line the groups up so there is an obvious one-to-one correspondence, as in Figure 5-2. Ask the child if the two groups have the same number of objects. If the child says yes, spread the objects apart in one of the groups. Ask the child if the two groups still have the same number of objects or if one

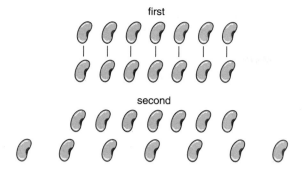

Figure 5–2 Bean configuration to test for conservation of number.

group now has more. If the child believes that one group has more objects, this child is not conserving number.

If the child is a nonconserver, try the same activity with smaller numbers of objects. Some children can conserve when there are only three or four objects but are overwhelmed by the visual configuration when there are more. A teacher should judge the readiness of each child individually, however, and not rely on a child's birth date. Some five-year-olds are able to conserve large numbers, and some seven- or eight-year-olds are not able to conserve at all.

Teachers should incorporate the use of dot cards without numerals in their classes with young children. A set of cards with up to five dots in several different configurations, such as the ones in Figure 5–3 or Appendix B, can be constructed. Later, cards with numerals may be added to the set so that children may match numerals to dots.

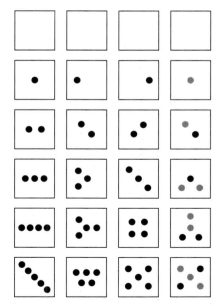

Figure 5–3 Dot cards for games.

Pre-Kindergarten – Kindergarten

OBJECTIVE: to develop early number concepts using dot cards.

1. Let the children play a matching game with the cards. Have them sort the cards into piles so that all the cards in one pile have the same number of dots.

2. Play the Alike and Different game or the One More or One Less game only this time use the dot cards.

3. Play a game of Go Fish or Old Maid, in which the children try to make books of three cards with the same number of dots.

4. To encourage the problem-posing abilities of children, let them make up their own games with the cards. Be sure that each child understands the rules before play starts. Let the children change the rules as they go along if everyone playing agrees. Similar games may be played with sets of objects.

Subitizing, the ability to immediately recognize a certain number of objects on sight (usually up to four or five), is an important skill for children to develop as they develop their number sense. Children should have a variety of experiences where they quickly look at a small number of objects and either tell you the number of objects they see, or tell you if the amount is larger or smaller than another amount. Try showing the children a set number of objects, say 10, and then give them several other sets of objects to compare to the first. Ask them if the other sets have more or fewer, or ask them to estimate the amounts in the other sets by comparing to the amount that they know. Let the children discuss how they make their decisions. With experience, children are frequently better than adults at this skill.

The following activities give more suggestions for children to develop their skills at subitizing.

OBJECTIVE: to develop sight number concepts.

5. Play a Magic Number game in which small objects are hidden under a box. When the objects are uncovered, the children must tell you how many objects there are. Uncover the objects for only a short while so that the children do not have time to count them. Children should learn to recognize up to four or five objects on sight.

6. To expand sight-number concepts to the semiconcrete level, play the Magic Number game with the dot cards. Use the cards as flash cards, and have the children tell you the number of dots on a card without counting. You may wish to try this with more dots, although most adults can recognize only about five things without having to count.

In addition to making flash cards with up to five dots in random order, make flash cards by copying the five frames from Appendix B. After seeing these a few times, children should be able to very quickly recognize any amount up to five by using the five as a benchmark and noting numbers that are one or two more or less than five.

Once children are comfortable with amounts up to five, make flash cards by copying the ten frames from Appendix B. For these, students will use both five and ten as benchmarks for recognizing amounts.

7. Children's dice and board games often give them the opportunity to use sight numbers. Any game in which a child rolls one or two dice and then moves the number of spaces shown encourages him or her to recognize the number of dots on the dice and then to match the number to moves that are similar to moves on the number line. These games may be played at home and during indoor recess as well as during the mathematics class.

Combinations

As numbers larger than 5 are introduced, the children may begin to see them as combinations of groups of smaller objects. For example, 7 may be seen as 3 and 4 or as 2 and 5. Students should be encouraged to look for patterns in the combinations that add to 7 or any other given number. This grouping should be encouraged because it will greatly facilitate the later learning of addition and subtraction facts. If a child has learned to recognize 8 as 5 and 3, there will be no need to memorize $5 + 3 = 8$ or $8 - 5 = 3$. The child will simply need to learn the symbols +, −, and =; the facts will already be known. The following activities are designed to help children learn larger numbers by partitioning and combining sets.

A   C   T   I   V   I   T   I   E   S

Pre-Kindergarten – Grade 2

OBJECTIVE: to use partitioning of sets to develop concepts of larger numbers.

1. Make a shake box out of a small box with a partition in the middle. Place 6 to 10 beans in the box (see Figure 5–4).

Put the lid on the box and shake it. Then remove the lid. Record the number of beans on each side of the partition. For instance, with 7 beans, you may have 6 and 1, 4 and 3, 5 and 2, and so on.

2. Give each child 6 to 10 buttons. Let the children separate the buttons into groups as many ways as possible. For instance, 6 may be 5 and 1, 2 and 4, 3 and 3,

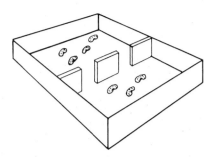

Figure 5 – 4   Shake box for partitioning small sets of objects.

and so on. Encourage the children to recognize these amounts without counting, but they may use counting to check the answers, if necessary. Ask the children to record the groups in some orderly fashion and to look for patterns in the groupings.

OBJECTIVE: to increase visual number concepts.

3. For this activity, you may copy the dominoes from Appendix B or use a set of double-six dominoes. Let each child sort the dominoes into piles with the same number of total dots. There may be piles such as those in Figure 5–5. The Magic Number game described in #5 of the previous activity set may also be played, using the dominoes as flash cards.

4. Name a number between 2 and 10 and ask students to hold up that many fingers. When you name a number such as 5, ask the students to look around at the other students' representations. Ask them if everyone is showing 5 in the same way. They should realize that there are a number of different ways to show 5, such as 1 and 4, 2 and 3, or even 0 and 5.

Note that using fingers to represent numbers reinforces the use of 5 and 10 as benchmarks and has the added

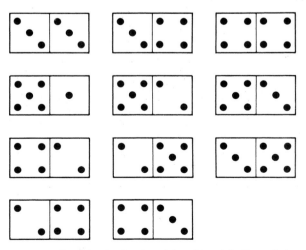

Figure 5 – 5   Double six dominoes in piles of 6, 7, or 8 dots.

benefit of activating the part of the brain, the left parietal lobe, where recent brain research has shown that many number concepts are developed. Unlike the advice not to use our fingers to count that many of us may have heard when we were children, new brain research indicates that this concrete representation of numbers using fingers actually enhances the development of number sense (Butterworth, 1999; Dehaene, 1997).

Zero

Zero is often a difficult concept for children. It is easier to recognize that there are no elephants in the room than it is to realize that there are zero elephants. The idea of "having zero" seems to be a more difficult concept than the idea of "not having any." The following activities are designed to help children learn the concept of zero.

A C T I V I T I E S

Pre-Kindergarten – Grade 2

OBJECTIVE: to introduce the concept of zero concretely.

1. Read the book *Zero Is Not Nothing* (Sitomer and Sitomer, 1978) and let the children name things that they "have zero of" in the classroom. The answers may range from pink elephants to a rug on the floor to sit on.

2. Collect several small empty boxes and put pennies in every box but one. Leave that box empty. Tape the boxes shut. Ask the children to guess which box has zero pennies without peeking inside. If you used cotton balls instead of pennies, could they still guess?

3. When you take attendance, talk about the number of children absent. How many are absent if you have perfect attendance? What will happen if zero children enter the room? What if zero children leave?

4. During physical education time or recess, talk about the number of times you jump rope or bounce a ball. Can you jump zero times? Bounce the ball zero times?

5. Play a dice game where each child rolls one die. Put a sticker over the six on the die so one side of each die has zero dots. The child with the larger amount of dots is the winner of the round. Will the child who rolls zero dots ever be the winner?

OBJECTIVE: to introduce the concept of zero on a semiconcrete level.

6. Add blank cards to either the set of dot cards or the set of picture cards used before. Have the child sort them as before. Tell the child the number of dots on the blank card is zero.

One-to-One Correspondence and Counting

As the number of children attending preschool and watching programs such as *Sesame Street* increases, the number of children entering kindergarten with some ability to count also increases. These children may be counting either **rotely,** just reciting words memorized in order, or **rationally,** with understanding. Some children with the ability to rote count can complete a counting sequence only if they use the "sing-song" pattern that they used in learning to count. Other children chant the counting sequence, becoming progressively faster at repeating the number names. Initially, children develop the ability to count groups of objects, at first pointing and reciting the number names, sometimes skipping numbers, or, at other times, skipping objects. Rational counting occurs when a child can count a set of objects and realizes that the last number name spoken in the counting sequence tells how many objects there are all together—for example, "One, two, three, four, five, six, seven. There are seven buttons." And, when asked again how many objects there are, the child can confidently repeat just the last number name in the sequence, "Seven, there are seven buttons."

The following activities give children a variety of counting experiences based on putting two sets of objects or objects and pictures in one-to-one correspondence. In this way, the children connect the counting numbers to objects and do not just recite them rotely. They learn that each word goes with only one object and that the final word spoken when counting aloud gives the number of objects in the entire set.

A C T I V I T I E S

Pre-Kindergarten – Kindergarten

OBJECTIVE: to use one-to-one correspondence and counting to determine the number of objects in a set.

1. Draw and cut out five garages and collect five toy cars or trucks. Tell the children that one vehicle may park in each garage. Randomly set out from one to five garages on the table. Ask the children to match a vehicle to each garage and to count as they make the matches. After the vehicles have been matched to the garages and counted, ask the children to tell you how many vehicles there are altogether. How many garages are there?

The activity may be varied to use boats and docks or airplanes and hangars. Let the children suggest other things to match. As the children gain the ability to match and count, increase the number of objects to be counted.

2. Using the dot cards from earlier activities and some bingo chips, tell the children to cover each dot on the card with a chip and to count as they make the matches. Ask them how many dots are on each card. Is that the same as the number of chips on the card? Increase the number of dots on the cards when the children are ready.

3. Collect five small cans for flower pots, such as juice cans (be sure there are no sharp edges). Make 15 flowers using pipe cleaners for the stems and construction paper for the petals. Put one to five dots on the outside of each can. Ask the children to match the number of flowers to the number of dots on the can. Let the children count to tell you how many dots and flowers there are. Later, you can increase the numbers of flowers and dots.

4. Children should practice counting several times during the day, whenever the opportunity arises. For example, if you ask the children to set up the chairs for the reading group, observe them to see if they count the number of children in the group and count out the same number of chairs or solve the problem in another way.

Children can also practice counting on from a given number. If there are already 5 chairs in the circle and they need 8 chairs, ask them to count beginning with 5. As they get more chairs, they can count forward—6, 7, 8. If there are too many chairs in the circle, they can count backward as they remove chairs. If there are 10 chairs and they need only 7, they can count back from 10 as they take the chairs away—9, 8, 7. The ability to count forward and backward will help them later when they learn addition and subtraction.

5. Children do not always need to count physical objects and may count backward as well as forward. They may count the number of days until a special holiday, the number of seconds in the countdown on a microwave, or the number of claps of thunder they hear. For young children, calendar time first thing each morning gives them a chance to relate counting days to the calendar. A party on the hundredth day of school on which all children bring in 100 objects to count in a variety of ways reinforces these concepts of rational counting.

In all of these activities, it is fine if children can tell you the numbers without counting; they should not be required to count. After the children are proficient at matching two sets of objects or a set of dots and a set of objects, numerals may be substituted.

Measuring Length

Thus far, the discussion has focused on number as related to sets of discrete or individual objects. Number may also refer to the length of an object, a measurement concept. Number lines, rulers, and Cuisenaire rods depend upon this measurement idea. We also use number in a measurement sense when we say "He is four years old" or "She is three blocks from home." Measurement concepts are discussed in detail later but are mentioned here briefly as they relate to number concepts.

Difficulties arise as children move from associating numbers with sets of discrete objects to associating numbers with lengths. First, children may not understand the number 2 to be two units long; they may understand 2 to be simply two objects. Second, many children do not conserve length. They believe a rod changes in length when its position changes. They have difficulty understanding that 2 is twice as long as 1. To introduce number concepts using measurement, the teacher should first ascertain whether the children can conserve length.

One good model for length is Cuisenaire rods. For young children, Cuisenaire rods may be used to discuss such ideas as longer than, shorter than, and the same length. After discussing these concepts, children who can conserve length may begin to associate the rods with numbers. The children may use the white rod, which is the shortest one, to represent one. Using this white rod to measure, the children may then determine the length of each of the other rods. They will find that if the white rod is 1 unit long, then the red is 2, the light green is 3, the purple is 4, the yellow is 5, the dark green is 6, the black is 7, the brown is 8, the blue is 9, and the orange is 10. Once children have determined these lengths, they should try some of the following activities to reinforce the number concepts.

> ### A C T I V I T I E S

Pre-Kindergarten – Grade 2

OBJECTIVE: to introduce ordering concepts involving length.

1. Make a staircase using one rod of each color. Construct the staircase so that the rod on top is a white rod, the rod on the bottom is orange, and the rods in between are arranged in order of length (see Figure 5–6). What will happen if you put a white rod next to each rod in your staircase?

OBJECTIVE: to reinforce the concept of equivalent lengths as an introduction to addition.

2. Find the yellow rod. Make trains of rods that are the same length as the yellow rod, such as those shown in Figure 5–7. Have the children record every combination whose length equals the length of the yellow

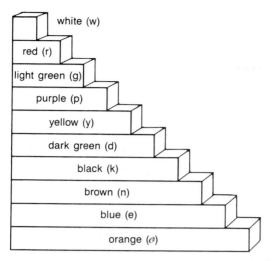

Figure 5–6 Staircase of Cuisenaire rods from the shortest rod (a one-centimeter white rod) to the longest rod (a ten-centimeter orange rod).

rod, beginning with the colors and later using the numbers to represent the rods. You may wish to use interlocking Cuisenaire rods for this activity so that the trains will remain together when students pick them up for discussion. Ask the students to compare their trains to those of a partner. Did anyone find a train that you did not find? How do you know if you have found all the possibilities?

3. After children are comfortable finding several combinations of two rods that equal a single rod, ask them to find all the possible combinations of two rods that are equal in length to any rod other than the white rod. Challenge them to find a way to determine the

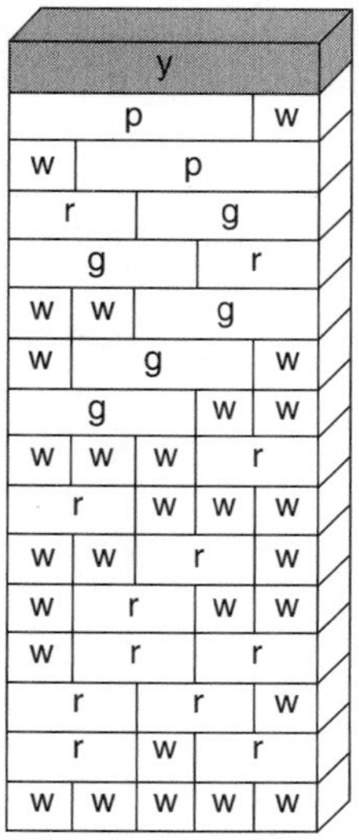

Figure 5–7 All the trains of Cuisenaire rods equal in length to a yellow rod.

number of different combinations of two rods. Note that the yellow rod in #2 has 4 combinations of 2 rods that give the same length—purple and white, white and purple, red and green, and green and red. For any rod of length N, there are $N - 1$ combinations of two rods that will give the same length.

Children may determine the number values of their trains after they become proficient at using the colors.

4. Have one child make a train of two rods and challenge another child to find one rod that is the same length as the train. What happens with a train such as brown and black? Let the children play the game for several days before asking them to associate numbers with the rods.

The rods may also be used in an introduction to the **number line.** Construct a number line so that the numbers are one centimeter apart. Mark zero and number the line up to 10 or so, as shown in Figure 5–8.

Give each child a number line in which the numbers are drawn 1 centimeter apart and obtain a transparency of a number line and translucent Cuisenaire rods made for the overhead projector to use yourself. Because children often do not associate the numbers on the number line with lengths, using Cuisenaire rods helps them see that 2 is the distance from 0 (zero) to 2 and not just the point half way between 1 and 3. For this reason, it is important to have 0 (zero) on the number line. Using the Cuisenaire rods on a centimeter ruler in the same manner as the number line gives students a chance to practice measuring while they are learning to associate numbers with the concept of length. A clear centimeter ruler can be used with translucent Cuisenaire rods on the overhead projector.

Points to the left of 0 need not be marked at this time, but there should be an arrow pointing to the left from 0 as well as an arrow pointing to the right from the last positive number marked. If the children ask the meaning of the arrows or ask if there are other numbers to the left of 0, answer that the numbers go on forever in both directions.

Decide if the children are ready for a detailed discussion of the concepts of **infinity** or **negative numbers** at this time. If they are, show them that one everyday use of negative numbers is as low-temperature values on the thermometer. Or, let them use a calculator to

Figure 5–8 Cuisenaire rods showing a length of 5 on the number line.

see what happens if they try to subtract 6 from 4. In general, however, do not introduce a detailed study of negative integers or infinity in the primary grades.

The following activities are designed to introduce the child to the use of the number line.

A C T I V I T I E S

Pre-Kindergarten–Grade 2

OBJECTIVE: to introduce the concept of measurement on the number line.

1. Let the children choose a Cuisenaire rod at random. Place the rod on the number line with the left end of the rod on 0 (zero). Where is the right end? How does this number compare to the value of the rod? Try this with several different rods.

2. Choose two rods to line up on the number line in a train, as shown in Figure 5–9. Place the left end of the first rod on 0 (zero). Can you predict where the right end of the second rod will be?

After working with the Cuisenaire rods on the number line, children should understand the concept of length on the number line and should be able to move on to number-line activities that do not require the use of the rods. The following are examples of other number-line activities.

A C T I V I T I E S

Pre-Kindergarten–Grade 2

OBJECTIVE: to develop number line concepts through body movements.

1. Make a large number line on the floor with masking tape. Make sure the starting point is marked 0 (zero) to show that no steps have been taken at this point. On the number line, mark intervals that are about the size of a child's step (about 25 centimeters). Make sure that each interval is the same size.

Have the children take turns starting at 0 (zero) and walking a given number of steps. Have them confirm that the point at which they finish corresponds to the number of steps they took. In this way, the number of

discrete steps is associated with the distance walked on the number line.

2. Using the 1-centimeter number lines, let the children use their fingers to count a certain number of spaces, beginning at zero. What number is on the point where the children land? Emphasize counting spaces rather than points.

OBJECTIVE: to practice skills on the number line.

3. Use Freddie the frog with the number line. Let Freddie start at zero and hop a certain number of spaces. Where does he land?

Grouping

Grouping is an important concept in the Hindu-Arabic system of numeration. Many older systems of numeration, such as the Roman and the Egyptian, did not use grouping, and thus they were awkward for writing and manipulating symbols for large numbers. Because place value is so important in our system of numeration and because grouping is essential to place value, young children should begin grouping even while they are learning the numbers from 1 to 9. They should have experience grouping by twos, threes, fours—all the way to tens—for two good reasons. First, the notion of an exchange point is a key to understanding place value. Second, regrouping using smaller numbers provides valuable practice that is more important to have than waiting until 10 objects have been collected to make an exchange.

Research has shown that students frequently have a very shallow understanding of the use of grouping in our base ten place-value system. This is not surprising since many developed societies continued to use numeration systems lacking place value for thousands of years after the concept of place value was developed in regions such as Mesopotamia and India. Despite the fact that a numeration system using place value greatly simplifies representation and computation with all types of numbers, it is not as intuitive as a system that uses repetition of symbols, such as the Egyptian system. Students might be able to fill in the blanks in an exercise that is commonly seen in primary mathematics textbooks such as 23 = _____ tens _____ ones and might correctly count out 23 chips when asked to show what 23 stands for. However, when these same children are asked to show with the chips what the 2 in the number represents, many of them will show you 2 chips rather than 20. They have not internalized the critical concept that the 2 represents 2 tens, not 2 ones. It is difficult for them to think of the 10 as a single entity, not just as 10 separate ones. With

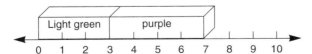

Figure 5–9 Cuisenaire rods showing a combination of a length of 3 and a length of 4.

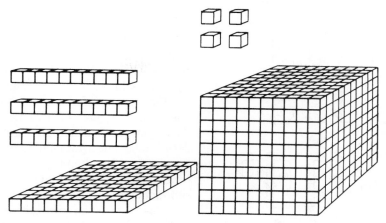

Figure 5–10   An example of proportional grouping materials for base ten.

experience trading for groups of varying sizes, students can begin to understand this important concept.

There are two basic types of grouping materials: **proportional** and **nonproportional.** Proportional materials are constructed so that if the grouping is by tens, the material that shows 10 is 10 times as large as the material that shows 1 and the material for 100 is 10 times as large as the material for 10, and so forth. Proportional materials include multibase blocks (see Figure 5–10), tongue depressors, coffee stirrers or straws, counting cups and beans, and Cuisenaire cubes, squares, and rods.

Nonproportional materials, such as money, do not show consistent size changes. A dime is not 10 times as large as a penny and a dollar is not 10 times the size of a dime. Nonproportional aids include chip trading, money, and the abacus. Allow children to explore with the proportional grouping materials freely before you begin formal instruction. Let the children discover the size differences and the trades that are possible as they build houses or make designs with the blocks.

The following activities are designed to give children thorough experiences in grouping. This becomes the foundation for later work with place value.

A C T I V I T I E S

Pre-Kindergarten – Grade 2

OBJECTIVE: to introduce trading games using proportional materials.

1. Multibase blocks are proportional grouping materials that consist of various sizes of wooden or plastic blocks representing the powers of particular grouping points. Multibase blocks are commercially available in sets with grouping points of 2, 3, 4, 5, 6, and 10. A set of blocks with a grouping point of 3 is shown in Figure 5–11. Regardless of the grouping point, the smallest

pieces are called units; the remaining pieces are called, in order, longs, flats, and cubes. You may make your own set of multibase blocks using self-adhesive paper (such as contact paper) printed with a grid approximately 1 centimeter square and railroad board. Cut out units, longs, and flats to match the grouping point desired.

After the children have had an opportunity to play with the materials and to discover the grouping point, give them a handful of units and ask them to make all of the trades possible. For example, the blocks in Figure 5–12a can be traded for the blocks in Figure 5–12b because the blocks represent the same amount of material. If children have difficulty making the exchanges, instruct them to make groups of three units until all units are used and then to exchange each group of three for a long, as shown in Figure 5–13.

2. After the children have played some grouping games, let them play the Build-a-House game. For this

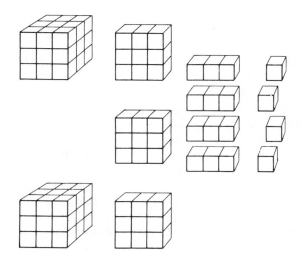

Figure 5–11   An example of proportional grouping materials with a grouping point of 3.

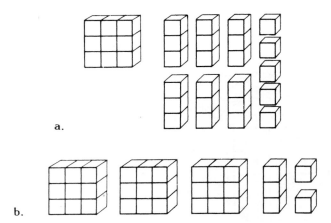

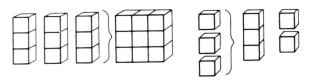

Figure 5–12   An example of trading with blocks with a grouping point of 3.

Figure 5–13   An example of trading units for longs and longs for flats.

game, children form two families. Each family is trying to build a house before the other. To begin the game, the children agree which city they will live in, Three for One, Four for One, or Five for One, and choose multibase blocks to match the city.

To play, each team rolls one die to determine the paycheck for the week. The dots showing on the die tell the child the number of single units earned that week. Children should trade in single units for a long as soon as possible, trade longs for a flat, and trade flats for a cube. A cube is the house, and a team "wins" as soon as it completes a house.

Children should also play the game in reverse. In this game, they begin with a large cube and try to spend it. The dots showing on the die tell the child the number of single units to spend on that round. In this game, the first team to spend all its money loses.

The second game is usually much more difficult for the children than the Build-a-House game, especially in the beginning. The first move is the most difficult. Having one large cube and needing to spend two units is similar to the problem 1,000 − 2. Children who realize that they must make several trades before they can spend two units have very good place-value concepts. Discuss with the children the trades that they must make, both as they play the game and after they have finished.

After the children have played the games for awhile, ask them to record their plays. Encourage them to cre-

ate their own methods for recording. Some children might use numbers while others use drawings to represent their trades. Ask them to explain how their moves in the game are related to what they are recording. This activity will give them a good basis for later constructing algorithms for addition and subtraction with regrouping.

Students should also be encouraged to ask the questions of an investigative mathematician as they play these games. They might discuss such things as: Why does it take longer to build a house if we are playing in Five for One City than it does in Three for One City? What if we played in Twelve for One City? How is playing the subtraction game like playing the addition game? How is it different? or When might there be a time when you can make more than one trade on the same roll of the die?

3. Teachers may construct proportional materials from railroad board or other firm construction material. Figure 5–14 illustrates one such set, with a grouping point of 3, and Figure 5–15 illustrates a set with a grouping point of 4.

Use dot cards with these triangular materials. Place the dot cards face down in a pile in the center of the table. Let the children take turns drawing a card and picking up that many small triangles. Make trades whenever possible. The first team or child to get two large triangles wins.

Repeat the game with squares. Activities suggested for the multibase blocks may also be used with these materials.

4. Another material that you may use is the counting cup and beans. For a grouping point of 5, a cup with five beans represents a first grouping, five cups of five in

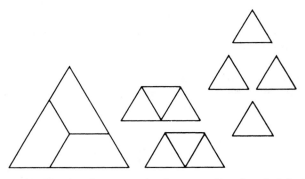

Figure 5–14   Another example of a proportional material with a grouping point of 3.

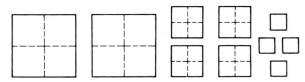

Figure 5–15   A proportional material with a grouping point of 4.

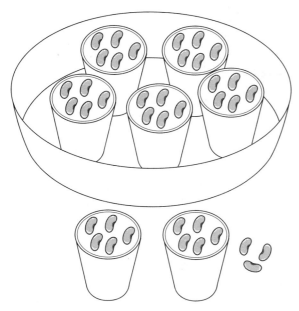

Figure 5–16   Counting cups and beans with a grouping point of 5.

a larger container represent a second grouping, and so forth, as shown in Figure 5–16.

The counting cups and beans may be used to play a store game. A single bean represents a penny, a cup with five beans is a nickel, and five cups of five beans represent a quarter. Put price tags on small objects, such as 37¢ for a hair ribbon and 7¢ for a pencil.

Ask the children to count out individual beans to represent a price and then to make any trades possible. Is the pencil more than a nickel? Is the ribbon less than a quarter? Encourage the children to set prices and make up questions of their own. This game may also be played using pennies, nickels, and quarters in place of the beans.

Again, each of the activities described for any of the grouping materials may be used with the counting cups. So far, each grouping activity suggested has focused on only one or two exchanges. If you have students who demonstrate a strong understanding of these trades, encourage them to try similar games requiring more exchanges or using other grouping points. Ask them to record their thinking along with their trades in their journals.

OBJECTIVE: to introduce grouping concepts using sets of discrete objects and charts and tallies to keep track of experimentations.

5. Begin with eight buttons. Have the child place them in groups of 3 (***) and record the results on a chart, as shown in Figure 5–17.

Repeat the activity with grouping points of 2 (**), 4 (****), 5 (*****), and 6 (******). Chart the results. Discuss with the children what happens as the grouping point changes.

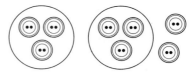

groups	ones
2	2

Figure 5–17   Recording trades with buttons with a grouping point of 3.

super-groups	groups	ones
2	2	1

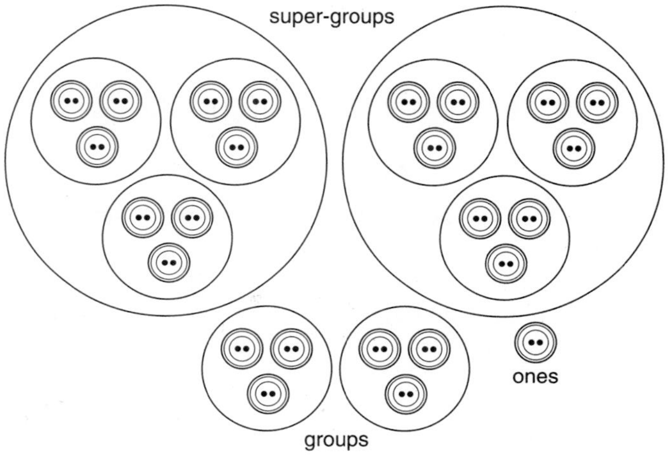

Figure 5–18   Recording larger trades with buttons with a grouping point of 3.

Repeat the activity but use more buttons, say 25. Put all of the groups of 3 (***) together and label these groups. Next, group together three groups of 3 and label these supergroups. Record the results in a tally box with three sections, such as the one shown in Figure 5–18.

Repeat the activity with other grouping points and starting amounts. Record the results. There may be times when you will need super-supergroups, or more, especially for small grouping points such as 2.

Colored chips are convenient nonproportional teaching aids. They may be purchased commercially or constructed by the teacher.

OBJECTIVE: to introduce grouping concepts using nonproportional materials.

6. Gather about 120 colored chips. You should have about 40 orange chips, 30 yellow chips, 20 green chips, 20 red chips, and 10 blue chips.

Choose a magic number for trading. Let the children take turns rolling a die and collecting the orange chips. When the magic number is reached, exchange orange chips for yellow chips. For example, if the magic number is 3, three orange chips may be traded for one yellow, three yellows for one green, three greens for one red, and three reds for one blue. Set the goal as either a red or a blue chip. Discuss the children's trades as they play and ask questions such as, "How many more will you need to reach the goal?" or "Who is winning and by how much?"

The chips may be used for the same games as the proportional materials.

After the students have used several different grouping points with the materials, expand the activities to include base ten activities. Be sure to encourage the children to record their activities as they work and to discuss the strategies they use.

A C T I V I T I E S

Grades 3 – 8

OBJECTIVE: to compare and contrast different numeration systems.

📖 **1.** Ask the students to read a book that looks at other numeration systems such as Adler's *Base Five* (1975) or *Roman Numerals* (1977) or St. John's *How to Count Like a Martian* (1975). Compare and contrast the Hindu-Arabic system with other systems studied. Talk about such features as whether or not there is a zero in the system, whether the system uses grouping by tens or some other number, and whether it is an additive system or a place-value system. Discuss the pros and cons of each feature. For students who have a good understanding, ask them to record their findings in a Venn diagram such as the one in Figure 5–19. After students have studied other systems, challenge them to create a system of their own and teach it to others in their group.

OBJECTIVE: to apply study of other number bases to everyday problems.

2. Encourage students interested in computers to read about binary or hexadecimal numbers and report their findings. Some students might wish to talk to postal workers about the binary code that is used in bar codes to separate items based on zip codes.

Very Large and Very Small Numbers

As students become comfortable with our numeration system and its foundation in base ten, they should begin to ask questions about numbers that are larger

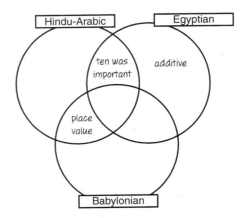

Figure 5–19 Using a Venn diagram to compare numeration systems.

than a million or smaller than zero. Frequently, they will encounter these numbers on a calculator. Depending on the type of calculator, different notations may be displayed as students explore various operations. Most will show negative numbers such as -3 or $-2,345$, but when these get very small, exponential notation may be used. Some calculators will simply display an error message if numbers get too large or too small, but others may show something like 5.5 E20, 1.5−13, or even −3.7 E15. Students will ask you for the meanings when these things appear on the calculator. Depending on the age and experience of the students, you should be prepared to explain the concepts behind these symbols. 5.5 E20 means that the answer is written in scientific notation and this stands for 5.5×10^{20}, or 550,000,000,000,000,000,000; 1.5−13 would mean that this is the very small positive decimal, .00000000000015; and −3.7E15 is −3,700,000,000,000,000. You should not begin any explanation of exponents with these large numbers, however. When students are working with the base ten materials, they should realize that the square that is 10 units on a side has an area of 100 (square units) and the cube with 10 units on a side has a volume of 1,000 (cubic units). When we write 10^2, this is read as "ten squared" and 10^3 is read as "ten cubed." These exponents tell us the number of times that the base number (in this case, ten) is multiplied by itself. We could read 10^2 as "ten to the second power" or read 10^3 as "ten to the third power," but reading these as "ten squared" and "ten cubed" reminds us that we can find their values by making a 10×10 square or a $10 \times 10 \times 10$ cube and determining the number of square or cubic units in the figure. Later students will realize that ten to any power is a one with that many zeros behind it. For example, 10^{15} is 1,000,000,000,000,000. You should not tell the students this as a rule, however. They should have several concrete investigations to help them figure this out for themselves.

In a similar manner, students should investigate negative numbers when they arise in their world. Even young children should be familiar with negative numbers from, for example, scores in games, temperatures, losing or borrowing money, being below sea level, and perhaps reports on the stock market. They may have encountered negative numbers on a number line when they explored what happens if you subtract 5 from 3; the answer is found to the left of zero on the number line. Danny, a first grader, learned about negative numbers quite well when he borrowed a dollar to buy an action figure and then had to pay it back out of his allowance a week later.

A C T I V I T I E S

Grades 3–5

OBJECTIVE: to become acquainted with integers on a number line.

1. Make a large number line on the floor with masking tape, placing zero in the center. Make the numerals to the right of the zero in blue and the numerals to the left of zero in red. Explain to the children that these numerals represent distances in blocks east (blue numerals) and blocks west (red numerals) from City Hall in Anytown, U.S.A. (see Figure 5–20). (You can use landmarks in your own town for this activity.) Place a picture or model of City Hall on zero and place pictures or models of other buildings or landmarks on the red and blue numerals. Pose questions to the students such as "How many blocks is it from school to the zoo?" and "If you start at the library and go five blocks east, where are you?" This activity can later be linked to integers by designating movement toward the east as adding, movement toward the west as subtracting, blue numerals as positive, and red numerals as negative. For example, the question "If the zoo is on the blue five and you go seven blocks west, where are you?" corresponds to the equation $5 - 7 = $ **n**. You would land on the red 2 (−2), which may be the location of the drug store. Encourage the students to make up similar problems for each other. Younger children do not need to worry about writing equations for their situations, but you may wish to ask third or fourth graders to begin to use the integer notation. The important

thing at this stage is for students to have a concrete understanding of integers.

DEVELOPING FLUENCY WITH NUMBERS

Once children can orally associate numbers with sets, introduce written numerals. The fact that written numerals are often introduced too early may be one reason we picture numerals instead of sets when we hear a number; therefore, we should be sure children can orally associate the numbers with sets before they are asked to learn written numerals.

> During the early years teachers must help students strengthen their sense of number, moving from the initial development of basic counting techniques to more-sophisticated understandings of the size of numbers, number relationships, patterns, operations, and place value. (NCTM, 2000, p. 79)

The NCTM *Principles and Standards for School Mathematics* (2000) state that primary students should be able to use multiple models to represent understanding of place value, to connect these to number words and numerals, and to develop understanding of relative position and magnitude of cardinal and ordinal numbers. Older elementary students should recognize and generate equivalent representations of the same number by composing and decomposing numbers and explore numbers less than 0. In this section, we will investigate ways to help students as they further develop these understandings.

Matching Numerals to Sets and Number Names

Children should be familiar with seeing written numerals before being asked to write them. Numerals are not something children can discover on their own. If we want children to learn Hindu-Arabic numerals, we must teach them.

The following activities are designed to help the child match numerals with sets. These activities may begin with the numerals from 1 to 5 and be expanded

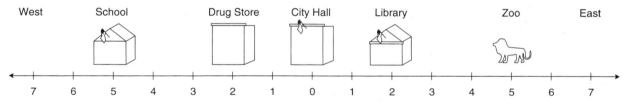

Figure 5–20 Floor number line to introduce making sense of integers.

later to include other numerals as well as the written words for the numbers.

Pre-Kindergarten – Grade 2

OBJECTIVE: to match written numerals to sets.

1. Play a Treasure Hunt game. Give each child a numeral and have the child look around the room for sets of objects that match the numeral. For instance, the child with the numeral 3 may find three cars, three pencils, and three chairs in the learning center.

2. Make several sets of cards for different card games similar to Old Maid or Go Fish. The cards should give children a chance to practice matching numerals, sets, and dots, such as those in Figure 5–21. Later add cards for number names.

3. Dominoes with numerals on one side and dots on the other are useful for matching numerals and dots.

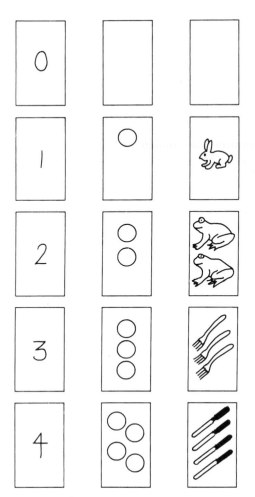

Figure 5–21 Sample cards for matching card games.

Children can play dominoes, matching the numerals on the dominoes to corresponding dots.

4. Even very young children can begin to use a calculator as they learn to recognize numerals, but this should be done in conjunction with concrete materials and oral discussions in order to develop solid concepts of the numbers that they are using. Understanding leads to number sense, the ability to recognize number relationships, and the ability to interpret numbers used in daily life. For young children, this may mean using a calculator as they count a pile of pennies they have saved. For this activity, children should work in pairs, one with a simple calculator and one with a pile of pennies to count. Ask the first child to count the pennies as he or she moves one penny at a time from one pile to another. The second child should push +1 on the calculator as each penny is moved. After all the pennies have been counted, the first child should announce the number of pennies in the pile while the second child pushes the = button on the calculator. The two children should then compare to see if the number in the display on the calculator matches the number of pennies counted.

As the children are playing the game, special notice should be taken when the number in the tens place changes as a result of adding one. Ask the children to predict what the next number will be if you begin at 19 and press +1.

5. Cut strips of paper about 4-inches × 11 inches (regular computer paper cut in half) and fold the paper into thirds so each section is roughly a 4-inch square. Put numerals from 1 to 9 (or larger) on the right-hand third of the paper and put dots to total that number in the other two sections. For example, for the number 7, you might have something like that shown in Figure 5–22.

Ask the students to make several different strips for each of the numbers. Pair the students and ask the two to combine all their number strips. Students should then take turns showing the strips to each other while the student showing the strip covers up one of the three sections. The other student then has to guess what is covered. For example, on this strip, if the second section is covered, the student has to think, "I can see five dots and I know that the total is seven. I have to figure out how many dots would need to be added to five to get seven." Some students might do this by counting on; others may use their fingers, holding up five fingers on one hand and determining that two more must be

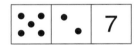

Figure 5–22 One example of a number strip for building fluency with numbers.

added to get seven; and still others might just know that 5 + 2 = 7. Encourage the children to discuss their reasoning with each other as they play the game.

OBJECTIVE: to reinforce number concepts.

6. Play riddle games with the children using what they know about numbers. For example, you might give the following clues:

I am less than ten.
I am an even number.
I am more than seven.
What number am I?

As children become more proficient at this game, you might use more complex clues such as:

I am less than the number of toes on one foot.
If you double me, I am less than ten.
I am double an even number.
What number am I?

When a student correctly answers your riddle, that student should choose a new number and make up a riddle with clues for the other students. Students can discuss which riddles have exactly one right answer, which riddles have more than one answer, and which riddles have no right answers. Children can write up their riddles and publish them in the class newsletter or leave them in a learning center for other students to guess.

After children have experience with writing riddles to guess a single number, they can try clues to finding a pair of numbers such as:

I am thinking of two numbers.
My numbers are both even.
My numbers add to ten.
What are my numbers?

Again, students should write riddles for each other and discuss which riddles have zero, one, or more than one correct answer.

Number Names

After children have learned to match numerals to sets and have learned to count rationally to at least 5, introduce written words for the numerals. Expand many of the same activities used to introduce the numerals to include the number names. In card games, add cards with the number names on them for the children to include in the matches. Mark the number line with the number names as well as with the numerals.

Children's literature is a good source for teaching numerals and number names. Several good children's books introduce numerals and number names. Encourage children to find the number names in stories and to check the pictures to see if the pictures show the correct number of objects.

Children also enjoy finger plays using poems such as "Ten Little Monkeys" and "Five Birds on a Fence," in which they recite the poem and show numbers with their fingers. Children's music also is a good source of ideas for reinforcing counting. Music can be a great memory aid for many children. Librarians and music teachers can help you find excellent children's books, stories, finger plays, and songs.

A C T I V I T I E S

Pre-Kindergarten – Grade 2

OBJECTIVE: to investigate counting in other cultures.

1. Read *Moja Means One* (Feelings, 1971) or *Count on Your Fingers African Style* (Zaslavsky, 1980) to the students and ask them to compare their own styles of counting to those in the books. Children may wish to read other counting books from around the world and compare them to the more familiar counting books from the United States. If you are fortunate enough to have students who were raised in other cultures or for whom English is not the first language, you might invite them or their parents to talk to the class about the words and techniques used to count in their native lands.

Writing Numerals

After children can match numerals to sets, they can begin to learn to write numerals. Children at this age often do not have good fine motor control and may need to use very large materials in the beginning. The following are a few suggestions for writing numerals with materials other than paper and pencil.

A C T I V I T I E S

Pre-Kindergarten – Grade 2

OBJECTIVE: to use bodily/kinesthetic abilities to write numerals.

1. Cover the bottom of a box lid with sand or salt. Let the children practice writing numerals in the sand. After you check the work, have the children simply shake the box lid to erase their efforts and begin again.

2. Cut large numerals out of sandpaper and let the children run their fingers gently over the numerals. Have them do this blindfolded and try to guess what the numeral is. Then have them draw what they have just felt.

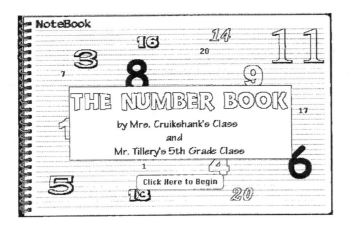
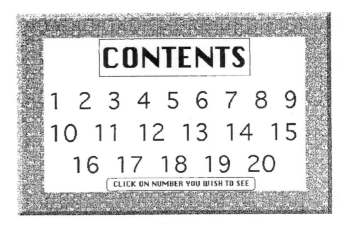

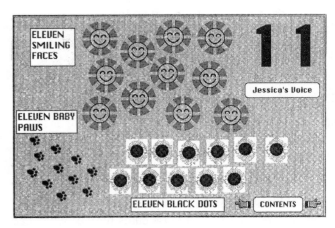

Figure 5–23 *HyperStudio* stack developed cooperatively by fifth grade and kindergarten classes.

OBJECTIVE: to reinforce writing numerals.

3. Draw numerals on large squares of posterboard. Use arrows to show the direction to move to write the numerals. Laminate the numerals and let the children copy them with a grease pencil or washable crayon.

The computer can also be used to reinforce children's number concepts as well as the writing of numerals and number words. Programs such as PowerPoint or *Hyper-Studio,* computer applications that allow students to develop a series of cards that can be used to display or explain information, give students a chance to develop their computer skills as they develop their number sense.

HyperStudio allows students to use text, pictures drawn by the student, scanned pictures or photographs, photographs from digital cameras, pictures, and other graphics found on the Internet, recorded sound, and animation to present information. Direct links to the Internet may be incorporated in a stack. For example, a group of fifth-grade students prepared a report on erosion in a nearby nature area using a *HyperStudio* stack

on the computer and projected the cards in the stack on a screen for the rest of the class. In another fifth-grade class, students Rachel and Don were paired with kindergarten students Jessica and Richard. Each kindergartner was given a number and worked with the fifth grader, who helped record the information given by the younger student into a *HyperStudio* stack. The result was a class book featuring the numbers 1 through 20. Figure 5–23 shows selected pages from the number book. If you were to "click" on the button with Richard's name on it you would hear Richard briefly talking about the number 2. Likewise, Jessica talks about the number 11. *HyperStudio* can be effectively used to present and illustrate a variety of mathematics-related material. Encourage the creativity of your students.

Developing Fluency with Rational Counting and Ordering

Children are ready to further develop their fluency with rational counting and ordering once they have a good understanding of number concepts from zero to ten; can associate numbers with sets of objects, pictures, and dot cards, first orally, then using written numerals, and finally using written number words; can determine whether sets have the same number of objects or whether one set has more or fewer objects than another; and can put sets of objects in order from a set with the fewest objects to a set with the most. In this section, we present a number of activities that extend these concepts, including counting backward as well as forward; skip counting and looking for patterns; recognizing the symbols for greater than, less than, and equal to; and developing ordinal number concepts.

A C T I V I T I E S

Pre-Kindergarten – Grade 2

OBJECTIVE: to introduce the concepts *greater than* and *less than*.

1. An adaptation of the card game War may be played with a deck of cards having from zero to nine dots on a card. When constructing the cards, make four or five cards for each number of dots. The game is played by two or more children. The cards are shuffled, and all are dealt. Each player turns over one card and places it face up on the table. The player with the card showing the most dots wins all the cards on this round. If there is more than one card showing the greatest number of dots, the two players with those cards have a "war." Each of these players then places a card face down on his or her first card and another card face up on top of the second card. The new face-up cards are compared. The player whose card has the most dots wins all the cards in the war as well as any other players' cards on this round. Play continues until one player has all the cards or a time limit expires. If the children question which card has the most dots, they should establish a one-to-one correspondence between the dots to decide.

The second phase in this game is to use a regular deck of cards or the numerals without the dots. Play continues as before.

2. Another variation of this game is for each child to turn up two cards rather than one on each turn. The child with the greatest total on the two cards wins the round. If the totals are the same, the "war" is played by turning up two more cards.

3. After the children have had experience with the words *greater than* and *less than*, the symbols may be introduced. A popular idea for introducing the symbols is the use of a "hungry fish" (see Figure 5–24). The fish always wants to eat as much as possible, so its mouth is always open toward the greater amount. The children may use blocks to represent the fish's food. Set up two groups of blocks with between one and nine blocks in each group and let the children place the

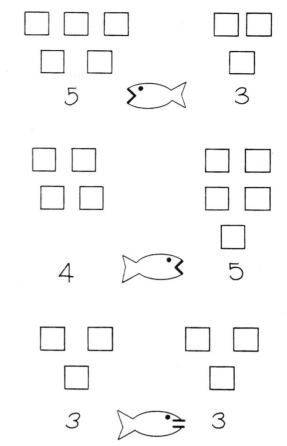

Figure 5–24 Hungry fish used to illustrate >, <, and =.

corresponding numeral under each set. The children then decide which set is greater, using one-to-one correspondence if necessary, and place the fish between the numerals with its mouth open toward the larger numeral. If the activity is done on paper, the children may trace inside the fish's mouth to keep a permanent record of the larger number. Discuss the terms *greater than* and *less than* as the symbols are introduced.

The symbol for *equals* (=) may be introduced at the same time. The fish cannot decide which group to eat because both are the same size. It keeps its mouth neither wide open nor closed (see Figure 5–24).

After children are comfortable putting numbers in order to count the cardinal number of objects in a set, they may begin to use numbers in an ordinal sense. Ordinal numbers should be used throughout the day just as cardinal numbers should. As children line up for any activities, discuss who is first in line, second, last, and so on. Talk about the first thing on the schedule each morning. Let the children suggest other times they use ordinal numbers.

Grades 3–5

OBJECTIVE: to reinforce counting and patterns by skip counting forward and backward.

1. Play a skip-counting game in which the first child chooses any number to begin with and then the second child chooses a number from two to five to skip count by. (In the beginning, you will probably want to count by twos and fives beginning with 2 or 5 and discuss the patterns that you find with the children.) After children are proficient with simple skip counting, challenge them to find patterns with such directions as "Start at 7 and skip count by twos" or "Start at 45 and skip count backward by fives."

2. Play Skip Count Ping Pong. In this game, students stand in a circle and count by ones, but if the number is one that you would say if you are counting by threes (such as 3, 6, 9, 12), the student whose turn it is says "Ping" rather than the number. You can also play this for fives, where you say "Pong" instead of the number you would say if skip counting by fives (5, 10, 15, 20, etc.). Once students are comfortable playing either the Ping version or the Pong version, challenge them to play Ping Pong, where both rules apply at once and students must remember to say "Ping Pong" when they hit numbers such as 15 and 30. This is a good lead-in to common multiples and should be discussed with the students.

OBJECTIVE: to explore patterns on a hundreds chart.

3. Make a large hundreds chart out of pegboard, with cup hooks from which to hang numerals (see Figure 5–25). Hang all 100 numerals in their proper places. Let the children discuss the patterns they notice.

Now turn the cards over so that they are still on the proper hooks but the children cannot see the numerals. Ask a child to guess where the 3 should be and then to check by turning the card over. If the child is correct, leave the numeral showing. If the child is incorrect, turn the card over and let another child guess. Continue by guessing other numbers such as 23 or 30. Let each child have a turn to guess.

Discuss the patterns as you go along. This activity can also be used with copied hundreds charts and small squares of paper to cover the numerals. (A hundreds chart is included in Appendix B for you to copy.) Let the children remove the square of paper when they guess where the number is.

Discuss the strategies used to find the numbers. Ask questions such as: Where is the number that is 10 more than 23? Where is the number that is 20 less than 45? Where would I find a number ending in 5? Where would I find a number beginning with 7? What number would be two rows directly under 37? If I start at 3 and turn over

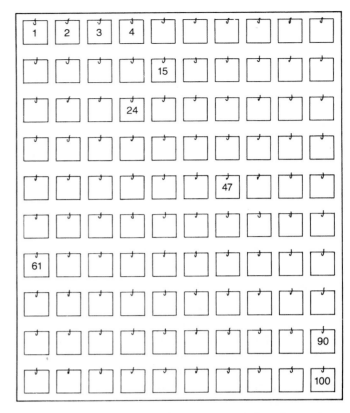

Figure 5–25 Hundreds chart with numerals hanging on cup hooks to reinforce pattern concepts.

every third number (skip count by threes), will I turn over the 50? What if I skip count by twos—will I turn over the 50? What other numbers might I skip count by and turn over the 50? What patterns do you notice when turning over numbers skip counting by any amount?

4. Look at Weblink 5–1. Using the online calculator and hundreds board, ask the students to skip count by different amounts and predict the numbers that will be marked on the hundreds board. Encourage the students to work with a partner and discuss the patterns that they see.

Several computer and calculator activities are designed to help a child with early number concepts. The following examples include programs and activities for both number recognition and counting.

Pre-Kindergarten–Grade 2

OBJECTIVE: to use the computer to reinforce matching numerals to pictures of sets of objects.

1. *Sticky Bear Numbers Deluxe*, available from Optimum Resources, is a program for preschool and kindergarten children. It consists of sets of objects

that appear in response to a child's pressing either the space bar or a numeral on the keyboard. The child may make a new set of objects appear by pressing a new numeral or may increase or decrease the set by one by pressing the space bar. For example, by pressing the space bar once, the child makes a train appear. Each additional time the child presses the space bar, another train appears until nine trains are showing on the screen. After nine trains have appeared, the trains disappear one by one as the space bar is pressed until all trains have disappeared. The numeral 0 (zero) then appears on the screen. A numeral accompanies each set shown on the screen. When the space bar is pressed again, new sets of objects appear. Children as young as 18 months old can enjoy the graphics, and older children can begin to associate numerals with sets. The program also illustrates how to draw the numerals from 0 to 100 and connects these to pictures and the number words.

Other software that you might want to investigate for young children as they learn number concepts includes *Millie's Math House* and *Reader Rabbit's Math PreK–3* from Riverdeep, *Sunbuddy Math Playhouse* from Sunburst, and *Huggly Saves the Turtles* and *Clifford Thinking Adventures* from Tom Snyder.

Even very young children can use a calculator to develop counting skills. As children first learn to count, they may use a calculator to help them keep track of their counting. For example, a child counting a pile of chips can push "+ 1" on the calculator each time he or she moves a chip. Having finished counting the pile of chips, the child can push "=" on the calculator to check if his or her calculator will show the numeral just said.

Children can explore with a calculator to see what happens when they push "+ 1 = = = =." Later, children may start with any number and then try "+ 5" or "+ 2." What happens when you start with a larger number and push "− 2 = = ="? Children may encounter negative numbers doing this. (Calculators work differently, and you may need to explore this with yours before you try this with the children.)

Building Fluency with Large and Small Numbers

PLACE VALUE   Be certain that children have had many experiences with grouping activities before you formally introduce the numeral 10. It is difficult for young children to understand that 10 represents ● ● ● ● ● ● ● ● ● objects and not ● object. Children may logically assume that if you put a 1 and a 0 (zero) together, you should have 1 plus 0 objects, not 10. Early experience with grouping smaller amounts should help

children understand why "ten" is written as 10. The 1 here means one group and the 0 means zero units.

Extensive work on this concept when it is first introduced can help children avoid problems later. Many teachers in the intermediate and middle grades can tell you that place value remains a major difficulty as children learn operations that require regrouping. Even high school students often repeat lessons on addition and subtraction in general math classes because they never fully understood the meaning of place value.

As place value in base ten is introduced, the previous activities that involved grouping materials in other bases should be expanded to grouping by tens. Children should have extensive experience using both proportional and nonproportional materials to group by tens, hundreds, thousands, and so on. Encourage the children to record the results of their work using such things as place-value charts. The following are some additional activities to be used in base ten.

A C T I V I T I E S

Pre-Kindergarten – Grade 2

OBJECTIVE: to reinforce concretely place-value concepts in base ten.

1. With a large box of coffee stirrers or tongue depressors, have a contest to see who can pick up the largest handful of sticks. After the first student has taken a handful, ask the entire class to estimate how many sticks there are in the handful. Choose two students to be the counters—one to count and one to double-check. Once the children have counted the sticks, ask them how many bundles of 10 they think that you can make from the sticks. For example, if the children have counted out 87 sticks, tell them that you are going to put a rubber band around 10 sticks to make a bundle and ask how many bundles of 10 they think you can make. You might be surprised at the number of students who do not guess 8 bundles. Choose several children to be the bundlers and give each a rubber band for each bundle of 10 that they make. Once they make 8 bundles and have 7 sticks left over, record this on a chart similar to the one in Figure 5–27.

Separate the children into groups of four; give each child a table to record the number of sticks that the child can pick up. After each child has grabbed a handful of sticks, count the number of sticks and record this with the child's name on the chart. Then ask the children to record the number of bundles and singles that can be made. Tell the children that if anyone gets more than 10 bundles of 10 that these should be put together in a bundle of 100.

Grade K — Raft Game

Strand Numeration

Skills Practice counting by 5s and exchanging five 1s for one 5 and five 5s for one 25

OPTIONS FOR INDIVIDUALIZING						
GRADES	**K**	**1**	**2**	**3**	**4**	**5**	**6**
ENRICHMENT						
CORE PROGRAM	✔					
RETEACHING AND PRACTICE		✔				

Games Kit Materials (per group)
- 1 die

Additional Materials (per group)
- 15 beans
- 20 planks made from a craft stick with 5 beans glued to it
- 4 rafts made from 5 planks and 2 craft sticks
- 4 small toys

Players 2

Object of the game To exchange beans for planks and to exchange planks for rafts.

Directions

Advance Preparation Each student glues 5 beans on each craft stick to make planks. Then they glue 5 planks to 2 craft sticks as shown below to make a raft (each with 25 beans).

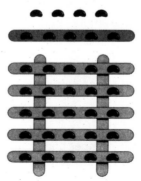

1. Players take turns rolling the die and picking up the number of beans shown by the number on the die.

2. When a player collects 5 beans, he or she exchanges them for a plank. Similarly, a player exchanges 5 planks for a raft.

3. As players acquire rafts, they can take a counting bear (or another toy) and float it across a pretend river.

2 Game Directions

Figure 5–26 From Grades K-6 Everyday Mathematics: Teacher's Guide to Games Copyright © 2003 by SRA/McGraw-Hill, reproduced with permission of the McGraw-Hill Companies.

MATH PROGRAM

The activity shown in Figure 5–26 is a kindergarten activity from the *Teacher's Guide to Games* with the *Everyday Math* program. Games are an integral part of the Everyday Math curriculum for a number of reasons. They add to the enjoyment of the program, help students develop their critical reasoning and problem-solving abilities, and give students a chance to practice and master basic skills. These are used to reduce the number of repetitious worksheets and to help students strengthen their number sense and mental computation abilities.

In this activity, students play a trading game with a grouping point of five. They trade five loose beans for a plank and trade five planks for a raft. In this way, students are building their concepts of place value and grouping with small numbers before they have had much experience with base ten. This gives them a stronger foundation for grouping in base ten when that is introduced.

In addition to the games, many of the lessons are "Explorations" giving students a chance to work in small groups using concrete materials to explore a concept. In addition, students are engaged in projects that include observing; communicating; identifying; reading for mathematical content; and collecting, organizing, and graphing data.

Name	Number of Sticks	Bundles of 100	Bundles of 10	Singles
Rajeev	87	0	8	7

Figure 5–27 Chart for recording bundles of sticks.

After all the children have had a chance to pick up sticks, bring them back together to discuss who had the biggest handful. Discuss the relationship of the bundles and singles to the number of sticks. Many children will be surprised to see that the number of bundles matches the number of tens (or hundreds).

2. Give children several ten strips and units from base ten blocks. You may copy the Base Ten Patterns from Appendix B and have the students cut out the tens and ones so each child has at least 10 tens and 100 ones. Challenge the children to show 54 with the pieces in as many ways as possible. Encourage them to record their results in an organized fashion. This may be difficult for some children, who may be stumped after 54 singles and 5 tens and 4 ones. If they are stuck, show them 4 ten strips and 14 ones and ask for the total value.

If children don't suggest it themselves, you might want to introduce a chart to keep track of their answers. See if the children use a pattern such as the one in Figure 5–28 or if they have difficulty organizing their thinking.

Try this periodically with different numbers. If children begin to find this too easy, challenge them to try to find all the ways to make 143 using hundreds, tens, or ones pieces. After students have had a chance to explore, bring them together to talk about their observations and patterns that they have noticed.

Pose riddles such as, "I used 24 pieces to make my number. I am less than 100. What might my number

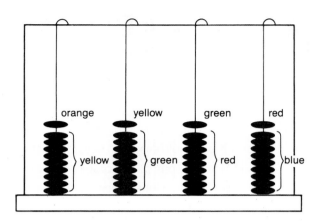

Figure 5–29 Base ten abacus.

be?" (24, 33, 42, 51, 60, 69, 78, 87, 96) "I used 14 pieces and I have two more tens than I do ones. What number am I?" (86) After you have posed a few riddles, let the children make up their own riddles for each other.

3. Purchase or construct several simple base ten abaci. Among the most useful are those with 10 beads on each bar, with the first 9 beads of one color and the tenth bead the color of the first 9 beads on the next bar (see Figure 5–29).

When the children fill up one bar with 10 beads, the color of the tenth bead should remind them to trade in all 10 beads for 1 bead on the next bar. Thus, 10 ones are traded for 1 ten, 10 tens for 1 hundred, and so on. Let the children use the abacus to record results from work with other place-value materials.

OBJECTIVE: to extend sight numbers to amounts between 10 and 20.

4. Use chips placed on tens frames such as the ones shown in Figure 5–30. You should have transparent grids for the overhead projector, and each student should have grids of his or her own. You may use the Blackline Masters in Appendix B to make these. Ask the students to explore by placing varying amounts of chips on the frames and determining the total. When children are comfortable finding the total, place a secret amount of

Number	Tens	Ones
54	5	4
	4	14
	3	24
	2	34
	1	44
	0	54

Figure 5–28 Chart for recording the number of ways to make 54.

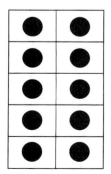 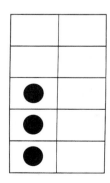

Figure 5–30 Example of tens frames showing 13 chips.

chips on the grids and flash them briefly on the overhead projector. Discuss with the students their methods of determining the total.

After the children have had much experience with physical models and with recording base ten numerals, concepts on the abstract level may be reinforced with materials that use only numerals. These materials may include hundreds charts, place-value charts, Bingo games, flash cards, and playing cards. The following activities are designed to be used after the children have a good concrete understanding of grouping in base ten.

A C T I V I T I E S

Grades 2–5

OBJECTIVE: to provide for practice in forming numerals as they are spoken and to allow for rapid checking of children's responses.

1. Let each child make a place-value chart that includes the hundreds or thousands, depending on the level of practice the child needs. This chart may be made from heavy manila paper by folding up the bottom part of the paper and stapling pockets to hold numeral cards. Label the pockets ones, tens, hundreds, and so on. Let each child make three cards for each numeral from 0 through 9.

Read a numeral you wish the children to form, such as 346 (three hundred forty-six), and let the children form the numeral by placing cards in the correct pockets and then holding the place-value chart up for you to see (see Figure 5–31). Quickly check to see whether or not each child has the correct response. This way, each child can get immediate feedback on the response and will not practice incorrect techniques. You may also use "magic slates" or individual whiteboards; the children write their responses, hold them up for you to check, and then erase them to prepare for the next problem. Include riddles such as, "I have the same number of hundreds and ones and twice as many tens. The total of the digits in my number is 8. Who am I?" (242) Let children take turns making up and asking riddles for the others to answer.

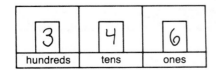

Figure 5–31 Individual pocket chart for displaying three-digit numerals.

OBJECTIVE: to provide for practice in recognizing numerals and place values.

2. Use 3-by-5 cards to make a deck of playing cards with values such as:

600	six hundred	6 hundreds
30	thirty	3 tens
4	four	4 ones

These cards may be used in a variety of card games that require the children to make matches, such as Concentration, Go Fish, Rummy, and Old Maid. After children become proficient with these cards, add others such as 3 tens, 14 ones, and 44; 2 hundreds, 15 tens, 6 ones, and 356. These cards may also be used for games such as Bingo. The Bingo cards should look like regular Bingo cards but with numerals to match the calling cards. The rules are the same as those for regular Bingo.

Calculators may also be used to reinforce place-value concepts. Let children predict what will show on the display if they press 3 × 100 or 7 × 1000. Be careful if you try 3 × 100 + 5 × 10 + 7 =. On a scientific calculator, you will get 357, but on many other calculators you will get 3,057. Children may wish to discuss why this happens and try several examples to test their hypotheses. This is a good time to discuss the order of operations and the use of parentheses.

The TI-10 calculator includes the ability to show place value using keys for hundreds, tens, and ones and has games to help students increase their number sense.

Children may also play games such as Go Fish on the calculator. Three or more children may play this game at a time. Play begins with each child putting a secret six-digit number into his or her calculator. All six digits should be different to begin the game. To play, one child asks another for a number, say 6. If the child asked has a 6 in any place, then it is given to the child who asked for it. If the 6 is in the tens place, the child being asked will say, "Take 60." That child will then subtract 60 from his or her number and the other child will add 60 to his or her number.

After the game has progressed, it is possible that the child being asked may have two 6s showing in the number. If this happens, the child must give up only one digit and should choose to give up the 6 in the place with the least value. For example, a child with 236,762 should say, "Take 60" and subtract only 60, not 6,060. Play continues until one player's score goes above six digits, or 1,000,000, or until one player's score goes to zero. The player with the highest score is declared the winner.

Integers

Students will become more comfortable with integers as they encounter uses for them in everyday situations. In addition to using negative numbers to show such things as temperatures below zero, altitudes below sea level, spending more money than you earn, or losing yards on the football field—situations that students might have encountered in the elementary grades—middle grades students should become familiar with such uses of integers as using a negative number to show a decrease in a variety of situations such as a loss in the stock market (negative earnings), a decrease in speed when driving (negative acceleration), or a decline in population (negative population growth). As students learn to use a broken-line graph to graph trends, they should make the connection between a negative slope on a graph and real-world experiences such as these. Operations with integers and their graphic representations will be explored further in future chapters.

Exponents and Scientific Notation

Because very large and very small numbers are becoming increasingly important in our world, it is necessary to have a convenient way to record them. It is quite difficult to read a number such as 235,000,000,000,000,000,000 or 0.0000000000000000456. Mathematicians, scientists, journalists, and others often use a simpler method of representing these very large or very small numbers that is based on our base ten numeration system; this method is called scientific notation. In scientific notation, numerals are expressed as a product of two numbers where the first number is greater than or equal to 1 but less than 10 and the second number is a power of 10. The numbers above would be written as 2.35×10^{20} and 4.56×10^{-17}. The following activities are designed to give students a basis for understanding scientific notation and the use of exponents.

A C T I V I T I E S

Grades 6–8

OBJECTIVE: to develop an understanding of very large and very small numbers and appropriately use exponential and scientific notation to represent them.

1. Ask students to complete the chart in Figure 5–32 by noting patterns. Ask the students how they might write the common form of any power of 10 by just knowing whether the exponent is positive, negative, or zero. By following the patterns on the chart, students should be able to predict that $10^0 = 1$, but they may have trouble predicting that 10^{-1} is 0.1 or

Exponential Form	Common Form
10^5	100 000
10^4	10 000
10^3	
	100
10^1	
10^0	
10^{-1}	
10^{-2}	
	0.001
10^{-4}	

Figure 5–32 Chart showing patterns in powers of ten.

that 10^{-2} is 0.01. Note that 10 to any negative power is the same as the unit fraction with that power of 10 in the denominator. That is, 10^{-4} is the same as $1/10^4$, or 0.0001. This means that on the chart in Figure 5–32, the pattern continues by moving the decimal point one place to the left each time the exponent decreases by one. After some discussion, students should recognize that a positive exponent tells you the number of zeros after the 1 for any positive power of 10 and a negative exponent is one more than the number of zeros after the decimal point and before the 1 for any negative power of 10. Encourage the students to discuss why this is true.

2. Ask students to use a calculator to explore what happens with the display for very large or very small numbers. Some calculators will simply display an error message if the number gets too large or too small. Other calculators might round very small numbers to zero. Still others will use some calculator version of scientific notation. Ask students to explore this on their own calculators to see if everyone has the same display. You might have students complete the chart in Figure 5-33 to determine what is displayed by the calculator when they type in the numbers given these in either common form or scientific notation. Encourage students to look for patterns on the chart to find the common form when given scientific notation and vice versa.

ESTIMATING AND USING BENCHMARKS

Often, it is more important for a child to be able to estimate a reasonable response than it is to have an exact answer. Politicians and newspapers may estimate the number of people in a crowd at a rally, or a store

Common Form	Scientific Notation	Calculator Display
251 000 000 000	2.5×10^{11}	
25 100 000	2.5×10^{7}	
0.0000000251	2.51×10^{-8}	
251 000 000 000 000		
0.00000251		
	$2.51 \quad 10^{-12}$	
	2.51×10^{1}	

Figure 5-33 Chart for recording calculator representations of scientific notation.

manager may estimate the number of pounds of hamburger to have on hand for the big sale, but, in both of these cases, an exact answer may not be necessary or even possible. As we continue to use calculators and computers, estimation skills become even more crucial. Calculators may give an exact answer, but children need to be able to estimate to determine whether that response makes sense. Estimating, therefore, should be a major part of all strands of mathematics.

We have suggested ways to incorporate estimation with each topic presented in this text. Another successful procedure is to have a special estimation activity once a week at the beginning of a math lesson. For example, using the same glass jar, one with a capacity of 250–450 milliliters, place a different type of material in the jar each week. Begin with larger objects, such as colored cubes, shell macaroni, marshmallows, individually wrapped candies, unshelled peanuts, and bottle caps. On estimation day, distribute slips of paper to the children and have each child write down his or her name and estimation of how many objects are in the jar. Make up a small certificate to award to the student or students with the closest estimate.

As time passes, decrease the size of the objects placed in the jar. For example, the following items work well: pennies, beans, buttons, various sizes of Cuisenaire rods, breakfast cereal, and paper clips. Toward the end of the school year, try rice and split peas. Every now and then, vary the type of estimation. For example, for three or four weeks, use different sizes of jars but use the same objects.

You might want to read stories or poems to the children that encourage estimation. If you have a jar full of jelly beans, the children might enjoy hearing *The Jelly Bean Contest* by Kathy Darling. The poem, "How Many, How Much," by Shel Silverstein is a good introduction to children making up their own estimation questions about things they may not have thought of before.

One week, put a golf ball in the jar with instructions to estimate the number of dimples on the ball (380 to 500, depending on the brand). Another week, place a small box from some household product on a table and ask how many centimeter cubes it would take to fill the box (the volume of the box).

Gulley (1998) describes a highly motivating "estimate of the week" contest at a middle school in which she has been involved. In this case all students at the school are invited to participate in estimating objects such as the length of a piece of rope on the wall or ceiling, the area of the school, the volume of a sleeping bag stuff sack, the number of a particular kind of cereal in a box, the combined ages of the faculty, the mass of a pumpkin, the percent of pink paper to the total paper in a stack, and the time it takes to melt a punch bowl of solid ice at room temperature.

Keep looking for objects to challenge the estimation skills of your students. It will not be too difficult to provide something for each week of the year.

The following are a few examples of estimating activities related to number concepts.

A C T I V I T I E S

Pre-Kindergarten–Grade 5

OBJECTIVE: to practice estimating large numbers of concrete objects.

1. Make a set of large flash cards (about 25 centimeters by 25 centimeters) and put various numbers of bright dots on each one. Doman (1980) uses up to 100 dots on a card for children under the age of four, but most elementary school children (and most adults) have difficulty actually recognizing more than about five dots. Using larger numbers of dots and flashing the cards briefly force the children to use estimation and grouping skills to guess the number of dots on a card. With only a few odd minutes per day of practice, children can become quite accurate in their guesses, and although exact answers are not a goal of estimation activities, a few children may be able to tell you the exact number of dots each time. With this activity, all children should improve visualization skills and develop a better concept of number.

2. Look at Weblinks 5–2, 5–3, and 5–4. In each of these, students practice estimation skills by determining the number of objects, length, or area. In Weblink 5–3, students compare two sets of objects. Weblink 5–4 states a quantity and asks the user to estimate whether the set of objects is more or less than the number given. All of these present problems that are challenging for adults as well as students.

Figure 5–34 Example of a number line for estimation of smaller numbers.

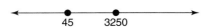

Figure 5–35 Example of a number line for estimation of larger numbers.

OBJECTIVE: to build number concepts related to measurement.

3. Bodily/kinesthetic children are often not given the opportunity to use some of their best abilities. This activity gives bodily/kinesthetic children a chance to shine and helps other children develop tactile skills.

Children should work in pairs. Let the children put a pile of Cuisenaire rods on the table. One child should close his or her eyes and the other child should select a Cuisenaire rod and place it in the hand of the first child. The first child should put that hand behind his or her back and open his or her eyes. The child with the rod should try to guess the color or length of the rod. Looking at the rods on the table, the child tries to match the rod felt with the rods seen.

Let the partners change roles and try the activity again. Children are often better at this activity than adults after only a few tries.

4. Place two numbers on a number line and ask children to estimate the location of others. For example, you might have a number line such as the one shown in Figure 5–34. Ask the students to place other numbers, such as 12, 25, and zero. This might also be extended to larger numbers using a number line such as the one shown in Figure 5–35. In Figure 5–35, you might ask students to find 100, 1,000, 5,000, or 1,000,000. For numbers such as 1,000,000, students would have to determine how far off the page the number would be.

Older children can also develop estimation skills with numbers. For these children, the numbers should include thousands and even millions.

A C T I V I T I E S

Grades 5–8

OBJECTIVE: to develop concrete ideas of large numbers.

1. Send the children on a scavenger hunt for 1 million of something. They may decide to look for grains of sand in the sandbox or blades of grass in the yard. This activity will cause them to search for methods other than counting. They may measure 5 milliliters (ml) of sand and count the grains in that amount and then estimate how many milliliters it takes to make 1 million grains, or they may count the blades of grass in 4 square centimeters (cm^2) and estimate the number of square centimeters it takes to make 1 million blades of grass.

2. Children may try to collect 1 million of something, such as bottle caps or twist ties. They must devise a method of keeping track of their collection. They may put 10 caps or ties in a small bag and 10 small bags in a larger bag. Ten bags of 100 may be placed in an even larger bag, and so on. After collecting for a while, the children may try to predict how long it will take to obtain 1 million of the item and may try to estimate how much space such an amount will occupy.

3. Children can do research to discover the current national debt. They then may determine how high a stack of $1 bills the debt would make or how long a row of $100 bills the debt would make if the bills were laid end to end. Children will probably wish to use a calculator to aid in computations but will discover that the numbers may be larger than what the calculator can display. Then they will need to discuss what to do.

The children's books *Is a Blue Whale the Biggest Thing There Is?* by Robert Wells (1993) and *If You Made a Million* (1989) and *How Much Is a Million* (1986) by David M. Schwartz contain some excellent ideas for teaching the concepts of large numbers, money, banking, and interest. They could be used as an introduction to these topics. The book *Innumeracy* (1988) by John Allen Paulos also has several suggestions for estimation topics that would help students (and adults) better understand today's world.

4. Let the children predict how many seconds they have been alive and then use a calculator to check their guesses.

5. Check with a local manufacturer or a restaurant. Ask how many gadgets they produced or hamburgers they sold in the last week. How many would this be per hour? Per month? Per year? If the restaurant is part of a chain, can you estimate how many hamburgers were sold by the entire chain in one year? Use your calculator to assist you.

6. Ask the children to predict how long it would take for all of the children in the school to read a total of 1 million pages in trade books. Ask them to devise a method for keeping track of the number of pages read and for involving all of the students.

7. View the Annenberg video *Animals in Yellowstone.* (Parts of this can also be found on the Annenberg Elementary Assessment video and in the Annenberg Reasoning video. More information can be found at Weblink 5–5.) Discuss ways in which the students estimated the total number of elk, bison, and pronghorn sheep in Yellowstone National Park. Ask the students to design an experiment to estimate the number of animals or birds in a local park. You may be able to find parents who have the interest and skills to help you with this task. Local conservation societies might also be interested in having the students assist them in some of their work that involves assessing the impact of various projects on the local wildlife.

Work with estimation will probably help children realize a need for rounding numbers. Often, exact answers are not required or even sensible. One cannot tell exactly how many grains of sand there are in a bucket or exactly how many stars are in the sky, but approximate answers involving rounded numbers may be useful.

Number lines may be used for rounding numbers less than 100 to the nearest 10. Children can locate a number such as 47 and determine whether it is closer to the 50 or to the 40. For a number such as 45, determine whether it is more sensible to round up or round down. Base ten blocks are also useful for rounding numbers. Children may show a number such as 287 with the blocks and then determine whether the amount is closer to 280 or 290 if they are rounding to the nearest 10, or closer to 200 or 300 if they are rounding to the nearest 100. Notice that rules for rounding numbers often do not apply in real life. If 63 students and 3 teachers are going on a field trip in buses with a maximum capacity of 30, finding you need 2 buses when rounded to the nearest whole number will leave 6 people stranded. Use several real-life situations and discuss when it is reasonable to round up and when it makes more sense to round down.

REASONING, SOLVING AND POSING NUMBER PROBLEMS

As children develop concepts and skills, they should use their problem-solving abilities to construct knowledge for themselves. Many of the activities presented earlier were presented in a problem format. Following are activities to encourage children to seek and define problems as well as to solve them.

A C T I V I T I E S

Grades 3–5

OBJECTIVE: to reinforce the concepts of greater than and less than and to encourage the development of strategies.

1. The game Guess My Number can be played in several ways. One variation of the game found on many computer programs can also be played by two children without a computer. It involves one player who writes down a secret number from 1 to 100. The second player tries to guess the number with the fewest possible guesses. After each guess, the first player tells the second whether the guess was too high or too low.

- *Understanding the problem.* I need to know that I am trying to guess a number my partner has chosen. This number may be as small as 1 or as large as 100. I will be told if my guesses are too large or too small.

- *Devising a plan.* The number could be even or odd, prime or not prime, but guessing a particular number will not give this information. What I will do, then, is to guess the number 50 and eliminate half of the numbers (eliminate possibilities).

- *Carrying out the plan.* I guess the number 50 and find that I am too high. Therefore, I know the number is from 1 to 49. I have eliminated 51 numbers. Next, I will guess the number 25 and see if I can eliminate more numbers. After six guesses, I discover that my partner's number was 17.

- *Looking back.* I was able to find the number quickly. I did not waste any guesses. I can use this strategy again. I can generalize this process to find that it should never take more than seven guesses to discover a whole number from 1 to 100.

Children can develop several strategies as Guess My Number progresses. They learn that wrong guesses can be valuable. The knowledge that guessing and wrong answers can be quite useful in mathematics is important to a child's willingness to tackle new problems.

One major skill in problem solving is finding a pattern. Working with numbers provides a good opportunity to practice finding patterns. Provide patterns such as 2, 4, 6, 8, —, — or 97, 94, 91, 88, —, —, —. After children understand the process, let them make up patterns for each other and place them in a learning center or copy them for everyone to work. Children may wish to use the constant feature on the calculator as they explore these patterns. An electronic example of this is available at Weblink 5–6 (click e-examples).

After children have worked with patterns of their own, they may be ready for such patterns as Pascal's triangle, Fibonacci numbers, and sequences involving finite differences. For ideas on presenting these topics, see *Teaching Children Mathematics* and *Mathematics Teaching in the Middle School* or the references for this chapter. Encourage children to do further research on their own both with concrete materials and in books.

Study the patterns in Figure 5–36. Make a list of the patterns the children find in the table. The patterns may include the following:

Pascal's Triangle

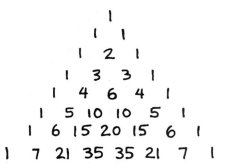

Figure 5–36 Pascal's triangle.

- Each number is the sum of the two numbers diagonally above it.
- The sum of the numbers in each row is a power of 2. The first row is just 1, 2^0; the sum of $1 + 1$ in the second row is 2, 2^1; the sum of $1 + 2 + 1$ in the third row is 4, 2^2; and so on.
- Diagonals that intersect in the middle of the triangle are identical, and each of these diagonals has an interesting pattern. The diagonal on the outside is all ones. In the next diagonal, the numbers have a difference of 1. The difference between numbers in a diagonal is equal to the closest number in the next diagonal to the outside.
- Each row is symmetrical.

There are many other patterns as well.

Many interesting activities that relate to the triangle can be found or created. The following are just a few. Children may create more of their own.

Grades 6–8

OBJECTIVE: to relate patterns in Pascal's triangle to everyday life.

1. Flip a penny five times. How many ways can you get five heads? Only one way, right? How many ways can you get one head and four tails? Five ways, right? List them. How many ways can you get two heads and three tails? Three heads and two tails? Four heads and one tail? Five tails? Do you see a pattern? Is it related to Pascal's triangle? Test your hypothesis to see if this pattern holds for flipping coins other numbers of times.

2. How many ways can you select three children for the safety patrol from five volunteers? How is this related to Pascal's triangle?

3. Study the map in Figure 5–37. Danny lives at Main and 1st Street. He has a crush on Maureen, who lives at Grand and 6th Street. Maureen says Danny may visit each afternoon as long as he takes a different path each time. He may travel only north and east and must stay on the labeled streets. For how many afternoons may Danny visit Maureen?

Try to discover how Pascal's triangle is related to each of these activities. Encourage children to make up

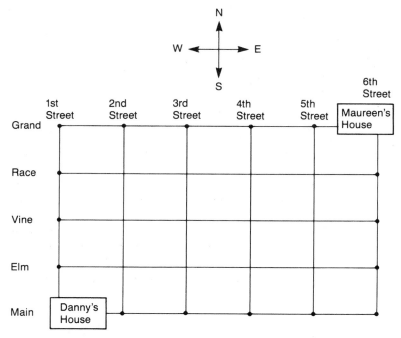

Figure 5–37 Applying Pascal's triangle to a map problem.

other patterns by asking themselves such questions as "What would happen if . . . ?" or "What if this were not true?" or "How else may I look at this?"

After working with Pascal's triangle, students might decide to investigate what happens when the odd counting numbers are listed in the same format as Pascal's triangle, as discussed in Chapter 4.

Fibonacci Numbers

Study the following pattern:

1,1,2,3,5,8,13,21,34,55, ...

How was this pattern formed?

As the Italian geometrician Leonardo Fibonacci studied natural objects such as spirals on a pine cone and petals on a flower, he discovered that the number of parts was often a number in this sequence. Let the children go on a scavenger hunt to find natural occurrences of Fibonacci numbers.

Intermediate and middle school children might enjoy videos that make use of patterns such as Pascal's triangle and the Fibonacci sequence. Three good ones that you might use include *Donald in Mathmagic Land*, *Math Vantage Unit I: Patterns*, and *The Phantom of the Bell Tower*. Further information on these and other technology and print materials for exploring patterns in more depth is available in the reference list.

The following activity uses Fibonacci numbers. Try to discover how this pattern may help you solve the problem.

A C T I V I T I E S

Grades 6–8

OBJECTIVE: to apply Fibonacci numbers to problem solving.

1. Antonio works at a soda fountain. He mixes milk shakes after school. He makes either regular shakes or extra-large shakes. An extra-large shake is twice the size of a regular shake. How many different ways can Antonio fill shake orders to use the equivalent of 10 regular shakes? For example, Antonio might first make 2 regular shakes and then 4 extra-large shakes, or he could first make 4 extra-large shakes and then 2 regular shakes; these two combinations are considered different. List all the possibilities. Do you see a relationship to Fibonacci numbers? Try your hypothesis out on different shake orders.

OBJECTIVES: to reinforce place-value concepts and to encourage logical thinking.

2. The game Pica-Fermi is an old one, but more recent versions of it may be seen in *Mastermind* and in computer and calculator games. This game is similar to Guess My Number in that it has two players. One player writes down a secret number that the other tries to guess with the least possible number of guesses. This time, the first player may write down a two-, three-, or four-digit number (the number of digits should be agreed upon ahead of time), which the second player tries to guess by naming a number with the number of digits. The first player then tells the guesser the number of correct digits in the wrong place and the number of correct digits in the correct place by saying *pica* for the digits correct and in the wrong place and *fermi* for the digits correct and in the correct place. A sample game follows.

The secret number is 482.

The player guesses	Pica	Fermi
123	1	0
456	0	1
789	0	1
147	1	0
519	0	0
736	0	0
482	0	3

The score is 7 for this round, the number of guesses used to find 482. Try the game yourself with a partner. Discuss the strategies you used.

OBJECTIVES: to reinforce concepts of consecutive numbers and to encourage problem-solving strategies.

3. Number Shuffle is played by placing the digits 1–8 in a diagram such as Figure 5–38. No two consecutive digits may be touching horizontally, vertically, or diagonally.

Encourage students to ask themselves questions such as "Are any positions basically the same because of symmetry?" and "Are any numbers special in terms

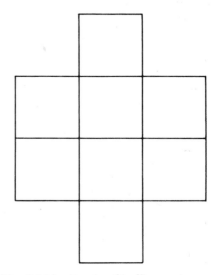

Figure 5–38 Grid for Number Shuffle puzzle.

of consecutive digits?" The last question should prompt the students to place the 1 and the 8 in the two center squares, which is a key to solving this problem.

OBJECTIVES: to reinforce place value, give practice with a calculator, and encourage logical thinking.

 4. Challenge the students to make their telephone numbers show on their calculators using only the 1, 0, +, and = keys. No telephone number should require pressing the "+" more than eight times. Many students begin by pressing $1 + 1 + 1 + 1 + 1 \ldots$, but they should soon realize this will be futile. Others will try $1\,000\,000 + 1\,000\,000 + 100\,000 \ldots$, but they should quickly realize that while this may result in the telephone number, the + was pressed more than eight times. Some hints may be needed before the child realizes that he or she may use $1\,111\,111 + 1\,011\,111 + \ldots$.

OBJECTIVE: to develop a combination of spatial and numerical problem-solving abilities.

5. Estelle Dickens and Jeffrey Sellon (1981) have developed a set of activities called *Cuisenaire Roddles*, which include games and puzzles for use by one or more children. The children place the Cuisenaire rods on game boards to solve brainteasers or play strategy games that involve such skills as finding number patterns and completing "magic triangles." Children enjoy solving these puzzles and creating puzzles of their own for each other.

OBJECTIVES: to encourage historical research, to introduce non-place-value systems of numeration, and to aid in the development of new systems of numeration.

6. Introduce systems of numeration that do not use a base ten system. Roman numerals may be evaluated in terms of using both an additive and a subtractive system and compared to the Egyptian system, which was strictly additive. The Chinese system, which uses both multiplication and addition, may then be introduced. These systems may be compared to the Babylonian and Mayan systems, which were both place-value systems, although neither used base ten.

Children may research how our Hindu-Arabic numerals were developed. Encourage children to make up systems of their own and share them with other students. Children may look at the use of binary numbers in computers and perhaps create a tertiary number system, which might be more efficient.

7. Ask your students to read about the lives of female mathematicians who studied number theory and to demonstrate some of their findings. A good place to begin the research is *Women and Numbers: Lives of Women Mathematicians Plus Discovery Activities* by Teri Perl (1993). This book describes their lives in language that is very readable by intermediate and middle grades students; it also suggests a variety of activities that students can do to understand the areas of mathematics that these women explored. For example, after a description of Ada Lovelace is a problem involving triangular numbers. Sonya Kovalevsky's description includes an activity involving prime numbers, Evelyn Boyd Granville's chapter has a problem with Pascal's triangle, and Fanya Montalvo's has work with Fibonacci numbers. These descriptions give girls good role models of women who found their life's work in the mathematical field, and they also give them an opportunity to expand their mathematical horizons.

For more information on women mathematicians and scientists, see Weblink 5–7.

ORGANIZING FOR NUMBER TLC

Many of the activities in this chapter can be done by two children working as partners, while others may be done individually or in larger groups. Because the meaning of numbers must be constructed by the children themselves, they must be given time to work with materials and to think about questions that the teacher or other students have asked. It is important to give the students enough time to argue with each other about their work. Group time should be as important as individual time for working on problems and for discussing meanings with the teacher.

The games described in this chapter may be led by the children as well as the teacher. They give the children the opportunity to discuss meanings and understanding without trying to match an answer in a book. Be sure to give children plenty of time to work together on activities to develop grouping concepts. These concepts are crucial to the understanding of place value, and they will take a great deal of time to develop.

COMMUNICATING NUMBER SENSE

As students work with a partner and in groups, the discussion that goes on is essential to the development of the concept of number and the idea of place value. Kamii states:

> A characteristic of logico-mathematical knowledge is that there is absolutely nothing arbitrary in it. Two plus two makes four in all cultures. It follows that in the logico-mathematical realm, children *will* arrive at the truth if they debate long enough. They need to talk about their number experiences in everyday life, during games, and as they work with the development of place value concepts. The social interaction that goes on is an important part of the construction of the number concepts. (1990, p. 27)

It is important that the teacher focus on the children's understanding and not try to impose an arbitrary notion of number on the children. The only way the teacher will know what the children understand about numbers is to ask them. The teacher must take the time to listen to the children and to ask them questions that cause them to reach disequilibrium and construct their own concepts of number. In this way, oral communication becomes an integral and necessary part of every lesson.

Older children can communicate their reasoning in written form. They can keep logs about what they have learned and write out their methods of solving different types of problems. They can write down the new concepts they have learned and what areas may still be confusing.

Some of this writing may be expanded into portfolio entries. Students in the middle grades may write a portfolio entry based on their methods of determining the best way to approximate the number of blades of grass on the football field. They might take sample plots of 100 square centimeters each from a number of different parts of the field and explain how this can be used to estimate the number of blades of grass in the whole field. They might explain that parts of the field are bare from overuse and other parts have much thicker grass. They might divide the field into a half-dozen plots with different amounts of grass growth, sample each plot four times, find the average number of blades of grass in each sample, approximate the number of blades of grass in each plot, and total the number of blades of grass from all the plots. Extensions of this activity might include determining the best type of grass seed to replant parts of the field and finding the cost of doing this. Students should suggest other connections and extensions as they work on the problem.

CONNECTING AND REPRESENTING NUMBER LEARNING

Mr. Green's primary class is studying Native Americans. They have found that Native Americans used popcorn, and they are reading *The Popcorn Book* by Tomie de Paola (1978). Through this study, they have learned that $\frac{1}{2}$ cup of unpopped popcorn will make 12 cups of popped popcorn. They plan to have a popcorn party for their parents and are trying to figure out how much popcorn to buy. This will only be a small fraction of the 18.5 billion quarts of popcorn eaten in America each year.

Ms. Paulin's fourth-grade class is investigating the use of numbers in the daily newspaper. Each student has cut out 10 sentences from the paper that make use of numbers. The students are now grouping the sentences according to the numbers in them. They have made a large chart on the wall with the headings 0–9, 10–99, 100–999, 1,000–9,999, and greater than 10,000. So far, the heading with the most sentences under it is greater than 10,000. The students are discussing reasons why there are so many large numbers. They have noticed that there were several articles on the spending habits of citizens of the United States and the federal debt. They are now searching to determine who has found the sentence with the largest number. This is complicated by the fact that some numbers are expressed as numerals and some consist of a combination of numerals and words such as "8 billion."

After the students have completed the task of pasting the numbers on the chart, Ms. Paulin gathers them all on the floor around the chart to discuss their work. Students practice reading some of the numbers in the articles and discuss how large some of them really are. Their homework for the evening is to listen to television or radio for one half-hour and to write down a sentence for every number they hear. These will be sorted and investigated tomorrow according to the type of program that contained the numbers. Students brainstorm questions they would like to investigate, such as "Are there more numbers on the news or more numbers in a sitcom?" and "Are numbers stated in television news programs larger or smaller on average than numbers they found in the newspaper?" These questions are recorded on chart paper for the students to look at after they have collected their data.

Ms. Baker has just finished reading *Counting on Frank* (Clement, 1991) to her sixth graders. Will comments that the pictures in the book look like a picture book for his little brother. However, Dan says that he likes the numbers in the book. He wonders if they are really true. Ms. Baker is pleased that Dan has mentioned that because she plans to have the students take some of the events in the story and determine if the mathematics is reasonable. She divides the class into pairs and assigns each pair a different "fact" from the book to investigate. After all the groups have reported on their findings, Ms. Baker tells the class that they are going to write their own book for Mr. Meier's primary class to read. Each of the pairs must come up with a new mathematical statement to include in the book. Sabatina is already thinking about a fact based on the number of hairs on her dog. She can hardly wait to get home and have Geraldine help her count hairs on her Dalmatian Gypsy.

Ms. Baker decides that tomorrow would be a good time to introduce the new *Counting on Frank* software that she has just received.

ASSESSING NUMBER LEARNING

As in any assessment, begin assessing number learning by looking at goals and objectives. Begin by examining the goals and objectives from the NCTM *Standards,* those set by your state or school district, and those of the textbook series being used. Review standardized tests that the students are required to take. These are often incomplete, however. Many of the conceptual and attitudinal goals and objectives of the teacher and learner are not tested by current standardized tests. Many of these tests are changing, however, to include more conceptual and performance-based items.

Take advantage of the tests provided in the children's textbook for assessing achievement of the objectives of that series. Texts often have pre- and post-tests for the students in the teacher's manual or related materials and practice tests for the students in their own books. Please keep in mind that written tests, especially tests that only look for one right answer, cannot give you all the information that you need about your students.

Your observations of students should provide much additional information. Look for what the child does well and for what the child may be having difficulty with. It is probably more important to look at the child's *processes* than it is to look at the child's *products.* A teacher can learn much more about the child by watching him or her work than by looking at the answers to a test. To aid in keeping track of children's individual work, the teacher should jot down anecdotal records each day. The teacher will probably not be able to observe each child each day but should make a point of seeing each child at least once per week. Ask the children to keep a portfolio of some of their best work, also. They may keep a written log, noting what they have learned and what is still not understood.

When studying number concepts, look for the following as the children manipulate concrete materials:

1. *Conservation.* With young children, be sure to determine whether the child can conserve both number and length.
2. *Counting.* Again, with young children, look for common counting errors. Can the child count rationally? That is, does the child say one number for each object counted or are numbers simply recited in order with no regard for the material being counted? Does the child realize that the sequence of the counting numbers does not change? Does the child understand that objects may be counted in any order? Does the child realize that the number named last when counting refers to the total number of objects in the set and not just to the last object? Can the child start counting with any number or only with 1? Can the child skip count by twos, fives, tens, and so on? Can the child count past the "hard numbers"—for example, 29 to 30, 99 to 100, 999 to 1,000, and so on? Can the child count backward from any number?
3. *Number concepts.* Does the child associate a number with a set of objects or is the number only a word to recite? Does a child recognize amounts up to at least 5 by sight?
4. *Grouping concepts.* Does the child understand trading units for groups and groups for supergroups, and so forth? Can the child record the results of trading?
5. *Place-value concepts.* Does the child understand the meaning of numerals written in standard Hindu-Arabic notation? Can the child model numerals with place value materials such as multibase blocks and chips for trading? Check this understanding by asking the child to count out 25 chips or other small objects. Circle the 5 in 25 and ask the child to show you that many chips. Then circle the 2 in 25 and ask the child to show you how many chips the 2 represents. If the child shows you 2 chips rather than 20, you will know that place-value is not clearly understood. You may wish to view the videotapes by Marilyn Burns and Kathy Richardson (listed in the references) to watch them interviewing children on this concept. You might be surprised at some of the very common misconceptions.
6. *Estimation and approximation concepts.* Can the child use numbers to make reasonable estimates or approximate results using a variety of representations?
7. *Problem creating and problem solving.* Can the child use numbers and strategies to create and solve problems?
8. *Uses in everyday life.* Is the child aware of numbers in the world around him or her and can the child use numbers rationally outside of school?

SOMETHING FOR EVERYONE

Physical models described in this chapter, such as Cuisenaire rods, multibase blocks, chips for trading, bean cups, the abacus, and bundling sticks, are excellent aids for tactile learners, while visual learners may wish to combine these materials with drawings. Auditory learners will wish to discuss what they are doing as they manipulate the objects. Music is an excellent aid for auditory learners, and they will enjoy counting songs and poems.

Students who learn well sequentially and in discrete units often like recipes and rules and tend not to estimate. They see the parts better than the whole. These students can count forward well and prefer discrete materials such as chips to spatial materials such as Cuisenaire rods and multibase blocks when learning number concepts.

Students who tend to be more spatial and holistic see the whole rather than the parts. They may estimate well and see the answer without knowing how they got it. They prefer Cuisenaire rods and multibase blocks to chips or other discrete objects for learning number concepts. They often can count backward better than forward.

Children who need more challenge should be given many opportunities for both problem solving and problem creating. Topics such as Pascal's triangle, Fibonacci numbers, and other numeration systems, such as the Egyptian, Roman, or Babylonian systems, are a good starting point. Students can find a wealth of information and interesting problems in these areas with some research on the Internet or in a good library, in the Ideas section of *Teaching Children Mathematics,* in articles in *Mathematics Teaching in the Middle School,* in the calendar section of the *Mathematics Teacher,* or in the student section of the newsletter of the National Council of Teachers of Mathematics (see Appendix A for the address). Encourage gifted students to make up problems of their own after solving some of these.

Children having difficulty with number concepts should not be rushed to work with numbers on an abstract level. Whether the difficulty is with beginning number concepts, perhaps due to the inability to conserve numbers or to counting misunderstandings, or with later ideas such as place value, the children need to work with physical models. After the children feel comfortable with the models and seem to have grasped the concepts, be sure to have the children write the numerals with the models still in front of them. For many children, it is very difficult to make the transition from the physical models to the abstract numerals. Do not expect them to be able to remember what you did with the models yesterday if you ask them to work solely with numerals today. The two must be used together.

FOR YOU AS A TEACHER: IDEAS FOR DISCUSSION AND YOUR PROFESSIONAL PORTFOLIO

This section is intended to provide you the opportunity to read, write, and reflect on key elements of this chapter. We have listed several discussion ideas. We hope that one or more of these ideas will prove interesting to you and that you will choose to investigate and write about the ideas. The results of your work should be considered as part of your professional portfolio. You might consider these two questions as guides for your writing: "What does the material in this chapter mean for you as a teacher?" or "How can what you are reading be translated into a teaching practice for you as a teacher?"

DISCUSSION IDEAS

1. Analyze several of the counting books listed in the references or other favorites of your own. Compare books from different countries. Discuss the use of books from a variety of cultures in an elementary mathematics class. Will the use of different counting systems enhance the class or do you think children will be confused by the different use of numbers? Justify your position.

2. Choose two or three children between the ages of four and nine, and ask them several questions about conservation of numbers, counting, and place value. Analyze any mistakes that they make, and determine whether they can conserve number. Compare any mistakes in counting or place-value concepts to those described in this chapter or those that you see in a video such as the ones by Annenberg/CPB, Kathy Richardson, or Marilyn Burns that are listed in the references. Design individualized instruction based upon the results of your observations.

3. Choose and analyze a piece of software designed to help young children learn counting or number concepts. Do you think the software would be a help or a hindrance for a child in the early stages of learning numbers? If possible, watch a young child using the software and interview him or her to determine if new concepts are being developed accurately.

4. Choose a textbook series and examine the sections on place value for grades one through four. What physical models are suggested? How does the development of concepts move from the concrete to the connecting to the abstract level? How much repetition is there from one year of the program to the next? Do concepts build in complexity as the students get older? Compare your results to those of a classmate who has studied another program.

5. Choose a famous number pattern such as Pascal's triangle, triangular numbers, or Fibonacci numbers and research its historical development. What patterns can you find in these numbers that made them so famous? Explore some of the questions that are raised in the history books, and try to find a new pattern that is not mentioned in any of the books. Report on your findings to the class.

ADDITIONAL RESOURCES

REFERENCES

Baroody, Arthur J., "Basic Counting Principles Used by Mentally Retarded Children," *Journal for Research in Mathematics Education,* 17, no. 5 (November 1986), 382–89.

Barta, James, and Diane Schaelling, "Games We Play: Connecting Mathematics and Culture in the Classroom," *Teaching Children Mathematics,* 4, no. 7 (March 1998), 388–93.

Bresser, Rusty, and Caren Holtzman, *Developing Number Sense Grades 3–6.* Sausalito, CA: Math Solutions Publications, 1999.

Burns, Marilyn, *Mathematics: Assessing Understanding.* New Rochelle, NY: Cuisenaire, 1993.

Butterworth, Brian, *What Counts: How Every Brain Is Hardwired for Math.* New York: Free Press, 1999.

Dehaene, Stanislas, *The Number Sense: How the Mind Creates Mathematics.* New York: Oxford University Press, 1997.

Dickens, Estelle, and Jeffrey Sellon, *Cuisenaire Roddles.* New Rochelle, NY: Cuisenaire, 1981.

Doman, Glenn, *Teach Your Baby Math.* Philadelphia: Better Baby Press, 1980.

Dossey, John A., Ina V. S. Mullis, Mary M. Lindquist, and Donald L. Chambers, *The Mathematics Report Card: Are We Measuring Up? Trends and Achievement Based on the 1986 National Assessment.* Princeton, NJ: Educational Testing Service, 1988.

Education Development Center, *Seeing and Thinking Mathematically in the Middle Grades: The Language of Numbers.* Portsmouth, NH: Heinemann, 1996.

Fuson, Karen C., and J. W. Hall, "The Acquisition of Early Number Word Meanings: A Conceptual Analysis and Review," in *The Development of Mathematical Thinking,* ed. H. P. Ginsburg. New York: Academic Press, 1983.

Ginsburg, Herbert P., *Children's Arithmetic: The Learning Process.* New York: Van Nostrand, 1977.

———, "Children's Surprising Knowledge of Arithmetic," *Arithmetic Teacher,* 28, no. 1 (September 1980), 42–44.

Gulley, Wendy, "Estimate of the Week," *Mathematics Teaching in the Middle School,* 3, No. 5 (February 1998), 324–328.

Hiebert, James, "Children's Thinking," in *Research in Mathematics Education,* ed. Richard J. Shumway. Reston, VA: National Council of Teachers of Mathematics, 1980.

Kamii, Constance, "Constructivism and Beginning Arithmetic (K–2)," in *Teaching and Learning Math in the 1990s,* ed. Thomas J. Cooney and Christian Hirsch. Reston, VA: National Council of Teachers of Mathematics, 1990.

Karp, Karen S., and Robert N. Ronau, "Birthdays and the Binary System: A Magical Mixture," *Mathematics Teaching in the Middle School,* 3, no. 1 (September 1997), 6–12.

Leutzinger, Larry P., Edward C. Rathmell, and Tonya D. Urbalsch, "Developing Estimation Skills in the Primary Grades," in *Estimation and Mental Computation* (National Council of Teachers of Mathematics, 1986 Yearbook). Reston, VA: NCTM, 1986.

McIntosh, Alistair, Barbara Reys, and Robert Reys, *Number Sense: Simple Effective Number Sense Experiences.* White Plains, NY: Dale Seymour, 1997. (series of four books for grades 1–2, 3–4, 4–6, and 6–8)

National Council of Teachers of Mathematics, *Principles and Standards for School Mathematics.* Reston, VA: NCTM, 2000.

National Research Council, *Everybody Counts: A Report to the Nation on the Future of Mathematics Education.* Washington, DC: National Academy Press, 1989.

Paulos, John Allen, *Innumeracy: Mathematical Illiteracy and Its Consequences.* New York: Hill & Wang, 1988.

Perl, Teri, *Women and Numbers: Lives of Women Mathematicians Plus Discovery Activities.* San Carlos, CA: Wide World Publishing Tetra, 1993.

Piaget, Jean, *The Child's Concept of Number.* New York: Norton, 1965.

Roper, Ann, *Cooperative Problem Solving with Unifix Cubes.* Sunnyvale, CA: Creative Publications, 1990.

Roper, Ann, Shirley Hoogeboom, and Judy Goodnow, *Cooperative Problem Solving with Calculators.* Sunnyvale, CA: Creative Publications, 1991.

Schielack, Jane F., and Dinah Chancellor, *Uncovering Mathematics with Manipulatives and Calculators: Levels 1, 2 & 3.* Dallas: Texas Instruments, 1995.

Sheffield, L. J. *Extending the Challenge in Mathematics: Developing Mathematical Promise in K–8 Students.* Thousand Oaks, CA: Corwin, 2002.

Sheffield, L. J., C. Findell, C. Gavin, and C. Greenes, *Awesome Math Problems for Creative Thinking.* Chicago: Creative Publications, 2002. (Series of six mathematics problem solving books for grades 3–8)

Skemp, Richard R., *The Psychology of Learning Mathematics.* Hillsdale, NJ: Erlbaum, 1987.

Stokes, William T., *Notable Numbers.* Los Altos, CA: Covington Middle School, Los Altos School District, 1972.

Taverner, Nixie, *Unifix Structural Material.* North Way, England: Philograph Publications, 1977.

Watson, Clyde, *Binary Numbers.* New York: Crowell, 1977.

Wilcutt, Robert, Carole Greenes, and Mark Spikell, *Base Ten Activities.* Palo Alto, CA: Creative Publications, 1975.

Zaslavsky, Claudia, *The Multicultural Math Classroom: Bringing in the World.* Portsmouth, NH: Heinemann, 1996.

CHILDREN'S LITERATURE

Adler, David A., *Base Five.* New York: Crowell, 1975.

———, *Roman Numerals.* New York: Crowell, 1977.

Anno, Mitsumasa, *Anno's Counting House.* New York: Philomel, 1982.

Brent, Jan, *The Twelve Days of Christmas.* New York: Putnam, 1990.

Carle, Eric, *The Very Hungry Caterpillar.* New York: Putnam, 1969.

Clement, Rod, *Counting on Frank.* Milwaukee, WI: Gareth Stevens, 1991.

Crews, Donald, *Ten Black Dots.* New York: Greenwillow, 1986.

Darling, Kathy, *The Jelly Bean Contest,* Champaign, IL: Garrard Publ. Co, 1972.

Dee, Ruby, *Two Ways to Count to Ten.* New York: Holt, 1988.

dePaola, Tomie, *The Popcorn Book.* New York: Holiday, 1978.

Feelings, Muriel, *Moja Means One: A Swahili Counting Book.* New York: Dial, 1971.

Friedman, Aileen, *The King's Commissioners.* New York: Scholastic, 1994.

Giganti, Paul, Jr., *How Many Snails? A Counting Book.* New York: Greenwillow, 1988.

Hamm, Diane J., *How Many Feet in the Bed?* New York: Simon & Schuster, 1991.

Hulme, Joy, *Sea Squares.* New York: Hyperion, 1991.

McKissack, Patricia, *A Million Fish . . . More or Less.* New York: Knopf, 1992.

Merriam, Eve, *12 Ways to Count to 11.* New York: Simon & Schuster, 1993.

Pinczes, Elinor J., *One Hundred Hungry Ants.* Boston: Houghton Mifflin, 1993.

Reese, Mary, *Ten in a Bed.* Boston: Little, Brown, 1988.

Schwartz, David M., *How Much Is a Million?* New York: Lothrop, Lee, & Shepard, 1986.

———, *If You Made a Million.* New York: Lothrop, Lee, & Shepard, 1989.

Schwartz, David M., and Paul Meisel, *On Beyond a Million: An Amazing Math Journey.* Danvers, MA: Bantam Doubleday Dell, 1999.

Scieszka, Jon, and Lane Smith, *Math Curse.* Bergenfield, NJ: Viking, Penguin Books, 1995.

Silverstein, Shel, "How Many, How Much?" In *A Light in the Attic.* New York, Harper & Row, 1981.

Sitomer, Mindel, and Harry Sitomer, *Zero Is Not Nothing.* New York: Crowell, 1978.

St. John, Glory, *How to Count Like a Martian.* New York: Walck, 1975.

Tang, Greg, and Harry Briggs, *Grapes of Math: Mind Stretching Math Riddles.* New York: Scholastic, 2001.

Wahl, John, and Stacey Wahl, *I Can Count the Petals of a Flower.* Reston, VA: National Council of Teachers of Mathematics, 1976.

Wells, Robert E., *Is a Blue Whale the Biggest Thing There Is?* Morton Grove, IL: Whiltman, 1993.

Williams, Vera B., *Cherries and Cherry Pits.* New York: Mulberry, 1986.

Wood, Audrey, and Don Wood, *Piggies.* San Diego: Harcourt Brace Jovanovich, 1991.

Zaslavsky, Claudia, *Count on Your Fingers African Style.* New York: Crowell, 1980.

TECHNOLOGY

Annenberg/CPB, *Teaching Math: A Video Library, K–4.* Boston: WGBH Educational Foundation, 1995.

———, *Mathematics Assessment: A Video Library, K–12.* Boston: WGBH Educational Foundation, 1995.

Banta, Milt, Bill Berg, and Heinz Haber, *Donald in Mathmagic Land.* Burbank, CA: Walt Disney Home Video, 1989. (video)

Broderbund, *Carmen Sandiego Math Detective.* Novato, CA: Broderbund, 1998. (software)

Burns, Marilyn, *Mathematics: Assessing Understanding.* White Plains, NY: Cuisenaire. (set of 3 videos and discussion guide)

Children's Television Network, *Mathnet Mysteries: The View from the Rear Terrace.* Lincoln, NE: GPN, 1991. (video kit)

Creative Wonder, *Counting on Frank.* Minneapolis, MN: The Learning Company. 1996 (software)

Davidson, *Math Blaster Jr.* Torrance, CA: Davidson, 1997. (software)

Edmark, *Mighty Math Calculating Crew.* Orlando, FL: Harcourt Brace, 1996. (software)

———, *Mighty Math Carnival Countdown.* Orlando, FL: Harcourt Brace, 1996. (software)

———, *Millie's Math House.* Orlando, FL: Harcourt Brace, 1995. (software)

GPN, *Math Vantage: Unit 1: Patterns.* Lincoln, NE: GPN, 1997. (video and print materials)

HRM, *The Phantom of the Bell Tower.* Pleasantville, NY: Human Relations Media, 1992.

Learning Company, *Reader Rabbit's Math PreK–3.* Novato, CA: Riverdeep, 1998. (software)

MECC, *MathKeys.* Minneapolis, MN: The Learning Company, 1995. (software)

Morrison, Philip, Phylis Morrison, and the Office of Charles and Ray Eames, *Powers of Ten.* New York: Scientific American, 1982. (video and book)

Richardson, Kathy, *A Look at Children's Thinking Video I, Assessment Techniques: Beginning Number Concepts.* Norman, OK: Educational Enrichment, 1990.

———, *A Look at Children's Thinking Video II, Assessment Techniques: Number Combinations and Place Value.* Norman, OK: Educational Enrichment, 1990.

Scholastic, *Clifford Thinking Adventures.* Watertown, MA: Tom Snyder, 2000. (software)

Tom Snyder, *Huggly Saves the Turtles,* Watertown, MA: Tom Snyder, 2000. (software)

Stickybear Software, *Stickybear Numbers Deluxe.* Hilton Head Island, SC: Optimum Resource, Inc. 2000.

Sunburst, *Sunbuddy Math Playhouse.* Pleasantville, NY: Sunburst, 1997. (software)

WEBLINKS

Weblink 5–1 Learning about Number Relationships and Properties of Numbers Using Calculators and Hundred Boards: Displaying Number Patterns: E-Example from Illuminations from NCTM. http://standards.nctm.org/document/eexamples/chap4/4.5/index.htm#applet

Weblink 5–2 Estimator. Students practice estimation skills by determining the number of objects, length, or area. http://shodor.org/interactivate/activities/estim/index.html

Weblink 5–3 Comparison Estimator. Similar to Estimator but compares two sets of objects. http://shodor.org/interactivate/ activities/estim2/index.html

Weblink 5–4 More or Less Estimator. Similar to Estimator activity but states a quantity and asks the user to estimate whether the set of objects is more or less than the number given. http://shodor.org/interactivate/activities/estim3/ index.html

Weblink 5–5 The Annenberg/CPB Math and Science Collection. http://www.learner.org/

Weblink 5–6 NCTM electronic version of the NCTM *Principles and Standards.* http://standards-e.nctm.org

Weblink 5–7 4000 Years of Women in Science. http://crux.astr.ua.edu/4000ws/4000ws.html

TEACHING AND LEARNING ADDITION AND SUBTRACTION OF WHOLE NUMBERS AND INTEGERS

As you read the following pages, consider these guiding questions:

1. What is an operation, and how does it differ from a specific operation like addition or subtraction?
2. What is the sequence for helping children make sense of the concepts and skills of addition and subtraction?

3. What are several physical objects useful in presenting the concepts of addition and subtraction?

4. What does it mean to "develop fluency with addition and subtraction"?

5. What are some different activities to help children remember the basic addition and subtraction combinations?

6. Why should students develop skill in estimating, using benchmarks, and mental calculating?

7. What are some reasons that students make mistakes in their computation?

NCTM Principles and Standards for School Mathematics

Number and Operations

Instructional programs from prekindergarten through grade 12 should enable all students to:

Understand meanings of operations and how they relate to one another

Pre-K to 2

- understand various meanings of addition and subtraction of whole numbers and the relationship between the two operations;
- understand the effects of adding and subtracting whole numbers.

Grades 6–8

- understand the meaning and effects of arithmetic operations with fractions, decimals, and integers;
- use the associative and commutative properties of addition and multiplication and the distributive property of multiplication over addition to simplify computations with integers, fractions, and decimals.

Compute fluently and make reasonable estimates

Pre-K to 2

- develop and use strategies for whole-number computations, with a focus on addition and subtraction;

- develop fluency with basic number combinations for addition and subtraction;
- use a variety of methods and tools to compute, including objects, mental computation, estimation, paper and pencil, and calculators.

Grades 3–5

- develop fluency in adding, subtracting, multiplying, and dividing whole numbers;
- develop and use strategies to estimate the results of whole-number computations and to judge the reasonableness of such results;
- select appropriate methods and tools for computing with whole numbers from among mental computation, estimation, calculators, and paper and pencil according to the context and nature of the computation and use the selected method or tool.

Grades 6–8

- develop and analyze algorithms for computing with integers and develop fluency in their use.

NCTM (2000), pp. 78, 148. Reprinted by permission.

Make a copy of the Table for Addition in Appendix B and complete it. Describe as many patterns as you can find in the table. Include such things as drawing a square around 4, 9, or 16 cells anywhere in the table and looking for sums and differences of the numbers in the cells. As you write your descriptions, be sure to explain your thinking.

REFLECTIONS AND REFINEMENT: After you have completed this task, compare your work with that of some of your classmates. How did your response differ from those of others? As you continue through this term, see if you can find additional patterns to describe. Write what you have found here.

Addition and subtraction are commonly used in our daily lives. From adding change at the market to updating our checkbook, these operations serve us well. Studying addition and subtraction as part of the school mathematics curriculum in the early grades prepares our students to be productive, thoughtful citizens. It also prepares them to continue their study of mathematics. Once students make sense of addition and subtraction and become fluent in their use, they can more easily engage in challenging mathematical problem solving.

With the advent of computational alternatives, time devoted to paper-and-pencil computation in the elementary school mathematics curriculum has been reduced. Alternatives to paper-and-pencil computation include using mental calculation, estimation, and the calculator. Children growing up in a time of electronic computation need to be skillful in estimation and mental computation. They will need to know when answers are reasonable and when they are not.

When performing computations, students should be able to decide whether to use paper and pencil, mental calculation, estimation, or calculators. This decision is made when a particular calculation is needed. Students skilled in using a variety of computational techniques have at their command the power and efficiency of mathematics. We should provide children many opportunities to make decisions regarding which computational technique to employ. This chapter is written to suggest ways to help students think about addition and subtraction of whole numbers and integers and to create in students the habit of making thoughtful decisions.

> [U]nderstanding number and operations, developing number sense, and gaining fluency in arithmetic computation form the core of mathematics education for the elementary grades. (NCTM, 2000, p. 32)

Children begin learning addition and subtraction long before they are introduced to the **basic addition combinations,** the whole-number sums from $0 + 0$ to $9 + 9$.

First, children develop understanding of everyday relationships. They gain some meaning of whole numbers before they attend school. Through their explorations, youngsters invent informal systems of mathematics. Children use counting procedures to find how many things are in a collection of objects and counting strategies to solve simple word problems.

Our job as teachers is to determine how children think about numbers. One thing we may do is to pose simple word problems and observe how the children solve them. For example, "Sarah has four tiles; David gives her two more. Now, how many does she have?"

The responses can serve as a basis for beginning number work. Perhaps the child **counts all**—that is, counts 1, 2, 3, 4, using fingers to keep track; and then 5, 6, continuing to count fingers; and gives the answer 6 by reporting how many fingers were counted. Perhaps the child **counts on**—that is, says 4, and then 5, 6, counting two more fingers. Perhaps the child uses tiles or beans to count out the answer. Perhaps all counting is done in the child's head with lip movement as the only sign of counting. Perhaps the child visualizes a set of four objects joined with a set of two objects and responds without counting. For children having difficulty, we can provide practice in counting and grouping. We are challenged to build on what children bring to the classroom and provide activities that help children further grow and develop their mathematical thinking and their understanding of the concepts of addition and subtraction.

This work with oral word problems is very important and should precede any written work with number sentences. Students should have extensive work in posing and answering each other's story situations orally and with materials before they ever see an abstract addition or subtraction number sentence. They should use many physical models: tiles, base ten blocks, Cuisenaire rods, beans, and cubes are among the most useful. Other counting objects, like milk jug caps, nuts and bolts, buttons, and washers, are ideal for illustrating operations. Calculators and computers help in learning basic arithmetic operations as well. Children beginning to make sense of the basic operations are active learners.

> Representing numbers with various physical materials should be a major part of mathematics instruction in the elementary school grades. (NCTM, 2000, p. 33)

MAKING SENSE OF ADDITION AND SUBTRACTION CONCEPTS

In the early grades children should be introduced to the concepts of addition and subtraction using stories, activities, games, and physical objects. As mentioned above, children will typically respond to addition and subtraction questions using their own devices, including counting. That children know to count comes from their early experiences at home and in everyday life. That children develop an understanding of addition and subtraction comes from their ability to observe events and establish relationships. Kamii has termed the process of "making mental relationships between and among objects" **constructive abstraction** (2000, p. 9). Through constructive abstraction, children develop an initial understanding of addition and subtraction. Addition of whole numbers is the mental action of joining or combining two amounts, resulting in a larger single amount. Subtraction of whole numbers is the mental action of removing an amount from a larger amount, resulting in a smaller single amount. Subtraction is more difficult for younger children to grasp because the part-whole relationship is more complex and class inclusion has not been established. Early work with subtraction will find students using addition and counting to arrive at a solution. Eventually, we move away from the physical experiences with sets of objects toward the pictorial and abstract. Children learn that addition renames a pair of numbers with a single equivalent number. For example, the pair (4, 2) is associated with 6 under the operation of addition. Learning how addition works is learning the concept of addition. Learning that 4 + 2 = 6 is learning a basic addition combination.

Each of the following sections—on addition, subtraction, properties of addition and subtraction, and adding and subtracting integers—presents activities for helping students make sense of concepts and alternative algorithms.

Making Sense of Addition Concepts and Alternative Algorithms

Sorting, classifying, and reversibility of thought are necessary for children to understand both addition and subtraction. **Classifying** is the process of grouping or sorting objects into classes or categories according to some systematic scheme or principle. For example, sorting attribute blocks by shape is classifying. Children use specific properties of the objects to be classified and make comparisons between objects in order to decide on their proper categories. **Reversibility of thought** occurs when children are able to reverse their thinking process. An example from the Piaget task to check class inclusion is provided here: Suppose you have a set of 10 colored cubes, 7 green and 3 yellow. A child who is observing the cubes is asked if there are more cubes or more green cubes. This question is asked to determine if the child perceives that the total collection of cubes includes the green cubes and is larger than the subset of green cubes. When asked if there are more cubes or more green cubes, children who have not achieved reversibility of thought respond that there are more green cubes. These children are comparing the subset of green cubes with the subset of yellow cubes. When their perception shifts from the whole set (cubes) to the subset (green cubes), they ignore the whole set, the set of cubes, and cannot reverse their thought back to it from the subsets.

The ability to recognize subsets of objects as included in a larger set occurs at about the age of seven. As a result, we sometimes try to teach the concepts of addition and subtraction to children before children can fully comprehend them. Take care to provide a variety of sorting and grouping experiences when the concept of addition is introduced.

A useful early addition experience is to have children respond to number stories. For example, give Missy three oranges and give Loren two. Start with, "Loren has two oranges and Missy gives him three more. How many oranges does Loren have?" Prompt Missy to give Loren her three oranges. Some children will know the answer without counting oranges, while others will need to count. Invite the children to explain how they found the answer.

Along the same lines but subtly different is this story: "Jacob has three computer games and Margo has four computer games. How many do they have together?" Again, invite students to explain how they determined the answer.

The difference between the two number stories is that the first story suggests an operation and the second merely describes a state of affairs. While both stories are useful, the first one provides a somewhat stronger foundation for understanding joining, or combining, the basis of addition.

With encouragement, children can tell number stories of their own, using real or imaginary situations. Telling or writing these stories provides language experience. The final result may be a bulletin board, a class number stories book, or a *HyperStudio* stack with number stories.

Colored cubes, beans, milk jug caps, color tiles, multibase blocks, Cuisenaire rods, and other counting objects can serve as bases for developing the concept of addition. The operation initially presented is *join* or *combine* (an operation for sets of objects), to prepare children for addition (an operation on number). We use *join* or *combine* because we believe these words are easier for children to understand. Of particular importance is to have children discuss their thinking and the procedures they use to reach solutions. The following activities include various ways to present the addition concept.

A C T I V I T I E S

Pre-Kindergarten – Grade 2
OBJECTIVE: to develop addition number stories.

1. Introduce to the whole class an addition number story that can be acted out. Be prepared by collecting several books from the reading corner and other objects in the room. Begin by saying, "Samantha has four books from the reading corner and Jennelle gives her three more books. Now how many books does Samantha have?" Encourage discussion. Ask several children to explain how they found the number of books that Samantha now has after Jennelle had given her three more. Then have Samantha and Jennelle act out the story.

Next, invite students to make up stories in which a student in the class gives some objects to another student. Have them ask, "How many (objects) does (student name) have altogether?" Have students act out the stories.

2. Once students can easily make up addition stories, have them make up stories that they can dictate or write down. There should be many types of people, pets, or objects in the students' experiences that can be the basis of the stories. Be sure to have the students illustrate their stories. This may be a station set up during stations time. If writing is a challenge, have parent helpers or older students at the school assist in the writing. When the stories are completed, have students share their addition stories with the other students. Collect the stories and make a class book to share with parents or with other classes.

OBJECTIVE: to use addition in the class store.

3. During the time the students play in the class store, have them "buy" several items (not more than 10) and explain how they were able to determine how much they will cost altogether. The amount of each item should be established based on the ability levels of the students. Again, have the students dictate or write stories about what they bought, what they will do with what they bought, and how much it cost to buy the items. If they are able, the students should explain what coins were necessary to pay for the items.

OBJECTIVE: to use Cuisenaire rods to model addition.

4. The jumbo Cuisenaire rods or the connecting Cuisenaire rods are ideal for this activity. Two or more Cuisenaire rods placed end to end form a train. Invite the children to make a train using a light green rod and a yellow rod. Next, have them find another rod that is the same length as the light green and yellow rods combined; they will soon discover the brown rod. Have the children place the brown rod beside the light green-yellow train as in Figure 6–1. Explain that light green plus yellow equals brown.

Encourage the children to find another train that is the same length as the brown rod. Expect a variety of answers. Seven two-rod trains are possible if reversals, such as red plus dark green and dark green plus red, are considered different trains. There are also three-rod

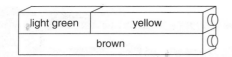

Figure 6–1   Cuisenaire rods illustrating light green + yellow = brown.

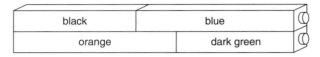

Figure 6–2   Cuisenaire rods illustrating black + blue = orange + dark green.

trains (for example, red plus red plus purple) as well as four-, five-, six-, and seven-rod trains, and there is even an eight-rod train. When the children have discovered the trains, have them say what the trains are.

At this point, numbers are not directly associated with the Cuisenaire rods. Number values will be assigned to the rods later.

Children soon find two-rod trains that are longer than the longest single rod, orange. Here, ask them to make a train using orange plus whatever rod is necessary to equal the length of the original two rods. For example, Figure 6–2 shows a two-rod train, black plus blue, which is equal to orange plus dark green. Other trains may be equal to more than two orange rods; for example, purple plus dark green plus yellow plus black equals orange plus orange plus red.

As children become more proficient at adding rods they produce more complex sums. To shortcut writing the names of all the rods, use the symbols used by the developers of Cuisenaire rods: w (white), r (red), g (light green), p (purple), y (yellow), d (dark green), k (black), n (brown), e (blue), *o* (orange).

The first four activities present ways to introduce the concept of addition. Next, we begin the transition toward more abstract work. The transition to using symbols should be presented slowly and with concrete models representing the symbolic expressions.

A C T I V I T I E S

Pre-Kindergarten – Grade 2

OBJECTIVE: to introduce the symbolism of addition.

1. Draw three loops on a large sheet of paper or place them directly on the floor with yarn or masking tape. Place several objects in the top two loops, as in

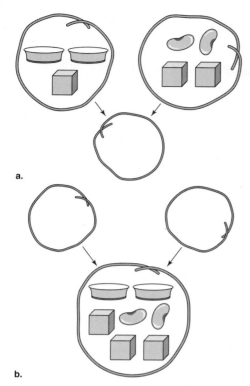

a.

b.

Figure 6−3 Two groups of objects are combined to help develop the symbolism of addition.

Figure 6−3a. Indicate to the children that they are to combine or join the objects and put them in the third loop. Be sure you introduce the word *combine* or the word *join*.

Begin the transition from joining objects to adding numbers by asking the children how many objects are in the first loop. In Figure 6−3a, the first loop has 3 objects. The second loop has 4 objects. The loop with the objects combined (Figure 6−3b) has 7 objects. Explain that this diagram shows 3 plus 4 equals 7.

Encourage the children to develop other examples and invite the children to tell what addition combinations the various diagrams show. The children read the diagrams at this point rather than actually add the numbers.

Soon, you can use the symbols for addition. Introduce the symbols in an addition sentence, such as 3 + 4 = 7. Then introduce them in the vertical form:

$$\begin{array}{r} 3 \\ + 4 \\ \hline 7 \end{array}$$

Help the children read these sentences and become familiar with them.

2. With the Cuisenaire rods, establish a value for the white rod. For example, if the white rod is 1, what is the

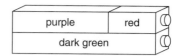

Figure 6−4 Cuisenaire rods used to help develop the symbolism of addition.

value of the red rod, the light green rod, the purple rod, and so on? Challenge the children to find the rod values if the white rod has a value of 1. Children may determine these rod values by finding how many white rods it takes to make the red rod (2), the light green rod (3), and the purple rod (4). Be open to other suggestions for determining the rod values. Give children additional experience with the rods to allow them to be at ease in symbolizing the rod values.

Later, particularly in work with fractions, other rod values will be established. Be careful not to declare 1 the permanent value of white, 2 the permanent value of red, 3 the permanent value of green, and so on. If white equals 1, the train in Figure 6−4 is 4 plus 2 and is equal to 6, or 4 + 2 = 6.

To this point, we have introduced the concept of addition using several embodiments and the symbols that describe addition. As we continue, we introduce an important property of addition, the commutative property, along with a new embodiment for addition.

A C T I V I T I E S

Pre-Kindergarten−Grade 2

OBJECTIVE: to use dominoes as a model for addition.

1. Use sets of double-six dominoes for this activity. These may be the commercial sets or teacher constructed sets. A set of double-six dominoes consists of 28 dominoes showing all combinations from blank-blank to six-six. To begin, explain that a domino such as the one in Figure 6−5a is read as "3 plus 5." If all of the dots are counted, we can complete the number sentence by supplying the sum, 8; thus, 3 + 5 = 8. If the same domino is picked up differently or rotated, it may be read as "5 plus 3 equals 8," and will appear as in Figure 6−5b.

Soon, children will pick up a domino, read it as either "3 + 5 = 8" or "5 + 3 = 8", and will know that no matter which way it is read, the sum is still 8. This important characteristic of addition is the **commutative property of addition.** Knowing that order has no effect on the sum reduces the number of addition combinations to be remembered.

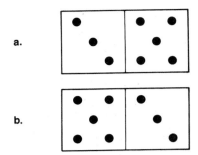

Figure 6−5 Dominoes showing the commutative property of addition.

When the students can read the dominoes, let them spread the dominoes face down, mix them up, and select them one at a time and explain to other group members or the whole class what they "say." Any domino portion that is blank is read as "zero," meaning that it has zero dots. The domino blank-four is read as "0 plus 4" or "4 plus 0," depending on how it is held. As the children become confident reading dominoes, change to a double-nine set.

To vary this activity, change the standard domino dot pattern to a more random pattern. This will require that you construct your own dominoes. Thus, the dot pattern for three may be three dots in a triangular configuration rather than the traditional diagonal line of three dots and four also may be a different pattern as in Figure 6−6. Using different configurations helps children to visualize various dot patterns and to attach number values to those different patterns. Burton et al. (1993) describe a series of clever domino activities that help develop number sense and operations for kindergarten, first-, and second-grade students. You are encouraged to consider using them.

There are many ways in which children make sense of addition. Besides activities that help advance the concept of addition, there are other learning situations that assist children in establishing numerical relationships. For example, in the daily classroom routines such as distributing snacks, taking and recording lunch counts, discussing the calendar, voting during class meetings, telling time, and counting money, students develop an understanding of relationships among numbers that serves as a foundation for addition. Children's explanations and discussions help teachers see

how they are constructing their mathematical knowledge. As a student explains a process or a procedure, the personal logic of the student emerges. Often these are alternative processes or algorithms; that is, they are processes unique to the individual giving the explanation. This type of thinking should be embraced.

Further, as problems, projects, and games are introduced, students build their understanding of addition (and subtraction, multiplication, and division as well). The number stories mentioned earlier serve as a beginning of problem solving. They may present a problem or question that invites several approaches and may have several solutions.

Kamii provides valuable guidelines for choosing and/or inventing word problems:

1. Give problems that are closely related to children's lives.
2. Give problems involving a variety of operations.
3. Give problems involving a variety of contents and situations.
4. At times, give problems involving large numbers.
5. At times, give problems for which there is more than one correct answer.
6. At times, give problems that require especially careful logico-mathematization. (2000, pp. 133−140)

The term *logico-mathematization* refers to the process of developing mathematical relationships in one's mind. The process is unique to each individual. With reference to word problems, the term suggests that some problems should require analytical thinking. Here is an example from Kamii: "Grandpa said he grew up in a house where there were 12 feet and one tail. Who could have lived with Grandpa?" (2000, p. 122). Children will devise a variety of solutions to this problem, including the possibility of family members, birds, dogs, cats, and fish living with grandpa. The solution requires thoughtful decisions.

Students engage in rich discussions as they explain how they approached a problem. In addition, children are talented authors of number stories and problems. A good example of number stories that first-grade children have invented may be found on Weblink 6−1.

Projects or multiday lessons engage students in activities built around a single theme or physical object. For example, two pre-kindergarten−grade 2 units in the NCTM Illuminations series focus on addition and subtraction. They are Do It with Dominoes and Begin with Buttons (Weblinks 6−2 and 6−3). A text-based resource for project learning is *Math Excursions K* (Burk et al., 1993). *Math Excursions* levels one and two have also been produced. These units of study provide direction for students and teachers as they look in depth at

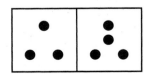

Figure 6−6 Domino dot configurations altered to help children visualize various dot patterns.

a topic like addition or subtraction or work on a theme that requires addition or subtraction.

Number games interest children because they are fun to play. Depending on the game, various number ideas and operations are involved. Kamii describes an easy addition game, One More, for kindergartners. It involves a game board with 35 spaces, each containing a numeral 2 through 7. Students roll a die and have several transparent chips of the same color. Kamii explains the way the game is played: "The players take turns rolling the die and placing a chip on the number rolled plus one, anywhere on the board. For example, if a person rolls a 4, she puts a chip on a 5. The person who uses up all her chips first is the winner" (2000, pp. 170–171). One More helps children develop the relationship "one more than" and helps them remember the plus-one addition relationships. You will find number games in the activities throughout this and other chapters of this book. Be sure to invite children to invent games of their own or reinvent rules for games that they already play. A good source for number games invented by teachers is Wakefield (1998).

The concept of addition has been presented with a model that uses joining or combining sets of objects. While the children were still at the concrete level, number was attached to the operation to assist the children in seeing the relationship between joining objects and adding numbers. We continue by introducing the concept of subtraction in a similar manner.

Making Sense of Subtraction Concepts and Alternative Algorithms

Teaching the concept of subtraction is much like teaching the concept of addition. The materials, models, and approach are the same. The concept, however, is different and much more difficult than addition. Eventually we want children to be able to see that subtraction is the inverse of addition. To achieve this, we need to ensure that students have a firm understanding of addition. Subtraction can be fully understood only when children can classify and sort objects by their attributes and achieve reversibility of thought. Children must be able to see the relationship between a collection of objects and a subset of that collection in order to understand subtraction. When a subset is removed from a collection, the idea of subtraction is understood if children realize that returning the subset to the collection restores the collection to its original state. Thus, the student is doing more than merely following the teacher's direction to remove a subset and count the elements in the resulting collection. For the children who cannot yet classify and have not achieved reversibility of thought, you will need to provide additional material, time, and encouragement.

Number stories that introduce children to addition should also be used to introduce children to subtraction. For example, "Cindy has 6 model horses. Trisha takes 2 of the horses to play with. Now, how many horses does Cindy have?" This story, an example of *take away or remove,* may be acted out to find the solution.

We begin another story: "Chris has 5 books. Ken has 2 books. How many more books does Chris have than Ken?" Here, the books can be compared and the difference can be determined.

Still another approach is this: "Jack has 3 cookies and Nicole has 7. How many more cookies does Jack need to have as many as Nicole?" This is an example of a *missing addend* approach to subtraction. These latter two approaches, comparing and missing addend, can be difficult for children to learn. Considerable use of word problems provides worthwhile thinking practice for these subtraction ideas.

Include stories with too much or too little information. For example, "Robert has 4 pencils. Corrie has some pencils. How many more pencils does Corrie have than Robert?" Encourage children to develop their own number stories, and see if other children can solve them. You may place copies of number stories children have written in a learning center for other students to work on. The following activities offer additional ways to present the concept of subtraction to students.

A C T I V I T I E S

Pre-Kindergarten – Grade 2
OBJECTIVE: to introduce the concept of subtraction using sets of objects.

1. Draw a loop on a large sheet of paper or use a loop of yarn. Place nine objects in the loop (Figure 6–7a). Then, with yarn or string of a different color, form another loop inside of the first loop, surrounding some of the objects (Figure 6–7b). Ask the children to remove all objects that are inside the smaller loop (Figure 6–7c). Practice this activity a number of times and discuss the results with the children to see if they understand that they have removed some of the objects they had when they started, and that if they returned the objects, the collection of objects would be the same as the original collection.

Next, let the children indicate how many objects there are at each step of the activity. For example, "How many cubes did we start with?" There were 9 cubes. "How many did we take away?" We took away 4 cubes. "How many do we have left?" We have 5 cubes left. "How can we say what we just did in a number sentence?" Nine take away 4 equals 5.

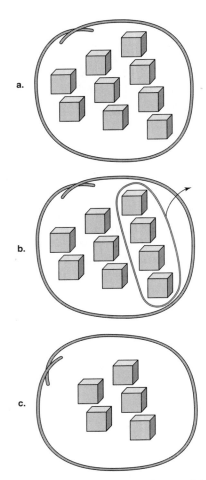

Figure 6–7 Yarn loops and cubes used to model subtraction.

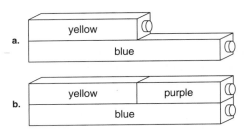

Figure 6–8 Cuisenaire rods illustrating blue − yellow = purple.

Children can invent and work out many other examples of the subtraction operation as part of learning about subtraction. This "take away" model is the most direct way to show the meaning of subtraction. It should be used considerably in the beginning stages of learning subtraction. Combine this procedure with number stories describing what is happening.

OBJECTIVE: to use Cuisenaire rods as a model for subtraction.

2. After considerable play with the Cuisenaire rods, have the children place a blue rod in front of them. Then have them put a yellow rod beside the blue rod, with one end even with an end of the blue rod, as in Figure 6–8a.

Ask the children to find a rod that will form a train with the yellow rod and will make that train as long as the blue rod. You may say, "See if you can find a rod that will go here." as you point to the space at the end of the yellow rod. Children will find that the purple rod will fill the space (Figure 6–8b). Explain that blue minus yellow equals purple.

Ask, "What is blue minus green?" Have the children place the rods as described above and find the rod to fill the space. Then invite the children to "read" the subtraction sentence that is illustrated.

The Cuisenaire rods model used here emphasizes the **missing addend concept.** In the abstract version of the missing addends problem 5 + ? = 9, children ask themselves, "What added to 5 makes 9?" With the rods, we are asking, "What added to yellow makes blue?" when solving the problem blue minus yellow equals what? Be sure students have the opportunity to discuss the ideas presented and that they make sense to them.

OBJECTIVE: to use dominoes to illustrate the concept of subtraction.

3. When dominoes are used as a model for subtraction, children are encouraged to find the difference between the number of dots on one side of the domino and the number of dots on the other side. Help children make a comparison: "Suppose we want as many dots on this side of the domino (side with two dots) as on the other side (side with six dots). How many more do we need?" In the case of the two-six or six-two domino, shown in Figure 6–9a, we need four more dots on the two-side.

Let the children explain how they found the difference. For example, some children make the comparison by matching the dots on one side of the domino with those on the other side. The dots left over represent the difference. Other students may count the number of dots needed. Still other children may be more comfortable mentally removing the dots found on the lesser side (2) from the dots found on the greater side (6). Of course, when each side has the same number of dots, as in Figure 6–9b, the difference is zero. How do the children explain this difference?

Children can describe this operation after they devise a way to find the difference. The number sentence that describes the domino in Figure 6–9a is "6 minus 2 equals 4." Students should be able to pick up any domino and quickly give the number sentence that is shown.

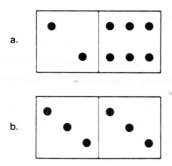

Figure 6−9 Dominoes used to illustrate subtraction.

OBJECTIVE: to symbolize subtraction.

4. Once the language describing subtraction has been introduced and used, the operation can be symbolized. The loops in Figure 6−10 may be used to illustrate the transition from the concrete to the abstract. Children are asked, "How many cubes are in the first loop?" They respond by counting them. There are 7 cubes. "How many cubes are we removing or taking away?" We are removing 2 cubes. "How many cubes are there left?" There are 5 cubes. "We say this using numbers by writing 7 − 2 = 5."

The transition to the abstract symbols should take place as soon as using the loops and using the language that describes the operation they are performing makes sense to the children. Practicing subtraction and discussing and recording the results in learning groups will strengthen the children's abilities in subtraction.

5. Activity 2 in this section used the Cuisenaire rods. The language the students are using is "blue minus yellow equals purple"; thus, the change to numbers is quick. If the white rod equals 1, blue has the value of 9, yellow has the value of 5, and purple has the value

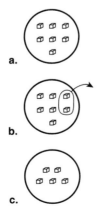

Figure 6−10 Loops and cubes used to develop the symbolism of subtraction.

of 4. Thus, the number sentence 9 − 5 = 4 results directly from the sentence using colors.

Again, be cautious by reminding the children, "In this case, the white rod is 1." Later, the value of the white rod may change. Considerable experience is necessary for children to become skilled with the abstract numerical description of the rods.

The following example illustrates how once students make sense of an operation like subtraction they can communicate their understanding of the process. Diane, a second-grade teacher, told her students that an imaginary student named George was going to be joining their class and asked the students to write a letter to George explaining how they used the traditional subtraction algorithm when regrouping was involved. Ben's letter to George is shown in Figure 6−11.

The discussion presented in the earlier section on children inventing alternative addition algorithms is appropriate for subtraction. Besides the activities presented for helping make sense of subtraction concepts, there are other important activities that involve children in subtraction situations. Daily classroom routines that introduce subtraction stories and problems are particularly helpful. Children's explanations and discussions let us see how they are developing their understanding of subtraction. Often we find that students are providing alternative processes or algorithms; that is, they are finding processes that are unique to

Figure 6−11 Ben's letter to George.

their individual thinking processes. We should be sure to provide opportunities for inventing these alternative algorithms.

Again, projects or multiday lessons that include subtraction can provide valuable practice for thinking about and discussing addition and subtraction. Games that incorporate addition and subtraction are useful because children often employ counting and addition to find solutions involving subtraction.

Properties of Addition and Subtraction

While presenting the concept of an operation and the concepts of addition and subtraction, take the opportunity to include examples of important properties of these operations. We have already mentioned the commutative property of addition. During the modeling of addition and subtraction, include situations in which no objects are joined to an existing set of objects and in which no objects are removed from a set. These are models of the **identity element** for addition and subtraction; that is, any number plus zero or minus zero results in the number you started with. With this background, $6 + 0 = 6$, $0 + 6 = 6$, and $6 - 0 = 6$ will be easy to remember. Allow children to discover that $0 - 6$ (left-hand identity) does not hold for subtraction.

We have already demonstrated the commutative property of addition using dominoes; however, this property can be clearly shown with any of the preceding models. For example, with Cuisenaire rods, the train dark green plus purple can be reconstructed as the train purple plus dark green. Then both can be shown to be equal to orange, as in Figure 6–12. Thus, we have the numerical examples $6 + 4 = 10$ and $4 + 6 = 10$ when the white rod is equal to 1.

Give children the opportunity to discover that in operations with whole numbers, the commutative property does not hold for subtraction. That is, $6 - 4 = 2$, but $4 - 6$ does not have a solution.

Another useful pattern is **adding or subtracting one**. Again, examples from any of the models already presented can illustrate this pattern. After a number of examples, children discover that adding one to a number results in the next number in the counting sequence. For example, $6 + 1 = 7$ and $12 + 1 = 13$. Likewise, children discover that subtracting one from a

number results in the previous number in the counting sequence, $9 - 1 = 8$ and $2 - 1 = 1$.

Just as adding zero, using the commutative property of addition, and adding one can help in learning the basic addition combinations, the **associative property of addition** can help children as they determine sums such as $9 + 6$. If children are in the habit of making mental groupings of 10, they will likely find that the answer is easier to determine. For example, $9 + 6 = 9 + (1 + 5) = (9 + 1) + 5 = 10 + 5 = 15$. The associative property is shown in $9 + (1 + 5) = (9 + 1) + 5$; how the numbers are grouped to add does not affect the sum.

A good way to show the associative property of addition is to have children place beans or chips on number strips like those in Figure 6–13. For a larger sum, more than two strips may be necessary.

Have the children put beans for the addends on the first and second number strips. Then have them fill up the first strip to complete the ten, using the last beans on the second strip. Here, we see $9 + 6 = 10 + 5 = 15$. This procedure will reinforce the groupings of ten that the students made as they were attaching meaning to number.

This is a good procedure to use with problems with three or more addends and with larger problems that require regrouping. Use the associative property to make the learning of certain number combinations easier. Avoid presenting it as simply an abstract property of addition.

The time students spend discussing properties of addition and subtraction is very important to making sense of the properties. After the students understand the concepts of addition and subtraction and are comfortable posing story problems and solving each other's story problems using physical models, they should begin to analyze the operations and discover properties that make it easier to remember the basic combinations. The commutative property, the identity element, and the associative property are just a few of the patterns children should discover and discuss. They may notice many patterns of addition and subtraction combinations other than the pattern of adding and subtracting 1. They may notice that if they know the doubles, they can find

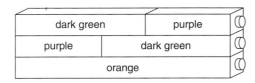

Figure 6–12 Cuisenaire rods showing the commutative property of addition.

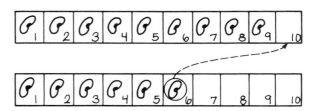

Figure 6–13 Bean strips used to develop the associative property of addition.

the answer to the fact 6 + 7 by taking the double 6 + 6 and adding 1 or by taking the double 7 + 7 and subtracting 1. Encourage the children to keep a written record of the properties and patterns they have discovered. These may all be combined in a class book, bulletin board, or math journal for the students to refer to.

Adding and Subtracting Integers

Integers—the positive and negative whole numbers and zero—play an important role in mathematics learning as students study algebra and coordinate geometry. Making sense of integers begins in informal settings in the early elementary grades. Informal models for integers include thermometers, number lines, colored chips, money, and calculators. In Chapter 5, we suggested introducing integers using the number line and buildings on a "street." Red and blue numerals were used to represent the negative and positive whole numbers.

Once integers make sense, students may begin adding and subtracting integers. There are several types of activities that provide initial understanding of integers and of adding and subtracting integers. Discovering and discussing the rules for adding and subtracting integers provides an understanding that cannot be matched by memorizing the rules. Thoughtful students will look for patterns to help make sense of the rules. The activities that follow should encourage looking for patterns.

A C T I V I T I E S

Grades 3 – 5

OBJECTIVE: to help children determine the greater value of two integers.

1. The game Top It (Integers) uses a deck of cards representing two each of various integers, ranging from $^-10$ to $+10$. The game is for two to four players. One player deals all of the cards. Each player neatly stacks the cards that are dealt. Each player turns over a card and places it face up. The player with the highest integer claims all of the cards played. If any players are tied with high cards, the cards remain in front of the players and those who are tied each draw another card. The player with the highest integer takes all of the cards. The winner of the game is the player with the most cards after all of the cards have been turned over.

Intially, it may prove helpful to have a number line available as the game is played. Later, the number line will be unnecessary. The game may also be played with the lowest integer winning the hand.

A variation of this game may be played by having each player draw two cards, finding the sum (or difference), and comparing the result with the other player(s). The highest sum wins the hand.

OBJECTIVE: to use a calculator to predict patterns involving integers.

2. Give students calculators and let them explore using the constant feature. Let them begin with addition. Start by pressing 3 + 4 = = = =. Challenge the children to explain what is happening. Do they notice that the calculator adds 4 each time they press "equals"? Encourage them to predict the next number before they press "equals." After they are comfortable with addition, try 12 − 3 = = = = =. Again, ask the children to explain what is occurring. Can they continue to predict the next number when the results are negative? Let the children work with a partner to explore other patterns. Third- to fifth-grade students should be asked to write down and to discuss any generalizations they can make about adding or subtracting integers.

Grades 6 – 8

OBJECTIVE: to add and subtract integers on a number line.

1. Make a large vertical number line (see Figure 6 – 14) that resembles a thermometer for the following number-line problems. As with all new concepts, negative numbers should be introduced using concepts with which the children are already familiar. Temperature makes a good model for beginning work with integers because many students have experienced negative numbers on the thermometer. To find the difference in two temperatures such as the difference between 4 degrees and $^-2$ degrees, have the students find 4 degrees and count down the thermometer to $^-2$ degrees. This difference of 6 degrees corresponds to the equation $4 - (^-2) = 6$. The thermometer is also useful when you ask the students to begin at 5 degrees and determine the temperature after a drop of 7 degrees, as in Figure 6 – 14 ($5 + (^-7) = ^-2$). Begin at $^-4$ degrees and determine the temperature after an increase of 8 degrees ($^-4 + 8 = 4$). Ask the students to make up other number stories for each other and to demonstrate solutions on the number line. After the students have worked several problems, ask them to discuss with one another any patterns that they have found. Keep a written record of the rules the children discover in a prominent place in the classroom. One of the first rules the children may discover is the **additive inverse.** That is, the sum of any number and its opposite is zero; these opposites are called additive inverses. For example, 1 and $^-1$ are additive inverses because $1 + (^-1) = 0$ and $(^-1) + 1 = 0$. Patterns for operating with integers will be needed as students work with signed

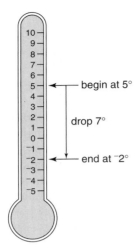

Figure 6–14 A vertical number line for adding and subtracting integers.

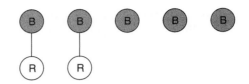

Figure 6–15 Bingo markers showing 5 + (⁻2) = 3.

numbers, not only for integers, but also for rational numbers, algebraic expressions, and coordinate geometry.

As with all concepts, it is useful to experience integers in a number of different contexts. Another real-life situation involving integers is Danny's experience borrowing money.

OBJECTIVE: to add and subtract integers using discrete objects.

2. Each student will need a handful of Bingo chips of two different colors for the following activities. This example uses blue and red chips. Set up a bank using blue chips for positive amounts ($) and red chips for negative amounts (IOUs). If you earn $2, you take 2 blue chips. This adds a positive amount to your account. If you owe $3, you take 3 red chips. This adds a negative amount to your account. If you buy a toy for $5, you take away 5 blue chips, thus subtracting a positive amount from your account. If you pay off a debt, you subtract IOUs or red chips, a negative amount, from your account. For example, Danny normally gets an allowance of $1 each week (adding a positive amount). The week he paid off his debt, instead of receiving $1 and adding it to his negative $1 for a net total of zero, his debt of $1 was taken away, again leaving him with a net total of zero. Therefore, subtracting a negative amount had the same outcome as adding a positive amount. Here are some problems to try with the chips.

a. Julie has $5. She owes Sam $2. What is her net worth? The number sentence is 5 + (⁻2) = _____. She has $5 and adds a $2 IOU. Take 5 blue chips for the positive $5 and 2 red chips for the IOU. Each red chip can be added to a blue chip, its additive inverse, to make $0. When the

zeros are taken away, what is left? Three blue chips or a positive $3 (see Figure 6–15).

b. Jorge owes his dad $6. His father tells Jorge that he will take away $5 of the debt if Jorge rakes the yard. How much will Jorge have or owe after he rakes the yard? The number sentence is ⁻6 − (⁻5) = _____. He has a $6 debt and his father will take away a $5 debt. Take 6 red chips for the ⁻6. When his father takes away the $5 debt, he will take 5 of the red chips. One red chip is left, signifying a debt to his father of $1 (see Figure 6–16).

c. What if Jorge decides the following week to again rake the yard when he is only $1 in debt? If his father again agrees to take away a $5 debt, how much will he have or owe? The number sentence is ⁻1 − (⁻5) = _____. He has a $1 debt and his father will take away a $5 debt. You start with 1 red chip to signify the $1 debt. Immediately you recognize that you have a problem; you do not have 5 red chips for Jorge's father to take away. You remember that a positive chip and a negative chip add to zero. You decide to add several zeros to the ⁻1. You can add as many zeros as you want without changing the value of the chips, ⁻1. Since you only need 5 red chips for Jorge's father to take away, you decide to add 4 zeros—4 blue chips and 4 red chips. You now have a total of 5 red chips and 4 blue chips. Verify that the chips still have a value of ⁻1. Now you can take away 5 red chips. What is left? The 4 blue chips, signifying a positive $4. Jorge now has $4 (see Figure 6–17).

d. Marta has $4. She wants to buy a used video game for $9. How much will she owe if she buys the game? The number sentence is 4 − 9 = _____. Start with 4 blue chips to signify the $4 she has to begin with. You immediately recognize that to spend $9, you need to take away 9 blue chips and you do not have enough blue chips. Again, you add zeros to your starting amount of 4 blue chips. This time you add 5 zeros—5 red chips and 5 blue chips—to your starting amount of 4 blue chips.

Figure 6–16 Bingo markers illustrating ⁻6 − (⁻5) = ⁻1.

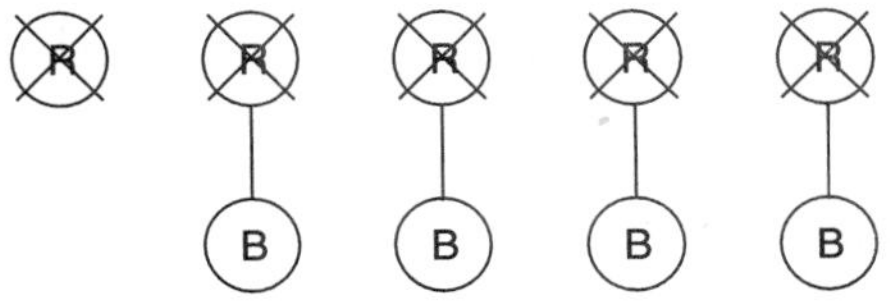

Figure 6–17 Bingo markers representing $^{-}1 - (^{-}5) = 4$.

At this point, you have 9 blue chips and 5 red chips. You take away the 9 blue chips to pay for the video game, and you are left with 5 red chips, or a debt of $5.

Ask the students to make up similar word problems of their own. Be sure they discuss their solutions. After they have worked several problems, they will probably not need to use the chips any more. Encourage the students to just write the equation for the problem and then explain to each other (and you) how they would go about solving it. Remember that it is the method, not the answer, that you are interested in here. After the students have worked several problems, ask them if they notice any patterns. Can they generate any rules? What happens if you subtract a negative number? Is the result always the same as that of adding a positive number? Students will find that this is true. They should also notice that subtracting a positive number has the same result as adding a negative number.

OBJECTIVE: to use everyday situations to create integer word problems.

3. Encourage the students to make up number stories of their own using integers. Be on the alert for other types of real-life situations involving positive and negative amounts. You might want to follow the ups and downs of the stock market for experience with positive and negative numbers. Decimals will be prevalent in stock market values. Looking at gains and losses of yardage on the football field makes for some interesting problems. What happens if a penalty of 5 yards is taken away (subtracting a negative number)? Does this have the same effect as a gain of 5 yards? Have the students' number stories available for other students to work on or put them on worksheets and use them instead of examples in the textbook.

Negative integers are appropriately introduced to children in grades 3–5 when they are presented informally. Temperature and money and the number line provide models that can be used to explore and make sense of integers. In grades 6–8, learning operations with integers and recognizing the applications of integers in algebra and geometry become important. The properties of addition and subtraction that were mentioned in the previous section should be explored with integers as soon as students are comfortable with both the properties and integer addition and subtraction.

DEVELOPING FLUENCY WITH ADDITION AND SUBTRACTION

Computational fluency is a phrase that refers to knowing the basic number combinations and using effective methods for computing. Children should learn the basic addition and subtraction number combinations and the skills associated with adding and subtracting. The **basic addition combinations,** of which there are 100, are those ranging from $0 + 0$ to $9 + 9$. They are shown in Table 6–1. The **basic subtraction combinations,** again numbering 100, are those ranging from $18 - 9$ to $0 - 0$.

Algorithms are methods used to calculate; mathematics consists of numerous algorithms for addition and subtraction. As children learn the basic combinations and algorithms for addition and subtraction, they can make use of paper-and-pencil procedures, mental strategies, calculators, and computers. The NCTM reminds us: "Regardless of the particular method used, students should be able to explain their method, understand that many methods exist, and see the usefulness of methods that are efficient, accurate, and general. Students also need to be able to estimate and judge the reasonableness of results" (2000, p. 32). Underlying computational fluency is children's understanding of operations and algorithms.

> By the end of grade 2, students should know the basic addition and subtraction combinations, should be fluent in adding two-digit numbers, and should have methods for subtracting two-digit numbers. (NCTM, 2000, p. 35)

TABLE 6–1 The Basic Addition Combinations

		Addend									
	+	0	1	2	3	4	5	6	7	8	9
Addend	0	0	1	2	3	4	5	6	7	8	9
	1	1	2	3	4	5	6	7	8	9	10
	2	2	3	4	5	6	7	8	9	10	11
	3	3	4	5	6	7	8	9	10	11	12
	4	4	5	6	7	8	9	10	11	12	13
	5	5	6	7	8	9	10	11	12	13	14
	6	6	7	8	9	10	11	12	13	14	15
	7	7	8	9	10	11	12	13	14	15	16
	8	8	9	10	11	12	13	14	15	16	17
	9	9	10	11	12	13	14	15	16	17	18

Basic Addition and Subtraction Combinations

For quick recall, children should be expected to visualize and/or remember the basic addition and subtraction combinations. Begin this memorization when children understand the concepts of addition and subtraction. Your efforts to develop the concepts will pay off as the combinations are learned. Because the children have a physical model to which they can refer, they will be able to determine a basic combination temporarily forgotten. They can successfully use a variety of counters, including fingers. They can use Cuisenaire rods, Unifix cubes, number lines, or calculators.

The addition and subtraction combinations may be presented almost simultaneously. The join or combine model used with objects is easier to grasp than the take-away or remove model. We recommend you start first with join, later introducing take away. As the children understand the concepts, they will be able to work with both addition and subtraction at the same time.

Many math textbooks show relationships between addition and subtraction combinations. A family includes several combinations each of which relates the same three numbers through addition or subtraction. One such family follows:

$$8 + 5 = 13$$
$$5 + 8 = 13$$
$$13 - 8 = 5$$
$$13 - 5 = 8$$

Word or story problems commonly appear in mathematics textbooks. Those that ask students to compute an immediate answer provide students with an avenue for practicing addition and subtraction skills. For example, in the following word problem, students are asked to find the sum of three numbers: "Crystal has 3 boxes of breakfast cereal at home. Her friend Jennifer has 2 boxes of cereal at home and her friend Megan has 2 boxes of cereal at home. How many boxes of cereal do they have altogether?" Students solve these word problems in a variety of ways. Among methods they may use are mentally counting, counting out loud, counting on their fingers, finding objects to lay out to represent the cereal boxes, drawing pictures, and acting out the word problem. The action students use to find answers is predicated on their understanding the problem, that is, what does the problem ask? what information is given? how am I going to solve this word problem? what operation(s) is called for? does the answer make sense? Some students need to be guided through these questions so they may establish a systematic approach to word problems. They find that terms such as *altogether* and *in all* generally refer to addition. Terms such as *are left* and *how many more* suggest using subtraction. Students should be able to differentiate between the meaning of these words and phrases. Because there are exceptions to each word clue students should be aware of how important thoughtful reading is as they solve word problems.

The classroom should contain tools with which to perform simple calculations. The most basic tools for calculating are the many counters already mentioned. When children are first learning the basic addition combinations, encourage them to use beans, cubes, milk jug caps, nuts and washers, or chips to find the answer. Let them put some objects down, join others with them, and count the result or recognize the answer by sight. Let them use fingers as counters as well. As the work becomes more abstract and the children use mental strategies, paper and pencil, or calculators, let them make marks on paper to help reinforce the basic addition combinations. The NCTM noted, "Young children often initially compute by using objects and counting; however, prekindergarten through grade 2 teachers need to encourage them to shift, over time, to solving many computation problems mentally or with paper and pencil to record their thinking" (NCTM, 2000, p. 84).

The number line is useful for learning addition combinations. For younger children, a walk-on number line provides large motor experiences. Its use in building the concept of number provides familiarity. For older children, a number line on the wall or chalkboard or attached to a desktop is useful. The procedure for use is the same. When children wish to add $8 + 4$, they begin at 0 on the number line and take eight steps or move directly to 8 (Figure 6–18a). Next, they take four steps in the same direction along the number line. Where they stop, 12, is the sum of $8 + 4$.

Another effective way to use the number line is to have it calibrated in centimeters. Cuisenaire rods may then be placed along the number line to help illustrate that the number line represents a continuous length and not just points where the numbers appear. For example, if the white rod has the value of 1, $8 + 4$ may be shown by placing a brown rod followed by a purple rod along the number line beginning at 0 as in Figure 6–18b. The result, 12, is clearly seen.

When students wish to subtract $9 - 5$, they again begin at 0 on the walk-on number line and take nine steps or move directly to 9 (Figure 6–18c). Next, they take away by reversing their direction and moving five spaces back, to 4.

With the Cuisenaire rods, a blue rod (representing 9) is placed along the number line, beginning at 0. Then a yellow rod (representing 5) is placed along the blue rod beginning at the point marked 9. The difference, 4, can be seen by reading the number line, as in Figure 6–18d.

Children need careful instruction in working on a number line because they commonly forget to count spaces and instead count marks on the line. The walk-on and Cuisenaire rod number lines provide direct experience in counting spaces.

The calculator is another tool for learning addition combinations. It should be used periodically to quickly produce facts that are forgotten or unlearned. Simple four-function (addition, subtraction, multiplication, division), light-activated calculators should be available for pre-kindergarten through grade 2 classroom use. Calculators speed up computations during games and activities intended to help children memorize basic addition combinations. Set up races with basic combinations in which some students have calculators and others do not. Students will quickly learn that it is faster to remember 8 + 7 than it is to push the buttons on the calculator.

Computer games and activities are available to help children to learn and reinforce basic addition and subtraction combinations. Often a particular software presents more that just computation practice. It may also include work with problem solving, fractions, geometry, measurement, and so on. The activities tend to be fast paced, challenging, colorful, and enjoyable. Examples of such computer activities are *Mighty Math Number Heroes* (Edmark), *How the West Was One + Three × Four* (Sunburst), and *Treasure MathStorm!* (The Learning Company).

The activities that follow are specifically designed for addition but may be used as effectively for subtraction by making simple changes in the materials.

A C T I V I T I E S

Pre-Kindergarten – Grade 2

OBJECTIVE: to help children remember the basic addition combinations.

1. Provide children with frequent practice in mental arithmetic. Because the main focus of learning the basic combinations is mental, this type of activity is particularly useful. Limit practice periods to five or ten minutes. Orally present addition combinations to children while the children write on a piece of paper or a small individual whiteboard only the answer to the problem. The difficulty of the problems should be determined by the age and experience of the children. Initially, speedy responses are not necessary. Children need an opportunity to practice using their mental faculties.

Ask the children to number from 1 to 5 on their papers. Explain that you are going to give them a problem and they should think of what the answer is and then write the answer down; they should not use their pencils to find the answer. Here are examples of mental exercises: What is 4 plus 7? What is 3 plus 3 plus 2? Answer yes or no; 3 plus 8 is more than 10. Four plus 5 equals 9; what else equals 9? As the children become more proficient, increase the number of questions from 5 to 10, 15, or 20. Expand the questions from just basic combinations to other, related mathematical topics, such as place value.

2. Pic-addition, short for picture addition, appeals to children. Pic-addition requires construction of activity

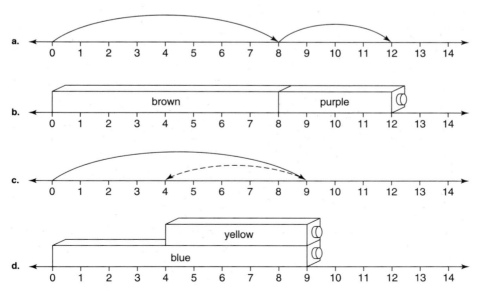

Figure 6–18 Cuisenaire rods placed along a number line showing that the number line represents a continuous length.

materials. The first step is to select a picture of an animal, cartoon character, or athlete that is popular with the children.

Next, glue the picture to a piece of oaktag or posterboard. Spread the glue thinly over the entire back of the picture. There should be no border (see Figure 6–19a).

In the next step, draw square or rectangular regions with pencil on the back of the oaktag or posterboard holding the picture. Within these regions, draw circular and square frames. With marking pen, write an addition

problem in each circular or square frame on the back of the picture. Make sure problems with the same answer, such as 1 + 2 and 2 + 1, are placed in different-shaped frames (Figure 6–19b).

Finally, draw regions on the inside of a box lid or on a piece of oaktag to make an answer board. The lines should form regions the same size and shape as those on the back of the picture. Within these regions, draw circular and square frames to match those on the back of the picture. In each circular or square frame, write the answer to the addition problem in the position opposite that of the problem (Figure 6–19c). (When the problem is correctly answered, the problem card is flipped over and the regions are moved to different positions.) Cut the picture apart using the lines on the back to form individual cards.

Have students select one of the individual cards. Instruct them to look at the problem and solve it, then place the card in the answer frame in the region corresponding to the answer, turning the card picture side up. As they complete the solutions, the picture emerges in its entirety.

3. Concentration games are another source of basic fact practice. A popular version is called "Peopletration" because children are important participants in the game. Provide 12 large cards (22 centimeters by 30 centimeters) constructed from oaktag or posterboard. Each card should have five problems or answers to problems written on one side and a large alphabet letter, *A* through *L,* on the other side. To assure corresponding sets, the first set of problems and answers on each card should be written with black ink, the second set with red, then blue, green, and purple. Figure 6–20 illustrates two such cards, front and back.

Select 12 children to hold the cards. Give each child one of the cards identified with the large alphabet letters. Have the 12 children stand side by side across the front of the room, holding the cards so the letters face the rest of the class.

Designate which game color to use—green, for example. Instruct one of the other children to select two letters, hoping for a match. For example, a student might say "*C*" and "*H.*" Whoever is holding card *C* reads whatever is written in green on the back of the card, in this case, "5 + 2." Whoever is holding card *H* reads whatever is written in green on the back of that card, in

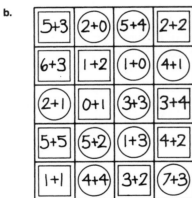

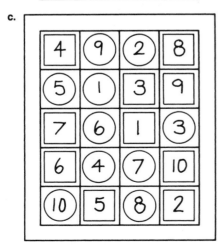

Figure 6–19 Sample of a Pic-addition game.

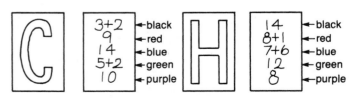

Figure 6–20 Sample of the concentration game Peopletration.

this case, "12." Because 5 + 2 does not equal 12, there is no match. Play continues until there is a match. When a match occurs, the two cards are laid down or the children holding them sit down and the game continues. The game is over when all of the cards have been matched.

The conventional concentration game consists of two arrays of cards (10 centimeters by 12 centimeters). Each array contains 16 cards. One side of each card is unmarked. The other side of one array has basic combinations such as 2 + 9. The opposite side of the second array has answers such as 11. When an individual points to pairs of cards, the cards are turned over and compared. If the combination and the answer match, the child scores a point and gets another turn. Otherwise, the next player takes a turn. The game ends when all of the cards have been matched.

4. Bingo activities provide opportunities for children to review number combinations. **Bugs Bingo** is a popular activity. Two to four players participate. Each group needs three regular dice or dice showing the numerals 1 to 6, as well as about 25 bingo markers (small squares of paper work well) and a Bingo board. The board for this game is shaped like a ladybug, from which the name originates. Figure 6–21 shows one of the game boards and numeral patterns for three others.

Each player puts a marker on the FREE square and then rolls a die. The player with the highest number on the die begins. The first player rolls all three dice and adds the number of dots showing. The other players check that the sum is correct.

All players cover that numeral on their boards. Although the numeral may appear more than once on the board, only one numeral is covered at each turn. Once a marker is placed on a numeral, it cannot be moved to another region.

The dice are passed to the next player, and play continues until someone has 5 markers in a row, horizontally, vertically, or diagonally.

If additional boards are needed, they should be made with different numeral patterns. For each board, however, there is one FREE region and there are 24 regions with these numerals:

> one each of 4, 5, 6, 15, 16, 17
> two each of 7, 8, 9, 12, 13, 14
> three each of 10, 11

5. The game Top It uses a deck of cards representing the basic addition combinations. Figure 6–22 shows a deck of easy cards and a deck of hard cards. Choose the deck that matches the children's ability levels, or combine the decks into a single deck representing nearly all of the basic addition combinations.

The game is for two or four players. One player deals all of the cards. Each player neatly stacks the cards that are dealt. Each player turns over a card and places it face up. The player with the highest sum claims all of the cards played. If any players are tied with high cards, the cards remain in front of the players and those who are tied each draw another card. The player with the highest sum takes all of the cards. The winner of the game is the player with the most cards after all of the cards have been turned over.

This section has presented a few of the many activities that can be employed to help children practice the basic addition combinations. Each activity can be easily adapted to include subtraction practice.

There are also unique opportunities to incorporate literature that focuses on addition and subtraction. It may be in the form of counting forward and backward as in *Dorobō the Dangerous*, by Vaughan (1995). Crane finds that someone is eating the fish from her pond and children can count along with Crane as she has fewer each day. The story continues as Crane solves her problem and ends as it began with her counting song. Along the same line are the delightful *Ten, Nine, Eight* by Bang (1983) and *Seven Little Hippos* by Thaler (1991). Both involve counting backward and use well-illustrated themes to do so. The goal is to have children able to accurately and quickly respond to all basic addition and subtraction combinations. Other activities and games are presented in the chapter references.

Figure 6–21 Game board and numeral patterns for Bugs Bingo.

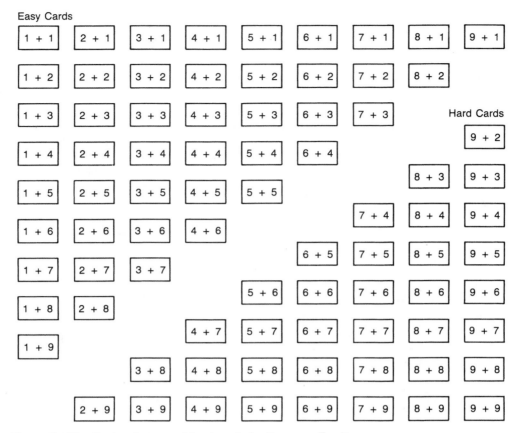

Figure 6–22 Decks of easy and hard cards for the game Top It.

Algorithms

As children learn algorithms, some will likely find ways to modify standard or alternative algorithms so that they make more sense to them. Some children will invent their own algorithms using their personal logic. When this occurs, students should be encouraged to write down their algorithms and share them with the other students. Discussions will follow as students attempt to understand or challenge the explanations of the algorithm inventors.

It is helpful if children know the basic addition and subtraction combinations as they begin to work with algorithms. In addition, children should have available physical materials with which to work. The base ten blocks are a useful set of materials for modeling addition and subtraction. For example, provide the students with the base ten blocks and other materials and a problem such as: "Jack wants to buy a 39¢ top and a 59¢ airplane. How much will they cost altogether?" Have the children work in small groups to find a solution, and have them write down their method using words and symbols. When all the groups are finished, ask each group to share its solution with the whole class. Discuss the merits of each solution. This gives students the opportunity to explore and invent algorithms. Let the students decide which algorithm they prefer and when they no longer need to use the physical models. It is likely that the students will devise some algorithms similar to the standard addition and subtraction algorithms, but be ready for algorithms that are different. The process of inventing algorithms is an important part of developing computational fluency.

> [W]hen children in the elementary grades are encouraged to develop, record, explain, and critique one another's strategies for solving computational problems, a number of important kinds of learning can occur. (NCTM, 2000, p. 35)

In mathematics textbooks, addition and subtraction algorithms are usually taught sequentially, beginning with the simplest problems, which require no regrouping (carrying or borrowing). The difficulty and complexity increase until multidigit problems with regrouping are presented. However, when students begin multidigit addition and subtraction using physical models, there is no need to separate problems that require regrouping from those that do not. Avoid assigning page after page of laborious addition and subtraction problems. When children can demonstrate paper-and-pencil algorithms for addition and subtraction, it is time to let them use calculators to speed up computations. Using the calculator is the most efficient procedure for performing an arithmetic operation that may be too complex for mental computation.

> As students encounter problem situations in which computations are more cumbersome or tedious, they should be encouraged to use calculators to aid in problem solving. (NCTM, 2000, pp. 87–88)

On the following pages, paper-and-pencil algorithms for addition and subtraction are presented in turn. We begin with the standard paper-and-pencil algorithm that is generally considered most efficient for each operation. Alternative algorithms are then presented. Alternative procedures often serve as teaching algorithms and help to bridge the gap between physical models and the abstract. Sometimes alternative algorithms are the most efficient paper-and-pencil algorithms for children. It was mentioned above that students sometimes invent algorithms similar to the standard addition and subtraction algorithms. Likewise, they may invent algorithms similar to the alternative algorithms presented below. While the standard algorithm is presented first, followed by alternative algorithms, we are not suggesting that children will invent algorithms in this order. You should not introduce standard algorithms until students have explored, invented, and discussed their own algorithms.

ADDITION. The standard addition algorithm is generally considered the most efficient paper-and-pencil procedure for adding. The algorithm has been applied to the six problems below, each of which has at least one two-digit addend. The problems are presented in order of difficulty. The first three algorithms involve no regrouping. The others have regrouping in one or more of the place value positions.

$$
\begin{array}{ccc}
10 & 34 & 22 \\
+\ 8 & +10 & +14 \\
\hline
18 & 44 & 36 \\
\end{array}
$$

$$
\begin{array}{ccc}
^{1}19 & ^{1}37 & ^{1}63 \\
+\ 2 & +\ 28 & +\ 59 \\
\hline
21 & 65 & 122 \\
\end{array}
$$

The first two problems involve adding a number to 10 and adding 10 to a number. Sums involving 10 are important to know because they occur continually during computation. Being able to recognize sums involving 10 and make groupings of 10 while solving problems saves considerable time and energy during computation. The latter three algorithms display the regrouping numeral 1, indicating regrouping has taken place. In these cases, 10 ones have been grouped for one 10. While the algorithm would be simpler without the regrouping numeral, most who use this algorithm include it.

It is important that children understand what happens when regrouping occurs. Work with place value provides this understanding, and children can be taught the standard addition algorithm with little more than a set of base ten blocks or a picture of them. Most math texts include illustrations of counting devices and step-by-step procedures for teaching the algorithm. You are encouraged to use physical materials as models for textbook algorithms.

For example, Figure 6–23 shows both the numeral representation and the pictorial representation of 22 + 14. The joining of unit cubes and longs (Figure 6–18b) is accompanied by the teacher asking, "How many ones are there?" There are 2 ones plus 4 ones, or 6 ones. The children put the 6 beneath the 2 + 4 and make sure there are as many cubes on the place-value board. Next, the teacher asks, "How many tens are there?" There are 2 plus 1, or 3. The children place the 3 beneath the 2 tens + 1 ten and make sure there are as many longs on the place-value board. The transition from the concrete to the abstract should be made as often as necessary for the concepts to make sense to the children.

An algorithm that requires regrouping is only slightly more difficult than one that does not require regrouping when children have the proper foundation, that is, when they have learned about grouping various materials, including the base ten blocks, during the initial study of place value. When an algorithm requiring regrouping is accompanied by an illustration that reinforces earlier skills, children pick up the process quickly (see Figures 6–24a, b, and c).

The teacher asks, "How many ones are there?" There are 3 ones plus 7 ones, or 10 ones; that is, there is one group of tens and there are 0 ones. It is important here that the unit cubes be grouped and exchanged for one long, even if just pictorially. "How many units do we have after the exchange?" We have 0. The students write down the 0 beneath the 3 + 7. They record a 1 in the tens column to remind them that they have exchanged 10 ones and now have 1 ten. "How many tens are there?" There are 6 tens plus 5 tens plus 1 ten, or 12 tens; that is, there is one group of 100 (1 hundred) and there are 2 tens. The longs should be put together and exchanged for one flat and two longs. "How many tens do we have after

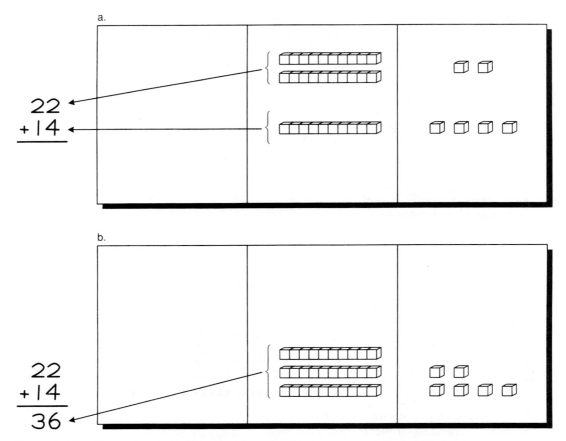

Figure 6–23 Numeral representation and base ten blocks representation of 22 + 14.

the exchange?" We have 2 tens. The students write down the 2 beneath the 6 + 5. They also record the 1 hundred because they have no more place-value positions in the problem. They check to make sure the multibase blocks show 120.

The addition algorithms for larger numbers are extensions of the above process. They take more time to perform but are not substantively different.

As soon as children can perform the algorithm without physical or pictorial models, they should be encouraged to do so. Math texts provide plenty of practice exercises. Children should practice for several days after they are able to perform the algorithm without materials. While there may be 30 problems on a page, 10 to 20 problems will give children the necessary practice. If children continue to have difficulty reaching the correct answer, you should diagnose the difficulty. Assigning more problems to solve is unlikely to be the best strategy. We discuss diagnosing computational errors in the section on assessment.

The following activities differ from those presented earlier. Their primary focus is ways to present alternative addition algorithms.

A C T I V I T I E S

Pre-Kindergarten – Grade 2

OBJECTIVE: to invent algorithms for addition problems.

1. Introduce "solve it any way you can" problems. Present a problem and invite students to solve the problem using any technique they may choose. For example, "Yesterday during sharing time, students in the morning kindergarten class brought 7 items to share and students in the afternoon kindergarten class brought 9 items to share. How many items were brought by students to share? Suppose this happened for three more days—how many items would be shared altogether?" Be ready to provide children with materials that they may ask for. When the students have finished working, have them discuss how they found their solution and share any materials that they may have used.

OBJECTIVE: to add columns of three or more numbers.

2. When children are competent with the basic addition combinations, challenge them to add three digits. At first, the numbers should be no larger than

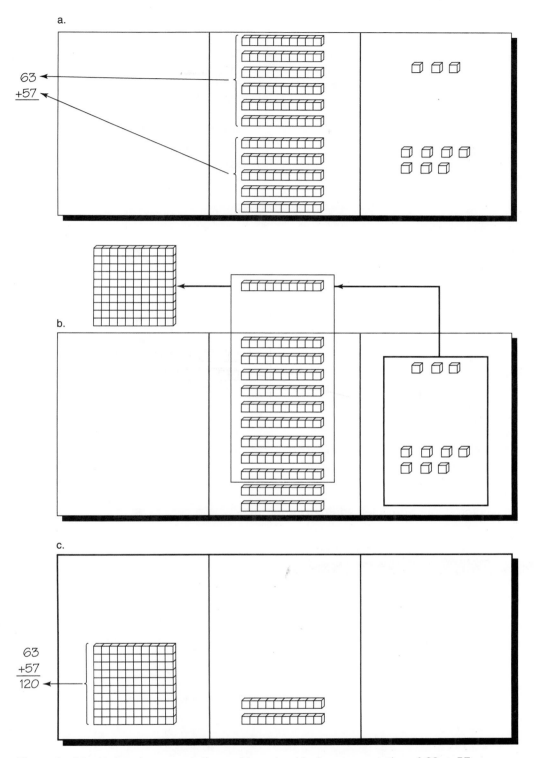

Figure 6 – 24 Numeral representation and base ten blocks representation of 63 + 57.

basic combinations, such as 3 + 4 + 8 or 8 + 1 + 5. Present the problems in the format the children are used to seeing, most likely the vertical format. When the problems become more difficult, help students develop an algorithm that works for them. A column addition algorithm is shown in row a below.

$$
\text{a.}\quad
\begin{array}{r} 6 \\ 7 \\ +4 \\ \hline \end{array}
\quad
\begin{array}{r} 6 \\ 4 \\ +7 \\ \hline \end{array}
\quad
\begin{array}{r} 10 \\ +7 \\ \hline 17 \end{array}
$$

$$
\text{b.}\quad
\begin{array}{r} 6 \\ 7 \\ +4 \\ \hline \end{array}
\quad
\begin{array}{r} 6 \\ 7 \\ +4 \\ \hline \end{array}
\quad
\begin{array}{r} >13 \\ +4 \\ \hline 17 \end{array}
$$

To approach this problem, find numbers that add to 10 and reorder the problem to put those numbers together. The numbers adding to 10 can then be combined and the final sum calculated. After some practice, most children can group the tens by reordering the problem mentally. They see groups of 10 in the problem and group numbers mentally, shortcutting the algorithm.

A second approach is shown in b. Beginning at the top or bottom of the column, add successive numbers, keeping the intermediate sum in mind until reaching the last number. The last calculation provides the answer to the problem. Let children choose the algorithm they are most comfortable with when adding columns of numbers.

OBJECTIVE: to use the expanded notation algorithm.

3. **Expanded notation** is a direct outgrowth of work with place value. Children recognize that two flats, four longs, and six small cubes represent 200 + 40 + 6, or 2 hundreds + 4 tens + 6 ones. An alternative addition algorithm uses this knowledge. The problems below show two solutions using expanded notation. In problem a, no regrouping is necessary. The problem is rewritten from standard into expanded notation. The columns are added and the expanded notation is rewritten into standard notation.

$$
\text{a.}\quad
\begin{array}{r} 63 \\ +24 \\ \hline \end{array}
\qquad
\begin{array}{r} 60+3 \\ +20+4 \\ \hline 80+7 = 87 \end{array}
$$

$$
\text{b.}\quad
\begin{array}{r} 58 \\ +29 \\ \hline \end{array}
\qquad
\begin{array}{r} 50+8 \\ +20+9 \\ \hline 70+17 = 80+7 = 87 \end{array}
$$

Problem b requires regrouping in the ones column. As in the earlier example, the problem is rewritten from standard into expanded notation. Each column is added. Finally, regrouping takes place as the answer is rewritten into standard notation. The algorithm used with problem b is advantageous because children never lose sight of the numbers they are regrouping. It is important to point out this fact and let the students discuss regrouping.

OBJECTIVE: to use the loop abacus as a tool in learning the addition algorithm.

4. The abacus is useful as a tool. As children learn about place value, the abacus is handy in teaching the regrouping process. Any time ten counters appear on a given loop, they must be exchanged for one counter on the adjacent loop. Students need to discuss why this exchange is necessary. The regrouping process is demonstrated as we solve a problem on the abacus. In the first frame of Figure 6–25, an abacus is ready to add 746 + 285. The counters below the holding clips represent 285; the counters above represent 746.

In the second frame, we remove the holding clip in the ones column and exchange ten counters on the ones

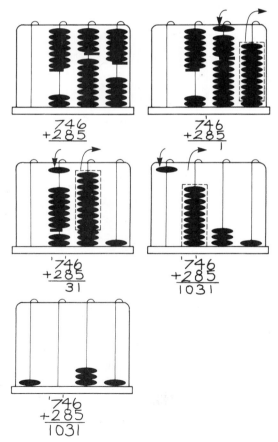

Figure 6–25 Numeral representation and abacus representation of 746 + 285.

loop for one counter on the tens loop. We have one counter left in the ones column.

In the third frame, we remove the holding clip in the tens column and exchange ten counters on the tens loop for one counter on the hundreds loop. We have three counters left in the tens column.

In the fourth frame, we remove the holding clip in the hundreds column and exchange ten counters on the hundreds loop for one counter on the thousands loop. We have no counters left in the hundreds column.

In the fifth frame, we see the abacus after all the exchanges have been made.

OBJECTIVE: to use the partial sums algorithm for addition.

5. Another algorithm that helps children through the process of regrouping or carrying is the **partial sums algorithm.** It may be used whether or not regrouping is necessary. To illustrate this algorithm, note the problem below (48 + 39). The first step in the solution is to add the numbers in the ones column, 8 + 9. The answer, 17, is the first partial sum and is placed beneath the problem.

$$
\begin{array}{r} 48 \\ +39 \\ \hline \end{array}
\quad
\begin{array}{r} 48 \\ +39 \\ \hline 17 \end{array}
\quad
\begin{array}{r} 48 \\ +39 \\ \hline 17 \\ 70 \end{array}
\quad
\begin{array}{r} 48 \\ +39 \\ \hline 17 \\ 70 \\ \hline 87 \end{array}
$$

The next step is to add the numbers in the tens column, 40 + 30, or 4 tens + 3 tens. The result, 70, is the second partial sum and is placed beneath the 17.

Finally, the partial sums are added to arrive at the answer, 87. You may also add the tens first and then the ones using this algorithm. This is very useful for mental computation. Take care with this algorithm to assure that the correct place value positions in the partial sums are maintained.

SUBTRACTION. Again, for subtraction, give the students a real-life situation such as spending 18¢ out of 25¢ and determining the amount of change they have left. Allow the children to work in groups to determine the solution and record their methods. Discuss the various methods used by the different groups before presenting the standard algorithm. Of course, the concept of subtraction is considerably different.

The standard paper-and-pencil algorithm for subtraction relies on children's knowing the basic subtraction combinations and being well versed in place-value concepts. You recall that the basic subtraction combinations are related to the basic addition combination. Thus, for the addition combination 4 + 7 = 11, we have the corresponding subtraction combinations, 11 − 4 = 7 and 11 − 7 = 4. Techniques for helping children memorize these combinations were discussed in the section on basic combinations.

Six examples of the standard subtraction algorithm are presented below.

$$
\begin{array}{r} 18 \\ -10 \\ \hline 8 \end{array}
\quad
\begin{array}{r} 44 \\ -34 \\ \hline 10 \end{array}
\quad
\begin{array}{r} 36 \\ -22 \\ \hline 14 \end{array}
$$

$$
\begin{array}{r} \overset{1}{2}\overset{1}{1} \\ -9 \\ \hline 12 \end{array}
\quad
\begin{array}{r} \overset{5}{6}\overset{15}{5} \\ -37 \\ \hline 28 \end{array}
\quad
\begin{array}{r} \overset{2}{3}\overset{11}{2}\overset{12}{2} \\ -63 \\ \hline 259 \end{array}
$$

The first three examples involve no regrouping, or borrowing. The last three require that regrouping take place. The first two problems involve subtracting 10 and subtracting so that 10 is the difference. The third problem is solved by applying basic subtraction combinations to the ones and tens columns in the problem.

The fourth example necessitates regrouping from the tens place to the ones place. This is shown by crossing out the 2 tens and replacing them with 1 ten. The ones place is increased from 1 to 11, reflecting the exchange of 1 ten for 10 ones. The subtraction is then carried out.

The fifth example is similar to the fourth because there is regrouping from the tens to the ones place. In this case, 6 tens and 5 tens are exchanged for 5 tens and 15 ones.

In the final example, there is regrouping from the tens to the ones place and from the hundreds to the tens place. Thus, 2 tens and 2 ones become 1 ten and 12 ones; then, 3 hundreds and 1 ten become 2 hundreds and 11 tens. The markings have been shown in the procedure as they are used by most who employ this standard algorithm.

When students develop a subtraction algorithm, it is important that they use physical models. At this point, we demonstrate with base ten blocks. The first example is 65 − 37. Figures 6–26a, b, and c illustrate how to construct the problem using the blocks.

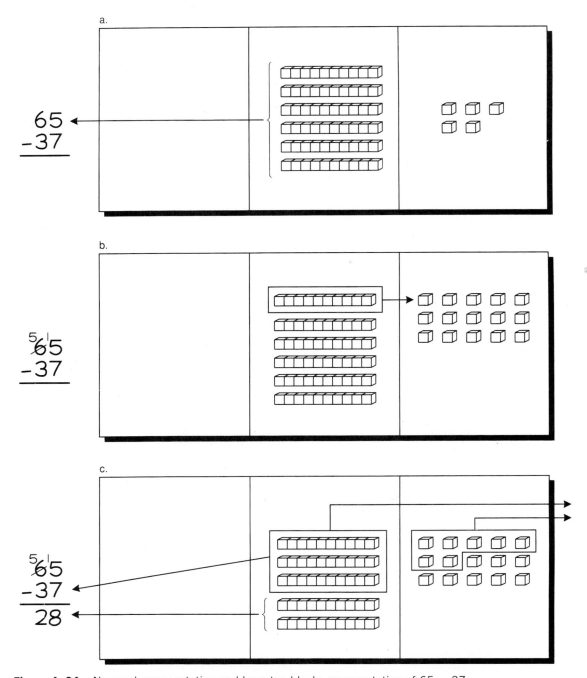

Figure 6–26   Numeral representation and base ten blocks representation of 65 − 37.

First, attempt to remove 7 small cubes from 5 small cubes. Finding this impossible, perform an exchange (see Figure 6–26b). Trade 1 long for 10 small cubes. Now, from the collection of 15 small cubes, remove 7, leaving 8 small cubes. Moving to the tens, remove 3 longs from 5 longs; this leaves 2 longs. Having finished the algorithm, you find the difference is 2 longs and 8 small cubes, or 28 (see Figure 6–26).

The first few times children encounter subtraction involving regrouping with the base ten blocks, they should use only the blocks. Once the procedure is mastered, use the written algorithm along with the blocks. Finally, as soon as the children are able, use only the written algorithm, bringing the blocks back if there is some difficulty in solving a particular problem. The base ten blocks, or any physical models, clearly show what happens at each step in an algorithm.

Once each step is understood and discussed, children should practice the symbolic algorithm.

Children working with physical models or practicing paper and pencil algorithms may discover clever shortcuts or original procedures. Children should be encouraged to create and demonstrate to the class their own algorithms.

As in the case of addition, the activities that follow include alternative algorithms and approaches for subtraction. If some children find an alternative that is superior for them, let them adopt it as their standard algorithm.

A C T I V I T I E S

Pre-Kindergarten – Grade 2

OBJECTIVE: to use the expanded notation algorithm for subtraction.

1. When the **expanded notation algorithm** is used, children see what happens in the process of regrouping, or *borrowing*. The first example below, 43 − 22, does not require regrouping. Both numbers are rewritten in expanded form. In the ones column, 2 is subtracted from 3, resulting in 1. In the tens column, 40 − 20 or 4 tens − 2 tens results in 20, or 2 tens. Then 20 + 1 is rewritten into standard form, 21.

a.
$$\begin{array}{rr} 43 & 40+3 \\ -22 & -(20+2) \\ \hline & 20+1 = 21 \end{array}$$

b.
$$\begin{array}{rrr} 43 & 40+3 & 30+13 \\ -27 & -(20+7) & -(20+7) \\ \hline & & 10+6 = 16 \end{array}$$

In the second example (b), regrouping is necessary. Children cannot subtract 7 from 3 after the problem is written in expanded form. They must rewrite 40 + 3 as 30 + 13. This process regroups 1 ten to 10 ones. Children can subtract 7 from 13, with the result of 6. They may also subtract 30 − 20 or 3 tens − 2 tens, with the result of 10. Then 10 + 6 is rewritten into standard form, 16.

You may find it necessary to help children work through several examples of the expanded notation algorithm with concrete objects such as base ten blocks, beansticks, and Cuisenaire rods before you move to symbols. Work first with problems that don't require regrouping, then advance to the more complicated regrouping problems.

OBJECTIVE: to use the abacus as a model to illustrate the standard subtraction algorithm.

2. Children who have used the abacus when learning place value and addition have the exchanging skills necessary for subtraction. To solve 342 − 164, begin with 342 on the abacus as shown in the first frame of Figure 6–27. As in the second frame, exchange 1 ten for 10 ones, resulting in 12 ones. Then remove 4 ones, as shown in the third frame, resulting in 8 ones. Then exchange 1 hundred for 10 tens as in the fourth frame; there are 2 hundreds and 13 tens remaining. As in the fifth frame, remove 6 tens, leaving 7 tens. Because no further regrouping is necessary, remove 1 hundred, completing the problem. Frame six shows how the abacus looks after 164 has been subtracted from 342. The answer, 178, is easily read.

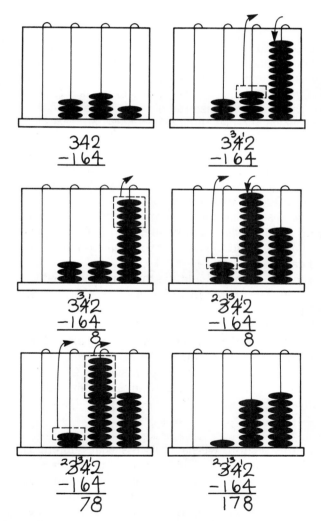

Figure 6–27 Numeral representation and abacus representation of 342 − 164.

OBJECTIVE: to use the "How much more do I add" (HMMDIA) algorithm to subtract.

3. The **"How much more do I add" (HMMDIA) algorithm** is a subtraction algorithm that uses an additive component. We demonstrate with the following example (168 − 49). The algorithm consists of adding to the subtrahend, 49, until you reach the minuend, 168. At each step of this adding process, the number added is recorded. Later, all of the written numbers are added together.

$$
\begin{array}{cccc}
168 & 168 & 168 & 168 \\
-49 & -49 & -49 & -49 \\
\hline
 & 1 & 1 & 1 \\
 & & 50 & 50 \\
 & & & +68 \\
\hline
 & & & 119
\end{array}
$$

Explain to the children using the example that they will be adding from 49 to 168. Begin with 49. Ask yourself, "How much more do I add to 49 to reach the next group of 10?" The next group of ten is 5 tens, or 50. The answer in this example is 1. Write down the 1 as shown and now think 50 because you have just added one to 49 and gotten 50.

Now ask, "How much more do I add to 50 to reach 100?" In this case, the answer is 50. Write down the 50 as shown and think 100 because you have just added 50 to 50 and gotten 100.

Next, ask, "How much more do I add to 100 to reach 168?" The answer is 68. Write down the 68 as shown. You have reached the number you were adding to, 168, and can stop.

The final step is to add the three numbers that were recorded. The answer to 168 − 49 is 1 + 50 + 68, or 119.

You may find it necessary to review this algorithm several times before the process becomes clear. Once you have done this example, give other examples, particularly some that are simpler, such as 25 − 8. This unusual subtraction algorithm surprises and motivates children.

In this section, we have discussed developing computational fluency for addition and subtraction. First, that involved having recall of the addition and subtraction combinations. Second, it involved using effective procedures or algorithms for adding and subtracting. Current math texts present thorough instruction on how to develop standard algorithms, and they contain ample problems for practice. Be sure to invite students to invent and discuss their own algorithms before using those in the text.

Developing Fluency with Integers

Operations with integers should be practiced and mastered in the middle grades. After considerable experience with simple additions and subtractions of integers, especially with various models such as number lines (vertical and horizontal), colored chips, and money, students should have made sense of how the operations behave. Thus, students should have discovered a number of properties of operations with integers. After exploring questions such as "When is the sum of two addends smaller than either addend?" or "What happens if I subtract a negative number?", students should make a number of observations, such as that when two positive numbers are added, the result is a larger positive number. For example, $(+4) + (+3) = +7$. When two negative numbers are added the result is a negative number with a larger absolute value. For example, $(^-5) + (^-6) = ^-11$. When one positive number and one negative number (or one negative number and one positive number) are added, the difference between the two numbers is found and assigned the sign of the larger of the two numbers. For example, $(^-8) + (+5) = ^-3$. That is, $8 − 5 = 3$; the 3 is assigned the negative sign because the sign of 8 (the larger number) is negative. This assumes, of course, that when we say the larger of the two numbers, we mean the absolute values of the two numbers. As another example, $(+7) + (^-5) = +2$.

When two positive numbers are subtracted, the result is the same as in whole-number subtraction if the subtrahend is equal to or less than the minuend. For example, $(+7) − (+1) = 7 − 1 = 6$. If the subtrahend is greater than the minuend, the difference between the two numbers is found and the result is negative. For example, $(+4) − (+9) = ^-5$. When a negative number is subtracted from a positive number, the result is a larger positive number. For example, $(+7) − (^-3) = +10$. When a positive number is subtracted from a negative number, the result is a smaller negative number. For example, $(^-2) − (+6) = ^-8$.

All of the above examples may be shown with Bingo markers in the same way as the activities focusing on money in the Adding and Subtracting Integers section earlier in this chapter. For students to be fluent with adding and subtracting integers, they need a variety of meaningful problems and investigations and an opportunity to discuss their findings with peers. Students should develop procedures that build on understanding what they are doing and understanding why each procedure works. During the learning process for operations on integers, students should be encouraged to develop algorithms that work for them and make sense to them. Following are activities that help develop skill with adding and subtracting integers.

A C T I V I T I E S

Grades 6–8

OBJECTIVE: to practice skills in operating with integers.

1. Use a regular deck of playing cards without the jokers and face cards, or make your own deck with 10 red cards (numbered 1 through 10) and 10 black cards (numbered 1 through 10). The black cards are worth positive amounts, and the red cards are worth negative amounts. This is a game best played by four players, but it can be adjusted for other numbers of players by adding more cards. Begin the game by shuffling the cards and dealing five cards face down to each player. Each player then picks up his or her five cards, adds the numbers shown on the cards, and writes down the total number of points. This is the score for round one. On each turn, each player draws one card from the player on the left. If you take a red 5, you must add a negative 5 to your score. What happens to the player who lost the red 5? That person will subtract a negative 5. Does this have the same effect as adding a black 5? Round two ends when each player has drawn one card from the player on the left. At this point, everyone again adds the points shown on his or her five cards. The score from round two is added to the score from round one. Play continues in the same manner until someone has a score greater in absolute value than 50 or until time is called. The player with the score greatest in absolute value at the end of the game wins.

Note: An easy way to check that everyone has added correctly on each round is to check the total score for the four players. This should always be zero. Ask the students to explain why this is so. If you are using a different number of players and a different number of cards, determine the sum of all the cards before you begin.

2. Students might enjoy practicing their skills with operations with integers using the computer program by Bonnie Seiler, *The Great Signed Number Race.* This program builds on a similar program by the same developer, *How the West Was One + Three × Four.* The earlier program gives students the opportunity to construct and solve arithmetic equations as they practice learning the order of operations for expressions such as $(2 + 3) \times 4$. In *The Great Signed Number Race,* students work with positive and negative integers and all operations in a race through the Old West.

Activities described in the section Basic Addition and Subtraction Combinations may be modified to include integers. Invite students to make the modifications or to develop activities that help reinforce integer relationships. It may take longer for students to develop a conceptual understanding of negative numbers than to just memorize the rules, but the goal of operations with integers is understanding, not rule memorization. If you recall the hierarchy of goals in the section Solving and Posing Problems in Chapter 4, you will remember that the "doers"— those who can remember rules but do not understand the mathematics—are toward the bottom of the diagram. You want students who understand the mathematics; the calculator knows the rules.

ESTIMATING, USING BENCHMARKS, AND MENTAL CALCULATING

Whether working with pencil and paper or working with calculators and computers, children should develop skill in estimating and mental calculating. When estimation is applied, overall accuracy should improve. For example, a fifth grader who is adding $383 + 792$ should be able to determine that the answer will be close to but less than $400 + 800$, or 1,200. If that student adds and gets 4,800 or 840, it should be apparent that an error was made. Estimating will not eliminate all errors, but it will help in many cases.

Just as there are strategies in problem solving, there are also strategies in estimating. Reys (1986) reports five such strategies from her research. They include the front-end strategy, clustering, rounding, compatible numbers, and special numbers. The **front-end strategy** has two steps: (1) perform the operation using only the most significant digits, and (2) adjust or refine the estimate by performing the operation on the remaining digits. For example, to estimate $193 + 428 + 253$, children should think that 1 (hundred) + 4 (hundred) + 2 (hundred) = 7 (hundred), using the most significant digits first. Then, to adjust the estimate, they should think that 93 is about 100 and 28 + 53 is about 75. The final estimate is 700 + 100 + 75, or 875.

The **clustering strategy** is used to estimate the sum of several numbers that cluster around a particular value. The strategy involves estimating the average of the numbers and then multiplying the average by how many numbers there are. For example, to estimate 23 + 28 + 22 + 25 + 29 + 27, children can estimate the average of the numbers as 25 and then multiply by 6. The result, 150, is a good estimate of the actual sum.

The **rounding strategy** may be used for any operation. The process involves rounding the numbers being used and then performing the operation. It is important to round carefully in order to provide the best estimate. For example, to estimate 43 × 57, children can round and then multiply 40 × 60 to give an estimate of 2,400. The 43 is rounded down, and the 57 is rounded up. If both numbers are rounded down, the result is an underestimate. If both numbers are rounded up, the result is an overestimate. In such cases, mental adjustments up or down should be made.

The **compatible numbers strategy** refers to looking for numbers that seem to fit together. For example, to estimate 2 + 8 + 5 + 2 + 3 + 9 + 4, children can search for pairs of numbers whose sums are close to 5 and 10. Thus, 2 + 8 = 10, 5 + 2 + 3 = 10, 9 is close to 10, and 4 is near 5, so the estimated sum is 10 + 10 + 10 + 5, or 35.

The **special numbers strategy** refers to seeking values that are easy to use in mental computation. This strategy is best used with fractions, decimals, and percentages. For example, to estimate 0.9 + 5.8, children can think that 1 + 6 = 7. Children should look for values near 1, 10, and 100 as part of the special numbers strategy.

To become competent estimators, children must be carefully taught the estimation strategies and must be given time to practice the strategies. Periodic checks should be made to confirm that students are remembering estimation strategies. Skill in mental calculation means that children are able to answer number questions in their heads without relying on paper and pencil or a calculator. Using benchmarks facilitates mental calculation. Children should be instructed on how to use benchmarks as they perform mental calculations. That is, they should seek ways to use decades (10, 20, 30, etc.), hundreds, or thousands to simplify calculations. For example, to add 6 + 7 + 4, use 6 + 4 = 10 followed by adding 7. To add 58 + 29, use 57 + 30 = 87 by adding 1 to the 29 to make 30 and subtracting 1 from the 58 to make 57. By adding 1 and subtracting 1 the total remains the same. For subtraction, 43 − 22 could be thought of as 41 − 20 = 21. Subtracting 2 from 22 results in 20, and subtracting 2 from 43 results in 41. By subtracting 2 from each number, the difference remains

the same. To subtract 168 − 49, use 169 − 50 = 119. In this case, 1 is added to both the minuend and the subtrahend. In learning skills of mental calculating, students will develop their own techniques of mental calculating and should be encouraged to do so.

> Viewed as a basic skill for computation or estimation, mental computation is seen as a set of procedures applied mentally . . . . But when students generate their own computation strategies, mental computation can be seen as a higher-order thinking skill. (NCTM, 1994, p. 12)

Facility with mental calculation helps children perform computations more quickly and demonstrates children's understanding of the basic arithmetic operations. The following activities are intended to strengthen children's skill in estimating, using benchmarks, and mental calculating.

ACTIVITIES

Pre-Kindergarten – Grade 2

OBJECTIVE: to practice estimation with addition and subtraction.

1. Use a set of double-six or double-nine dominoes. Large-format dominoes work well if this activity is done with the whole class. Constructed from railroad board and approximately 10 cm by 20 cm in size, large-format dominoes, as in Figure 6–28, appeal to students. A complete set of dominoes is displayed in Appendix B. To practice estimating with addition, hold a domino before the class for three to five seconds, then ask the children if they believe there are 10 dots, more than 10 dots, or fewer than 10 dots on the domino. Let them signal to you that there are 10 dots by putting a hand flat on the table or floor. A hand with thumb up means more than 10; a hand with thumb down means fewer than 10.

To practice estimating with subtraction, have the children find the difference between the number of dots on one end of a domino and the number of dots on the other end. Have them indicate whether the

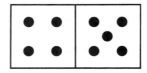

Figure 6–28 Sample large-format domino for estimation practice.

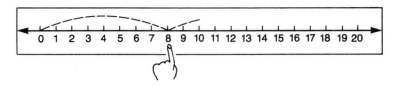

Figure 6–29 Practicing mental calculation using a number line.

difference is equal to 3 dots, more than 3 dots, or fewer than 3 dots. They can use the same hand signs as before.

OBJECTIVE: to use the number line to practice mental calculation with addition and subtraction.

2. Use this activity with a wall number line, smaller desk number lines, or a walk-on number line. For addition, begin with an initial jump to the first addend and then explain the next jump, letting the children mentally calculate where the second jump will land. After the children answer, let them perform the second jump. Figure 6–29 shows a number line and the position of a finger after the children have been told to start at 0 and to jump to 8.

Ask them, "If we make a jump of 6, where do you think we will land?" Let them mentally calculate. Then let them make the jump of 6 to find the answer.

For subtraction, follow a similar procedure. Let the children make the beginning jump, for example, to 15. Then ask, "If we jump back (subtract) 4, where do you think we will land?" Let them mentally calculate, and then subtract 4 to find the answer. To vary this activity, have the children estimate if the answer will be equal to, more than, or less than a particular number, such as 10, 15, or 20. At the end of the activity, invite students to explain how they calculated their answers.

OBJECTIVE: to use the benchmark 10 for mental addition and subtraction.

3. To begin, use base ten blocks, beans, or Unifix cubes to present combinations of objects that add to 10. For example, $0 + 10$, $1 + 9$, $2 + 8$, and $3 + 7$ each equals 10. Have the children estimate the sum of combinations of objects.

Next, present combinations such as $8 + 7$ and challenge the children to make a grouping of 10 plus a second number to result in the same amount. As in Figure 6–30, $8 + 7$ could be changed to $(8 + 2) + 5$, then to $10 + 5$. Beginning with physical models helps make the grouping to 10 more meaningful and slows the process so most children can successfully participate.

For subtraction, round numbers to 10 for easier calculation. For example, write $12 - 5$ on the chalkboard. Explain that sometimes you forget a basic subtraction fact and need a way to figure the answer in your head. One way is to make the larger number a 10 or a 20, whichever is closer. Ask, "Is 12 closer to 10 or 20?" Twelve is closer to 10. Ask, "What do you have to do to 12 to make it 10?" Subtract 2 from 12. Explain, "If you subtract 2 from 12, you must also subtract 2 from 5 so the difference will be the same." Encourage the students to discuss why this is always true. Continue, "What is $5 - 2$?" The answer is 3. Summarize, "We have changed $12 - 5$ to $10 - 3$.

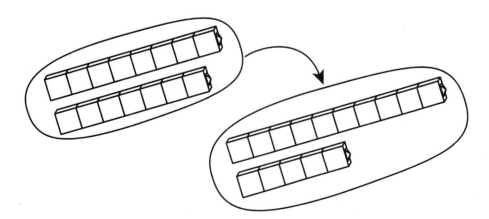

Figure 6–30 Regrouping Unifix cubes using the benchmark 10.

What is the answer?" The answer is 7; therefore, 12 − 5 is 7. Review the process several times. The mental process of subtracting or adding to make the larger number (minuend) a multiple of 10 is quicker than the oral explanation.

The problem 12 − 5 also may be solved by adding 5 to the subtrahend, 5, to reach 10. Then 5 must also be added to 12 to maintain the difference. The new problem becomes 17 − 10. By changing either the minuend or the subtrahend to 10, students may find problems easier to solve. These mental shortcuts are particularly useful when they are performed with larger subtractions in such problems as 36 − 18; the problem may be restated as 38 − 20.

Estimation and mental calculation activities for primary children should be informal and concrete. You can use more formal techniques with older children. The more formal procedures may require children to round numbers to the nearest 10, 100, or 1,000 and to add and subtract numbers that have been rounded to 10, 100, or 1,000.

As you move from topic to topic in the math text, you can quickly prepare questions. Mental arithmetic problems should be presented to students each week, alternating with other warm-up activities. Over time, children will show considerable improvement in their ability to handle mental arithmetic.

A C T I V I T I E S

Grades 3−5 and Grades 6−8

OBJECTIVE: to use estimation to determine if certain purchases can be made.

1. This activity consists of a series of questions that should be answered without paper and pencil. Have students number from 1 to 5 on a sheet of paper. As each question is presented, ask them to estimate the answer by rounding off; then have them record their answer. The questions below ask whether or not certain items can be purchased with a fixed amount of money. You can say, "Answer yes or no. You have $50. Can you buy

- A wristwatch for $28.95 and a basketball for $24.00?
- An umbrella for $19.99 and a case of apples for $19.99?
- A ring for $37.50 and a chess set for $14.95?
- A radio for $21.89 and some tapes for $29.50?
- Three books for $15.00 each?"

Such questions take little time. Discuss the solutions before going on to another topic. Ask students to explain to the class what they were thinking as they solved a particular problem. One student explained that as she worked on question 1 above, she thought the wristwatch was about $30.00 and the basketball was about $25.00. The sum of the two items was $55.00. You can't buy that much with $50.00. Other students agreed that they had solved question 1 in the same way. Bill spoke up and said he thought the wristwatch was about $28.00 and he knew the basketball was $24.00. He added the two amounts together and found the sum was $52.00. He agreed that you can't buy both with $50.

OBJECTIVE: to use historical material to motivate estimation and mental arithmetic.

2. Textbooks from the past (usually available from municipal or college libraries) provide interesting and amusing mental exercises that students enjoy hearing and attempting to solve. One such textbook is Greenleaf's *Mental Arithmetic*, published in 1859 (see Figure 6−31). Its formal title is much more impressive: *A Mental Arithmetic, Upon the Inductive Plan; Being an Advanced Intellectual Course, Designed for Schools and Academies.* Examples of the exercises Greenleaf included in his book follow. The page on which each problem can be found is provided in parentheses.

- A farmer sold 6 bushels of wheat, 7 bushels of rye, and 8 bushels of corn; how many bushels did he sell? (p. 12)
- A lady expended for silk 4 dollars, for gloves 1 dollar, and for a bonnet 9 dollars; how many dollars did she expend in all? (p. 12)
- How many are 8 and 9? 8 and 19? 8 and 29? 8 and 39? 8 and 49? 8 and 59? 8 and 69? 8 and 79? 8 and 89? 8 and 99? (p. 15)
- George spent 19 cents for candy and 21 cents for fruit; how much more would he have to spend to make 50 cents? (p. 23)

OBJECTIVE: to use the calculator to improve mental calculation of addition and subtraction.

3. Select two teams of students. Each team may have as few as one member or as many as half of the class. Provide one calculator for each team.

As play begins, one member from Team A says a three-digit number. A player from Team B says another three-digit number. Both players silently write the sum of the two numbers. Give a limit of 5 seconds to make calculations.

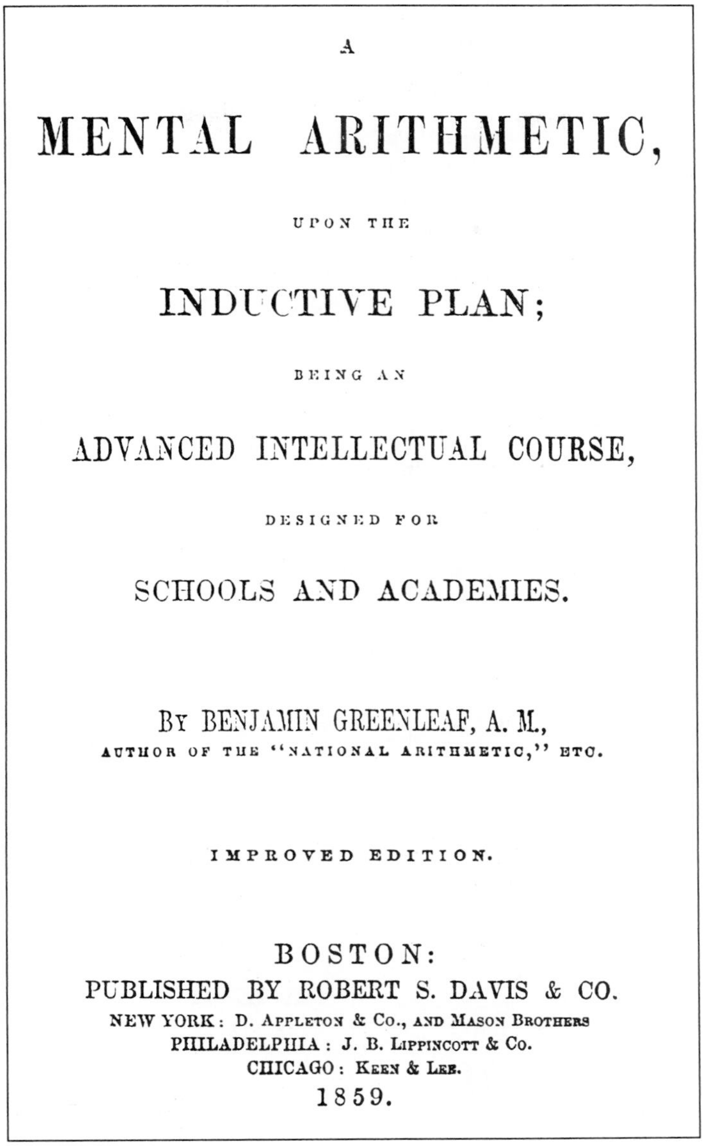

A

MENTAL ARITHMETIC,

UPON THE

INDUCTIVE PLAN;

BEING AN

ADVANCED INTELLECTUAL COURSE,

DESIGNED FOR

SCHOOLS AND ACADEMIES.

BY BENJAMIN GREENLEAF, A. M.,
AUTHOR OF THE "NATIONAL ARITHMETIC," ETC.

IMPROVED EDITION.

BOSTON:
PUBLISHED BY ROBERT S. DAVIS & CO.
NEW YORK: D. APPLETON & Co., AND MASON BROTHERS
PHILADELPHIA : J. B. LIPPINCOTT & Co.
CHICAGO: KEEN & LEE.
1859.

Figure 6–31   Title page of Greenleaf's 1859 *Mental Arithmetic* book.

Then have both players use the calculator to determine the sum. The player whose calculation is closest to the actual sum scores a point for the team. In the case of a tie, both teams earn a point. The next player on each team should name and calculate in the next round.

You or the students may suggest other rules, depending on the age and ability of the students. For example, you may stipulate that only two-digit numbers be used or that the number must end in zero or have a zero in the tens place.

The rules for the subtraction activity are similar to those for the addition. One player each from Teams A and B names a three-digit number. Both players then write down the difference between the two numbers. They use a calculator to determine the answer. Again, the player whose calculation is closest to the actual difference earns a point for the team. Children who engage in this activity for a while develop calculation strategies that benefit them in the game.

Many calculator activities that call for estimation not only strengthen estimation skills but also improve calculator skill. A sampling of calculator activity books is included in the chapter references.

REASONING, SOLVING AND POSING ADDITION AND SUBTRACTION PROBLEMS

Addition and subtraction are important skills in problem solving. Many problem situations require repeated additions and subtractions. Following are some activities that provide practice in problem solving and cause students to use addition and subtraction.

A C T I V I T I E S

Pre-Kindergarten – Grade 2

OBJECTIVE: to use "magic squares" for problem-solving and computational practice.

1. "Magic squares" have been popular and engaging puzzles for many centuries. A magic square is a square array of numbers that produce the same sum when added along each row, column, and diagonal. For younger children, start with a 3-by-3 frame on the chalkboard or provide children with a worksheet with several such frames. Figure 6–32a shows how the frames look.

Ask the children to use the numbers 1, 1, 1, 2, 2, 2, 3, 3, 3 and to put one number in each region of the frame. It does not matter how the children decide to place the numbers. Initially, do not attempt to make the square "magic," as the sums of rows, columns, and diagonals are unlikely to be the same. Figure 6–32b shows how one child placed the numbers.

Next, ask the children to add each row and write each sum at the end of the row. Then have them add each column and put each sum at the bottom of the column. Finally, have them add each diagonal and put the sums at the corners.

Talk to the children about some of their answers. Ask, "What is the largest sum you found in your square?" Expect several different answers. The largest would be 9. Ask, "What is the smallest sum you found in your square?" Again, several answers are possible. The smallest would be 3. Ask, "What number do you have the most of?" Six would be the sum found most often.

At the next stage, provide frames and ask the children to put a 1 in each row and to arrange the 1s so that no more than one 1 appears in each column. Ask the children to put a 2 in each row and to arrange the 2s so that no more than one 2 appears in each column. Then have the children put a 3 in each of the empty regions. Figure 6–32c shows one such arrangement.

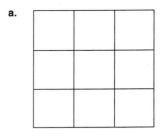

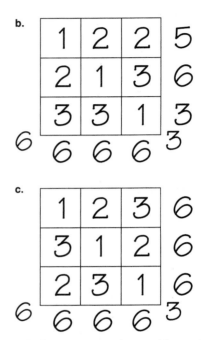

Figure 6–32 Magic squares used as problem-solving activities.

Again, ask the children to add up each row, column, and diagonal. One of two possible results will occur. All but one diagonal will add to 6, or all rows, columns, and diagonals will add to 6. Discuss what numbers a diagonal needs to add to 6. Invite the children to figure out what numbers to put in the diagonals. Complete the magic square so all of the sums are 6.

Extend magic squares by providing children with a new series of numbers to use in the square. For example, 2, 2, 2, 3, 3, 3, 4, 4, 4 can be used. This time the sum is 9. Challenge the children to put the numbers in the frame to make a magic square. Here is a possible solution using Polya's problem-solving steps.

- *Understanding the problem.* This is just like the problem we solved using 1s, 2s, and 3s, but now we are using three different numbers. The sum will be 9.

- *Devising a plan.* We will try the same plan that worked when we used smaller numbers. We will put a 2 in each row so that no more than one 2 appears in each column. Then we will do the same thing with 3 and 4. We need to make sure both diagonals add to 9 (guess and check).

- *Carrying out the plan.* When we fill in the numbers as we planned, we get a sum of 9 everywhere but in one diagonal, where we get 4 + 4 + 4, or 12. To get three of the same number that add to 9, the numbers need to be 3. So the diagonal needs to be 3 + 3 + 3. We will exchange the 4s for 3s and see if it works. It does!

- *Looking back.* We'll check again to make sure all the rows and columns and both diagonals add to 9. They do. For both the magic squares we have solved, the second of the three different numbers in the sequence fills one of the diagonals. It was 2 + 2 + 2 in the first magic square and 3 + 3 + 3 in the second magic square. We think it will be 4 + 4 + 4 in a magic square that uses 3, 3, 3, 4, 4, 4, 5, 5, 5 for its numbers. Let's try it.

Have the children name a number series, using three consecutive numbers three times each. Have the children solve the magic square.

Objective: to construct and solve problems involving addition.

2. Provide the children with a worksheet that contains several frames, each with nine numerals and an empty box at the top. Figure 6–34a illustrates one of these frames.

Ask the children to choose two numbers in the frame, add them together, and put the answer in the box at the top. Have them do the same thing for each frame on the worksheet. When the worksheet is done, the children will have made problem boxes for other children to solve.

Have the children exchange worksheets and see if they can find the pair of numbers that have the sum that equals the number on top. Instruct them to circle the two numbers. The children may check their solutions with a calculator. Figure 6–34b shows one solution. With the same set of numbers in a frame, many different problems can be made. It is also possible to have more than one solution for a single problem.

To extend this activity, have the children use subtraction instead of addition. Have them place the difference in the box at the top, with the operation sign on either side. Figure 6–34c shows an example. The circled numerals represent two numbers whose difference equals 13.

To further extend the activity, have the children determine all of the numbers for the frame as well as the solution number and the operation. You will find the problems become more difficult and challenging. Collect the solutions and display them on the bulletin board.

OBJECTIVE: to use a Bingo activity involving problem solving, addition, and subtraction.

3. Plus/Minus Bingo may be played with two players or with the two halves of a class. Each player needs a Plus/Minus Bingo card. The card shown in Figure 6–35a is for a game involving addition; that shown in Figure 6–35b, a game involving subtraction. Each addition card should be a different combination of the same numerals; subtraction cards should be similarly varied. Develop the Bingo cards from the sums and differences of numbers found in Groups A and B (See Figure 6–35c). Select the numerals in Groups A and B to match the level of the children's arithmetic abilities.

In turn, players select one numeral from Group A and one from Group B. As the numbers are called, they should be recorded on the board, on the overhead, or on paper to avoid duplications. The players use calculators or paper and pencil to add the two numbers; then they put a marker (bean or Bingo marker) on the numeral representing the sum. Four markers in a row, column, or diagonal represent a win.

To vary this activity, construct combination cards with some numerals taken from the addition card and some numerals taken from the subtraction card. Play proceeds as described above except players must announce whether they are adding or subtracting at the beginning of each turn. Because of the number of possible answers, let three markers in a row, column, or diagonal represent a win.

A C T I V I T I E S

Grades 3–5 and Grades 6–8

OBJECTIVE: to use "magic squares" for problem-solving and computation practice.

1. Begin by challenging the students to complete a 3-by-3 magic square using the numbers 1, 2, 3, 4, 5, 6, 7, 8, 9. The sum for each row, column, and diagonal of that square is 15.

When that magic square has been solved, ask the students to try another 3-by-3 magic square using the numbers 1, 3, 5, 7, 9, 11, 13, 15, 17. The sum for that magic square is 27. Clever students will be able

GOAL

LEARN HOW TO...
◆ use a model to work with integers

AS YOU...
◆ take hikes along a number line

Exploration 1

Modeling INTEGER Operations

SET UP *Work in a group of four. You will need:*
• Labsheets 3A, 3B, and 3C • scissors • three paper clips

▶ In this activity, you'll explore what happens when you move in different ways along a number line.

3 **Use Labsheets 3A and 3B.** Follow the directions on Labsheets 3A and 3B to set up a number line and build three spinners. Then follow the steps below to practice hiking on the number line. Each group member should have a turn as the hiker.

First Three members of the group spin the spinners and give the directions to the hiker in the following order.

1 Start at the number shown on the START spinner.

START
```
0  -3
2      1
3     -2
-1  0
```

2 Face the direction shown on the DIRECTION spinner.

DIRECTION

FACE THE – DIRECTION | FACE THE + DIRECTION

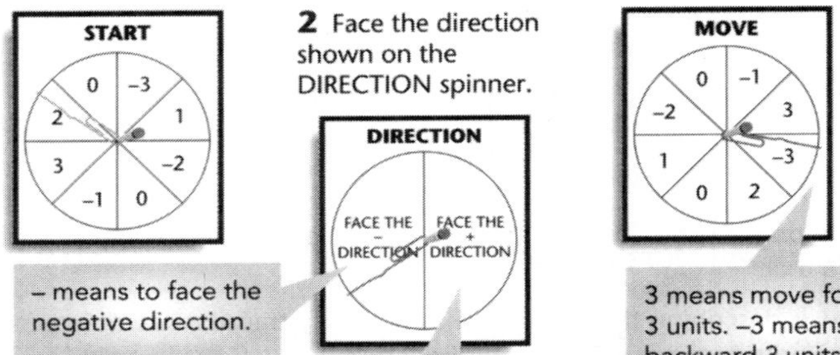

– means to face the negative direction.

+ means to face the positive direction.

3 Move in the way described on the MOVE spinner.

MOVE
```
0  -1
-2     3
1     -3
0   2
```

3 means move forward 3 units. –3 means move backward 3 units.

| NEGATIVE DIRECTION | –6 | –5 | –4 | –3 | –2 | –1 | 0 | 1 | 2 | 3 | 4 | 5 | 6 | POSITIVE DIRECTION |

Then The hiker follows the instructions and calls out the number he or she finishes at on the number line.

102 **Module 2** Search and Rescue

Figure 6–33 From Math Thematics by Rick Billstein and Jim Williamson. Copyright 2002 by McDougal Littell, a division of Houghton Mifflin Company.

MATH PROGRAM

The page in Figure 6–33 shows a group activity from the seventh-grade *Math Thematics* series to introduce operations with integers using a hike on the number line. Students in the group take turns hiking on the number line according to the directions on the spinner. They first spin one spinner to tell them a starting point between ⁻3 and 3, then spin another spinner to tell them which direction to face, and then spin a third spinner to tell them the number of units to walk either forward or backward. As they walk, this information is recorded on a Table of Hikes for later observations and discussion. Homework consists of practice and application problems that build on these ideas.

This series is designed around thematic modules that connect mathematical concepts to real-world applications. Later in this chapter, problems with integers include the use of a wind-chill index chart, gains and losses in a football game, and profits and losses for a large company. Many of the lessons actively involve students in exploring, modeling, and communicating mathematics using a variety of tools, including technology, where appropriate.

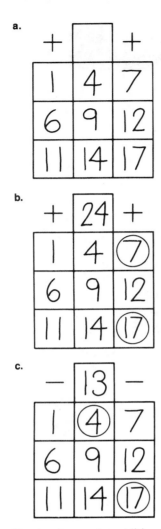

Figure 6–34 Number frames for addition and subtraction problem-solving practice.

a.

PLUS/MINUS BINGO					
63	95	55	71	39	44
35	61	77	99	50	82
91	45	88	67	52	75
86	73	37	53	97	48
57	89	46	80	41	59
43	93	84	42	69	90

b.

PLUS/MINUS BINGO					
21	48	5	57	31	12
3	10	58	23	50	37
43	63	14	54	7	25
20	35	9	65	29	52
61	39	56	16	59	13
45	11	27	67	18	41

c.

GROUP A   GROUP B

69 42   11 13 19
   31
24 56 75   15 21 17

Figure 6–35 Plus/Minus Bingo cards and number cards.

to use the solution pattern in the first magic square to guide them in solving the second magic square. Figure 6–36a and b show the completed magic squares.

There are solutions other than the ones shown, representing rotations and reflections of the square. Can you find another solution?

2. To extend work with magic squares, let the students select series of nine digits and try them in 3-by-3 magic squares. Have the students discover sequences that do not work. For example, any nine numbers in an arithmetic sequence can be successfully used in a magic square, but those in a geometric sequence seldom can be used.

Challenge students to determine what the sum of each row, column, and diagonal will be. Three times the middle number of a usable nine-number sequence is the sum for the magic square containing that sequence. Encourage students to make up magic square problems for other students.

Next, present challenge problems, such as a 5-by-5 magic square using the numbers from 1 to 25. The sum here is 65. Unless students discover a solution pattern, this is difficult to solve.

Try a 4-by-4 magic square, using the numbers 1 to 16. The sum is 34. A partially completed 4-by-4 magic square is shown in Figure 6–36c. Sometimes, providing partial solutions is an incentive for students who otherwise might not seek a solution.

OBJECTIVE: to use problem-solving skills in an addition and subtraction context.

3. The guidelines for this activity are simple. Present to the students a format for addition or subtraction with nine empty regions, as in Figure 6–37a. Explain that the object is to put each of the numbers from 1 to 9 in one of the regions so the correct sum results. Figure 6–37b shows a solution

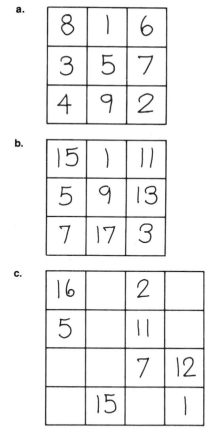

Figure 6–36 Magic squares for problem-solving and computation practice.

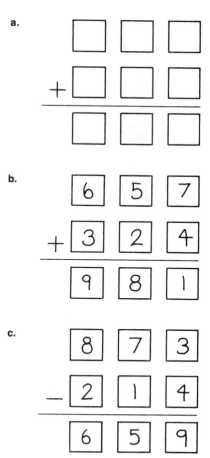

Figure 6–37 Using nine regions for addition and subtraction problem solving.

to the problem; Figure 6–37c is a solution to the corresponding subtraction problem.

A number of solutions are possible for both the addition and the subtraction problem. To encourage students, begin a collection on a bulletin board or chalkboard of the different solutions. Have the students look for patterns to help them find solutions. For example, if the three digits in the sum add to 18, the other digits can be arranged in the addends to solve the problem. On the board, outline an area in which to place nonsolutions. Nonsolutions often provide insight to help solve the problem.

ORGANIZING FOR ADDITION AND SUBTRACTION TLC

Organizing for teaching, learning, and curriculum for addition and subtraction is not significantly different from organizing for teaching, learning, and curriculum for multiplication and division. To avoid repetition, we present the teaching, learning, and curriculum discussion for all four basic operations in the Organizing for TLC section in Chapter 7.

COMMUNICATING LEARNING OF ADDITION AND SUBTRACTION CONCEPTS

For students to communicate in a variety of ways as they explore the concepts of addition and subtraction is an integral part of learning these topics. The discussion of communication for addition and subtraction does not differ from the same discussion for multiplication and division. To avoid repetition, we again present the discussion of communication in the Communicating section in Chapter 7.

CONNECTING AND REPRESENTING ADDITION AND SUBTRACTION LEARNING

The students in Mr. Thompson's second-grade class were sitting on the carpet as Mr. T, as the children called him, read the poem "Smart" from *Where the Sidewalk Ends* by Shel Silverstein (1974).

He began,

"My dad gave me one dollar bill

'Cause I'm his smartest son,

And I swapped it for two shiny quarters

'Cause two is more than one!"

As the poem continued, the students chuckled and laughed and made an occasional comment about the coin trading that takes place. The two quarters are traded for three dimes, the three dimes for four nickels, and, finally, the four nickels for five pennies. In the final stanza, the boy's father gets red in the face and shakes his head. Mr. T asked the students to return to their desks and in their math journals explain whether the father was happy (as the boy thought) or sad and why they thought so.

Following this writing activity, Mr. Thompson read *Alexander, Who Used to Be Rich Last Sunday* by Viorst (1978). In this story, Alexander is given a dollar. The story tells how he is parted from his money through a series of events in his life. It is a humorous account of how money disappears. After the story was read, the class discussed the events leading to Alexander losing his dollar. And they were challenged to compare Alexander's plight with that of the son in "Smart." Mr. Thompson asked, "How were the stories alike and how were they different? How did each boy feel at the end of their respective stories? What are other ways that cause money to slip away from us?" Many students participated in the discussion.

The students in Ms. Robinson's fifth-grade class worked together in cooperative groups to prepare a menu for a Thanksgiving dinner. Each group prepared its own menu. After the menus were finished, lists of the ingredients were made and estimates of individual ingredients and the total cost of the food were made. Next, the class took a trip to a local grocery store to price the items that were needed to prepare their menus. When the students returned they wrote about their menus and how the actual cost for the ingredients compared with their estimates.

In Ms. Collin's eighth-grade class the students participated in a holiday extravaganza gift-buying simulation. Each student had up to $250 to spend for five gifts. The students brought department store merchandise catalogs and used them to "purchase" gifts for friends and members of their families. After perusing the catalogs and deciding on their purchases, the students completed a catalog order form, wrote checks to "pay" for their purchases, and balanced their checkbooks.

These activities are intended to involve students in applications of adding and subtracting in a context that helps show how mathematics is connected with and represented in a student's daily life. Notice that using the Silverstein poem and the Viorst story helps connect mathematics with literature. There are excellent sources that suggest how topics in mathematics are integrated with children's literature and how teachers may use children's literature to enrich quantitative and visual thinking. Several are listed in the bibliography at the end of this and other chapters of this book.

This is one way that connections and representations are made between the mathematics that students are learning and other aspects of school and daily life. Another powerful way to make connections is to integrate math with other school subjects. *Math Excursions #2* (Burk et al., 1991) introduces a set of clever integrated units for primary students. One such unit is "The Popcorn Party," in which students plan and put on a popcorn party for up to 100 people. As students work through the unit, they perform a variety of mathematical tasks and include work in language arts, science, and social studies. For students to see how mathematical connections and representations are made helps them to better understand how mathematics is an integral part of their lives.

ASSESSING LEARNING OF ADDITION AND SUBTRACTION

Most of the addition and subtraction concepts and skills children learn have been presented by the time children finish the third grade. This is not to say that all children are fluent in addition and subtraction when they enter the fourth or even fifth grade.

What is a teacher to do in such cases? Individual or small group instruction is necessary. You will need to determine why there is an inability to add or subtract. Is it because the student does not know what addition or subtraction is (concept)? Does the student not know the basic addition or subtraction combinations (skill)? Could it be that the student cannot perform an algorithm (skill)? Does the student lack interest because of past failure with addition and subtraction (affect)? Are assignments with too many problems causing discouragement (affect)? Does the student bring to school a negative attitude about school work and achievement (affect)?

There are many ways addition and subtraction learning is assessed. If students are given the opportunity to construct and discuss their own algorithms, then assessment may be based, in part, on the reasoning that went into constructing the algorithm and the validity of the algorithm. Of course, mathematics textbooks and supplemental materials accompanying the textbooks offer options for assessment. Chapter pretests and posttests, mid-chapter checkups, and unit tests are common in math texts. Such tests provide information about how children add and subtract relative to the material contained in the chapter. Have the students collect samples of their work in their math portfolio (see Chapter 3) so progress is documented over the course of a school term.

While testing programs are well established for addition and subtraction, diagnostic teaching techniques are not so well established. Diagnostic procedures require teacher observations of children's daily work to pinpoint error patterns that lead to low computational success. Teachers need to talk with students and have them discuss their thinking processes. Too often, children who make mistakes are told to redo a problem or to work more problems of the same type, but no one determines the source of the errors. Reworking incorrect problems may reinforce incorrect methods. Discover the cause of the problem to correct the process, not just the result.

Reasons that a child is making mistakes may include

1. *Social, physical, or emotional problems.* Children may be hampered in cognitive skills by noncognitive problems such as a short attention span, hunger, fear of reprisal for getting the incorrect answer or not completing the work, or the desire to be "like everyone else." Ask for information about such children from the parents, previous teachers, or behavior specialists. Those who have worked with a particular youngster in the past may be able to offer advice about how to assist the youngster. Make your own observations. If you are the first to observe this behavior, report your concern to a behavior specialist, resource teacher, or principal. Generally, extra time, care, and patience are necessary to provide the environment in which mathematical growth can take place.

2. *Lack of prerequisite skills or appropriate state of development.* Children may not be ready to learn a particular concept because they have not mastered previous skills or because they have not reached the appropriate developmental stage. Children may not be ready to learn missing addends, the inverse of addition, because they have not yet reached that stage of development and cannot comprehend the reversibility concept.

   By having children explain their thinking as they work, you will be able to pinpoint where their skills fail them. Reteach faulty prerequisite skills to students having difficulty. Give additional time and materials to children who are developmentally unready to learn.

3. *Weak knowledge of basic combinations.* This is a common diagnosis. For example, children may know how to perform an addition algorithm but be unable to recall basic addition combinations. Children are then frustrated and unmotivated to even try. You can spot children with a weak command of basic combinations by reviewing their paper-and-pencil work, administering combination tests, and listening to them as they explain how they perform operations.

   Work with children who need help. Provide activities that assist memorization of basic combinations. Also, check to make sure children understand the concept of the operation for which they are practicing skills. The children may need to return to physical materials to build necessary foundations.

4. *Incorrect or incomplete algorithm.* Teacher diagnosis is particularly important in this area. To help diagnose incorrect algorithms, have children show you their work and explain how they arrived at a particular solution. Their thinking is usually revealing. Children tend to make systematic errors. For example, in subtraction, a common error is subtracting the smaller digit from the larger digit regardless of whether it is the minuend or subtrahend. VanLehn (1983) describes many of these faulty procedures, called **bugs.**

   Remember, algorithms created by children are very often valid, whereas those memorized by rote may not be valid. Pinpoint the source of the error; have the children reconstruct the algorithm with physical models, and discuss their procedures.

5. *Wrong operation.* Children may use the wrong operation because they have misread the operation sign or because they have chosen the wrong operation in solving a word problem. The latter error is more serious. Continue the work with word problems. Discuss word problems with children having difficulty and encourage them to explain the operation to perform even if they do not work the problem. Practical situations and problems written by the children help children having difficulty understand the appropriate operations to use.

Once children's strengths and weaknesses have been diagnosed, group the children for at least part of their instructional time according to this diagnosis. At other times, let children with strong skills in a particular area help children with weaker skills; use cooperative learning groups; teach the class as a whole group or work with individuals. When grouping, keep the following points in mind:

- *Keep the groups flexible.* Do not group in October and expect to have the same groups in May. Groups should change as skills and concepts change.
- *Avoid labeling children.* Even if they are called eagles and seahawks, children know if the teacher thinks of them as slow and fast.
- *Avoid giving one group busy work while working with another group.* Let groups work independently with materials, games, a computer, the math text, or challenging problems, but make sure the tasks are meaningful.

- *Have interesting tasks appropriate to the level of the group.* Each group may have different material, but all materials should be carefully thought out. What may be uninteresting for one group may be just what another group needs.

Your ability to diagnose the cause or causes of difficulty and to remediate the difficulty depends on your own familiarity with mathematics, the learning process, and your students. You will need patience. The students will need support and encouragement.

Children's activities must seem worth doing for them to gain the most. Fourth graders should be convinced that they are not doing second- or third-grade work. To avoid boredom, try to choose aids or algorithms that are new to the child. Encourage the students to share their own algorithms with others. Construct an algorithm bulletin board to display the students' original algorithms. Children who have previously failed may be visual/spatial or bodily/kinesthetic learners, so be sure to include experiences for visualizing and manipulating. Allow children to use calculators so that they may learn more advanced mathematics and not always be frustrated by their weaknesses with basic combinations. Finally, be willing to set aside the regular textbook assignments that can pile up and, over time, overwhelm the slow, discouraged students.

SOMETHING FOR EVERYONE

Teaching operations with whole numbers and integers requires attention to various learning modes. The styles of children learning addition and subtraction do not differ appreciably from the styles of children learning multiplication and division. To avoid repetition, we present a discussion of learning modes for all four basic operations in the Something for Everyone section at the end of Chapter 7.

FOR YOU AS A TEACHER: IDEAS FOR DISCUSSION AND YOUR PROFESSIONAL PORTFOLIO

This section is intended to provide you the opportunity to read, write, and reflect on key elements of this chapter. We list several discussion ideas. We hope that one or more of these ideas will prove interesting to you and that you will choose to investigate and write about the ideas. The results of your work should be considered as part of your professional portfolio. You might consider these two questions as guides for your writing: "What does the material in this chapter mean for you as a teacher?" or "How can what you are reading be translated into a teaching practice for you as a teacher?"

DISCUSSION IDEAS

1. Compare the way you learned addition and subtraction, both concepts and skills, with the discussion and activities presented in Chapter 6.

2. Read the "Guidelines for Choosing and/or Inventing Word Problems" section of Kamii's text, *Young Children Reinvent Arithmetic* (2000, pp. 133–140). Using the guidelines, begin to develop an original collection of word problems for your own classroom.

3. Review the section on Basic Addition and Subtraction Combinations. Then consider the table of basic addition combinations, Table 6–1, and discuss how you can help children remember the addition combinations by reducing the total number of combinations needed to be memorized. You may start by using some of the properties of addition.

4. Develop an alternative algorithm for subtracting 45 − 18, one that is new to you and not mentioned in the text. Describe your algorithm to someone else to see if that person can understand how to perform it.

5. Choose either Silverstein's poem "Smart" from *Where the Sidewalk Ends* (1974) or Viorst's story *Alexander, Who Used to Be Rich Last Sunday* (1978) and read it. Then, write a letter to either the boy or Alexander and discuss how things might have been made to come out more profitably.

ADDITIONAL RESOURCES

REFERENCES

Abrohms, Alison, *Literature-Based Math Activities: An Integrated Approach*. New York: Scholastic Professional Books, 1992.

Ashlock, Robert B., *Error Patterns in Computation: Using Error Patterns to Improve Instruction*. Saddle River, NJ: Merrill/Prentice Hall, 2002.

Braddon, Kathryn L., Nancy J. Hall, and Dale Taylor, *Math through Children's Literature: Making the NCTM Standards Come Alive*. Englewood, CO: Teacher Ideas Press, 1993.

Browning, Christine A., and Channell, Dwayne, *Explorations: Graphing Calculator Activities for Enriching Middle School Mathematics*. Austin, TX: Texas Instruments, 1997.

Burk, Donna, Allyn Snider, and Paula Symonds, *Math Excursions K*. Portsmouth, NH: Heinemann, 1993.

———, *Math Excursions 2*. Portsmouth, NH: Heinemann, 1991.

Burns, Marilyn, *Math and Literature (K–3)*. Sausalito, CA: Math Solutions Publications, 1995.

Burton, Grace M., Ann Mills, Carolyn Lennon, and Cynthia Parker, *Number Sense and Operations*. Reston, VA: National Council of Teachers of Mathematics, 1993.

Carpenter, Thomas P., James M. Moser, and Thomas A. Romberg, eds., *Addition and Subtraction: A Cognitive Perspective*. Hillsdale, NJ: Erlbaum, 1982.

Davidson, Jessica, *Idea Book for Cuisenaire Rods at the Primary Level*. White Plains, NY: Cuisenaire Co. of America, 1977.

Greenleaf, Benjamin, *A Mental Arithmetic. Upon the Inductive Plan; Being an Advanced Intellectual Course, Designed for Schools and Academies*. Boston: Robert S. Davis, 1859.

Griffiths, Rachel, and Margaret Clyne, *Books You Can Count On*. Portsmouth, NH: Heinemann, 1988.

Jones, Graham, and Roger Day, *Algebra, Data, and Probability Explorations for Middle School: A Graphics Calculator Approach*. Menlo Park, CA: Seymour, 1997.

Kamii, Constance, with Leslie Baker Housman, *Young Children Reinvent Arithmetic*. New York: Teachers College Press, 2000.

Kolakowski, Jane Steffen, *Linking Math with Literature*. Greensboro, NC: Carson-Dellosa, 1992.

National Council of Teachers of Mathematics, *Computational Alternatives for the Twenty-first Century*. Reston, VA: NCTM, 1994.

———, *Principles and Standards for School Mathematics*. Reston, VA: NCTM, 2000.

Reys, Barbara J., "Mental Computation," *Arithmetic Teacher*, 32, no. 6 (February 1985), 43–46.

———, "Teaching Computational Estimation: Concepts and Strategies," in *Estimation and Mental Computation*, ed. Harold L. Schoen and Marilyn J. Qweng. Reston, VA: National Council of Teachers of Mathematics, 1986.

Reys, Robert, and Nobuhiko Nohda, eds., *Computational Alternatives for the Twenty-first Century: Cross-Cultural Perspectives from Japan and the United States*. Reston, VA: National Council of Teachers of Mathematics, 1994.

Satariano, Patricia, *Storytime Mathtime: Math Exploration in Children's Literature*. Palo Alto, CA.: Dale Seymour, 1994.

Schielack, Jane F., and Dinah Chancellor, *Uncovering Mathematics with Manipulatives and Calculators: Level 1*. Dallas, TX: Texas Instruments, 1995.

Schoen, Harold L., and Marilyn J. Zweng, *Estimation and Mental Computation*. Reston, VA: National Council of Teachers of Mathematics, 1986.

Sheffield, Stephanie, *Math and Literature (K–3) Book Two*. Sausalito, CA: Math Solutions Publications, 1995.

Sparrow, Len, and Paul Swam, *Learning Math with Calculators: Math Activities for Grades 3–8*. Sausalito, CA: Math Solutions Publications, 2001.

Thiessen, Diane, and Margaret Matthias, eds., *The Wonderful World of Mathematics*. Reston, VA: National Council of Teachers of Mathematics, 1992.

VanLehn, Kurt, "On the Representation of Procedures in Repair Theory," in *The Development of Mathematical Thinking*, ed. Herbert P. Ginsburg. New York: Academic Press, 1983.

Wakefield, Alice P., *Early Childhood Number Games: Teachers Reinvent Math Instruction*. Boston: Allyn & Bacon, 1998.

Whitin, David J., and Sandra Wilde, *Read Any Good Math Lately?* Portsmouth, NH: Heinemann, 1992.

Williams, Susan, and George W. Bright, *Investigating Mathematics with Calculators in the Middle Grades: Activities with the Math Explorer and Explorer Plus Calculators*. Dallas, TX: Texas Instruments, 1998.

CHILDREN'S LITERATURE

Bang, Molly, *Ten, Nine, Eight*. New York: Greenwillow, 1983.

Silverstein, Shel, *Where the Sidewalk Ends*. New York: HarperCollins, 1974.

Thaler, Mike, *Seven Little Hippos*. New York: Simon & Schuster, 1991.

Vaughan, Marcia, *Dorobō the Dangerous*. Morristown, NJ: Silver Burdett Press, 1955.

Viorst, Judith, *Alexander, Who Used to Be Rich Last Sunday*. New York: Aladdin, 1978.

TECHNOLOGY

Edmark, *Mighty Math Carnival*. Novato, CA: Riverdeep Interactive Learning, 1996. (software)

———, *Mighty Math Number Heroes*. Novato, CA: Riverdeep Interactive Learning, 1996. (software)

Sunburst, *How the West Was One + Three × Four*. Pleasantville, NY: Sunburst Communications, 1996. (software)

Seiler, Bonnie A., *The Great Signed Number Race: How Integers Won the West*. Pleasantville, NY: Sunburst Communications, 1997. (software)

The Learning Company, *Treasure MathStorm!* Novato, CA: Riverdeep Interactive Learning, 1993. (software)

Tom Snyder Productions, *Fizz & Martina's Math Adventures*. Watertown, MA: Tom Synder Productions, 1999. (video kit)

WEBLINKS

Weblink 6–1: First-grade number stories from the University of Chicago School Mathematics Project. http://everydaymath.uchicago.edu/students/1stgrademuseum.shtml

Weblink 6–2: NCTM Illumination series Do It with Dominoes. http://illuminations.nctm.org/lessonplans/prek-2/dominoes/index.html#11

Weblink 6–3: NCTM Illumination series Begin with Buttons. http://illuminations.nctm.org/lessonplans/prek-2/begin_with_buttons/index.html

Additional Weblink

Weblink 6–4: A rich resource for math teaching ideas from PBS. http://www.pbs.org/teachersource/math.html

TEACHING AND LEARNING MULTIPLICATION AND DIVISION OF WHOLE NUMBERS AND INTEGERS

GUIDING QUESTIONS

As you read the following pages, consider these guiding questions:

1. How are multiplication and division used in activities of daily life?
2. What is a possible sequence of teaching the concepts and skills of multiplication and division?
3. What are several embodiments for presenting the concepts of multiplication and division?
4. What are some different activities to help children memorize the basic multiplication and division combinations?

NCTM Principles and Standards for School Mathematics

Number and Operations

Instructional programs from prekindergarten through grade 12 should enable all students to:

Understand meanings of operations and how they relate to one another

Pre-K to 2

• understand situations that entail multiplication and division, such as equal groupings of objects and sharing equally.

Grades 3–5

• understand various meanings of multiplication and division;

• understand the effects of multiplying and dividing whole numbers;

• identify and use relationships between operations, such as division as the inverse of multiplication, to solve problems;

• understand and use properties of operations, such as the distributivity of multiplication over addition.

Grades 6–8

• understand the meaning and effects of arithmetic operations with integers;

• use the associative and commutative properties of addition and multiplication and the distributive property of multiplication over addition to simplify computations with integers.

NCTM (2000), pp. 78, 148, 214. Reprinted by permission.

Compute fluently and make reasonable estimates

Pre-K to 2

• use a variety of methods and tools to compute, including objects, mental computation, estimation, paper and pencil, and calculators.

Grades 3–5

• develop fluency with basic number combinations for multiplication and division and use these combinations to mentally compute related problems, such as 30×50;

• develop fluency in adding, subtracting, multiplying, and dividing whole numbers;

• develop and use strategies to estimate the results of whole-number computations and to judge the reasonableness of such results;

• select appropriate methods and tools for computing with whole numbers from among mental computation, estimation, calculators, and paper and pencil according to the context and nature of the computation and use the selected method or tool.

Grades 6–8

• develop and analyze algorithms for computing with integers and develop fluency in their use.

My Math Journal

The representation below may be used to model 13 × 14. How can you use a representation such as this to mentally multiply any two numbers between 10 and 20? Write a description below that you could use to teach a 10-year-old to become proficient at this mental multiplication. Be sure to explain all of your thinking.

REFLECTIONS AND REFINEMENT: After you have completed this task, compare your work with that of some of your classmates. How did your response differ from those of others? Write what you have found here.

Like addition and subtraction, multiplication and division are commonly used in our daily lives. From purchasing multiple items such as camera film and bedding plants to determining how many cookies and brownies are necessary for a group of children, these operations serve us well. Studying multiplication and division as part of the school mathematics curriculum in the early and middle grades prepares students to be productive, thoughtful citizens. It also prepares them to continue their study of mathematics. Once students make sense of multiplication and division, along with addition and subtraction, and become fluent in their use, they can more easily engage in challenging mathematical work.

Computation, however, is seldom performed with pencil and paper except in school. Calculators or computers do the work, or the computation is performed mentally. The efficiency and accuracy of electronic computation has been a convincing argument for its use. Children growing up in a time of electronic computation need to be skillful in estimation and mental calculation. They need to know what information a problem is presenting and what operations are required to solve that problem. Again, students should have the opportunity to decide whether to use paper and pencil, mental calculation, estimation, or a calculator.

> The teacher plays an important role in helping students develop and select an appropriate computational tool (calculator, paper-and-pencil algorithm, or mental strategy). (NCTM, 2000, p. 156)

As with addition and subtraction, teaching multiplication and division begins well before children actually start memorizing the basic combinations, which are, for multiplication, the whole number products from 0×0 to 9×9. As children informally begin to manipulate objects and count, they develop relationships and ideas associated with the concept of number. They are also establishing the foundations for learning the concepts of multiplication and division. The activities for learning the concepts of addition and subtraction mentioned in Chapter 6 are useful for learning the concepts of multiplication and division as well. The skills of adding and subtracting are important prerequisites for performing the multiplication and division algorithms.

Teachers are responsible for determining if children are developing skills that provide a basis for multiplication and division. Word problems help to check children's thinking. For example, "Lori, Julie, and Greg decided to pick clover for a bouquet. Each of them picked four clovers. How many clovers were there altogether? Young children are able to solve such problems using a variety of procedures that emerge from their personal logic. Children with well-developed counting abilities will be able to count out the answer by **counting all,** or using fingers or objects. Some children may **skip count;** for example, count by saying, "four, eight, twelve." Other children may count in their heads. Opportunities to count and skip count should be provided as part of the mathematics program. For children having difficulty, provide practice in grouping objects and counting. Be sure to allow students time to discuss how they solved their problems and encourage questions to those who are explaining.

The physical models that help children develop understanding and skill with multiplication and division include attribute materials, base ten blocks, Cuisenaire rods, beans, and cubes. Collections of objects such as milk jug caps, shell-shaped macaroni, tiles, and buttons are useful in the early stages of learning about operations. Calculators are helpful for learning multiplication and division. Children should be active as they learn about these operations.

MAKING SENSE OF MULTIPLICATION AND DIVISION CONCEPTS

Children should experience multiplication and division in the early grades. Number stories and word problems provide the opportunity for them to begin thinking about and making sense of multiplication and division. Multiplication word problems are initially presented until children can easily solve them. Then, division word problems are introduced. Children use a variety of approaches to solve the word problems, often inventing novel solutions. Physical objects should be available for children to use.

> In prekindergarten through grade 2, students should also begin to develop an understanding of the concepts of multiplication and division. (NCTM, 2000, p. 84)

Later, we move away from concrete experiences with sets of objects to the pictorial and abstract. Children learn that *multiplication* is renaming a pair of numbers by a single equivalent number. For example, the pair (3, 6) is associated with 18 under the operation of multiplication. Learning how multiplication works is learning the concept of multiplication. Learning that $3 \times 6 = 18$ is learning a basic multiplication combination, a skill that is dealt with later.

Each of the following sections on multiplication, division, and properties of multiplication and division present activities for helping students make sense of concepts and alternative algorithms.

Making Sense of Multiplication Concepts and Alternative Algorithms

Sorting, classifying by two or more attributes, and arriving at reversibility of thought are necessary in order for children to understand multiplication and division. Sorting and classifying are presented in Chapter 13. Diagrams are used to assist children using attribute blocks in their sorting. Eventually, children are challenged to show ways of sorting using two attributes simultaneously, such as red and rectangular. **Reversibility of thought** occurs when children construct the knowledge that $2 \times 3 = 6$ also implies that $6 \div 2 = 3$. Achieving reversibility of thought means that children can understand the processes of doing and undoing exemplified in the inverse operations of multiplication and division.

With buttons or cubes, let children construct two groups of three and indicate that there are a total of six as in Figure 7–1a. If, at the same time, the children can begin with a group of six and separate it into two equivalent collections (Figure 7–1b), reversibility of thought is illustrated. Children need a variety of grouping experiences when multiplication and division are being introduced.

Have children continue to respond to number stories as they did while learning addition and subtraction. For example, "Jody is having a birthday party. She has invited six of her friends. She wants to play a game that requires five stickers for each player. How many stickers does she need for the game?" Some children will add 5 plus 5 plus 5 plus 5 plus 5 plus 5 plus 5 or count by 5s. Others will know the answer without counting. Still others will draw and count the stickers to find the answer. The counting or adding strategies typically precede the response, "7 times 5." Expect some discussion about how many groups of stickers are needed at the party.

The operation presented initially to serve as a basis for understanding multiplication joins multiple sets of equal size. Arithmetically, it involves adding several numbers of equal size to determine a product of two factors. For example, 3×4 may be thought of as three groups of four. The product, 12, can be determined by $4 + 4 + 4$. When young children participate in the following activity, they tend to count or use repeated addition to determine the answer. Counting and repeated addition are valuable models for multiplication. They are among the easiest approaches for young children to use and understand.

A C T I V I T I E S

Pre-Kindergarten – Grade 2

OBJECTIVE: to use repeated addition as a model for multiplication.

1. Select a favorite flower such as a daffodil and display it. The flower may be real, artificial, or in a photograph. Ask the children how many petals are on a daffodil. If they are unable to tell or do not know, let them count the petals. Respond, "Yes, there are six petals on a daffodil. Here is another daffodil. How many petals are there on two daffodils?" The students may count the additional six petals, they may add 6 plus 6, or they may seem to just know that 2 sixes are 12. Ask, "How many petals would I have if there were three daffodils?" Continue this line of questioning for as long as it is fairly easy for the children to determine an answer. Encourage the children to discuss how they found their answers.

As a variation of this activity, display other flowers with different numbers of petals. The NCTM has published an attractive book entitled *I Can Count the Petals of a Flower*, by John Wahl and Stacey Wahl (1977). It provides many examples of flowers with varying numbers of petals. Garden catalogs usually picture many varieties of flowers. The children may have favorite flowers they would like to talk about. Children enjoy not only talking about flowers but also drawing and coloring them. A colorful display can result from a discussion that includes the foundations of multiplication.

2. You may extend the above activity by using materials that are found in small groups. Flashlight batteries are commonly found in groups of two, four, and eight. Some pencils are packaged in pairs or dozens. Shoes and gloves come in pairs. Tennis balls are usually packaged in threes, as in Figure 7–2. Some soaps are found in groups of four. These examples and others that children will name provide opportunities to skip count and use equal addends.

You may also find children's books that suggest counting by various numbers or illustrate objects

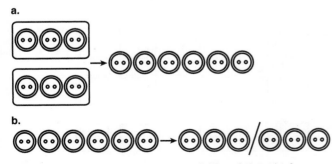

Figure 7–1 Buttons showing reversibility of thought for multiplication and division.

Figure 7–2 Tennis balls packaged in threes.

that come in various sized collections. For example, *How Many Feet in the Bed,* by Hamm (1991) tells a humorous story of a family climbing in bed with father and then climbing out and how the number of feet are counted forward and backward. Another book, *What Comes in 2s, 3s, & 4s?* by Aker (1990) describes and illustrates many common objects that are found in groupings of 2, 3, and 4. Both help to develop the skip counting that is important in learning multiplication and division.

OBJECTIVE: to use groups and number of objects in each group to model multiplication

3. Use children's experiences to discuss multiplication. For example, "Let's name some animals". Responses might include dog, cat, bird, spider, ant, tiger, and buffalo. Pick examples that the children have mentioned to make word problems. "There are three ants. Ants have six legs. How many legs are there altogether?" or "Ants have six legs. We have three ants. How many legs are there altogether?" Note that three (ants) represents the number of "groups" and six (legs) represents the number in each group. Invite the children to pick an animal, draw a picture of it, and write a multiplication question about the animal. Students may pick any number of attributes of the animal to write about (eyes, tails, ears, teeth, as well as legs).

Each Orange Had 8 Slices is a counting book by Paul Giganti, Jr. (1992) and another excellent way to introduce multiplication. This book has statements with matching drawings, such as "On my way to the playground I saw 3 red flowers. Each red flower had 6 pretty petals. Each petal had 2 tiny black bugs. How many red flowers were there? How many pretty petals were there? How many tiny black bugs were there in all?" (Giganti, 1992, p. 1). There are many other examples from children's lives, including children on tricycles, circus clowns with balloons, ducks in a zoo, and, of course, the orange slices. Asking children to write their own pages with accompanying drawings to add to this book would be a good way to develop a deeper number sense.

Modeling multiplication problems can help students make sense of multiplication. A question like "How many toes are found on four children?" will suggest to students different ways to represent the question. Tiles or other objects representing toes may be laid out. Drawings of toes may be made. Tally marks may be made on paper. Some students may count by 10s or add 10s. Other students may count on their fingers. As children begin to discover the meaning of multiplication, physical and mental models will serve to remind them of its meaning. Rectangular arrays are models that may be introduced to assist in visualizing multiplication. These are also a good introduction to finding the area of a rectangle. While these are not better models than those invented by children, they are likely to be somewhat different. The next two activities use rectangular arrays to help children make sense of multiplication.

Grades 3–5

OBJECTIVE: to use rectangular arrays as models for multiplication.

1. Provide children with objects such as cubes, washers, or tiles. Ask the children to make a row with seven tiles. Invite the students to tell a number story that is illustrated by the tiles. For example, a student might suggest that each tile is a day of the week. The first tile is Monday, the second tile is Tuesday, and so on. Another student might say that the tiles represent seven children at ballet practice. Yet another student might indicate that the tiles are trading cards. Continue the story of one of the students. "If the tiles represent the days of the week and you have a chore to do each day, how would you use your tiles to show all of your chores for three weeks?" There will likely be several representations of three weeks. While accepting all of the responses, guide the students to show the weeks with seven tiles in one row, seven in the second row, and seven tiles in the third row (Figure 7–3). Discuss with the students how this representation shows three weeks, each with seven days, and the fact that they have made 3 groups of 7 tiles; there are 3 tiles along one side and 7 tiles along

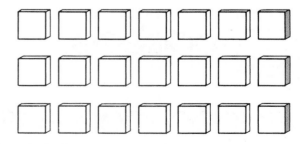

Figure 7–3 Rectangular array of tiles as a model for multiplication.

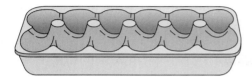

Figure 7–4 Egg carton used as a rectangular array.

Figure 7–5 An array used to help symbolize multiplication.

the other. The children can describe their arrangement as "3 by 7." Ask, "How many tiles are there altogether? Let's count them." There are 21 tiles.

Now, ask the children to make a similar pattern of tiles but using different numbers. This time they should think of a number story that is illustrated by the array that they have made. When the arrays are finished, have the children share the story that they thought of for their array. Next, have the students make another array with different numbers, draw the array on paper, and write the number story for the array on the paper.

2. Collect items that are configured in arrays—for example, an egg carton, a muffin tin, a plastic carrier for soda cans, pudding pack, and so on. Make a display of them. Invite the children to draw pictures of three of the containers and make up word problems represented by the arrays. Encourage the students to think beyond the items that originally were packaged or "belonged" to the container. For example, with the egg carton in the configuration shown in Figure 7–4, the story might be "For January, February, March, April, May, and June I have two toys I can choose to play with each month. How many toys can I choose altogether?"

The array model may be used later as a pictorial model for multiplication. The pictorial array in Figure 7–5 shows a 3-by-6 group, or the product 3 times 6. This model works particularly well when children begin to develop skill with basic multiplication combinations.

Arrays may be read symbolically. In Figure 7–5, the number of rows determines the first factor and the number in each row determines the second factor. The product is determined by counting the number of regions. This example represents 3 times 6 equals 18, or $3 \times 6 = 18$.

Before long, children easily use the symbols for multiplication. Introduce the symbols in a multiplication sentence, $3 \times 6 = 18$, and in the vertical form

$$
\begin{array}{r}
6 \\
\times 3 \\
\hline
18
\end{array}
$$

Help the children read these sentences and become familiar with them.

Children who have had extensive experience with the Cuisenaire rods can extend their work with the rods to help make sense of multiplication. Capitalizing on the idea of repeated addition, students may begin by finding the value of three light green rods and then finding the single rod that will match this train. Thus, a blue rod is equivalent to three light-green rods.

In the beginning stages of learning how to multiply with the Cuisenaire rods, do not assign number values to the rods. Only when the concept of multiplication has been presented and children are comfortable with the manipulation and language associated with the concept is it time to introduce the symbolism of multiplication. The transition from concrete to abstract requires that the models and symbols be used simultaneously.

A C T I V I T I E S

Grades 3–5

OBJECTIVE: to use Cuisenaire rods as a model for multiplication.

1. Cross two rods that are to be multiplied, one on top of the other, as illustrated in Figure 7–6a. Here, we have a purple rod on top of a dark-green rod. It is read from the bottom up, "dark green times purple."

To perform the multiplication, ask the children to place dark-green rods side by side until the purple rod reaches from one edge of the dark-green rods to the other. This is shown in Figure 7–6b. Then, place the dark-green rods end to end in a train (Figure 7–7). Finally, place two orange rods and a purple rod beside this train to show its value. Thus, dark green times purple equals two orange plus purple.

As this model is shared with students, encourage discussion to help clarify any questions that may arise. Each step in the process needs to be clearly presented and discussed so it makes sense to the children. Encourage the children to relate this model to finding the area of a rectangle with the length and width of the two Cuisenaire rods and then to relate this to repeated addition.

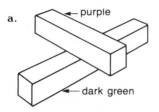

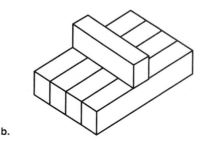

Figure 7–6 Cuisenaire rods illustrating dark green times purple.

OBJECTIVE: to introduce the symbolism of multiplication.

2. With the Cuisenaire rods, establish a value for the white rod (again, be careful not to declare 1 the permanent value of white). "If the white rod equals 1, what is the value of yellow? (5) What is the value of light green? (3) A tower of yellow and light-green rods is 5 times 3 (yellow times light green) and is equal to 15 (orange plus yellow)." One effective way to determine the product is to put the rods side by side on centimeter grid paper, outline the rods, and count the number of centimeter squares that are contained in the outline. This technique uses the array model discussed earlier. Additional time and experience with the rods will be needed to allow children to be at ease in symbolizing the rod values.

There are many ways in which children make sense of multiplication. Besides activities that help advance the concept of multiplication, there are other learning situations that assist children in establishing numerical relationships. The classroom routines mentioned in Chapter 6 may also be used to present multiplication and division. Those include distributing snacks, taking and recording lunch counts, discussing the calendar, voting during class meetings, telling time, and counting money. Children's explanations and discussions help teachers see how they are constructing their mathematical knowledge. As a student explains a process or a procedure, the personal logic of the student emerges. Often these are alternative processes or algorithms; that is, they are processes unique to the individual giving the explanation. Again, this type of thinking should be embraced.

The concept of multiplication has been presented using several embodiments. Groups containing the same number of objects were joined in some way. Numbers were then attached to the models to assist children in discovering the relationship between joining sets and multiplying numbers. We continue by introducing the concept of division in a similar manner.

Making Sense of Division Concepts and Alternative Algorithms

Teaching the concept of division is similar to teaching the concept of multiplication. The materials are the same, as is the approach. The concept, however, is different. We believe that if children are taught the concepts of multiplication and division at nearly the same time, the process of learning division becomes easier; the fact that one operation is the inverse of the other can more readily be seen. The operations can be directly compared and the differences noted.

The prerequisites for division are the same as those for multiplication. For the children who cannot yet sort objects by two or more attributes simultaneously and for those who have not achieved reversibility of thought, we must provide additional materials, time, and encouragement.

Continue to introduce number stories. For example, "Mr. Thompson's class of 29 children will be working in the plant sale booth for the school's spring fair. Five children at a time can work each shift in the booth. How many shifts can Mr. Thompson's class volunteer to work?" Students will present a variety of solutions. Some children will start with 29 students and subtract 5 students several times until no more subtractions can be made, then count the number of subtractions. Others will know the answer by counting forward by 5s. Still others will draw and group the

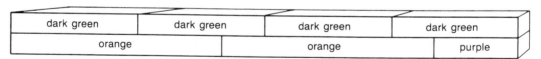

Figure 7–7 Cuisenaire rods showing the answer to dark green times purple.

students to find the answer. These strategies typically precede the response, "29 divided by 5." Expect discussion about how many groups of students can be formed. What if the story, instead of saying that 5 children at a time could work in the booth, said that there were 5 shifts that needed students and asked how many students could work together in each shift? As you read about measurement and partition problems in the following paragraphs, you will recognize that these two versions of the number story represent measurement and partition division, respectively.

The operation presented initially to serve as a basis for understanding division involves removing multiple sets of equal size from a larger set. Arithmetically, it involves subtracting several numbers of equal size from a larger number to determine a quotient. For example, $18 \div 6$ may be thought of as seeking the number of 6s that is contained in 18. The quotient, 3, can be determined by subtracting $18 - 6 - 6 - 6$. Counting and repeated subtraction are valuable models for division. They are among the easiest approaches for young children to use and understand.

Division problems typically fall into two categories: measurement problems and partition problems. In a **measurement problem,** the total number of objects is provided along with the number of objects to be put into each group. It is then necessary to find the number of groups that can be made. For example, if there are 15 pieces of paper and each child is given 3 pieces, how many children receive paper? Five children receive paper.

In a **partition problem,** the total number of objects is provided along with the number of groups that are to be made. It is then necessary to find how many objects will go into each group. For example, if there are 15 pieces of paper and 3 children, how many pieces are given each child? The paper is partitioned into 3 sets of 5 pieces. Children should be encouraged to make up problems of their own using real-life situations to help them better understand measurement and partition division.

A C T I V I T I E S

Pre-Kindergarten – Grade 2

OBJECTIVE: to use objects as a model for division.

1. Begin by reading *The Doorbell Rang* by Hutchins (1986). Mother has baked some cookies that can be shared by two children, but the doorbell rings and another child arrives. That is not a problem because the twelve cookies can still be evenly shared. More children join the party and soon there is just one cookie for each child. The doorbell rings again, and this time it is

grandma with a whole tray of cookies. This story lends itself to a discussion of how the cookies can be evenly shared as more children arrive at the party. Physical objects can be used to simulate the cookies and the sharing can be demonstrated by the students as the discussion proceeds.

A rich extension of this activity is the project described by Burk et al. (1991). The project, called "Cookies," uses *The Doorbell Rang* and other books about cookies over the course of eight days. Every aspect of the project is carefully outlined and the teacher is given hints about making it successful. The children write story problems, create a drama around the story, make cookies (as props) and serving trays, and then reenact the story. A class story on chart paper is created as the mathematics of *The Doorbell Rang* is examined, followed by individual cookie problems written by the students. The project concludes as children share their story problems.

2. Use objects that the children know to make word problems. "In our classroom there are 124 chair legs. Each chair has 4 legs. How many chairs are there altogether?" or "We have 42 pencils for work stations in the room. Each station will have 6 pencils. How many work stations can we have?" or "There are 48 coat sleeves hanging on our coat hooks. How many coats are there altogether?" Challenge the students to devise solutions to the word problem and explain the solutions to others in the class. Invite the children to pick objects, draw a picture of them, and write a division question about the objects. Students may pick any number of attributes of the objects to write about. Share the word problems in class.

3. Have the children place brown Cuisenaire rods in front of them. Ask, "How many red rods does it take to make a brown rod?" Let the children experiment to discover that 4 red rods are contained in a brown rod. The result will be similar to the rods in Figure 7–8a.

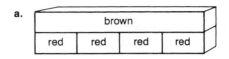

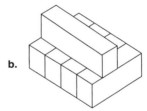

Figure 7–8   Using Cuisenaire rods to illustrate division.

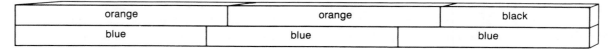

orange		orange		black	
blue		blue		blue	

Figure 7–9 Cuisenaire rods showing the solution to orange plus orange plus black divided by blue.

The division question we have just posed is "brown divided by red equals what?" We found that the answer is 4. If we think of division as the inverse operation to multiplication, we are asking the question "Red times what equals brown?" Here, we do just the opposite of what we did in performing multiplication; we put the brown rod down, lay red rods end to end along the brown rod (Figure 7–8a), and then place the red rods side by side, searching for the rod that equals the width of the red rods, as in Figure 7–8b. It is the purple rod, so $n \div r = p$. If the white rod has the value of 1, then the purple rod has the value of 4.

4. The problem $(o + o + k) \div e$ (orange plus orange plus black divided by blue) is solved by placing the rods together in a train and then finding the number of blue rods it takes to make that same length. It takes 3 blue rods as shown in Figure 7–9.

Had we divided by yellow, we would have found the result to be 5 yellow rods plus a red rod (Figure 7–10). The red rod represents the remainder. It is evaluated by comparing it to the white rod, which has the value of 1. Thus, $(o + o + k) \div y = 5$ remainder 2. Children who have used Cuisenaire rods while learning other number operations will find that division fits well with their other work.

OBJECTIVE: to practice measurement and partition division using objects.

5. Provide children with a handful of beans. Have them count out twenty-four beans. Tell the students, "Make as many groups of six beans as you can." They will make four groups. This is a measurement problem.

Next, request that the children make six equal groups using the twenty-four beans. Ask, "How many beans are there in each group?" There will be four beans in each group. This is a partition problem.

Give the children plenty of practice using both measurement and partition problems. They should be able to recognize the difference between the two kinds of division and to use physical objects to illustrate the meaning of each.

Once the language describing division has been introduced, practiced, and discussed, the operation can be symbolized. It is important that division make sense to children. Students should know and be able to explain what division is, how it relates to multiplication, and when it is appropriate to use different approaches to solve a problem: physical objects, paper and pencil, mental calculations, and calculators. The transition to the abstract symbols should take place as soon as the children are competent using objects and using the language that describes the operation they are performing.

Activities on pages 194–196 employed the Cuisenaire rods. The language the students are using is "brown divided by red equals purple, or 4." The change to number occurs quickly. If the white rod equals 1, brown has the value of 8, red has the value of 2, and purple has the value of 4. Thus, the number sentence $8 \div 2 = 4$ results directly from the sentence using colors. Children need additional experiences with the rods to become proficient using the numerical descriptions of the rods.

In the bean activity in activity 5, students had 24 beans and were asked to make as many groups of 6 beans as they could. The children counted them and indicated that there were 24 altogether. Repeat the activity, saying, "We are going to find out how many groups of what size?" We are going to find out how many groups of 6. Ask, "How many groups of 6 are there?" There are 4. Explain, "We say this using numbers by writing $24 \div 6 = 4$." The symbols should be written to show the operation. Using models of division to introduce and reinforce the symbolism of division will strengthen the meaning of the symbols. Several models should be used as the symbols are introduced.

Properties of Multiplication and Division

Earlier, we mentioned that you should take the opportunity to include examples of important properties of the operations being presented. There are some that are important to know when working with

orange		orange		black	
yellow	yellow	yellow	yellow	yellow	red

Figure 7–10 Cuisenaire rods showing the solution to orange plus orange plus black divided by yellow.

multiplication and division. Give the students ample opportunities to discover and discuss these properties using physical models. The first of these is the **identity element for multiplication and division.** That is, any number times 1 or divided by 1 results in the number you start with. With this information, $6 \times 1 = 6$, $1 \times 6 = 6$, and $6 \div 1 = 6$ are easy basic combinations to remember. Children should discover that $1 \div 6$ (left-hand identity) does not hold for division of whole numbers.

A second important property is the **commutative property of multiplication.** This can be shown using any of the models presented above. For example, with an array of tiles, ask a child to stand in position A as shown in Figure 7–11 and describe the array. In that case, the array would be read 3 by 6, or 3 times 6. There are 18 tiles. Then ask the child to move to position B and describe the array. In this second case, the array should be read 6 by 3, or 6 times 3. The number of tiles stays the same. Students should realize that $3 \times 6 = 18$ and $6 \times 3 = 18$.

Knowing that the order has no effect on the product reduces the number of multiplication combinations to be remembered. Children should have the opportunity to discover that the commutative property does not hold for division; that is, $8 \div 4 = 2$, but $4 \div 8$ does not have a whole-number solution.

A third useful pattern multiplies a number by zero or divides zero by a number. While the results are similar for both of these examples, the ideas are quite different.

Ask the children to make 4 rows of tiles with 3 tiles in each row. They should be able to describe their work as 4 times 3 equals 12. Next, have the children make 4 rows of tiles with 2 tiles in each row and describe the result (4 times 2 equals 8). Then, have them make 4 rows of tiles with 1 tile in each row and describes the result (4 times 1 equals 4). Finally, ask the children to make four rows with zero tiles in each row and describe the result (4 times 0 equals 0).

Have the students experiment with this activity, invent their own activities, and discuss the results any time zero tiles are put into rows. See if the children can make a generalization regarding the result any time there are zero rows.

Encourage the children to act out these situations and to create situations of their own that involve zero. The children will soon discover that any number times zero is zero. For example, $8 \times 0 = 0$ and $0 \times 5 = 0$.

In division, zero cannot be the divisor. To find how many groups of zero are contained in 24 makes no sense and is *undefined* in mathematics. Thus, $27 \div 0$, $6 \div 0$, and $0 \div 0$ are all undefined. On the other hand, dividing zero by any number is possible. Have the children act out this situation: If there are 0 (zero) pieces of clay and you wish to give each child 3 pieces, how many children will receive clay? The children can decide how this situation is described in division (0 divided by 3 equals 0).

Similarly, describe this situation: If there are 0 pieces of clay and 3 children, how many pieces can be given to each child? Again, the children will see that 0 divided by 3 equals 0. After a number of examples, the children realize that zero divided by any number is zero. Time spent discovering and discussing these properties will make remembering the multiplication and division combinations easier.

> In grades 3–5, students should focus on the meanings of, and relationship between, multiplication and division. (NCTM, 2000, p. 151)

Multiplying and Dividing Integers

In Chapter 6 we mentioned the importance of learning about and making sense of integers, the positive and negative whole numbers and zero. Understanding the nature of integers and how operations on integers work is fundamental for success in algebra and coordinate geometry. Models for integers include thermometers, number lines, colored chips, money, and calculators. Children should begin making sense of integers in informal settings in the early elementary grades.

Once integers make sense and adding and subtracting integers have been introduced, students will be ready for multiplying and dividing integers. Discovering and discussing patterns that result from multiplying and dividing integers will provide a foundation for understanding. The rules for multiplying and dividing integers will emerge from the patterns. The activities that follow should encourage looking for patterns.

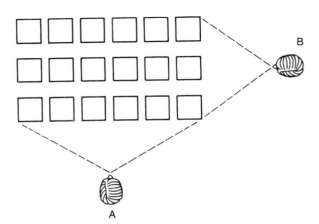

Figure 7–11 Two views of an array as a model for the commutative property of multiplication.

A C T I V I T I E S

Grades 6 – 8

OBJECTIVE: to find patterns when multiplying integers.

1. An NCTM web-based Illuminations lesson plan (Weblink 7–1) focuses on multiplying. The lesson plan is based on a 1993 *Arithmetic Teacher* article that describes how teacher Marcia Cooke used a videotaping project to explore the multiplication of integers. Students videotaped one another walking forward and backward. Then, using the tape, played forward and backward, they discovered the patterns associated with multiplying integers. You are encouraged to read and consider using the ideas that were described.

2. Use a large vertical number line similar to the one shown in Figure 6–14, which resembles a thermometer, for these number-line problems. Earlier we introduced addition and subtraction of integers using the vertical number line. Now, we present multiplication. Future time may be indicated by a positive number and past time may be indicated by a negative number. If the temperature rises at a rate of 3 degrees per hour (positive amount) and the temperature is now 0 degrees, what will the temperature be in 4 hours (positive number)? Here, we are multiplying a positive number by a positive number of $4 \times 3 = 12$. The temperature will be 12 degrees in 4 hours. Suppose it was 55 degrees when we started. What will the temperature be in 4 hours? If the temperature drops steadily at a rate of 5 degrees per hour (negative amount) and the temperature is now 0 degrees, what will the temperature be in 3 hours (positive number)? Figure 7–12 illustrates the problem. Here we are multiplying a negative number by a positive number or $3 \times {}^-5 = {}^-15$. The temperature will be $^-15$ degrees in 3 hours. What was the temperature 4 hours ago? [$({}^-4) \times ({}^-5) = {}^+20$]. Suppose it was 55 degrees when we started. What will the temperature be in 3 hours? Ask the students to make up

other questions for each other and to demonstrate solutions on the number line. After the students have worked several problems, ask them whether they have discovered any patterns in their work. Keep a written record of the rules the children discover in a prominent place in the classroom.

OBJECTIVE: to multiply and divide integers using discrete objects.

3. After working several problems involving addition and subtraction of integers, using red and blue chips, try some problems involving multiplication and division of integers. Again, time in the future is represented by a positive number and time in the past by a negative number. Having a debt of $3 for 5 weeks in a row can be thought of as $5 \times ({}^-3) = $ _____. You would add 3 red chips every week for 5 weeks. Asking how your finances stood 5 weeks ago relative to today after these 5 weeks of debt would be $({}^-5) \times ({}^-3) = $ _____. You would have to start at some representation of zero and take away 3 red chips 5 times to find the answer (see Figure 7–13).

Because division is the inverse operation of multiplication, the problem $15 \div ({}^-3) = $ _____ can be thought of as the inverse of the problem above. When would you have $15 more than you have today if you add a debt of $3 each week? You know that if you continue to add the debt of $3 every week into the future, you will always have less money than you have today. You cannot go into the future; that is, the number of weeks cannot be positive. To have more money when you add a debt every week, you must go into the past. Therefore, $15 \div ({}^-3)$ must equal $^-5$, representing 5 weeks ago. After working several multiplication and division problems with the students, ask them to note any patterns and to generate rules for multiplying and dividing integers. They should notice that multiplying or dividing two negative integers has the same result as multiplying or dividing two positive integers; when multiplying or dividing a positive integer by a negative integer or a negative integer by a positive integer, the result will always be negative.

In grades 6–8, learning addition, subtraction, multiplication, and division with integers and recognizing applications of integers in algebra and geometry are important objectives. Modeling and discussing integer operations are very useful aspects of this learning. The

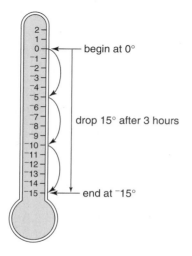

Figure 7–12 Thermometer as a model for $3 \times {}^-5 = {}^-15$.

begin at 0°

drop 15° after 3 hours

end at $^-15$°

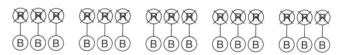

Figure 7–13 Red and blue chips representing $({}^-5) \times ({}^-3) = {}^+15$.

properties of multiplication and division that were mentioned in the previous section should be explored with integers as soon as students are comfortable with both the properties and integer multiplication and division.

DEVELOPING FLUENCY WITH MULTIPLICATION AND DIVISION

Computational fluency is a phrase that refers to knowing the basic number combinations and using effective methods for computing. Children should learn the basic multiplication and division number combinations and the skills associated with multiplying and dividing. The **basic multiplication facts,** of which there are 100, are those ranging from 0×0 to 9×9. The **basic division facts,** of which there are 90, are those ranging from $81 \div 9$ to $0 \div 1$.

As mentioned earlier, *algorithms* are methods used to calculate; mathematics includes numerous algorithms for multiplication and division. As children learn multiplication and division, they can make use of paper-and-pencil procedures, mental arithmetic, calculators, and computers. We begin our discussion of skills with basic combinations and follow with algorithms.

Basic Multiplication and Division Combinations

For quick recall, children should be expected to visualize and/or remember the basic multiplication and division combinations. Memorization should begin when children understand the concepts of multiplication and division. Helping children to associate meaning with these operations is rewarded as the combinations are learned. With experience using physical models, children will be able to reconstruct a basic combination that they have forgotten. They can use a variety of objects as counters. They also may use arrays, Cuisenaire rods, or calculators.

The multiplication and division combinations may be presented almost simultaneously. Typically, elementary mathematics textbooks present multiplication followed by division, with some illustration of how they are related. You may wish to start with the multiplication concept models, and follow shortly by the division concept models. As children understand the concepts, they will work comfortably with both multiplication and division at the same time. Because the multiplication and division combinations are closely related, they can be learned together effectively. A family of related combinations includes several combinations related by the numbers being multiplied and divided. One such family follows:

$$3 \times 6 = 18$$
$$6 \times 3 = 18$$
$$18 \div 3 = 6$$
$$18 \div 6 = 3$$

The classroom should contain tools with which to perform simple calculations. The most basic tools for calculating are the counters mentioned throughout earlier chapters. In the initial stages of learning the multiplication and division combinations, encourage children to use cubes, beans, milk jug caps, buttons, or tiles to find the answer by forming the specified number of groups, each containing a given number of objects, such as three groups of seven tiles. As the work becomes more abstract and paper and pencil or calculators are used, marks on paper help reinforce basic multiplication and division combinations. Children will develop personal strategies for solving multiplication and division problems. Those should be encouraged and discussed.

The number line, introduced earlier for addition and subtraction, is useful for multiplication and division. For children with little number-line experience, the walk-on number line is a good place to start. Another alternative is the number line calibrated in centimeters, beside which Cuisenaire rods can be placed. Model multiplication and division using a number line on which you take jumps using your finger or a pencil. When children wish to multiply 3×4, begin at 0 on the number line and take 3 jumps of 4, as in Figure 7–14a. The point at which you stop, 12, is the product of 3 and 4. The number line serves as an example of the repeated addition model for multiplication.

When students wish to divide 14 by 7, explain, "We are going to find how many 7s are contained in 14. Put your finger on your number line at 14." Continue, "We are going to find how many jumps of 7 we can make as we move from 14 to 0. Let's all make one jump of 7 toward 0. Are we at 0 yet? No, so let's make another jump of 7. Are we at 0 yet? Yes, how many jumps did we make?" There were 2 jumps (see Figure 7–14b). Ask, "How many 7s are contained in 14?" There are 2. Summarize, "We can say $14 \div 7 = 2$. Now let's try $12 \div 3$." This is an example of measurement division.

The calculator can play an important role during the learning of multiplication and division combinations. It

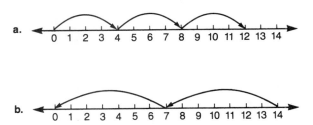

Figure 7–14 Number line illustrating multiplication and division.

should be used to quickly produce combinations that are forgotten, particularly during games and activities intended to help children memorize basic combinations. Using the calculator should not replace the memorization of combinations. It can, however, assist children by providing immediate feedback and allowing them to continue their activity.

Computer games and activities are available to assist children as they learn and reinforce basic multiplication and division combinations. In many cases the same software used in reinforcing the basic combinations in addition and subtraction also reinforces multiplication and division. Games such as *Mighty Math Calculating Crew* (Edmark) are designed to strengthen children's abilities in multiplication and division.

You can help children prepare for learning the multiplication and division combinations. For example, skip counting forward and backward using various numbers helps children become familiar with the multiples of these numbers. The first 10 multiples of the numbers from 0 to 9 are the basic multiplication combinations.

Another way to prepare children for the basic multiplication combinations is to have them collect objects and record how many objects there are. For example, put groups of 4 beans in portion cups. Record the number of beans in 1 cup, then 2 cups, 3 cups, and so on, up to 10 cups.

The multiplication table can help children learn the multiplication combinations. The table, shown in Table 7–1, has ten rows and ten columns. The multiplication table is read by selecting the first factor from the left side and the second factor from the top. The product of the two factors is found in the table where that row and that column meet. The combinations 8 × 6 is shown in the figure. Use the properties discussed earlier, the identity, zero, and commutative properties, and known combinations such as the twos and fives to eliminate all the combinations students already know. They will be pleasantly surprised to see how few combinations remain to be memorized.

The activities that follow are specifically designed for multiplication. Some are modifications of the activities presented in Chapter 6 for addition. Each activity may be used just as effectively for division by making simple changes in the materials.

A C T I V I T I E S

Grades 3–5

OBJECTIVE: to help children memorize the basic multiplication facts.

1. Provide practice in mental arithmetic. Practice periods should be limited to 5 or 10 minutes. Orally

TABLE 7–1   The Basic Multiplication Combinations

X	0	1	2	3	4	5	6	7	8	9
0	0	0	0	0	0	0	0	0	0	0
1	0	1	2	3	4	5	6	7	8	9
2	0	2	4	6	8	10	12	14	16	18
3	0	3	6	9	12	15	18	21	24	27
4	0	4	8	12	16	20	24	28	32	36
5	0	5	10	15	20	25	30	35	40	45
6	0	6	12	18	24	30	36	42	48	54
7	0	7	14	21	28	35	42	49	56	63
8	0	8	16	24	32	40	(48)	56	64	72
9	0	9	18	27	36	45	54	63	72	81

The table header "Factor" appears across the top columns and "Factor" appears vertically along the left side.

present the multiplication combinations to children and have the children write on a piece of paper only the answer to the problem.

An alternative approach is to provide children with numeral cards (0–9) or marking boards and have them hold up the appropriate answer for you to see as in Figure 7–15. Determine the difficulty of the problems based on the age and experience of the students. Initially, speedy responses are not necessary. Students need an opportunity to practice using their minds.

Ask the students to number from 1 to 5 or 10 on their papers. Explain that you are going to give them a problem and they should think of the answer and then write it down. At first, they may need to use their pencils to determine the answer; after a few sessions, they should not. Examples of mental exercises follow: What is 3 times 2? What is 2 times 4 times 3? Yes or no, 4 times 6 is more than 20? Three times 4 equals 12, what else equals 12?

As the students become more proficient, insist that they not use pencils to determine the answer. Increase the number of questions. Expand the questions to include mixed operations. For example, begin with 5, multiply by 3, now add 5.

Figure 7–15 Student showing the answer to a mental arithmetic problem.

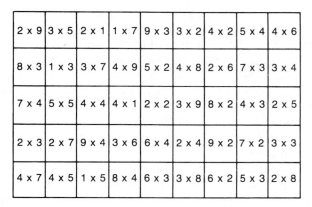

2 x 9	3 x 5	2 x 1	1 x 7	9 x 3	3 x 2	4 x 2	5 x 4	4 x 6
8 x 3	1 x 3	3 x 7	4 x 9	5 x 2	4 x 8	2 x 6	7 x 3	3 x 4
7 x 4	5 x 5	4 x 4	4 x 1	2 x 2	3 x 9	8 x 2	4 x 3	2 x 5
2 x 3	2 x 7	9 x 4	3 x 6	6 x 4	2 x 4	9 x 2	7 x 2	3 x 3
4 x 7	4 x 5	1 x 5	8 x 4	6 x 3	3 x 8	6 x 2	5 x 3	2 x 8

Figure 7–16   Game board for Times Up.

1	2	3	4	5	6
2	4	6	8	10	12
3	6	9	12	15	18
4	8	12	16	20	24
5	10	15	20	25	30
6	12	18	24	30	36

Figure 7–17   Game board for Four-in-a-Row Multiplication.

2. Times Up is a game for two players that helps children learn the multiplication combinations. Times Up requires construction of activity materials. First, construct a board with 45 regions, each containing a multiplication expression (see Figure 7–16).

Make two sets of 24 markers, each of a different color—for example, yellow and blue. In each set of markers, there should be one marker with each of the following numerals: 2, 3, 4, 5, 6, 7, 8, 9, 12, 14, 15, 16, 18, 20, 24, 25, 27, 28, 32, and 36. There should be two markers with each of the numerals 10 and 21.

To play this game, each player selects one set of markers and turns them numeral side down, mixing them together. Each player then turns over one marker to determine who will begin the game. The player with the highest number begins.

On each turn, a player turns over one marker, notes the number, and places it on a region of the playing board that corresponds to the number. For example, if a marker with the numeral 6 is drawn, it should be placed on a region containing 2 × 3 or 3 × 2. Only one marker may be placed on a region. If the marker cannot be played, it is laid aside face up. Play continues until all of the regions are covered or until no more markers can be placed on the board. The player who has placed the most markers is the winner.

This activity is unusual in that children are given the answer and are expected to find the problem. This allows children to establish a different set of associations with the basic multiplication combinations. Competition in this activity is limited to the "luck of the draw." Thus, the opportunity to win is accorded all who play.

3. The game Four-in-a-Row Multiplication is a variation of tic-tac-toe. Two to four students may play. This game requires a game board like the one shown in Figure 7–17 and a pair of dice with the numerals 1 to 6. Blank dice are available on which numerals may be written, or standard dice may be used for this game. Each player should be supplied with a set of unique

markers, 18 each for 2 players, 12 each for 3 players, and 9 each for 4 players.

To start play, each player rolls the pair of dice; the numbers that show are used as factors to form a product. For example, if 3 and 4 are showing, the product is 12. The player with the largest product takes the first turn.

Each player rolls the pair of dice in turn, multiplies the two numbers together, and places a marker on the playing board to cover the product. If the product is already covered, the turn is lost. The winner is the first player to get four markers in a row horizontally, vertically, or diagonally.

To extend this game, dice with the numerals 2 to 7, 3 to 8, or 4 to 9 may be used. For each new pair of dice, a new game board is necessary. For dice with the numerals 2 to 7, the game board contains the numerals 4 to 49. The game board is the section from the multiplication table corresponding to the numbers on the dice.

4. This is a Bingo activity called MULTI Bingo. This game may be played with a small group or the entire class. Each player will need a MULTI Bingo card and a number of markers. A sample card is shown in Figure 7–18. Each Bingo card has one happy face region

M	U	L	T	I
5	7	12	20	42
2	10	18	24	30
1	6	☺	25	32
4	8	15	28	35
3	9	14	21	36

Figure 7–18   Sample MULTI Bingo card.

(free space) and twenty-four regions with numerals. The numerals are randomly placed in each column. Following are the numerals for each column on the card:

M: 1, 2, 3, 4, 5
U: 6, 7, 8, 9, 10
L: 12, 14, 15, 16, 18
T: 20, 21, 24, 25, 28
I: 30, 32, 35, 36, 42

The leader draws a calling card from a shuffled deck and calls out the letter and multiplication expression on the card. The calling cards have the following letters and expressions:

M: 1×1, 2×1, 3×1, 4×1, 5×1
U: 2×3, 7×1, 2×4, 3×3, 2×5
L: 2×6, 2×7, 5×3, 4×4, 9×2
T: 4×5, 3×7, 8×3, 5×5, 4×7
I: 6×5, 4×8, 5×7, 6×6, 7×6

Players complete the multiplication and place a marker on the corresponding answer in the appropriate column. The first player to get five markers in a row horizontally, vertically, or diagonally wins the game.

5. This activity, Top It, was introduced earlier to help practice the addition and subtraction combinations. Figure 7–19 shows a deck of easy and a deck of hard multiplication cards designed to accommodate the children's skill levels. The decks may be combined into a single deck representing nearly all of the basic multiplication combinations.

Begin play with the stack of cards face down. The first player turns over a card and places it face up, giving the product. The second, third, and fourth players do the same. The player with the highest product claims all of the cards played. If any players are tied with high cards, the cards remain in front of the players and those who are tied each draw another card. The player with the highest product takes all of the cards. The winner is the player with the most cards at the end of the game.

Grades 6–8

OBJECTIVE: to help students develop multiplication fluency.

1. The Product Game is one of the NCTM Illuminations activities (see Weblink 7–2). There are four different activities. First is the Product Game, where students start with two factors and find their product. The game board consists of a list of factors and a grid of

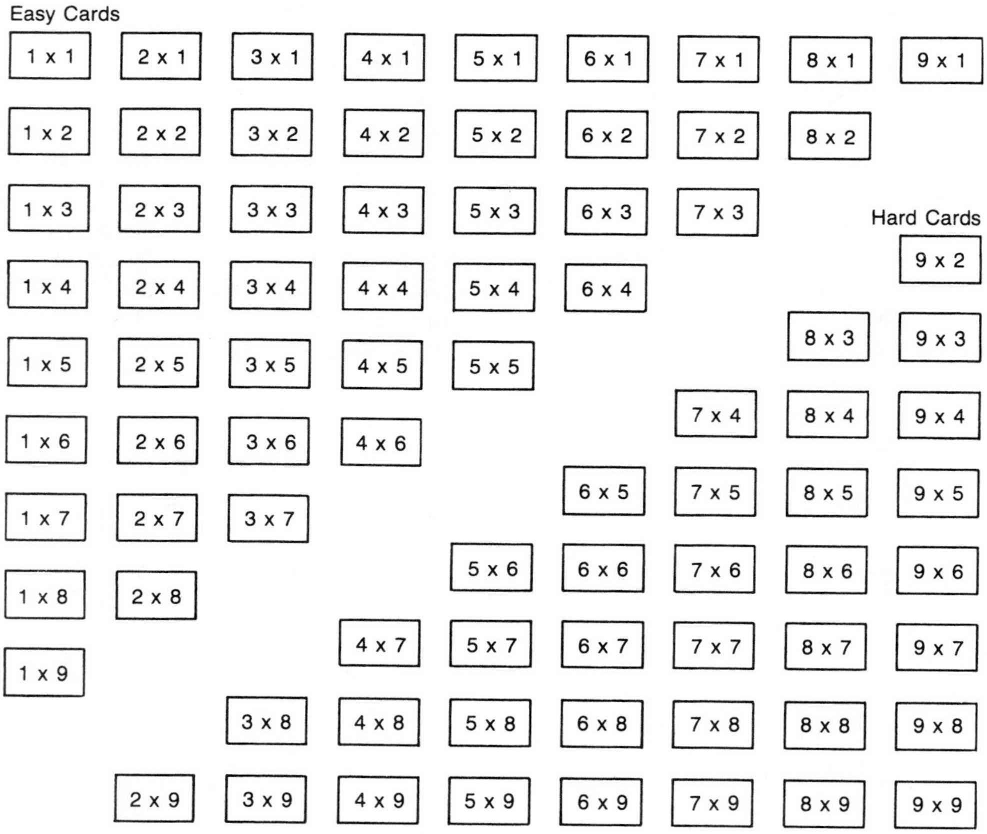

Figure 7–19 Decks of easy and hard cards for multiplication Top It.

products. Two players compete to place four squares in a row—vertically, horizontally, or diagonally. The second activity gives a player the chance to build a product game by changing the grid size, adding new factors, and providing new numbers in the grid. The third activity invites students to explore how factors and multiples of numbers are related using Venn diagrams. The fourth activity involves strategies that are connections and extensions of the Product Game. You are encouraged to investigate the Product Game for possible use in your classroom.

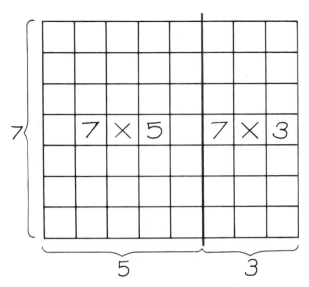

Figure 7–20   Arrays to help illustrate the distributive property of multiplication over addition.

This section has presented a few of the numerous activities that can be used to help children practice the basic multiplication combinations. Each activity can be adapted to include division practice. The goal is for the children to be able to accurately and quickly respond to all basic multiplication and division combinations. Sources of other activities and games have been included in the references at the end of this chapter.

Although the properties of multiplying by one, the commutative property of multiplication, and multiplying by zero can be helpful in learning the basic multiplication combinations, the **associative property of multiplication** can also be helpful for children as they multiply numbers like 4×16. If children rename the larger factor and apply the associative property, the problem can be made easier. For example, 4×16 may be renamed as $4 \times (2 \times 8)$. Using the associative property, the problem may be restated as $(4 \times 2) \times 8$, then 8×8, which is a basic combination and equals 64.

The associative property is shown in $4 \times (2 \times 8) = (4 \times 2) \times 8$; how the numbers are grouped to multiply does not affect the product. As children learn this property, give them repeated simple examples that they can calculate from memory or with a calculator. These examples should allow them to discover that the product is unchanged regardless of the order in which the numbers are multiplied.

A property that is helpful when mentally multiplying numbers is the **distributive property of multiplication over addition**. For example, when multiplying 7×8, we can think of 8 as $5 + 3$, multiply 7×5 and 7×3, and then add the products. Thus, $7 \times 8 = 7 \times (5 + 3)$, which then equals $(7 \times 5) + (7 \times 3)$, or $35 + 21 = 56$. An illustration using arrays helps children visualize an application of the distributive property. Figure 7–20 shows $7 \times (5 + 3)$. Children can move the dividing line to see that they could use $7 \times (4 + 4)$ or $7 \times (6 + 2)$ as well.

While not very efficient with paper and pencil, the distributive property helps us recall basic combinations and simplify the larger problems we do in our heads. Later, students will find knowing the distributive property to be essential as they simplify algebraic

expressions. To multiply 8×74 mentally, think $8 \times (70 + 4)$ is $560 + 32$, or 592. Find the product of a larger multiplication problem by adding the products of two smaller problems. There are other variations of the distributive property, such as distributing over subtraction, but the property just described is the one most widely used. Materials for teaching multiplication, including base ten squares and an addition/multiplication grid, may be found in Appendix B.

Algorithms

As with learning addition and subtraction, children will likely find ways to modify standard or alternative multiplication and division algorithms so they can make more sense of them. Invented algorithms should be encouraged, and children should be urged to write down their algorithms and share them with the other students. Rich discussions can emerge as students attempt to understand or challenge the explanations of the algorithm inventors.

It is helpful if children know the basic multiplication and division combinations as they begin to work with algorithms. In addition, children should have available physical materials with which to work. The base ten blocks are a useful set of materials for modeling multiplication and division. For example, provide the students with the base ten blocks and other materials and a problem such as: "Hannah has collected 42 figures and toys for her playhouse. She wants to share them with her brother and her sister. How many will each child have when she has shared them?" Have the children work in small groups to find a solution and have them write down their method using words and symbols.

When all the groups are finished, ask each group to share its solution with the whole class. Discuss the merits of each solution. This gives students the opportunity to explore and invent algorithms. Let the students decide which algorithm they prefer and when they no longer need to use the physical models. It is likely that the students will devise some algorithms similar to the standard multiplication and division algorithms, but be ready for algorithms that are different. The process of inventing algorithms is an important part of developing computational fluency.

> At the grades 3–5 level, as students develop the basic number combinations for multiplication and division, they should also develop reliable algorithms to solve arithmetic problems efficiently and accurately. (NCTM, 2000, p. 35)

In mathematics textbooks, multiplication and division algorithms are usually taught sequentially, beginning with the simplest problems, which require no regrouping (carrying). The difficulty and complexity increase until multidigit problems with regrouping are presented. However, when students begin multidigit multiplication and division using physical models, there is no need to separate problems that require regrouping from those that do not. When children can demonstrate paper-and-pencil algorithms for multiplication and division, it is time to let them use calculators to speed up computations. Using the calculator is the most efficient procedure for performing an arithmetic operation.

> [C]alculators do not replace fluency with basic number combinations, conceptual understanding, or the ability to formulate and use efficient and accurate methods of computing. (NCTM, 2000, p. 145)

On the following pages, paper-and-pencil algorithms for multiplication and division are presented in turn. We begin with the standard paper-and-pencil algorithm that is generally considered most efficient for each operation. Alternative algorithms are then presented. Alternative procedures often serve as teaching algorithms and help to bridge the gap between physical models and the abstract. Sometimes alternative algorithms are the most efficient paper-and-pencil algorithms for children. It was mentioned above that students sometimes invent algorithms similar to the standard multiplication and division algorithms. Likewise, they may invent algorithms similar to the alternative algorithms presented below. While the standard algorithm is presented first, followed by alternative algorithms, we are not suggesting that children will invent algorithms in this order. You should not introduce standard algorithms until students have explored, invented, and discussed their own algorithms.

Multiplication. The standard paper-and-pencil multiplication algorithm is applied to the six problems below, each of which has at least one two-digit factor.

$$
\begin{array}{cccccc}
12 & 62 & {}^{2}25 & 34 & 43 & {}^{3}{}^{4}38 \\
\times 3 & \times 4 & \times 5 & \times 10 & \times 12 & \times 45 \\
\hline
36 & 248 & 125 & 340 & 86 & {}^{1}190 \\
& & & & {}^{1}43 & 152 \\
\cline{5-6}
& & & & 516 & 1{,}710 \\
\end{array}
$$

The first example shows multiplying by a one-digit number with no regrouping. The second problem involves multiplying by a one-digit number with regrouping from the tens to the hundreds place. The third example shows multiplying by a one-digit number with regrouping from the ones to the tens place. Typically, when a single-digit number and a multiple-digit number are multiplied, the multiple-digit number is placed on the top in the standard algorithm, as shown in the first three examples.

The last three examples show multiplying by two-digit numbers. The fourth example shows multiplying by a two-digit number that is a multiple of 10 with no regrouping. The fifth example shows multiplying by a two-digit number with no regrouping. The final example shows multiplying by a two-digit number with regrouping.

In the examples with regrouping from the ones to the tens place the regrouping numeral has been shown. Most who use this algorithm include it. It is important that children understand what happens when regrouping occurs. This is an extension of their work with place value.

Typically, it is at the fourth-grade level that children are introduced to the multiplication and division algorithms. At this time, with a sound foundation of preparation, children can construct the procedures necessary for performing successfully their own or the standard algorithms. Using physical models such as base ten blocks or similar models assists in the effort. Most math texts illustrate the algorithms as they are presented. You are encouraged to use physical models for textbook algorithms.

We illustrate using an example stated as a word problem. Miss Jensen's class has completed work on a language arts project. Each student has written two poems and made an illustration of one of the poems. The 26 students believe they have turned in all their work. Just to check, Miss Jensen asks Shelley to count the papers. Because each student used a separate sheet for each part of the project, there should be 3 sheets for each person. Shelley counts 76 papers. Miss Jensen asks the class to verify that 76 is the correct answer.

Figure 7–21 shows a method the class might use to solve the problem 3 × 26 with multibase blocks representing the papers and a place-value board.

In this example, the repeated addition model is used first. What the student sees is 26 + 26 + 26 (see Figure 7–21a). Since there are 26 students and each student should have 3 sheets of paper, three groups of 26 represent the total number of sheets in all. The unit cubes are combined into a group of 10 with 8 remaining. The

10 cubes are exchanged for 1 long (see Figure 7–21b). Then the longs are joined. The result, 7 tens and 8 ones, or 78, is the product of 3 and 26 (see Figure 7–21c).

A second procedure, shown in Figure 7–22, follows the standard paper-and-pencil algorithm. The first step is to multiply 3 × 6. This is illustrated by 3 groups of 6 small cubes. Ten cubes are then exchanged for 1 long (see Figure 7–22a). The next step is to multiply 3 × 20.

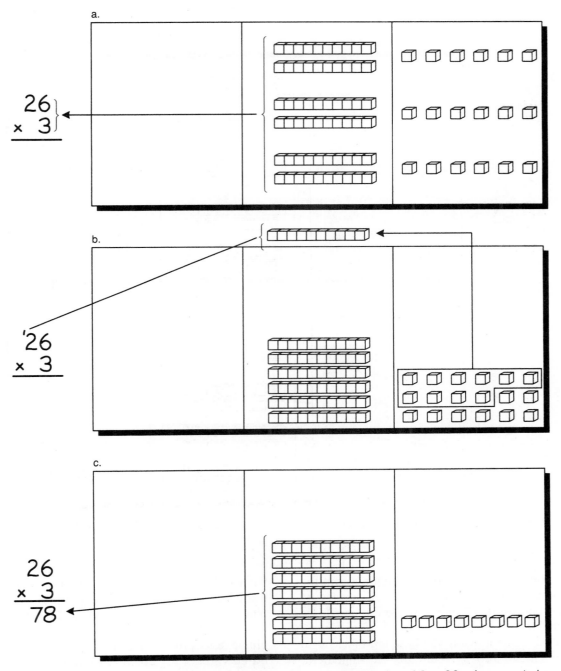

Figure 7–21   Numeral representation and base ten blocks representation of 3 × 26 using repeated addition.

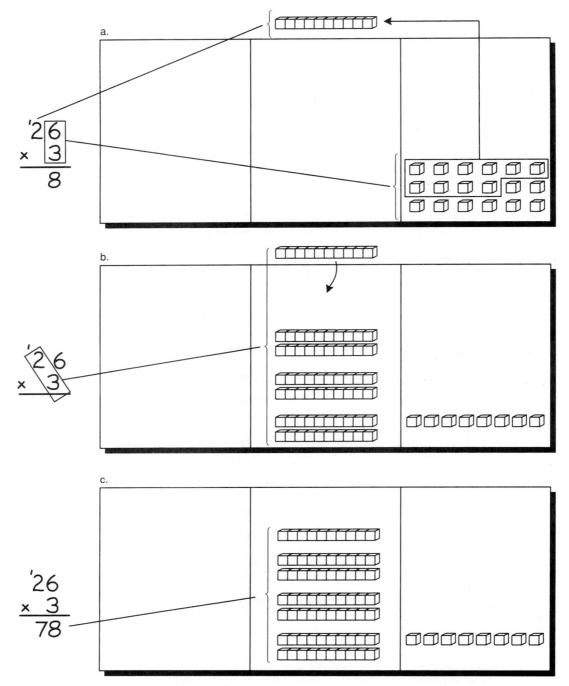

Figure 7–22 Numeral representation and base ten blocks representation of 3 × 26 using a standard algorithm.

This is shown by 3 groups of 2 longs. The long from the exchange above is joined to these 6 longs (see Figure 7–22b). The final result is 7 tens and 8 ones, or 78 (see Figure 7–22c).

Another useful model using the base ten blocks is to organize the blocks into a rectangular arrangement, with each dimension representing one of the factors being multiplied. For example, to multiply 12 × 14,

we would construct a rectangular region showing 12 in one dimension and 14 in the other dimension, as in Figure 7–23. The product of 12 and 14 is found by describing the pieces that make up the rectangle, 100 plus 6 tens plus 8 ones (168). For the problem illustrated earlier, 3 × 26, we would construct a rectangle showing 3 in one dimension and 26 in the other dimension, as in Figure 7–24. The final product is

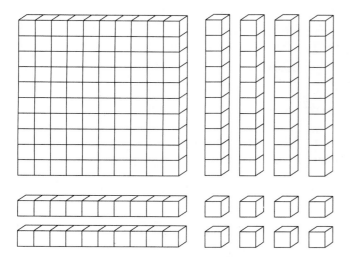

Figure 7–23 12 × 14 modeled using a rectangular arrangement with base ten blocks.

found by describing the pieces, 6 tens plus 18 ones (60 + 18, or 78). Whether using the repeated addition approach or the standard paper-and-pencil algorithm, the base ten blocks help to show how the algorithm works. A similar material, the algebra blocks, can be used in place of the base ten blocks. The algebra blocks are introduced in Chapter 10.

Regardless of which procedure is used, the class finds that not all the language arts papers have been turned in. The papers are soon located.

After students have constructed their own algorithms and compared them to those of other students, you may want to introduce the algorithms in the textbook. The multiplication algorithms presented in various math texts tend to be similar and quite easy to follow. The texts provide slow, step-by-step progressions from the easiest to the more difficult multiplication problems. And, texts provide plenty of practice exercises. Children should practice for several days after they are able to perform the algorithm without assistance. It is unnecessary for children to be assigned all of the problems on a textbook page. If children continue to have difficulty accurately completing algorithms, diagnose the difficulty. Assigning additional problems before children's error patterns are corrected is counterproductive. At this point, children need special assistance and perhaps a

new approach to help them learn the algorithms. Once children have learned the algorithms and the algorithms make sense to them, they need periodic practice to reinforce their skill.

The activities that follow differ from those presented earlier. Their primary focus is on ways to present alternative multiplication algorithms.

ACTIVITIES

Grades 3–5

OBJECTIVE: to invent algorithms for multiplication problems.

1. Introduce "solve it any way you can" problems. Present a problem and invite students to solve the problem using any technique they may choose. For example, "We have been watching a new home being built on a lot across the street from the school. On each of the 4 sides of the house we have found 4 windows. How many windows are there in the house? There are 2 more empty home lots nearby. Suppose 2 more homes, each with 4 windows on a side, are built on these lots. How many windows will there be in all of the new houses altogether?" Be ready to provide children with materials that they may ask for. When the students have finished working, have them discuss how they found their solution and share any materials that they may have used. You may also invite students to devise their own "solve it any way you can" problems.

OBJECTIVE: to use a variety of multiplication algorithms.

2. The **expanded notation algorithm** is an outgrowth of the work with place value. Two solutions using expanded notation follow. In problem a, no regrouping is necessary to solve 3 × 23.

The problem is rewritten from standard into expanded notation. The 3 ones and the 2 tens are each multiplied by 3. Then the expanded notation is rewritten into standard notation.

In problem b, 4 × 27 is figured in a similar manner, multiplying the 7 ones and the 2 tens by 4. As the answer is rewritten into standard form, regrouping must occur. The 28 must be expanded to 20 + 8 and the 20 added to the 80, resulting in 100 + 8, or 108. The

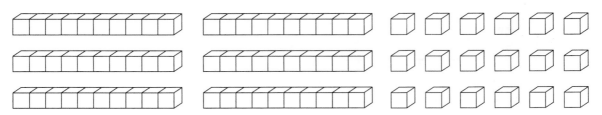

Figure 7–24 3 × 26 modeled using a rectangular arrangement with base ten blocks.

expanded notation algorithm is similar to the standard multiplication algorithm except that regrouping occurs at a different time. The expanded notation algorithm is advantageous because children never lose sight of the numbers they are regrouping.

a.
$$\begin{array}{r} 23 \\ \times\ 3 \\ \hline \end{array} \qquad \begin{array}{r} 20+3 \\ \times\quad\ 3 \\ \hline 60+9=69 \end{array}$$

b.
$$\begin{array}{r} 27 \\ \times\ 4 \\ \hline \end{array} \qquad \begin{array}{r} 20+7 \\ \times\quad\ 4 \\ \hline 80+28= \end{array}$$
$$=(80+20)+8=100+8=108$$

3. Children who have had experience working with the loop abacus should know that any time 10 counters appear on a given loop, the counters must be exchanged for 1 counter on the loop immediately to the left. This is demonstrated as we solve 3 × 35 on the abacus. In the first frame of Figure 7−25, an abacus shows 3 × 35.

The clips separate three representations of 35. In the second frame, we remove the holding clips in the ones column and exchange 10 counters on the ones loop for 1 counter on the tens loop. Five counters are left in the ones column.

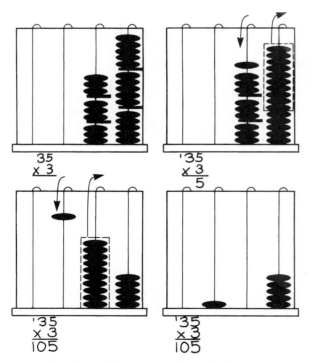

Figure 7−25 Numeral representation and abacus representation of 3 × 35.

In the third frame, we remove the holding clips in the tens column and exchange 10 counters on the tens loop for 1 counter on the hundreds loop. No counters are left in the tens column.

The fourth frame illustrates the abacus after all the exchanges have been made. The standard algorithm shows the progression from start to finish.

4. The **partial products algorithm** is another procedure that helps children through the process of regrouping. It may be used whether or not regrouping is necessary. The problem below illustrates the partial products algorithm by multiplying 8 × 57.

$$\begin{array}{r} 57 \\ \times\ 8 \\ \hline \end{array} \qquad \begin{array}{r} 57 \\ \times\ 8 \\ \hline 56\ (8\times7) \end{array}$$

$$\begin{array}{r} 57 \\ \times\ 8 \\ \hline 56 \\ 400\ (8\times50) \end{array} \qquad \begin{array}{r} 57 \\ \times\ 8 \\ \hline 56 \\ 400 \\ \hline 456 \end{array}$$

The first step in the solution is to multiply the number in the ones column, 7, by the multiplier, 8. The answer, 56, is the first partial product and is placed beneath the problem.

The next step is to multiply the number in the tens column, 5, by the multiplier, 8. The result, 40 tens, or 400, is placed beneath the 56.

Finally, the partial products are added to arrive at the answer, 456. Take care with this algorithm to ensure that the partial products are written in the correct place-value positions.

The partial products algorithm may be illustrated using physical models. In Figure 7−23, the base ten blocks were used to show 12 × 14. In describing the pieces that make up the rectangular region in Figure 7−23, we found that 12 × 14 was equal to one hundred plus 6 tens plus 8 ones. The partial products algorithm for 12 × 14 is shown below.

$$\begin{array}{r} 14 \\ \times 12 \\ \hline 8\quad \}\ 8\ \text{ones} \\ 20 \\ 40\quad \}\ 6\ \text{tens} \\ \hline 100\quad \}\ 1\ \text{hundred} \\ \hline 168 \end{array}$$

In this algorithm, we find the same product that we found with the base ten blocks—100 plus 6 tens plus

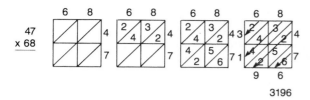

Figure 7–26   Using lattice multiplication to show 68 × 47.

8 ones. It is important for students to make such connections as they learn mathematics.

Incidentally, the same partial products are found when the horizontal *FOIL* algorithm is used to solve (10 + 2) (10 + 4). This algorithm is presented in Chapter 10.

5. The **lattice algorithm** for multiplication has been around for several hundred years. For each pair of numbers multiplied, a lattice is constructed. The lattice shown first in Figure 7–26 illustrates the problem 68 × 47.

For each place-value position in the factors, a region divided diagonally is provided. Begin by multiplying 4 times 8 and writing the product, 32, in the regions where 4 and 8 intersect. Then multiply 4 times 6 and write the product, 24, where 4 and 6 intersect. Continue by multiplying 7 times 8 and 7 times 6, recording each answer in the appropriate regions.

Finally, beginning at the lower right, add diagonally from right to left (see arrows) to determine the digits in the product of 68 and 47. Note that regrouping occurs from the third diagonal to the fourth diagonal (hundreds place to thousands place). The answer is read beginning at the upper left, down the left side of the lattice and across the bottom—the answer is 3,196.

This very different algorithm provides a clever approach to long multiplication problems. It can be worked easily with factors of any size.

John Napier, a Scottish mathematician who lived from 1550 to 1617, created a unique multiplication tool for peasant workers who had little education and little knowledge of the basic multiplication combinations. The tool, *Napier's rods,* consisted of a series of rods on which the multiplication tables had been written. A person could carry the rods in a pocket.

The technique of lattice multiplication was used with the rods. Patterns for constructing the rods are shown in Figure 7–27. The first rod is the index rod and contains a vertical listing of factors. The first digit at the top of each rod is another index factor.

Napier's rods resembled the orange Cuisenaire rod in size and shape. We find it easier to use tongue depressors or strips of oaktag to construct the rods.

When multiplying two numbers, lay the appropriate rods side by side next to the index rod. Then add along the diagonals. For example, Figure 7–28 shows how to multiply 5 × 36. The 3 rod and the 6 rod are placed side by side next to the index rod. Move down the index rod to 5. Then add diagonally as we did with lattice multiplication. The result, 180, is read in the same way as a result is read from the lattice.

Children enjoy taking a break to construct and use Napier's rods. See if they can discover how to perform multiplication such as 26 × 365.

Division. The procedure used to perform division is quite different from that used to perform multiplication. Division does, however, rely heavily on knowledge of multiplication as well as subtraction. Skill with the basic subtraction, multiplication, and division combinations is a key to success in performing division algorithms.

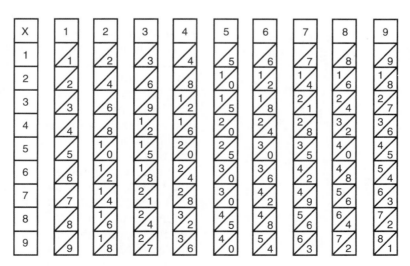

Figure 7–27   Pattern for constructing Napier's rods.

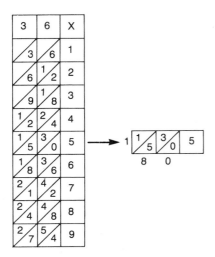

Figure 7–28   Napier's rods illustrating 5 × 36.

Recall that the basic division combinations are related to the basic multiplication combinations. Thus, for the multiplication combination 3 × 7 = 21, we have the corresponding division combinations 21 ÷ 3 = 7 and 21 ÷ 7 = 3. Techniques for helping children memorize these combinations were discussed earlier, in the section on basic combinations.

When introducing division algorithms, be sure to let students use real-life situations and physical models to construct their own algorithms. For example, a box of mixed party favors for a birthday party has 50 favors. On your birthday you have invited 7 of your friends. How many favors can each child at the party be given if all of the favors need to be given out? Allow plenty of time for students to work on the problem and to discuss their solutions with each other. There may be some surprising results.

Five examples of the standard paper-and-pencil division algorithm are presented below.

$$\begin{array}{r} 13 \\ 3\overline{)39} \end{array} \qquad \begin{array}{r} 44 \\ 3\overline{)132} \\ \underline{12} \\ 12 \\ \underline{12} \\ 0 \end{array} \qquad \begin{array}{r} 44\ r2 \\ 3\overline{)134} \\ \underline{12} \\ 14 \\ \underline{12} \\ 2 \end{array}$$

$$\begin{array}{r} 12 \\ 15\overline{)180} \\ \underline{15} \\ 30 \\ \underline{30} \\ 0 \end{array} \qquad \begin{array}{r} 16\ r13 \\ 27\overline{)445} \\ \underline{27} \\ 175 \\ \underline{162} \\ 13 \end{array}$$

The first three examples have one-digit divisors. The first of these has no regrouping, the second has regrouping, and the third has regrouping and a remainder. The last two examples have two-digit divisors; both have regrouping, and the last one has a remainder. The only markings that appear are in the last example, where regrouping was necessary during the first subtraction.

When the division algorithm is presented and discussed, it is important to accompany the instruction initially with physical models. We demonstrate with base ten blocks. The first example is 39 ÷ 3. How the problem is presented determines whether children will solve it with measurement or partition division.

In a measurement problem, the total number of objects is provided along with the number of objects to be put into each group. It is then necessary to find the number of groups that can be made. In a partition problem, the total number of objects is provided along with the number of groups to be made. It is then necessary to find how many objects will go into each group.

The first example is stated as a partition problem: We have 39 tomato seeds and 3 planting groups for a science project. How many seeds will each planting group receive? Figure 7–29 shows how to go about solving this problem.

Using the base ten blocks and the place value board, lay out 3 longs and 9 cubes to represent 39, as in Figure 7–29a. Next, separate the pieces into three groups, each of which contains the same number of pieces, as in Figure 7–29b. We find we have 1 long and 3 cubes in each group, or 13 cubes, as in Figure 7–29c. Each planting group will receive 13 seeds.

The example is now stated as a measurement problem: We have 39 tomato seeds. Each student will get 3 seeds for a science project. How many students will get seeds? The solution to this problem requires that the children form groups of 3 cubes and see how many such groups can be made. It is necessary to exchange each long for 10 cubes so the grouping by 3 can be completed. In the end, 13 groups of 3 will be made. Thus, 13 students will get seeds.

While the manipulation is different for each of these problems, the algorithm is the same. How the problem is presented, however, determines how to interpret the result. In the first case, the answer is 13 seeds; in the second case, 13 students.

When regrouping is necessary in the algorithm, as in 132 ÷ 3, the partition problem is most appropriate. Suppose a collection of 132 stamps is being divided among 3 children, how many stamps will each child receive? Using the base ten blocks, show 132 by displaying 1 flat, 3 longs, and 2 cubes as in Figure 7–30a.

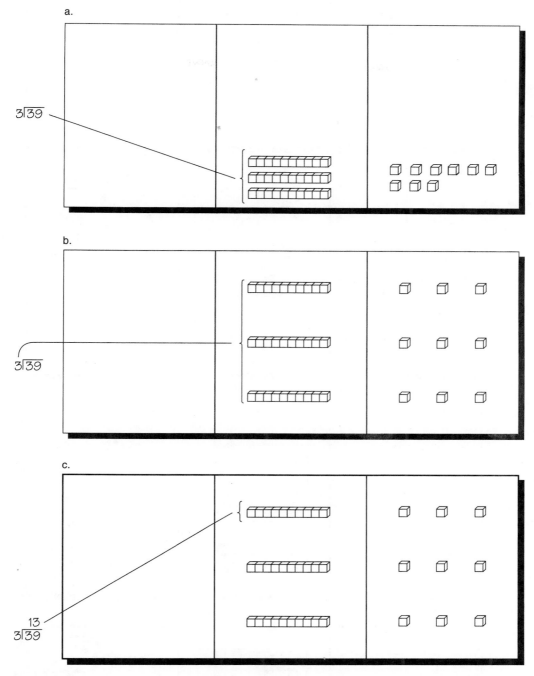

Figure 7–29 Numeral representation and base ten blocks representation of 39 ÷ 3 using partition division.

In order to separate the pieces into 3 groups, exchange the flat for 10 longs and exchange 1 long for 10 cubes as in Figure 7–30b. Then complete the operation by separating the pieces into three groups, as shown in Figure 7–30c. Figure 7–30d shows the final result. Thus, each child will receive 44 stamps. The exchanges, from hundreds to tens and from tens to ones, represent the regrouping in this division problem.

This work with physical models should not last long. Once the students have constructed algorithms and can perform the standard algorithm with manipulatives, encourage them to practice at the abstract level. As in the case of multiplication, the activities presented include alternative algorithms and approaches for division. Some children find that an alternative is superior for them and adopt

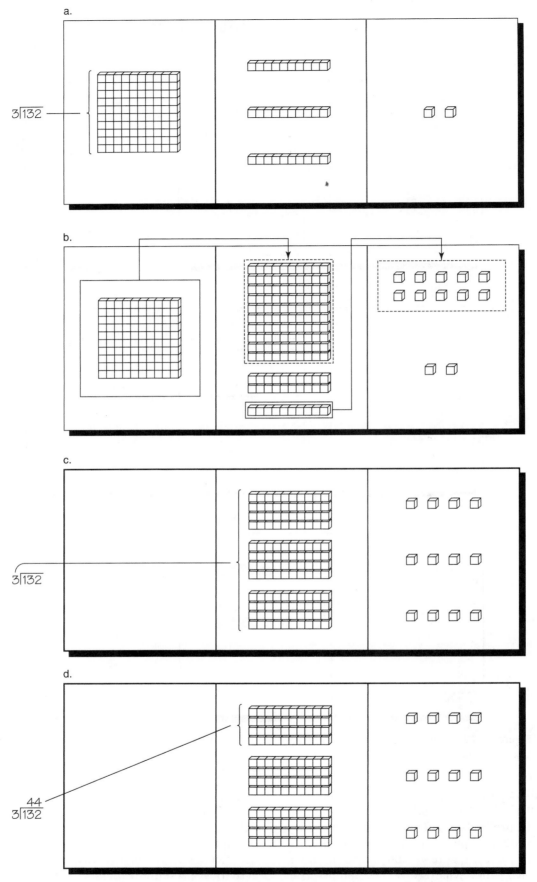

Figure 7–30 Numeral representation and base ten blocks representation of 132 ÷ 3 using partition division.

it as their standard algorithm. It is appropriate for children to create their own algorithms; encourage them to do so.

A C T I V I T I E S

Grades 3–5

OBJECTIVE: to invent algorithms for division problems.

1. Introduce "solve it any way you can" problems. Present a problem and invite students to solve the problem using any technique they may choose. For example, "Tomorrow we are going to make small pizzas in class. Four children can share a pizza. We have 26 children in our class. How many pizzas should we make?" Be ready to provide children materials that they may ask for. When the students have finished working, have them discuss how they found the solution and share any materials that they may have used.

OBJECTIVE: to use various algorithms for division.

2. When the **expanded notation algorithm** is used, children are better able to see what happens in each place-value position of the dividend. The problem below shows 96 ÷ 4.

$$4\overline{)96} \quad 4\overline{)90+6} \quad 4\overline{)80+16}$$

$$4\overline{)80+16}^{\,20+4} \quad 4\overline{)96}^{\,24}$$

The number in the dividend, 96, is rewritten in expanded form. Because 4 does not evenly divide into 90, regrouping is required from the tens to the ones place. Thus, 90 + 6 is regrouped to 80 + 16. Then the 80 is divided by 4 and the 16 is divided by 4, resulting in 20 + 4. Then 20 + 4 is rewritten into standard form, 24.

You may find it necessary to help children work through several examples of the expanded notation algorithm with physical models such as base ten blocks, beans, and Cuisenaire rods while performing the algorithm. Work first with problems that do not require regrouping, such as 48 ÷ 4. With some practice, children should gain understanding of the division process.

3. Repeated subtraction may be used as an algorithm. The division problem 48 ÷ 12 may be thought of as asking, "how many 12s are contained in 48?" This is the measurement concept of division. We may solve the problem by seeing how many times 12 may be subtracted from 48. This is illustrated by the problem

below. Here, we see that there are four 12s in 48 because it took four subtractions of 12 to reach zero.

$$
12\overline{)48} \qquad
\begin{array}{r}
48 \\
-12 \ (1) \\
\hline
36 \\
-12 \ (2) \\
\hline
24 \\
-12 \ (3) \\
\hline
12 \\
-12 \ (4) \\
\hline
0
\end{array}
$$

It takes many separate subtractions to solve a problem like 48 ÷ 4. It is much more efficient to subtract multiples of 4. The problem below shows that the first subtraction is 10 × 4 and that the second subtraction is 2 × 4. The final result is that 10 + 2, or twelve, 4s are contained in 48. If children had to perform 12 or more subtractions, it is questionable they would maintain much interest. Subtracting using multiples of the divisor helps eliminate this difficulty.

$$
4\overline{)48} \qquad
\begin{array}{r}
48 \\
-40 \ (10\times4) \\
\hline
8 \\
-8 \ (2\times4) \\
\hline
0
\end{array}
$$

4. The **Greenwood,** or **down the side,** algorithm is particularly useful because it helps avoid one of the pitfalls of long division, incorrect estimation of quotient figures. The Greenwood algorithm incorporates the repeated subtraction idea presented above. The following problem illustrates this algorithm for the division 597 ÷ 27.

The first step is to estimate a multiple of the divisor, 27. In this case, we have estimated 10 × 27. The product 10 × 27, or 270, is subtracted from 597, leaving 327. We again estimate the multiple 10 × 27 in the second step. After subtracting 270 again, 57 remains. Our final estimate is 2 × 27, or 54. Subtracting 54 results in 3. Because 3 is less than the divisor, 3 is the remainder for this problem. We then add 10 + 10 + 2, which results in the quotient figure, 22. Thus, 597 ÷ 27 = 22 r3.

When the partial quotient figures were estimated, the multiples were 10 times the divisor. Using 10 or 100 times the divisor simplifies the estimation. As children gain experience with estimating, they can estimate

2 Follow the Laws of Order

Order matters when you're putting on your shoes and socks, baking a cake, or setting a VCR to record your favorite program. You will see how the order in which you do addition, subtraction, multiplication, and division also makes a difference.

Evaluate an Expression in Different Ways

How does the order in which you perform operations affect the answer?

In the steps below, you will investigate different ways of evaluating the same expression. After you complete step 2, stop and participate in a class discussion before going on to step 3.

1 Use your calculator to evaluate the following expression: $14 \div 2 - 4 + 1 \times 6 \div 3 \times 2 + 10$. Enter the numbers and operation symbols from left to right. Press the $=$ key only after you enter the entire expression. Record your answer.

2 Try to figure out in what order the calculator evaluated the expression in step 1. Describe what you think is actually going on "inside" the calculator. Hint: One way to discover the order of operations a calculator uses is to record the number your calculator shows each time you press an operation sign.

3 Evaluate the expression in step 1 in a way that is different from the way you think your calculator did it. Explain your answer.

4 Exchange papers with a partner.

   a. Try to figure out what was going on inside your partner's calculator.

   b. Try to figure out how your partner evaluated the expression in a different way.

   c. Do you agree with the two ways your partner evaluated the expression? Why?

Figure 7–31 From *MathScape: Seeing and Thinking Mathematically, Sixth Grade,* copyright ©1998 by Creative Publications. All rights reserved. Reprinted by permission of The McGraw-Hill Companies.

Figure 7–31 shows a page from a sixth-grade student guide designed to introduce a need for developing consistent rules for the order of operations. In this activity, students are encouraged to evaluate the same expressions using different calculators. Students are encouraged to record the number that is shown on the calculator each time an operation sign is pressed and to press the equal sign only at the end of the entire expression. Students are usually quite surprised that not all calculators give the same response even when they have correctly pressed all the same keys. After realizing that different calculators give different answers, students are encouraged to work with a partner to determine what is going on inside the calculator and asked whether they agree with the results. It is only after a thorough discussion with a partner and then as a class that students discuss the need for mathematicians to have an agreed-upon method of evaluating expressions. After this discussion, the students are told which expression uses the correct order of operations and are asked to determine what the rules for this are and to suggest ways to remember these rules. There is also a warning that if the mnemonic PEMDAS (Please Excuse My Dear Aunt Sally: Parentheses—Exponents—Multiplication—Division—Addition—Subtraction) is used, students must know that multiplication and division are at the same level and done from left to right and that the same is true of addition and subtraction. This middle grades mathematics program, *MathScape: Seeing and Thinking Mathematically,* was developed under a grant from the National Science Foundation and is designed to implement the recommendations of the National Council of Teachers of Mathematics *Principles and Standards for School Mathematics.* Activities stress classroom discourse and students making sense of the mathematics rather than simply memorizing rules. This activity follows activities that emphasize "Start with what you know" and playing a "What must be true?" game. Sample student work is included with each lesson and is frequently used to identify common student misconceptions. Each activity focuses on developing student power, and the series includes a wide variety of assessment strategies.

partial quotients that are close to but less than the dividend.

A variation of the Greenwood algorithm is one in which children put their partial quotients above the dividend in the proper place-value position. When all estimates have been made, the final quotient is determined by adding up. The problem below shows how this **pyramid method** works for 597 ÷ 27.

The first estimate is 10, which is placed above the dividend, 597. Then 10 × 27, or 270, is subtracted from 597. The second estimate also is 10, which is placed above the first estimate. Then 270 is subtracted from 327, leaving 57. The final estimate, 2, is placed above the other two estimates. Then 54 is subtracted from 57, leaving 3, the remainder. The sum of the partial products, 10 + 10 + 2, is found, with the final result of 22 r3.

When performing the standard division algorithm, four basic steps must be completed, sometimes several times for a given problem. These steps are: (1) estimating the quotient figure, (2) multiplying the partial quotient times the divisor, (3) subtracting the product from the dividend, and (4) checking the difference to make sure it is less than the divisor and, if it is not, revising the quotient figure. Each of these steps provides opportunities for mistakes and frustration.

Hallmarks of the division algorithm are erasure marks on students' papers. Calculators can help students estimate quotient figures. Accord time and patience to children as they develop skill with the division algorithm. Encourage them and provide them with careful teaching and reteaching.

Engage in discussions so students have an opportunity to share their thinking. In this section, we have discussed developing computational fluency for multiplication and division. First, it involves having recall of the multiplication and division combinations. Second, it involves using effective procedures or algorithms for multiplying and dividing. Current math texts present thorough instruction on how to develop standard algorithms, and they contain ample problems for practice. Be sure to invite students to invent and discuss their own algorithms before using those in the text.

Developing Fluency with Integers

Operations with integers should be practiced and mastered in the middle grades. When students are fluent with addition, subtraction, multiplication, and division of integers, they know how to perform the operations and they know why and how the answers are positive or negative. Using models such as number lines, colored chips, and money helps students see patterns that can be generalized into rules for operations. After exploring questions like "When is the product of two factors always positive?" or "What happens if I divide a negative number by a positive number?", students should make observations such as when two positive numbers are multiplied, the result is a larger positive number. For example, $(^+3) \times (^+4) = {^+}12$. When two negative numbers are multiplied, the result is a positive number. For example, $(^-6) \times (^-5) = {^+}30$. There have been many ways suggested about how to picture what is going on when a negative number is multiplied by a negative number; for example, using patterns, highway models, number lines, bill paying, mathematical explanations, and proofs. A variety of these models are presented on Weblink 7−3. When one positive number and one negative number (or one negative number and one positive number) are multiplied, the product is negative. For example, $(^+4) \times (^-6) = {^-}24$.

When two positive numbers are divided, the result is a positive number. For example, $(^+18) \div (^+3) = {^+}6$. There are cases, of course, when the quotient is a whole number with a remainder or when the quotient is a rational number. In all cases, the results are positive. When two negative numbers are divided, the result is a positive number. For example, $(^-28) \div (^-7) = 4$. Again, there are cases when the quotient is a whole number with a remainder or when the quotient is a rational number, but all cases are positive. When a negative number is divided by a positive number or when a positive number is divided by a negative number, the result is a negative number. For example, $(^-22) \div (^+2) = ^-11$. This case may also result in a whole number with a remainder or a rational number, but all cases are negative. Students should discuss why this is true.

For students to be fluent with multiplying and dividing integers, they need to develop procedures that build on understanding what they are doing and understanding why each procedure works. During the learning process for operations on integers, students should be encouraged to develop algorithms that are comfortable for them and make sense. Following are activities that help develop proficiency multiplying and dividing integers.

A C T I V I T I E S

Grades 6–8

OBJECTIVE: to practice multiplying and dividing integers.

1. Use a regular deck of playing cards without the jokers and face cards, or make your own deck with ten red cards (numbered 1 through 10) and ten black cards (numbered 1 through 10). The black cards are worth positive amounts, and the red cards are worth negative amounts. This is a game best played by four players, but it can be adjusted for other numbers of players by adding more cards. Begin the game by shuffling the cards and dealing three cards face down to each player. Each player then picks up his or her three cards, looks at the cards, and passes one of the cards to the player on the left. Next, each player multiplies the numbers shown on the three cards, taking into account whether the product is positive or negative. This is the score for round one. On each turn, a player passes one card to the player on the left. If you receive a red 5, you must multiply the other two numbers shown are your cards by a negative 5. Can the score for a single hand be 1,000? What is the highest score for a single hand? What is the lowest score for a single hand? Round two and subsequent rounds are played in the same way. At the end of round two, the score from round two is added to the score from round one. Play continues in the same manner until someone has a score greater in absolute value than 1,500 or until time is called. If time is called, the player with the score greatest in absolute value at the end of the game wins. Rules may be established about whether mental calculations, paper and pencil, or calculators should be used.

A variation of this game for division is to have each player draw two cards from the stack that are placed face down in front of the players. In this game, the card with the greater absolute value is divided by the card with the lower absolute value (or either card if they are the same). The remainder is the score for the round. If the numbers on two black cards are divided, the remainder is assigned a positive value. If the numbers on two red cards are divided, the remainder is assigned a positive value. If the numbers on one red card and one black card are divided, the remainder is assigned a negative value. The scores for each round are totaled. The first player to have a score greater in absolute value than 30 is the winner. To make the game more challenging, a set of cards could be constructed so that there are black numbers from 1 to 30 and red numbers from 1 to 30.

2. As was suggested in Chapter 6, students may use the computer program *The Great Signed Number Race* to practice working with positive and negative integers and all operations in a race through the Old West.

ESTIMATING, USING BENCHMARKS, AND MENTAL CALCULATING

Estimation and mental arithmetic play an important role in both paper-and-pencil and calculator computation involving multiplication and division. Students should know if their answers are reasonable. This is done by estimating products or quotients just before or just after working an algorithm or using a calculator, and comparing the estimated results to the calculated results. If the results vary considerably, the students should recalculate the results. The procedure takes just a few moments, and it should develop into a lifelong habit. Estimator Four from the Number and Operation Concepts section of the Shodor Education Foundation interactive website gives you a choice of addition, multiplication, and percentage estimation practice in a game format. It can be found on Weblink 7–4.

Estimating quotient figures in the standard division algorithm is a skill that challenges many children. For example, below are two division problems that for most fifth graders require estimation. An older student may be able to look at the divisor, realize that $2 \times 64 = 128$, and estimate the quotient figure in the first example at 1 and the quotient figure in the second example at 2.

$$64\overline{)1279} \qquad 64\overline{)1289}$$

We examine two ways to estimate the quotient figure. The first is to round the divisor up or down, depending on the units digit. The numbers 61 to 64 would be rounded down to the benchmark 60, while 65 to 69 would be rounded up to the benchmark 70. In our problem, 64 would be rounded to 60. The guide number, 6, is used to determine the first quotient figure in $1,279 \div 64$. We ask, "How many 6s are contained in 12?" Our estimate is 2. We soon discover that 2 is too large and revise the estimate to 1, which is correct. Using the same procedure for $1,289 \div 64$, we estimate a quotient figure of 2; this one is correct. With this rounding procedure, students should be willing to revise their estimates.

The second way to estimate the quotient figure is to construct a table of multiples of the divisor. Using a calculator, this takes a few moments. These multiples become benchmarks for determining quotient figures. The multiples of 64 are:

$1 \times 64 = 64$ $4 \times 64 = 256$ $7 \times 64 = 448$
$2 \times 64 = 128$ $5 \times 64 = 320$ $8 \times 64 = 512$
$3 \times 64 = 192$ $6 \times 64 = 384$ $9 \times 64 = 576$

By examining the dividend of the first problem, the student will realize that 2×64 in the table of multiples is too large, and therefore the estimate must be 1. For the second problem, the estimate 2 is correct because $2 \times 64 = 128$. Not only is the first quotient figure easy to estimate, the other quotient figures in the problem are also easy to estimate.

A variation of this approach is to estimate the entire quotient using the multiples of 64 in combination with the powers of 10. Thus, the first estimated quotient figure is 10, to which you add 9 as you continue the problem. This is similar to the approach used in the Greenwood algorithm discussed earlier.

No single method of estimating quotient figures has been shown to be superior. Encourage the children to construct their own algorithms and let the children select the one they find most comfortable.

A C T I V I T I E S

Grade 3 – 5

OBJECTIVE: to practice estimating multiplication and division.

1. Use a set of double-nine dominoes. The large-format dominoes work well if this activity is done with the whole class. Hold up a domino for about three seconds. Ask the children if they believe the product of the two sides of the domino is more than, less than, or equal to 40. Let them signal to you that the product is 40 by putting a hand flat on the table or floor. A hand with thumb up means more than 40. A hand with thumb down means less than 40.

For division estimation, put a numeral such as 50 on the chalkboard. Hold up a domino for about three seconds, and have the students find the sum of the two sides and then divide 50 by the sum. Have them indicate whether the quotient is more than, less than, or equal to 5. The students can use the same hand signs as before.

2. On occasion, we need to multiply large numbers or estimate their product in our heads. Sometimes these numbers are powers of 10 or multiples of powers of 10, as in 50×70 or 30×600. Other times, the numbers are not even decades, as in 38×19 or 53×691. In the first case, numbers like 50 and 70 may be multiplied by counting the zeros (there are two) and then multiplying the remaining numbers, 5 and 7. When the result, 35, is rejoined with the two zeros, we have $50 \times 70 = 3,500$.

With 30×600, follow the same procedure. Count the zeros (there are 3) and multiply the remaining numbers, 3 and 6, to get 18. Rejoin the 3 zeros to produce the answer, 18,000.

In the case in which the numbers are not powers of 10 or multiples of powers of 10, use the rounding strategy described in Chapter 6. The numbers are rounded up or down, then multiplied, and then the product is adjusted. For example, with 38×19, round 38 to 40, and round 19 to 20. Then multiply 40×20. The result, 800, is an estimation of the product of 38×19. Because both numbers were rounded up, the estimation is somewhat higher than the actual product of 38×19, which is 722.

For the problem 53×691, round 53 down to 50 and round 691 up to 700. Then compute the product of 50×700, which is 35,000. Because one number was rounded up and one was rounded down, it is more difficult to tell whether our estimation is too high or too low. The actual product of 53×691 is 36,623 and shows us the estimate was low. If both numbers had been rounded down, the estimate would have been below the actual product.

Another type of problem requiring mental calculation is sometimes presented. If 6×49 or 6×51 requires an exact answer, remember that 6×49 is 6 less than 6×50. Without difficulty, we know $6 \times 50 = 300$; six less is 294. Likewise, 6×51 is 6 greater than 6×50, or 306. It is helpful for children to practice multiplying numbers that are even decades, one less, or one greater.

OBJECTIVE: to use historical material to motivate estimation and mental arithmetic.

3. Chapter 6 presented several mental exercises that appeared in an 1859 text by Greenleaf. Here are mental exercises prescribed by Daniel Fish in *Arithmetical Problems, Oral and Written,* copyrighted in 1874 (see Figure 7–32). Just before he presents 73 mental exercises and 120 written exercises, Fish notes:

> Any class or pupil that has gone over the Elementary Rules, in regular course of any textbook on these subjects, should be prepared for test, drill, and review in the examples of this chapter. (p. 47)

Examples of the exercises Fish included in his book follow. The page on which each problem can be found is provided in parentheses.

- $8 \times 9 \div 12 + 3 \times 5 + 10 \div 11 \times 8 + 20 \div 12 + 4 \times 7 - 3 =$ how many? (p. 49)
- A number multiplied by 8, divided by 6, multiplied by 10, and the product increased by 5 equals 45; what is the number? (p. 49)

- A farmer sold a grocer 15 bushels of potatoes at $1 a bushel, and bought 20 pounds of sugar at 15 cents a pound, and 10 pounds of coffee at 30 cents a pound; how many pounds of tea at 75 cents a pound could he buy for what was still due him? (p. 51)
- If it costs $56 for bricks to build a cistern when bricks are worth $8 a thousand, what will it cost for bricks to build it when they are worth $10 a thousand? (p. 52)

OBJECTIVE: to use the calculator to improve multiplication and division estimation skills.

4. Four to six players and one calculator are needed. One player is *it* for the first round. That player generates a number on the calculator by entering and multiplying four numbers equal to or less than 12,

Figure 7–32   Title page of Fish's 1874 *Arithmetical Problems* book.

such as $11 \times 8 \times 6 \times 9 = 4,752$. The object of the game is to find numbers that will divide the number generated and then to divide by those numbers, generating new numbers. Play continues until a player correctly announces "prime," indicating that only two factors are left, 1 and the number itself.

Play begins as soon as the initial number is generated. The calculator is passed to the player to the left of the person who is it and continues to the left. The player who is it does not play in that round. The first player divides 4,752 by a number he or she thinks will divide evenly by pressing the divide sign, entering the number, and pressing the equals sign. Neither 1 nor the number itself may be used as a divisor. If the number is correct, the calculator is passed to the next player. If it is incorrect, that is, if the answer is not a whole number, the player restores the previous number, by multiplying by the number used to divide, and passes the calculator to the next player. It may be necessary to round the product to restore the previous number.

For each correct division, a point is scored. The player whose division results in a prime number and who declares "prime" is awarded another point. Each player must either divide or declare "prime." The person correctly declaring "prime" generates a new number. After three rounds, the player with the most points wins.

REASONING, SOLVING AND POSING MULTIPLICATION AND DIVISION PROBLEMS

Multiplication and division are important skills in problem solving. These operations are often necessary to help solve problems. For example, in Mr. Edwin's class, the students are constructing a cardboard geodesic dome like the one described in Chapter 11 (see Figure 11–35). The dome radius is to be 125 centimeters. The dome is constructed using triangles of two different sizes; some triangles are equilateral with side 0.6180 times the dome radius, and the other triangles have one side 0.6180 times the dome radius and two sides 0.5465 times the dome radius. Appliance cartons are available at the local dealer. It takes 15 of the equilateral triangles and 45 of the other triangles to make the dome. How many dishwasher cartons should be requested? Generate discussion about the size of each triangle and the additional information needed in order to request the cartons. Following are more problem situations that require the use of multiplication or division.

Grades 3–5

OBJECTIVE: to construct and solve problems involving multiplication and division.

1. Provide children with a worksheet that contains several frames, each with nine numerals and an empty box at the top. Figure 7–33a illustrates one of these frames.

Ask the children to choose any two numbers in the frame, multiply them together, and put the answer in the box at the top. Have them do this for each frame on the worksheet. When this is done, the children will have made problem boxes for other children to solve.

Have the children exchange the worksheets and see if they can find the pair whose product equals the number on top. Instruct them to circle the two numbers. The children may check their solutions with the calculator.

Figure 7–33b shows one solution. With the same set of numbers in the frame, many different problems can be made. It is also possible to have more than one solution for a single problem.

To extend this activity to division, have the children divide any number in the box by a smaller number in the box and put the remainder in the box at the top. Figure 7–33c shows an example. We solve the problem below:

- *Understanding the problem.* The object here is to divide a larger number by a smaller number to produce a quotient with the remainder 7. The divisor must be greater than 7 because a divisor equal to or smaller than 7 cannot have a remainder of 7.

- *Devising a plan.* We should not use 7 as a divisor because it cannot result in a remainder of 7. Thus, we begin with the smallest possible divisor, 8, and the smallest dividend, 9, and work up through each of the dividends to be sure to try all combinations. After 9, we try these dividends: 24, 29, 35, 38, 50, and then 55 (numbers from the problem). Next, we use 9 as a divisor and work up through the dividends beginning with 24. We make a systematic list, continuing this way until we find the number with a remainder of 7.

  Is it possible that none of the divisions has a remainder of 7? Is it possible that more than one of the divisions have a remainder of 7?

- *Carrying out the plan.* We begin by dividing 24 by 8, 29 by 8, and 35 by 8, finding remainders of 0, 5, and 3. It occurs to us that if we can think of the greatest multiple of the divisor less than the dividend, we can just subtract that multiple from the dividend to get the remainder. For example, we

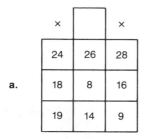

Figure 7–33   Frames for multiplication and division problem boxes.

subtract 24 − 24 = 0, 29 − 24 = 5, and 35 − 32 = 3 to find the first three remainders. Going on, we subtract 38 − 32 = 6, 50 − 48 = 2, and 55 − 48 = 7. There is an answer!

Is it the only answer? We continue working and find another solution, 55 divided by 24.

- *Looking back.* We take the two number pairs we found, 55 ÷ 8 and 55 ÷ 24, and divide again to make sure the remainder is 7. It is in both cases. We have satisfied the problem.

Further extend the activity by having the children determine all the numbers for the frame as well as the solution number and operation. The problems will become difficult and challenging. Make a display of problems and solutions.

OBJECTIVE: to develop a winning strategy.

2. This activity is called **High to Low.** Two players may play. The players mix up double-six dominoes and place them face down on the floor or a table. Each player turns over a domino. The player with the higher product goes first.

Each player draws 10 dominoes, keeping them face down. The first player turns over two dominoes as in Figure 7–34a.

Using each domino to represent a two-digit factor, the player decides which factor each domino will represent. For example, the four-two domino may be used as 42 or, reversed, 24. The three-zero domino may be used as 30 or 3. Once the two factors have been chosen, the player multiplies them together, using paper and pencil or a calculator. The player then puts the product on a scoring sheet similar to the one in Figure 7–34b.

The object is to put the product in one of the spaces so the other products will eventually be in order from highest to lowest. Suppose our first player, Harry, selected 23 and 3 as his two factors. He finds the product is 69 and places it in space number 2 on his scoring sheet as in Figure 7–34b.

The second player, Roberta, turns over two dominoes, selects two factors, multiplies them, and records the answer on her scoring sheet. Because five pairs of dominoes are selected, each player may discard one pair during play. However, the pair must be discarded before the player records the product on the scoring sheet. The player declares that turn a pass. Once a player passes, he or she must play all of the remaining dominoes.

Play continues until all of the spaces on the scoring cards of both players are filled. The players calculate their final scores by marking out any products not in order and adding the remaining products. If all four numbers are in order from highest to lowest, the player doubles the score. The player with the higher score wins.

For division, have the players proceed as above except the two dominoes represent a dividend and a divisor. Have them divide the larger number (dividend)

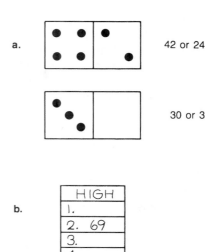

Figure 7–34   Sample dominoes and scoring sheet for High to Low.

a.

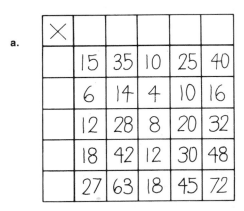

b.

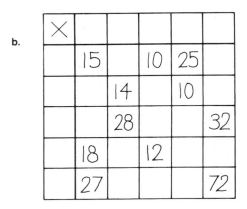

Figure 7–35 Problem table for multiplication practice.

by the smaller (divisor) and put the remainder on the scoring sheet. The other rules, including those for scoring, remain the same.

OBJECTIVE: to make and use problem tables.

3. This activity serves, in part, as a review of the multiplication and division combinations. Begin by putting on the chalkboard, an overhead projector, or worksheets a mixed-up multiplication table with no factors along the left side or across the top. An example is shown in Figure 7–35a.

Explain that all the numbers in the table are in the right place. The students must find the factor that belongs to the left of each row and at the top of each column to make the table correct.

To make this activity more challenging, present a table missing some of the numbers as well as the factors, as shown in Figure 7–35b. Have the children both complete the table and insert the factors.

Notice that the examples use single-digit factors. Extend this activity by introducing numbers each of which is the product of a single-digit factor and a two-digit factor or the product of two two-digit factors.

Encourage the children to make up tables of their own to see if they can stump other students. See who can construct the most difficult table puzzle. Display the results on a bulletin board.

ORGANIZING FOR ADDITION, SUBTRACTION, MULTIPLICATION, AND DIVISION TLC

When students are learning the concepts of the basic operations, the activities in which they are engaged should be problem-based, often emerging from word problems, challenging them to reflect on and discuss their solutions. For example, we might present this problem: "As you follow the Yukon Quest sled dog race between Fairbanks, Alaska, and Whitehorse, Yukon Territory, on its website [Weblink 7–5], you notice that a particular musher, Darren, is running 12 dogs at the fourth checkpoint. The trail is rough and the dogs have been fitted with "booties" to keep ice crystals from getting between their toes. Suppose you need to carry a dozen booties for each dog, as they sometimes lose them along the way. This team started the race with 13 dogs. How many booties did Darren have at the start of the race?" Be sure students have a chance to work on the problem individually at first. Then, initiate a discussion on how students went about solving the problem. Encourage questions among students and discussion of procedures. Perhaps a student or a table group may demonstrate a solution to the whole class, for example, using base ten blocks on the overhead projector, showing how they found 12×13. This provides children the chance to ask questions of the presenter and to clarify their thinking regarding the model being used. In this case, the class is organized in individual, small-group, and whole-class sessions during the course of working on the problem and discussing the results.

Having the students work in groups may be most appropriate when scarce materials are being used. A variety of materials may be used simultaneously, in keeping with the principle of multiple embodiment. The conversations among group members as they work together help individuals clarify their thinking and the thinking of others as they construct new concepts and algorithms.

As students learn the skills of the basic operations, the activities in which they are engaged lend themselves, by and large, to cooperative learning groups, pair work, or individual learning. A cooperative group goal may be to ensure that all group members have facility with some or all of the basic combinations in addition, subtraction, multiplication, or division. Considerable energy will likely be put forth, and the resulting pride in achieving the "basic combinations" goal will be long-lasting. When students engage in games and activities, they are often engaged as pairs, threes, or fours. When practicing with the computer or calculator, students will likely work individually or in pairs.

Students who are participating in estimating and mental-calculating activities may be organized in any fashion. You may find whole-group instruction efficient for practicing mental arithmetic so that you can instruct, provide examples, present practice problems, and invite discussion among students. When individuals need or desire special work in estimating and mental calculating, then small-group or individual participation may be most appropriate.

Because considerable time is spent developing the computational fluency in elementary school, you are encouraged to provide instruction in a variety of group settings to help maintain student interest. The activities suggested in Chapters 6 and 7 provide you with activities that can be adapted to various modes of instruction.

COMMUNICATING ADDITION, SUBTRACTION, MULTIPLICATION, AND DIVISION LEARNING

Oral and written communication provide ways for children to learn mathematics and thinking processes. Concepts and skills associated with the basic operations can be clarified, as well as illustrated, by children communicating with one another as well as with the teacher. Number stories were mentioned early in the process of developing the concepts of all the basic operations. Oral communication that includes the necessity for children to decide what is being asked, if information is missing, or if a passage or story makes sense, as well as accompanying mental calculation, should be a regular part of instruction.

Books that engage students in mathematical thinking such as *Anno's Mysterious Multiplying Jar* (Anno and Anno, 1983) and *Math Curse* (Scieszka and Smith, 1995) provide chances for students to use logic and problem solving as they read and listen to these delightful stories. There should be many opportunities for students to listen to and respond to stories involving calculating.

The constructivist theory of learning mathematics discussed in Chapter 2 stresses that students should be asked to share their theories about concepts, that students should be engaged in dialogue with the teacher and with one another, that the teacher should have students elaborate on their initial responses to questions, and that the teacher should ask thoughtful, open-ended questions and encourage students to ask questions of each other. All of these suggestions are intended to develop students' abilities to communicate mathematically.

Students are sometimes asked to keep journals as part of their language arts program. It is just as appropriate to keep a journal in mathematics. The math journal may be kept in the students' individual portfolios (see Chapter 3), along with math assignments, assessment material, and projects. Topics for writing include algorithms that students use to perform various calculations, whether these methods involve paper and pencil, mental calculation, estimation, or the calculator or computer. These journal entries may include the standard algorithms or those invented by individuals. Further, attitudes about mathematics or learning mathematics are appropriate topics for mathematics journals.

Creative stories about number may be episodes written as part of composition practice or as a journal entry. Reading Norton Juster's delightful book *The Phantom Tollbooth* (1961) will surely inspire students in grades 5–8 to write some wonderfully imaginative stories.

Cooperative and individual writing are appropriate activities for cooperative learning groups. As group members explore a mathematical problem, the group recorder provides a chronicle of the thinking process. These records are then shared with other groups during the "debriefing" time at the end of the activity. Discussion is then invited. Excellent examples of written descriptions of calculations and thinking are presented by Marilyn Burns in her books: *A Collection of Math Lessons from Grades 1 through 3* (Burns and Tank, 1988), *A Collection of Math Lessons from Grades 3 through 6* (Burns, 1987), and *A Collection of Math Lessons from Grades 6 through 8* (Burns and Humphreys, 1990).

CONNECTING AND REPRESENTING LEARNING OF MULTIPLICATION AND DIVISION

Ms. Roberts gathered her fourth-grade class together in the reading corner and began her lesson by asking what the word *mysterious* means. There were only three students who indicated that they knew for sure what the word means. Carlos responded that mysterious meant something that people could not figure out, like a mystery story. Others joined in and added that mysterious meant some thing like a robbery or something that was curious. Ms. Roberts asked if it could be about a jar and some math. The students looked puzzled and quickly responded that probably a jar and math were not very mysterious.

Then, Ms. Roberts opened the book *Anno's Mysterious Multiplying Jar* (Anno and Anno, 1983) and began reading, "This story is about one jar and what was inside it." After reading and showing the children the beautiful illustrations on the next two pages, Ms. Roberts continued, "On the sea was 1 island. On the island there were 2 countries. Within each country were 3 mountains. On each mountain there were 4 walled kingdoms." The students were captivated by the story as it continued. Finally, the story came to the lines, "Within each box there were 10 jars. But how many jars were in all the boxes together?"

Ms. Roberts then challenged the students to see if they could figure out how many jars there were. They were to work for 10 minutes in their table groups to get started on the problem and then take the problem home to complete. "That's just like the multiplying that we have been doing," commented Jennifer. Ms. Roberts agreed that that might be a good place to start. The students began their work.

That Jennifer was able to see the connection between her work in multiplication and the challenge set forth in *Anno's Mysterious Multiplying Jar* pleased Ms. Roberts. It also meant that the groups that began working on the problem were likely to devise plans to solve the problem and would soon find the solution. Mr. Christner's eight-grade mathematics students welcomed the announcement that they would be viewing a video on Tuesday. The short video, *Powers of Ten* (Eames, 1989), sparked the imagination of the students. This remarkable video shows a series of 42 views of the universe, ranging from 1 billion light-years (a square measuring 10^{25} meters on a side) to 0.1 fermi (a square measuring 10^{-16} meters on a side). Each successive view is 10 times narrower than the previous view. Thus, the video begins with a view of space that shows distant galaxies and narrows to eventually show the Milky Way, then the sun and planets, the earth, Lake Michigan, a park in Chicago, a man in the park, the man's hand, a capillary vessel in the man's hand, molecules in a cell in the man's hand, atoms that form the molecular structure in the man's hand, and finally the core of the atom.

To help the students understand the measures, Mr. Christner led a discussion about the meaning of *light-year* (the distance that light travels in one year, approximately 6,000,000,000,000 miles), kilometers, meters, millimeters, microns, angstroms, and fermis (the length 10^{-13} centimeters). The students were very impressed with the sizes of the views they had seen in the video. To give the students time to further grasp the information that they had seen and discussed, Mr. Christner made the Morrisons' book, *Powers of Ten* (1982), available for students to look at and read. The book was popular with the students for several weeks.

These activities are intended to involve students in applications of multiplying and dividing in a context that helps show how mathematics is connected with events in their world. Notice that using the Anno story helps connect mathematics and problem solving with literature. *Powers of Ten* set in two media, film and text, help to show clear connections among the elements of the universe. The book may be read and viewed from front to back or from back to front with the same enriching impact.

Another way to make connections is described by the National Research Council in its book *Measuring Up* (1993). In an interesting assessment activity entitled "How Many Buttons?" students are asked to estimate the number of buttons there are in their school. Prior to working on the problem, students have estimated the number of buttons in their class and then carefully counted and recorded their data on a line plot. Using their data and assumptions they must make that arise from questions, the students work in pairs to solve the problem and record their solution strategies, justifying why they chose particular strategies. This activity involves sampling procedures, multiplication and division, graphing, statistics, and use of calculators. For students to see how mathematical connections are made helps them to better understand how mathematics is an integral part of their lives.

ASSESSING LEARNING OF MULTIPLICATION AND DIVISION

Learning the basic multiplication and division combinations begins in the primary grades, generally in grades 2 and 3. Learning the algorithms for multiplication and division generally begins in earnest in grade 4. That is why the algorithm activities have been focused at grades 3–5.

Not all students who reach or even leave grade 6 can multiply or divide proficiently. What should you as a teacher do when students are not performing at your level of expectation? Use individual or small-group instruction. Determine why there is an inability to multiply or divide. Is it because the student does not know what multiplication or division is (concept)? Does the student not know the basic combinations (skill)? Can it be that the student cannot perform an algorithm (skill)? Does the student lack interest because of past failure with multiplication and division (affect)? Are assignments with too many problems causing discouragement (affect)?

There are many ways multiplication and division learning are assessed. As students construct their own algorithms, the opportunity to assess their work arises by questioning the students or reading the descriptions of how they discovered a solution. Math texts include carefully designed testing programs. Virtually every step of the learning process is tested and retested. Students should periodically submit a work sample to be placed in their portfolios. These work samples will document the growth the students are making. Part of the teacher's responsibility is to assure learning takes place at the appropriate developmental level.

In Chapter 6, we discussed several reasons children make mistakes. You may wish to review those reasons for they are the same for children performing multiplication and division. Some children will have difficulty completing algorithms, whether their own or those from the textbook. Your diagnostic skills will be challenged as soon as you enter the classroom. From the time of your first activity and thereafter, there will be children's hands in the air or children lining up by your desk requesting help.

The first comment you may hear is "I don't get it." This means the student does not know what the assignment is, did not listen to your explanation, wants your attention, does not want to try, or is unable to do an algorithm. You must decide what caused the student to say, "I don't get it."

The diagnosis has begun. Generally, you must individually reteach part or all of an algorithm or look at a partially or fully completed algorithm and decide where the student made an error. Most teacher's guides list only the answers to the problems from the student texts. They do not show each step in the algorithm, particularly if the students developed the algorithm. Thus, with only the answer at hand, you must listen to the student work through the algorithm with which the student is having difficulty to see where the error is.

In a multiplication problem such as 24 × 54, you may find one or more of these errors: (a) problem miscopied from the text, (b) basic combination error, (c) regrouping was not done, (d) regrouping took place when not needed, (e) student forgot to add the regrouped amount after multiplying, (f) problem not completed, (g) partial products not lined up, and (h) error in adding partial products. Each of these errors is illustrated in problems a–h below. Problem i shows a "standard" algorithm.

a.
$$\begin{array}{r} {}^{12}45 \\ \times 24 \\ \hline 180 \\ 90 \\ \hline 1{,}080 \end{array}$$

b.
$$\begin{array}{r} {}^{1}54 \\ \times 24 \\ \hline 218 \\ 108 \\ \hline 1{,}298 \end{array}$$

c.
$$\begin{array}{r} 54 \\ \times 24 \\ \hline 206 \\ 108 \\ \hline 1{,}286 \end{array}$$

d.
$$\begin{array}{r} {}^{1}54 \\ \times 24 \\ \hline 216 \\ 118 \\ \hline 1{,}396 \end{array}$$

e.
$$\begin{array}{r} {}^{1}54 \\ \times 24 \\ \hline 206 \\ 108 \\ \hline 1{,}286 \end{array}$$

f.
$$\begin{array}{r} {}^{1}54 \\ \times 24 \\ \hline 216 \end{array}$$

g.
$$\begin{array}{r} {}^{1}54 \\ \times 24 \\ \hline 216 \\ 108 \\ \hline 324 \end{array}$$

h.
$$\begin{array}{r} {}^{1}54 \\ \times 24 \\ \hline 216 \\ 108 \\ \hline 1{,}276 \end{array}$$

i.
$$\begin{array}{r} {}^{1}54 \\ \times 24 \\ \hline 216 \\ 108 \\ \hline 1{,}296 \end{array}$$

All of this assumes that you and the students are using the same algorithm. For students who use an alternative algorithm or an individually constructed algorithm, there may be other types of errors. It is well worth exploring with the students how they are going about reaching their solutions.

Coping with the "I don't get it" students demands teaching time. Besides diagnosing and correcting students' written errors, students may need to return to physical models to illustrate whatever is not clear from the abstract or pictorial approach. Above all, you must be supportive and encouraging. Let the students know you are working with them for the same ends.

Skillful diagnosis of the cause or causes of students' difficulties requires you to be proficient in mathematics and knowledgeable about children and the learning process. Take advantage of resource people in your school who may be able to assist in diagnosing. Sometimes students need extra time or a new approach for learning basic combinations. Sometimes algorithms must be carefully retaught, perhaps using grid paper to emphasize proper alignment of digits as in Figure 7–36.

For students to gain the most from them, activities must seem worth doing. A sixth grader should be convinced that she or he is not doing fourth- or fifth grade work. Allow students to use calculators so they may continue to learn other or more advanced mathematics and not always be frustrated by their weaknesses with basic combinations. Finally, be willing to set aside certain textbook assignments; assignments can pile up and turn students away from mathematics.

The communication between you and your students, whether it be from conversations or from journal entries, can be the basis for assessing their progress in mathematics. Being a willing and compassionate listener will benefit both you and your students. It may well be that both of you are thinking alike and merely expressing the ideas differently.

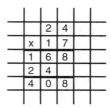

Figure 7–36 Using grid paper for aligning a multiplication problem.

SOMETHING FOR EVERYONE

Teaching operations with whole numbers and integers involves considerable work with abstract symbols. The activities in Chapters 6 and 7 are intended to supplement and enrich the math text. In the mathematics textbook, operations are usually carefully presented using pictorial and abstract modes. Teacher's manuals recommend that teachers use physical models, as well. All of these approaches, the manipulative, pictorial, and abstract, are presented because we know that children tend to learn from the concrete to the abstract.

There are other modes of learning, however, that should be attended to as children learn whole-number operations. Children who learn most effectively in a visual/spatial mode should be provided with pictures and encouraged to draw pictures and diagrams as they develop concepts and skills involving operations with whole numbers. Representing operations on the number line and drawing arrays to illustrate multiplication combinations may be especially useful for visual/spatial learners. The math text can be helpful for these learners as well when attractive illustrations are accompanied by careful instructions, but be aware that children do not always interpret diagrams the way textbook authors intend them to. Ask the children to tell you what they think the drawings mean. Talk about the mathematics that is being presented.

Bodily/kinesthetic learners find materials such as colored cubes, base ten blocks, Cuisenaire rods, and abaci useful in learning operations with whole numbers. Bodily/kinesthetic learners should see and manipulate physical models of the operations as they are simultaneously writing down the abstract symbols. This manipulation helps them to connect what they are doing to the abstract algorithms they are learning in the books. Be sure that these children understand that the particular material they are using is not important. Encourage them to use several different materials to model the same exercise.

Challenge bodily/kinesthetic learners to create their own algorithms for the operations and then test them using physical models to see if their methods will work for all kinds of problems. Let these students teach their algorithms to other students in the class and keep a record of the favorite methods.

Children who learn most effectively in the verbal/linguistic mode should find it fairly easy to learn basic combinations and algorithms by oral means. These children will likely be able to understand oral instructions and suggestions for correcting faulty algorithms more easily than other children. They can sometimes help in explaining adult instructions to other students. They may enjoy listening to tapes or records of songs and poems designed to help children memorize basic combinations. They may even make up their own mnemonic devices to remember combinations or the steps in an algorithm.

Children who are logical/mathematical learners benefit from an emphasis on following each step in an algorithm. These children can often work comfortably at an abstract level by fifth or sixth grade and may be able to follow the written instructions in the book if accompanied by careful oral directions from the teacher. These children often do well with a traditional approach to instruction, but even these children can benefit from some work with physical models. Although such children may appear to be doing well, they may not have a concrete understanding of what they are doing. They should be encouraged to illustrate each step of an algorithm with physical models such as chips for trading, an abacus, or bundling sticks.

Children who process information existentially are more apt to visualize an answer without going through a step-by-step process. Even though these children often have a superior number sense, they may not do well in a traditional mathematics program because they have difficulty in memorizing isolated facts or in following an algorithm with several steps.

Such children should be encouraged to explore the relationships among combinations both concretely and abstractly. For example, they may be able to find the answer to $6 + 7$ because they know the doubles and they know that $6 + 7$ is 1 more than $6 + 6$ or 1 less than $7 + 7$. Some children even hide these abilities because they believe they are cheating if they use the answer to a previous combination to find a new answer instead of memorizing each combination in isolation. Be sure to let such children know that it is good to relate combinations. The best mathematicians are those who can find the greatest number of relationships among known ideas and use them to discover new relationships. Visual/spatial learners should be able to work well with materials such as base ten blocks and Cuisenaire rods.

Be sure to have children with different learning styles share their methods with each other. All students can benefit by learning to work in different modes and can strengthen their own abilities to learn by being able to choose among a number of different learning strategies.

Promising students should be provided with enriching experiences that extend their thinking abilities. Challenge them with problem-solving activities that use operations with whole numbers and integers (the ones suggested in Chapters 6 and 7 may provide a starting point). Let promising students make up problems for each other and the rest of the class or explore patterns in the addition and multiplication tables or in multidigit algorithms.

Use the pre- or posttests provided in textbooks to assess students before you assign work with a given unit. The tests can tell you if there are any gaps in the students' knowledge of the information you are about to present. If the children have already mastered the concepts, provide them with new challenges. Never force the promising students to work every problem on a page when the other children are working only the even exercises; promising students soon learn to hide their talents to avoid boring busywork.

Challenge promising students by exploring algorithms that have been used historically for operations with whole numbers. Children sometimes believe that there is only one right way to work a problem, and they are amazed to find that people in other times or even today in other parts of the world use algorithms quite different from the ones found in American textbooks. Ask the children to explain why these algorithms work. Encourage them to make up other algorithms of their own. After they master operations with whole numbers in base ten, introduce operations in other bases.

Children who have difficulty with operations in base ten may need a slower, more individualized approach. If children do not seem to understand the standard algorithm, try a different method. Children who have trouble with the traditional multiplication algorithm may have more success with lattice multiplication. Children having difficulty dividing may be more successful using the Greenwood method. Or, these students may find success by inventing their own algorithms.

Children having difficulty may need more time to work with physical models. They need to make sense of the basic operations. Do not rush them to learn abstract algorithms. Encourage them to write down the algorithm as they manipulate the objects. When the objects are no longer needed, most children give up the objects by themselves because it is faster to write the algorithm without manipulating the objects.

Children's learning styles and abilities should help determine how you present mathematics. Be sensitive to the individual needs of all children with whom you work. Be sure, however, to include enriching and pleasurable activities for all students.

FOR YOU AS A TEACHER: IDEAS FOR DISCUSSION AND YOUR PROFESSIONAL PORTFOLIO

This section is intended to provide you the opportunity to read, write, and reflect on key elements of this chapter. We list several discussion ideas. We hope that one or more of these ideas will prove interesting to you and that you will choose to investigate and write

about the ideas. The results of your work should be considered as part of your professional portfolio. You might consider these two questions as guides for your writing: "What does the material in this chapter mean for you as a teacher?" or "How can what you are reading be translated into a teaching practice for you as a teacher?"

DISCUSSION IDEAS

1. Select either the concept of multiplication or the concept of division. Discuss how that concept can be presented to a class of second-grade students in a way that leads to conceptual understanding.

2. Compare the array model for multiplication with the Cuisenaire rod model. How are they alike and how are they different? Discuss your ability to teach multiplication using either model.

3. Construct a division basic combinations table. How can you help children memorize the basic division combinations by first introducing the families of related facts for multiplication and division?

4. Construct one of the games designed to help students remember the basic multiplication and division combinations. Play the game with a classmate or two and discuss the strengths of that game for helping students.

5. Become proficient with multiplication on the Napier's rods. Teach someone else how to multiply 26 × 365 using the rods. You may need to prepare the other person by showing him or her an easier problem first.

6. Visit Weblink 7–6. On this website you will find many activities that focus on number and operations for students in grades 3–5. Explore the site and the many links to other sites. Make a record of activities that will help you as a teacher.

ADDITIONAL RESOURCES

REFERENCES

Burk, Donna, Allyn Snider, and Paula Symonds, *Math Excursions 2: Project-Based Mathematics for Second Graders.* Portsmouth, NH: Heinemann, 1991.

Burns, Marilyn, *A Collection of Math Lessons from Grades 3 through 6.* White Plains, NY: Cuisenaire Co. of America, 1987.

Burns, Marilyn, and Cathy Humphreys, *A Collection of Math Lessons from Grades 6 through 8.* New Rochelle, NY: Math Solutions, 1990.

Burns, Marilyn, and Barbara Tank, *A Collection of Math Lessons from Grades 1 through 3.* White Plains, NY: Cuisenaire Co. of America, 1988.

Cooke, Marcia B, "A Videotaping Project to Explore the Multiplication of Integers," *Arithmetic Teacher,* 41 (November 1993), 170–171.

Creative Publications, *MathScape: Seeing and Thinking Mathematically.* Mountain View, CA: Creative Publications, 1998.

Fish, Daniel W., *Arithmetical Problems, Oral and Written; with Numerous Tables of Money, Weights, Measures, Etc.* New York: Ivison, Blakeman, Taylor & Co., 1874.

Morrison, Philip, and Phylis Morrison, *Powers of Ten.* New York: Scientific American Library, 1982.

National Council of Teachers of Mathematics, *Principles and Standards for School Mathematics.* Reston, VA: NCTM, 2000.

National Research Council, *Measuring Up.* Washington, DC: National Academy Press, 1993.

Reys, Robert E., et al., *Keystrokes: Multiplication and Division.* Palo Alto, CA: Creative Publications, 1979.

Schoen, Harold L., and Marilyn J. Zweng, eds., *Estimation and Mental Computation.* Reston, VA: National Council of Teachers of Mathematics, 1986.

Seymour, Dale, *Developing Skills in Estimation, Book A.* Palo Alto, CA: Dale Seymour, 1981.

Sheffield, Linda Jensen, *Problem Solving in Math, Book D.* New York: Scholastic, 1982.

CHILDREN'S LITERATURE

Aker, Suzanne, *What Comes in 2s, 3s, & 4s?* New York: Simon & Schuster, 1990.

Anno, Masaichiro, and Mitsumasa Anno, *Anno's Mysterious Multiplying Jar.* New York: Philomel, 1983.

Giganti, Paul, Jr., *Each Orange Had 8 Slices: A Counting Book.* Hong Kong: Greenwillow, 1992.

Hamm, Diane Johnson, *How Many Feet in the Bed?* New York: Simon & Schuster, 1991.

Hutchins, Pat, *The Doorbell Rang.* New York: Mulberry, 1986.

Juster, Norton, *The Phantom Tollbooth.* New York: Random House, 1961.

Scieszka, Jon, and Lane Smith, *Math Curse.* New York: Penguin, 1995.

Wahl, John, and Stacey Wahl, *I Can Count the Petals of a Flower.* Reston, VA: National Council of Teachers of Mathematics, 1977.

TECHNOLOGY

Eames, Charles, *Powers of Ten.* Santa Monica, CA, Pyramid Film &, 1989. (video)

Edmark. *Mighty Math Calculating Crew.* Redmond, WA: Edmark, 1997. (software)

Seiler, Bonnie A., *The Great Signed Number Race How Integers Won the West.* Pleasantville, NY: Sunburst Communications, 1997. (software)

WEBLINKS

Weblink 7–1: NCTM Illuminations lesson plan: A Videotaping Project to Explore the Multiplication of Integers. http://Illuminations.nctm.org/lessonplans/6–8/videotaping/index.html

Weblink 7–2: NCTM Illuminations activity: The Product Game. http://Illuminations.nctm.org/imath/6–8/Product Game/ product1.html

Weblink 7–3: Ask Dr. Math: FAQ, Negative × Negative = Positive. http://mathforum.org/dr.math/faq/faq.negxneg.html

Weblink 7–4: Estimator Four from the Number and Operation Concepts section gives you a choice of addition, multiplication, and percentage estimation practice. http://www.shodor.org/interactivate/activities/egame/index.html

Weblink 7–5: Website of the Yukon Quest International Sled Dog Race. http://www.yukonquest.org

Weblink 7–6: NCTM Illuminations selected web resources for number and operation for grades 3–5. http://Illuminations.nctm.org/swr/list.asp?Ref=1&Std=0&Grd=3

ATTACHING MEANING TO RATIONAL NUMBERS

GUIDING QUESTIONS

As you read the following pages, consider these guiding questions:

1. What applications and physical models might you use to help students develop part-whole, ratio, and division models for common fractions?

2. How can you use children's understanding of place value for whole numbers as a basis for introducing decimal fractions?

3. What strategies and physical models might you use to help children understand that there are an infinite number of ways to write equivalent fractions in common and decimal form?

4. Why is it preferable to talk about simplest terms rather than reduced terms, and how might you help children develop this concept?

5. What is the difference between a ratio and a proportion and how might you use examples from children's everyday life to help them understand these concepts?

6. What are some common errors students make as they learn concepts of rational numbers and how might you help them correct these misconceptions?

NCTM Principles and Standards for School Mathematics

Number and Operations

Instructional programs from prekindergarten through grade 12 should enable all students to:

Understand numbers, ways of representing numbers, relationships among numbers, and number systems

Pre-K to 2

- understand and represent commonly used fractions, such as $\frac{1}{4}$, $\frac{1}{3}$, and $\frac{1}{2}$.

Grades 3–5

- recognize equivalent representations for the same number and generate them by decomposing and composing numbers;
- develop understanding of fractions as parts of unit wholes, as parts of a collection, as locations on number lines, and as divisions of whole numbers;
- use models, benchmarks, and equivalent forms to judge the size of fractions;

NCTM (2000), pp. 78, 148, 214. Reprinted by permission.

- recognize and generate equivalent forms of commonly used fractions, decimals, and percents.

Grades 6–8

- work flexibly with fractions, decimals, and percents to solve problems;
- compare and order fractions, decimals, and percents efficiently and find their approximate locations on a number line;
- develop meaning for percents greater than 100 and less than 1;
- understand and use ratios and proportions to represent quantitative relationships.
- use factors, multiples, prime factorization, and relatively prime numbers to solve problems.

My Math Journal

Divide each geoboard below in half in a different way, using just one rubber band. Sketch where you would place the rubber band on each geoboard to indicate how you would divide it, and then shade one-half. Remember that each half must have the same area but need not be congruent to the other half. A sample has been drawn for you in Figure 8–1.

What methods did you use to divide the geoboards in half? Write a complete description that could be understood by your fellow students.

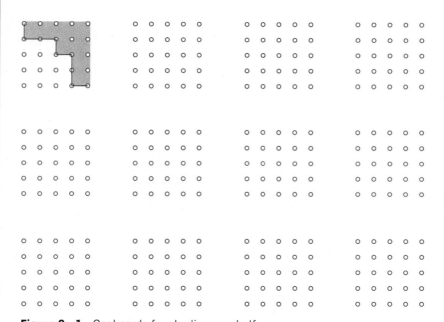

Figure 8–1   Geoboards for shading one-half.

REFLECTIONS AND REFINEMENT: *After you have completed this task, compare your work with that of some of your classmates. Did you find solutions that they did not have? Did they find solutions that you did not have? As you continue through this term, see if you can find additional ways to divide a geoboard in half. What if you were not restricted to using just one rubber band? Write your hypotheses and discoveries here.*

Concepts about rational numbers begin to develop long before children enter school. When children are asked to share a granola bar fairly with a brother or sister, they begin to intuitively grasp the idea of $\frac{1}{2}$. In kindergarten, these intuitive ideas may be introduced more formally but the emphasis should continue to be on situations from the child's life that utilize a variety of concrete materials. Children should realize that rational numbers are very much a part of their everyday lives, and they will need a thorough understanding of them in order to function as intelligent adult consumers.

Ask the children to keep a record of all the times rational numbers are used in their everyday lives. You may be surprised at the large number of uses they find. Create a bulletin board with the uses the children find at home, in newspapers and magazines, and from interviewing people about the uses in their careers. Interviews may reveal such things as the baker using common fractions when preparing recipes or formulas, the bus driver using decimal fractions when buying gas and figuring mileage, the store manager using percents when planning a sale, the car salesperson using percents to figure the commission earned, the nurse using decimal fractions to measure out the medicine to give to a patient, the teacher using percents to figure students' grades, and the government official using percents to determine budgets.

Children themselves must use rational numbers when they cook a meal, sew an apron, measure a garden, build a birdhouse, tip a waiter, or figure the amount they earn for $2\frac{1}{3}$ hours of baby-sitting. The United States' system of money and the metric system of measurement are based on decimal fractions. Conventional measures of length, area, weight, volume, and time make extensive use of common fractions. Sales and sales tax commonly use percents. It is important, therefore, for children to have a solid understanding of all types of rational numbers.

Some people have argued that the proliferation of calculators and the move toward using the metric rather than the conventional system of measure may make it unnecessary to use common fractions, but common fractions will continue to be used to describe such everyday occurrences as eating $\frac{1}{2}$ of an apple, and operations with common fractions must be understood for later work with algebraic fractions, so we present rational numbers in common fraction as well as decimal fraction form.

It is important to remember that common fraction notation and decimal fraction notation are ways of naming the same rational number. The concept of the number is the same regardless of the form in which it is written. Before continuing, we give a formal definition of a rational number.

A **rational number** is one that can be expressed as $\frac{p}{q}$ where p and q are both integers and $q \neq 0$. Rational numbers can be expressed in different ways; they may be written as **common fractions** ($\frac{1}{2}$, $\frac{3}{4}$, . . .); as **decimal fractions,** commonly called decimals (0.5, 0.75, . . .); or as **percents** (50 percent, 75 percent, . . .). Any rational number may be represented by an infinite number of numerals. For example, $\frac{1}{2} = 0.5 = 50$ percent $= \frac{2}{4} = \frac{3}{6} = \frac{4}{8} = \frac{5}{10} = $ . . . . Common fractions may also have several different meanings. They may represent:

1. The part-whole model, where the whole is a unit of measure, a geometric shape, or a set of objects.
2. A ratio between two subsets.
3. Division.

Given the wide range of ways to represent rational numbers and the variety of meanings, it is not surprising that children often are confused when dealing with rational numbers in any form.

Children should use physical models when learning new concepts, and fortunately there are many good materials. Both commercial and teacher-made materials can aid learning of rational number concepts. These materials should be used in the primary grades as children begin to formalize fraction concepts and should also be used in the intermediate and middle school grades, when students learn to operate with common fractions, decimal fractions, and percents. The materials described in this chapter include Fraction Tiles, Fraction Factory, rectangular and circular fraction regions, Decimal Squares, base ten blocks, rulers, number lines, fraction strips, Fraction Bars, colored chips, Cuisenaire rods and arrays. Computer programs, such as *Fraction Attraction* (Sunburst, 1998) and *Mighty Math Number Heroes* (Edmark, 1996), and calculators are also useful in the development of skills with rational numbers. As children use these materials, ask them to explore, question, discover relationships, and discuss their findings with each other. Learning should be both active and related to the child's world.

MAKING SENSE OF RATIONAL NUMBER CONCEPTS

As mentioned in the introduction, rational numbers can be represented in a variety of ways, and the representations may have a variety of meanings. Therefore, it is important that students have an understanding of the meanings of a fraction or decimal before we introduce the abstract numerals that represent them. We want children to have a number of concrete experiences in familiar settings with fractions, such as one-half or two-thirds or one-tenth of familiar objects, before representing them as $\frac{1}{2}$ or $\frac{2}{3}$ or 0.1. This section begins with a description of several meanings for common fractions and several materials that may be used to develop those meanings. We then compare common fractions to decimal fractions and percents. The section ends with a discussion of equivalent fractions and ordering fractions.

Part-Whole Model for a Common Fraction

The first model for a fraction that children typically encounter in school is the **part-whole model.** In this model, the **denominator** represents the number of parts the whole or unit has been divided into and the **numerator** represents the number of parts currently under consideration. If the unit is a unit of measure such as length, area, or volume, each of the parts must be of equal size, even though they need not be congruent. If the unit consists of discrete objects such as chips or children, the objects need not be the same size. However, when children are first introduced to fractions, it is common to use congruent parts or discrete objects of the same size. The following are examples of activities and materials that can be used to help children develop the part-whole concept of a common fraction using area, length, volume, and discrete objects as the unit.

A C T I V I T I E S

Pre-Kindergarten – Grade 2

OBJECTIVE: to develop the concept of a fraction as part of a region divided into equal-sized pieces.

1. Give each child a number of squares cut out of paper. Ask the children to fold a square in two sections. Unfold the square, and examine the sections. Are they the same size? If the square represents a candy bar to be split among two children, would each child receive the same amount? Compare squares that were folded in half to those that were not and discuss the differences. Be sure that children understand that when they have half a candy bar, each child must have the same amount of candy. There is no such thing as "the bigger half."

Using another of the squares, ask the children to fold it in half another way. Tell them to color one of the halves and to cut it out to compare the sections. These will probably be similar to the pieces shown in Figures 8–2a and b.

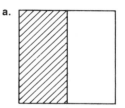

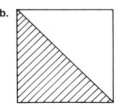

Figure 8–2 Squares showing one-half in two different ways.

Fold a square as shown in Figure 8–3. Then unfold it and color the two end pieces. Ask the children if the colored pieces are still $\frac{1}{2}$. Let the children cut out the pieces to prove that the two halves do indeed cover the same area.

Challenge the children to find other ways to color $\frac{1}{2}$ of the square. Have them prove the answer by cutting the pieces out and showing that the colored pieces do fill the same area as the noncolored pieces. Figure 8–4 shows other responses that the children may give.

After children have shown $\frac{1}{2}$ in many different ways, ask them to repeat the process for other fractions.

2. Use plastic or cardboard regions that have been divided into halves, thirds, and fourths. You may use commercial sets such as Fraction Tiles or Fraction Factory, which are sets made of plastic. A whole square region is one color, and congruent parts are other colors to represent various fractions (available from Creative Publications). Or, using the masters included in the

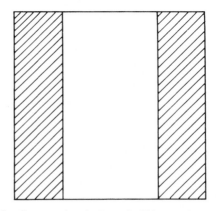

Figure 8–3 Square showing one-half in another way.

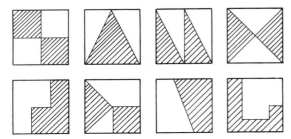

Figure 8–4 Additional ways to show one-half of a square.

appendix, make your own sets out of colored railroad board or run off copies of the regions onto colored paper and let the children cut out their own sets. It is helpful to have several units of the same color and the halves, thirds, and fourths each of a different color. Your pieces may look like those in Figure 8–5 or Figure 8–6. You may also use the square or circular fraction dies on the Ellison lettering machine to make a set of fraction pieces.

Let the children explore with the materials. Challenge the children to make a complete region using pieces that are all the same color. Ask what each piece is called. Ask how many thirds, fourths, or halves it takes to make a whole region. Count $\frac{1}{3}, \frac{2}{3}, \frac{3}{3}$ or $\frac{1}{4}, \frac{2}{4}, \frac{3}{4}, \frac{4}{4}$ as you make a whole. Let the children predict the number of sixths, eighths, and tenths it will take to make the whole region. Encourage the children to make up their own questions using the pieces. Add pieces of other sizes to the group. Sixths, eighths, and twelfths are good sizes to work with. Notice that you should ask students to make the whole when given a fractional part as well as to find the fraction when given a whole.

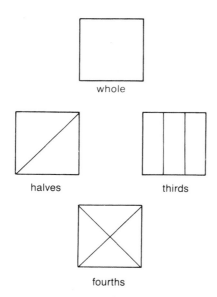

Figure 8–5 Square fraction pieces.

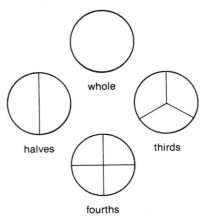

Figure 8–6 Circular fraction pieces.

Make up word problems using the pieces. Use problems such as: "Mrs. Jensen has a granola bar that she wants to split evenly among her three grandchildren. Show the pieces you would use so that each child gets a piece the same size. What is each piece called?" Let the children make up their own word problems.

3. The fraction one-tenth should receive special attention because of the frequent use of decimal fractions with calculators, computers, and metric measures. With young children, introduce the fractions such as halves, thirds, and fourths first because it is easier for such children to divide a unit region into 2, 3, or 4 pieces than it is to divide the region into 10 pieces. The reason is similar to that for teaching children to group by threes and fours before grouping by tens when teaching the concept of place value. When tenths are introduced, you may use commercial materials such as Decimal Squares or base ten blocks or you may make your own materials, similar to those described in the last activity. The decimal patterns in Appendix B can be used for this activity.

The activities described in the previous example may be repeated using tenths. Introduce tenths as common fractions before you introduce them as decimal fractions, since children will be more familiar with the common fraction form after their work with halves, thirds, and fourths. You may also introduce fifths at this time, since children are probably discovering a number of equivalent fractions as they work with the pieces.

Grades 3–5

OBJECTIVE: to develop the concept of a common fraction as part of a whole unit of length.

1. Rulers, number lines, fraction strips, and Fraction Bars show fractions based on a unit of length. In each of these, a unit is chosen and then subdivided into equal-sized parts (see Figure 8–7). Fraction Bars (available from Scott Resources) are vinyl strips divided into

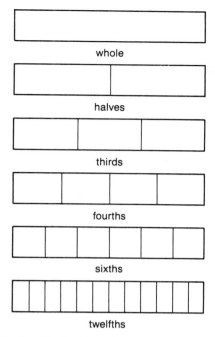

Figure 8–7 Fraction bars.

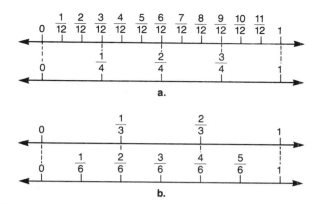

Figure 8–8 Number lines showing equivalent fractions.

units, halves, thirds, fourths, fifths, sixths, tenths, and twelfths, with each division printed on a different color of vinyl. The Fraction Bars are all the same length but have different amounts shaded to represent the various fractions. Teachers and students may make similar sets of fraction strips by copying the masters in the appendix onto colored construction paper or railroad board. Again, it is useful to use different colors for each fraction piece. You may also use the masters in the appendix to make fraction number lines. With either the teacher-made fraction strips or the Fraction Bars, the children may repeat the activities described above for the regions.

Fraction Bars come with sets of cards with numerals written on them and Bingo cards with pictures of fractions shown as parts of circular regions. Children can play several games in which they match the numerals to the bars or the circular regions. The teacher's guides that come with the bars describe a wide variety of activities, and the children can make up others of their own. When numerals for fractions are first introduced, children may have difficulty relating the symbols to the spoken words and concepts with which they are familiar. The written symbols should be introduced only after the children have the concepts and oral language necessary to understand them. Be sure to give students plenty of experiences to understand the written symbols.

After the children have had a number of experiences with the Fraction Bars or the fraction strips, they can draw the corresponding number lines such

as the ones shown in Figures 8–8a and b. Later the children will be asked to transfer this skill to using the fraction number lines without the fraction strips or Fraction Bars. Often, textbooks show only work on the number line, and children should be able to use number lines with rational numbers as well as whole numbers.

When the children are comfortable finding fractional parts of various unit lengths, they should study the marks on a conventional ruler and discuss the meaning of the various parts. They may find that some rulers show $\frac{1}{4}$ inch, others show $\frac{1}{8}$ inch, and still others may show $\frac{1}{16}$ inch. Then have children compare conventional rulers to metric rulers, which show tenths of a centimeter.

2. After students have developed a good concept of using common fractions to show part of a whole unit of length or area, challenge them with problems such as the following: (1) "This line segment (Figure 8–9) represents $\frac{2}{3}$ of the length of rope needed in the school gym. How would you show the entire rope needed?" (2) "This rectangle (Figure 8–10) represents $\frac{1}{2}$ ($\frac{3}{4}$, $\frac{4}{5}$) of my garden. Draw a sketch of what my whole garden might look like." Note that students might use a variety of methods to solve these problems and they should be given the opportunity to explain these methods. These challenges are designed to help students develop a deeper understanding of the fraction concepts.

Figure 8–9 Line segment representing $\frac{2}{3}$ of a piece of rope.

Figure 8–10 Rectangle representing $\frac{1}{2}$ of a garden.

OBJECTIVE: to develop the concept of a fraction as part of a whole unit of volume.

3. Common fractions are often used in everyday life to refer to parts of units other than those for area or length. These include units of time, weight, mass, money, capacity, and volume. Children should have experience using fractions for all of these measures.

The following are a few ideas for using common fractions to describe parts of a unit of volume. Measuring cups are good for exploring fraction concepts in connection with volume. Children should be given the opportunity to explore pouring water, sand, beans, or rice from one measuring cup into another. Ask the children to predict how many $\frac{1}{2}$ cups it will take to fill a whole cup. Will four $\frac{1}{3}$ cups be more or less than one cup? Is $\frac{1}{2}$ cup more or less than $\frac{1}{3}$ cup? After the prediction, let the children pour to see if they were right. Let the children pose questions to each other. Find simple recipes and let the children do the measuring. Discuss their observations about the fractional parts they have measured.

OBJECTIVE: to develop the concept of common fractions as part of a set of discrete objects.

4. Often, a common fraction is used to refer to part of a set of discrete objects. A mother may refer to half a dozen eggs, or the teacher may say that $\frac{1}{4}$ of the children may go to the learning center. When a common fraction is used in this way, the denominator refers to the number of equal-sized groups into which the set is divided, and the numerator refers to the number of groups currently under consideration.

Colored cubes, Bingo chips, or even the children themselves are good manipulative materials for this type of fractional representation. A child may start with 12 chips to represent 1 dozen eggs and then discuss what must be done in order to find $\frac{1}{2}$. The separation of the set into two equal parts should be related to earlier work separating regions, lengths, and volumes into two equal parts. After children work with halves, they may find thirds, fourths, sixths, and twelfths of the dozen eggs. Children may then use other units of discrete objects, such as finding $\frac{1}{4}$ of the children in the class or $\frac{1}{3}$ of the books in their desks.

Children may have some difficulty with the fact that fractional parts do not always contain the same number of objects. Half a dozen eggs is not the same number as half the children in the class. Have children compare this to the fact that half of a large circle (or half a large pizza) is not the same size as half of a small circle (or half a small pizza). However, children should realize that half of a dozen eggs is the same number as the other half of the dozen.

Ratio Model for a Common Fraction

The activities just described involve using common fractions to describe a part-whole relationship. Common fractions may also be used to describe a ratio between two sets. In the **ratio model,** the denominator and the numerator each represent the number of parts under consideration. The denominator does not represent the parts of the whole, as in the part-whole model. The numerator and denominator represent subsets that are being compared.

In fact, some young children have difficulty with the part-whole concept because they have difficulty with the class inclusion concept. They want to compare one subset to another subset rather than compare a subset to a whole. They may identify each of the pictures in Figure 8–11 as $\frac{1}{2}$ because they are comparing the one shaded section to the two nonshaded sections.

This is a correct concept of the fraction $\frac{1}{2}$, but only if the fraction is used in a ratio sense. It is true that the shaded section in each picture is $\frac{1}{2}$ the size of the nonshaded section, but because they are looking for a part-whole response and not a ratio response, most textbooks and most standardized tests say the child was wrong in giving the response of $\frac{1}{2}$. Teachers should encourage children to compare the two.

The following activities suggest ways that ratio concepts may be introduced and compared to part-whole models. The activities are suggested for the intermediate grades because that is when ratios are commonly introduced in textbooks. Often, only a few physical models for ratios are included in the textbooks, and you will probably need to supplement children's work in the books. Many younger children may benefit from activities comparing ratio models and part-whole models because the ratio model fits their own intuitive concepts of common fractions.

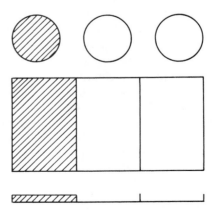

Figure 8–11 Shaded amount shows $\frac{1}{2}$ used as ratio. The shaded portion is $\frac{1}{2}$ of the unshaded portion in each drawing.

Grades 3–5

OBJECTIVE: to develop the ratio concept of a fraction using objects.

1. Children encounter ratio ideas in everyday life, especially ratios used to describe relationships between discrete objects. The teacher may say that there are two girls for every three boys in a group or there are two cookies for each child at a birthday party.

Use chips or colored cubes to represent the situations. The chips shown in Figure 8–12 may be used to show that there are two girls for every three boys in the group. Let green chips represent the girls and blue chips represent the boys. Ask the children what part of the whole class is girls. How is the ratio concept of a fraction related to the part-whole concept?

2. Another common use of ratio is with gears. Children may observe gears. In Figure 8–13, note that there are 5 teeth on the small gear and 10 teeth on the large gear.

You may buy gears from a hardware store, obtain gears from factories (which may give you some of their old ones), or use a commercial set such as TECHNIC™ from Lego. Mark each gear so the children can count the number of turns of each gear. Ask the children to turn the large gear one complete turn and count the numbers of turns of the small gear. Compare the number of turns to the ratio of the teeth on the large gear to the teeth on the small gear.

The children should note that the small gear in Figure 8–13 will go around twice while the large gear goes around once. The ratio of the teeth on the large gear to the teeth on the small gear is 10:5, while the ratio of the number of turns of the large gear to the number of turns of the small gear is 1:2.

Let the children make hypotheses about what will happen with gears of other sizes. Get these gears and test the hypotheses.

OBJECTIVE: to develop the concept of ratio using length.

3. Cuisenaire rods are a good material to use to represent a common fraction as a ratio between two lengths. Use them with children who have had previous experience using the rods. Ask the children to find several pairs of rods for which one rod is half the length of the other. Possibilities are shown in Figure 8–14.

Figure 8–12 Chips showing a ratio of two girls for every three boys.

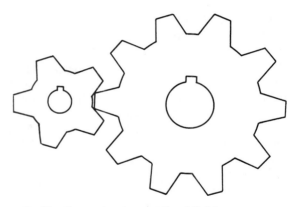

Figure 8–13 Gears showing a ratio of 5:10.

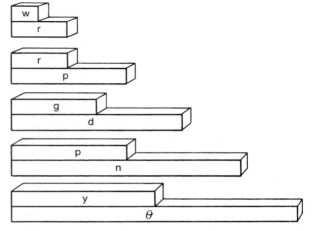

Figure 8–14 Cuisenaire rods showing a ratio of 1:2.

Note that children are comparing the length of one rod to the length of the other and not comparing one rod to the total length of the two. Let the children suggest other fractions to display with the rods such as $\frac{2}{3}$ and $\frac{3}{4}$. Encourage comparing the other rods to the orange rod for the concept of tenths. Being comfortable with finding tenths helps children make the transition to writing decimal fractions.

Ask the children to measure something such as the length of their desk using only orange Cuisenaire rods. They should first estimate and then measure to check how close their estimates are. After measuring the desk in orange rods, ask them to estimate the number of yellow rods to measure the same length. Encourage the students to discuss their estimates in small groups. Observe to see if they realize that it takes twice the number of yellow rods as orange rods, because the yellow rods are half the length of orange rods.

OBJECTIVE: to develop the concept of ratio using volume.

4. Ask children to try to find examples of ratios used at home. They may notice that salad dressing calls for 1 part vinegar for 5 parts oil or that iced tea mix calls for 1 teaspoon of iced tea mix for 1 cup of water. Bring in ingredients to let the children make the solutions or mixtures at school. Ask questions about the ratios as you mix. If the mixture is 1 part vinegar for 5 parts oil, what part of the total mixture is vinegar? Note that if the ratio is 1:5, the vinegar is $\frac{1}{6}$ of the total because the whole mixture has 6 parts. Have the children compare this work to earlier work with ratios with discrete objects.

Using Common Fractions to Indicate Division

So far, we have discussed two different concepts that may be represented by common fractions, part-whole and ratio. Common fractions may also be used to indicate a division problem. When fractions are used to indicate division, the division problem $5 \div 6$ is shown as $\frac{5}{6}$. The models used may be similar to those used for the partition division problems with whole numbers in Chapter 7. Therefore, introduce activities using common fractions to indicate division after children have learned to divide with whole numbers and after they understand the part-whole concept of a fraction. The following activities focus on the division concept of common fractions.

A   C   T   I   V   I   T   I   E   S

Grades 3 – 5

OBJECTIVE: to develop the concept of a common fraction representing division using discrete objects.

1. Begin with problems such as $6 \div 2$, which have whole-number answers. Tell the children you have 6 cookies and wish to put them into 2 equal groups. The children may wish to use chips to show that $6 \div 2 = \frac{6}{2} = 3$.

Ask the children what they would do if you had 7 cookies and wished to put them into 2 equal groups. Again, let the children model this with the chips. They will find that they have one chip left over. Some of the children may decide that they can divide the last cookie in half so that each group will have $3\frac{1}{2}$ cookies. Therefore, $7 \div 2 = \frac{7}{2} = 3\frac{1}{2}$.

These experiences with the division model for common fractions are good for explaining the renaming of improper fractions as mixed numerals. Ask the children to use materials to explain why $\frac{8}{3} = 2\frac{2}{3}$.

OBJECTIVE: to develop the division concept for common fractions using length.

2. Chips are not a good material to use for many of the division problems involving fractions because they cannot be broken into fractional pieces. Models involving measures of length, area, or volume are often preferable because they can be broken into smaller parts. Using these materials, start with a story situation and let the children discover the answer on their own. Give each of the children some blank 3-by-5 index cards and tell them the 3-inch and the 5-inch sides of the cards represent 3 yards and 5 yards, respectively.

Tell the children that you have 3 yards of material from which to make puppets for a play. You need to make 4 puppets and wish to use the same amount of material for each one. What part of a yard of material can you use for each puppet? Ask the children to fold the 3-by-5 index cards and measure to find the answer. Many children will be surprised to find that you will have $\frac{3}{4}$ yard of material for each puppet, $3 \div 4 = \frac{3}{4}$ (see Figure 8–15).

Ask the children to make up a story situation for the problem $5 \div 3$ and to again fold a 3-by-5 card and measure to find the result (see Figure 8–16). Repeat the activity with several different measures until the children can generalize that $a \div b = \frac{a}{b}$.

3. After children have had several experiences folding paper to show the division model for a fraction, they can transfer to a number line. Again, begin with the problem $3 \div 4$. Give each child a number line 3 inches

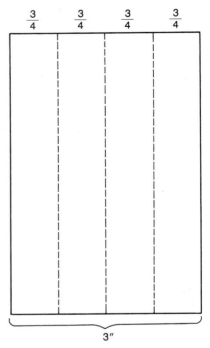

Figure 8–15   Index card folded to show $3 \div 4 = \frac{3}{4}$.

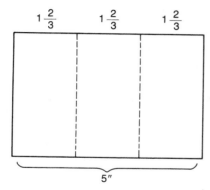

$1\frac{2}{3}$ $1\frac{2}{3}$ $1\frac{2}{3}$

5"

Figure 8–16 Index card folded to show $5 \div 3 = \frac{5}{3}$.

long. Ask the children to divide the number line into 4 equal parts. They will probably find that this is difficult to do unless each unit on the number line is broken into smaller parts.

Suggest that the children break each unit into 4 equal parts. Ask the children how many small parts there are in 3 units. There are 12. Now ask the children to break the number line into 4 equal parts. The children should discover that each of the parts will be $\frac{3}{4}$ inch long (see Figure 8–17).

Ask the children to compare this work to the work folding the index cards. Repeat the activity with number lines of different sizes and with different fractions. Ask the children to make up story situations illustrated by their number lines.

OBJECTIVE: to reinforce the division concept of a common fraction using a variety of measures.

4. Discrete objects and length are not the only models used to show the division concept of a common fraction. Many other units of measure such as time, money, volume, area, and mass may also be used. Make up story situations for other units of measure and let children choose their own methods and materials for solving the problems. Here are a few suggestions:

- *Money.* Mrs. Jackson has $5 to buy favors for a birthday party. She needs 10 favors and wishes to spend the same amount on each one. What part of a dollar should she spend on each favor?
- *Time.* The Moyer relay team wishes to run the 1-mile relay in 5 minutes. If the 4 girls on the relay team each run the same distance in the same amount of time, how fast should each girl run her $\frac{1}{4}$ mile?

Figure 8–17 Number line showing $3 \div 4 = \frac{3}{4}$.

- *Volume.* The Coleys have a 2-liter bottle of soda. If Amy wants to split the soda evenly into 10 glasses, what part of a liter should she pour into each glass?
- *Area.* The Sheffields have a 2-acre plot of ground that they wish to plant with corn, tomatoes, and peppers. If they use the same amount of land for each vegetable, how much land will be used for each?

Encourage the children to make up their own situations and trade with each other to solve them.

Decimal Fractions

If you are using a textbook series, decimal fractions may be introduced before, along with, or after common fractions. You will probably wish to follow the textbook guidelines, but there are advantages to introducing decimals earlier because of the use of the decimal in place-value notation, in our money system, in the metric system of measurement, and on calculators and computers, as well as the relative ease of computation with decimal fractions. Conceptually, however, it is probably easier to understand the meaning of halves, thirds, and fourths than it is to understand tenths and hundredths because there are fewer partitions involved. Whenever you decide to introduce common and decimal fractions, be sure the children realize they are simply different notation systems for the same concepts.

We focus here on the use of decimal fractions and percents to represent parts of whole units. Again, a unit may be a set of discrete objects or any unit of measure (length, area, volume, mass, money, or time). Children should have a good concept of tenths before they begin work with written decimal fractions. Work with decimals may begin as soon as children understand the concept of dividing a unit into 10 equal-sized parts.

Because the money system in the United States is based on decimals, children also may be introduced to hundredths at a fairly young age. Most six-or seven-year olds can understand that there are 100 pennies in a dollar and that 1 penny may be written as $.01. This represents $\frac{1}{100}$ of a dollar.

When decimal fractions are introduced, place value for whole numbers should be reviewed. Let the children study the following place-value chart and tell you what happens as you move one place to the right on the chart.

thousands   hundreds   tens   ones . __ __

Children should notice that the value of the position on the right is one-tenth of the value of the position directly to the left of it. Ask the children to predict the value of the place to the right of the ones place—that is, the first place after the decimal point. (Note that in countries outside the United States, a comma may be used in place of a decimal point, for example, $1,7 = 1\frac{7}{10}$) Children should realize that this place will have one-tenth the value of the ones place and therefore is the tenths place.

The activities for teaching the concept of a common fraction as part of a whole may be repeated for decimal fractions, beginning with tenths and later expanding to hundredths, thousandths, and so on. The following activities suggest other ways in which decimal fractions may be introduced.

A C T I V I T I E S

Grades 3–5

OBJECTIVE: to develop the concept of a decimal fraction using a length, area, or volume model.

1. Take out the white and orange Cuisenaire rods and tell the children that the orange rod represents 1. Ask the children to tell you the value of one of the white rods. Use the decimal notation to represent the value 0.1.

After the children understand the concept of tenths using the rods, add the orange flats from the base ten blocks and tell the children that the orange flat now represents 1. What is the new value of the orange rod (long)? What is the value of each white rod? What is the value shown by the rods in Figure 8–18 if the flat is 1? (1.34)

Ask the children to show 0.45, 0.89, and so on. Let the children make up problems for each other and discuss how they found the answers. After the children are proficient at working with both tenths and hundredths, add the orange cube to the set. If the cube is 1, the flat becomes 0.1, the long becomes 0.01, and the white

rod becomes 0.001. Repeat the activities with thousandths.

2. After the children have worked with the base ten blocks, they may do the same activities using paper or cardboard models. You may use a commercial set such as Decimal Squares, or make a set out of paper. If you make your own set, a convenient size is 1 square decimeter for a unit. Mark squares with 10 columns for tenths, and mark columns with 10 rows for hundredths (see Figure 8–19). (A master for this square is included in Appendix B.)

Laminate the decimal squares so that the children may write on them with erasable markers. Make a separate set of cards with various decimal fractions written on them, and ask the children to shade the squares to match the decimal fractions written on the cards. The children may then use the cards to play various games that involve matching the numerals to the pictures, such as Go Fish or Old Maid.

3. Because the metric system is a decimal system, it provides good examples of decimal fractions. Children learning the concept of 0.1 may take strips of paper each 1 decimeter long (or they may use orange Cuisenaire rods) and line them up on a meter stick. Ask, "How many strips of paper or rods does it take to make 1 meter?" Ten. Ask, "How could you express three strips?" 0.3 meter.

Extend the activity to hundredths by using strips each 1 centimeter long or by using the white Cuisenaire rods. Ask, "What part of a meter is represented by 23 white rods? What part of a meter is represented by five orange rods and two white rods?" Let the children make

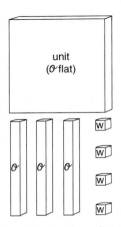

Figure 8–18   Base ten blocks where flat represents one whole unit.

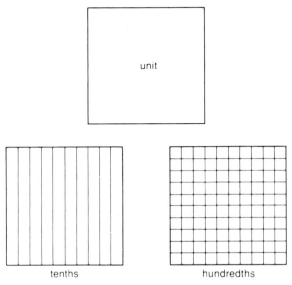

Figure 8–19   Decimal squares for one unit, tenths, and hundreds.

up their own questions for each other and discuss their methods of solution. Thousandths may be introduced by using millimeters or by using grams and kilograms or milliliters and liters.

Percent

After children are comfortable using decimal fractions as well as common fractions, introduce them to the concept of *percent.* Percent simply means "per hundred," or "out of 100." A percent may be thought of as a ratio between some number and 100. For example, 18 percent is 18 out of 100. Have children practice writing percents as ratios, common fractions, and decimal fractions. Eighteen out of 100 may be written as $\frac{18}{100}$, 0.18, or 18 percent. Different notations are useful at different times; you might use $\frac{18}{100}$ when writing out the fractional part of a dollar on a bank check, $\frac{9}{50}$ to tell the probability of winning a game, $0.18 to give the price of an apple, or 18 percent to note the discount on a recent purchase.

Note that *percent* and *percentage* are not the same thing. Children (and teachers) often confuse the two. A **percent** indicates a rate, while a **percentage** indicates an amount. For example, if you take out a loan of $500 for one year at 10 percent, the rate is 10 percent, the base is $500, and the $50 you pay in interest is the percentage. The percentage and the base are amounts, and the percent is the ratio between these two amounts.

Materials and activities for introducing percent are similar to those for introducing decimal fractions. You may repeat any of the activities involving hundredths using a percent representation. The following activities give a few additional ideas.

A C T I V I T I E S

Grades 6 – 8

OBJECTIVE: to develop the concept of percent.

1. The Decimal Squares with 10 rows of 10 squares each may be used again for this activity. Make an overhead transparency of one of the Decimal Squares, and on the overhead projector, let the children watch you shade part of the square red. Ask the children what percent of the square is shaded red.

A hundreds board without the numbers is also useful for developing the concept of percent. Hang different colored markers on the hooks. For example, if you have 15 green markers on the pegs and 85 red markers, ask the children what percent of the board has green markers and what percent has red markers.

Let children make up different examples for each other. Ask them to compare their answers in common and decimal fractions to their answers in percents.

2. Money is a good tool to use in introducing percent since the United States currency is based on the decimal system. Ask the children to express 18¢ as a percent of 1 dollar. Set up a chart such as the following:

Amount	Percent of 1 Dollar
$0.18	18
$0.26	–
$0.35	–
$0.92	–
$2.96	–

Ask the children to make up other examples for each other and discuss how they found their answers.

Naming and Representing Fractions in Multiple Ways

After children understand the concept of a common fraction as part of a unit, they may begin to explore the concept of **equivalent fractions.** Unlike whole numbers, each fraction has an infinite number of symbolic representations. The common fractions that name the same number are called equivalent fractions.

A C T I V I T I E S

Grades 3 – 5

OBJECTIVE: to develop the concept of equivalent fractions.

1. This is a game for two to six players using the Fraction Bars. Begin by turning all the Fraction Bars face down and letting each child choose six bars. Each child may look at his or her own bars but should not show them to the other players. To begin play, one player should choose one Fraction Bar and place it face up in the center of the table. The next player may then play all the fraction bars in his or her hand that are equivalent to the first one by placing them in a pile on top of the first bar. If the second player has no equivalent Fraction Bars or after all the equivalent fractions have been played, the second player should start a new pile by placing another Fraction Bar face up next to the first one. The next player may then play all Fraction Bars that are equivalent to either of the two amounts showing and then start another pile with a new Fraction Bar. The first player to play all of his or her bars is the winner. Ask the children to write down all the sets of equivalent fractions they find.

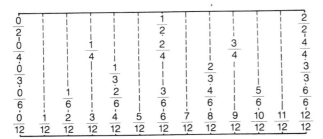

Figure 8–20   Strip of paper folded to show equivalent fractions.

When the children get a list such as $\frac{1}{2} = \frac{2}{4} = \frac{3}{6} = \frac{6}{12}$, ask them if they notice any patterns in the list. They should realize that to convert from one fraction to an equivalent fraction, they can either multiply or divide the numerator and denominator by the same number. Let the children repeat the activity with other materials such as the Fraction Tiles or the fraction strips to see that the same rules are true regardless of the material used.

2. Give each child a strip of adding machine tape 1 foot long. If you do not have adding machine tape, you might cut a plain sheet of computer paper in thirds the long way so you have a strip of paper that is approximately 3 inches by 12 inches. Have the children label the left end of the strip with a 0 and the right end with a 1.

Ask the children to fold the strip in half. Have them now label the left end $\frac{0}{2}$, the middle $\frac{1}{2}$, and the right end $\frac{2}{2}$.

Ask the children to fold the tape in half again and to relabel it. They should now have $\frac{0}{4}, \frac{1}{4}, \frac{2}{4}, \frac{3}{4}$, and $\frac{4}{4}$.

Unfold the tape and label the thirds, and then fold the tape in half again and label the sixths. Fold it in half once more and label the twelfths. The final strip should look like the one in Figure 8–20.

Ask the children to list all the fractions that name the same fold on the strip. Ask them how the lists may be extended by continuing to fold the paper. Ask if there is ever an end to the number of equivalent fractions.

After students have worked with the folded paper, ask them to place various fractions in the appropriate place on a number line. Stress the importance of the 1 and the 0 on the number line when determining the correct location of each fraction. Where is $\frac{1}{2}$ in relation to $\frac{3}{8}$ or $\frac{4}{3}$? How does this compare to the paper strip or fractions on a ruler?

Ordering Fractions

After the children have worked with equivalent fractions, have them use the same materials to order fractions. Following are a few activities for developing the concept of ordering fractions.

Grades 3–5

OBJECTIVE: to develop the concept of ordering fractions.

1. Use one of the sets of fractional regions such as the pie pieces or the rectangular regions for each pair of students. Ask one student in each pair to name two common fractions and ask the second student to predict which of the two is bigger. The students should then find the fraction pieces corresponding to the fractions named and place them on top of each other to determine whether the prediction was correct by comparing the areas of the two regions.

2. Use the folded adding machine tape that the children have labeled with common fractions. Ask the children to locate $\frac{1}{4}$ and $\frac{1}{2}$ on the tape. Ask the children which is smaller and have them write the answer using the symbol for less than. They should write $\frac{1}{4} < \frac{1}{2}$.

Let the children suggest several other pairs of numbers from the number line and write comparisons using $<$, $=$, or $>$. Are there any pairs of common fractions that cannot be compared using one of these three symbols? Can any pairs be compared using more than one of these symbols? This is called the **trichotomy principle:** Any rational number is greater than, less than, or equal to any other rational number.

After the children have compared pairs of numbers, ask them to compare several numbers at once using $<$. They may write $\frac{1}{12} < \frac{1}{6} < \frac{1}{4} < \frac{1}{3} < \frac{5}{12} < \frac{1}{2} < \frac{7}{12} < \frac{3}{4} < \frac{5}{6} < \frac{11}{12} < 1$. Is it possible to make a longer chain of numbers? Are there any fractions between $\frac{1}{12}$ and $\frac{2}{12}$? The fact that there is always another rational number between any two rational numbers is called the **density property.**

3. Show the students a number line with two points marked, as in Figure 8–21. Ask the students to place other points on the number line, such as zero, $\frac{1}{2}, \frac{3}{4}$, and 2.

After children have a good concrete understanding of the rational number concepts, develop more abstract skills with the numbers in different forms. Be sure you do not rush the children into this abstract work before they have mastered the ideas concretely. The following section focuses on developing skills with rational numbers written as common fractions, decimal fractions, and percents.

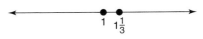

Figure 8–21   Number line indicating location of two rational numbers.

DEVELOPING FLUENCY WITH RATIONAL NUMBERS

The skills associated with rational numbers are renaming equivalent common fractions, reading and writing decimal fractions, converting common fractions to decimal fractions and percents and vice versa, ordering both common and decimal fractions, and using proportions. These skills involve making the transition from work with manipulative materials to abstract work using either mental calculation, paper and pencil, or calculators or computers. We begin with procedures for renaming common fractions.

Renaming, Reading, and Writing Common Fractions

After children can find equivalent fractions using a variety of concrete models, they are ready to discover more abstract procedures for finding equivalent fractions. Children should have made lists of the equivalent fractions that they found using materials and should have generalized the fact that equivalent fractions may be found by multiplying or dividing the numerator and the denominator by the same number. Ask the children to make a list of at least 10 ways to name 1 ($\frac{1}{1}$, $\frac{2}{2}$, $\frac{3}{3}$, . . .). Ask the children what they notice about the numerator and the denominator of each fraction that is equivalent to 1.

Notice that when you have $\frac{a}{b} \times \frac{c}{c}$ or $\frac{a}{b} \div \frac{c}{c}$ you are multiplying by the identity or dividing by the right-hand identity 1. Multiplying or dividing by the identity does not change the value of the original number. Let the children make up tables with several names for different common fractions, such as $\frac{1}{2}$, $\frac{1}{3}$, $\frac{1}{4}$, $\frac{2}{3}$, and $\frac{3}{4}$.

After children can list several equivalent fractions for any given fraction, have them practice writing fractions in **simplest terms.** We prefer using *simplest terms* or *simplest form* rather than *reduced*, or *lowest, terms*, because some children will think a fraction has gotten smaller when it is reduced even if they have been working with equivalent fractions.

To find fractions in simplest terms, return to the concrete materials you worked with for finding several ways to name a fraction. Tell the children that when you have a list of equivalent fractions, the one in simplest terms has the smallest number in the denominator, and it is not possible to divide both the numerator and the denominator evenly by a whole number greater than 1. It is in simplest terms because it uses the fewest parts.

After working with physical models, challenge students to simplify a fraction abstractly. The children might suggest looking for any numbers that will divide evenly into both the numerator and the denominator and then continue dividing until no more numbers will divide into both. If you are using a calculator such

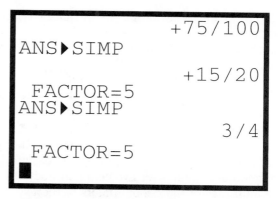

Figure 8–22 Calculator display showing simplification of fraction $\frac{75}{100}$ to $\frac{3}{4}$.

as the Math Explorer, or the TI73 or TI80 experiment by pushing the "simp" button and the "equals" button when the calculator is displaying a common fraction. What happens if you push the "simp" button more than once? Try it for several different fractions and discuss the results (see Figure 8–22).

Children should find the **greatest common factor** (greatest common divisor) of the numerator and denominator to simplify the fraction in one step. If c is the greatest common factor, then dividing both the numerator and the denominator by c gives you a fraction in simplest form.

After children are comfortable with finding equivalent fractions for a given fraction, have them find equivalent fractions with a common denominator for two or more common fractions. Have children reverse the process used to simplify fractions, that is, have them multiply a fraction by $\frac{a}{a}$ in order to find equivalent fractions. This skill is used in working with addition, subtraction, and division of common fractions, when it is often necessary to write fractions in a form with a common denominator before any operation can be performed. There are several ways to find common fractions with a common denominator, and three of them are discussed here.

A C T I V I T I E S

Grades 3–5

OBJECTIVE: to find a common denominator for two common fractions.

1. Ask the children to find a common denominator for the fractions $\frac{2}{3}$ and $\frac{3}{4}$. First, ask the children to get out their lists of the equivalence classes of these two common fractions. Find examples of equivalent fractions for $\frac{2}{3}$ that have denominators that also appear on the list of equivalent fractions for $\frac{3}{4}$. The children may find denominators of 12, 24, 36, and 48.

Tell the children that twelfths are the **least common denominator** since 12 is the smallest number that appears as a denominator in both equivalence classes. Therefore, to write $\frac{2}{3}$ and $\frac{3}{4}$ with the least common denominator, the children would write that $\frac{2}{3} = \frac{8}{12}$ and $\frac{3}{4} = \frac{9}{12}$. Let the children find common denominators for other pairs of fractions and discuss their methods.

2. Sometimes a common denominator is the denominator of one of two common fractions that you wish to add together. At other times, it is easy to find a common denominator for two common fractions by listing multiples of the denominators of the two fractions and finding the multiples that they have in common. Sometimes it is necessary to find a common denominator for two fractions when one denominator is not a multiple of the other and it is laborious to list equivalence classes until a common denominator appears. Thus, it is often most efficient to use prime factorization to find the **least common multiple** of the two denominators. Remember that prime numbers are those that have exactly two divisors, the number itself and one. The least common multiple is also the least common denominator.

For example, if you wish to add $\frac{5}{12}$ and $\frac{7}{30}$, first find the prime factorization of the two denominators, 12 and 30. $12 = 2 \times 2 \times 3$ and $30 = 2 \times 3 \times 5$. Put these factors into a Venn diagram such as the one in Figure 8–23.

The union of the two sets is the least common denominator, $2 \times 2 \times 3 \times 5$, or 60. (Notice that the intersection of the two sets gives the greatest common factor.) Each of the fractions must be written in sixtieths, the least common multiple. Each numerator is multiplied by the number or numbers in the Venn diagram that do not appear in the denominator of that fraction. The numerator of $\frac{5}{12}$ is multiplied by 5, and the numerator of $\frac{7}{30}$ is multiplied by 2. Thus, $\frac{5}{12} = \frac{5}{2 \times 2 \times 3} = \frac{5 \times 5}{2 \times 2 \times 3 \times 5} = \frac{25}{60}$; and $\frac{7}{30} = \frac{7}{2 \times 3 \times 5} = \frac{7 \times 2}{2 \times 3 \times 5 \times 2} = \frac{14}{60}$. Let the children make up other problems for each other and discuss their solutions.

3. For a fraction with a large number in the denominator, children will probably need to use a factor tree

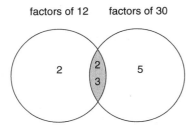

factors of 12   factors of 30

2   2
     3   5

Figure 8–23 Venn diagram illustrating finding the greatest common factor and least common multiple (least common denominator of 12 and 30).

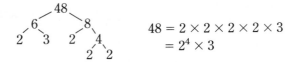

$$48 = 2 \times 2 \times 2 \times 2 \times 3$$
$$= 2^4 \times 3$$

Figure 8–24 One way to factor 48 into prime factors.

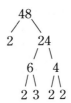

Figure 8–25 Another way to factor 48 into prime factors, illustrating the Fundamental Law of Arithmetic.

to find the prime factors. To make a factor tree, place the number to be factored at the top and choose two factors that when multiplied give you the original number. Continue until all factors are prime numbers. For example, for 48, begin with 6×8 as shown in Figure 8–24.

Notice that the order in which the factors are found does not matter. You still end up with the same prime factors. (see Figure 8–25) This is called the **Fundamental Law of Arithmetic.**

Most textbooks include a chapter on number theory that precedes the unit on operations with common fractions and includes lessons in finding least common multiples and greatest common factors. We also discuss the necessity for finding common denominators in the next chapter when we talk about operations with common fractions.

We invite you to visit Weblink 8–1, the National Library for Virtual Manipulatives for Interactive Mathematics and investigate the Factor Tree activity. This activity includes an interactive computer applet that challenges students to find all the prime factors of two numbers and place them in a Venn diagram similar to the one in Figure 8–23.

Also, look again at Weblink 8–2, which we mentioned in Chapter 7, the NCTM Illuminations site, and play the Product Game and the Factor Game. In the Factor Game, students start with a number and find its factors. In the Product Game, students start with factors and multiply to find the product. The two games work well together because they help students to see the relationship between products and factors. Both games give students an enjoyable way to build concepts of factors and multiples.

After children understand renaming fractions and can rename fractions in simplest terms and rename two fractions with a common denominator, let them play games that reinforce those skills. Card games, board games, and Bingo are good for this. The following activities are designed to give children practice in renaming common fractions.

A   C   T   I   V   I   T   I   E   S

Grades 3–5 and Grades 6–8

OBJECTIVE: to determine fraction combinations that total one whole

1. Divide students into groups of two or three and give each group a set of fraction circles that are divided into halves, thirds, fourths, eighths, and twelfths. (You may use commercial pieces or give the students copies of the fraction circle page in the appendix.) Challenge the students to find as many ways as possible to make one whole using these pieces. Remind them that they may use such combinations as $\frac{1}{2} + \frac{1}{3} + \frac{1}{6}$ in addition to such things as $\frac{6}{6}$ or $\frac{4}{4}$. Encourage students to use organized lists to determine whether they have exhausted all the possibilities. An additional challenge for students who have solved this problem is to add fifths and tenths. Other students might wish to start with halves, thirds, and sixths and gradually add other pieces.

2. After students are competent at finding equivalent fractions, ask them how they would determine if two fractions such as $\frac{18}{24}$ and $\frac{75}{100}$ are equivalent. The students may try to find a common denominator, which is very time consuming; they may try simplifying both fractions, which in this case would work very well; or they may get out their calculators and divide to determine if both common fractions are equivalent to the same decimal fraction (see Figure 8–26).

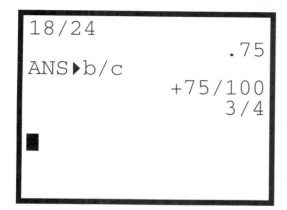

Figure 8–26 Calculator display showing equivalent fractions.

Ask the students to list several pairs of common fractions that they know are equivalent. They should have fractions in the form $\frac{a}{b} = \frac{c}{d}$. Ask them if they notice anything about the relationship among a, b, c, and d. Encourage the use of calculators so students may check several pairs of fractions without being bogged down by the computations. If the students don't try it, you might suggest that they multiply $a \times d$ and compare it to $b \times c$. This is called cross-multiplying.

After students have cross-multiplied with several pairs of equivalent fractions, ask them to compare the findings. Does $a \times d$ always equal $b \times c$? What happens if the original fractions are not equivalent? More advanced students may wish to find out why this works.

Naming and Representing Rational Numbers in Multiple Ways

After students understand the concepts of decimal fractions and can extend the place value into hundredths and thousandths, have them practice both reading and writing decimal fractions. Be sure this abstract work is based on a solid concrete foundation. The following activities are designed to give students practice reading and writing decimal fractions.

A   C   T   I   V   I   T   I   E   S

Grades 3–5

OBJECTIVE: to practice reading and displaying decimal fractions.

1. Make a set of cards with decimal fractions written in both numerals and words. On one card, write a decimal fraction in words and on another write the same decimal fraction in numerals, such as three hundredths and 0.03. Make about 15 such pairs.

Let the students use the cards to play the Match Game. Turn all the cards face down on the table in front of the students. The students should take turns turning over a pair of cards. The goal is to get one numeral card and one word card that show the same decimal fraction. If the two cards match, the student gets to keep the cards and takes another turn. If the cards do not match, they are placed face down on the table in their original positions and it is the next person's turn. Play continues until all the cards have been matched. The player with the most matches at the end is the winner.

Students who still need work on matching the decimal fractions to pictorial representations can play this same game matching pictures and numerals or words. It is helpful in both variations of the game to have an answer key with which to check any matches that the players are not sure of.

2. Ask each student to make a decimal place-value chart. Have each student fold a piece of tagboard or make a pocket chart like the one in Figure 8–27 by folding and stapling a piece of oaktag.

Give each student two sets of cards with the numerals 0–9 on them. The caller should then read numbers such as thirty-five and four hundred twenty-six thousandths. The players should place the numeral cards in the correct positions and hold the chart up for the caller to check. The teacher or student caller may then quickly check to see which students are correctly displaying the number.

This activity may be done by the whole class, small groups, or a pair of children working alone. For another variation of this activity, furnish each child with a calculator and ask the children to put the numbers in the calculator as they are read. You or a caller may then check each calculator display, or the children may compare their displays.

After children understand the concepts of fractions in common, decimal, and percent form and are proficient at naming equivalent fractions and reading and writing decimal fractions, they are ready to learn to rename fractions as decimals or percents and vice versa. Results from the Fourth National Assessment of Educational Progress show that students have difficulty with this. Only 30 percent of seventh-graders could express 0.9 as a percent and 8 percent as a decimal (Kouba et al., 1988).

Results from the 1996 National Assessment of Educational Progress (NAEP) showed general progress in the United States over earlier mathematics assessments, but improvement is still needed (Weblink 8–3). Results of the Third International Mathematics and Science Study show that middle school students in the United States have difficulty in renaming simple fractions. When presented with a grid of 24 squares and asked to shade $\frac{5}{8}$ of them, only 43 percent of U.S. eighth graders did this correctly. Nearly $\frac{1}{4}$ of the eighth graders shaded in 5 squares rather than the correct 15 squares. By contrast, 92 percent of students in Singapore, 81 percent of Korean students and 80 percent of Japanese students answered this correctly. The international average was 52 percent correct (Weblink 8–4). On a similar question from the 1996 National Assessment of Educational Progress, 65 percent of the eighth graders correctly identified 4 shaded squares on a grid of 12 squares as $\frac{1}{3}$ on a multiple choice item where the other choices were $\frac{1}{6}$, $\frac{1}{5}$, $\frac{1}{4}$, $\frac{1}{3}$, or $\frac{1}{2}$ (Weblink 8–3).

Children who can read a decimal fraction should also be able to write it in common fraction form. Children who can tell you that 0.23 is 23 hundredths should also be able to write it as $\frac{23}{100}$. When they realize that *percent* simply means "per hundred," they can also write it as 23 percent, or 23%. Some fractions must be simplified once they are written in common fraction form, and children should be reminded of that.

Converting a common fraction to a decimal may not be as easy as converting a decimal to a common fraction because just reading a common fraction may not tell you its decimal form. Reminding the children that one meaning for a common fraction is division can help them make the conversion. The common fraction $\frac{5}{6}$ is the same as 5 divided by 6. The division may be done very quickly on the calculator or slightly more laboriously by hand.

Dividing fractions may be the children's first introduction to nonterminating decimals. Children will realize as they divide 5 by 6 that they could go on forever and never reach a point where there is no remainder. Their answer of .8333333 . . . will end in 3 no matter how long they continue the division. Other fractions such as $\frac{1}{2}$, $\frac{1}{4}$, $\frac{3}{5}$, and $\frac{7}{10}$ terminate in a few places.

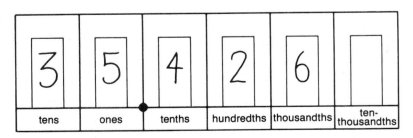

Figure 8–27 Decimal place-value chart.

Have students explore converting common fractions to decimal fractions to see if they can predict which common fractions will terminate and which will not. They may need the hint that it will help to first write each fraction in simplest terms and then to factor the denominator into prime factors. Compare the prime factors to the factors of the powers of ten. Using a calculator will help the students explore a greater number of conversions. Lead students to the generalization that whenever the denominator has only 2s and/or 5s as factors, the decimal equivalent will terminate. Otherwise, the common fraction will be equivalent to a repeating decimal. Children who are learning to write computer programs may wish to write a program to convert common fractions to decimals and percents and vice versa.

Note that all rational numbers can be written either as terminating or repeating decimals. Nonrepeating decimals such as the decimal expansion of pi or the square root of 2 or decimals such as 0.101001000100001 . . . are irrational numbers.

After students are comfortable converting decimal fractions to common fractions and common fractions to decimal fractions, they may learn to convert decimal fractions to percents. Begin with decimal fractions in hundredths. These are very easy to convert to percents, since *percent* means per hundred. For example, 0.16 is simply 16 percent (16%).

When students can convert hundredths to percent, ask them to try fractions that are in tenths. They may notice that 0.3 = 0.30 and is therefore equal to 30 percent (30%). (You may need to ask them how many hundredths are equal to 0.3 if they do not notice this on their own.)

After students can convert tenths and hundredths to percents, try other decimal fractions, such as 0.005. Ask the students if this is more or less than 1%. They may need to return to the decimal squares or other pictorial materials to determine that this is $\frac{1}{2}$ of 0.01 and is therefore $\frac{1}{2}$% or 0.5%.

When the students can successfully convert several decimal fractions to percents, ask the students what they notice about the decimal point as they move from a decimal fraction to a percent. Yes, it moves two places to the right. Ask, "How do you convert a percent back to a decimal?" Move the decimal point two places back to the left. If students have a "%" key on their calculators, have them explore its use at this point.

After students can easily convert decimal fractions to percents and vice versa, ask them how they would convert a common fraction to a percent. For most, the easiest method is probably to convert the common fraction to a decimal fraction and then to convert the decimal fraction to a percent. Calculators come in handy when using this method.

The following activities are designed to give students practice in converting decimal fractions, common fractions, and percents.

ACTIVITIES

Grades 6 – 8

OBJECTIVE: to practice converting decimal fractions, common fractions, and percents.

1. The games described earlier for practice with renaming common fractions and with reading and writing decimal fractions may be adapted for practice with renaming decimal fractions, common fractions, and percents. Bingo cards can be made with common fractions on the calling cards and decimal fractions and/or percents on the Bingo cards. Children can play a match game in which they match a card with a common fraction to a card with an equivalent decimal fraction to a card with an equivalent percent. Card games such as Old Maid can also be adapted so that children match these three types of cards.

Encourage students to create other games of their own to practice making conversions. Keep calculators handy as the children play the games so that the children may check their work.

Ordering Rational Numbers

After students can find equivalent common fractions and read and write decimal fractions, they are ready to practice ordering both common and decimal fractions. Often, children must determine such things as which of two fractions is greater or whether a given fraction is greater, less than, equal to, or between other fractions. Many children do not have accurate strategies for determining the relative sizes of rational numbers. They may have difficulty because of the infinite number of ways of writing equivalent fractions or because of the denseness of rational numbers. It is difficult for children to realize that there is always another rational number between any two given rational numbers, which is not true for whole numbers.

Children may need to return to some of the work with concrete materials before they begin to practice ordering fractions on an abstract level. The following activities are designed to give the children practice in ordering both common and decimal fractions. Be sure to discuss strategies with the children as they work. Note that it is not always possible to determine incorrect strategies by simply looking at mistakes on the children's papers.

A C T I V I T I E S

Grades 3–5

OBJECTIVE: to practice ordering common and decimal fractions.

1. Ask the children to predict, and then use a concrete material such as the circular regions to determine, which fraction in each of the following pairs is the greater:

$$\frac{1}{2} \quad \frac{3}{4}$$

$$\frac{2}{3} \quad \frac{5}{6}$$

$$\frac{3}{8} \quad \frac{3}{5}$$

$$\frac{3}{8} \quad \frac{2}{5}$$

$$\frac{1}{3} \quad \frac{3}{8}$$

Have the children explain why they made the predictions that they did and tell whether or not they were right. Ask children whose predictions were wrong to explain why the predictions were wrong. Can you tell which is larger by looking only at the numerator or only at the denominator?

When children can make fairly accurate estimates of the sizes of the fractions, ask them to cross-multiply each pair of fractions the way they did to determine if the two fractions were equivalent and to observe the findings. Ask, "For each pair of common fractions $\frac{a}{b}$ and $\frac{c}{d}$, what is the relationship of the fractions if $ad > bc$? What is the relationship if $ad < bc$?" Cross-multiply with several pairs of fractions and check the results by using concrete materials, converting both fractions to a common denominator or using a calculator to convert both common fractions to decimal fractions. Let the children come up with a generalization. Does the generalization fit their intuitive ideas about ordering fractions?

2. A computer program that students might enjoy using to learn fraction, decimal, and percent concepts is *Fraction Attraction*, available from Sunburst (1998). In this program, students visit a multimedia amusement park where they engage in four activities designed to build and reinforce concepts of rational numbers. Frac-Track is a racetrack game where horses move around the track based on fractions, decimals, and percents that students choose. In Frac-o-Wheel, varying representations of equivalent fractions are chosen to move a Ferris wheel to load or unload passengers. Whack-a-Frac builds further on the idea of equivalent fractions, and Fuzzy Fracs requires that students understand concepts of ordering and relative size as they attempt to knock down figures in a carnival game in size order.

You also might wish to view the Annenburg middle grades assessment video to watch fifth-grade students play a Fraction Track game where students must use equivalent fractions to move game pieces from one side of the game board to the other.

3. The game *Pyramid* can be played by two or more children. The first child must name a common fraction between 0 and 1 and write it on the bottom line of a sheet of paper. This child should then use the calculator to convert the common fraction to a decimal fraction and write the decimal fraction on the same line next to the common fraction. The next child must then name another common fraction that is greater than the first but still less than 1. This common fraction and its decimal fraction equivalent are then written on the next line of the pyramid. Play continues with larger and larger common fractions until the fraction named is not larger than the previous one, until the fraction named is larger than 1, until a time limit is reached, or until the children realize that the game could go on for an infinite number of moves and they tire of it. The beginning of a game is shown below:

$$\frac{1}{2} = 0.5$$

$$\frac{2}{5} = 0.4$$

$$\frac{3}{8} = 0.375$$

$$\frac{1}{3} = 0.333 \ldots$$

$$\frac{1}{4} = 0.25$$

$$\frac{2}{9} = 0.222 \ldots$$

$$\frac{1}{6} = 0.1666 \ldots$$

$$\frac{1}{8} = 0.125$$

$$0$$

Children may make the game harder by not allowing denominators that are powers of ten or not allowing unit fractions. To play this game well, some children may need to return to the activities for building the concepts of ordering common and decimal fractions.

Children may explore what happens to a repeating decimal when it is displayed on the calculator, since the calculator obviously cannot show an infinite number of decimal places. Calculators either round or truncate the decimals. When the calculator *truncates* a decimal, it merely cuts off all the decimal places beyond those that it can display. When the calculator *rounds* a decimal, if the first digit beyond the last digit on the display is less than 5, the last digit is not changed. If the first digit beyond the last digit on the display is greater than 5, the last digit is rounded up. If the first digit beyond the last digit on the display is 5, most calculators round up, although the rules vary.

Let the children try a fraction such as $\frac{2}{3}$ to see the response on the calculator. Some calculators will display 0.6666666, and some will display 0.6666667. Ask the children which is more accurate. The calculator function may be compared to a computer that continues to divide until told to stop when converting common fractions to repeating decimals.

Rates, Ratios, and Proportions

One of the uses of common fractions is to show a ratio of one part to another part. A **proportion** consists of two equal ratios. If you know that there are 2 girls for every 3 boys in the class and you know the whole class has 10 girls, you may use a proportion to find the total number of boys in the class. Set up the proportion as follows:

$$\frac{2 \text{ girls}}{3 \text{ boys}} = \frac{10 \text{ girls}}{n \text{ boys}}$$

The technique of cross-multiplying works in solving a proportion. In this example, when you cross-multiply, you get $2 \times n = 3 \times 10$. If $2n = 30$, then $n = 15$. The total number of boys in the class is 15.

Children may use proportions to solve problems involving percents and inverse proportions to solve problems involving more complex relationships such as comparing the number of teeth in a gear to the number of rotations it will make. Textbooks for the middle grades give several more examples. However, don't assume that children understand proportions after working these examples abstractly. Proportional reasoning is one of the signs of formal operational thinking, and many adults have difficulty with formal operational thinking. Try some of the following questions yourself (assume letters not mentioned will remain the same):

$\frac{a}{b} = \frac{c}{d}$ What will happen to *c* if *a* gets larger?

$\frac{e}{f} = \frac{g}{h}$ What will happen to *h* if *e* gets larger?

$\frac{j}{k} = \frac{l}{m}$ What will happen to *l* if *k* gets smaller?

Did you have difficulty with any of these? Try to explain your reasoning to a classmate. Do you feel that you could explain proportions well to children? Explain-

ing on an abstract level is difficult. Try returning to concrete examples for your explanations. You may need to substitute numerals for the letters. Now try this one:

The red string is 3 paper clips long. The blue string is 5 paper clips long. If you measure the red string in Bingo chips, you find it is 6 chips long. How many chips will it take to measure the blue string?

Was this any easier? Did you draw a picture or visualize the answer mentally? How does this question compare to the earlier ones? Keep these activities in mind as you introduce proportions to the children. Be sure to include concrete examples to help children develop the concepts. The following activities give a very brief idea of some of the uses for proportions. Be sure to add other ideas of your own.

A C T I V I T I E S

Grades 6–8

OBJECTIVE: to practice using proportions.

1. Proportions are used frequently in children's everyday lives. Give the children some examples of their uses and ask them to make up their own problems using proportions or to collect examples of problems they encounter, say, in the grocery store or while reading the newspaper. The following are a few examples:

- José is baking a birthday cake. The recipe feeds 12 and calls for 3 eggs. José is planning a large party and wants to make a cake for 36 people. How many eggs does he need? Use the ratio $\frac{3}{12} = \frac{n}{36}$ or $\frac{3}{n} = \frac{12}{36}$. Discuss with the children how to set up the proportion. There are two other proportions the children may set up that would be equivalent to these. Can you find them?

- Mrs. Montoya is buying prizes for José's party. The prizes are 3 for $.50. Mrs. Montoya wishes to buy 36 prizes. How much will they cost? How do you decide on the proportions $\frac{3}{\$.50} = \frac{36}{n}$ or $\frac{3}{36} = \frac{\$.50}{n}$?

- Mishon is building a scale model of a car to give José for his birthday. The scale is 5 centimeters per meter. If the model is 30 centimeters long, how long is the car?

$$\frac{5 \text{ centimeters}}{1 \text{ meter}} = \frac{30 \text{ centimeters}}{n \text{ meters}}$$

or

$$\frac{5}{30} = \frac{1}{n}$$

Children may wish to use physical materials to model each of these problems. Be sure to connect the work they are doing concretely to the abstract solution of the equations.

2. Read the book *If You Hopped Like a Frog* by David Schwartz (1999) and discuss the proportions that were used to determine the statements such as "If you hopped like a frog, you could jump from home plate to first base in one mighty leap." Challenge the students to do some research and make up their own pages to the book.

OBJECTIVE: to practice using proportions to solve percent problems.

3. One method of solving problems involving percents is through the use of the following proportion:

$$\frac{\text{rate}}{100} = \frac{\text{percentage}}{\text{base}}$$

This proportion works regardless of whether the children need to find the rate, the percentage, or the base in a given problem. For example, a store may be having a sale on all its jeans. In one case, the jeans originally cost $20 (base). They have been reduced by $5 (percentage) and you wish to find the percent of the original cost that the reduction represents. Use the proportion $\frac{n}{100} = \frac{\$5}{\$20}$. By cross-multiplying, you find that $\$20 \times n = 100 \times \$5$, or $20n = 500$, or $n = 25$ percent. The jeans are marked down by 25 percent of the original cost.

In another problem, you see a sign that says "20% off everything on this rack." You wish to buy a pair of jeans that were originally $30 and want to find out how much you will save buying them on sale. Again, you can use the proportion to solve the problem. This time, you know the percent and the base and wish to find the percentage. The proportion is $\frac{20}{100} = \frac{\$n}{\$30}$. By cross-multiplying, you find that $20 \times \$30 = \$n \times 100$, or $100n = 600$, or $n = \$6$. You will save $6 on the jeans.

In the third case, the sign says that the jeans have been marked down 40% and that you will save $10 on each pair. What was the original cost of the jeans? This time, you know the percent and the percentage and you wish to find the base. Use the same proportion. The proportion is $\frac{40}{100} = \frac{\$10}{\$n}$. By cross-multiplying, you find that $40 \times \$n = 100 \times \$10$, or $40n = 1,000$, or $n = \$25$. The jeans originally cost $25. The children will find many more examples of ways proportions can be used, not only in their textbooks but also in their own shopping. You may wish to introduce a unit on becoming a wise consumer and ask children to bring in examples of percent problems from their own experiences. The newspaper is a rich source of problems. The children may be surprised to find the number of examples of store sales that do not report the percents correctly. Challenge the children to find examples of misleading or incorrect ads in the paper. They may even wish to inform the store managers of their mistakes.

Ask the children if it makes a difference if the percents are reported as a percent of the original cost or as a percent of the discounted cost. Let the children work several examples to see that it does indeed make a difference. Encourage children to ask questions and explore other aspects of percents. They may even be able to teach their parents and other adults some aspects of becoming wise consumers.

OBJECTIVE: to practice using proportions with inverse relationships.

4. If children have worked with the gears mentioned earlier in the chapter, they should have noticed that the larger gears with more teeth went around fewer times. If a gear with 10 teeth turned a gear with 5 teeth, the larger gear went around only $\frac{1}{2}$ the number of times that the smaller gear went around. The proportion for the gears is

$$\frac{\text{the number of teeth in the first gear}}{\text{the number of teeth in the second gear}} = \frac{\text{the number of turns of the second gear}}{\text{the number of turns of the first gear}}$$

If the larger gear turns 3 times, the proportion is $\frac{10}{5} = \frac{n}{3}$, where n is the number of turns for the smaller gear. By cross-multiplying, you get $10 \times 3 = 5 \times n$, or $30 = 5n$, or $n = 6$. The smaller gear turns 6 times as the larger gear turns 3 times. This works because the number of teeth on one gear multiplied by the number of turns that gear makes is a constant. Therefore, the number of teeth on the first gear times the number of turns of the first gear is equal to the number of teeth on the second gear times the number of turns of the second gear.

ESTIMATING AND USING BENCHMARKS

Test results from the Fourth National Assessment of Educational Progress (Kouba et al., 1988) show that students generally are poor at estimations that involve common or decimal fractions. As we rely more on calculators and computers, estimation and mental calculation skills become increasingly important. The 1992 National Assessment of Educational Progress showed that calculator usage had increased since 1990, and that at grades 8 and 12, students who used a calculator at least weekly had higher mathematics proficiency than their counterparts who never or hardly ever used a calculator in math class (Dossey, Mullis, Gorman, and Latham, 1994, p. 89). The Third International Mathematics and Science Study showed that 98 percent of eighth graders in the United States reported having a calculator available at home and

59 percent had a computer available. Over 60 percent of the students reported using calculators nearly every day in class (Beaton et al., 1996, p. 163–164). Children should be encouraged to estimate or calculate mentally in activities involving rational numbers just as they were in whole number activities.

Some of the activities mentioned earlier, such as the Pyramid Game, require that children be able to estimate whether one fraction is larger than another. There are also a number of times when children should be able to accurately calculate an answer mentally. For example, they should know the common fraction equivalents for percents that they encounter every day. Children should have several estimation and mental calculation experiences as they learn rational number skills. The activities presented below give a few more ideas for practicing estimation and mental calculation skills. The activities are listed for a wide range of grade levels because although children should ideally learn to estimate at the same time that they first learn fractions, many children do not. Therefore, the activities may be used with students in the middle grades as well.

A C T I V I T I E S

Grades 3–5 and Grades 6–8

OBJECTIVE: to develop estimation skills with common fractions.

1. Children should be able to use certain model fractions to compare various amounts. Give children experiences with benchmarks such as $\frac{1}{2}$, $\frac{1}{4}$, and $\frac{3}{4}$ so that they may estimate whether other amounts are more or less than these. Begin by letting children estimate when something is half full. Use a glass container and let children pour beans into it until they believe it is half full. After they fill it to what they think is half full, have them empty the beans into another container and again fill the container half full with different beans. Leave these beans in the container and then pour the first amount of beans back into the container. If both estimates were good, the container should be full. Or, measure the total container and the amount poured into it to see how close the amount is to $\frac{1}{2}$ of the container.

After the children can estimate $\frac{1}{2}$ fairly well, pour varying amounts into the container and ask the children if the amounts are more or less than $\frac{1}{2}$. When the children can accurately compare amounts to $\frac{1}{2}$, then repeat the activity with $\frac{1}{4}$ and $\frac{3}{4}$. Older children with more estimation experience may use a liter and estimate amounts in tenths of a liter (deciliters).

2. Ask children to keep a list of the times outside of school that they need to use common or decimal fractions to estimate. They may include some of the following:

- Part of an hour to eat breakfast, take a bath, do homework, and so on.
- Part of a mile or kilometer to walk to a friend's house, the store, or to school.
- Part of a quart or liter of milk drunk for dinner.
- Part of a cake or pie eaten for dessert.
- Part of a pound or kilogram of meat or cheese to buy for lunch.

Children can think of many other examples themselves. Encourage them to share the techniques they use to estimate.

OBJECTIVE: to practice mental conversion of percents to common fractions.

3. Older students should have experience in converting percents to common fractions mentally because of the widespread use of percents in everyday life. Bring in ads from department store sales and look for the percents that are used. Ask the students to tally how often different percents are used in the ads. They will probably find frequent use of percents that convert to tenths, thirds, fourths, and halves.

4. In many parts of the country, it is common practice to leave a 15 percent tip at a restaurant. Ask the students to determine a method for finding a 15 percent tip based on knowing 10 percent. They will probably tell you that 5 percent is $\frac{1}{2}$ of 10 percent, and therefore, to find 15 percent, you can add 10 percent and 5 percent. Ask students to bring in restaurant receipts and practice finding 15 percent of the total. Challenge the students to find 15 percent of a number in a variety of ways. In addition to this method, a students might suggest that you could divide the number by 20 and then multiply by 3 or you could find $\frac{1}{4}$ of a number and then subtract $\frac{1}{10}$ of the number. Be sure to ask students to justify each of their methods.

Ask the children the benefits of knowing the common fraction equivalents. Discuss how to use proportions to find discounts if you know the common fraction equivalents of the commonly used percents. Ask the children how they convert 20 percent, 30 percent, 40 percent, . . . to common fractions if they know that 10 percent is $\frac{1}{10}$. If 33.3 percent is $\frac{1}{3}$, what is $\frac{2}{3}$? If 25 percent is $\frac{1}{4}$, what is $\frac{3}{4}$? If an item is marked 25 percent off, how can you use the common fraction equivalent to find the discount? Let the children ask similar questions of their own and share their strategies with each other.

REASONING, SOLVING, AND POSING RATIONAL NUMBER PROBLEMS

Throughout this chapter, we have mentioned a number of opportunities for children to solve problems and to create problems of their own, which they will then solve or which their classmates will solve. Because of the importance of this topic, more ideas for problem solving and problem creating are included here. As with any other topic, problem creating and solving should become the child's natural approach to work with rational numbers.

A C T I V I T I E S

Grades 3–5 and Grades 6–8

OBJECTIVE: to explore relationships among common fractions, recognizing that each fraction may be represented in a number of different ways.

1. Pattern blocks are designed so that the areas of many of the blocks are multiples of the areas of other blocks. This makes them well-designed for exploring fractional relationships. The book *Fractions with Pattern Blocks*, by Mathew E. Zullie (1975), suggests many activities for the exploration of these relationships. Many of the activities require that the children use problem-solving and higher-level thinking strategies.

Have the children use orange squares, uncolored parallelograms, green triangles, blue rhombuses, red trapezoids, and yellow hexagons for these activities. Ask, "If the yellow hexagon represents 1, what are the values of each of the other pieces?" If the children have difficulty determining the other values, ask, "How many green triangles does it take to cover the yellow hexagon? How many red trapezoids does it take to cover the hexagon? How many triangles does it take to cover the parallelogram?"

Next, challenge the children to find as many examples as they can that show $\frac{1}{3}$ using any number of pattern blocks.

- *Understanding the problem.* I will need to find ways to show $\frac{1}{3}$ using pattern blocks. This means that I should look for single blocks or groups of blocks that can represent the value of 1 (unit). Then I will try to find blocks to represent $\frac{1}{3}$. I will try also to find other ways to make a unit.

- *Devising a plan.* One way I can solve this problem is to take 3 blocks of one shape—for example, 3 orange squares. Then I place them together to form a row. This rectangular row will have the value of 1. Any orange square is $\frac{1}{3}$ of the row. Another way to solve the problem is to look for combinations of

blocks that can be placed together into shapes to represent 1. For example, a blue rhombus combined with a green triangle can have the value of 1. Then a green triangle has the value of $\frac{1}{3}$. I will try some of these ways.

- *Carrying out the plan.* I can place 3 of the uncolored parallelograms together to make a shape with the value of 1. One of the parallelograms represents $\frac{1}{3}$ of the unit shape. That works also with 3 green triangles, orange squares, blue rhombuses, red trapezoids, and yellow hexagons.

I can also use a single red trapezoid as the unit. Then a green triangle represents $\frac{1}{3}$. Another combination representing the value of 1 is 2 red trapezoids. Then a blue rhombus represents $\frac{1}{3}$. If a yellow hexagon and a red trapezoid are combined into a unit, a red trapezoid represents $\frac{1}{3}$. Still another solution is to see 6 green triangles as a unit; then 2 green triangles represent $\frac{1}{3}$. I have found at least ten different ways to show $\frac{1}{3}$ using the pattern blocks.

- *Looking back.* I need to check to make sure each of the fraction models I made shows the fraction $\frac{1}{3}$. I will then try to generalize my solutions. I can continue to use more blocks to show the unit and try to find other examples in which more than one block is used to show the fraction $\frac{1}{3}$.

Encourage the children to make up questions of their own. Children can make designs to represent the unit and trace the outline. Have them trade outlines and challenge each other to find various fractional amounts of the unit designs. Is there more than one solution for each design? Let the children find out.

2. Earlier in this chapter, we suggested that you have the children explore many ways to show $\frac{1}{2}$ using paper folding and Cuisenaire rods. A similar activity should be repeated using other materials and other fractions.

Ask the children to make two trains of Cuisenaire rods such that one train is $\frac{1}{2}$ the length of the other train, as in Figure 8–28. This will help the children

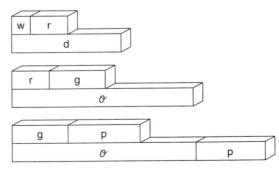

Figure 8–28 Trains of Cuisenaire rods where the top train is $\frac{1}{2}$ the length of the bottom rod or rods.

later when they learn to use the rods to show addition of fractions. Ask the children to use the rods to show other fractional relationships, such as $\frac{2}{3}$, $\frac{3}{4}$, and 0.6.

After the children can find these relationships, tell them that the dark-green rod represents 1 and ask them to find the rod for $\frac{1}{3}$. If the dark-green rod represents 2, which rod is $\frac{1}{3}$? Let the children challenge each other with problems of their own. Is it always possible to find a rod to represent a given fraction? Why not?

ORGANIZING FOR RATIONAL NUMBER TLC

Because the concepts of rational numbers and the rules for operations with them frequently are different from the concepts and rules that students have for whole numbers, it is important that students be encouraged to explore these ideas concretely in small groups to encourage open discussion of ideas. When younger students are first discovering the concepts of fractions, they can work in groups of two, three, or more to find ways to divide different amounts of materials equally among the members of the group. For example, three students may be given a large sheet of paper and asked to fold it and then cut along the folds so that each person in the group has the same amount of paper, or four students may be given a bottle of juice or a bag of peanuts to share equally. In each case, discuss the fractional parts that are found and compare the methods used by one group to those used by another.

When students have mastered the concepts of rational numbers, they may work in groups to expand upon these ideas. Ask a group of four to brainstorm everything they know about the fraction $\frac{3}{4}$ or to write equivalent names for $\frac{3}{4}$ in as many ways as possible. They may also list all the ways in which they see rational numbers being used every day.

COMMUNICATING LEARNING OF RATIONAL NUMBER CONCEPTS

Payne and Towsley (1990) state that work with fractions and decimals should be mostly oral in grades K–4 and that it should be only oral in grades K–2, using models and realistic problems. Children of this age are not ready for the abstract symbolic notation of fractions. Even in grades 5–8, they recommend that all work begin with concrete models, realistic problems, and oral language. This oral communication of ideas is essential to the development of the concepts of rational numbers. Mack (1990) notes that while students bring a rich informal background to the study of rational numbers through real-life situations, this knowledge is not connected to the abstract symbols and procedures. Indeed, knowledge of rote procedures may actually hinder students in building on prior knowledge. If students try to learn abstract symbols and procedures before they are given a chance to discuss their understanding of rational number concepts orally, they may never develop a true understanding of rational numbers.

Children could write about fractions in their daily journals. Younger children might draw or collect pictures of things that represent one-half. This might include a picture of a half-full glass of milk, a drawing of a half-dollar, a clock that shows half past the hour, and a line segment that is $\frac{1}{2}$-inch long. Third- or fourth-grade students might write a journal entry describing how to find $\frac{1}{2}$ or $\frac{1}{3}$ of a set of objects such as 1 dozen eggs, all the students in the class, or all the cookies on a plate.

CONNECTING AND REPRESENTING RATIONAL NUMBER LEARNING

Mr. Winkler's primary class has just finished reading *The Doorbell Rang* by Pat Hutchins (1986). In the story, Mom has just finished making a batch of cookies that two children are getting ready to share when the doorbell rings and a third child enters. Just as the three children get ready to share the cookies, a fourth child rings the bell. Before these children can eat, two more children arrive. Each time children arrive in the story, the class has discussed new fractions. They are using a dozen counters to represent the cookies, and they are determining how many cookies each child would get if they had $\frac{1}{2}$, $\frac{1}{3}$, $\frac{1}{4}$, $\frac{1}{6}$, or $\frac{1}{12}$ of the total number of cookies. Mustapha says that this is just like the problems they did with division last month. When Mr. Winkler finishes reading the story, the class decides they would like to act the story out with real cookies. Mr. Winkler agrees to bring in a simple cookie recipe and talk to the cooks in the school cafeteria about using the oven. Each child will talk to their parents about furnishing one of the ingredients for the cookies. Mr. Winkler knows that the recipes will give the students even more work with fractions.

Other children's books that can be used to introduce fraction concepts include *Gator Pie* by Louise Mathews (1979) and *Eating Fractions* by Bruce MacMillan (1991). You might also wish to view the *Communication* or *Cookies to Share* videos from Annenburg Video Library to observe a group of fourth graders as they explore fraction and decimal concepts.

Mr. Howsam's seventh- and eighth-grade academic team has entered a statewide competition involving the stock market sponsored by the Economic Council. They

Pieces of Eighths

Jerome wanted to share a
pizza with seven friends. He
said, "I will cut the pizza into
eighths. I will make eight
pieces." This picture shows
how Jerome's pizza looked
when he finished.

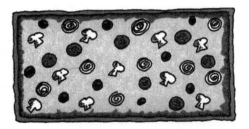

1. On the lines below, tell what you think about the way
   Jerome cut the pizza. Did he cut the pizza into eighths?

   _____

   _____

   _____

2. Show how you would divide the pizza fairly among
   eight children.

Figure 8–29 From *Math Trailblazers* Student Guide, Grade One, by TIMS. Copyright ©1997
by Kendall/Hunt Publishing Company, Used with permission.

MATH PROGRAM

The first-grade page shown in Figure 8–29 is from the Student Guide of *Math Trailblazers,* an elementary mathematics curriculum project funded by the National Science Foundation and developed as part of the Teaching Integrated Mathematics and Science Project (TIMS). This program is based on the belief that children deserve a challenging mathematics curriculum and that mathematics is best learned through solving many different kinds of problems. Many of the problems involve making connections between the mathematics learned in school and that used in everyday life as seen in this problem.

One of the homework assignments associated with this chapter includes asking students and their families to find and discuss six items at home that come in halves or fourths. Some of the suggestions include crackers, milk (half gallon), and butter (quarter pound sticks). In addition, students fold and color paper shapes as they explore halves, fourths, and eighths.

Notice that even the first graders are expected to write about their mathematical understanding. Reading, writing, and talking are all used in the mathematics classes to help students construct mathematical concepts on a higher level. This is in keeping with the philosophy of the program that children can handle more difficult mathematics and science than is often assumed. In addition to the fraction concepts shown here, the program also includes measurement, data collection, statistics, geometry, ratio, probability, graphing, algebra, and patterns and relationships, all introduced through problem solving and applications.

have been number one in the district and number five in the state for the last five weeks. They have had many heated discussions about buying and selling stocks that rise or fall fractions of a point. Today, Geraldine enters the team meeting with a long face. Their best stock has fallen 11.25 points, and they know that this big drop will cause their team to drop off the list of the top 10 teams. The academic team spends most of the meeting trying to decide what to do about this stock.

A stock market project designed for middle-grade students using real-time data from the New York Stock Exchange is available online at Weblink 8–5.

ASSESSING LEARNING OF RATIONAL NUMBERS

As with other concepts, children should be assessed informally as well as formally on their rational number concepts. As children work with concrete materials, keep track of which children demonstrate competence with the rational number concepts and skills and which children are still having difficulty. For additional instruction, group together children having difficulty with the same concepts or skills. Let the other students explore some of the applications of rational numbers.

Dorgan (1994) in a study of three 1992 textbook series for grades 1–5 noted that while textbooks offer opportunities for making connections between pictorial and symbolic representations, there are several areas in which the texts have limited value, including "the development of qualitative reasoning, the building of connections among various modes of representation, and the growth of communication skills" (p. 155). She noted that a student's development of a strong foundation in fraction concepts depends more on the way in which the teacher chooses to use the text than on the text itself.

As you assess children, present problems in a variety of ways, since some children may be able to perform satisfactorily using one model or one type of presentation but not another. Differences are found in performance when children are asked to create their own models for a given rational number rather than to select a model from a number of choices, or when they are asked to write the correct common fraction to match a given picture rather than to select or create a picture to match the fraction. Some children can select the correct model from concrete materials but not from pictures, or can draw a picture but not create a concrete model such as paper folding. Children may select or create the correct model using areas but not using a number line. It is therefore important to present rational number tasks to children using a variety of models and a variety of methods of presentation.

For students in the intermediate grades and beyond, be sure to include portfolio tasks that look at students' concepts of rational numbers. You might ask students to write a detailed description of how they decide on relative size of two different fractions or other rational numbers. They should include diagrams of a variety of different models in their descriptions, such as number lines, area models, volume models, and sets of discrete objects, as well as descriptions of times in everyday life when this concept is important, such as deciding how much stocks have gone up or down as they move from .62 to .75 and estimating which sweater is the better buy if one was $30 and is marked down 25 percent and the other was $33 and is marked down 33 percent.

Some assessment tasks may be paper-and-pencil or calculator tests but others should be individual interviews in order to get the clearest picture of the child's conceptions or misconceptions about rational numbers. Following are some of the common problems that arise as children work with rational numbers.

1. Some children do not realize that in the part-whole model of a fraction, the parts must be of equal size. They may give some of the responses shown in Figure 8–30. Children having difficulty with the part-whole concept should return to work with concrete materials such as paper folding. Have them cut out the regions to show that all halves, thirds, fourths, and so on take up the same amount of area even if they are not congruent.

2. Some children give a ratio answer when a part-whole answer is expected. They may give the responses shown in Figure 8–31.

   This problem is related to difficulty with the Piagetian tasks of class inclusion and reversibility. Children may have difficulty realizing that in the part-whole model, the fractional part must be compared back to the whole that includes it; they compare one part to the other parts. Or they may not realize that something divided into two halves will again

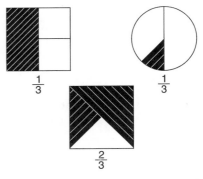

Figure 8–30   Example of children's misconceptions about the part-whole model of a fraction.

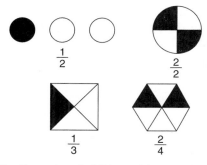

Figure 8–31 Examples of children giving a ratio response when a part-whole response is expected.

become one whole when you put the two halves back together. Such children need more experience manipulating concrete models and discussing their meanings before they continue with abstract work with fractions.

3. Some children have difficulty writing a common fraction as a division problem. They think that $\frac{2}{3}$ means $3 \div 2$ rather than the other way around. This misunderstanding is particularly troublesome as children attempt to convert common fractions to decimal fractions.

    Children will also need instruction on which number to put into the calculator first when they divide. Remind them that the numerator is the dividend and the denominator is the divisor. You may also need to return to the concrete models and remind them that the number in the numerator tells you the number you begin with and the number in the denominator tells the number of parts it is being divided into.

4. Some children do not realize that a common fraction is a single number. They think of it as two numbers, one sitting on top of the other. This causes them to work with the numbers separately when they perform operations with common fractions; they may add together numerators and denominators when they attempt to add two common fractions. Work with concrete materials and with renaming common fractions as decimal fractions helps children realize that common fractions represent only one number.

5. Some children have difficulty ordering rational numbers, even unit fractions. They think that $\frac{1}{3}$ is bigger than $\frac{1}{2}$ because 3 is bigger than 2. These children may need to return to work with concrete materials to discover that there is an inverse relationship between the size of the denominator in a unit fraction and the size of the piece that the fraction represents. The activities suggested for estimation should help these children.

    Vance (1986) has found that similar problems arise when children order decimal fractions, especially

when the numbers do not contain the same number of decimal places. When ordering .5, .34, and .257, some children decide that .257 is the largest because it uses the most digits or that it is the smallest because it is written in thousandths, which are smaller than tenths or hundredths. Such reasoning would work for the problem above but not for .5 and .678.

Children having difficulty ordering decimals should return to work with physical models and with estimation. They should work with rewriting decimals so that all the decimal fractions contain the same number of decimal places.

Calculators can be useful here. Vance suggests a calculator game in which the students try to "wipe out" a digit in the calculator display. For example, if the calculator shows 23.9876, wipe out the 7 by subtracting .007. Ask students to see if the same thing happens when they subtract .0007 or .0070.

6. Some students have difficulty understanding that rational numbers are dense. It is hard to understand that with rational numbers there is no next number as there is with whole numbers; there is always another rational number between any two rational numbers. Students who find it hard to give a rational number between $\frac{1}{4}$ and $\frac{2}{4}$ or between 0.1 and 0.2 may need to return to work with concrete materials and with renaming rational numbers. If $\frac{1}{4}$ and $\frac{2}{4}$ are renamed as $\frac{2}{8}$ and $\frac{4}{8}$, or if 0.1 and 0.2 are renamed as 0.10 and 0.20, it is easier for students to find another number between them. The Pyramid Game described earlier also will help students practice finding a rational number between two other rational numbers.

7. Some children understand unit fraction concepts but not concepts of fractions with numerators greater than 1 or concepts of mixed numbers. Children who have a concrete understanding of these concepts may still have difficulty with improper fractions. Such children should return to a variety of models, including concrete regions and the number line, to develop a better understanding of improper fractions.

8. Some students have difficulty converting decimals to percents. They remember that they should move the decimal point two places, but they move it the wrong direction. This is especially true for percents that are less than 1 or greater than 100.

    This problem with the decimal point also arises in writing dollars and cents. A number of adults seem not to realize that when used with a cent sign, the decimal point represents hundredths of a cent. It is tempting to offer the grocer a penny for four oranges when the sign above the oranges reads .25¢ for one orange. Children enjoy looking for mistakes such as this.

    Similar mistakes involving the decimal point arise when children are using a calculator. Be sure children use their estimation skills to determine whether or not their answers make sense. Examples from real life can be useful here. Misplacing the decimal point when solving a real-life problem involving money can be very costly.

9. Some students have difficulty with proportional reasoning. Tasks involving proportions are often difficult on the abstract level, even for adults. Be sure to include concrete work on these concepts and encourage students to discuss their reasoning with each other.

SOMETHING FOR EVERYONE

Again, we recognize that while children learn in a variety of modes, some children may learn more comfortably in a particular mode, such as visually or auditorily. Because both Chapters 8 and 9 are directed at teaching rational numbers, the specific learning modes associated with rational numbers are discussed at the end of Chapter 9.

FOR YOU AS A TEACHER: IDEAS FOR DISCUSSION AND YOUR PROFESSIONAL PORTFOLIO

This section is intended to provide you the opportunity to read, write, and reflect on key elements of this chapter. We list several discussion ideas. We hope that one or more of these ideas will prove interesting to you and that you will choose to investigate and write about the ideas. The results of your work should be considered as part of your professional portfolio. You might consider these two questions as guides for your writing: "What does the material in this chapter mean for you as a teacher?" or "How can what you are reading be translated into a teaching practice for you as a teacher?"

DISCUSSION IDEAS

1. Analyze two different elementary mathematics textbook series to see how fraction and decimal concepts are introduced. Which concept is introduced first? Are there connections made between fraction and decimal concepts or are these treated as separate topics? Compare your findings to those of a classmate.

2. Describe how you might introduce common fractions using the part-whole model. What physical models might you use? What errors would you expect children to make when first learning these concepts? How will you help students make the transition from physical models to drawings to abstract concepts?

3. Find at least two different computer programs that are designed to help children learn fraction concepts. Analyze each for the clarity of the mathematics presented. If possible, watch a child using at least one of the programs, and interview the child to determine if any learning took place because of using the program.

4. Design a lesson to help children practice the conversion of fractions to equivalent decimals and percents. Be sure to include physical models.

5. Develop an open-ended problem to assess student understanding of proportional reasoning. Be sure that the problem allows students to use different methods of solution and requires them to use higher-level thinking. Include a scoring rubric for your problem.

ADDITIONAL RESOURCES

REFERENCES

Allinger, Glenn D., and Joseph N. Payne, "Estimation and Mental Arithmetic with Percent," in *Estimation and Mental Computation* (National Council of Teachers of Mathematics, 1986 Yearbook). Reston, VA: NCTM, 1986.

Beaton, Albert E., Ina V. S. Mullis, Michael O. Martin, Eugenio J. Gonzalez, Dana L. Kelly, and Teresa A. Smith, *Mathematics Achievement in the Middle School Years: IEA's Third International Mathematics and Science Study.* Chestnut Hill, MA: Boston College TIMSS International Study Center, November 1996.

Behr, Merlyn J., et al., "Order and Equivalence of Rational Numbers: A Clinical Teaching Experiment," *Journal for Research in Mathematics Education,* 15, no. 4 (November 1984), 323–341.

Behr, Merlyn J., Thomas R. Post, and Ipke Wachsmuth, "Estimation and Children's Concept of Rational Number Size," in *Estimation and Mental Computation* (National Council of Teachers of Mathematics, 1986 Yearbook). Reston, VA: NCTM, 1986.

Bennett, Albert B., Jr., *Decimal Squares.* Fort Collins, CO: Scott Resources, 1982.

Bennett, Albert B., Jr., and Patricia A. Davidson, *Fraction Bars.* Fort Collins, CO: Scott Resources, 1973.

Bezuk, Nadine, and Kathleen Cramer, "Teaching about Fractions: What, When, and How?" in *New Directions for Elementary School Mathematics,* ed. Paul R. Trafton and Albert P. Shulte. Reston, VA: National Council of Teachers of Mathematics, 1989.

Bradford, John, *Everything's Coming Up Fractions with Cuisenaire Rods.* New Rochelle, NY: Cuisenaire Co. of America, 1981.

Burns, Marilyn. *Teaching Arithmetic: Lessons for Introducing Fractions, Grades 4–5.* Sausalito, CA: Math Solutions, 2001.

Carpenter, Thomas P., et al., "Decimals: Results and Implications from National Assessment," *Arithmetic Teacher,* 28, no. 8 (April 1981), 34–37.

Cook, Marci, *Fractions: Try-A-Tile.* Sunnyvale, CA: Creative Publications, 1988.

De Francisco, Carrie, and Marilyn Burns, *Teaching Arithmetic: Lessons for Decimals and Percents, Grades 5–6*. Sausalito, CA: Math Solutions, 2002.

Dorgan, Karen, "What Textbooks Offer for Instruction in Fraction Concepts," *Teaching Children Mathematics*, 1, no. 3 (November 1994), 150–155.

Dossey, John A., Ina V. S. Mullis, Steven Gorman, and Andrew S. Latham, *How School Mathematics Functions: Perspectives from the NAEP 1990 and 1992 Assessments*. Washington, DC: National Center for Educational Statistics, 1994.

Dossey, John A., Ina V. S. Mullis, Mary M. Lindquist, and Donald L. Chambers, *The Mathematics Report Card: Are We Measuring Up? Trends and Achievement Based on the 1986 National Assessment*. Princeton, NJ: Educational Testing Service, 1988.

Eicholz, Robert E., et al., *Addison-Wesley Mathematics, Book 7*. Menlo Park, CA: Addison-Wesley, 1987.

Erickson, Sheldon, *Proportional Reasoning: AIMS Activities Grades 6–9*. Fresno, CA: AIMS Education Foundation, 2000.

Head, Debby, and Libby Pollett, *Count on Kids, Cluster One: Pattern Blocks Parts and Wholes*. Shelbyville, KY: bby Publications, 1994.

Holden, Linda, *The Fraction Factory*. Sunnyvale, CA: Creative Publications, 1986.

Jenkins, Lee, and Peggy McLean, *Fraction Tiles: A Manipulative Fraction Program*. Hayward, CA: Activity Resources, 1972.

Kouba, Vicky L., Catherine A. Brown, Thomas P. Carpenter, Mary M. Lindquist, Edward A. Silver, and Jane O. Swafford, "Results of the Fourth NAEP Assessment of Mathematics: Number, Operations, and Word Problems." *Arithmetic Teacher*, 35, no. 8 (April 1988), 14–19.

Lichtenberg, Betty K., and Donovan R. Lichtenberg, "Decimals Deserve Distinction," in *Mathematics for the Middle Grades (5–9)* (National Council of Teachers of Mathematics, 1982 Yearbook). Reston, VA: NCTM, 1982.

Mack, Nancy K., "Learning Fractions with Understanding: Building on Informal Knowledge," *Journal for Research in Mathematics Education*, 21, no. 1 (January 1990), 16–32.

Manfre, Edward, and Judy Vandegrift. *A Clear View of Decimals*. Nashua, NH: Delta Education, 1999.

———, *A Clear View of Fractions*. Nashua, NH: Delta Education, 1999.

———, *A Clear View of Percent*. Nashua, NH: Delta Education, 1999.

———, *A Clear View of Ratio and Proportion*. Nashua, NH: Delta Education, 1999.

McClain, Kay, ed., "Not One, but Six Fractions Equivalent to One-Third!" *Mathematics Teaching in the Middle School*, 3, no. 3 (November–December 1997), 213–214.

National Council of Teachers of Mathematics, *Principles and Standards for School Mathematics*. Reston, VA: NCTM, 2000.

Payne, Joseph N., and Ann E. Towsley, "Implications of NCTM's *Standards* for Teaching Fractions and Decimals," *Arithmetic Teacher*, 37, no. 8 (April 1990), 23–26.

Post, Thomas R., "Fractions: Results and Implications from National Assessment," *Arithmetic Teacher*, 28, no. 8 (May 1981), 26–31.

Post, Thomas R., Merlyn J. Behr, and Richard Lesh, "Research-Based Observations about Children's Learning of Rational Number Concepts," *Focus on Learning Problems in Mathematics*, 8, no. 1 (Winter 1986), 39–48.

Post, Thomas R., et al., "Order and Equivalence of Rational Numbers: A Cognitive Analysis," *Journal for Research in Mathematics Education*, 16, no. 1 (January 1985), 18–36.

"Rational Numbers (Focus Issue)," *Arithmetic Teacher*, 31, no. 6 (February 1984).

Roper, Ann, and Linda H. Charles, *Fraction Squares Plus Jobcards*. Sunnyvale, CA: Creative Publications, 1990.

Vance, James, "Ordering Decimals and Fractions: A Diagnostic Study," *Focus on Learning Problems in Mathematics*, 8, no. 2 (Spring 1986), 51–59.

Zullie, Mathew E., *Fractions with Pattern Blocks*. Palo Alto, CA: Creative Publications, 1975.

CHILDREN'S LITERATURE

Clement, Rod, *Counting on Frank*. Milwaukee, WI: Gareth Stevens, 1991.

Hutchins, Pat, *The Doorbell Rang*. New York: Greenwillow, 1986.

Mathews, Louise, *Gator Pie*. New York: Dodd, Mead, 1979.

McMillan, Bruce, *Eating Fractions*. New York: Scholastic, 1991.

Schwartz, David M. *If You Hopped Like a Frog*. New York: Scholastic, 1999.

TECHNOLOGY

Annenberg/CPB, *Teaching Math: A Video Library, K–4*. Boston: WGBH Educational Foundation, 1995.

Broderbund, *Math Workshop Deluxe*. Novato, CA: Broderbund, 1998. (software)

Edmark, *Mighty Math Number Heroes*. Orlando, FL: Harcourt Brace, 1996. (software)

Eisenhower National Clearinghouse, *Tools for Discussion: Attaining Excellence through TIMSS*. Columbus, OH: Eisenhower National Clearinghouse for Mathematics and Science Education, 1998. (CD-ROM)

Sunburst, *Fraction Attraction*. Pleasantville, NY: Sunburst, 1998. (software)

WEBLINKS

Weblink 8–1: National Library for Virtual Manipulatives for Interactive Mathematics. See the Factor Tree Game. http://matti.usu.edu/nlvm/nav/category_g_3_t_2.html

Weblink 8–2: NCTM Illuminations. See the Product Game and the Factor Game. http://www.illuminations.nctm.org/pages/68.html

Weblink 8–3: National Center for Educational Statistics (NCES). The Nation's Report Card. http://nces.ed.gov/nationsreportcard/pubs/main1996/98481.asp

Weblink 8–4: National Center for Educational Statistics (NCES). Trends in International Mathematics and Science Study. http://nces.ed.gov/timss

Weblink 8–5: Interactive stock market project for middle school students available from the National Center for Supercomputing Applications. http://archive.ncsa.uiuc.edu/edu/RSE/RSEyellow/gnb.html

TEACHING AND LEARNING OPERATIONS WITH RATIONAL NUMBERS

As you read the following pages, consider these guiding questions:

1. How are operations with rational numbers used every day, and how might you write number stories for these operations that help students develop the concepts, skills, and algorithms necessary for understanding them?

2. What are some of the physical models that might be used to illustrate operations with rational numbers, and how might you use these with students?

3. How do operations with rational numbers compare with operations with whole numbers?

4. Why do rules such as "invert and multiply" work when dividing common fractions?

5. What are some common errors that students make when operating with rational numbers, and what might you do to help a student correct these errors?

NCTM Principles and Standards for School Mathematics

Number and Operations

Instructional programs from prekindergarten through grade 12 should enable all students to:

Understand meanings of operations and how they relate to one another

Grades 6–8

• understand the meaning and effects of arithmetic operations with fractions, decimals, and integers;

• use the associative and commutative properties of addition and multiplication and the distributive property of multiplication over addition to simplify computations with integers, fractions, and decimals;

• understand and use the inverse relationships of addition and subtraction, multiplication and division, and squaring and finding square roots to simplify computations and solve problems.

Compute fluently and make reasonable estimates

Grades 3–5

• develop and use strategies to estimate computations involving fractions and decimals in situations relevant to students' experience;

• use visual models, benchmarks, and equivalent forms to add and subtract commonly used fractions and decimals.

Grades 6–8

• select appropriate methods and tools for computing with fractions and decimals from among mental computation, estimation, calculators or computers, and paper and pencil, depending on the situation, and apply the selected methods;

• develop and analyze algorithms for computing with fractions, decimals, and integers and develop fluency in their use;

• develop and use strategies to estimate the results of rational-number computations and judge the reasonableness of the results;

• develop, analyze, and explain methods for solving problems involving proportions, such as scaling and finding equivalent ratios.

NCTM (2000), pp. 148, 214. Reprinted by permission.

Using only halves, thirds, fourths, sixths, eighths, and twelfths, list at least 15 different ways to make one whole. You may use combinations such as $\frac{1}{2} + \frac{1}{4} + \frac{2}{8}$ as well as $\frac{8}{8}$ or $\frac{3}{3}$. Remember to look for patterns and write your results in an organized list.

How do you know if you have found all the ways possible using only halves, thirds, fourths, sixths, eighths, and twelfths? Use your chart to predict how many total possible ways there are to find combinations equal to one whole. Write a convincing argument that your method will determine all possibilities.

REFLECTIONS AND REFINEMENT: *After you have completed this task, compare your work with that of some of your classmates. Did you find solutions that they did not have? Did they find solutions that you did not have? Did you use the same method to try to find all the possibilities? What do you think would happen if you could use other fractional pieces? Write your hypotheses and discoveries here.*

Operations with rational numbers are generally emphasized in the upper elementary and middle school grades. Operations with decimal fractions may be introduced earlier along with the decimal notation for money or perhaps with measurements in the metric system, but generally math programs wait until fourth or fifth grade to teach rational number operations.

There is some controversy over whether operations with common fractions should be delayed until seventh or eighth grade because of the increased use of decimal fractions and the difficulties many children experience with common fractions, but most textbooks do not delay the instruction that long. Many programs introduce operations with decimal fractions the same year in which they introduce operations with common fractions. That is one of the reasons we do not have separate chapters for common and decimal fractions.

Perhaps more importantly, we do not have these operations in separate chapters because conceptually the two represent the same situations. Children should be able to recognize that if they use three-tenths of a meter of material for a doll's blouse and seven-tenths of a meter of material for a doll's coat, it does not matter if they find the total amount of material by adding $\frac{3}{10} + \frac{7}{10}$ or by adding $0.3 + 0.7$. No matter how it is written, they have used a meter of material.

It is important that operations with rational numbers arise from examples in the "real world." Have children make a list of occasions in which rational numbers are used in their homes or everyday lives. The following are a few suggestions for events or places where rational numbers are used. Ask children to discuss situations in which rational numbers might be used and to make up story problems using these settings. Have the children add to the list as situations arise.

- Recipes
- Sewing
- Gardening
- Medicine
- Building
- Unit pricing
- Odometer
- Hourly wages
- Track and field events
- Kilowatt hours of electricity
- Stock market
- Scale drawings (architecture, engineering, drafting, surveying, mapmaking, etc.)
- Measurements of all types (time, length, area, volume, money, etc.)
- Probability and statistics
- Graphing

As we discuss the concepts of operations with rational numbers, we frequently draw examples from daily events. You and the children should do the same in your classroom.

Working with physical models continues to be important as children learn to operate with rational numbers. Even children in the seventh and eighth grades are generally concretely operational and cannot fully understand new concepts on an abstract level. Work with physical models helps children construct their knowledge about rational number operations. Continue to use the manipulative materials discussed in Chapter 8 for rational number concepts; these include Fraction Bars, circular and rectangular regions, pattern blocks, Cuisenaire rods, base ten blocks, Decimal Squares, number lines, fraction strips, paper for folding, colored chips, and arrays. Continue to stress calculator skills, especially with decimal fraction operations, and use appropriate computer programs to help the children develop skills with common and decimal fractions and percents.

As children develop understanding and skill in their work with rational numbers, they begin to explore some of the early concepts of operations with these numbers. When they find like denominators for two common fractions, they may notice that when two fractions have like denominators, it is very easy to add them together, to find how much bigger one is than the other, or even to find how many times bigger one is than the other. Encourage and expand on this intuitive understanding of operations with rational numbers as you introduce the operations more formally. Let children continue to question, explore, and discover relationships and algorithms of their own as they expand their knowledge of rational numbers to include operations.

MAKING SENSE OF CONCEPTS AND ALTERNATIVE ALGORITHMS FOR OPERATIONS WITH RATIONAL NUMBERS

After children understand the meaning of rational numbers written as both common and decimal fractions and can rename equivalent fractions, they are ready for operations with rational numbers. Operations with rational numbers should be understood before they are practiced abstractly. Too many students memorize rules such as "invert and multiply" but are not able to explain when or why this should be done. In this section, we concentrate on the meaning of operations with all types of rational numbers.

In the next section, we discuss developing and practicing skills with the operations. Be sure to allow children plenty of time for concept development before you move on to practicing skills. The more time children spend on the concepts, the less time they will need to practice the skills.

Addition of Common Fractions

When you first introduce children to the addition of common fractions, continue to use the physical models they used for learning the concepts of common fractions. Introduce addition using problems that are based on the children's experiences. Use problems that children can solve by exploring familiar materials.

Textbooks generally begin with problems involving common fractions with like denominators and later move to problems with unlike denominators. Children working with concrete materials may not need to separate problems with like from those with unlike denominators, however. If they have worked with renaming fractions concretely in developing concepts of common fractions, the addition and subtraction of common fractions should follow naturally. Following are some examples of situations that may be used to introduce addition of common fractions.

A   C   T   I   V   I   T   I   E   S

Grades 3–5

OBJECTIVE: to develop the concept of addition of common fractions with like denominators.

1. Give the children an example of a situation that would require the addition of common fractions, and let them use concrete materials such as the circular or rectangular regions (see Appendix B) to find the answer. A beginning example follows: Danny baked a pie and left it to cool. His sister Maureen came along and cut it into 6 equal pieces. She ate $\frac{1}{6}$ of the pie and gave her friend Suzanna $\frac{1}{6}$ of the pie. How much of the pie did they take altogether?

Let the children manipulate the pieces to show the answer of $\frac{2}{6}$. Then, have the children make up and illustrate other problems of their own. After children have worked several problems using the materials, ask them to write down what they have done using their own recording systems. They may initially write 1 sixth + 1 sixth = 2 sixths. After comparing this to earlier work with whole numbers, they may write the equation as $\frac{1}{6} + \frac{1}{6} = \frac{2}{6}$ or

$$\begin{array}{r} \frac{1}{6} \\ +\frac{1}{6} \\ \hline \frac{2}{6} \end{array}$$

Ask the children to write equations for all their work with the manipulatives. They may have some of the following:

$$\frac{1}{6} + \frac{1}{6} = \frac{2}{6}$$

$$\frac{1}{3} + \frac{1}{3} = \frac{2}{3}$$

$$\frac{1}{4} + \frac{2}{4} = \frac{3}{4}$$

$$\frac{2}{5} + \frac{3}{5} = \frac{5}{5}$$

Ask the children if they notice anything consistent about the problems. Lead them to discuss the fact that in each problem, the denominator remains the same and the numerators are added together. After the children have worked several problems using regions and have recorded the equations, ask them to show the same equations using another material such as the Cuisenaire rods, the number line, or the Fraction Bars. Figure 9–1 shows a few possibilities.

Discuss with the students the fact that the sum remains the same no matter what material is used to illustrate the equations. Ask the students to analyze what is wrong with examples such as $\frac{2}{3} + \frac{1}{3} = \frac{3}{6}$ and $\frac{2}{5} + \frac{1}{5} = \frac{3}{10}$. Ask how they can use the materials to help another child understand why those examples are incorrect. This explanation would make a good daily journal entry.

2. Children sometimes think that whenever you add two fractions, the answer will be less than 1 because that is often the case with the early examples. They need early exposure to problems for which the sum is

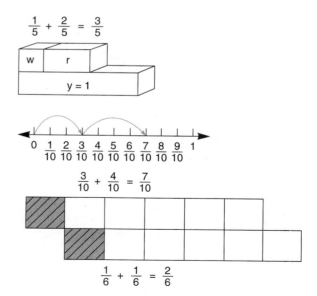

Figure 9–1 Various models for addition of common fractions.

greater than 1. Again, use examples from the children's everyday experiences. For example, for Danny's pie, he used $\frac{3}{4}$ cup of sugar for the crust and $\frac{3}{4}$ cup of sugar for the filling. How much sugar did he use altogether? Again, let the children use any of the familiar manipulatives to find the sum.

Some children may have difficulty when they realize that the answer is larger than 1 cup. Ask them how much larger than 1 cup the sum is. Say, "Yes, you have 1 whole cup and or $\frac{2}{4}$, or $\frac{1}{2}$, of another cup." Figure 9–2 shows some of the possible solutions with the materials.

Again, ask the children to write the equation for the problem. Discuss the fact that $\frac{6}{4}$ and $1\frac{2}{4}$ name the same amount (this should be familiar from the work with equivalent fractions). Let the children suggest other word problems, solve them with the manipulatives, and write the equations. Encourage the children to predict whether the answer to each example will be larger or smaller than 1. After the children have had some practice, let them work the problems mentally, without using the materials or writing the equations.

Some calculators show fractions in common as well as decimal form. Allow the students to use one of these calculators to explore the addition and subtraction of common fractions. What happens when you simplify a fraction or change from a mixed numeral to a fraction with a numerator greater than or equal to the denominator (an improper fraction)?

OBJECTIVE: to develop the concept of addition of common fractions with unlike denominators.

3. After the children have had experience adding common fractions with like denominators, suggest a problem that involves adding fractions with unlike denominators. Again, let the children choose a concrete material with which to solve the problem. Following is one example: After Danny's pie was eaten, he decided to bake a cake. His father said that the cake looked so good that he would like a huge piece. Danny's mom was on a diet, so she wanted only a small piece. Danny cut a piece $\frac{1}{4}$ of the whole cake for his dad and a piece $\frac{1}{8}$ of the cake for his mom. How much of the whole cake did Danny give his parents?

Figure 9–3a shows how the children may demonstrate this with the fraction pieces. Ask the children what they would call the answer. It is difficult to name the answer unless the pieces are all the same size. In Figure 9–3a, you have two pieces, but they are not two-fourths or two-eighths. It is not convenient to say you have one-fourth and one-eighth of the whole cake. Encourage children to draw on their experience with renaming common fractions to suggest that the fourth may be renamed as eighths. The children might exchange the fraction pieces as shown in Figure 9–3b.

Now ask the children to tell you the sum. The two pieces are divided into portions of the same size, eighths, so the sum is three-eighths. Encourage the

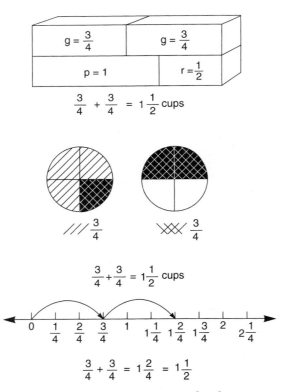

Figure 9–2 Various models to illustrate $\frac{3}{4} + \frac{3}{4}$.

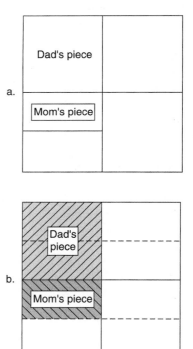

Figure 9–3 Illustration of showing a fourth plus an eighth of a piece of cake.

children to show their work in equation form. Ask the students to share the various ways of writing equations that they have devised. Let them try to use each other's methods and algorithms for a few days and discuss the benefits or drawbacks of each type of algorithm. If students have not discovered the conventional algorithm on their own, you might wish to introduce it. Several students may find that it is easiest to work with equations in vertical form, so show the conversion as

$$\frac{1}{4} = \frac{2}{8}$$
$$+\frac{1}{8} = +\frac{1}{8}$$
$$\overline{\hspace{2cm}\frac{3}{8}}$$

If students prefer another algorithm, do not force them to use the conventional algorithm as long as theirs works and is relatively simple to use and understand.

Let the children suggest other word problems and solve them using other concrete or semiconcrete aids. Some of the problems should involve common fractions that must be renamed with a common denominator. Remind children of their earlier work with renaming fractions. Ask children to write up word problems for each other to leave in the learning center or for you to use on worksheets for the whole class.

Encourage children to discuss their methods of solution with each other. If disagreements about the solutions arise, ask questions to lead the children to discover which solution is correct. They may find that several methods (or none) work. Compare the results to answers obtained using a calculator that shows common fractions (see Figure 9–4).

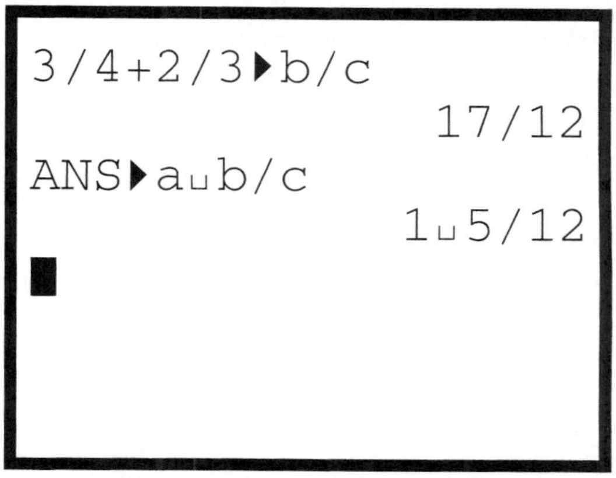

```
3/4+2/3▶b/c
                17/12
ANS▶a⌴b/c
                1⌴5/12
■
```

Figure 9–4 A calculator display showing addition of common fractions.

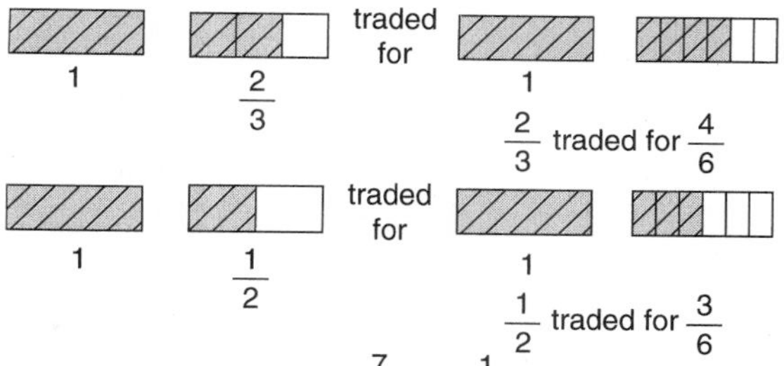

Figure 9–5 Using fraction strips to illustrate addition of common fractions.

OBJECTIVE: to develop the concept of addition of mixed numerals.

4. With mixed numerals as well as with proper fractions, students should develop addition concepts beginning with "real-life" situations. An example follows: Maria needs $1\frac{2}{3}$ yards of material to make a skirt and $1\frac{1}{2}$ yards of material to make a matching jacket. How much material should Maria buy for the outfit?

Again, the children should use the familiar fraction materials to work out the problem. Let the children discuss what to do with the fractions with unlike denominators. Encourage the children to begin by putting the whole sections together and then trading in the parts for amounts shown in sixths, the common denominator. Ask the children what to do with the sixths, since they make more than another whole yard. Encourage the children to write down the equations as they work with the materials to record what they are doing. The children's work with fraction strips may look like that in Figure 9–5.

After the children have added mixed numerals with the aid of one manipulative, encourage them to show the same problem with other manipulatives or pictures. Figure 9–6 shows other possibilities for $1\frac{2}{3} + 1\frac{1}{2}$.

Addition of Decimal Fractions

Depending on the mathematics program you use, you may decide to introduce addition with decimal fractions either before or after addition with common fractions. Many children find addition with decimal fractions easier than addition with common fractions because of their familiarity with adding amounts of money and the ease of adding decimal fractions on the calculator. As the metric system becomes more

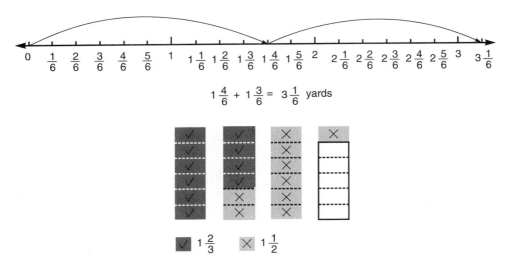

$$1\frac{4}{6} + 1\frac{3}{6} = 3\frac{1}{6} \text{ yards}$$

$\checkmark\ 1\frac{2}{3}$ $\times\ 1\frac{1}{2}$

Figure 9—6 Other models to illustrate addition of mixed numerals.

popular, even more examples of decimal fractions will be familiar from everyday life. Whether decimal fraction addition is introduced before or after common fraction addition, have students use the same physical models they used to understand the basic concepts of decimal fractions; these include Cuisenaire rods, Decimal Squares, number lines, arrays, and base ten blocks.

If addition of common fractions precedes addition of decimal fractions, have children write equations in both common and decimal fraction form and compare the results. If work with common fractions follows addition of decimal fractions, have children compare the two forms of addition when they learn to compute with common fractions. The activities described for common fraction addition can be repeated with decimal fractions. A few other suggestions follow.

A C T I V I T I E S

Grades 3—5

OBJECTIVE: to develop the concept of addition of decimal fractions in tenths using Cuisenaire rods and number lines.

1. As with common fractions, children should begin work with decimal fractions using a situation from everyday life. The following is one example: Amy bought

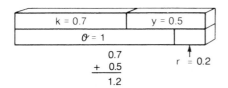

Figure 9—7 Using Cuisenaire rods to illustrate addition of decimal fractions.

a new odometer for her bike because she wanted to find out how far it was to her friends' homes. She put the odometer on her bike and saw that it was set at zero. After she rode to Maureen's house, the odometer read 0.7 kilometers. Amy rode from there to Ahmad's house and told Ahmad that he lives 0.5 kilometers from Maureen. What did Amy's odometer read when she arrived at Ahmad's?

Let the children use Cuisenaire rods to show the addition. Let the orange rod represent 1. Which rod shows 0.7? Which rod shows 0.5? Notice that once the children select the black and yellow rods, the addition is shown in the same manner that addition of whole numbers was illustrated.

Since the sum is more than the orange rod, we know that the odometer will show more than 1 kilometer. Ask the children how they can tell how much more than 1 kilometer will be shown. They should fill in the space next to the orange rod to match the total of the black and yellow rods. The total is an orange rod and a red rod. The red rod is 0.2 of the orange rod, so the odometer must show 1.2 kilometers (see Figure 9—7).

Let the children suggest other problems of their own and show them with the Cuisenaire rods.

2. After the children can use the Cuisenaire rods to show problems, they should transfer to the number line. Use a number line with 1 decimeter (10 centimeters) representing one unit. Each centimeter is then 0.1 of the unit. The children can lay the Cuisenaire rods on the number line to show the addition in the same way that they showed addition of whole numbers. When the children use the number line, they can simply read the answer off the number line, as shown in Figure 9—8.

3. After the children work several problems using Cuisenaire rods on the number line, they can show the

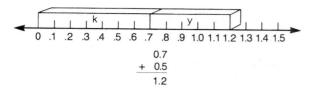

$$\begin{array}{r} 0.7 \\ +\ 0.5 \\ \hline 1.2 \end{array}$$

Figure 9–8 Using Cuisenaire rods on a number line to illustrate addition of decimal fractions.

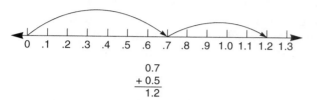

$$\begin{array}{r} 0.7 \\ +\ 0.5 \\ \hline 1.2 \end{array}$$

Figure 9–9 Using a number line to illustrate addition of decimal fractions.

addition on the number line by simply using arrows, as shown in Figure 9–9.

As children work the problems with any of the models, encourage them to write the algorithms in vertical form near the pictures. After the children have worked several problems, ask them what they notice about the addition algorithm. They should notice that the algorithm for adding decimal fractions is the same as that for adding whole numbers if the decimal points are lined up.

If children have constructed a different algorithm for adding decimals, encourage them to discuss their method. Does their method work if the decimals have differing place values, as in adding 0.232 and 0.2?

If the children have previously worked with adding common fractions, ask them to write the number sentence for the same exercise in common fraction form next to the number sentence in decimal fraction form, as shown below:

$$\begin{array}{cc} \dfrac{7}{10} & \begin{array}{r} 0.7 \\ +0.5 \\ \hline 1.2 \end{array} \\[2ex] +\ \dfrac{5}{10} & \\[2ex] \hline \dfrac{12}{10} = 1\dfrac{2}{10} & \end{array}$$

Ask them to compare the two examples and discuss their findings.

OBJECTIVE: to develop the concept of addition of decimal fractions in hundredths using base ten blocks, Decimal Squares, and arrays.

4. Children should be familiar with addition of hundredths because of their previous work in learning to add money. They may not relate this to a concrete model, however. Use the flat 10-by-10 base ten block to represent $1. Ask the children how they would show a dime and a penny. They should show you the long and the small cube, respectively. Ask the children to show amounts such as $.23, $.96, and $1.48.

Ask the children to use the blocks to determine Bill's total bill if he orders a hamburger for $1.39, a cola for $.55, and french fries for $.65. The blocks should initially look like those in Figure 9–10.

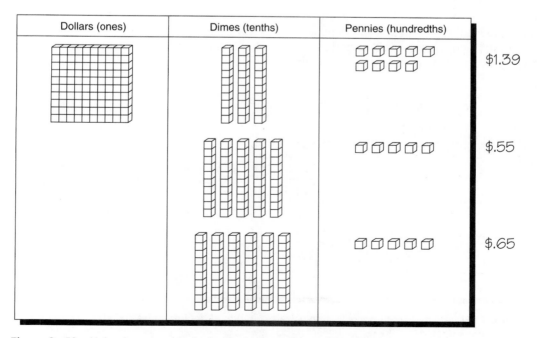

Figure 9–10 Using base ten blocks to illustrate addition of decimal fractions.

Have the children make all the trades possible to end up with the least number of separate blocks. After all the trades, the response should appear as in Figure 9–11.

Have the children write the number sentence near the work with the blocks and again allow them to develop their own algorithms for adding decimal fractions. Have they used the traditional vertical algorithm that mirrors addition of whole numbers as long as the decimal points remain in line or have they developed other methods?

Let the children suggest other problems of their own and work them with the blocks. After they have worked several problems with the blocks, have them work a few problems with other materials, such as the Decimal Squares or arrays that use 10-by-10 grid paper. Encourage the children to discuss their methods of solution. They should compare these to other methods, such as calculating mentally, working the example on a calculator, or computing with paper and pencil.

OBJECTIVE: to develop the concept of addition of decimal fractions with thousandths.

5. Once children are comfortable working problems involving tenths and hundredths, introduce problems involving thousandths. Following is one example: José is measuring chemicals for an experiment. He has measured 0.125 liter of water and 0.375 liter of oil into the same beaker. How much mixture is in the beaker?

Children may use actual beakers to work out the problem or they may model it using the base ten blocks or the Decimal Squares. If they use base ten blocks, the large cube should represent 1, and the smallest cube should be 0.001. Again, ask the children to write their addition algorithm near the work with the blocks and to compare this algorithm to the whole number algorithms.

Children should compare their work with decimal fractions to the algorithm for common fractions if they have had previous work with common fractions. Have children use calculators to compare the work with concrete objects. If you are using calculators that show both decimal and common forms, ask the students to work the problems in both forms and compare the results. Encourage the children to discuss their methods with each other and to estimate results without actually computing them.

OBJECTIVE: to develop the concept of addition with decimal fractions when some decimals are written in tenths and others are in hundredths or thousandths.

6. Children's main difficulties in adding decimal fractions come when the decimals are not all written to the same decimal place. If children are using the traditional algorithm for adding decimal fractions they may not realize that it is important to keep the decimal points lined up and they may try to write the numerals as shown below:

$$\begin{array}{r} 0.2 \\ 0.03 \\ 1 \\ \hline .06 \end{array}$$

Ask the children to use one of the concrete models to show the exercise. Using the base ten blocks, with the flat as 1, the materials would look like those in Figure 9–12. Have the children write the number sentence below their work with the blocks. Be sure that they realize the importance of lining up the decimal points and writing all decimal fractions in hundredths.

This is a good time to use a calculator to compare the results to paper-and-pencil computation. Ask the students to try examples such as .5 + .35 + .456 and .500 + .350 + .456. Do they obtain the same result? Ask the children to explain why this is true. If the students have previously added common fractions, ask them to compare this process to converting all common fractions to like denominators before adding.

Dollars (ones)	Dimes (tenths)	Pennies (hundredths)	
			$1.39
			.55
			.65
			$2.59

Figure 9–11 Using base ten blocks to illustrate addition of decimal fractions after the regrouping has been completed.

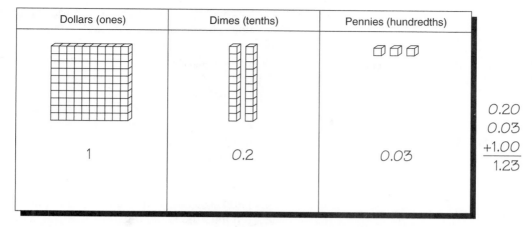

Dollars (ones)	Dimes (tenths)	Pennies (hundredths)	
1	0.2	0.03	0.20 0.03 +1.00 ——— 1.23

Figure 9–12   Using base ten blocks to illustrate addition of decimal fractions to correct misunderstandings with the abstract addition algorithm.

Subtraction of Common Fractions

When students begin work with subtraction of common fractions, again start with realistic situations. As with whole-number subtraction, problems may involve taking away one amount from another, comparing two amounts, or figuring out how much more is needed. Again, have children use manipulative materials to work out the examples when you first introduce subtraction of common fractions. Build on previous work with converting common fractions to equivalent fractions with like denominators and work with addition of common fractions.

Because addition and subtraction are inverse operations, you may introduce addition and subtraction of common fractions almost simultaneously. Students in third or fourth grade can generally reverse one operation to develop the other. Therefore, soon after children learn addition of common fractions, they may learn subtraction. Subtraction of mixed numerals may quickly follow addition of mixed numerals.

A few suggestions for teaching the concepts of subtraction of common fractions follow. You and the students should develop other ideas related to the earlier work with addition and the students' experiences outside of school.

A   C   T   I   V   I   T   I   E   S

Grades 3–5 and Grades 6–8

OBJECTIVE: to develop the concept of subtraction of common fractions with like denominators.

1. Suggest a problem such as the following and ask the children to work it using a manipulative such as the circular regions: Emilio had $\frac{3}{4}$ of a pound of cheese. He used $\frac{1}{4}$ of a pound to make macaroni and cheese. How much

cheese does Emilio have left? The children's regions should be similar to those in Figure 9–13.

Ask children to develop their own algorithms for subtracting fractions and to write the algorithm next to the pieces as they work the problem. Compare the various algorithms that the students have constructed and let them decide on the algorithms that they prefer. If they have not developed the traditional algorithm, you may wish to introduce it after they have developed their own understanding of subtraction of common fractions. Let the children suggest other word problems themselves and use other types of materials to work them. They should discuss their methods as they work.

One common mistake that children make when they write word problems for subtraction of common fractions is that they want to subtract a part of the first fraction rather than a part of a whole amount. For example, a child may say, "Jeff had $\frac{1}{2}$ of an apple. Amy ate $\frac{1}{4}$ of what Jeff had. How much does Jeff have left?"

Discuss with the children that $\frac{1}{4}$ of $\frac{1}{2}$ of an apple is only $\frac{1}{8}$ of the whole apple. This is less than $\frac{1}{4}$ of a whole apple. The equation for this problem would be $\frac{1}{2} - (\frac{1}{4} \times \frac{1}{2}) = n$. This is not $\frac{1}{2} - \frac{1}{4}$. Encourage children to show both problems with the manipulatives and to explain their solutions (more is said about problems involving multiplication in the section on multiplication of common fractions).

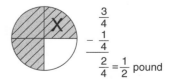

Figure 9–13   Using fraction circles to illustrate subtraction of common fractions as a take-away concept.

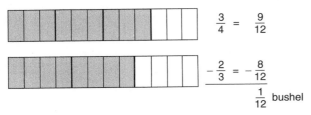

$$\frac{3}{4} = \frac{9}{12}$$

$$-\frac{2}{3} = -\frac{8}{12}$$

$$\frac{1}{12} \text{ bushel}$$

Figure 9–14 Using fraction bars to illustrate subtraction of common fractions as a comparison concept.

OBJECTIVE: to introduce subtraction of fractions with unlike denominators.

2. Use a word problem to introduce subtraction of fractions with unlike denominators. For example, Andreas has $\frac{3}{4}$ of a bushel of apples. Marlo has $\frac{2}{3}$ of a bushel of apples. What part of a bushel more does Andreas have than Marlo?

Notice that this is a comparison type of subtraction problem. Children can use number lines or Fraction Bars to compare the two amounts. If children do not convert the fractions to like denominators, they can tell that $\frac{3}{4}$ is greater than $\frac{2}{3}$ but they will have trouble determining how much greater.

Ask the children to always estimate which amount is greater before they begin to subtract and to estimate *about* how much greater that amount is. Compare this to adding $\frac{3}{4}$ and $\frac{2}{3}$. For addition, they first changed both fractions to like denominators. They should do the same when subtracting fractions with unlike denominators. Ask the children to write the algorithms they have developed beside the work with the number line or manipulatives as shown in Figure 9–14 and discuss their strategies of solution.

OBJECTIVE: to develop the concept of subtraction of mixed numerals.

3. Again, subtraction of mixed numerals should begin with an example from everyday life, such as: Cara has knitted $2\frac{3}{4}$ feet of a scarf. She wants the scarf to be $3\frac{1}{2}$ feet long. How many more feet does she need to knit?

This type of problem, which requires renaming one unit, often is difficult for children. Let the children use materials or a number line. On the number line, have the children show the $2\frac{3}{4}$ feet already completed and add on until they reach the $3\frac{1}{2}$ feet, as shown in Figure 9–15.

Have the children record the algorithm below the materials as they work. Work several problems with mixed numerals with the children, some that require renaming the whole number and some that do not. Have the children use other physical models to demonstrate exchanging the whole number for equivalent parts. Discuss with them the fact that the mathematics remains the same regardless of the concrete materials chosen to illustrate the equations. Figure 9–16 shows an example with pie pieces that some students may use. Other students may begin with $2\frac{3}{4}$ circular pieces and add on fourths until reaching $3\frac{1}{2}$.

Again, encourage the children to estimate or mentally compute several of the examples. Paper-and-pencil computations are not always necessary. Children should compare their various strategies as they work.

Subtraction of Decimal Fractions

Subtraction of decimal fractions may be introduced immediately following addition of decimal fractions. If subtraction of decimal fractions follows subtraction of common fractions, have the children compare the new work with decimal fractions to the previous work with common fractions. Have them write algorithms in both forms and compare the processes and answers. Let them also use calculators for comparison.

If the work with decimal fractions comes first, compare addition and subtraction of decimal fractions with the new work when you introduce addition and subtraction of common fractions. Use the same physical models for both addition and subtraction of decimal fractions. Compare the subtraction algorithms for

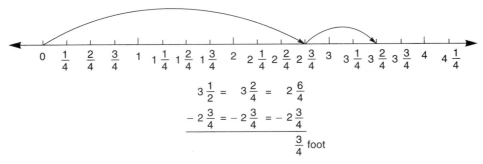

$$3\frac{1}{2} = 3\frac{2}{4} = 2\frac{6}{4}$$

$$-2\frac{3}{4} = -2\frac{3}{4} = -2\frac{3}{4}$$

$$\frac{3}{4} \text{ foot}$$

Figure 9–15 Using a number line to illustrate subtraction of common fractions as a missing addend concept.

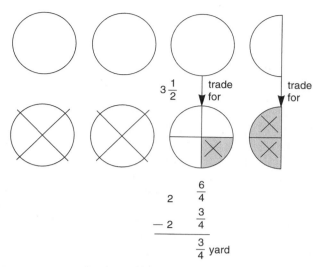

$$3\frac{1}{2} \quad \text{trade for} \quad \text{trade for}$$

$$2 \quad \frac{6}{4}$$
$$- 2 \quad \frac{3}{4}$$
$$\overline{\quad\quad \frac{3}{4} \text{ yard}}$$

Figure 9–16 Using fraction circles to illustrate subtraction of common fractions.

decimal fractions to the addition algorithms for decimal fractions and the subtraction algorithms for whole numbers. Use the same types of word problems for decimal fractions as you did for subtraction of whole numbers and for subtraction of common fractions. Money and metric measures are good sources of word problems because of the frequent use of decimals in these examples.

The activities for subtraction of common fractions and for addition of decimal fractions can be adapted to subtraction of decimal fractions. A few other ideas follow. You and your students should suggest others.

Grades 3–5

OBJECTIVE: to develop the concept of subtraction of decimal fractions.

1. Because dealing with money gives children a number of chances to add and subtract using decimals, have the children set up a store or restaurant. Initially, stock the cash register only with dollar bills, dimes, and pennies to reinforce the regrouping the children must do to perform the subtraction algorithm. For example, Ray is told that his bill for lunch comes to $2.57. He hands the cashier $3.00. Have the children make the change either by using the traditional decomposition algorithm or by counting forward from $2.57. Figure 9–17 shows the trades the cashier must make to give Ray his change if the decomposition algorithm is used.

Counting on from $2.57 has the advantage of helping the children learn to count back change (this seems to be a lost art in many stores). Encourage children to write down an algorithm for the method used. Let children create other algorithms of their own. Because so many stores now use computerized cash registers, encourage children to use calculators to compute the change. A parent or other adult in the community may be willing to come in to explain the use of various machines that aid clerks in making change.

2. Have children play an estimation game that also involves measurement and subtraction of decimal fractions. Make a set of cards that show amounts such as 5 centimeters, 6.2 centimeters, 8.4 centimeters, and 3 centimeters. Place the cards face down on the table.

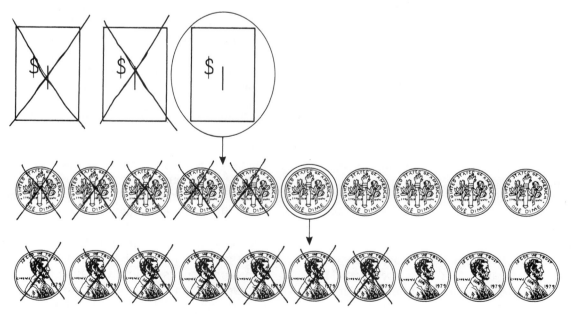

Figure 9–17 Using money to illustrate subtraction of decimal fractions.

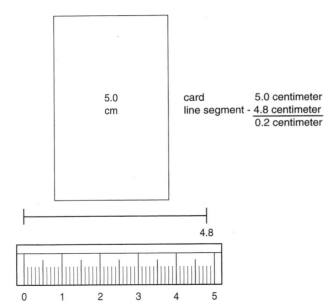

Figure 9 – 18   Using metric measurement to illustrate subtraction of decimal fractions.

Turn over one card and ask a child to draw a line segment approximately the length designated by the card. Then have the child measure the line segment to the nearest tenth of a centimeter (nearest millimeter) and subtract to find how close the length of the line segment is to the length specified on the card. The difference is the child's score for that round. Then turn over a card for the next child and repeat the activity.

After several rounds, the child with the lowest total is the winner. Children may find the difference on the ruler by comparing the length of the line segment to the length indicated by the card, or they may subtract as shown in Figure 9–18.

After children have had experience using the rulers, ask them to find the difference mentally, with a calculator, or by writing the subtraction algorithm.

Multiplication of Common Fractions

Too often, children memorize rules for multiplying and dividing common fractions but have very little concept of the meaning behind the rules. If the rule is forgotten, the children cannot reconstruct the algorithm because they have no understanding of the operation. Nor do they know which operation to choose when faced with a word problem involving fractions because they do not associate any real meaning with the operations. They can use a calculator to do the computation for them only if they know what computation is needed.

Unfortunately, this is also a problem for many adults. Ask anyone to give you a word problem that can be solved by $\frac{2}{3} \times \frac{3}{4}$ or $\frac{2}{3} \div \frac{3}{4}$. Perhaps this is a problem for you as well. After reading this section, you should not only be able to write word problems involving multiplication and division of common fractions but should also be able to demonstrate the solutions with a number of manipulatives.

Children usually begin by multiplying a common fraction by a whole number when they are introduced to multiplication of common fractions. This is perhaps the easiest type of problem to understand and to model with the manipulatives. Again, as with the other operations, the children should start with familiar examples and manipulatives or number lines.

The following activities begin with multiplying a common fraction by a whole number and then multiplying a whole number by a common fraction. Finally, we give ideas for multiplying two proper fractions and for multiplying two mixed numerals. If multiplication of decimal fractions has preceded multiplication of common fractions, have the children compare the processes and word problems to note the similarities. The concepts are not new, although the algorithms may be in a different form.

Grades 3 – 5 and Grades 6 – 8

OBJECTIVE: to develop the concept of multiplying a common fraction by a whole number.

1. Suggest a situation such as the following to the children when they are first learning to multiply common fractions. Ask the children to find the answer using any of the models with which they are familiar from earlier work with addition and subtraction of common fractions. The following example lends itself to being solved by repeated addition, so children who can add common fractions should be able to solve it. The school track is $\frac{3}{8}$ of a mile around. Sandy is on the track team, and she has run around the track three times in practice. How far has Sandy run?

Figure 9–19 shows some of the ways in which the children may work the problem. Ask them to write the multiplication sentence below their work and to write the answer as a mixed numeral.

Ask the children to suggest other examples of problems that can be solved by multiplying a common fraction by a whole number and to show the solution with the manipulatives. Have them exchange problems with each other as well as work their own problems. Encourage them to discuss their methods of solution with the author of the problem. If they have solved the problem in different ways, lead them to discover whether or not each solution works.

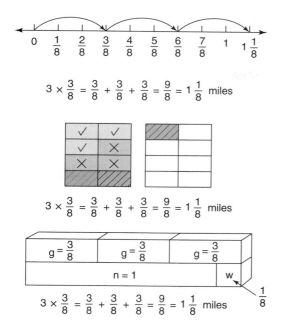

Figure 9–19 Multiple models to illustrate multiplication of a common fraction by a whole number.

OBJECTIVE: to develop the concept of multiplying a whole number by a common fraction.

2. This concept is one with which children should be familiar from earlier work with the concept of a common fraction as part of a set of discrete objects, but review it at this time. Suggest familiar examples such as finding $\frac{2}{3}$ of a dozen eggs, the number of ounces in $\frac{1}{2}$ of a pound, or the number of inches in $\frac{1}{4}$ of a foot. Point out that the word *of* in these examples indicates that the children should multiply. To find $\frac{2}{3}$ of a dozen, have the children multiply $\frac{2}{3} \times 12$. Since there are 16 ounces in a pound, $\frac{1}{2}$ of a pound is $\frac{1}{2} \times 16$, or 8 ounces. Let the children work these exercises using an array of concrete materials such as chips, if necessary, and discuss their thought processes with each other. Figure 9–20 shows $\frac{2}{3} \times 12$.

OBJECTIVE: to develop the concept of multiplying two proper fractions.

3. Just as arrays can illustrate multiplication of whole numbers and multiplication of a whole number by a common fraction, they can also illustrate multiplication of two common fractions. Again, introduce this multiplication with a "real" situation such as the following: Steve is planting a rectangular garden. He wants $\frac{1}{3}$ of his garden to be flowers. Steve likes roses, so $\frac{1}{2}$ of his flowers will be roses. What part of the total garden will be roses?

The array in Figure 9–21 represents the garden with $\frac{1}{3}$ planted in flowers and $\frac{1}{2}$ of that part planted in roses. Ask the children to record the corresponding number sentence $\frac{1}{2} \times \frac{1}{3} = \frac{1}{6}$ below the drawing.

Use several other examples, including ones that do not use unit fractions, and ask the students to show the solutions with arrays. Situations involving measurement, such as cooking, sewing, and building, are good sources of word problems. After the students have worked several examples and written the corresponding number sentences, ask them to compare the sentences to develop a rule for multiplying two common fractions.

After the students realize that they can multiply the numerators and the denominators, ask them if their rule works for multiplying a whole number by a common fraction. Remind children that they might write the whole number over 1 so that it is in fraction form before they multiply. Encourage the children to solve equations by computing mentally and then comparing their results to the results with the concrete models. They may also use a calculator that displays common fractions to compare results.

4. After the students have used arrays to illustrate multiplication of common fractions, have them use other manipulatives. A few examples follow.

- Fred sees $\frac{3}{4}$ of a pie on the counter. He is hungry, so he eats $\frac{1}{2}$ of the $\frac{3}{4}$ of the pie. How much of a whole pie does Fred eat?

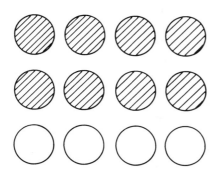

Figure 9–20 Using an array to illustrate multiplying a common fraction by a whole number.

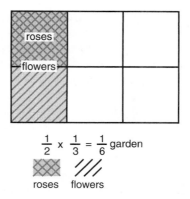

Figure 9–21 Array illustrating multiplication of common fractions.

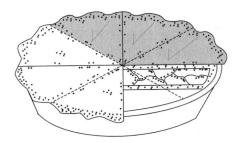

Figure 9-22 Using an area model to illustrate multiplication of common fractions.

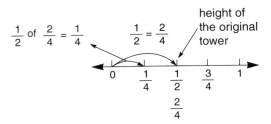

Figure 9-23 Using a number line to illustrate multiplication of common fractions.

Notice that Fred is eating $\frac{1}{2}$ of the $\frac{3}{4}$, not of the whole. Figure 9-22 shows the solution. Notice that Fred first cuts each of the fourths into halves; now he has 6 eighths. Then he takes $\frac{1}{2}$ of the 6 remaining pieces, or 3 eighths.

- Rachel is building a scale model of a toy tower. The original tower is $\frac{1}{2}$ of a foot tall. Rachel wants her tower to be $\frac{1}{2}$ of that height. How tall should Rachel build her tower?

  Use a number line to represent the original tower. Divide the number line into halves and mark the height of the original tower. Now divide that height into halves. Look at the number line and note that the original unit is now split into four equal pieces so each piece is $\frac{1}{4}$. The original tower takes up $\frac{2}{4}$ of the unit, and one-half of two-fourths is one-fourth. The scale model should be $\frac{1}{4}$ of a foot tall (see Figure 9-23).

- Brian is making punch. His recipe will serve three people, but Brian needs to serve only two, so he has decided to make $\frac{2}{3}$ of the recipe. The recipe calls for $\frac{1}{2}$ cup of sugar. Brian needs to know how much sugar to use for $\frac{2}{3}$ of the recipe.

  Use Cuisenaire rods to solve the problem (see Figure 9-24). Use the dark-green rod to represent 1 cup of sugar. Why? Can you use any other color rod to represent 1 cup? Try others and see what happens.

  If the dark-green rod is 1 cup, which rod represents the $\frac{1}{2}$ cup of sugar needed for the original recipe? The light-green rod is $\frac{1}{2}$ of the dark-green rod. Which rod is $\frac{1}{3}$ of the light-green rod? Which

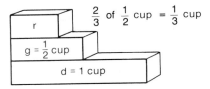

Figure 9-24 Using Cuisenaire rods to illustrate multiplication of common fractions.

rod(s) represents $\frac{2}{3}$ of the light green rod? Either the red rod or two white rods can be used to represent $\frac{2}{3}$ of the light green rod, but each representation is only $\frac{1}{3}$ of the dark green rod, which represents one cup. Therefore, Brian will need $\frac{1}{3}$ cup of sugar to make $\frac{2}{3}$ of the recipe.

Encourage the children to make up other problems and to discuss their methods of solution. They should realize that the concrete model used does not change the answer to the problem. The mathematics remains the same as the materials change.

OBJECTIVE: to develop the concept of multiplication of mixed numerals.

5. After students are comfortable multiplying two proper fractions, let them encounter situations involving the multiplication of a proper fraction by a mixed numeral or the multiplication of two mixed numerals. One example follows. You and the students should make up other examples of your own.

Raul is looking at a scale drawing of a flower. The scale says the actual flower is $2\frac{1}{2}$ times as large as the drawing. Raul measures the flower in the drawing and sees it is $1\frac{3}{4}$ inches long. How long is the actual flower?

Use a number line to solve the problem, as in Figure 9-25. Measure off $1\frac{3}{4}$ inches twice to show that the actual flower is 2 times as large. Then figure that $\frac{1}{2}$ of $1\frac{3}{4}$ inches is $\frac{7}{8}$ inch and go that much farther on the number line. The real flower must be $4\frac{3}{8}$ inches long.

Again, encourage the students to write the number sentence beneath the materials as they work. Allow students to develop their own algorithms for multiplying mixed numerals. If students try to multiply the whole numbers and then multiply the fractions and add the two parts, use the physical models and the word problems to lead students to discuss why this does not work. This might be a good time to discuss the distributive property by writing the problem as $(2 + \frac{1}{2}) \cdot (1 + \frac{3}{4})$. Some students might prefer an algorithm that tells them this can be solved by $(2 \times 1) + (2 \times \frac{3}{4}) + (\frac{1}{2} \times 1) + (\frac{1}{2} \times \frac{3}{4})$. Other students might discover that they can convert each of the mixed numerals to improper fractions before they multiply, then multiply as they did with proper fractions, and finally convert the answer back to a mixed numeral. Let the children create other problems for each other and

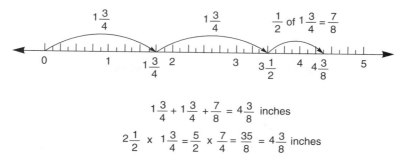

$$1\frac{3}{4} + 1\frac{3}{4} + \frac{7}{8} = 4\frac{3}{8} \text{ inches}$$

$$2\frac{1}{2} \times 1\frac{3}{4} = \frac{5}{2} \times \frac{7}{4} = \frac{35}{8} = 4\frac{3}{8} \text{ inches}$$

Figure 9–25 Using a number line to illustrate multiplication of mixed numerals.

solve them using a variety of models, comparing their methods of solution with each other.

Multiplication of Decimal Fractions

If multiplication of decimal fractions follows multiplication of common fractions, children should compare the two by writing number sentences in both forms and comparing the answers. Actual situations that give rise to multiplication of decimal fractions are very similar to those for common fractions. The main difference is that decimal fractions are always tenths, hundredths, or another power of 10. Because multiplying tenths by tenths results in an answer in the hundredths, we do not go beyond multiplying tenths using concrete models. A picture showing 0.52×0.63 must include 10 thousandths and is fairly difficult to draw.

Children multiplying decimal fractions should begin as they did when multiplying common fractions. Give examples of multiplying a whole number times a decimal and then of multiplying a decimal times a whole number. Multiply two decimal fractions later. Adapt the examples given for common fractions to decimal fractions. Have the children again use familiar manipulatives and add other ideas of their own. A few other suggestions follow.

Grades 3–5 and Grades 6–8

OBJECTIVE: to develop the concept of multiplying a decimal fraction by a whole number.

1. Money and metric measurement are good contexts for problems involving the multiplication of decimal fractions. Children may begin with the following situation: Kathi has 5 friends coming to her birthday party. She wants to give each friend and herself 0.3 liter of orange juice. How much orange juice will Kathi need so that the 6 children will each get 0.3 liter?

Work this problem as a repeated addition problem. Children who have had previous practice with addition of decimal fractions should have no difficulty in finding the product. Figure 9–26 shows some possible methods of solving the number sentence 6×0.3.

Have the children record the solution near the picture or materials as they work. Ask the children to compare their work to the addition problem $0.3 + 0.3 + 0.3 + 0.3 + 0.3 + 0.3 = n$. If children have previously multiplied common fractions, ask them also to compare their work to $6 \times \frac{3}{10} = n$.

This is a good time to use a calculator. Ask the students to compare entering $+ .3 = = = = = =$ to entering $.3 + .3 + .3 + .3 + .3 + .3$ and to entering

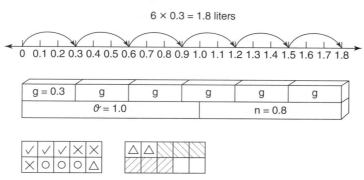

Figure 9–26 Using a variety of models to illustrate multiplication of a decimal fraction by a whole number.

0.5 x 5 milliliters = 2.5 milliliters

Figure 9–27 Using an area model to illustrate multiplication of a whole number by a decimal fraction.

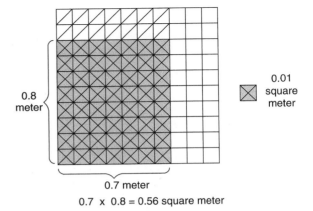

0.7 x 0.8 = 0.56 square meter

Figure 9–28 Using an array to illustrate multiplication of decimal fractions.

6. × .3. Have them try several examples to see if they always get the same answer with the three methods. Ask them to explain the results using concrete materials.

Encourage the students to suggest and work other word problems, discussing their results with you and each other.

OBJECTIVE: to develop the concept of multiplying a whole number by a decimal fraction.

2. The following is an example of a problem involving this concept: Jerry has a recipe calling for 5 milliliters of salt. He wants to make only 0.5 of the recipe. How much salt should Jerry use?

Figure 9–27 shows one possible method of solution. Notice that each of the 5 units representing the milliliters is split into 10 equal parts, and, in each case, Jerry takes 5 of the parts.

Again, ask the children to record the number sentence as they work. Let the children suggest and work similar word problems. Encourage them to estimate their answers and to use calculators to compare the results to their concrete work. Ask them to decide if the answer will be larger or smaller than the beginning amount and to explain why this is true.

OBJECTIVE: to develop the concept of multiplying two decimal fractions.

3. The following is one possible example to use to develop the concept of multiplying two decimal fractions: Marie is planting a small garden. It is 0.7 meter by 0.8 meter. How many square meters are there in Marie's garden?

Figure 9–28 shows a rectangular array for working this problem. Notice that the garden is less than 1 square meter. Ask the children to predict before working problems such as this whether the answer will be more or less than 1 and to explain their reasoning. In this case, the square meter is broken into hundredths, and the garden takes up 56 of those hundredths. Therefore, the garden covers 0.56 of a square meter.

Use other examples such as the following, which can be shown using string and a meter stick: Amy has a board 0.8 of a meter long. She needs 0.3 of the board for a project. How many meters of board will the project take?

Measure 0.8 meter of string and fold it into 10 equal parts. Take 3 of the parts, and measure that amount.

Ask children to work the following using dimes and pennies: Jeff has $.70. He is feeling generous and wants to give 0.4 of his money to his sister. How much should he give his sister?

Jeff can trade in all his money for pennies and then split the pennies into 10 equal piles. He can then give 4 of the piles to his sister.

Work with the children to make up other word problems. Notice that in each case, you need to take one part of the other part and want to know how the final answer relates to a unit. Children will need a great deal of practice with word problems and concrete materials before they become proficient at writing the word problems, but the time spent will pay off well in understanding. If the children have previously worked with multiplication of common fractions, they may also write the problem with common fractions and compare the results, for example, $0.4 \times 0.7 = \frac{4}{10} \times \frac{7}{10} = \frac{28}{100} = 0.28$. After students have worked several problems concretely with decimal fractions, ask them if they can make a generalization about the number of decimal places in the product.

Multiplication with Percent

Many percent problems can be solved as proportions. Another method of solving some problems involving percent is by using the formula $p = r \times b$. This stands for percentage = rate × base. The method is often useful for estimating or computing amounts mentally, such as figuring a 15-percent tip at a restaurant or deciding if you have enough money to buy pants that are 30 percent off the retail price.

The following activities give a few ideas for introducting the concept of multiplying a whole number or decimal fraction by a percent. Because a percent is simply another way of writing a common or decimal fraction, any of the activities described earlier for those forms may be adapted to percents.

A C T I V I T I E S

Grades 6–8

OBJECTIVE: to develop the concept of multiplying a whole number or decimal fraction by a percent.

1. Because *percent* means "per hundred," children should first practice finding percents of multiples of 100. Use the Decimal Squares or base ten blocks to introduce finding percents. Tell the children that you want to leave a 15-percent tip for your dinner. Your bill was $5.00.

Use the 10-by-10 square from the Decimal Squares or the 10-by-10 flat from the base ten blocks to represent $1.00. You now want to show 15 percent × $5.00. Ask the children to show 15 percent × $1.00. Do this for each of the dollars. How much do you have? Figure 9–29 shows one response. Ask the children to write a number sentence below the work with the squares or the blocks. Encourage the children to suggest and work other problems of their own. After the children have worked several problems with the materials, ask them to rewrite the number sentences using decimals instead of percents and to compare the answers. Use calculators to compute the same problems. If you have a "%" key on the calculator, compare its use to performing the calculation with the amount written in decimal form. Ask the children to practice finding the answers with mental calculation. This is certainly a skill adults frequently need.

2. When amounts are not multiples of 100, the task may not be so easy. Ask the children how they would find 25 percent of 16. Let the children suggest different solutions. They may need to be reminded that a percent is another way of writing a common or decimal fraction. Discuss the benefits of converting 25 percent to 0.25 and multiplying 0.25 × 16, or converting 25 percent to $\frac{1}{4}$ and multiplying $\frac{1}{4}$ × 16. Let the children suggest other problems of their own and decide whether to convert to a common fraction or a decimal fraction to find a solution.

In these examples, we were looking for the percentage each time. In the section on developing and practicing skills, we discuss problems involving percentage where the base or the rate needs to be found.

Division of Common Fractions

As mentioned earlier, children and adults often cannot give examples from "real life" of occasions when division of rational numbers is called for. They may vaguely recall that you invert one of the numbers and multiply, but they cannot tell you why this algorithm works or even which number should be inverted. Liping Ma (1999), in a study comparing mathematics teaching in the United States and China, noted that U.S. teachers often have difficulty giving a concrete example for division of fractions, while Chinese teachers can often give a variety of examples and physical models for the same

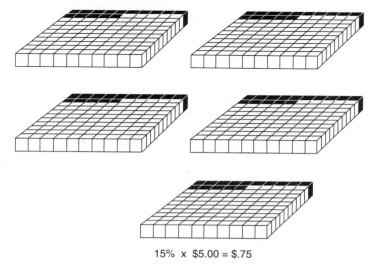

15% × $5.00 = $.75

Figure 9–29   Using arrays to illustrate multiplication involving percents.

problems. She notes that the Chinese teachers grew up learning mathematical concepts using a real-life context and physical models to make sense of the mathematics and that this carries over to their teaching. This section focuses on developing the meaning of division of rational numbers and understanding the *invert-and-multiply algorithm*. It introduces an algorithm for division of common fractions that builds on the measurement concept of division and previous work with finding a common denominator. We explore division of common fractions using both measurement and partition division situations, building on previous work with whole numbers. We then use similar situations to explore division of decimal fractions. If children divide decimal fractions before they divide common fractions, have them use this work as a basis for comparison when they begin dividing common fractions.

The following activities begin with the measurement concept of division of common fractions with a whole-number answer and move to fractional or mixed-numeral answers. The partition concept of division of common fractions follows the measurement idea, beginning with whole-number divisors and moving to fractional divisors. Appropriate algorithms are discussed for each type of division.

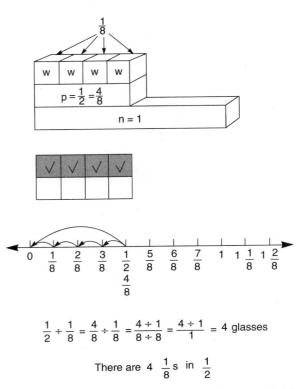

$$\frac{1}{2} \div \frac{1}{8} = \frac{4}{8} \div \frac{1}{8} = \frac{4 \div 1}{8 \div 8} = \frac{4 \div 1}{1} = 4 \text{ glasses}$$

There are $4 \frac{1}{8}$ s in $\frac{1}{2}$

Figure 9–30 Using a variety of models to illustrate division of common fractions.

A C T I V I T I E S

Grades 6–8

OBJECTIVE: to develop the measurement concept of division of common fractions with a whole-number quotient.

1. As with all other operations, begin division of common fractions with an example from the children's lives. The following is one possibility: Brittany has $\frac{1}{2}$ of a quart of orange juice. She wants to pour $\frac{1}{8}$ of a quart into each juice glass. How many juice glasses can Brittany fill?

Ask the children to compare this problem to earlier measurement division problems with whole numbers. A similar whole-number problem might have been: Brittany has 12 quarts of orange juice. She wants to put 3 quarts into each pitcher. How many pitchers can she fill?

Ask the children to first show the problem with whole numbers using materials. Then ask the children to work the problem with fractions. Figure 9–30 shows some possible solutions, using a variety of different familiar manipulatives or pictures.

Notice that in each case, the $\frac{1}{2}$ is exchanged for $\frac{4}{8}$ and the number of $\frac{1}{8}$s in $\frac{1}{2}$ is figured. The algorithm for this may be written as $\frac{1}{2} \div \frac{1}{8} = \frac{4}{8} \div \frac{1}{8} = \frac{4 \div 1}{8 \div 8} = \frac{4 \div 1}{1} = 4 \div 1 = 4$. When the fractions are written with like denominators and the numerators

and denominators are divided, the old denominators cancel out and the new denominator is 1. Then divide the numerators the same way you divide whole numbers.

This algorithm appears in an example from a textbook that refers to dividing numerators and denominators as an incorrect algorithm. Such division is actually quite proper and describes well the procedure for working measurement division problems with common fractions. For children familiar with renaming common fractions with like denominators, the method of dividing numerators and denominators is quite similar to the algorithm of multiplying numerators and denominators.

Even though textbooks may not mention this algorithm, children may create it on their own from work with materials. Children easily understand and remember this algorithm after they master algorithms for addition, subtraction, and multiplication of common fractions. We encourage you to use this common-denominator algorithm with your students, and if you decide to teach it in addition to the more traditional invert-and-multiply algorithm, be sure to send a note home to the parents to explain what you are doing and the reason for it.

Other suggestions for measurement situations involving the division of common fractions follow. Discuss the solutions with the children as they work the problems.

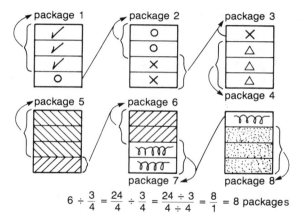

$$6 \div \frac{3}{4} = \frac{24}{4} \div \frac{3}{4} = \frac{24 \div 3}{4 \div 4} = \frac{8}{1} = 8 \text{ packages}$$

Figure 9–31 Area model illustrating division of common fractions.

Emma works for a cheese packing company. She puts $\frac{3}{4}$ of a pound of Swiss cheese into each party package. Emma has 6 pounds of Swiss cheese. How many party packages can Emma fill (see Figure 9–31)?

Erica is making doll clothes. She needs $\frac{2}{3}$ of a yard of materials for each outfit. She has $2\frac{2}{3}$ yards of material. How many outfits can she make (see Figure 9–32)?

Encourage children to make up other problems for each other. Ask the children to write the corresponding number sentences as they work.

OBJECTIVE: to develop the measurement concept of division of common fractions with a fractional or mixed-number quotient.

2. In the examples given earlier, the quotient was a whole number. Students are often confused when they must divide common fractions that do not have a whole-number quotient. They do not know what to do with the remainder. They may need to be reminded about the algorithm for division of whole numbers that allows them to write the remainder as part of the divisor. For example, the solution to $5 \div 2$ may be written as either 2 with a remainder of 1 or $2\frac{1}{2}$. When written as $2\frac{1}{2}$, the remainder 1 becomes the numerator of a fraction with the divisor 2 as the denominator. Thus, when we say $5 \div 2 = 2\frac{1}{2}$, the remainder 1 is

expressed as part of the divisor. In terms of fractions, the problem $5 \div 2$ may be thought of as $\frac{5}{2} = 2\frac{1}{2}$, which is consistent with the division concept of common fractions presented in Chapter 8. This also is the process used when children divide common fractions and the answer is not a whole number, as in the following example.

Danny has to take $\frac{2}{3}$ of a teaspoon of medicine in each dose. The doctor gave him a bottle containing 3 teaspoons of medicine. How many doses can Danny take? Figure 9–33 shows that Danny can take 4 full doses of medicine, and he will then have $\frac{1}{3}$ of a teaspoon of medicine left; that is, $\frac{1}{2}$ of another $\frac{2}{3}$ teaspoon dose of medicine.

Again, we show the common-denominator algorithm for division. Danny has $\frac{9}{3}$ teaspoons of medicine from the doctor and he wants to know how many doses of $\frac{2}{3}$ of a teaspoon each he can make. He can make 4 full doses and $\frac{1}{2}$ of another dose.

Children may wish to try to use a division algorithm similar to that for whole numbers. Study the following:

$$\frac{2}{3} \overline{\smash{\big)} \frac{9}{3}} \quad \begin{array}{c} 4r\frac{1}{3} \\ \hline \end{array} \qquad \text{or } 4\dfrac{\frac{1}{3}}{\frac{2}{3}} = 4\frac{1}{2}$$

$$\begin{array}{r} 4r\frac{1}{3} \\ \frac{2}{3} \overline{\smash{\big)} \frac{9}{3}} \\ -\frac{8}{3} \\ \hline \frac{1}{3} \end{array} \qquad \text{or } 4\dfrac{\frac{1}{3}}{\frac{2}{3}} = 4\frac{1}{2}$$

This algorithm will also work.

Encourage the students to suggest other examples and to solve them using the materials and the algorithm of their choice. Ask the students to predict whether the answers will be more or less than 1 before they compute the results. Note that whenever the divisor is larger than the dividend, the quotient will be less than 1. Ask students to discuss their methods of solution. They may use a calculator showing common fractions to compare results.

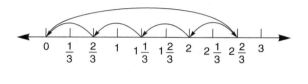

$$2\frac{2}{3} \div \frac{2}{3} = \frac{8}{3} \div \frac{2}{3} = \frac{8 \div 2}{3 \div 3} = \frac{4}{1} = 4 \text{ outfits}$$

Figure 9–32 Number line model illustrating division of common fractions.

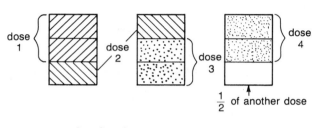

$$3 \div \frac{2}{3} = \frac{9}{3} \div \frac{2}{3} = \frac{9 \div 2}{3 \div 3} = \frac{9 \div 2}{1} = \frac{9}{2} = 4\frac{1}{2} \text{ doses}$$

Figure 9–33 Area model and alternative algorithm illustrating division of common fractions.

OBJECTIVE: to develop the partition concept of division of fractions with whole-number divisors.

3. Recall that division may be shown as either a measurement or a partition concept. In a partition problem, the total and the number of groups are known, and you are asked to find the amount in each group. Children should work a partition problem with whole numbers before they work a corresponding problem with fractions. Here is one suggestion: Neil plans to spend 4 hours on his homework this weekend. He plans to spend equal amounts of time on Saturday and Sunday. How many hours should Neil spend studying each day? Students should recognize this as a partition division problem; they divide the 4 into 2 equal parts to decide that Neil should spend 2 hours studying each day.

After working a problem with whole numbers, try the following: Jack plans to spend $\frac{1}{2}$ hour on his homework this weekend and wants to spend the same amount of time on Saturday and Sunday. How much time should Jack spend on his homework each day?

Figure 9–34 shows different materials used to solve this problem. Ask the children to compare this solution to $\frac{1}{2} \times \frac{1}{2}$. Jack will do $\frac{1}{2} \div 2$ of his homework on each day, or spend $\frac{1}{2}$ of $\frac{1}{2}$ hour.

Have children make up word problems for other number sentences and compare them to the corresponding multiplication problems. Each problem should be worked with concrete materials, with the number sentences written next to the work.

Following are a few other examples: Compare $\frac{2}{3} \div 3$ to $\frac{1}{3} \times \frac{2}{3}$. Bethany has $\frac{2}{3}$ of a pie. She wants to divide it equally among her two friends and herself.

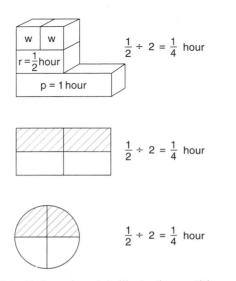

Figure 9–34 Variety of models illustrating partition concept of division of common fractions.

How much of the whole pie should each person get? Each will get $\frac{1}{3}$ of the $\frac{2}{3}$ pie, or $\frac{2}{9}$ of the whole pie.

Compare $\frac{3}{4} \div 5$ to $\frac{1}{5} \times \frac{3}{4}$. Antonio has $\frac{3}{4}$ of a pound of cheese. He wants to make 5 sandwiches and he wants to put the same amount of cheese on each sandwich. How much cheese should he put on each sandwich? Each sandwich should get $\frac{1}{5}$ of $\frac{3}{4}$ of a pound, or $\frac{3}{20}$ of a pound.

After you compare several multiplication and division problems, introduce the children to the invert-and-multiply algorithm for division of common fractions. Discuss why dividing by 3 gives the same answer as multiplying by $\frac{1}{3}$. Compare the results using the invert-and-multiply algorithm to the results using the common-denominator algorithm.

Let the children discuss which method they prefer. Do all children prefer the same algorithm? Does the preferred algorithm depend upon the type of problem being worked? Using the common-denominator algorithm fits the measurement problems better, while the invert-and-multiply method matches the partition word problems. As the teacher, you should determine whether the algorithm you prefer is based on the ease of understanding, the ease of use, or simply past familiarity.

The *partition concept of division* of fractions is not difficult to understand as long as the divisor is a whole number, but it can be fairly difficult to explain if the divisor is less than 1. We recommend that you use measurement examples for most of the problems with fractional divisors when students are initially learning to divide fractions. Some of the children may suggest partition word problems with fractional divisors, however, so we present them here. Encourage talented elementary children and middle school students to explore these problems further.

A   C   T   I   V   I   T   I   E   S

Grades 6–8

OBJECTIVE: to develop the partition concept of division of fractions with fractional divisors.

1. Following is a partition word problem for the number sentence $\frac{2}{3} \div \frac{1}{2} = n$: Mr. Washington has $\frac{2}{3}$ of a ton of grain. It is enough to feed $\frac{1}{2}$ of his herd of cattle. How much grain will it take to feed the whole herd?

Ask the children to compare this to a similar problem with whole numbers, such as: Mr. Ali has 6 tons of grain. This is enough to feed 3 herds of cattle. How much grain will it take to feed one herd of cattle?

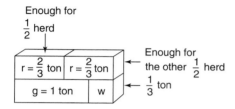

Need $1\frac{1}{3}$ tons for 1 herd

$$\frac{2}{3} \div \frac{1}{2} = 2 \times \frac{2}{3} = 1\frac{1}{3} \text{ tons}$$

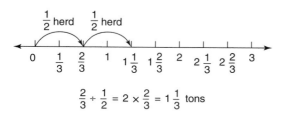

$$\frac{2}{3} \div \frac{1}{2} = 2 \times \frac{2}{3} = 1\frac{1}{3} \text{ tons}$$

Figure 9–35 Models illustrating partition concept of division of common fractions.

Have the children demonstrate how they would solve the problem with whole numbers using manipulatives. Then ask the children to show the fraction problem with the materials. Figure 9–35 shows two possible solutions.

Have the children write the number sentence below the work. Discuss with the children the similarity between solving this problem with the materials and showing $2 \times \frac{2}{3}$ with the materials. Repeat this process with other word problems and other manipulatives. Compare the results to those obtained using a calculator that works with common fractions.

2. Problems in which the divisor is not a unit fraction may pose more difficulties. Challenge the students who are ready to solve a problem such as the following using materials: Evelyn has $\frac{3}{4}$ of a pound of nuts. This is $\frac{2}{3}$ of the original package of nuts. How much did the original package weigh? Write the number sentence $\frac{2}{3} \times n = \frac{3}{4}$ or the sentence $\frac{3}{4} \div \frac{2}{3} = n$.

Children who think of this as a partition division problem may reason this way: "If $\frac{3}{4}$ of a pound is $\frac{2}{3}$ of the package, I should first find $\frac{1}{3}$ of the package and then multiply by 3 to find the whole package. To find $\frac{1}{3}$ of the package, I need to divide $\frac{3}{4}$ by 2. This tells me that $\frac{1}{3}$ of the original package was $\frac{3}{8}$ of a pound. I should now multiply this by 3, and this tells me that there must have been $\frac{9}{8}$, or $1\frac{1}{8}$ pounds of nuts in the package originally" (see Figure 9–36).

Note that by dividing by 2 and then multiplying by 3, the students have performed the same operation as inverting the $\frac{2}{3}$ and then multiplying by the inverse ($\frac{3}{2}$).

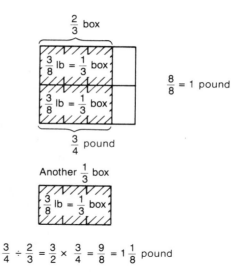

$$\frac{3}{4} \div \frac{2}{3} = \frac{3}{2} \times \frac{3}{4} = \frac{9}{8} = 1\frac{1}{8} \text{ pound}$$

Figure 9–36 Area model illustrating partition concept of division of common fractions.

The invert-and-multiply algorithm is discussed further in the section on skills. At this point, let the students work several examples using various materials, and encourage them to discuss their solutions.

Division of Decimal Fractions

If division of decimal fractions follows division of common fractions, the students should compare the two algorithms by solving number sentences in both common fraction and decimal fraction form and comparing the two quotients. Word problems and models for the two types of number sentences are essentially the same. Any of the suggestions given earlier for common fractions may be adapted for work with decimal fractions.

Review with children the algorithm for division of whole numbers before you attempt division of decimal fractions. Introduce division of decimal fractions with whole-number divisors first, and then move to divisors with one or two decimal places. A few suggestions for introducing division with decimal fractions follow.

A C T I V I T I E S

Grades 3–5 and Grades 6–8

OBJECTIVE: to develop the concept of division of a decimal fraction by a whole number.

1. Metric measures and money are good sources of problems. The following is one suggestion. Encourage children to create other word problems of their own and to discuss their methods of solution.

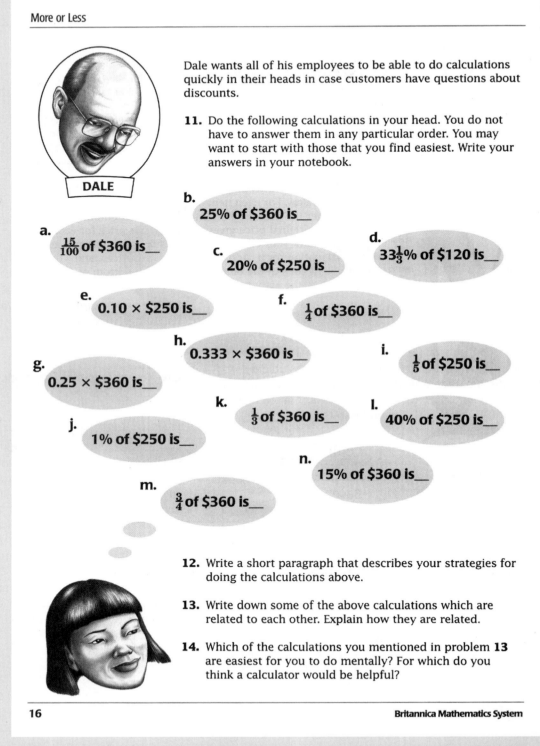

More or Less

Dale wants all of his employees to be able to do calculations quickly in their heads in case customers have questions about discounts.

11. Do the following calculations in your head. You do not have to answer them in any particular order. You may want to start with those that you find easiest. Write your answers in your notebook.

DALE

b.
25% of $360 is__

a.
$\frac{15}{100}$ of $360 is__

c.
20% of $250 is__

d.
$33\frac{1}{3}$% of $120 is__

e.
0.10 × $250 is__

f.
$\frac{1}{4}$ of $360 is__

h.
0.333 × $360 is__

g.
0.25 × $360 is__

i.
$\frac{1}{5}$ of $250 is__

k.
$\frac{1}{3}$ of $360 is__

l.
40% of $250 is__

j.
1% of $250 is__

n.
15% of $360 is__

m.
$\frac{3}{4}$ of $360 is__

12. Write a short paragraph that describes your strategies for doing the calculations above.

13. Write down some of the above calculations which are related to each other. Explain how they are related.

14. Which of the calculations you mentioned in problem **13** are easiest for you to do mentally? For which do you think a calculator would be helpful?

Figure 9–37 Reprinted with permission from *Mathematics in Context,* © 2003 by Encyclopedia Britannica, Inc.

This page (Figure 9–37) is from a sixth/seventh grade unit titled "More or Less" from the program *Mathematics in Context.* In this unit, students look at relationships among fractions, decimals, and percents as they learn to multiply with fractions and decimals and use percents in different situations. Most of the problems have a real-life context, and in this unit many of the problems are related to finding which price is best using estimation, mental computation, calculators, and paper-and-pencil computation. Note that students are asked to write about their strategies for doing the mental computation and to compare the problems that use similar strategies. Discourse about the different strategies is important as students compare their methods with each other to determine which work best in various situations.

This program was developed with a grant from the National Science Foundation to provide curriculum implementing the goals of the National Council of Teachers of Mathematics *'Principles and Standards for School Mathematics* (NCTM, 2000).' This four-year program consists of 40 units (10 per grade level) for grades 5–9 interwoven through the strands of number, algebra, geometry, and statistics. Teachers are encouraged to work through each unit themselves and to discuss them with other teachers, if possible, before working the units with the students. Assessments are varied, including observations, group work, and culminating projects as well as the more traditional homework problems and end-of-unit assessment. Students are encouraged to use self-evaluation and portfolios, and suggestions are included for evaluating student responses to the open-ended questions.

Sasha has a board that is 9.3 meters long. She wishes to make a bookshelf with three shelves of equal length from the board. How long should each shelf be?

Notice that this is a *partition type of division problem.* Model the problem. Cut a piece of string 9.3 meters long and then fold it into 3 equal parts. Ask the children to estimate how long each of the parts is. Will each part be longer than 1 meter? Will each one be longer than 10 meters? About how many meters long is each part? Is each longer or shorter than 3 meters? Ask the children to measure the parts to find the answer to the nearest 0.1 of a meter.

Ask the students to develop a division algorithm to solve 9.3 ÷ 3. Some of the students might use the following form:

$$\begin{array}{r} 3.1 \\ 3)\overline{9.3} \\ \underline{9} \\ 3 \\ \underline{3} \end{array}$$

Ask the children what should be done with the decimal point. After the children predict that the division algorithm is performed in the same manner as the algorithm for whole numbers, with the decimal point in the quotient directly above the decimal point in the dividend, ask them to work other problems with whole number divisors using that algorithm and to check the answer by measuring and folding string. Have them use a calculator to see if they get the same results.

OBJECTIVE: to develop the concept of division of decimal fractions with non-whole-number divisors.

2. After students have had experience dividing with whole-number divisors, give them a problem such as the following: Marta has a lemonade stand. She has made 2.4 liters of lemonade. She wants to sell glasses with 0.3 liter of lemonade in each one. How many glasses can she fill?

This *measurement type of division problem* can be shown using any of the materials familiar from the work with decimal fractions. Figure 9–38 shows several possibilities. Ask the children to write the number sentence below each example. They may also use a repeated subtraction algorithm to show the measurement idea of division.

If children have had previous experience with dividing common fractions, ask them to write the number sentence in common fraction form. They may show the problem as $2\frac{4}{10} \div \frac{3}{10} = \frac{24}{10} \div \frac{3}{10} = n$. Using the common-denominator algorithm, this becomes $\frac{24 \div 3}{10 \div 10}$. Since the denominators cancel, the problem is simply 24 ÷ 3 = 8. Discuss with the children that this has the same effect as moving the decimal point in both the divisor and the dividend one place to the right.

The children may also use the *division concept of common fractions* to show the problem as $\frac{2.4}{0.3}$. In this form, both the numerator and the denominator may be multiplied by 10 so the divisor will be a whole number. Thus, $\frac{2.4 \times 10}{0.3 \times 10} = \frac{24}{3}$.

This is a good time to use a calculator. Try the problem as 2.4 − .3 − .3 − .3 − .3 − .3 − .3 − .3 − .3 or 2.4 − .3 = = = = = = = =. How many

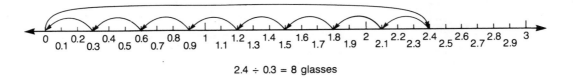

2.4 ÷ 0.3 = 8 glasses

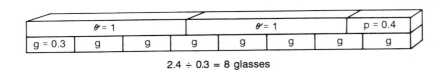

2.4 ÷ 0.3 = 8 glasses

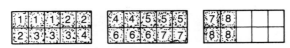

2.4 ÷ 0.3 = 8 glasses

Figure 9–38   Variety of models illustrating division of decimal fractions.

glasses of 0.3 liter each can you make? Compare this result to 2.4 ÷ 0.3.

After the children have worked several examples and have had an opportunity to create their own division algorithms, you might wish to show them the division algorithm that makes use of the carat to show the movement of the decimal point in both the divisor and the dividend. Ask the children to give you a rule for the number of places that the decimal point should be moved. Be sure the children have experience with divisors and dividends with varying numbers of decimal places so they can generalize that the number of places the decimal point moves in both the divisor and the dividend is equal to the number of decimal places in the divisor. They may need to add decimal places in the dividend to make this work.

Let the children use calculators to check their predictions about moving the decimal points. Using calculators allows them to make predictions and check a much larger number of examples than doing all the calculations with paper and pencil.

DEVELOPING FLUENCY WITH RATIONAL NUMBER OPERATIONS

After children understand the concepts behind the algorithms for operations with both common and decimal fractions, they can practice their skills with these operations. Do not rush the students into this practice. In many textbooks, one page explains how the algorithms work and then the next page includes 30 or 40 exercises for the children to practice the algorithm. It is more beneficial to spend more time on the development of understanding through the use of concrete materials than it is to rush to the abstract algorithms. Children who understand what they are doing often become much more proficient with the algorithms than children who have had a great deal more practice with the algorithms but did not understand the processes they were using.

Because of the proliferation of inexpensive calculators, it is not necessary to spend a great deal of time dividing by a divisor with five or six decimal places or adding two fractions with denominators such as 57 and 34. Very few of us as adults would do those problems with paper and pencil even if the occasion arose for us to work the problems at all. We would work the problems on a calculator. Even fractions with complicated denominators can be easily converted to decimals and the problem worked on a calculator, or the problem can be worked on a calculator that computes with common fractions.

Children should practice simpler problems with paper and pencil, however, and this section is devoted to developing those skills. It is also important that children learn to estimate and calculate mentally with rational numbers. The following section focuses on these skills.

Addition and Subtraction of Common Fractions

After children understand the algorithms for adding and subtracting common fractions, they may practice the two skills together. The activities for reinforcing operations with whole numbers may be adapted to reinforcing the same operations with rational numbers. Children enjoy inventing and playing their own card games, Bingo games, and board games, and they can make the playing cards with number sentences involving addition and subtraction of common fractions. A few other suggestions follow.

A C T I V I T I E S

Grades 3 – 5 and Grades 6 – 8

OBJECTIVE: to reinforce the skills of adding and subtracting common fractions.

1. Magic Squares, which have the same sum for each row, column, and diagonal, give the children a great deal of practice in both addition and subtraction of fractions. You may fill in as many or as few of the positions of the magic square as you wish, depending on the level of the children. For a real challenge, give the children a blank square and the list of fractions and ask the children to fill in all the spaces so that each row, column, and diagonal has the same sum. Figure 9–39 shows a partially completed square. Discuss with the children the best place to begin and strategies for completing the square. Fraction calculators may be useful here.

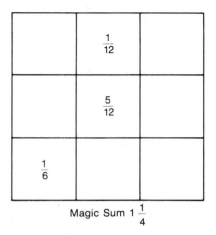

Magic Sum $1\frac{1}{4}$

Figure 9 – 39 Fraction Magic Square.

2. Children often enjoy using codes and solving puzzles. To solve the riddle in Figure 9–40, children must break the code by completing the addition and subtraction number sentences. Ask the children to make up other codes for each other and trade them.

3. Because computers can individualize work to the level of the children, many computer programs give children practice on the skills they need. Programs, such as *Fraction Operations* from Tenth Planet, *Fraction Attraction II* (1996) from Sunburst, and *Mighty Math Calculating Crew* (1996) and *Mighty Math Number Heroes* (1996) from Edmark, are designed to give the children more practice with the abstract algorithms. Look for programs that individualize instruction to the

needs of the children and explain, not just repeat, the algorithms that the children have missed.

4. Challenge students to find a way to name any unit fraction using two other unit fractions. (A unit fraction is a fraction with 1 in the numerator.) For example, you might say $\frac{1}{2} = \frac{1}{4} + \frac{1}{4}$. Students should be able to tell you fairly easily that any unit fraction $\frac{1}{n}$ might be obtained by taking $\frac{1}{2n} + \frac{1}{2n}$. Now challenge the students to name any unit fraction using two different unit fractions. For example, $\frac{1}{3} = \frac{1}{4} + \frac{1}{12}$. After students have explored this problem for a while, ask them to find a general rule for this. It will probably be a greater challenge for students to generalize that $\frac{1}{n} = \frac{1}{n+1} + \frac{1}{n(n+1)}$.

Use these values to solve the following riddle.

a $- \frac{1}{3}$	b $- \frac{2}{3}$	c $- 1$	d $- \frac{1}{4}$
e $- \frac{3}{4}$	f $- 0$	g $- \frac{1}{5}$	h $- \frac{2}{5}$
i $- \frac{3}{5}$	j $- \frac{4}{5}$	k $- \frac{1}{8}$	l $- \frac{3}{8}$
m $- \frac{5}{8}$	n $- \frac{7}{8}$	o $- \frac{1}{10}$	p $- \frac{3}{10}$
q $- \frac{7}{10}$	r $- \frac{9}{10}$	s $- \frac{1}{2}$	t $- 1\frac{1}{2}$
u $- 1\frac{1}{4}$	v $- 1\frac{3}{4}$	w $- 1\frac{1}{3}$	x $- 1\frac{2}{3}$
	y $- 1\frac{1}{5}$	z $- 1\frac{3}{5}$	

Why was the elephant wearing blue sneakers?

$\frac{1}{3}+\frac{1}{3}$ $1-\frac{1}{4}$ $\frac{1}{4}+\frac{3}{4}$ $\frac{1}{6}+\frac{1}{6}$ $\frac{3}{4}+\frac{1}{2}$ $\frac{1}{4}+\frac{1}{4}$ $\frac{1}{2}+\frac{1}{4}$ $\frac{1}{5}+\frac{1}{5}$ $1\frac{1}{5}-\frac{3}{5}$ $\frac{3}{4}-\frac{1}{4}$

$\frac{1}{2}+\frac{2}{5}$ $\frac{7}{8}-\frac{1}{8}$ $\frac{1}{2}-\frac{1}{4}$ $\frac{3}{5}-\frac{1}{2}$ $1\frac{1}{8}-\frac{1}{4}$ $\frac{1}{4}+\frac{1}{2}$ $\frac{3}{8}+\frac{1}{8}$

$\frac{2}{3}+\frac{2}{3}$ $\frac{1}{2}+\frac{1}{4}$ $1\frac{1}{10}-\frac{1}{5}$ $1\frac{1}{2}-\frac{3}{4}$ $1\frac{1}{2}-\frac{1}{6}$ $1\frac{1}{4}-\frac{1}{2}$ $\frac{3}{4}+\frac{3}{4}$

Figure 9–40 Fraction puzzle.

Addition and Subtraction of Decimal Fractions

After children understand the algorithms for addition and subtraction of decimal fractions using the concrete materials, have them begin to practice the algorithms more abstractly. Be sure to make full use of calculators and computers as the children are practicing these skills. Emphasize estimation and mental calculation, because once they leave school, the children will probably be performing more operations either mentally or with a calculator than they will with paper and pencil. A few activities for paper and pencil as well as for calculators and computers follow. Other ideas for estimating and mental calculating are described in that section.

ACTIVITIES

Grades 3–5

OBJECTIVE: to practice addition and subtraction of decimal fractions.

1. Make up a set of cards for the game Sum of One, as shown in Figure 9–41.

Children should shuffle the cards and deal them all out to the players. From two to six children may play. At a given signal, each player turns the top card on the dealt stack face up. If any player sees two or more cards that add to one, that player says, "Sum of one." If the player is correct, he or she keeps the cards that add to 1. If players disagree over whether the sum is correct, the children should use a calculator to check. Play continues with every player turning over his or her top card on each turn. The game ends when the designated time period ends or when one player has all the cards. The player with the most cards at the end of the game is the

winner. The game may be played with other sums or with differences.

2. Bring in newspaper ads or catalogs from different stores. Make up problems that require the children to add and subtract various amounts using money written as decimal fractions. Ask how much cheaper one item is than another or how much several items would cost altogether. Challenge the children to find exactly three items that would have a total cost of $10.00. See if the children can find two items with a difference in price of $.57. Ask the children to make up other problems of their own.

Encourage mental computation but allow children to use a calculator as they work, if necessary. Let them discuss their strategies for choosing the items and for performing the mental computations.

3. The Target Game allows children to use calculators but requires them to estimate and compute mentally in order to be successful. To play this game, one child begins by displaying a rational number on the calculator. A second child names another rational number as the target, and the third child tries to hit the target by adding to or subtracting from the number currently in the calculator. If the target is hit, the child hitting the target scores 1 point and begins a new game by leaving that number in the display and announcing a new target. The calculator is then passed to the next child, who attempts to hit the new target with addition or subtraction.

Each time the target is hit, a point is scored and a new target is named. If the target is not hit, the calculator is passed on, and the next player adds to or subtracts from whatever number is currently in the calculator display. A sample game is described below.

Maureen, Esteban, and Marlo are playing. Maureen puts 8.6 into the calculator and Esteban announces a target of 17.2. Marlo is given the calculator and thinks, "If I add 9, I will have 17.6; 17.2 is 0.4 less than that. I will add 0.4 less than 9, or 8.6." Marlo pushes "+8.6" and hits the target. She scores 1 point, announces a new target of 12.5, and hands the calculator to Maureen.

Maureen thinks, "12 is 5 less than 17 and 0.2 is 0.3 less than 0.5." She subtracts 5.3, and the calculator shows 11.9. Maureen realizes she did not figure the 0.3 correctly. It is now Esteban's turn, and the target is still 12.5.

Encourage the children to discuss their strategies aloud as they play the game. Strategies should be perfected as play continues. This game may also be played with common fractions, if you have a calculator that can handle them.

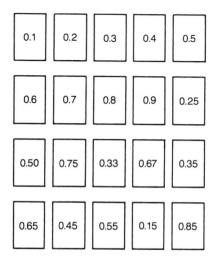

0.1	0.2	0.3	0.4	0.5
0.6	0.7	0.8	0.9	0.25
0.50	0.75	0.33	0.67	0.35
0.65	0.45	0.55	0.15	0.85

Figure 9–41 Cards for game Sum of One.

Multiplication and Division of Common Fractions

After children have a good concrete understanding of multiplication and division of common fractions and can relate the algorithms to both concrete and semi-concrete models, it is time to practice the algorithms more abstractly. As with addition and subtraction, emphasize understanding, not memorization of algorithms. Do not assign 30 or 40 exercises to be worked rotely each night in hopes of building greater proficiency. Be sure children understand any algorithm before they practice it because it is very difficult to "unteach" an incorrectly practiced algorithm. Encourage use of estimation and mental calculation, and teach the use of calculators to solve more difficult problems.

The reinforcement ideas described earlier for whole-number operations or for addition and subtraction of rational numbers may be adapted to multiplication and division of rational numbers. A few additional ideas for extending the algorithms and reinforcing the learning of multiplication and division of common fractions follow.

A C T I V I T I E S

Grades 6 – 8

OBJECTIVE: to extend the algorithm for multiplying or dividing common fractions by using cancellation.

1. After children have discovered and practiced the multiplication algorithm and the invert-and-multiply algorithm for common fractions, you can help them discover a shortcut for multiplying some fractions. Ask the children to complete the following number sentence and simplify the answer when they are finished:

$$\frac{3}{4} \times \frac{4}{5} = n$$

$$\frac{3}{4} \times \frac{4}{5} = \frac{3 \times 4}{4 \times 5} = \frac{12}{20} = \frac{12 \div 4}{20 \div 4} = \frac{3}{5}$$

Ask the children if there is an easier way to work the problem than to first multiply the 3 and the 5 by 4 and then to divide the 12 and the 20 by 4 to get the 3 and the 5 again. Ask the children to suggest a way to avoid having to multiply both the numerator and the denominator by the same number and then having to simplify the answer. Discuss with the students the relationship between the cancellation process and the use of the right-hand identity for division. Note that in each case you are dividing the numerator and the denominator by the same number; $\frac{a}{a} = 1$, the right-hand identity for division.

Have the children try their suggestions in solving the following problems:

$$\frac{8}{9} \times \frac{9}{15} = n$$

$$\frac{5}{6} \times \frac{7}{5} = n$$

Does the process work for problems such as

$$\frac{4}{5} \times \frac{3}{8} = n$$

$$\frac{2}{3} \times \frac{6}{7} = n$$

Suggest factoring the numerators and denominators before attempting the cancellation. Try to solve the following problem by factoring first:

$$\frac{24}{35} \times \frac{7}{36} = n$$

Let the students suggest other problems and use cancellation before they multiply. Let students use calculators to assist with the larger multiplication problems. In this way, they can explore more examples. (This skill will be very useful in algebra later on.)

Ask the children if they can also use cancellation for division when using the invert-and-multiply algorithm. Encourage them to explore what happens if they do not invert the divisor before they attempt to cancel.

OBJECTIVE: to develop the concept of reciprocals.

2. Ask the children to multiply several pairs of common fractions in the form $\frac{a}{b} \times \frac{b}{a}$. They may solve the following problems:

$$\frac{1}{2} \times \frac{2}{1} = n$$

$$\frac{2}{3} \times \frac{3}{2} = n$$

$$\frac{3}{4} \times \frac{4}{3} = n$$

Give the definition of a reciprocal. The *reciprocal* of any number *a* is the number that you must multiply *a* by to get 1, the multiplicative identity. Ask the children to find the missing number in each of the following:

$$\frac{5}{6} \times b = \frac{30}{30}$$

$$\frac{7}{8} \times c = \frac{56}{56}$$

$$1\frac{2}{3} \times d = \frac{15}{15}$$

You may need to suggest that the children first write $1\frac{2}{3}$ as an improper fraction. Ask them to give you a rule for finding the reciprocal of any common fraction.

OBJECTIVE: to develop the meaning of the invert-and-multiply algorithm.

3. After children understand the concept of reciprocals, ask those who seem to grasp the concept well to work a problem involving division of common fractions using a new algorithm. This will reinforce the idea that there are several ways to compute and that the children may choose the method easiest for them. Remind the children that common fractions can be used to represent division: $3 \div 4$ can be shown as $\frac{3}{4}$. Use this idea to show that $\frac{2}{3} \div \frac{4}{5}$ can be written as

$$\frac{\frac{2}{3}}{\frac{4}{5}}$$

How can children solve the number sentence written in this form? Suggest to the children that they multiply the numerator and the denominator by the same number to get a denominator of 1. This renames the fraction with an equivalent fraction and eliminates the messy denominator. (This skill is useful for later work with algebraic fractions.) Notice that it is necessary to multiply both the denominator and the numerator by the reciprocal of the denominator. This has the same effect as inverting the divisor and multiplying the inverted number by the dividend. See the following:

$$\frac{2}{3} \div \frac{4}{5} = \frac{\frac{2}{3}}{\frac{4}{5}} = \frac{\frac{2}{3} \times \frac{5}{4}}{\frac{4}{5} \times \frac{5}{4}} = \frac{\frac{2}{3} \times \frac{5}{4}}{1} = \frac{2}{3} \times \frac{5}{4}$$

Encourage the children to try other examples of their own. Ask them to explain in their own words why the invert-and-multiply algorithm works. This would make a good entry in the student's daily journal.

4. For students who enjoy games, the Fraction 24 game is a great way to practice computation with fractions. This is a commercial game, but you could devise a similar game of your own. This is based on the regular game 24, which consists of a deck of cards, each of which has with four numbers that can be combined to make 24. For example, if you have a card with the numbers 2, 2, 3, and 8, a student might say $(2 \div 2) \times 8 \times 3 = 24$. Note that each number on the card must be used exactly once with any operation to get an answer of 24. In the fraction version of this game, you might see the numbers $\frac{3}{4}$, 1, 2, and 6. A student might say $[(1 + 2) \div \frac{3}{4}] \times 6 = 24$. This is a great game for students to practice the correct order of operations

as well as operations with fractions. Students may wish to use calculators with the correct order of operations and the ability to perform operations on common fractions to check their work in this game.

Multiplication and Division of Decimal Fractions

After children understand the concepts of multiplying and dividing decimal fractions and can relate the abstract algorithms to both concrete and semiconcrete models, they can begin to practice the algorithms more abstractly. Again, we caution you against an overreliance on abstract practice without understanding. Be sure that children understand the concepts and are correctly working the algorithms before they take any practice work home.

We remind you that most adults work problems involving decimal fractions either mentally or with a calculator the majority of the time. This practice will certainly not lessen as our children enter adulthood. Use estimation, mental calculation, and calculators fully as children practice their skills. A few suggestions for practice follow.

A C T I V I T I E S

Grades 6 – 8

OBJECTIVE: to practice operations with decimal fractions.

1. Ask the students to predict which of the following will have an answer of 2.4 and to explain their predictions.

$$0.2 \times 12 = n$$
$$3.0 \times 0.08 = n$$
$$60 \times 4.0 = n$$
$$0.1 \times 240 = n$$
$$0.24 \times 10 = n$$
$$30.0 \times 8.0 = n$$
$$24.0 \div 10 = n$$
$$240 \div 0.1 = n$$
$$0.24 \div 0.1 = n$$

Ask the students to tell you why they made the predictions they did, and if they were correct. Students may use paper and pencil or a calculator to check, if necessary. Let the students make up other problems for each other.

2. Ask the students to describe the average person in each group of three or four. Tell the children to make several measurements (in meters) of each person in their group. They may measure each person's height; the length of each person's arms, legs, feet, and fingers; the circumference of each person's head, and so on. Avoid any measurements that may embarrass some of the children. After all the measurements are made, ask the children to find the mean of each measurement by totaling the measurements and dividing the total by the number of people in the group. Let the children compare groups to see which group has the smallest or largest mean on certain measures. Use the means to describe an average student. Can you find a student who matches this description? Let the children suggest other problems that involve any of the operations with decimal fractions. Use computer programs to help children practice their skills. The programs mentioned earlier for practicing addition and subtraction of decimal fractions also provide practice for multiplication and division and should be used for these skills as well.

Operations with Percents

Because percents are used so frequently in everyday life, children should develop their skills in this area. After the children understand the meaning of percent using concrete materials and can connect the algorithms to the models, they should practice their skills mentally and with calculators as well as with paper and pencil. Here are a few activities for developing this skill.

A   C   T   I   V   I   T   I   E   S

Grades 6–8

OBJECTIVE: to practice using percents.

1. Earlier, we mentioned using percent in the formula $p = r \times b$. In the earlier discussion, the problems involved knowing the rate and the base and finding the percentage. After mastering those problems, children should also work with problems in which the base or the rate is unknown. Allow children to use a calculator to solve problems such as the following:

- Juanita bought a coat that was marked $10.00 off. The coat was originally $50.00. What percent was taken off the original price? What percent is the discount of the selling price? Does the discount stay the same? Are the two percents the same? Why not?
- Fred bought a jacket that was $20.00 off. Fred said he saved 25 percent off the original price. What was the original price?

Ask the children to make up other problems and to trade the problems with each other. They can use ads from the newspaper as a resource. Children usually prefer solving each other's problems over solving the problems in the book. Discuss what to do with problems that have too much or too little information and the methods used to solve the problems that could be solved.

2. Another common use of percent is to figure the interest on a loan or savings account. Simple interest is figured using the formula $I = prt$; that is, interest = principal $\times$ rate $\times$ time. Ask the students to figure the amount of interest a savings account will pay if it pays simple interest at 5 percent for 2 years on $500.00. Students should take $500.00 $\times$ 5 percent $\times$ 2 to find the interest.

After students have worked several problems, some of them may wish to explore problems with compound interest or problems with a discount rate rather than simple interest. Children may wish to visit a bank or savings and loan to discuss ways to find the best interest rate on a savings account or on a car loan.

ESTIMATING, USING BENCHMARKS, AND MENTAL CALCULATING WITH RATIONAL NUMBER OPERATIONS

Throughout the chapter, we have discussed the importance of children using estimation and mental calculation skills. The Second National Assessment of Educational Progress found that only 24 percent of the 13-year-olds tested could correctly choose the number closest to the sum of $\frac{12}{13} + \frac{7}{8}$ from the choices 1, 2, 19, and 21 (Post, 1981). Both 19 and 21 were more popular choices. This demonstrates that most children do not realize that both $\frac{12}{13}$ and $\frac{7}{8}$ are fairly close to 1 and that, therefore, the sum must be almost 2. They are apparently trying to use some misunderstood algorithm that tells them to add either the numerators or the denominators. They probably do not realize that a fraction represents one number to be operated on as one entity and not two numbers, one on top of the other, to be operated on separately. They do not have the necessary understanding of the size of rational numbers. The Fourth National Assessment of Educational Progress found that fewer than 40 percent of the seventh graders tested could identify the largest and smallest of four fractions, and fewer than 50 percent recognized that $5\frac{1}{4}$ was the same as $5 + \frac{1}{4}$ (Kouba et al., 1988). This basic understanding of the size of rational numbers is crucial to understanding problems that require the use of rational numbers.

Reys and Bestgen (1981) found that students do not perform any better with decimals. Fewer than 30 percent of 13-year-olds could correctly estimate the sum of $95.0 + 865.2 + 1.583$ to the nearest power of 10.

It is therefore essential that we help children learn to estimate as well as calculate exactly with rational numbers. We cannot assume that children who can compute accurately with paper and pencil also can estimate. Many children who can correctly compute the product of two rational numbers cannot estimate whether the product will be larger or smaller than 1. The skills of estimation and mental calculation need to be specifically taught. Most children do not automatically transfer skills with paper-and-pencil calculation to mental estimation and calculation. The following activities are designed to help children develop these skills further.

A C T I V I T I E S

Grades 3 – 5 and Grades 6 – 8

OBJECTIVE: to develop estimation skills for addition and subtraction of rational numbers.

1. In Chapter 8, we mentioned activities for helping children estimate values of rational numbers by relating them to benchmarks of wholes, halves, and fourths. These skills help the children as they learn to add and subtract fractions. For example, if the children have an exercise such as $1\frac{15}{16} + \frac{12}{23}$, they may think the following way in order to estimate the sum: "$1\frac{15}{16}$ is almost 2. $\frac{12}{23}$ is about $\frac{1}{2}$. Therefore, the sum is about $2\frac{1}{2}$."

A similar activity that relates the problem to money is useful for decimal addition and subtraction because of the children's familiarity with the decimal notation of money. When given a problem such as $2.4876 - 1.98$, the children may think, "2.4876 is about \$2.50 and 1.98 is about \$2.00. Therefore, since \$2.50 − \$2.00 is \$.50, the answer is around 0.5."

Children may wish to use a calculator to see how close the estimates are. Estimates are also a good check on calculator work. Let children suggest other problems for each other to work. After they have worked several examples, children may suggest strategies for refining their estimates. Let them share strategies with each other and decide which ones work best for them.

OBJECTIVE: to develop estimation skills for multiplication and division of rational numbers.

2. Children are often surprised when they multiply two rational numbers and see that the product is smaller than either of the two factors or when they divide two rational numbers and get a quotient larger than either the dividend or the divisor. These experiences may go against generalizations they have made for whole numbers about the product being larger than either factor or the quotient being smaller than the dividend. Have the children return to the meaning of multiplication and division of rational numbers in order to help them

predict the size of the answer to a number sentence involving multiplication or division of rational numbers.

Give the children a word problem such as the following and ask them to tell you whether the scale drawing will be larger or smaller than the original: Jacque is making a scale drawing of his room. He wants the drawing to be 0.1 the size of his room. His room is 3.0 meters by 2.5 meters. How large should the drawing be?

The children should realize that the drawing will be smaller than the room. Ask the children to give you a number sentence for the word problem. Discuss with the children what happens when you take 0.1×3.0. Why is the answer less than 3? Ask the children to tell you the answer without using paper and pencil.

Have the children make up other word problems involving multiplication and predict the answer without using paper and pencil. Let them check using paper and pencil or a calculator if they wish. Encourage children to round mixed numerals to the nearest whole number to estimate their product or to mentally calculate the product of a whole number and a mixed numeral by multiplying the two whole numbers and then multiplying the first whole number times the fraction. For example, $3 \times 2\frac{1}{2} = (3 \times 2) + (3 \times \frac{1}{2})$.

Use word problems for estimation involving division of rational numbers also. Use a problem such as the following, and ask the children if the answer is more than 1 apple: Dan has $\frac{3}{4}$ of a pound of apples. Each apple weighs $\frac{1}{4}$ pound. How many apples does Dan have? Ask the children to write a number sentence for the word problem and to compute the answer mentally. Encourage the children to make up other word problems for each other and to predict the answers before using paper-and-pencil algorithms or a calculator.

OBJECTIVE: to use estimation skills to correctly place the decimal point in any problem involving operations with decimal fractions.

3. As the use of calculators becomes widespread, children need to become even better at estimating to determine whether or not the answer shown on the calculator is reasonable. One way to practice this skill is to give the children a list of number sentences along with their solutions, only without the decimal points. Ask the children to put the decimal point in the correct place without using paper and pencil or a calculator. Use a list such as the following:

$$6.9 \times 45.0 = 3105$$
$$8.14 \div 0.2 = 407$$
$$0.5 \times 26 = 130$$
$$0.18 \div 0.5 = 36$$
$$3.62 \times 54.789 = 19833618$$

Let students make up other problems on their own.

OBJECTIVE: to use mental calculations to answer problems involving percents.

4. Because we encounter percents frequently as consumers and often want to figure an amount exactly without using a calculator or paper and pencil, this area is an especially crucial one. Give children experience finding 1 percent and 10 percent of an amount. Ask the children to give you a rule for multiplying by these percents. Let them use calculators to see if the rule always works.

After the children can easily move the decimal point to find 1 percent or 10 percent, ask them for a way to find 5 percent or 15 percent. Good mental calculators might tell you that 5 percent is half of 10 percent and that to get 15 percent you should add 5 percent and 10 percent. Let the children practice finding the exact amount they should leave for a 15 percent tip for meals of varying amounts.

After children can easily find 1 percent, 5 percent, 10 percent, and 15 percent, ask them for an easy way to find 25 percent, 50 percent, and $33\frac{1}{3}$ percent. The children should know the fraction equivalents of these percents and practice finding $\frac{1}{4}$, $\frac{1}{2}$, and $\frac{1}{3}$ of varying amounts. Bring in sale ads from the paper and ask the children to figure how much they will save on sales of 25 percent, 50 percent, or $33\frac{1}{3}$ percent off.

After children are able to find these percents, ask them for 75 percent, $66\frac{2}{3}$ percent, and 40 percent. Good mental calculators will use 25 percent and/or 50 percent to find 75 percent, $33\frac{1}{3}$ percent to find $66\frac{2}{3}$ percent, and 10 percent and 50 percent to find 40 percent. Given these abilities, the children should be able to either find the exact amount or give a good estimate for any percents they encounter as consumers.

REASONING, SOLVING, AND POSING PROBLEMS WITH RATIONAL NUMBER OPERATIONS

Throughout the book, we have emphasized the importance of children both creating their own problems and solving the problems created by others. In this chapter, we have given suggestions for using problem creating and problem solving in teaching operations with rational numbers. Problem creating and solving should be the approaches to learning. Children should learn by asking questions, making mistakes, and finding the answers. Here are a few other suggestions for problems involving rational numbers.

A C T I V I T I E S

Grades 3–5 and Grades 6–8

OBJECTIVE: to use common fractions to describe data collected in an experiment.

1. Ask the children to suggest experiments they can conduct that involve rational numbers. They can use common fractions to describe the number of heads that come up when flipping a coin, the number of spades drawn from a deck of cards, or the number of times a sum of seven is shown when rolling two dice. Conduct one of the experiments 5 times, 10 times, and 100 times. For example, write fractions that represent the number of heads that come up when you flip a coin.

- *Understanding the problem.* If I flip a coin once, the fraction that represents the number of heads is either $\frac{1}{1}$ (one head, no tail out of the flip) or $\frac{0}{1}$ (no head, one tail out of one flip). Now, what I want to do is to flip a coin and see what I get. Each time I flip the coin I can write a new fraction based on one flip, two flips, three flips, and so on. Let's see, if I flip a coin five times I can get 5, 4, 3, 2, 1, or 0 heads. That is one of six fractions. I will need to try.

- *Devising a plan.* I will flip a coin and write a fraction describing the number of heads compared to the number of flips. The denominator will be 1. Then I will flip a coin again and write a different fraction describing the number of heads compared to the number of flips. The denominator will be 2. I will continue to flip the coin, recording a new fraction each time. The denominator will increase by 1 each time I flip the coin (make and use a drawing or model).

- *Carrying out the plan.* On the first flip, I have a head; my fraction is $\frac{1}{1}$. On the second flip, I have a head; my fraction is $\frac{2}{2}$. Next, a tail comes up; my fraction is $\frac{2}{3}$. I continue flipping the coin, and the fractions I get are $\frac{3}{4}$, $\frac{3}{5}$, $\frac{4}{6}$, $\frac{4}{7}$, $\frac{5}{8}$, $\frac{5}{9}$, $\frac{6}{10}$. Now, I want to flip the coin 10 more times to see if I get the same fractions. After that, I will attempt 100 flips.

- *Looking back.* Are all of my fractions written correctly? Do the denominators increase from 1 to 10? (I could write all of the denominators before I ever flip the coin.) Is there any pattern to the numerators? Can I predict the final numerator? Could I write a computer program to simulate the flips so I would not have to do all the work myself? If so, I can repeat the experiment as many times as I want and see if there is a pattern to the results.

Ask the children to describe the fractions they got each time. Which experiment would be the most accurate predictor in the long run? What would happen if they performed the task a thousand or a million times? These activities are a good introduction to teaching probability, which is described in Chapter 13.

OBJECTIVE: to solve problems involving spatial visualization and rational numbers.

2. Use the tangrams in Appendix B for the following activity. Tell the children that all seven pieces together have a value of 1. Ask them to find the value of each shape.

After the children have determined that the pieces have the values shown in Figure 9–42, ask the children to find the total value of each shape in Figure 9–43. Encourage the children to make other shapes of their own and to challenge each other to find the total values. How many different shapes can they make with the same value? Determine how much more one shape is than another.

OBJECTIVE: to use decimals and percents to describe data and make predictions.

3. Ask the children to design a survey and collect data on some area of interest to them, such as the food

offerings in the cafeteria. Let them list available offerings and suggest others and then ask students to select their favorites. When the survey is complete, have the children report the percent of children who chose each offering.

Have the children suggest uses for their data. They may wish to discuss the results with the head of the cafeteria service. Discuss with the children things that must be considered in planning menus, such as cost and nutrition. Have the children interview people from companies that are in charge of planning. How do they make decisions regarding the products or services they offer? The children may even wish to set up a company of their own and to keep records and collect data to plan for the future.

ORGANIZING FOR RATIONAL NUMBER OPERATIONS TLC

Several researchers recommend that more time be spent developing the concepts of rational number operations (Hiebert, 1987; Mack, 1990; Payne and Towsley, 1990). Students need to work in groups and discuss the concepts that they are constructing using concrete materials. Otherwise, students often have very incomplete or incorrect concepts of operations with rational numbers. They try to apply memorized algorithms to operations with rational numbers, and these algorithms are frequently remembered incorrectly, if at all. Symbols are poorly understood and introduced too early. If the symbols are not understood, and students have attempted to memorize rules rotely, they have nothing to fall back on when their memories fail them. They are not able to judge when they have an incorrect answer from mental estimation, written computation, or a calculator.

To construct correct algorithms, students need to work on real problems using the manipulatives and to discuss their findings with each other. Much of the early work on the development of algorithms should be spent in small cooperative learning groups working on real problems and constructing meaning for each of the operations. For example, to introduce multiplication and division of fractions, you might begin by giving a group a problem such as determining the number of pizzas you need to serve the whole class, if each student wants $\frac{1}{4}$ of a pizza. Let them work with circular fraction pieces to determine the answer. Later determine the number of servings you can get from $3\frac{3}{4}$ pizzas if each serving is $\frac{1}{4}$ of a pizza. Which operations were involved in these problems? Ask the students to write their findings and share them with the entire class. Did each group work the problems in the same way? Which method did they prefer? In this way, the grouping may move from a whole class with the teacher introducing the problem and the students

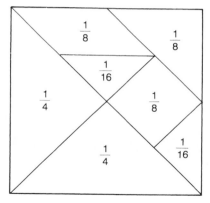

Figure 9–42   Tangram showing fractional amounts.

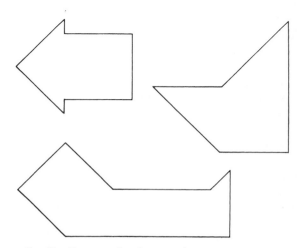

Figure 9–43   Tangram fraction puzzles.

discussing the background knowledge needed to get started, to small groups working cooperatively on the problems, back to the whole class listening to students in different groups explaining their methods of solution.

After the concepts have been constructed, other types of grouping may be used. Practice on the operations may be done in larger groups as students play a game to reinforce the computation skills, or individually as students work on puzzles and problems that require the application of these operations. At times, the teacher may need to work with a small group to remediate any difficulties they may be having, or the teacher may work with the talented students to challenge them to go beyond the explorations of the rest of the class.

COMMUNICATING LEARNING OF RATIONAL NUMBER OPERATIONS

Like the work with rational number concepts, the work with operations with rational numbers must include a heavy emphasis on verbal communication. The overreliance on rote memorization of symbol manipulation hinders students as they attempt to understand operations with rational numbers. As students work in groups solving problems that involve rational number operations, they should constantly be communicating with each other their understanding of the meaning of the problems. This oral communication frequently helps students make the necessary connections to the concepts they have already learned, such as operations with whole numbers and how they relate to operations with decimal fractions, or the connections between decimal fraction operations and operations with common fractions. When you circulate among the groups as they work on a problem, ask them how this problem relates to earlier ones.

In addition to the oral communication, ask the students to record what they are learning in daily logs and in work for their portfolios. Ask them to look for connections to earlier learning as well as for models that demonstrate what they have learned. Students should make use of concrete materials to exemplify meanings and use pictures in the logs and portfolios to illustrate the written messages.

CONNECTING AND REPRESENTING LEARNING OF RATIONAL NUMBER OPERATIONS

Mr. White's fifth-grade class is investigating the best offers on computer programs that they would like to purchase for their computer lab. They have found three companies that carry the software they want. The first company advertises a total price of $250 with a 10-percent charge for shipping and handling. The second company has a total price of $275 with free shipping and handling and a $25 discount for any purchases over $250. The third company offers the same programs for $300 with a 20-percent discount for schools, and a 5-percent charge for shipping and handling. The students are using the base ten blocks to help determine the best company for the software.

Ms. Willig's eighth-grade class is researching the best way to finance a new automobile. The class has split into teams of three or four, and each team is researching interest rates at different institutions. Jennifer's team has gone to three different car dealers to look at rates if the automobiles are financed at the dealership. Delisa's team has gone to two local banks and is comparing different rates based upon different down payments. Nathan's team has called three credit unions to compare the rates offered there, and Armondo's team is looking into finance companies. When all the data are collected each team will enter the information into a spreadsheet program and graph the results. The class will then analyze the information and make recommendations based on the results. Several students have indicated that they would like to include this information in their portfolios.

ASSESSING LEARNING OF RATIONAL NUMBER OPERATIONS

Use a number of means to assess the children as they add, subtract, multiply, and divide rational numbers. The textbook you use may contain both pre- and post-tests for the rational number chapters. Test the children before beginning a new unit to see which children already understand some of the concepts and which children need to begin at the beginning. If you use a test that pictures concrete materials and uses word problems, you will get a better idea of the children's abilities than if the test has only abstract number sentences for the children to complete. To get a better understanding of the children's levels, add a few questions on the concrete level.

As the children work through the unit, keep anecdotal records of their progress and note any areas of difficulty. Ask the children to explain their thinking processes as they work algorithms or manipulate concrete materials. Tell the children to record the algorithms they create and their solutions to problems in their math journals. They should keep examples of some of their best work in a portfolio.

Lembke and Reys (1994) found that students begin to develop intuitive concepts of percent before formal instruction and that formal instruction tended to make students' concepts of percent less intuitive and more rule driven, narrowing the variety of strategies that students use to solve percent problems. Be sure in your instruction of percent as well as other types of rational numbers that you build on students' intuitive concepts rather than break them down.

Check the children's written work for any patterns of errors. Some of the common errors children make are listed below. If you see children making any of these mistakes, talk to them about what they were thinking. You will often need to ask the children to return to the concrete models to correct any misunderstandings.

1. In addition and subtraction of common fractions, children add or subtract numerators and denominators.

2. To find like denominators, children add or subtract the same amount from the numerator and the denominator.

3. To multiply common fractions, children cross-multiply; that is, they multiply the numerator of one fraction by the denominator of the other.

4. To cancel when multiplying common fractions, children cancel two numbers from the numerators or two from the denominators.

5. Children cancel when dividing common fractions before they invert and multiply.

6. Children forget to invert when dividing common fractions, or they invert the dividend rather than the divisor.

7. When multiplying mixed numerals, children multiply the whole numbers, multiply the fractions, and then add the products together.

8. When adding or subtracting decimal fractions, children do not line up the decimal points.

9. When multiplying or dividing decimal fractions, children keep the same number of decimal places in the answer as appeared in one of the original numbers.

10. When multiplying or dividing a decimal fraction by a power of 10 or when converting a decimal to a percent or vice versa, children move the decimal point in the wrong direction.

If you see any of these errors, be sure to discuss them with the children. Do not just mark a problem incorrect without any feedback; that does not help the children make the necessary corrections. You will often find in talking to the children that they do not have a clear understanding of rational numbers or their usage in operations. If this is the case, return to the section on concept development in this chapter and use concrete materials with the children. Use word problems and materials that will help guide the children to correct the algorithms for themselves.

SOMETHING FOR EVERYONE

The physical models discussed in Chapters 8 and 9 should be used by all students initially when learning concepts and operations with rational numbers. Many teachers in the upper elementary grades seem to think that manipulative materials are for only the kindergartners and perhaps the first graders. They do not believe that older children need these "crutches." Indeed, many of the students in these grades also believe that the manipulatives are "baby stuff."

This is definitely not the case, however. Research has shown repeatedly that manipulatives are helpful for students of any age in learning mathematics and, specifically, in learning rational number concepts (Suydam, 1986). Visual, tactile, and kinesthetic learners need materials to develop a concrete understanding of the concepts. Students with bodily/kinesthetic strengths need to manipulate material such as region models, base ten blocks, Decimal Squares, Cuisenaire rods, and pattern blocks in order to internalize the concepts discussed in this chapter. They may have difficulty transferring this understanding to paper.

Allow children to devise their own methods of recording what they have learned with the materials. When children are presented with abstract rules or algorithms for such things as finding equivalent fractions, ordering common fractions, or converting a common fraction to a decimal fraction or a percent, be sure they have first modeled the rule with the concrete materials.

If the child is a verbal/linguistic learner, make sure the child is allowed to explain the rule to you after you explain it. For children who are visual learners, drawing models of the rational numbers is helpful. Make sure children have a variety of models, since some children may understand the concepts for a region model but not for a number-line model. Let these children draw pictures to explain why certain rules work, such as why you can multiply or divide the numerator and the denominator of a common fraction by the same number and not change the value of the fraction. Encourage children to write the algorithm or rule being demonstrated below the picture.

Some children who are able to manipulate symbols abstractly and perform the algorithms correctly may still not understand the meaning of the operations. Therefore, even children who seem to be performing well on an abstract level will benefit from being introduced to the materials.

Make sure to assist students in making the transition from the concrete materials to the abstract algorithms. They will probably not make this transfer automatically. Ask the children to write the algorithms as they manipulate the materials. Do not use the materials one day and expect the children to write the algorithms the next without the materials present. Let each child decide when he or she no longer needs to use the manipulatives. Children are usually good judges as to when the concrete knowledge has become internalized and the manipulation simply slows them down.

Depending on the students' maturational levels and abilities, a few children may only need to see the concepts demonstrated a few times to abstract the necessary information, while others will need to work individually with the materials for a long time as they work through the algorithms. Do not worry about covering all the pages in the textbook as the children learn. You are trying to teach children concepts, not a textbook.

If you find that some children are having difficulty, you may need to use a different concrete model. Some children may not be able to understand a length model such as the Cuisenaire rods or the number line but may be successful with an area model. Some children may not understand the concept of class inclusion or reversibility and may have difficulty with the part-whole model for common fractions. You must have a variety of models available for the children, and you should interview the children individually to determine the best method for teaching each one.

Children who can quickly understand and perform the operations with rational numbers will need more challenging work. Let them demonstrate that they can perform the algorithms correctly, but do not punish them by assigning more exercises from the book.

Many of the problem-solving and problem-creating activities described in this chapter are especially useful for gifted children. Be sure to encourage them to design problems and experiments of their own, but do not always expect them to work alone. They need interaction with their peers and with you. Here are a few other suggestions for avenues of exploration for promising students and any others who enjoy a challenge.

A C T I V I T I E S

Grades 3 – 5 and Grades 6 – 8

OBJECTIVE: to develop the concept of scientific notation.

1. In scientific notation, a number is written as a value from 1 to 10 multiplied by a power of 10.

For example, 3,245,654 can be written as 3.245654×10^6, and 0.000078 can be written as 7.8×10^{-5}.

Children should explore what happens to the exponent when you multiply and divide powers of 10. For example, $10^5 \times 10^6 = 10^{11}$; and $10^6 \div 10^5 = 10^1$. Ask the children to explain why these statements are true. They may wish to write out all the powers of 10 in expanded form and use the rules they know for multiplying and dividing by powers of 10.

Ask the children how this knowledge can help them estimate the product or quotient of two numbers written in scientific notation. What happens if you try to add or subtract two numbers written in scientific notation if the powers of 10 are not the same?

As children explore scientific notation, they can also explore the topic of significant digits. If you have one measurement accurate to four decimal places and another accurate to one decimal place, how many decimal places should you have in the sum, difference, product, or quotient of the two numbers?

OBJECTIVE: to understand why the invert-and-multiply algorithm works when dividing common fractions.

2. Children should constantly be challenged to discover why rules work, not just how they work. The invert-and-multiply rule for dividing common fractions is just one such example. Earlier in this chapter, we demonstrated this algorithm with numbers using the division concept of a fraction and the multiplicative inverse. Using the following, talented children could show that this algorithm would work for all rational numbers:

$$\frac{a}{b} \div \frac{c}{d} = \frac{\dfrac{a}{b}}{\dfrac{c}{d}} = \frac{\dfrac{a}{b} \times \dfrac{d}{c}}{\dfrac{c}{d} \times \dfrac{d}{c}}$$

$$= \frac{\dfrac{a}{b} \times \dfrac{d}{c}}{1} = \frac{a}{b} \times \frac{d}{c}$$

Another way to demonstrate the reason that the invert-and-multiply algorithm works is to use the fact that multiplication and division are inverse operations:

$$\frac{a}{b} \div \frac{c}{d} = n$$

Therefore,

$$\frac{c}{d} \times n = \frac{a}{b}$$

To solve for n, multiply both sides of the equation by the reciprocal of $\frac{c}{d}$:

$$\frac{d}{c} \times \frac{c}{d} n = \frac{d}{c} \times \frac{a}{b}$$

Because $\frac{d}{c} \times \frac{c}{d} = 1$, and 1 is the multiplicative identity,

$$n = \frac{d}{c} \times \frac{a}{b}$$

Use the commutative property of multiplication to show that this is the same as:

$$n = \frac{a}{b} \times \frac{d}{c}$$

Ask the children to explain other algorithms for rational numbers. For example, they could use the distributive property to show why, when multiplying two mixed numerals, you cannot just multiply the whole numbers together, multiply the proper fractions together, and then add the two products. Ask them to explain why cancellation works when multiplying or dividing common fractions. Encourage the children to discover and prove other rules for themselves.

Other topics children may be interested in exploring include operations with common fractions in other numeration systems, such as the Egyptian system. Reference books on the history of mathematics and mathematics activity books will give you and the children other ideas.

Many computer programs are designed to individualize instruction based on a child's knowledge and ability. If you have computers available, you should explore the possibilities. In any case, do not try to teach the whole class together from the book. That level of instruction will be inappropriate for most of your students.

FOR YOU AS A TEACHER: IDEAS FOR DISCUSSION AND YOUR PROFESSIONAL PORTFOLIO

This section is intended to provide you the opportunity to read, write, and reflect on key elements of this chapter. We list several discussion ideas. We hope that one or more of these ideas will prove interesting to you and that you will choose to investigate and write about the ideas. The results of your work should be considered as part of your professional portfolio. You might consider these two questions as guides for your writing: "What does the material in this chapter mean for you as a teacher?" or "How can what you are reading be translated into a teaching practice for you as a teacher?"

DISCUSSION IDEAS

1. Choose two common fractions such as $\frac{2}{3}$ and $\frac{3}{4}$, and write at least four different number stories using these numbers, each involving at least one of the operations of addition, subtraction, multiplication, and division. Trade problems with a friend, and use physical models, drawings, and equations to illustrate the solutions to each other's problems. Discuss your different methods of solution.

2. Develop an assessment for a fifth-, sixth-, or seventh-grade student on operations with rational numbers, and administer it to a student. Be sure to include application problems as well as computation. Analyze any errors that the student makes. Design a lesson plan based upon the results.

3. Look on the Internet for examples of problems involving operations with rational numbers that are used on a state, national, or international level, such as those from the Trends in International Mathematics and Science Study (TIMSS) (Weblink 9–1) and the National Assessment of Educational Progress (NAEP) (Weblink 9–2). What differences are there between problems given to elementary students and those designed for middle grade students? Report to the class some of your findings about the proficiency levels of the students tested.

4. Choose one of the pieces of software or one of the videos listed in the references and analyze how you might use it to teach concepts or skills with operations of rational numbers. Prepare a lesson plan using this technology in conjunction with physical models. Be sure to include the assessment that you will use to determine what concepts were learned.

5. A sixth-grade student says, "I have noticed that when we multiply, we always get a larger number and when we divide, we always get a smaller number." How would you respond to this? Be sure to include examples from whole numbers, fractions, and decimals. You might also think about integers in this explanation.

ADDITIONAL RESOURCES

REFERENCES

Behr, Merlyn J., Ipke Wachsmuth, and Thomas R. Post, "Construct a Sum: A Measure of Children's Understanding of Fraction Size," *Journal for Research in Mathematics Education,* 16, no. 2 (March 1985), 120–131.

Bennett, Albert B., Jr., *Decimal Squares.* Fort Collins, CO: Scott Resources, 1982.

Bennett, Albert B., Jr., and Patricia A. Davidson, *Fraction Bars*. Fort Collins, CO: Scott Resources, 1973.

Bradford, John, *Everything's Coming Up Fractions with Cuisenaire Rods*. New Rochelle, NY: Cuisenaire Co. of America, 1981.

Burns, Marilyn, *Teaching Arithmetic: Lessons for Introducing Fractions, Grades 4–5*. Sausalito, CA: Math Solutions, 2001.

Cook, Marci, *Fractions: Try-A-Tile*. Sunnyvale, CA: Creative Publications, 1988.

De Francisco, Carrie, and Marilyn Burns, *Teaching Arithmetic: Lessons for Decimals and Percents, Grades 5–6*. Sausalito, CA: Math Solutions, 2002.

Dossey, John A., Ina V. S. Mullis, Mary M. Lindquist, and Donald L. Chambers, *The Mathematics Report Card: Are We Measuring Up? Trends and Achievement Based on the 1986 National Assessment*. Princeton, NJ: Educational Testing Service, 1988.

Erickson, Sheldon, *Proportional Reasoning: AIMS Activities Grades 6–9*. Fresno, CA: AIMS Education Foundation, 2000.

Head, Debby, and Libby Pollett, *Count on Kids, Cluster One: Pattern Blocks Parts and Wholes*. Shelbyville, KY: bby Publications, 1994.

Hiebert, James, "Research Report: Decimal Fractions," *Arithmetic Teacher*, 34, no. 7 (March 1987), 22–23.

Holden, Linda, *The Fraction Factory*. Sunnyvale, CA: Creative Publications, 1986.

Jenkins, Lee, and Peggy McLean, *Fraction Tiles: A Manipulative Fraction Program*. Hayward, CA: Activity Resources, 1972.

Kouba, Vicky L., Catherine A. Brown, Thomas P. Carpenter, Mary M. Lindquist, Edward A. Silver, and Jane O. Swafford, "Results of the Fourth NAEP Assessment of Mathematics: Number, Operations, and Word Problems," *Arithmetic Teacher*, 35, no. 8 (April 1988), 14–19.

Lembke, Linda O., and Barbara J. Reys, "The Development of, and Interaction between, Intuitive and School-Taught Ideas about Percent," *Journal for Research in Mathematics Education*, 25, no. 3 (May 1994), 237–259.

Ma, Liping, *Knowing and Teaching Elementary Mathematics: Teachers' Understanding of Fundamental Mathematics in China and the United States (Studies in Mathematical Thinking and Learning)*, Mahwah, NJ: Erlbaum, 1999.

Mack, Nancy K., "Learning Fractions with Understanding: Building on Informal Knowledge," *Journal for Research in Mathematics Education*, 21, no. 1 (January 1990), 16–32.

Manfre, Edward, and Judy Vandegrift, *A Clear View of Decimals*. Nashua, NH: Delta Education, 1999.

———, *A Clear View of Fractions*. Nashua, NH: Delta Education, 1999.

———, *A Clear View of Percent*. Nashua, NH: Delta Education, 1999.

———, *A Clear View of Ratio and Proportion*. Nashua, NH: Delta Education, 1999.

McClain, Kay, ed., "Not One, but Six Fractions Equivalent to One-Third!" *Mathematics Teaching in the Middle School*, 3, no. 3 (November–December 1997), 213–214.

National Council of Teachers of Mathematics, *Principles and Standards for School Mathematics*. Reston, VA: NCTM, 2000.

Payne, Joseph N. & Ann E. Towsley, "Implications of NCTM Standards for Teaching Fractions & Decimals," *Arithmetic Teacher*, 37, no. 8 (April 1990), 23–26.

Post, Thomas R, "Fractions: Results and Implications from National Assessment," *Arithmetic Teacher*, 28, no. 8 (May 1981), 26–31.

Post, Thomas R., Merlyn J. Behr, and Richard Lesh, "Research-Based Observations about Children's Learning of Rational Number Concepts," *Focus on Learning Problems in Mathematics*, 8, no. 1 (Winter 1986), 39–48.

"Rational Numbers (Focus Issue)," *Arithmetic Teacher*, 31, no. 6 (February 1984).

Reys, Robert E., and Barbara J. Bestgen, "Teaching and Assessing Computational Estimation Skills," *Elementary School Journal*, 82 (November 1981), 117–127.

Roper, Ann, and Linda H. Charles, *Fraction Circles Plus Jobcards*. Sunnyvale, CA: Creative Publications, 1990. (includes Adding & Subtracting and Multiplying & Dividing)

———, *Fraction Squares Plus Jobcards*. Sunnyvale, CA: Creative Publications, 1990.

Suydam, Marilyn N., "Research Report: Manipulative Materials and Achievement," *Arithmetic Teacher*, 33, no. 6 (February 1986), 10, 32.

Thompson, Charles, "Teaching Division of Fractions with Understanding," *Arithmetic Teacher*, 26, no. 5 (January 1979), 24–27.

Vance, James, "Ordering Decimals and Fractions: A Diagnostic Study," *Focus on Learning Problems in Mathematics*, 8, no. 2 (Spring 1986), 51–59.

Vance, James H., "Estimating Decimal Products: An Instructional Sequence," in *Estimation and Mental Computation* (National Council of Teachers of Mathematics, 1986 Yearbook). Reston, VA: NCTM, 1986.

Williams, Susan E., and George W. Bright, *Investigating Mathematics with Calculators in the Middle Grades*. Austin, TX: Texas Instruments, 1998.

Zullie, Mathew E., *Fractions with Pattern Blocks*. Palo Alto, CA: Creative Publications, 1975.

CHILDREN'S LITERATURE

Cole, Joanna, *The Magic School Bus at the Waterworks*. New York: Scholastic, 1986.

TECHNOLOGY

Annenberg/CPB, *Teaching Math: A Video Library, K–4*. Boston: WGBH Educational Foundation, 1995.

Annenberg/CPB, *Mathematics Assessment: A Video Library, K–12*. Boston: WGBH Educational Foundation, 1995.

Broderbund, *Math Workshop Deluxe*. Novato, CA: Broderbund, 1998. (software)

Burns, Marilyn, *Mathematics for Middle School*. White Plains, NY: 1989. (series of videos and teacher's guides)

Davidson, *Math Blaster: Episode 1 — In Search of Spot*. Torrance, CA: Davidson, 1997. (software)

———, *Math Blaster: Episode 2 — Secret of the Lost City*. Torrance, CA: Davidson, 1997. (software)

———, *Mega Math Blaster*. Torrance, CA: Davidson, 1997. (software)

Edmark, *Mighty Math Calculating Crew*. Orlando, FL: Harcourt Brace, 1996. (software)

———, *Mighty Math Number Heroes.* Orlondo, FL: Harcourt Brace, 1996. (software)

HRM, *Algebra World CD-ROM.* Pleasantville, NY: Human Relations Media, 1998. (software)

Sunburst, *Gears.* Pleasantville, NY: Sunburst. 1995. (software)

———, *Tenth Planet Explores Math: Number Series Fraction Operations.* 1998. (software)

———, *Fraction Attraction II.* Pleasantville, NY: Sunburst, 1999. (software)

WEBLINKS

Weblink 9–1: Trends in International Mathematics and Science Study. http://www.nces.ed.gov/timss/

Weblink 9–2: National Center for Education Statistics (NCES). *NAEP Mathematics—Report Card for the Nation and the States: Findings from the National Assessment of Educational Progress.* http://nces.ed.gov/naep/

TEACHING AND LEARNING ALGEBRA

As you read the following pages, consider these guiding questions:

1. What is algebra, and why is it important for all students to know?

2. What are some of the algebraic reasoning skills and concepts that all elementary students should have to ensure a solid foundation for later algebraic ideas?

3. How might technology such as graphing calculators and computers be used to enhance the development of algebraic concepts?

4. How might an understanding of operations with whole and rational numbers be generalized to develop concepts of operations with variables and algebraic symbols?

5. What are some common misconceptions that students learning algebra might have, and what might you do to help students correct these?

Algebra

Instructional programs from prekindergarten through grade 12 should enable all students to:

Understand patterns, relations, and functions

Pre-K to 2

- sort, classify, and order objects by size, number, and other properties;
- recognize, describe, and extend patterns such as sequences of sounds and shapes or simple numeric patterns and translate from one representation to another;
- analyze how both repeating and growing patterns are generated.

Grades 3–5

- describe, extend, and make generalizations about geometric and numeric patterns;
- represent and analyze patterns and functions, using words, tables, and graphs.

Grades 6–8

- represent, analyze, and generalize a variety of patterns with tables, graphs, words, and, when possible, symbolic rules;
- relate and compare different forms of representation for a relationship;
- identify functions as linear or nonlinear and contrast their properties from tables, graphs, or equations.

Represent and analyze mathematical situations and structures using algebraic symbols

Pre-K to 2

- illustrate general principles and properties of operations, such as commutativity, using specific numbers;
- use concrete, pictorial, and verbal representations to develop an understanding of invented and conventional symbolic notations.

Grades 3–5

- identify such properties as commutativity, associativity, and distributivity and use them to compute with whole numbers;
- represent the idea of a variable as an unknown quantity using a letter or a symbol;
- express mathematical relationships using equations.

NCTM (2000), pp. 90, 158, 222. Reprinted by permission.

Grades 6–8

- develop an initial conceptual understanding of different uses of variables;
- explore relationships between symbolic expressions and graphs of lines, paying particular attention to the meaning of intercept and slope;
- use symbolic algebra to represent situations and to solve problems, especially those that involve linear relationships;
- recognize and generate equivalent forms for simple algebraic expressions and solve linear equations.

Use mathematical models to represent and understand quantitative relationships

Pre-K to 2

- model situations that involve the addition and subtraction of whole numbers, using objects, pictures, and symbols.

Grades 3–5

- model problem situations with objects and use representations such as graphs, tables, and equations to draw conclusions.

Grades 6–8

- model and solve contextualized problems using various representations, such as graphs, tables, and equations.

Analyze change in various contexts

Pre-K to 2

- describe qualitative change, such as a student's growing taller;
- describe quantitative change, such as a student's growing two inches in one year.

Grades 3–5

- investigate how a change in one variable relates to a change in a second variable;
- identify and describe situations with constant or varying rates of change and compare them.

Grades 6–8

- use graphs to analyze the nature of changes in quantities in linear relationships.

Draw an array below that shows $(x + 3) (x + 4)$. Use what you know about arrays for whole numbers and decimals such as 14×13 and 1.3×1.2. Explain how your array shows the product $x^2 + 7x + 12$.

REFLECTIONS AND REFINEMENT: How does the array you drew above compare to the one in the Math Journal problem at the beginning of Chapter 7 on page 189? How might you extend the meaning of your diagram to division and factoring? Compare your responses to those of others. What additional insights did this give you?

> The ideas included in the Algebra Standard constitute a major component of the school mathematics curriculum and help to unify it. (NCTM, 2000, p. 37)

We are all familiar with the word *algebra;* most of us probably took an algebra class or two in high school and perhaps another one or two in college. It has only been recently, however, that algebraic concepts have become an important part of an elementary and middle grade curricula. How would you define *algebra?* Take a few minutes to write down your definition of *algebra* before you move on with your reading.

Algebra is defined in the *Random House Word Menu* as the "theory and practice of arithmetic operations that uses symbols, especially letters, to represent unknown variables in equations" (Glazier, 1992, p. 143). Others define it more simply as generalized arithmetic. In this sense, algebra begins very early in the primary grades as students continue to develop the definition of mathematics in Chapter 1—namely, that mathematics is the science of pattern and order. The informal introduction to algebra in this chapter will continue to build upon the earlier concepts developed through the exploration of patterns.

> Algebra is frequently described as "generalized arithmetic," and indeed, algebraic thinking is a natural extension of arithmetical thinking. (Greenes, Cavanagh, Dacey, Findell, and Small, 2001, p. 1)

An understanding of algebra is increasingly important for success in our technological world, but algebra is frequently neglected in the mathematics curricula in the United States.

The *Third International Mathematics and Science Study* (Peak, 1996) showed that eighth-grade U.S. students performed at about the international average in algebra (defined as patterns, relations, expressions, and equations), although their performance was below several of the top-scoring countries such as Singapore, Japan, Hong Kong, Korea, the Russian Federation, and the Slovak Republic. This report also showed that topics taught in eighth grade U.S. mathematics classrooms were at a seventh grade level in comparison to other countries. Based on an examination of mathematics textbooks, it was found that especially in nonalgebra classes, there was a preoccupation with arithmetic at the expense of algebra, geometry, and measurement and that even in the algebra classes there was excessive attention to low-level knowledge and skills without sufficient attention to conceptual understanding and complex problem-solving (Silver, 1998, p. 5).

It is very important that middle grade students move beyond arithmetic and operations with rational numbers. The National Assessment of Educational Progress (NAEP) studies showed that in 2000, eighth-grade students who reported taking algebra or integrated mathematics scored significantly higher on the mathematics portion of the test than students who reported taking eighth-grade mathematics or pre-algebra. Approximately 37 percent of eighth graders took eighth-grade mathematics, while 31 percent took pre-algebra and 25 percent took algebra and an additional 6 percent took a math course above algebra I. In 1996, 8 percent of 17-year-olds reported that the highest mathematics course taken in high school was general mathematics or pre-algebra, and 13 percent had taken either pre-calculus or calculus. By 2000, 14 percent of high school seniors reported taking pre-calculus, and an additional 12 percent reported taking calculus. Not surprisingly, NAEP mathematics scores rose with the number of higher-level math courses taken (see Weblink 10–1). Even with the rising level of mathematics courses and mathematics test scores, international test scores for high school mathematics students in the United States continue to lag behind those of students in many other countries.

Robert Moses (Moses and Cobb, 2001), a civil rights leader in the 1960s, compares the importance of taking higher-level mathematics courses to the importance of the civil rights movement. He notes that the level of mathematics courses taken is one of the main indicators of successful transition into college and other high-level postsecondary endeavors. He compares telling students that they are not capable of understanding complex mathematics to telling blacks that they were not capable of voting. He has started a math literacy program, the Algebra Project, to prepare all students for high-level mathematics and thus high-level careers.

It is critical that all students be well prepared for algebra and other advanced mathematics before they complete middle school. In this chapter, we will focus on activities that are designed to help students develop these algebraic reasoning and thinking skills; recognizing, extending, and generalizing patterns and using models, symbols, variables, and equations to describe patterns, generalizations, and relationships.

MAKING SENSE OF ALGEBRAIC CONCEPTS

Patterns and Relationships

Understanding patterns, relations, and functions is noted in the NCTM *Principles and Standards* as one of the critical aspects of algebraic reasoning that should begin in preschool and continue throughout the K–12 mathematics curricula. The human brain is designed to make sense of patterns and even has a brain wave, the P-300 wave, that has been shown to search out patterns in the world around us. This aspect of algebra is the perfect place to strengthen that part of our brains, beginning with preschool children. (For more information on ways to strengthen and enhance brain functioning, see Weblinks 10–2, 10–3, and 10–4.) This ability to see patterns and make generalizations builds on the definition of *algebra* as generalized arithmetic.

Children should have experiences with both repeating and growing patterns. We will begin with activities for repeating patterns and then extend these to growing patterns.

A C T I V I T I E S

Pre-Kindergarten – Grade 2

OBJECTIVE: to recognize, extend, and generalize repeating patterns.

1. Ask the students to make a pattern using materials such as the color tiles. For example, students might have something like Figure 10–1. Ask students to continue the pattern for several more tiles and then ask them to generalize the pattern with questions such as the following:

- If this pattern continues, what color will the 20th tile be? How could you figure this out?
- What if we had 101 tiles following this same pattern? What color would the 101st tile be? How do you know?
- What if the pattern used letters instead of colors, such as A, B, A, B, A, B . . .? How could you figure out what the 20th letter in the pattern is? What about the 101st letter?

2. Extend the pattern of color tiles in two directions as in Figure 10–2. Ask the students questions such as the following:

- If all the tiles are blue and yellow and follow the same pattern, what color would the tile with the A (or B or C) be? How do you know?

Extend the students' reasoning about these patterns with questions such as the following:

- What if you use three colors? How will that change the patterns?

Figure 10–1 Simple repeating pattern with colors.

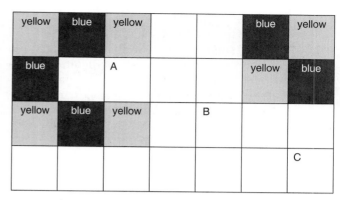

Figure 10–2 Repeating color pattern in two dimensions.

- What if you repeat the colors such as blue, yellow, yellow, blue, yellow, yellow? What color would the 20th tile be? How do you know?

3. Give each student a page of inch grid paper (you may copy the grid paper from Appendix B) and change from colors to words in a pattern. Ask each child to repeatedly write his or her first name in the grid. For example, Tyler might have something like Figure 10–3. Ask what letter will be in the last box on the page if this pattern continues. Can you figure this out without completing the entire page? What if the name is Dan or Virginia or Raphael? How could you predict the last letter for those names?

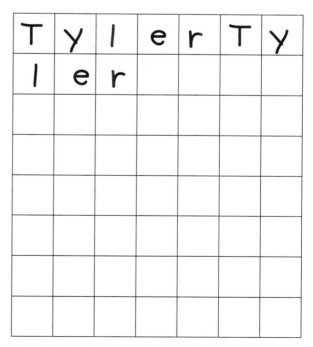

Figure 10–3 Repeating pattern of student's name in two-dimensions.

Young children sometimes have a lot of experience with repeating patterns. They see repeating patterns all around them in such things as wallpaper borders and the tiles on the floor, and it may be difficult for them to extend their understanding of repeating patterns to understanding growing patterns. The following activities are designed to give children experience with growing patterns.

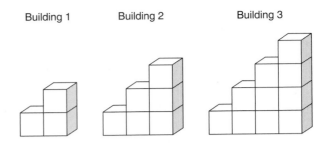

Figure 10–5 More complex growing pattern using interlocking cubes.

A C T I V I T I E S

Pre-Kindergarten – Grade 2

OBJECTIVE: to recognize, extend, and generalize growing patterns.

1. Give the students a set of interlocking cubes and ask them to build the structures shown in Figure 10–4. Ask them questions such as the following:

- How many blocks did it take to make the first building? The second building? The third building?
- If this pattern continues, how many blocks do you think it would take to make the 10th building? The 20th building? What about the 100th building? How do you know?

Encourage students to come up with a general rule. Some students might just say you have to add two each time, and they might continue to count by twos until they get to the answer. Other students might say that there are two cubes for each building number plus the one cube in the beginning. Encourage students to state the rules in their own words and to discuss their reasoning with one another.

Grades 3 – 5

OBJECTIVE: to recognize, extend, and generalize growing patterns.

1. Extend the difficulty of the problem for students who show a good understanding. Again, give the students a set of interlocking cubes and ask them to build the structures shown in Figure 10–5. Again, ask the students questions such as these:

- How many blocks did it take to make the first building? The second building? The third building?
- If this pattern continues, how many blocks do you think it would take to make the 10th

building? The 20th building? What about the 100th building?

Ask students to discuss how they determined these answers. Note that this problem is much more difficult than one that adds the same number of cubes each time. This is a pattern of triangular numbers, similar to the pattern of handshakes at the beginning of Chapter 4. It is easier for students to find that you add one more block each time than the time before than it is to realize that to find the total number of blocks you can take the building number, multiply it by the building number plus 1, and divide the answer by 2 [(n) $(n + 1)/2$].

2. After the students have had a number of experiences with patterns using physical models such as cubes, tiles, and pattern blocks, ask them to continue patterns such as the following:

$$4, 7, 10, 13, \text{_____}, \text{_____}, \text{_____}$$

After students have continued the pattern for several more instances, ask them what the 10th number in the pattern would be? What would the 20th number be? What about the 100th number? How do you know? Can you give a general rule? Note that the students might say that each time you add 3 and you just keep adding 3 until you get to the number that you want. Other students might say that to find the second number, you take 2 times 3 and add 1 and to get the third number, you take 3 times 3 and add 1, so to get the 20th number, you can take 20 times 3 and add 1. Students who have had previous experience with problems like this might even be able to represent this as $3n + 1$, where n is the number of the term. Don't rush students to writing algebraic expressions for this, however. Encourage them to express the rules in their own words.

> In general, if students engage extensively in symbolic manipulations before they develop a solid conceptual foundation for their work, they will be unable to do more than mechanical manipulations. The foundation for meaningful work with symbolic notation should be laid over a long time. (NCTM, 2000, p. 39)

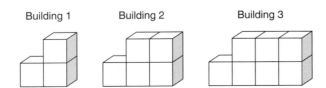

Figure 10–4 Simple growing pattern using interlocking cubes.

In addition to numerous experiences with repeating and growing patterns with physical models and with number sequences, students should look for patterns in everyday situations. The following activities are designed to give students experiences with algebraic reasoning related to their daily experiences.

A C T I V I T I E S

Grades 3 – 5

OBJECTIVE: to identify, describe, and extend patterns involving numerical situations.

1. Read a story involving transportation such as *Curious George Rides a Bike* (Rey, 1952), and ask the children to make a table showing the number of wheels and the number of bicycles such as in Table 10–1.

Completing the table would be good skill practice but does not require much complex reasoning. Students might use the constant feature on the calculator to add two each time to complete the second row on the table. To encourage deeper reasoning, ask the children to study the table and describe any patterns they notice. They should fill in the missing numbers on the table and explain how they knew where to put each number.

After the children have completed the table, ask them to make up a list of questions that could be answered by studying the table. Encourage them to include some questions that would require inferences where the answer is not on the table itself, such as "Would the number 23 appear as the number of wheels if the pattern were continued? Why or why not?" Let the children exchange questions with a classmate and try to answer them.

After the children have had experience with the patterns on the table for bicycles, ask them to make a similar chart for tricycles such as Table 10–2.

After the children have completed this chart, comparing it to the chart for the bicycles offers them greater opportunities to search for patterns and make generalizations. Are there any numbers that appear as the number of wheels on the bicycle chart that do not appear on the tricycle chart? Are there any numbers that appear as the number of wheels on the tricycle chart that do not appear

TABLE 10 – 2 Relationship between Number of Wheels and Number of Tricycles

Number of tricycles	1	2		4	5		...	25
Number of wheels	3	6	9			18	...	

on the bicycle chart? How do these numbers compare? What numbers appear on both charts?

Older students might expand this into a study of relatively prime numbers and common multiples. This question could also be expanded to questions such as "I have 25 wheels and they are all on either bicycles or tricycles. How many of each cycle might I have?" Children are often surprised to find that this question has several correct answers. Asking students to develop a method of finding all the combinations of bicycles and tricycles that have a total of 25 wheels gives them an opportunity to use an organized list or another strategy that involves patterns and predictions.

Encourage students who have a good understanding of patterns and generalizations to create other questions of their own such as: "What if we also look at the number of wheels on a car (or a unicycle)? Do we get the same answers to the earlier questions? Why or why not? How many combinations of vehicles are possible for 25 wheels if they can be cars, unicycles, bicycles, or tricycles?"

OBJECTIVE: to identify, describe, and extend patterns involving money.

2. A typical number story that you might see in a book shows four dimes and three pennies and asks students to find the total amount of money. To make this problem more interesting and to encourage deeper reasoning, use a book involving money such as *A Chair for My Mother* or *How the Second Grade Got $8,205.50 to Visit the Statue of Liberty,* and then pose a problem that encourages students to look for patterns. One such problem is: "I have 43 cents in my pocket. I have only dimes and pennies. What coins might I have?" If the children have done the previous problem, they might expect that again there are several correct answers. If children come up with only one possibility, you might suggest that they search for others. Challenge them to find all the possibilities. One of the ways that they might do this is by using a chart such as the following:

Dimes	Pennies	Total
0	43	43¢
1	33	43¢
2	23	43¢
3	13	43¢

TABLE 10 – 1 Relationship between Number of Wheels and Number of Bicycles

Number of bicycles	1	2		4	5		...	25
Number of wheels	2	4	6		12		...	

After children have analyzed the chart and have made some predictions about the total number of combinations possible, encourage them to ask other related questions. If they have trouble getting started, use some of the questions suggested in Chapter 4 for encouraging students to dig more deeply into problems such as why, why not, what if, and will that always work? In this case, students might notice that as the number of dimes decreases by 1, the number of pennies increases by 10 and ask if that will always be the case. They can then discuss why that will happen. Other questions students might ask include: What would happen to the number of combinations if there were nickels as well as dimes and pennies? What if there were also quarters? What if there were 48 cents or 97 cents?

What if you know I have 5 coins? What is the least amount of money I might have? What is the greatest amount? How many different combinations of money might I have?

What if I have 5 coins and 33 cents; how many possible combinations of coins might I have? Why is there only one possible combination of coins for this problem?

Encourage students to write their questions and then trade with their friends to solve them. Ask them to discuss the patterns that they noticed and the strategies that they used in their problem solving.

Grades 3 – 5 and Grades 6 – 8

OBJECTIVE: to extend and generalize proportional reasoning.

1. Students learning concepts of proportional reasoning might be asked to solve number stories such as "Sue can buy gum at 8 pieces for 3 cents and candy at 5 pieces for 2 cents. How much will it cost to buy 24 pieces of gum and 10 pieces of candy?" A problem that would require deeper reasoning is the following: "Chris and Tyler are pricing small wrapped candy. At the first store, they can get 8 pieces of candy for 3 cents. At the second store, they can get 5 pieces of the same candy for 2 cents. Which store has the better buy?" As students develop a variety of methods for solving the second problem, their understanding of proportional reasoning grows. One student may divide 8 by 3 and 5 by 2 to find the number of pieces of candy per cent. Another may divide 3 by 8 and 2 by 5 to find the number of cents per pieces of candy. Another may find how much of each type of candy could be bought for 6 cents. Yet another may find the price of 40 pieces of candy at each store. For problems such as this, students should be asked to compare and discuss a variety of methods and then asked to generalize their findings to other proportional reasoning problems. Other common proportional reasoning problems involve finding the best paying job per hour when rates are given for varying amounts of time or finding the best car mileage or the best crop yield when given yields and dimensions of fields. In each of these problems, the same methods used to solve the candy problem can be generalized and discussed in the new setting.

OBJECTIVE: to identify, describe, and extend patterns and make generalizations using money.

2. Older students also need experience working with money. A typical problem for intermediate students might give them the price of several objects and ask them to find the total price such as: "Dan has decided to buy tops, toy planes, and/or stuffed animals for the school fair. He must spend according to the following prices:

Tops	$ .50 apiece
Toy planes	$ 1.00 apiece
Stuffed animals	$10.00 apiece

If he buys 15 tops, 35 planes, and 50 stuffed animals, how much will he spend?"

A problem that would encourage deeper reasoning and lead to generalizations would be the following: "Latisha has exactly $100 to buy toys for the local children's charity and wants to buy exactly 100 toys. She has decided to buy tops, toy planes, and/or stuffed animals. She must spend according to the following prices:

Tops	$ .50 apiece
Toy planes	$ 1.00 apiece
Stuffed animals	$10.00 apiece

What combinations might she buy?"

Notice that this problem required only a slight change from the earlier problem but encourages far more reasoning and generalizations. Ask the students to find more than one answer to this. If they can do that, ask them to find all possible solutions and to convince you that no others are possible. Put these solutions in a chart and look for patterns. What generalizations might be made? What other questions might be asked to further extend this problem?

Variables, Functions, Equations, and Inequalities

> When children are encouraged to describe and represent quantities in different ways, they learn to recognize equivalent representations and expand their ability to use symbols to communicate their ideas. (Greenes et al., 2001, p. 3)

Very early in their school experiences, young children learn to represent mathematical situations using symbols for concepts of numbers (0, 1, 2, . . .), operations ($+$, $-$, $\div$, $\times$), and equality or inequality ($=$, $<$, $>$, etc.). Many of these are used to represent a specific situation. For example, students might write $7 + 8 = 15$ to represent a typical word problem such as "Kayla has 7 pieces of red candy and 8 pieces of yellow candy. How much candy does she have altogether?" All too often, problems such as this appear at the end of a chapter on addition, and children simply learn rotely to take the numbers in the word problem and add them together. The introduction of algebraic reasoning might be used to change specific, straightforward, skill-oriented problems into more interesting puzzle-type problems that encourage students to think rather than simply apply memorized algorithms. A simple change in the word problems might be all that is needed to encourage this algebraic reasoning about relationships among quantities and ways in which these quantities change relative to each other. The candy problem might be changed to "Julio has a bag of candy with only red and yellow candy in it. He has 15 pieces of candy altogether. There are twice as many pieces of red candy as yellow candy. How many red pieces and how many yellow pieces does Julio have?" Students in a formal algebra class might represent this as $x + y = 15$ and $2y = x$ where x represents the number of pieces of red candy and y represents the number of pieces of yellow candy. However, when algebraic reasoning is first introduced, students might use a variety of strategies to solve this problem, including guess and test.

Another simple change in the original problem designed to give students a deeper understanding of patterns and relationships would be the following question: "Katrina has 15 pieces of candy. Some are red and some are yellow. How many different combinations of red and yellow candy can you find that would give you a total of 15 pieces? How might you convince someone that you have found all the possible combinations?"

Whenever possible in your teaching, pose problems and questions such as those described with the 5 *W*s and an *H* for investigative mathematicians to encourage students to think deeply about the mathematics. Challenge students to use variables and other mathematical symbols along with a variety of models and other representations to describe the situations.

After students have experience writing mathematical symbols to represent relationships and equations, present problems that challenge students to describe a function.

A **function** is defined as a rule or process that sets up a correspondence between a first set (the **domain**) and a second set (the **range**) such that each element in the first set corresponds with *one and only one* element in the second set. Notice that this is not necessarily a one-to-one correspondence. A statement such as $y = x^2$ is a function of x, but it is not a function of y. For each x, there is one and only one y, but there are 2 x's for each y. For example, for $x = ^-3$, the only y is 9, but for $y = 9$, there are two possible x's, $x = 3$ and $x = ^-3$.

ACTIVITIES

Pre-Kindergarten – Grade 2

OBJECTIVE: to develop the concept of a function through the use of an input-output machine.

1. Guess My Rule is played by pairs of students using an input-output machine and the attribute blocks. Ask one student to be in charge of placing blocks in the input of the machine and ask the second student to think of a secret rule, such as "change only the color of the block." After the first student places a block in the input of the machine, the second student finds a block that fits his or her rule and places this block in the output of the machine. Try this several times, until the first student can guess the secret rule. Discuss whether more than one output was possible for each input. Ask the students to trade roles and make up a new rule. Was more than one output possible this time?

After playing the game with attribute blocks, play Guess My Rule with numbers and operations. Calculators are also useful in this activity. Students may place numeral cards in the input and output. The first student should choose a numeral card to place in the input while the second student decides on a secret rule. Begin with rules that use only one operation. The second student should place the numeral card that shows the result of the operation in the output. Do this several times, until the first student can guess the secret rule. Again, discuss whether more than one output was possible for each input. Ask the children to trade roles and choose another rule. Encourage them to discuss how they determined the rule each time.

Calculators from Texas Instruments such as the TI 10 and the TI 15 have a problem-solving feature that present students with simple operations and challenges them to find the missing numbers such as $7 + ? = 15$. Students guess the number to fill in for the ? and are told whether their responses are correct or are too large or too small.

OBJECTIVE: to develop the concept of a function using input-output machines.

Grades 3 – 5 and Grades 6 – 8

1. Use a computer applet such as the Number Cruncher game on Weblink 10–5, where the computer will generate simple input-output machines for the students to play a Guess My Rule game against the computer. A similar, even more challenging program is the Mystery Number game on Weblink 10–6 in the section on Patterns in Numbers. This site has a number of excellent activities for developing algebraic reasoning, especially students' abilities to recognize and generalize patterns with numbers, words, and attributes. In the Mystery Number game, the student chooses two numbers, and the computer performs a mystery operation that the student is challenged to discover. For example, the student might choose the numbers 3 and 4 and the computer might say 7. You might think that the operation is simple addition, but you decide to input the numbers 1 and 2 and the computer gives you and answer of ⁻3. You ask for more information by asking the computer to calculate an answer for 0 and 1 and you get a response of ⁻5. With each response, you have a choice of being tested on the rule or inputting two new numbers for more information. With a new input of 0 and 0, you again get a response of ⁻5. After a few more inputs, you ask the computer to test you and it gives you the numbers 13 and 7. You have decided that the function is to multiply the two numbers together and then subtract 5, so you tell the computer that the answer is 86 and are told that you have indeed figured out the rule of $a \times b - 5$.

Another problem-solving program that is available for either the computer or for graphing calculators is *Puzzle Tanks* (O'Brien, 1997). This game requires that students find the correct amounts of tank trucks to fill or empty tanks to reach a target amount.

OBJECTIVE: to develop the concept of a function through the use of a function machine and a table.

2. Draw a function machine and a table for recording inputs and outputs as in Figure 10–6 on an overhead transparency and put the transparency on the overhead projector for the students to use. Ask one student to write down a secret rule for the function machine on the transparency. Keep the rule hidden.

You may wish to begin with a rule involving only one operation, such as "subtract 7," but the activity becomes much more challenging if you allow more than one operation per rule, such as "subtract 7 and then multiply by 2." The other students will attempt to guess

the rule by determining what happens when different numbers are put into the function machine.

This is a good activity for using calculators. After the secret function has been written on the function machine and covered, the other students name an input, which is then written on the chart by the student with the secret rule. This student then puts the input into the calculator, performs the function, and records the output on the chart. This continues for several different inputs until the other students are confident that they know the secret rule. To avoid giving away the secret rule too early, when a student believes that he or she knows the rule, that student should predict the output for a given input, but not tell the rule. When most students can predict the output for a given input, ask the first student who predicted the output to tell the rule. If correct, this student is the next one to write a secret function. Figure 10–6 shows the inputs and outputs for the rule "divide by 2 and then subtract 3." Notice that if the game allows division and subtraction, you will frequently have outputs that are integers and other rational numbers, even if all the inputs are whole numbers.

> A thorough understanding of variable develops over a long time, and it needs to be grounded in extensive experience. (NCTM, 2000, p. 39)

The use of variables is another concept vital to the understanding of algebra. Algebra is often thought of by students as the area of mathematics that uses a lot of letters instead of numbers. These letters, however, are often not very well understood. Today, we generally use the term **variable** to mean a symbol for an element in a replacement set. This frequently does involve using a letter to stand for a number, but letters may also refer to points in geometry such as $\overline{AB} = \overline{BC}$, propositions in logic such as $p \wedge q$, or a matrix in algebra. The symbol used may not even be a letter. For example, $3 + x = 7$, $3 + \square = 7$, and $3 + ? = 7$ all have the same meaning, but the variable changes from x to $\square$ to ?. In this context, students have been studying variables since they began to work with symbols and operations. Primary and intermediate-level teachers should begin to use n or x to acquaint students with the idea of a variable and to help make the bridge to algebra, which formalizes these concepts. It is important that students in the middle grades continue to have many informal experiences with variables and begin to learn more formal symbolization.

A symbol or variable may stand for one or more numbers, which are called the values of the variable.

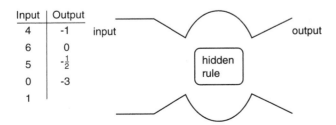

Input	Output
4	-1
6	0
5	$-\frac{1}{2}$
0	-3
1	

Figure 10–6 Function machine and table for Guess My Rule game.

The term *variable* may be used to mean a symbol that may have *two* or more values during a particular discussion, such as *area = l • w,* thus the concept of variance underlying the term variable. However, a variable may have only one value and students may have difficulty understanding why the *c* in $5c = 20$ is called a variable when the only amount it can stand for to make this a true statement is 4.

Another difficulty that students may have in working with variables is that they frequently think of a variable as a letter that stands for one particular number as in the Peanuts cartoon in Figure 10–7. If they see $2s + 5 = 9$ and $2c + 5 = 9$, they think that the *s* and the *c* must stand for different numbers. They may believe that it is all right to use *l* to stand for length and *w* to stand for width, but you cannot use *t* to stand for length. The variable *t* must stand for time, or turkeys, or tubas, or tambourines, but not length or width or dogs.

These misconceptions about using variables emphasize the importance of giving students a number of different experiences with variables in the middle grades so that they can build their own concepts. Just as a toddler may not understand that potatoes may be mashed, baked, or french fried and still remain potatoes, students in the middle grades need to experience variables in many different contexts before they begin to understand all the ways variables can be used.

One very important part of algebra is the solution of equations. Simple equations such as $x + 3 = 5$ might be introduced as early as first grade, but variables such as *x* are usually not used at this early stage. This type of equation commonly is introduced as an open sentence with an empty box used to denote where the missing number should go. Instead of $x + 3 = 5$, a primary textbook might show $\square + 3 = 5$. To **solve an equation,** you must find replacements for the variables that make the left side of the equation equal to the right side. For example, if you wish to solve the equation $x + 3 = 5$, you must find a value for *x* that will make this a true statement. In this case, we know the answer is 2, simply because we recognize the addition combination. It is not always that easy to solve an equation, however. The

following are a few examples of ways to introduce students to the idea of solving equations. Encourage the students to think of other examples of their own.

Pre-Kindergarten – Grade 2

OBJECTIVE: to use everyday situations to introduce the concept of writing and solving equations.

1. Begin the introduction to solving equations using number stories such as: There were 8 lizards playing in the sunshine. After a while, some of the lizards decided to crawl under the rock for a nap. Then there were only 5 lizards playing in the sunshine. How many lizards are under the rock?

The equation for this might be represented as $5 + n = 8$, where *n* represents the number of lizards under the rock.

Encourage the children to solve the problem using methods that make sense to them. Some children might decide to draw pictures of the lizards, others might act the problem out with counters, and others might reason through the problem and solve it mentally. After the children have solved the problem, let them share their methods of solution with each other.

After children are comfortable with simple problems such as these, move on to problems that require more reasoning, such as: Laronda saw 18 lizards playing on a rock. Some were brown and some were green. There were twice as many green lizards as brown lizards. How many of each color were there?

Again, students should select methods of solution that make sense to them. Some students will choose to use physical models for the problem, some might draw pictures, some might use guess and check, and advanced students might try using equations. If *b* is used for the number of brown lizards, then $2b$ would be the number of green lizards and the equation might be:

$$b + 2b = 18$$

Figure 10–7

Problem 2.1

In this problem, you will explore this question: If a square pool has sides of length s feet, how many tiles are needed to form the border?

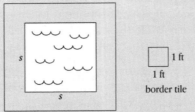

A. Make sketches on grid paper to help you figure out how many tiles are needed for the borders of square pools with sides of length 1, 2, 3, 4, 6, and 10 feet. Record your results in a table.

B. Write an equation for the number of tiles, N, needed to form a border for a square pool with sides of length s feet.

C. Try to write at least one more equation for the number of tiles needed for the border of the pool. How could you convince someone that your expressions for the number of tiles are equivalent?

■ **Problem 2.1 Follow-Up**

1. Make a table and a graph for each equation you wrote in part a of Problem 2.1. Do the table and the graph indicate that the equations are equivalent? Explain.

2. Is the relationship between the side length of the pool and the number of tiles linear, quadratic, exponential, or none of these? Explain your reasoning.

3. a. Write an equation for the area of the pool, A, in terms of the side length, s.
   b. Is the equation you wrote linear, quadratic, exponential, or none of these? Explain.

4. a. Write an equation for the combined area of the pool and its border, C, in terms of the side length, s.
   b. Is the equation you wrote linear, quadratic, exponential, or none of these? Explain.

Figure 10–8 From *Connected Mathematics Say it with Symbols* © 2002 by Michigan State University, Glenda Lappan, James T. Fey, William M. Fitzgerald, Susan N. Friel, and Elizabeth Phillips. Published by Pearson Education, Inc., publishing as Pearson Prentice Hall. Used by permission.

The activity shown in Figure 10–8 is from an eighth-grade lesson on equivalent expressions titled "Say It with Symbols" from the middle grades *Connected Mathematics* program. In this investigation, students use square tiles to investigate the border of a square pool. They are encouraged to find the border of a number of pools of differing sizes beginning with side lengths of 1, 2, and 3 units and then extending to pools with sides of length *s*. They are instructed to find the perimeter in a number of different ways and then to determine whether the different expressions are equivalent. Some of their solutions are expected to be $4s + 4$ (four sides and the four corners); $4(s + 1)$ (Four sides each with a length of $s + 1$); $4 (s + 2) - 4$ (four sides with a length of $s + 2$ minus the four corners that have been counted twice); and $2 (s + 2) + 2s$ (two sides with a length of $s + 2$ and two sides with a length of *s*). It is also expected that students will find their own solutions.

After students have found a number of different expressions, they make a table and graph of the information to determine whether the expressions are equivalent. This will lead to a discussion of properties of operations such as the distributive property to determine symbolically that these are equivalent. Note that these students previously have worked with graphs, tables, and equations to look at relationships and to determine whether equations are linear, quadratic, or exponential. They use that knowledge here to explain that the borders give linear equations but when the area of the pool is combined with the border, the equation then becomes quadratic.

Earlier in this unit, students explore rules for order of operations and later in this unit, they use mathematical properties to rewrite expressions and solve equations. Throughout this *Connected Mathematics* program, which was developed with the support by the National Science Foundation to implement the recommendations from the National Council of Teachers of Mathematics, students are encouraged to make sense of mathematics by building concrete models, discussing their reasoning with peers, and asking and answering questions related to the problems that they encounter. Assessment for each lesson includes application, connection, and extension problems, and each unit contains suggestions for culminating projects and unit exams.

Students might reason that $b + 2b = 3b$ and that if $3b = 18$, then b must be 6. Once the number of brown lizards is found, this number can be doubled or subtracted from 18 to find the number of green lizards. It is not important to teach formal methods of solving abstract equations in the elementary grades; the emphasis should be on making sense of the words and translating them into symbols and equations that represent this sense making.

The references at the end of this chapter list several books for elementary students to give them early practice in algebraic reasoning. Some of these are written for students as young as first grade. If work with algebraic reasoning is begun this early, students should develop a solid basis for later, more formal algebraic work.

Grades 3–5

OBJECTIVE: to use a balance to introduce the concept of solving equations.

1. For this activity, you will need a pan balance, some inch or 2-centimeter cubes, and a very lightweight paper or opaque plastic bag. (It should be light enough that its presence is not noticeable on the balance. If you cannot find a bag that is light enough, you can hold a screen in front of the balance to hide the secret number of cubes.) Have one student put a secret number of cubes in the bag. This may be named x cubes; or, perhaps, j cubes, if Joanna put the cubes in the bag. Place the bag on the left pan along with two other cubes that can be seen by the students. Now put enough cubes on the right pan to balance the left. Figure 10–9 shows a balance with the bag and 2 cubes on the left pan and 6 cubes on the right pan.

Ask the students to write an equation describing what they see. They might write $j + 2 = 6$. How can they tell how many cubes are in the bag? It would be easy if the bag were the only thing on the left pan. If they subtract two cubes from the left pan, what must they do to the right pan to keep the balance? Try it. Now you have only the bag on the left pan and four cubes on the right. This can be represented by $j = 4$. Look in the bag to see if you were right.

Ask other children to put different numbers of cubes in the bag and in plain sight on the left pan. Put cubes on the right pan to balance the left side and then determine the number of cubes in the bag. Do you always have to do the same thing to both pans to keep the balance? What if the bag is on the right side? Can you solve the equation $4 = x + 1$ in the same way that you solved the equation $x + 1 = 4$?

Try putting the same number of cubes in two bags along with another number of cubes in plain sight on one pan. What would you do if you saw $2c + 1 = 9$, as in Figure 10–10? If you begin by subtracting 1 cube from each pan, you then have $2c = 8$. Will the pans balance if you subtract 2 from each side? You cannot subtract 2 cubes from the side with the bags unless you open a bag. Can you take half the objects off each side? Yes, you can take off one of the bags and 4 of the cubes. What is left now? Is this the correct answer?

OBJECTIVE: to use a balance to introduce the concept of inequalities.

2. A balance may also be used to introduce the concept of inequalities. Repeat the activity above, only this time, put one too many cubes on one of the pans. Discuss with the children how you can tell by looking at the balance which side is heavier. Review the use of the greater than and less than signs. Does the balance change when you do the same thing to each side? Again, work the problem until you have only one bag on one of the pans. Ask the students to write the equation for each step. Leave the balance in the learning center so that students can pose different problems for each other.

As students learn to analyze mathematical situations and structures, challenge them to discover rules for operations that might help them better understand

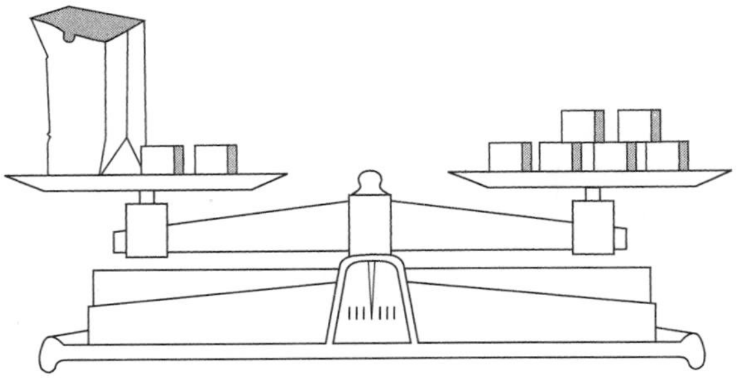

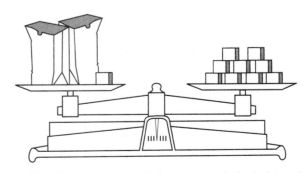

Figure 10–9 Using a pan balance to solve simple equations.

Figure 10–10 Solving a slightly more sophisticated equation using a pan balance.

computation. This is a good time to give students opportunities to deepen their understanding of the commutative, associative, and distributive properties and to apply them to a wide range of examples ranging from operations with whole numbers and rational numbers to operations involving symbolic algebra. For example, if students have a deep understanding that $a(b + c) = ab + ac$, they should be able to use this to help them mentally compute such varied problems as $8 \times 17 = 8 \times 10 + 8 \times 7$ and $3 \times 2\frac{1}{2}$ as $3 \times 2 + 3 \times \frac{1}{2}$ and $x(4y + 6)$ as $4\,xy + 6x$.

As students work with properties of operations, they will probably encounter equations such as $4 + 2 \times 7$. If they put this into their calculators, they may find that some calculators give an answer of 42 while others answer 18. Students should explore what is happening in these instances.

A C T I V I T I E S

Grades 3–5 and Grades 6–8

OBJECTIVE: to explore order of operations on different calculators.

1. Use different calculators to determine if you always get the same answer when working out equations. Try equations such as $3 + 4 \times 2 =$ _____ and $2 + 3 \div 4 =$ _____. Discuss with the students the difference between calculators that work the exercise in the order in which you put in the numbers and ones that use algebraic logic. If you have parentheses on your calculator, explore what happens when you use them. When using algebraic logic, you first compute the operations inside parentheses, beginning with the innermost parentheses, then you compute exponents, then you multiply and divide from left to right, and finally you add and subtract from left to right. This is called the **order of operations.**

Students might wish to continue the development of the concept of order of operations by playing *How the West Was One + Three × Four* by Bonnie Seiler (1996).

The order of operations is important to students not only for work with rational numbers, but also for simplifying algebraic expressions and solving equations. An **algebraic expression** is a symbolic form involving constants, variables, operations, and grouping symbols such as parentheses. Two or more algebraic expressions joined by addition or subtraction are called **terms,** and two or more algebraic expressions joined by multiplication or division are called **factors.** If two or more algebraic expressions containing at least one variable

are joined by an equal sign, it is called an **algebraic equation.**

The understanding of variables, expressions, and equations is one of the areas on which the NCTM *Standards* recommend an increased emphasis. Again, this understanding should be developed using concrete and pictorial materials.

Analyzing Change

Understanding change is fundamental to understanding functions and to understanding many ideas presented in the news. (NCTM, 2000, p. 40)

Calculus is the formal study of mathematical change, but understanding the concept of change should begin with preschool children. For young children, change can be examined qualitatively, such as realizing that they themselves have changed since they were babies. They have grown taller and they can do many things that they could not do a year or two earlier. Later, these changes can be examined quantitatively. For example, they might realize that they have grown 1 inch since last year. In this section, we look at ways that students might analyze change in various contexts both qualitatively and quantitatively. We begin with looking at functions with a constant change. Students should analyze these functions using a number of different representations, including everyday situations, charts, tables, and graphs.

A C T I V I T I E S

Grades 3–5

OBJECTIVE: to graph linear equations by plotting points.

1. Use information children may encounter as consumers or in other subjects as a basis for data to be graphed. For example, you may see an advertisement for corn at 15¢ per ear. Tell the children you want to make a graph to help you find the price of any number of ears. Show the children how to make a table that shows the number of ears of corn purchased and the total price. Figure 10–11 shows a table and the corresponding line graph for the data on the corn.

If n stands for the number of ears of corn and T stands for the total price, the equation $T = \$.15n$ can be written to show the relationship between the price and the number of ears of corn. A spreadsheet such as *Cruncher* or Excel might be used to help students make a table of cost per ear versus total cost. Students can experiment with changing a variable such as cost per ear or adding other factors such as the prices of other fruits or vegetables. If corn is 15¢ per ear and lettuce is 90¢ per head, how many different ways could you spend exactly $3 on corn and lettuce? A spreadsheet lets you explore this and many related questions. Articles by Edwards and Bitter (1989) and Edwards, Bitter, and Hatfield (1990) give you some ideas to get started.

Suggest that the children make up other graphs of their own. Can they write the equations for each other's graphs if they have not seen the original data? Can they add additional pairs to the table by looking at the graph? Ask the children how this work relates to the work with proportions, which was discussed in Chapter 9. Children now have an additional method of solving proportions.

Computer programs such as *Tabletop* from Broderbund, *The Cruncher* from Davidson, *Data Toolkit* and *Graph Links* from Harcourt Brace, and *Green Globs and Graphing Equations* by Sharon Dugdale and David Kibbey, available from Sunburst, can give the students additional practice in writing equations and graphing. Graphing calculators are also an excellent tool for the exploration of graphing equations for middle-grade students, as in Figure 10–12. Using a graphing calculator, you can very quickly see the effects of raising

the price of an ear of corn to 25¢, or you could plot two graphs to determine the number of ears of corn you could buy for $1.35. Students can explore with graphing calculators to determine when and why a slope changes or a graph shifts to the right or left.

Grades 6 – 8

OBJECTIVE: to use a graphing calculator and Calculator Based Laboratories (CBL™) or Calculator Based Ranger (CBR™) to analyze various types of graphs.

1. Set up a CBL™ or CBR™ attached to a graphing calculator. (If you have never done this, you might want to consult one of the books in the reference list.) Show the students the four graphs in Figure 10–13 and explain that they are going to reproduce the graphs by walking toward or away from the motion detector. Before actually trying this, ask the students to try to determine where to start, how fast to move, and when to stand

a.

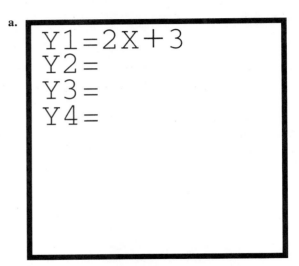

b.

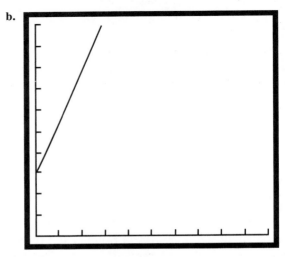

Figure 10 – 12 Graphing calculator display showing graph of linear equation.

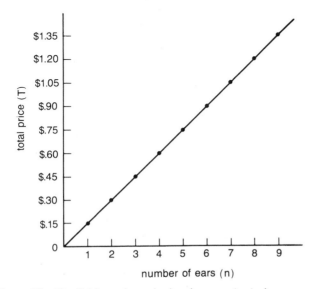

Corn	Prices
ears of corn	total price
1	$.15
2	$.30
3	$.45
n	$.15 n

Figure 10 – 11 Table and graph showing constant change.

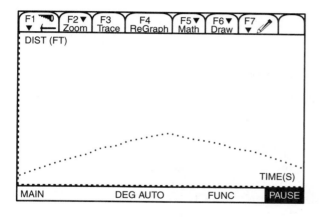
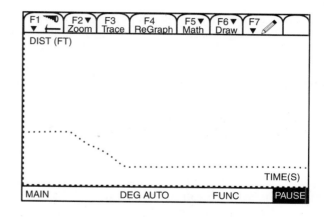
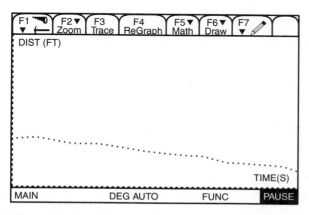
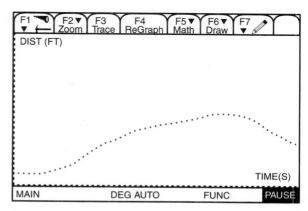

Figure 10–13   Calculator Based Laboratory (CBL™) display of distance graphs.

still. Ask for volunteers to try to match the graphs. If you have an overhead projection screen for the calculator, the class can help the volunteer out by giving suggestions as he or she walks. Discuss the importance of analyzing the slopes and direction of the graphs.

Notice that these graphs plot time on the *x*-axis and distance on the *y*-axis. What happens if the *y*-axis is speed instead of distance? How will that change the shape of the graphs?

OBJECTIVE: to use variables with functions and graphs.

2. Repeat the activity described earlier with the function machine, using variables instead of the terms *input* and *output* on the chart. The most common variables used are *x* for the input and *y* for the output. The function in the previous activity, where the rule was "divide by 2 and then subtract 3," would be written as $y = \frac{x}{2} - 3$. Ask the students to explore whether that is the same as the function $y = \frac{(x - 3)}{2}$. How do the graphs differ? Encourage the students to graph several functions, and then ask them if the function graph was always a line. Can they think of a function whose graph would not be a line?

OBJECTIVE: to explore the effects of changing amounts in equations using Cartesian graphs.

3. Begin with the equation $y = x$, and make a table of values such as the following:

x	y
2	2
5	5
−1	−1
0	0
$\frac{1}{2}$	

Ask the students to graph this equation using a Cartesian coordinate system. Now try the equation $y = 2x$. Make a table of values and then graph this equation on the same graph. Ask the students to make predictions for the graphs of $y = 3x$ and $y = \frac{1}{2}x$. Make a table of values for these equations and then graph them on the same graph. What do you notice? What happens to the slope as the coefficient of *x* changes? Encourage the students to ask other questions about the graph, such as what happens if the slope is negative? What if you add some value to the equation as in $y = x + 2$? Is the graph still a line? What has happened to the line?

OBJECTIVE: to explore the graphs of linear equations using a graphics calculator.

4. Try the previous activity, this time using a graphing calculator. You will not need to begin with the chart of values. Put the calculator in the graph mode and ask for the graph of $y = x$. Then ask for the graphs of $y = 2x$, $y = 3x$, $y = {}^-2x$, and $y = \frac{1}{2}x$ on the same graph. What do you notice? What is the effect of a negative coefficient of x? What happens as the coefficient gets larger? What happens if you add a constant to the equation? Can you make a graph that is nonlinear?

Representing, Analyzing, and Modeling Mathematical Situations and Relationships

> One of the most powerful uses of mathematics is the mathematical modeling of phenomena. (NCTM, 2000, p. 39)

In addition to using charts, tables, graphs, and equations to represent algebraic concepts, physical models are also quite useful in connecting concepts of algebraic and arithmetic operations. Algebra blocks are one such material that can be used for the development of algebraic ideas. They give the students a good picture of the concept, are related to earlier concepts learned with whole and rational numbers, and can be manipulated to determine answers to a variety of situations.

Algebra blocks can be purchased commercially, as *Algebra Lab Gear*, *Algeblocks*, or *Algebra Tiles*, or constructed out of railroad board. A master for algebra blocks is included in Appendix B. This set may be used with the large square having dimensions of x by x for an area of x^2, the medium-sized rectangle having dimensions of x by 1 for an area of x, and the small square having dimensions of 1 by 1 for an area of 1. You may change the representations so that the small square has dimensions of y by y for an area of y^2, which would then give the rectangle dimensions of y by x for an area of xy. Changing the values of the squares helps the students realize the variable nature of algebra. As you do the activities in this section, relate the work with the algebra blocks to the earlier work with base ten blocks. Earlier, the large square had dimensions of 10 by 10 for an area of 100, the

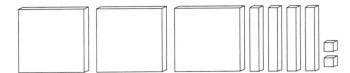

Figure 10–14   Using algebra blocks to represent algebraic expressions.

rectangle had dimensions of 10 by 1 for an area of 10, and the small square had dimensions of 1 by 1 for an area of 1. When we moved to decimals, the large square represented 1, the rectangle 0.1 and the small square 0.01.

Figure 10–14 shows the representation for $3x^2 + 4x + 2$ if the large square is x^2, the rectangle x, and the small square 1. Using the representation in which the small square is y^2, Figure 10–14 represents $3x^2 + 4xy + 2y^2$.

Students should also practice drawing graphs from a story such as a story about Nathan who is late to school and must run to get to school on time. If the students draw a graph with time on the horizontal axis and speed on the vertical axis, the graph will not be the same as one with time on the horizontal axis and distance on the vertical axis. Students in the middle grades should discuss the effects of such things as running at a fast, steady pace; speeding up; slowing down; stopping for traffic; and running at a slow, steady pace on both types of graphs.

A C T I V I T I E S

Grades 6–8

OBJECTIVE: to introduce concrete models for algebraic expressions.

1. Ask the students to each construct a set of algebra blocks using the master from Appendix B. The blocks may be made of either railroad board or laminated construction paper. It is helpful to make one set out of different colored construction paper to represent positive numbers and one set out of red construction paper to represent negative numbers. The *Algebra Tiles for the Overhead Projector* by Howden (1985), available from Cuisenaire Co., have blue x^2s, green xs, and yellow 1s. All of the negatives are red in that set.

Ask the students to use the blocks to show a variety of expressions. Begin by adding positive amounts. You might show $3x^2 + 2x + 5$, $4x^2 + 3x + 2$, and so on. After the students are comfortable with this activity, ask them to show negative amounts as well as positive amounts. Try $3x^2 + ({}^-2x) + ({}^-2)$. This might also be written as $3x^2 - 2x - 2$. After the students can

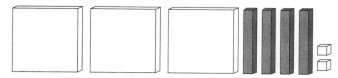

Figure 10–15 Using algebra blocks to represent algebraic expressions that include negative values.

represent amounts using the *x*s, tell them that they can use any letters to name the dimensions of the rectangles. Let them choose other letters for the dimensions and then tell you what the tiles represent. For example, Figure 10–15 shows $3z^2 - 4zw + 2w^2$ if the dimensions of the large square are *z* by *z* and those of the small square are *w* by *w*.

OBJECTIVE: to use algebra blocks to simplify expressions involving additive inverses.

2. Remind students of the rules they developed for additive inverses with integers. Ask them to predict what $x + (^-x)$ should be. Work this problem with the blocks. Use the blocks to show zero in a variety of ways. Figure 10–16 shows a few examples.

After the students are comfortable showing zero with the blocks, ask them to put down any combination of blocks, record the blocks they used, and then remove all the zeros. Figure 10–17 shows $3x^2 + (^-2x^2) + 2x + (^-3x) + 5 + (^-2)$. After the zeros are removed, the figure shows $x^2 - x + 3$.

Ask the students to model a number of different algebraic expressions. Let them make up problems for each other that involve the addition and subtraction of expressions. Discuss with them the rules for adding integers and how these rules are related to the addition and subtraction of algebraic expressions or **polynomials,** algebraic expressions built up from constants and variables by adding, subtracting, or multiplying. In a polynomial, a variable cannot appear in a denominator, in an exponent, or within a radical sign.

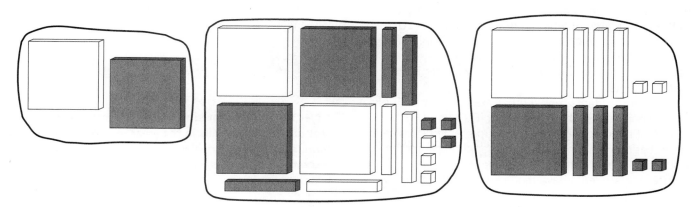

Figure 10–16 Representations of zero using the algebra blocks.

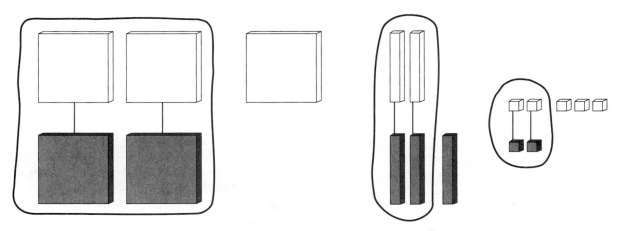

Figure 10–17 Simplifying expressions using algebra blocks.

OBJECTIVE: to multiply and factor polynomials using algebra blocks.

3. Review with the students the area model for multiplying whole numbers. In Figure 10–18, if the large square is 10 by 10 and the small square is 1 by 1, the picture represents 13 by 12. The area of the large square is 100, the area of the medium rectangle is 10, and the area of the small square is 1. When you add the values, you have $1(100) + 3(10) + 2(10) + 6 = 156$. If the large square is 1.0 by 1.0, the problem becomes $1.3 \times 1.2 = 1.56$. The same principles hold in algebra. If the large square is $x \times x$, the rectangle $x \times 1$, and the small square 1×1. Figure 10–18 now represents $(x + 3)(x + 2)$. The area is now $1(x^2) + 3x + 2x + 6$, or $x^2 + 5x + 6$.

Notice that this model relates to the distributive property using the **FOIL method,** which is frequently taught in algebra classes. **FOIL** is an acronym that stands for "first, outside, inside, and last." For $(x + 3)(x + 2)$, the FOIL method would involve multiplying the *first* terms in the parentheses $(x \bullet x)$, then the *outside* terms $(x \bullet 2)$, then the *inside* terms $(3 \bullet x)$, and, finally, the *last* terms $(3 \bullet 2)$. Locate each of these pairs of terms on the diagram. Try relating this to the multiplying of whole numbers, such as $(10 + 3)(10 + 2)$. Note that the FOIL method is simply an adaptation of the distributive property. Ask students to use the distributive property to show why the FOIL method works.

Have the students model other examples of multiplying polynomials, such as $(x + 3)(x + 4)$ and $(x + 1)(x + 3)$. Encourage them to make up problems for each other. Let one student make a model and ask another student to explain what is being shown.

After the students have modeled several problems involving the multiplication of two terms with positive amounts, ask them to reverse the operation and try factoring. Start with $x^2 + 5x + 4$ and ask the students to form a rectangle with the pieces. What are the dimensions of the rectangle? These are the **factors** of the polynomial. Figure 10–19 shows the results, $(x + 1)(x + 4)$.

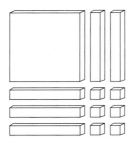

Figure 10–18 Multiplying polynomials using algebra blocks.

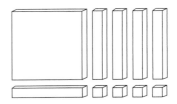

Figure 10–19 Factoring polynomials using algebra blocks.

DEVELOPING ALGEBRAIC FLUENCY

Many of the algebra concepts that are introduced in the elementary and middle grades will not be fully mastered until high school or later. Before that, however, students should know that patterns can be represented and analyzed mathematically, and they should have experience representing relations in a number of ways, including with physical models, tables, graphs, and verbal and symbolic rules. They should have a good understanding of linear functions and should have some experience with nonlinear relations as well. There are several computer programs that might be used to help students in the development of these concepts.

A C T I V I T I E S

Grades 6–8

OBJECTIVE: to present students with interesting challenges that develop their skills in the areas of solving linear equations, substituting variables, grouping like variables, solving systems of equations, and translating algebra word problems into equations.

1. *The Hidden Treasure of Al-Jabar* is a computer program available from Sunburst designed to give students interesting experiences with algebraic thinking. Each adventure in this program begins with students translating a word problem into an equation. Successful completion of the equation allows students to begin one of three types of challenges that involve systems of equations, balancing equations, or constructing linear equations. All challenges use visual models and puzzles and encourage students to write their reasoning in a journal as they progress through the problems. As a teacher, you can adjust the level of difficulty of the problems and even add problems from your own curriculum.

OBJECTIVE: to reinforce skills with graphing using the Cartesian coordinate system.

The computer program *Green Globs and Graphing Equations*, available from Sunburst, contains several activities that develop skills related to graphing and writing equations. For example, Equation Plotter allows the student to enter an equation from the keyboard. Promptly, the graph of the equation appears on a coordinate grid on the screen. This provides students with an opportunity to explore how equations will appear in graphic form. Activity sheets provided with the software lead students to make various observations. And teachers and students have the flexibility to experiment on their own.

Another activity is Linear and Quadratic Graphs, in which graphs are displayed on a coordinate grid and students enter equations that match the displayed graphs. Participants may select lines, parabolas, circles, ellipses, and hyperbolas to be displayed. When the students believe they have discovered the appropriate equation, they enter it, and immediately the graph of the equation is plotted on the screen along with the target plot. They may continue entering equations until the graphs match.

Green Globs is an activity that presents 13 "green globs" on the screen in a random fashion. The students attempt to explode all the globs by touching them with the graphs of equations that have been entered from the keyboard. The object is to use the fewest number of equations possible to explode the globs.

Calculators can now do many of the things that are taught in high school and college algebra courses, such as simplifying expressions, plotting functions, and solving equations. Just as there have been debates over whether elementary students should be allowed to use a calculator to do arithmetic computation, teachers are now debating whether calculators should be used to do algebraic and even calculus computations. Bernhard Kutzler, a mathematics professor at the University of Linz, Austria, has compared using a calculator to using a car. A calculator lets us go much further in the exploration of mathematics than does simply using mental calculation or paper and pencil, just as a car lets us go much further in exploring the world than does just walking or riding a bicycle. The fact that some people use a calculator inappropriately to do simple computation should not prompt us to ban calculators, just as the fact that people using a car inappropriately to drive to the corner grocery store has not prompted us to ban cars. We simply need to learn to maximize our use of our new tools. With the ever-growing capabilities of technological tools, we need to think about changing our traditional teaching styles to focus more on student development of reasoning and less on student memorization of poorly understood algorithms. Helping elementary and middle grade students build algebraic reasoning skills is a good place to start (see Weblink 10–7).

ESTIMATING AND MENTAL CALCULATING

Many algebraic equations can be solved mentally without writing out a lengthy series of equations. Encourage students to work these problems mentally whenever possible. A student should not need paper and pencil to find the solution for $x - 6 = 12$. If exact mental calculation is not possible, ask the students to estimate before working out an equation. Ask for justification for their estimates. For example, for the equation $4x + 920 = 256$, the students may have difficulty determining the exact answer mentally. One of the first questions they should ask themselves is whether x should be a positive or a negative number. How do you know? Is x greater or less than -100?

REASONING, SOLVING, AND POSING ALGEBRAIC PROBLEMS

Using algebra is an excellent way to explore real-life situations. It is not necessary to present these problems in type categories, however, such as age problems, money problems, and rate and ratio problems or even problems that use specific strategies such as guess-and-test problems, work-backward problems, and draw-a-picture problems. Several problem-solving books and websites with excellent suggestions for interesting problems are listed in the Additional Resources. Many of the problems can be investigated on a variety of levels and give students an excellent opportunity to deepen their understanding of algebra if they are encouraged to "question the answers, and not just answer the questions."

For example, one of the problems in the *Awesome Math Problems* books is the following: "The sum of five consecutive whole numbers is 90. What is the greatest of these five numbers?" (Sheffield et al., 2000, Grade 6, page 24). Students could use a number of strategies to solve the problem, including guess and test, or they could solve this using algebraic notation such as the following: "Let x stand for the largest of the five numbers: $(x - 4) + (x - 3) + (x - 2) + (x - 1) + x = 90$. Simplify this to $5x - 10 = 90$ and solve to find that $x = 20$."

A student who realizes that the middle of the five numbers is the mean of the sequence and must be $90 \div 5$, or 18, might show a deeper understanding of the structure of the problem than the student who can manipulate the symbols. Encourage all students to look more deeply into the problem asking questions like an investigative mathematician. For example, a student might ask the following:

- What if 90 is the sum of any number of consecutive whole numbers? What is the largest number that might be part of this set of consecutive numbers? What is the smallest number that might be part of a set of consecutive whole numbers that add up to 90?

- How many different ways might I get a sum of 90 using consecutive whole numbers?
- What if I use consecutive even numbers? Can I get a sum of 90?
- What type of numbers can I get using two consecutive whole numbers? What if I use three (four, five, *n*) consecutive whole numbers?
- Are there any numbers that are impossible to have as a sum of consecutive whole numbers? (Powers of 2 are not possible.) Why?

Use real situations to create other problems in the classroom. You might want to try looking at the stretchiness of a spring. Measure the length of a spring at rest and then measure the length again after hanging a heavy object such as a brick from it. What is the length of the spring now? Can you predict the length if you hang two bricks from it? What about three bricks? Make a graph of the results. What is the shape of the graph? Can you write an equation that would tell you the length of the spring for any given number of bricks? Encourage the students to ask other questions about the situation and explore the answers.

Other situations that are interesting to explore include looking at the distance a toy car travels beyond the end of a ramp compared to the angle on the ramp, the number of times a pendulum swings in 20 seconds compared to the length of the pendulum string, the time it takes water to empty from a paper cup with a hole in the bottom compared to the amount of water in the cup, and the length of time it takes a dropped object to hit the ground compared to the height of the drop. All of these lead to some very interesting physics concepts that can best be explored using very simple algebraic concepts. Encourage the students to carefully set up experiments in which they collect data to be organized in a table and then graphed. After the data are organized in this manner, ask the students to list all of the questions they can think of regarding the experiment. Which of these can be answered based on the data already collected and which need further exploration? Perhaps the science teacher would join you in this project. Make full use of technology such as graphing calculators, CBLs, and computers in these explorations.

ORGANIZING FOR ALGEBRAIC TLC

The activities described above that involve experimenting with different physical concepts would best be done in small groups. Three or four students working together can set up the experiment, collect data, and ask and answer a variety of questions about their information. They can also work collaboratively to present their data in an interesting and understandable fashion.

Other activities, such as exploring the effects of changing the constants on the graphs shown on a graphing calculator, would probably best be accomplished by two people working cooperatively. It is difficult for more than two students to work with one graphing calculator, but more students might get together to discuss results.

Other problems might initially be presented to the whole class at once for individual exploration. After students have had an opportunity to explore on their own, they could get together in small groups or as a class to share results.

If you are a middle-grade teacher or if you are preparing to become a middle-grade teacher, it is likely that one of the issues with which you must deal is whether to track some of the best students into an algebra class in seventh or eighth grade while the other students remain in a different track. Some states, such as California, require that all students take algebra by the end of eighth grade, while many others require that all students take one or two years of algebra in high school. Many programs developed under National Science Foundation grants to implement the NCTM *Standards* integrate algebra, geometry, probability, and statistics and several other concepts through middle and high school.

As you weigh the issues surrounding tracking some students into higher-level mathematics, you must look at all the implications of such a move. Does this mean that only some of the students will be exposed to higher-level mathematics by the time they leave school? If students take algebra in place of seventh- or eighth-grade mathematics, will they miss important geometry, probability, and statistics concepts? If there is no tracking, what other means are in place to ensure that interested students can learn calculus in high school? Which alternative will ensure that higher-level classes such as Advanced Placement Calculus and Advanced Placement Statistics or International Baccalaureate Mathematics Classes will be available to large numbers of students (males and females representing all races and socioeconomic groups) when they reach high school?

COMMUNICATING LEARNING OF ALGEBRAIC CONCEPTS

Students working on projects such as exploring the effects of changing the length of a pendulum string or the angle of a toy car ramp should be encouraged to create different means of presenting their data. They might want to build a model, make a chart, draw a graph, search for equations to describe the graphs, and present questions and answers in written form. Remember that others are interested in the process that they used and not just the results. Several of these projects may make very good exhibits for a math or science fair.

Ask students to generalize patterns that they notice during their explorations and to use a variety of representations to explain their reasoning. As students progress in their algebraic understanding, guide them to use proper language and algebraic notation to represent these generalizations. Encourage all students to keep a mathematician's journal where they record their burgeoning understanding.

CONNECTING AND REPRESENTING ALGEBRAIC LEARNING

Ms. Gonzalez's fourth-grade class has adopted a needy family for Thanksgiving and is planning to buy them some canned goods so they will have a healthy stock of food. Each group is pricing a different type of vegetables and determining the best price. Jennifer's group is looking at corn. They have found 3 12-ounce cans for $1.09 at one store and the same corn at 4 cans for $1.33 at another store. They want to buy 12 cans of the corn and are discussing different ways of determining the best buy. Lashonda has divided $1.09 by 3 and $1.33 by 4; Greg has divided 3 by $1.09 and 4 by $1.33; Whitney has subtracted $1.09 from $1.33; Millie has multiplied $1.09 by 4 and $1.33 by 3; and Jennifer has made a chart for each and drawn a graph. Each is convinced that he or she has found the best method of solving the problem. Mr. Gonzalez has asked each one to prepare a three-minute presentation of the method of solution, including a description of how this method could be used for any price and any number of cans. These presentations will be made to the whole class and followed by a discussion of how any of these methods could be used.

Ms. Washington is planning a lesson for her seventh-grade class on proportions. She knows how important this concept is for making a bridge between patterns in numerical expressions and the more abstract forms that students will experience in more formal algebra. She is working with Ms. Mazzocca, the science teacher, to make connections to the frequent use of ratios and proportions in the science class. They have begun a list of the science concepts that students will be studying this year that involve these concepts. So far, this list includes mixtures, density, scaling, temperature conversion, speed and acceleration, gravity and other forces, and pitch. They will team teach several of these topics to ensure that the students understand the concepts and do not just rotely apply rules to get the right answers.

ASSESSING ALGEBRAIC LEARNING

When assessing students' skills in algebra, it is important to remember that the process is at least as important as the answer. Ask the students to explain their reasoning and not just write down numerical answers when working algebraic problems or exercises.

If you use group projects, let the students assess their own work and that of the others in the group. They can list both what they contributed to the project and what they learned from it. They can also list two or three of the most important contributions from the others in the group. Many of these projects make good portfolio entries. Students who have explored some physical phenomena, used charts and graphs to collect and analyze data, made predictions based upon their data, and explored new questions related to this initial information, frequently have developed good problems for inclusion in portfolios.

Some common areas of misunderstanding or difficulty in algebra are listed below. Be on the lookout for these misunderstandings. You might ask students to be on the lookout for them in their own work and in the work of others in the groups in which they are working.

1. A number and a variable placed next to each other should be multiplied, not added. For example, many students think $2a$ means $2 + a$ rather than $2 \times a$. This is understandable, since 54 means $50 + 4$, not 50×4, and $4\frac{1}{2}$ means $4 + \frac{1}{2}$, not $4 \times \frac{1}{2}$.

2. Different variables may stand for the same number, and the same letter in a different equation may stand for a different number. If $2x + 3 = 7$ and $2y + 3 = 7$, both x and y stand for 2. If in one statement $x + 5 = 9$ and in another statement $x + 4 = 0$, x stands for 4 in the first statement and $^-4$ in the second.

3. Translating from a word problem to an equation is also difficult. If there are 4 apples for every orange in the bowl, the situation is not represented by $4a = o$. If a stands for the number of apples and o stands for the number of oranges, ask the students which there are more of in the bowl. The statement tells us there are more apples, 4 times as many as oranges. In the equation $4a = o$, which is larger, a or o? The o must be larger. Does this fit the statement from the word problem? Be on the alert for other incorrect methods of translating a written statement into an equation.

4. It is often easier for students to interpret information in physical, pictorial, or graphical form than in equation form. Be sure to use multiple representations, such as physical, geometric, or graphical models, whenever possible.

5. Some students may believe that every relationship is a linear one. Let them try graphing $y = x^2$ on the

calculator or the relationship of the acceleration of a falling object to the distance traveled to see that not all relationships can be graphed with a line.

6. The concept of a variable is a difficult one and students frequently struggle to correctly use symbols, variables, expressions, equations, and inequalities. Give them plenty of experience in defining and illustrating for you the meanings of these terms and symbols.

SOMETHING FOR EVERYONE

Algebra provides a challenge for students who excel in abstract mathematical work; on the other hand, when physical models are used to illustrate concepts and to reinforce skills, students who have strengths in visual and spatial areas are quite able to grasp the concepts and develop the skills. Because students may be beginning their study of algebra in the early grades, it is important to use a variety of instructional techniques.

Verbal/linguistic learners will be able to describe and explain algebraic processes. They may, however, have some difficulty in displaying spatially the concepts that are being presented unless clear verbal explanations are provided. In cooperative group activities, students who are verbal/linguistic learners may be very helpful in describing the problem situations. They will also be very helpful when it comes to writing the results of the experiments and the solutions to the problems.

Those who do well in bodily/kinesthetic situations will succeed when materials such as algebra blocks and balance scales are used to model algebraic equations. Having the chance to move the materials around and discuss the relationship between one configuration and another will help provide the link between the concrete and abstract aspects of algebra.

Students with special talent in mathematics will likely discover algebraic relationships and patterns quickly. Because the work in algebra is at the introductory level, there is plenty of room for these students to excel and move ahead. For example, when using *Green Globs and Graphing Equations,* students will be able to work at several levels and will be able to solve increasingly challenging problems. Talented students can select more difficult problems on which to work. Further, when working with manipulatives, talented students will be able to develop complex examples and solutions. These students should also be helpful when it comes to discussing and explaining concepts and skills in their cooperative work groups.

Those who have difficulty in learning algebra should be encouraged to work with the models that illustrate the concepts. Provide opportunities for them to be successful and to demonstrate to the whole class and to members of their cooperative work group those ideas that they do grasp. Allow these students more time as they begin to learn algebra. Be willing to seek out alternative methods and materials for reteaching concepts and skills that were not immediately learned.

FOR YOU AS A TEACHER: IDEAS FOR DISCUSSION AND YOUR PROFESSIONAL PORTFOLIO

This section is intended to provide you the opportunity to read, write, and reflect on key elements of this chapter. We list several discussion ideas. We hope that one or more of these ideas will prove interesting to you and that you will choose to investigate and write about the ideas. The results of your work should be considered as part of your professional portfolio. You might consider these two questions as guides for your writing: "What does the material in this chapter mean for you as a teacher?" or "How can what you are reading be translated into a teaching practice for you as a teacher?"

DISCUSSION IDEAS

1. Set up a debate on the issue of whether all middle grade students should take algebra I before the end of eighth grade. Look at studies such as the National Assessment of Educational Progress (Weblink 10–1) and the Trends in International Mathematics and Science Study (see Weblink 10–8) as you prepare the debate. Look at the November 1998 NCTM *Mathematics Education Dialogues,* an issue devoted to the topic of tracking, on Weblink 10–9. Interview elementary, middle school, high school, and college mathematics instructors and analyze their responses. Find an Internet site where algebra teaching and learning are discussed and ask the same questions. Take a position on whether algebra should be a separate course or should be integrated into the rest of the mathematics curriculum, and be prepared to support your position.

2. Choose one of the algebra programs that makes extensive use of physical models such as *Algebra Lab Gear* (Picciotto), *Algebra Tiles* (Howden) or *Algeblocks* (Johnston Hills). Learn how to add, subtract, and multiply algebraic expressions using the materials and then teach a middle-grade student to do the same thing. Compare the strategies that you and the student use when learning the concepts. How do these strategies compare to learning algebra more abstractly? Which method did you prefer? Which method did the student

prefer? You also might want to try this on the computer using a program such as *Computer Interactive Algeblocks* (Johnson, 1996) and compare this to learning with the physical models.

3. Talk to middle school teachers and administrators in your area about whether algebra is taught as a separate mathematics class in middle school. If so, is it available to all students? If not, is algebra integrated into every year of middle school mathematics? What do the teachers and administrators see as the benefits and drawbacks of their policies on this issue? How do middle school teachers and administrators discuss the issues with the high school teachers and administrators to ensure smooth transition from one level to the next level?

4. Choose a middle school mathematics series and compare the algebra part of the series to the recommendations from the *NCTM Principles and Standards*. Is algebra covered in the depth recommended by the *Principles and Standards*? Is the program conceptually oriented, making use of physical models and everyday applications, or is it more abstract? If possible, compare your series to one of the series developed under a National Science Foundation grant to implement the *NCTM Standards*. (At the middle-grade level, these programs include the *Connected Mathematics Project* (CMP), *Math in Context*, *MathScape*, and *Math Thematics*. More information on these programs can be found on Weblink 10–10.

5. Find an algebra (or calculus) book, video, or piece of software that was written for elementary students. (There are several in the reference list.) How do the elementary algebra concepts compare to concepts expected from middle school and high school students? If possible, choose one or more of these materials, design a lesson for primary or intermediate students, and try it out. Compare the algebra learned by these young students to the way you learned algebra. Which method would you prefer as a student? As a teacher? Why?

ADDITIONAL RESOURCES

REFERENCES

Austin, Richard A., and Denisse R. Thompson, "Exploring Algebraic Patterns through Literature," *Mathematics Teaching in the Middle School,* 2, No. 4. (February 1997), 274–291.

Battista, Michael T., and Caroline Van Auken Borrow, "Using Spreadsheets to Promote Algebraic Thinking," *Teaching Children Mathematics,* 4, no. 8 (April 1998), 470–478.

Berman, Barbara, and Fredda Friederwitzer, "Algebra Can Be Elementary . . . When It's Concrete," *Arithmetic Teacher,* 36, no. 8 (April 1989), 21–24.

Brueningsen, Chris, Bill Bower, Linda Antinone, and Elisa Brueningsen, *Real-World Math with the CBL System.* Austin, TX: Texas Instruments, 1994.

Brueningsen, Chris, Elisa Brueningsen, and Bill Bower, *CBR Explorations: Math and Science in Motion: Activities for Middle School.* Austin, TX: Texas Instruments, 1997.

Burrill, Gail F., Miriam Clifford, and Richard Scheaffer, *Data-Driven Mathematics.* White Plains, NY: 1998. (a series of 11 modules on algebra, geometry and advanced mathematics)

Carlson, Ronald J., and Mary Jean Winter, *Algebra Experiments II: Exploring Nonlinear Functions.* Menlo Park, CA: Addison-Wesley, 1993.

Charles, Linda H., *Algebra Thinking: First Experiences.* Mountain View, CA: Creative Publications, 1990.

Clark, Anita, *Algebra Activities, K–9.* Lansing: Michigan Council of Teachers of Mathematics, 1990.

Cook, Marcy, *Try-A-Tile: Logic with Algebra.* Mountain View, CA: Creative Publications, 1990.

Coxford, A. F., ed., *The Ideas of Algebra, K–12.* Reston, VA: National Council of Teachers of Mathematics, 1988.

Cuevas, Gilbert J., and Karol Yeatts. *Navigating through Algebra in Grades 3–5.* Reston, VA: NCTM, 2001.

Cuisenaire Company of America, *Algeblocks for Middle School.* Vernon Hills, IL: ETA/Cuisenaire, 2001.

Dossey, John A., Ina V. S. Mullis, Mary M. Lindquist, and Donald L. Chambers, *The Mathematics Report Card: Are We Measuring Up? Trends and Achievement Based on the 1986 National Assessment.* Princeton, NJ: Educational Testing Service, 1988.

Dossey, John A., Ina V. S. Mullis, Steven Gorman, and Andrew S. Latham, *How School Mathematics Functions: Perspectives from the NAEP 1990 and 1992 Assessments.* Washington, DC: National Center for Education Statistics, 1994.

Educational Testing Service, *Algebridge.* Providence, RI: Janson, 1990.

Ferrini-Mundy, Joan, Glenda Lappan, and Elizabeth D. Phillips. "Experiences with Patterning," *Teaching Children Mathematics,* 3, no. 6 (February, 1997), 282–288.

Friel, Susan, Sid Rachlin, and Dot Doyle. *Navigating through Algebra in Grades 6–8.* Reston, VA: NCTM, 2001.

Fulton, Brad S., and Bill Lombard, *The Pattern and Function Connection.* Millville, CA: Teacher to Teacher Press, 1994.

Glazier, Stephen, *Random House Word Menu.* New York: Random House, 1992.

Goodnow, Judy, *Beginning Algebra Thinking for Grades 5–6.* Oak Lawn, IL: Ideal School Supply, 1994.

Gray, Virginia, *The Write Tool to Teach Algebra.* Berkeley, CA: Key Curriculum Press, 1993.

Greenes, Carole, and Carol Findell, *Groundworks Algebra Puzzles and Problems.* Mountain View, CA: Creative Publications, 1998. (series of books, grades 4–7)

Greenes, Carole, Mary Cavanagh, Linda Dacey, Carol Findell, and Marian Small, *Navigating through Algebra in PreKindergarten–Grade 2.* Reston, VA: NCTM, 2001.

———*Groundworks Algebraic Thinking.* Mountain View, CA: Creative Publications, 2000. (series of books, grades 1–3)

Hoogeboom, Shirley, and Judy Goodnow, *Beginning Algebra Thinking for Grades 3–4.* Oak Lawn, IL: Ideal School Supply, 1994.

Howden, H. *Algebra Tiles for the Overhead Projector.* New Rochelle, NY: Cuisenaire Co. of America, 1985.

Johnston, Anita, *Algeblocks,* Cincinnati, OH: South-Western Pub. Co. 1994.

Jones, Graham A., and Roger Day, *Algebra, Data, and Probability Explorations for Middle School: A Graphics Calculator Approach.* Menlo Park, CA: Dale Seymour, 1998.

Kalman-Stoveland, Stacy, *Beginning Algebra Thinking for Grades 1–2.* Oak Lawn, IL: Ideal School Supply, 1996.

Lappan, Glenda, James T. Fey, William M. Fitzgerald, Susan N. Friel, and Elizabeth D. Phillips, *Moving Straight Ahead: Linear Relationships.* Palo Alto, CA: Dale Seymour, 1997.

——, *Variables and Patterns: Introducing Algebra.* Palo Alto, CA: Dale Seymour, 1997.

——, *Frogs, Fleas, and Painted Cubes: Quadratic Relationships.* Palo Alto, CA: Dale Seymour, 1998.

——, *Growing, Growing, Growing: Exponential Relationships.* Palo Alto, CA: Dale Seymour, 1998.

——, *Say It with Symbols: Algebraic Reasoning.* Palo Alto, CA: Dale Seymour, 1998.

——, *Thinking with Mathematical Models: Representing Relationships.* Palo Alto, CA: Dale Seymour, 1998.

Lawrence, Ann, and Charlie Hennessy, *Lessons for Algebraic Thinking Grades 6–8.* Sausalito, CA: Math Solutions Publications, 2002.

Lubinski, Cheryl A., and Albert D. Otto, "Literature and Algebraic Reasoning," *Teaching Children Mathematics,* 3, no. 6 (February, 1997), 290–295.

MacDonell, Alan, ed., *The Super Source: Patterns and Functions Grades 7–8.* White Plains, NY: Cuisenaire Company of America, Inc., 1998.

McKnight, C. C., F. J. Crosswhite, J. A. Dossey, E. Kifer, J. J. O. Swafford, K. J. Travers, and T. J. Cooney, *The Underachieving Curriculum: Assessing U.S. School Mathematics from an International Perspective.* Champaign, IL: Stipes, 1987.

Moses, Robert P., and Charles E. Cobb, Jr., *Radical Equations: Civil Rights from Mississippi to the Algebra Project* Boston: Beacon Press, 2001.

National Council of Teachers of Mathematics, *Mathematics Education Dialogues,* Reston, VA: NCTM, November, 1998.

——, *Principles and Standards for School Mathematics.* Reston, VA: NCTM, 2000.

Peak, Lois, *Pursuing Excellence: A Study of U.S. Eighth-Grade Mathematics and Science Teaching, Learning, Curriculum, and Achievement in International Context.* Washington, DC: Office of Educational Research and Improvement, U.S. Department of Education, November, 1996.

Picciotto, Henry, *The Algebra Lab Middle School: Exploring Algebra Concepts with Manipulatives.* Worth, IL: Creative Publications, 1990.

Picciotto, Henry, and Anita Wah, *Algebra: Themes, Concepts, and Tools.* Mountain View, CA: Creative, 1994.

Saxelby-Jennings, Jo, ed., *Algebra Impacts Math Homework: Key Stage One and Two.* Leamington Spa, Warwickshire, England: Scholastic, 1994.

Sheffield, Linda J., *Extending the Challenge in Mathematics: Developing Mathematical Promise in K–8 Students.* Thousand Oaks, CA: Corwin Press, 2002.

Sheffield, Linda Jensen, Carol R. Findell, M. Katherine Gavin, and Carole E. Greenes, *Awesome Math Problems for Creative Thinking.* Chicago: Creative Publications, 2000. (six books, grades 3–8)

Sherard, Wade H., *Logic Algebra Problems.* Palo Alto, CA: Dale Seymour, 1990.

Silver, Edward, *Improving Mathematics in Middle School: Lessons from TIMSS and Related Research.* Washington, DC: U.S. Department of Education Office of Educational Research and Improvement, 1998.

Speer, William, David Hayes, and Daniel Brahier, "Becoming Very-Able with Variables," *Teaching Children Mathematics,* 3, no. 6 (February, 1997), 305–308.

Stone, Bob, and Peter Patilla, *Toward Algebra through Structures: Multilink Middle School Mathematics.* Glen Burnie, MD: NES Arnold, 1995.

Texas Instruments, *Getting Started with the CBR.* Austin, TX: Texas Instruments, 1997.

——, *CBL System Experiment Workbook.* Austin, TX: Texas Instruments, 1997.

Van Dyke, Frances, *A Visual Approach to Algebra.* Orangeburg, NY: Dale Seymour, 1998.

Von Rotz, Leyani, and Marilyn Burns, *Lessons for Algebraic Thinking Grades K–2.* Sausalito, CA: Math Solutions Publications, 2002.

Wickett, Maryann, Katharine Kharas, and Marilyn Burns, *Lessons for Algebraic Thinking Grades 3–5.* Sausalito, CA: Math Solutions Publications, 2002.

Widmer, Connie, and Linda Sheffield, "Modeling Mathematics Concepts Using Physical, Calculator, and Computer Models to Teach Area and Perimeter," *Learning and Leading with Technology,* 25, no. 5 (February, 1998), 32–35.

——, "Putting the Fun into Functions through the Use of Manipulatives, Computers, and Calculators," *School Science and Mathematics,* 94, no. 7 (February, 1998), 350–355.

Wiebe, Arthur, Michelle Youngs, Sheldon Erickson, and Cheryl Hartshorn, *Multiplication the Algebra Way.* Fresno, CA: AIMS Education Foundation, 2001.

Willcutt, Robert, *Building Algebraic Thinking with Progressive Patterns: Pattern Blocks, Rods, and Cubes.* Pacific Grove, CA: Critical Thinking Press and Software, 1995. (series of three books)

Willoughby, Stephen, "Functions from Kindergarten through Sixth Grade," *Teaching Children Mathematics,* 3, no. 6 (February, 1997), 314–318.

Willoughby, Stephen S., Carl Bereiter, Peter Hilton, and Joseph H. Rubinstein, *Real Math.* La Salle, IL: Open Court, 1991.

Winter, Mary Jean, and Ronald J. Carlson, *Algebra Experiments I: Exploring Linear Functions.* Menlo Park, CA: Addison-Wesley, 1993.

CHILDREN'S LITERATURE

Burmingham, John, *Mr. Gumpy's Outing.* New York: Scholastic Press, 1970.

Juster, Norton, *The Phantom Tollbooth.* New York: Random House, 1975.

Rey, Henry A. *Curious George Rides a Bike.* Boston: Houghton Mifflin, 1952.

Williams, Vera. *A Chair for My Mother*. New York: Hooper Trophy, 1989.

Wood, Audrey, *The Napping House*. Orlando, FL: Harcourt, 1984.

Zimelman, Nathan. *How the Second Grade Got $8,205.50 to visit the Statue of Liberty*, Pacific Grove, Albert Whitman & Co. 1992.

TECHNOLOGY

Broderbund, *Tabletop*, Novato, CA: Broderbund, 1995. (software)

Cohen, Don, *Calculus by and for Young People*. Champaign, IL: Don Cohen—The Mathman, 1991. (kit with two videos, book, and worksheets)

Davidson, *The Cruncher*. Torrance, CA: Davidson, 1997. (software)

———, *Alge-Blaster*. Torrance, CA: Davidson, 1997. (software)

Dugdale, Sharon, and David Kibbey, *Green Globs and Graphing Equations*. Pleasantville, NY: Sunburst Communications, 1999. (software)

Edmark, *Mighty Math Astro Algebra*. Orlando, FL: Harcourt Brace, 1996. (software)

———, *Millie's Math House*. Orlando, FL: Harcourt Brace, 1995. (software)

Edwards, Edgar L., Jr., ed., *Algebra for Everyone*. Reston, VA: National Council of Teachers of Mathematics, 1990. (video, discussion guide, and book; software)

GPN, *Math Vantage: Unit I: Patterns*. Lincoln, NE: GPN, 1997. (video and print materials)

———, *Math Vantage: Unit V: The Language of Mathematics*. Lincoln, NE: GPN, 1997. (video and print materials)

Harcourt Brace, *Data ToolKit*. Orlando, FL: Harcourt Brace, 1996. (software)

———, *Graph Links Grades 1–6*. Orlando, FL: Harcourt Brace, 1996. (software)

HRM, *Algebra World CD-ROM*. Pleasantville, NY: Human Relations Media, 1998. (software)

Johnson, Anita, *Computer Interactive Algeblocks*. Cincinnati, OH: South-Western, 1996. (software)

Marshall, Gail, and associates, *Balancing Bear*. Pleasantville, NY: Sunburst Communications, 1996. (software)

O'Brien, Thomas, *Puzzle Tanks*. Pleasantville, NY: Sunburst Communications, 1997. (software available for computer and calculator)

Seiler Bonnie. How the West was One + Three × Four. Pleasantville, NY: Sunburst Communications, 1996. (software)

Sunburst, *The Hidden Treasure of Al-Jabar*. Pleasantville, NY: Sunburst Communications, 2001. (software)

———, *Sequencing Fun!* Pleasantville, NY: Sunburst Communications, 1998. (software)

———, *Zap! Around Town*. Pleasantville, NY: Sunburst Communications, 1998. (software)

———, *Tenth Planet, Introduction to Patterns*. Pleasantville, NY: Sunburst Communications, 1998. (software)

WEBLINKS

Weblink 10–1: National Assessment of Educational Progress: Mathematics Homepage http://nces.ed.gov/nations reportcard/mathematics/

Weblink 10–2: The Brain Lab, a compendium of full-text articles and resources sponsored by New Horizons: http://www.newhorizons.org/neuro/front_neuro.html

Weblink 10–3: The Dana Alliance for Brain Initiatives: http://www.dana.org/

Weblink 10–4: Neuroscience for Kids, sponsored by the National Institutes of Health's National Center for Research Resources: http://faculty.washington.edu/chudler/neurok.html

Weblink 10–5: Shodor Project Interactivate: http://shodor.org/interactivate/

Weblink 10–6: The Annenberg CPB Math and Science Project Teachers' Lab Patterns in Mathematics: http://www.learner.org/teacherslab/math/patterns/

Weblink 10–7: The Algebraic Calculator as a Pedagogical Tool for Teaching Mathematics by Bernhard Kutzler: http://b.kutzler.com/article/art_paed/ped-tool.html

Weblink 10–8: Trends in International Mathematics and Science Study: http://ustimss.msu.edu/

Weblink 10–9: NCTM *Mathematics Education Dialogues*: http://www.nctm.org/dialogues/

Weblink 10–10: Show Me Center: Supporting Standards Based Middle Grades Mathematics Curricula: http://showmecenter.missouri.edu/

TEACHING AND LEARNING GEOMETRY

As you read the following pages, consider these guiding questions:

1. What implications for teaching and learning geometry come from the van Hieles?
2. How are topology and projective geometry related to students learning Euclidean geometry?
3. How might you sequence the use of geoboards in teaching and learning geometry?
4. What geometry skills are developed as students use *Logo* to discover geometry?
5. What investigations in coordinate geometry are appropriate for elementary and middle-level students?
6. What geometry activities can you present that enhance the problem solving skills of students?
7. How are teachers able to connect the learning of geometry with the daily lives of their students?

Geometry

Instructional programs from prekindergarten through grade 12 should enable all students to:

Analyze characteristics and properties of two- and three-dimensional geometric shapes and develop mathematical arguments about geometric relationships

Pre-K to 2

- recognize, name, build, draw, compare, and sort two- and three-dimensional shapes;
- describe attributes and parts of two- and three-dimensional shapes;
- investigate and predict the results of putting together and taking apart two- and three-dimensional shapes.

Grades 3–5

- identify, compare, and analyze attributes of two- and three-dimensional shapes and develop vocabulary to describe the attributes;
- classify two- and three-dimensional shapes according to their properties and develop definitions of classes of shapes such as triangles and pyramids;
- investigate, describe, and reason about the results of subdividing, combining, and transforming shapes;
- explore congruence and similarity;
- make and test conjectures about geometric properties and relationships and develop logical arguments to justify conclusions.

Grades 6–8

- precisely describe, classify, and understand relationships among types of two- and three-dimensional objects (e.g., angles, triangles, quadrilaterals, cylinders, cones) using their defining properties;
- understand relationships among the angles, side lengths, perimeters, areas, and volumes of similar objects;
- create and critique inductive and deductive arguments concerning geometric ideas and relationships, such as congruence, similarity, and the Pythagorean relationship.

Specify locations and describe spatial relationships using coordinate geometry and other representational systems

Pre-K to 2

- describe, name, and interpret relative positions in space and apply ideas about relative position;
- describe, name, and interpret direction and distance in navigating space and apply ideas about direction and distance;
- find and name locations with simple relationships such as "near to" and in coordinate systems such as maps.

Grades 3–5

- describe location and movement using common language and geometric vocabulary;
- make and use coordinate systems to specify locations and to describe paths;
- find the distance between points along horizontal and vertical lines of a coordinate system.

Grades 6–8

- use coordinate geometry to represent and examine the properties of geometric shapes;
- use coordinate geometry to examine special geometric shapes, such as regular polygons or those with pairs of parallel or perpendicular sides.

Apply transformations and use symmetry to analyze mathematical situations

Pre-K to 2

- recognize and apply slides, flips, and turns;
- recognize and create shapes that have symmetry.

Grades 3–5

- predict and describe the results of sliding, flipping, and turning two-dimpensional shapes;
- describe a motion or a series of motions that will show that two shapes are congruent;
- identify and describe line and rotational symmetry in two- and three-dimensional shapes and designs.

Grades 6–8

- describe sizes, positions, and orientations of shapes under informal transformations such as flips, turns, slides, and scaling;
- examine the congruence, similarity, and line or rotational symmetry of objects using transformations.

Use visualization, spatial reasoning, and geometric modeling to solve problems

Pre-K to 2

- create mental images of geometric shapes using spatial memory and spatial visualization;
- recognize and represent shapes from different perspectives;
- relate ideas in geometry to ideas in number and measurement;
- recognize geometric shapes and structures in the environment and specify their location.

Grades 3–5

- build and draw geometric objects;
- create and describe mental images of objects, patterns, and paths;
- identify and build a three-dimensional object from two-dimensional representations of that object;
- identify and build a two-dimensional representation of a three-dimensional object;
- use geometric models to solve problems in other areas of mathematics, such as number and measurement;
- recognize geometric ideas and relationships and apply them to other disciplines and to problems that arise in the classroom or in everyday life.

NCTM (2000), pp. 96, 164, 232. Reprinted by permission.

Grades 6–8

- draw geometric objects with specified properties, such as side lengths or angle measures;
- use two-dimensional representations of three-dimensional objects to visualize and solve problems such as those involving surface area and volume;
- use visual tools such as networks to represent and solve problems;
- use geometric models to represent and explain numerical and algebraic relationships;
- recognize and apply geometric ideas and relationships in areas outside the mathematics classroom, such as art, science, and everyday life.

A pentomino is made by connecting five squares of the same size so that each square shares at least one complete side with another square. Copy two pages of the inch graph paper from Appendix B, cut five squares apart, and try to find all of the possible pentominoes. If you find a shape that can be flipped or rotated to make another shape, it is considered to be the same shape. As you find different shapes, outline them on the graph paper. Work with others in your class to find all 12 pentominoes.

Color each of your 12 pentominoes a different color and cut them out. Try to put all of your pentominoes together in one large rectangle. It is possible to make rectangles that are 3 by 20, 4 by 15, 5 by 12, and 6 by 10. Sketch any of your successes. If you cannot get the large rectangles, try using 6 of the pentominoes to get rectangles that are 3 by 10 or 5 by 6.

As you discuss your work be sure to explain all of your thinking.

REFLECTIONS AND REFINEMENT: After you have completed this task, compare your work with that of some of your classmates. How did your solution differ from those of others? As you continue through this term, see if you can find additional rectangles or other shapes to construct using the pentominoes. Write what you have found here.

Most of our buildings and decorations are based on geometric forms. And, much of nature can be described in geometric terms; this accounts, in part, for the origin of geometry. The work of Babylonian astronomers and Egyptian surveyors laid the foundations for geometry. It is appropriate, then, to help children recognize the geometry that surrounds them.

The environments most familiar to children are those of the home, neighborhood, and school. By and large, the objects in these environments are the products of human effort. The products of nature are evident, as well, and provide rich, intriguing objects of study. Once children are made aware of various shapes and geometric forms, they will find them everywhere. The patterns and forms in nature may not be as obvious but will capture children's interests for long periods of time. Peter Stevens noted in his book *Patterns in Nature* that

> [W]hen we see how the branching of trees resembles the branching of arteries and the branching of rivers, how crystal grains look like soap bubbles and the plates of a tortoise's shell, how the fiddleheads of ferns, stellar galaxies, and water emptying from the bathtub spiral in a similar manner, then we cannot help but wonder why .nature uses only a few kindred forms in so many different contexts. Why do meandering snakes, meandering rivers, and loops of string adopt the same pattern, and why do cracks in mud and markings on a giraffe arrange themselves like films in a froth of bubbles? (1974, p. 3)

A children's book that highlights patterns in nature is *Echoes for the Eye: Poems to Celebrate Patterns in Nature,* (Esbensen, 1996), a collection of poems and illustrations of shapes in the natural world. Read the book to students and discuss the images. Children's awareness of geometry in the environment is heightened considerably as teachers focus their attention on various applications of geometry. This awareness also strengthens students' appreciation for and understanding of geometry and helps develop students' spatial sense.

The foundations for learning geometry lie in informal experiences from pre-kindergarten through middle school. These experiences should be carefully planned and structured to provide youngsters with a variety of concepts and skills. These concepts and skills serve as a basis for later, more formal work in geometry. That is why it is important to provide pre-extensive, systematic exposure to geometric ideas from pre-kindergarten through grade 8.

Infants explore space initially by thrashing about in a crib or playpen and crawling toward objects or open doors. Children discover that some objects are close, while others are far. They discover that rooms have boundaries, and that sometimes, if a door is left open, the boundaries can be crossed. They discover that certain items belong inside boundaries—for example, father's nose belongs within the boundaries of his face, or the bathtub belongs within the confines of the bathroom.

Children also discover that events occur in a sequence or an order. Early in their lives, they learned that their own crying was often followed by the appearance of a parent, who then attended to their needs. Later, children notice that a stacking toy is put together by putting certain parts in a particular order.

These examples illustrate children's initial experiences in space. They are far removed from school experiences with geometric shapes but nonetheless help show how children discover spatial relationships. Children learn first about the common objects in their environments. Piaget and Inhelder (1967) found that young children view space from a **topological** perspective. For example, shapes are not seen as rigid; they may readily change as they are moved about. Later, children use projective viewpoints as they make the transition to a Euclidean point of view. Shadows provide an example of **projective geometry.** In projective geometry, distances and dimensions are not conserved, but the relative positions of parts of figures and the positions of figures relative to one another are conserved. Employing projective viewpoints helps children, by ages five to seven, to begin to perceive space from a Euclidean point of view when they see shapes as rigid—the shapes do not change as they are moved about.

There are many physical models available that enhance the learning environment for geometry. Among those that we recommend are pattern blocks, geoblocks, geoboards, reflective tools, paper models, and *Logo* (the computer language of turtle graphics). These and other useful materials are described and illustrated as they are presented in this chapter.

Geometry also serves as an instructional medium in its own right. Geometric models are used to introduce and illustrate a variety of mathematical topics. For example, geometric models are used to illustrate algorithms in Chapters 6 and 7 and geometric models are used to illustrate the concept of fractions in Chapter 8. Visualizing mathematics through models is well established as a teaching method. Materials such as *Math and the Mind's Eye* (Bennett et al., 1987) and *Visual Mathematics* (Bennett and Foreman, 1995, 1996) have been designed for use in grades 4–10 to help students develop their visual thinking. You are encouraged to explore these and other materials that employ geometry to model other mathematical topics.

MAKING SENSE OF GEOMETRIC CONCEPTS

The concepts upon which geometry is built begin with the simplest figure, the point, and expand to lines, line segments, rays, curves, plane figures, and space figures. We briefly discuss each of these.

The **point,** like all geometric figures, is an abstract idea. A point has no dimensions. It may be thought of as a location in space. For example, the tip of a pencil, the corner of a table, or a dot on a sheet of paper can represent a point.

A **line** is determined by two points and consists of a set of points connecting the two points and continuing endlessly in both directions. Figure 11–1a represents the line AB, defined by the points A and B.

Line segments and **rays** are subsets of a line. Like the line, each is determined by two points. The line segment, however, has two end points and the ray has only one end point. Line segment AB in Figure 11–1b is described by the two points A and B. Ray AB in Figure 11–1c includes end point A and a set of points continuing endlessly beyond point B. The arrowhead indicates the direction of a ray.

Lines, line segments, and rays have one dimension, length. When three or more points are not on the same line, a different kind of geometric figure results. It is a **plane figure,** or a figure in two dimensions. Figures such as *angles* (the union of two rays) and *triangles* (the union of three segments) are plane figures. We now consider curves and other plane figures.

A **curve** is a set of points that can be traced on paper without lifting the pencil. Figure 11–1d shows a simple curve between points A and B. It is **simple** because it does not cross over itself as it is drawn. The curve in Figure 11–1e is not simple because it crosses over itself as it is drawn from point A to point B. These two curves are not closed because they both have end points. When a curve has no end points, it is a **closed curve.** Figure 11–1f illustrates a simple closed curve.

Plane figures that are simple closed curves formed by joining line segments are called **polygons.** A polygon is named by the number of segments joined to make it. There are **triangles** (3 sides), **quadrilaterals** (4 sides), **pentagons** (5 sides), **hexagons** (6 sides), and so on. Figure 11–1g shows several polygons. A common simple closed curve not formed by joining line segments is the **circle.**

The prefixes of the words that name the polygons—**tri, quadri, penta, hexa, octa,** and **deca**—are of Latin or Greek origin and tell the reader how many sides a figure contains. Thus, *tri* means "three"; *quadri,* "four"; *penta,* "five"; *hexa,* "six"; *octa,* "eight"; and *deca,* "ten."

A polygon may have certain properties that provide a more specific description. For example, a **regular figure,** such as a square or an equilateral triangle, has sides that are the same length and angles of the same measure. Having sides that are parallel and having right angles are other descriptive characteristics of plane figures. A **square** is a quadrilateral with all sides the same length and all angles the same size. A **rectangle** is a quadrilateral with opposite sides parallel and the same length and all angles the same size. A **parallelogram** is a quadrilateral with opposite sides parallel and the same length. A **rhombus** is a quadrilateral with opposite sides parallel and all sides the same length. A rhombus is sometimes called a diamond.

A **space figure** is one that does not lie wholly in a plane. A soup can represents one such figure, called a **cylinder,** shown in Figure 11–1h. Other space figures include spheres, pyramids, prisms, and cones. The playground ball serves as a model of a **sphere,** the set of all points in space equidistant from a given point. A **pyramid** is a figure with a base the shape of a polygon and sloping triangular sides that meet at a common vertex. A **prism** is a figure whose ends are congruent polygons and parallel with each other, and whose sides are parallelograms. A **cone** is a figure with a circular base and a curved surface that tapers to a point.

Polyhedrons are space figures that have four or more plane surfaces. **Regular polyhedrons** are those in which each face is a regular polygon of the same size and shape and in which the same number of edges join at each corner or vertex. There are only five regular polyhedrons: the **tetrahedron** (4 faces), the **cube** (6 faces), the **octahedron** (8 faces), the **dodecahedron** (12 faces), and the **icosahedron** (20 faces). These are shown in Figure 11–1i.

The geometric concepts described above form a major part of the elementary and middle school mathematics curriculum. How these ideas are presented to children is important. *Principles and Standards for School Mathematics* suggested:

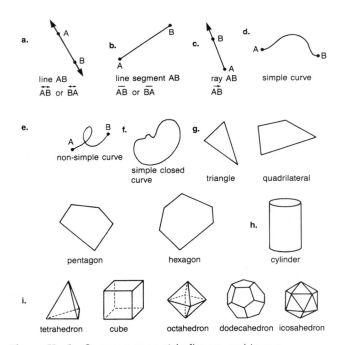

a.
line AB
$\overleftrightarrow{AB}$ or $\overleftrightarrow{BA}$

b.
line segment AB
$\overline{AB}$ or $\overline{BA}$

c.
ray AB
$\overrightarrow{AB}$

d.
simple curve

e.
non-simple curve

f.
simple closed curve

g.
triangle

quadrilateral

pentagon

hexagon

h.
cylinder

i.
tetrahedron   cube   octahedron   dodecahedron   icosahedron

Figure 11–1 Common geometric figures and terms.

Beginning in the early years of schooling, students should develop visualization skills through hands-on experiences with a variety of geometric objects and through the use of technology that allows them to turn, shrink, and deform two- and three-dimensional objects. Later, they should become comfortable analyzing and drawing perspective views, counting component parts, and describing attributes that cannot be seen but can be inferred. Students need to learn to physically and mentally change the position, orientation, and size of objects in systematic ways as they develop their understandings about congruence, similarity, and transformations. (NCTM, 2000, p. 43)

The following development of geometric concepts expands on the elementary or middle school textbook presentation of recognition of shapes and definition of terms. We begin with a description of the van Hiele levels of geometric thinking, followed by views young children have of the world when they enter school, activities that introduce projective geometry, plane figures and their properties, symmetry and transformations, space figures and their properties, and fractal geometry.

The van Hiele Levels

Pre-kindergarten through middle school instruction plays an important developmental role as children learn geometry. The work of Pierre M. van Hiele and Dieke van Hiele-Geldof has influenced the teaching of geometry in various parts of the world. The van Hieles were Dutch middle-level mathematics teachers who studied the students with whom they worked. As an outgrowth of their research, P. M. van Hiele (1986) and Teppo (1991) described a model of instruction that included three levels through which individuals pass as they learn to work comfortably in the most abstract geometries. Between the levels are learning periods during which the student gains the background for moving to the next level. Each learning period has the same structure. The van Hiele levels are the following:

- *Level 1: Visual.* Students learn to recognize various shapes globally after repeatedly seeing them as separate objects. Students do not notice the common characteristics of similar figures.
- *Learning Period 1:* Overview of geometric content, exploring content, discussing content with a special focus on language and communication, applying knowledge of content, and developing an overview of the learning.
- *Level 2: Descriptive.* Students observe and manipulate figures, thus determining the properties necessary for identifying various shapes. Measuring is one way students learn the necessary properties.

- *Learning Period 2:* Overview of geometric content, exploring content, discussing content with a special focus on language and communication, applying knowledge of content, and developing an overview of the learning.
- *Level 3: Theoretical.* Students use deduction while working with postulates, theorems, and proof.

Many high school geometry courses begin work at the third level. Burger (1985) noted, however, that many high school students are working at the levels of younger children—levels 1 and 2. Thus, teachers and students may have difficulty understanding each other. It is important, therefore, for pre-kindergarten through middle school mathematics programs to provide informal geometry experiences to help students progress through the first and second levels. The activities suggested in this chapter illustrate the types of geometric experiences that assist students through the early van Hiele levels.

Young Children's Views of the World

The perceptions of children before they are five to seven years old are topological. **Topology** is the study of space concerned with position or location, where length and shape may be altered without affecting a figure's basic property of being open or closed. For example, a five-year-old shown a triangle and asked to make several copies of it may draw several simple closed curves but not necessarily triangles, as in Figure 11–2a. To the child, all of the drawings are the same, because the child perceives that the triangle has only the property of being closed (younger children often draw figures that are not closed). As well, a triangle may be stretched into any closed figure, as in Figure 11–2b (Copeland, 1984, p. 216).

The study of space in which a figure or any enclosed space must remain rigid or unchanged is called **Euclidean geometry.** The historical development of geometry was Euclidean; that is, geometry developed from ideas such as points, lines, and polygons.

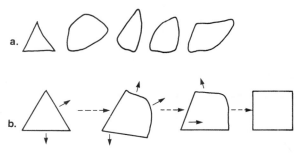

Figure 11–2 Examples of children's topological thinking.

Some of Piaget's research has implied that children do not develop geometric concepts in a Euclidean manner. Because of their topological perspectives, children need active, exploratory time when they enter school (1953, p. 75).

In Chapter 5, relationships among objects and numbers were discussed as the concept of number was developed. Likewise, spatial relationships can be identified as the concepts associated with space are developed. Children who perceive the world from a topological point of view are developing an understanding of four basic relationships:

1. *Is close to* or *is far from*
2. *Is a part of* or *is not a part of*
3. *Comes before* or *comes after*
4. *Is inside of, is outside of,* or *is on*

During kindergarten and first grade, children develop to the point where they can understand the meaning of Euclidean space. That is, children develop their abilities to reproduce shapes without significantly altering the characteristics of those shapes. For example, in the earlier topological stage, children copy a figure but allow corners to become round and distances to change. At the stage of Euclidean understanding, corners remain corners and distances are unchanged—the figure is considered rigid.

The shift from topological to Euclidean thinking is not sudden. It may occur over a period of two years. Thus, usually between the ages of four and six, children can recognize and name the more common figures: square, triangle, rectangle, circle. Other figures are neither identified nor differentiated from these shapes. For example, the square and other rhombuses may be confused, as may the rectangle and other parallelograms. Even more difficult for children is copying various shapes from blocks or drawings. Children may be able to accurately identify shapes long before they are able to produce their own examples.

During kindergarten and first grade, it is important to continue activities that relate to topological space. The following are typical activities that extend topological ideas.

A C T I V I T I E S

Pre-Kindergarten – Grade 2

OBJECTIVE: to develop and reinforce the concepts of near, far, on, in, under, over, inside, and outside.

1. Developing language in concert with activities is a natural part of teaching. Have children sit in small groups at tables on which numerous objects are placed. Give directions to various children. For example, "Julia, please put the red block as far away from the plastic cup as you can," or "David, please put the short pencil in the tin can." Several children may participate simultaneously. Check the understanding of the language and the concept. Engage the children in discussion about the activity.

2. Draw three regions on the playground or on the floor of the multipurpose room. The regions represent a red base, a green base, and a catchers' region. Select two groups of children: those who attempt to change from the red base to the green base when a signal is given and those who begin at the catchers' region. As the children are changing from the red to the green base, the catchers run from their region and tag those who are changing.

The catchers may tag the changers as long as they are outside of both the red and green bases. Once the changers reach the green base, they try to return to the red base. They continue running back and forth between bases as long as possible. Children who are tagged join the catchers. The game is over whenever there are no more children to run between the red and green bases.

Children participating in this activity are concerned about being inside or outside of the various regions. Occasionally during the activity, have the children "freeze." Tell the children, "Raise your hand if you are inside the green region. Raise your hand if you are outside the green region. Raise your hand if you are inside the red region. Raise your hand if you are outside the red region. Raise your hand if you are outside both the red and green regions."

3. Construct the following activity on the playground or on paper. Put large drawings such as those in Figure 11–3 on the ground and invite the children to stand *inside* and to see if they can get to the outside by walking. There is one rule: you cannot step over a boundary line.

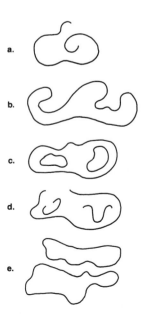

Figure 11–3 Examples of boundary figures for inside and outside activity.

Students unable to get outside are inside a closed curve. All other students are outside the closed curve or are standing on the curve itself, or the region is not closed. Have the children experiment with several curves until they can easily determine if they are inside or outside a region, or if there is a closed region at all.

A simple curve like that in Figure 11–3a does not divide the plane in which it is drawn. Thus, only one region exists, whereas in Figure 11–3b, two regions exist because the simple closed curve separates the plane into two regions. In Figure 11–3c, there are four regions and the curve itself. The region outside the figure is counted. Figure 11–3d shows one region; Figure 11–3e shows three regions.

If these activities are performed on paper, the children may benefit from coloring each region a different color. Devise variations of this sort of boundary exercise. Discuss the activity, encouraging the children to explain what happens in each case.

4. Another type of boundary activity is the maze. The object of this activity is to see if two children are in the same region. On the playground, the children attempt to walk to one another without walking on or across a boundary. On paper, have children trace the regions with their fingers. The variations and the complexity of these designs are nearly unlimited. Figure 11–4 provides two examples of simple mazes. The children in Figure 11–4a are able to walk to each other because they are in the same region. In Figure 11–4b, the children cannot reach each other because they are in different regions. Let the children explain the differences in each maze.

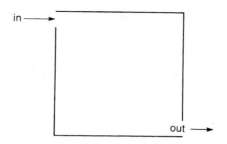

Figure 11–5   Frame for beginning maze construction.

5. A third, more complex boundary activity involves having children construct maze puzzles for themselves and other children. Maze puzzles may be constructed by beginning with a simple frame with a door to go in and a door to go out, as in Figure 11–5.

To complete the maze, draw lines from any wall. The only rule is that no line can connect one wall with another wall. Steps a, b, and c in Figure 11–6 show how a maze puzzle was constructed. Children are fascinated by the construction of mazes and they enjoy challenging one another to solve their mazes.

OBJECTIVE: to develop the ability to verbalize about geometric figures and patterns.

6. Encourage children to draw construct and manipulate space figures. Materials may include tiles,

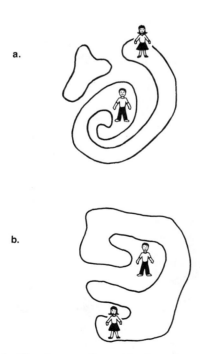

Figure 11–4   Simple maze figures for boundary activity.

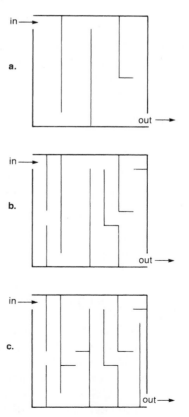

Figure 11–6   Steps in completing a maze.

attribute blocks, geoblocks, cubes, cans, empty milk cartons, Unifix cubes, Cuisenaire rods, pattern blocks, parquetry blocks, and clay. **Geoblocks** are pieces of unfinished hardwood, cut into a wide variety of space figures. Have the children talk with one another as they work. During that time, circulate and ask individuals, "Tell me what your picture shows. Can you find another shape like this one? How would you describe this piece? How are the buildings the same?"

Children can learn to be analytical when questions are carefully phrased. For example, "Can you make another house just like the one you have made there? I would like you to try." At the same time, the questions can serve to gather information for the teacher. Be sure to allow children to explain an answer.

OBJECTIVE: to use visual clues in matching shapes.

7. Encourage children to construct picture jigsaw puzzles. Challenge the students with difficult puzzles, and discuss informally with individuals or small groups how they have gone about putting the puzzle together. It should be evident that strategies are developed as puzzles are completed. Edge pieces are generally put together first, followed by pieces that form distinct images or those that have easily matched colors. Pieces are added to the puzzle when their shapes fit a region that has been surrounded by other pieces. Finally, all other pieces are put into place by the process of elimination.

The preceding activities have been presented to help reinforce the early geometry ideas of youngsters. They serve as preparation for the following activities, which help introduce children to the Euclidean shapes.

Projective Geometry

As children investigate figures and their properties through shadow geometry, they are involved in the transition from a topological perspective of their world to a Euclidean perspective. Piaget and Inhelder (1967, p. 467) noted that "Projective concepts take account, not only of internal topological relationships, but also of the shapes of figures, their relative positions and apparent distances, though always in relation to a specific point of view." Children explore what happens to shapes held in front of a point source of light, such as a spotlight or a bright flashlight. They also explore what happens to shapes held in the sunlight when the sun's rays are nearly parallel. They discover which characteristics of the shapes are maintained under varying conditions. Children need to make observations, sketch the results of their work, and discuss their observations. As a result, children develop a viewpoint that is not part of a topological perspective.

The activities that follow are intended to provide children with experience with projective geometry.

A C T I V I T I E S

Pre-Kindergarten – Grade 2

OBJECTIVE: to produce and describe the shadows of squares and other shapes, using the sun as a source of light.

1. Provide pairs of children with square regions such as wooden or plastic geoboards or regions cut from railroad board. Take the children to an area of the playground that has a flat, smooth surface such as blacktop or concrete. Have the children hold the square regions so that shadows are cast on the ground, as in Figure 11–7.

Encourage the children to move the square regions so that the shadow changes. Be sure both members of a pair have a chance to experiment with shadow-making. After a few minutes, gather the children around you and ask them to talk about the shadows they found as they moved their square regions. If it is difficult for a child to explain the shape of the shadow, have the child illustrate the shadow for the others. Let the children discuss how they were able to make the shapes larger and smaller. See what other observations they have made.

To make a permanent record of shapes, have one member of each pair of children put a piece of paper on the ground and let the shadow fall on the paper. Have that child draw around the outline of the shadow on the sheet of paper. When each student has had a chance to draw a favorite shape, there will be a collection of interesting drawings that can serve as a source for discussion, sorting, and display.

2. Using the square regions from Activity 1, challenge the children to make the shadow into a square. Ask the students what they had to do to produce a square shadow. Give the children square regions that

Figure 11–7 Examining shadows of squares and other shapes.

have been cut from paper to put on the ground. Have the children use their square regions to make a shadow just large enough to exactly cover the paper square on the ground. Have them make a square smaller than the paper square, then one larger than the paper square. Let the children discuss how they were able to make their shadows different sizes.

Next, give pairs of children a paper diamond region that is not a square to put on the ground and ask them to try to make the same shape using the square region. Have them exactly cover the diamond shape, then make diamond shapes smaller and larger than the paper diamond.

See if the children can make a triangle or a pentagon shadow using the square region. See if they can make a rectangle or another parallelogram. It will be necessary to provide paper shapes as models for the children to use. Be sure to have the children sketch their results and discuss their findings.

3. Introduce diamond, triangular, and hexagonal regions to see what kinds of shapes their shadows are. Can a diamond shadow be made with a diamond region? Can a square shadow be made? What other shadow shapes can be made? Can a triangular shadow be made with a triangular region? Can square or diamond shadows be made?

Other shapes should be available with which the children can experiment. Again, outlining the shadows will produce a permanent record of the shadow shapes. Expect the children to make discoveries that you had not thought of, and join in the excitement of such discoveries.

4. Using the outlines that the children drew of shadows cast by square regions, see if the children can find things that are alike and things that are different in the drawings. Encourage the students to count the number of corners and the number of sides of each shadow shape and to compare those numbers. Write down the conclusions made based on these observations.

Pose problems such as: "Suppose we take one of our shadow drawings and cut it out and glue it to a piece of railroad board cut exactly like the outline. Would it be possible to use that shape to make a shadow that would just match the square region that we started with? How do you think it could be done? Why do you believe that it can't be done?" Let the children perform the experiment to see if they can do this. Have them put their square regions on the ground and see if they can exactly cover the square region with a shadow from the outline region.

OBJECTIVE: to produce and describe the shadows of squares and other shapes, using a point source of light.

5. Set up a spotlight or use a flashlight so that the light is projected onto a screen or wall. Let the children play in the light by making shadows using their hands or by holding small objects. After this introductory activity,

provide the children with square regions and encourage them to explore the different ways that shadows can be produced. Tape paper to the wall and have the children outline the shadows to provide a record of their work that can be displayed on a bulletin board and discussed.

As an extension, introduce other shapes such as triangular, rectangular, and hexagonal regions and let the students find out what their shadows look like. Let the children describe their shadow shapes and explain how various shadows were made.

6. Compare the outline drawings of the shadows of the square regions made using the sun as a source of light with those made using a point source of light. A bulletin board display can have the shadows sorted, with shadows made using the sun on one side and those made using the projector or flashlight on the other side. Can all of the same shadow shapes be made? Do the shapes look similar? For those shadows that are different, would it be possible to make that shape if we tried again using the sun or a point source of light?

To extend this activity, cut out the outline of a shadow of a square region made with a point source of light, glue it to a piece of railroad board cut to exactly the same shape, and see if it is possible to make a shadow that matches the original square region. Are the results of this activity the same as the results obtained using the sun as a source of light?

7. Take a square region and place it on a block or paper cup so that the square region is supported parallel to the floor as in Figure 11−8. Have the children hold a flashlight above the square region, moving it from side to side, and ask them to observe the shadow that is produced.

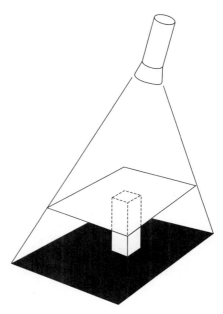

Figure 11−8 Setup for a shadow activity using a flashlight as a light source.

What characteristics of the shadow shape are noted? If a sheet of paper is placed beneath the block, an outline of the shadow shape can be drawn. Then direct comparisons can be made between the square region and its shadow, such as comparing the sizes of the corners and the lengths of the sides.

Is it possible to make diamonds or rectangles by moving the light to various positions? As the flashlight is moved higher and lower how does the size of the shadow change? Next, use triangular and rectangular regions and explore their shadows.

The preceding activities in projective geometry have been presented to help children as they make the transition from topological notions to Euclidean notions. You may also wish to examine the activities suggested by Dienes and Golding (1967) and by Mansfield (1985) in the works listed in the references at the end of the chapter.

Plane Figures and Their Characteristics and Properties

Children's abilities to learn the names and properties of common plane figures, such as triangles, squares, rectangles, circles, parallelograms, rhombuses, hexagons, and so forth, vary considerably within any group of children. Those who are able to observe a shape and then easily find another like it or those who are able to look at a figure and then draw it maintaining the characteristics essential to the figure are ready to proceed with more systematic instruction on Euclidean shapes.

Piaget and Inhelder (1967, p. 43) indicated that learning shapes requires two coordinated actions. The first is the physical handling of the shape, being able to run fingers along the boundaries of the shape. The second is the visual perception of the shape itself. It is insufficient for children merely to see drawings or photographs of the shapes. A variety of materials and activities can help to present plane figures to children. Some of these materials and activities are presented below.

Pre-Kindergarten – Grade 2

OBJECTIVE: to develop tactile understanding of common plane figures.

1. Give children flat shapes to explore. The shapes may be commercially produced, such as attribute blocks, or they may be teacher-constructed from colorful railroad

board. Allow the children time for free play with little or no teacher direction. Perhaps the children will construct houses, people, cars, animals, patterns, or larger shapes.

After having plenty of free time with the shapes, the children will be ready for the teacher to ask a few questions or to compliment them on their work. If someone has constructed a truck, ask several children to construct others just like it. Challenge the children to make an object that is the same except upside down.

If a pattern is made, perhaps it can be extended. Encourage children and ask, "What shapes have you used to make your picture? What would happen if we changed all of the triangles to squares? What would happen if all the pieces were exchanged for larger pieces of the same shape? Let's try it."

2. Construct models of various shapes for the children to handle. One way to construct a model is to bend heavy wire in the shape of a triangle, square, rectangle, circle, parallelogram, rhombus, or hexagon. A touch of solder should hold the ends together. Another way is to glue small doweling to a piece of railroad board. The children can then develop a tactile understanding of the shapes.

Once the children have handled the shapes, encourage them to describe the shapes. Ask, "How many corners does it have? How many sides does it have? What else do you notice?" Ask them to draw a particular shape while looking at and feeling the model. Later, ask them to draw the shapes while only feeling or seeing the models. Finally, ask the children to draw the shapes without either seeing or feeling the models.

OBJECTIVE: to make patterns using geometric shapes.

3. Parquetry blocks (Figure 11–9) are a unique material to use to learn about plane figures. **Parquetry blocks** are geometric shapes of varying colors and sizes. The first attempt to use them should be in a free-play activity. Then, there are several ways to use the blocks to present shapes.

- Copy activities include holding up one of the shapes and having children find another block of the same or a different shape. Next, put three or four of the blocks together in a simple design and ask the children to copy the design. It may be

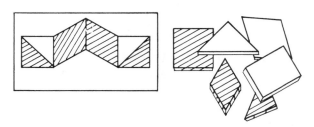

Figure 11–9 Parquetry blocks and sample work card.

copied exactly or with a slight variation, such as with different colors. Finally, put the blocks into a simple design but separate them from each other. Copying this design requires the children to visualize across the separations.

- Present outlines of parquetry blocks and ask the children to find a piece the same color, shape, and size and place it on the outline. Later, have them match just shape and size. Present more complicated outlines, using designs of two or more blocks, after the children have worked with single blocks.
- Ask children to make their own outlines for others to fill in either by drawing around the various shapes or by putting all the shapes down and drawing around the entire design. The latter variation produces a challenging puzzle for children to complete.

While our discussion has centered on the parquetry blocks, another learning aid, pattern blocks, works equally well for the activities just mentioned.

OBJECTIVE: to construct common geometric figures.

4. The **geoboard** is a dynamic aid for use in teaching geometry. It consists of a board 20 to 25 centimeters square with five rows of five escutcheon pins in each row (Figure 11–10). Students can stretch rubber bands around the pins to form various figures.

After a period of free play during which children can discover some of the patterns, shapes, and pictures that can be constructed, direct some copying activities. Construct a particular configuration or shape and show it to the children, asking them to copy it. Initially, construct a line segment, then perhaps combinations of two, three, or more line segments (Figure 11–10). Next, construct simple shapes. Gradually make the shapes more complex and challenging, as in Figure 11–11. As soon as the children understand the nature of the copying exercises, allow them to construct shapes for others to copy. Be sure students have the opportunity to discuss the characteristics of their figures.

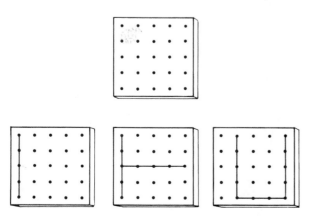

Figure 11–10 Geoboards and simple rubber band shapes.

Figure 11–11 Examples of shapes to copy on the geoboard.

As the children gain experience in recognizing and naming shapes, use the names to describe shapes for the children to construct. Say, for example, "Let's make triangles on our geoboards. If we look at everyone's triangles, can we find some things that are the same? Are there any triangles that are completely different? Who has the biggest triangle? Who has the smallest? Who has the triangle with the most nails inside the rubber band? Who can make a shape that is not a triangle? Now, let's make some squares."

An extension of this activity may be employed using dynamic geometry software. A good example is found on Weblink 11–1. Interactive geoboards are used. The first activity has the students work with triangles, developing the idea of congruence. The second activity has the students make and compare a variety of polygons.

OBJECTIVE: to discover characteristics of various shapes.

5. Shapes Inside Out, for pre-kindergarten–grade 2, may be found on Weblink 11–2. The lesson plan for this activity focuses on spatial sense. Teachers ask students to identify geometric shapes based on their attributes and place teddy bear counters in various locations. For example, "Put the teddy bear inside a shape that has a square corner" or "Put the teddy bear outside a shape that has more than four sides." As an extension, students may be asked to describe the locations of teddy bears that have already been situated.

OBJECTIVE: to discover characteristics of various shapes.

6. Tessellating is covering or tiling a region with many pieces of the same shape. Countertops and floors are often tessellated with square pieces. Of the regular Euclidean figures (that is, those with sides of equal length and angles of equal measure), only triangles, squares, and hexagons will completely cover a region without the need for additional pieces to fill in gaps. There are, however, many irregular shapes with which a region may be tessellated. Figure 11–12 shows a tessellation of quadrilaterals. All quadrilaterals will tessellate.

Give children a sheet of paper to serve as a region and numerous pieces of some shape with which to tessellate. Pattern blocks are a handy and colorful material to use in tessellating. Ask the children to cover the paper with a particular shape and to decide which shapes will work. Have them discuss their work. Later, ask them to try to use a combination of two or three shapes to tessellate.

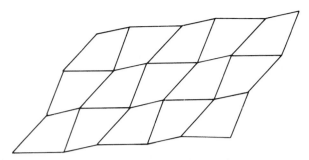

Figure 11–12 A tessellation of quadrilaterals.

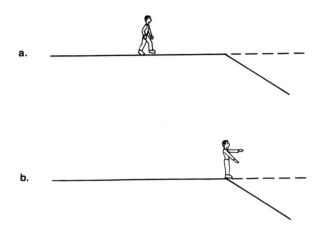

Figure 11–13 Developing the concept of an angle.

Before they begin, have the children estimate whether or not they can use the shapes to tessellate.

7. Books that feature shapes can help children become aware of how commonplace geometry is in our surroundings. In *Shapes, Shapes, Shapes,* Hoban (1986) invites children to identify a variety of shapes from photographs that they should recognize. *The Button Box* (Reid, 1990) displays a multitude of buttons that illustrate shape and pattern and describes their uses. Bread in a variety of shapes is presented by Morris (1989) in *Bread, Bread, Bread.* This description of bread from many cultures helps children identify many unusual shapes. Grifalconi (1986) tells a story of west Africa in which the shapes of houses are important. *The Village of Round and Square Houses* is a beautifully written and illustrated book about a real place. After reading books such as these to the students and discussing them, leave the books out for the students to peruse on their own.

OBJECTIVE: to develop the concept of an angle.

8. An **angle** may be thought of as a change in direction along a line. On the floor or playground, have children walk along a line that at some point changes direction, however slightly or sharply, as in Figure 11–13a. Discuss with the children that the change in direction forms an angle.

Ask the children if they can think of a figure that has an angle or corner. Children discussing the characteristics of a plane figure will mention the corners or bends that help give the figure its shape. The concept of an angle is being developed at an intuitive level.

Later, more formally define an angle as two rays sharing a common end point. Have children walk along chalk or tape lines that form a zigzag path. By pointing one arm in the direction in which they have been walking and the other arm in the direction of change, children can form the angle of change. Figure 11–13b illustrates using the arms.

Then, have the children walk on large polygons. This activity serves as an introduction to one aspect of the computer language *Logo. Logo* activities are presented in a later section.

OBJECTIVE: to practice making polygons and discover now their properties may change.

9. Provide the members of a learning group with a 10-foot length of yarn that has been knotted at the ends to form a large loop. First, have two members of the group each hold it with both hands so that 4 vertices are formed, as in Figure 11–14. The other members of the group serve as observers and recorders. The holders pull the yarn taut, producing a quadrilateral, then they explore what happens to the shape as they change the sizes of the angles and the lengths of the sides of the figure. An observer's job is to describe what happens and a recorder's job is to sketch the shape as it changes. Will it be possible to produce a triangle? How about a pentagon? What must be done to make a square, a rectangle, and a parallelogram? When the children have had a chance to discuss their findings and to look at the sketches of the figures, ask them what they can conclude about changing the angles, changing the lengths of the sides, and making other types of geometric figures.

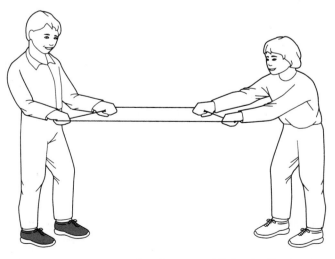

Figure 11–14 Students forming a quadrilateral with yarn.

To extend this activity, have a third student hold the yarn so that there are 6 vertices. Now, what different shapes can they make and how does changing the angles and the lengths of the sides affect the appearance of the figure? Does changing the length of the yarn affect the results of this activity? Again, discussion helps children share their observations and their sketches help to verify their conclusions.

The activities just presented are intended to give primary children experiences with plane figures to complement work in the mathematics program. A number of activities can be combined to develop a thematic unit about shapes. As a part of her work with kindergarten children, student teacher Nicole Erwert designed a week of shape activities. On **Monday,** each student constructed a shape book with four pages, featuring, in turn, triangles, circles, squares, and other rectangles. Then the children looked through magazines for examples of the shapes to cut out and glue on the appropriate page of their book. On **Tuesday,** the students took a shape walk in the school neighborhood, recognizing shapes on buildings, various structures, and in nature. On **Wednesday,** the children constructed a "town" by using common boxes onto which they had glued shapes that they had cut out. All of the buildings were placed on a "street" drawn on a large sheet of butcher paper. On **Thursday,** the students constructed geometric "people" by cutting out shapes and gluing them onto pieces of construction paper as in Figure 11–15. That afternoon a bulletin board was arranged using the geometric people. On **Friday,** a listening activity was introduced. Each student had a worksheet with several triangles, squares, circles, and other rectangles drawn on it. Instructions such as "color all of the triangles blue" were given. This quiet activity provided an opportunity for assessment of both shape recognition and listening ability.

Further, center activities were provided throughout the week. Students rotated from centers featuring geoboards on which to construct shapes, building blocks, a game of shape Bingo, and shapes used to build patterns.

This was a successful week and raised the shape awareness of the children. They talked about various shapes each day.

Most of the following activities are intended to support children as they work in the first and second of the van Hiele levels, visual and descriptive. This means the students will continue to analyze the properties of Euclidean figures and will begin to understand the characteristics of the figures in terms of definitions.

Figure 11–15 A geometric person formed by gluing shapes together.

A C T I V I T I E S

Grades 3–5 and Grades 6–8

OBJECTIVE: to discover important properties that define a variety of polygons.

1. Periodically designate a bulletin board as a shape board. Attach a label such as "quadrilaterals" and invite the children to put as many different quadrilaterals as they can on the board. Encourage a discussion about the meaning of quadrilateral. Let the students generate a list of characteristics of a quadrilateral. After two or three days, have the children describe the ways in which the shapes are different. Thus, the children look at the defining properties of quadrilaterals. Ask the children to classify the quadrilaterals as squares, rhombuses, rectangles, parallelograms, and trapezoids. Which categories overlap? How do the shapes relate? At other times, the board theme may be triangles, hexagons, or octagons.

2. Introduce students to dynamic geometry software by having them go to Weblink 11–3. Here, students explore properties of rectangles and parallelograms by dragging corners and sides of the figures and changing their shape and size. Students are encouraged to make conjectures about the properties and characteristics of the dynamic figures. The conjectures are then

_____ , 19____

Dear Family,

Our class is beginning a mathematics unit called *Flips, Turns, and Area*. The ideas in this unit may be new to you. Your child will learn about special shapes called *tetrominoes*—different arrangements of four squares:

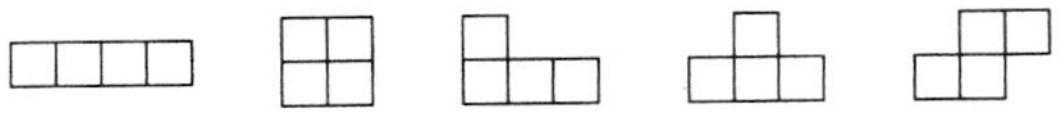

We'll be talking about three ways we can move these shapes—

by sliding: by flipping: 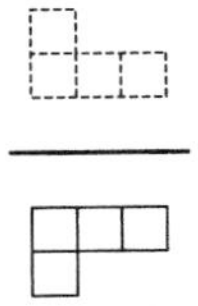   and by turning:

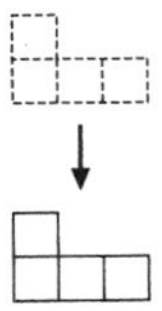

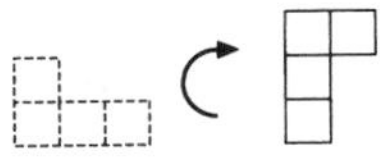

We'll work with these ideas using paper cutouts and a computer game called Tumbling Tetrominoes. After we've started the unit, ask your child to explain the game to you.

Being able to visualize how different shapes fit in space is an important geometric skill. It also has a lot of practical aspects. For example, think of how hard it is to get a couch up a stairway and into the living room—it's really a matter of slides, flips, and turns!

Part of this unit is all about discovering *area* as a measure of a flat surface. Look for opportunities at home to talk about area with your child. For example:

Do you have square tiles covering a floor or bathroom wall? How many squares are there?

Suppose you make roll-out cookies with your child. This poses a problem of area: How can you place the cookie cutters so that you cover the most area, and have the least amount of dough leftover? Do you have to rotate the cookie cutter to get the best fit?

Have a good time exploring these ideas with your child!

Sincerely,

Figure 11–16 From *Investigations in Number, Data and Space: Flips, Turns, and Area*, by Douglas H. Clements, Susan Jo Russel, Cornelia Tierney, Michael T. Battista & Julie Sarama; Copyright © 1998. Reprinted by permission of Pearson Education, Inc.

The family math page from the third-grade book shown in Figure 11–16 is designed to be sent home at the beginning of this unit entitled *Flips, Turns, and Area.* This page is available in several different languages so that teachers can communicate with parents for whom English is a second language. As you can see from this page, students in this section will be designing tetrominoes and then studying transformations of these shapes as they look at area and tessellation concepts. As part of this unit, students will use an included computer program that is similar to the commercial game Tetris. In this game, however, students attempt to completely cover rectangles with an area of 120 square units. In doing this, students investigate all the factors of 120 and cut out rectangles to determine all the possible 120 square unit rectangles. They then work with paper tetrominoes to try to cover these rectangles.

This *Flips, Turns, and Area* unit is one of 10 units in this third-grade program. It is part of a series for kindergarten through fifth grade entitled *Investigations in Number, Data and Space.* These units could be used as replacement units in conjunction with another program, but they are designed to be a complete, self-contained program. Each unit has a teacher's book, and some contain software, but there are no student books. Students frequently use black-line masters from the teacher's book but are generally involved in active investigations with objects and experiences from their environments. These activities include pair and small-group work, individual tasks, and whole-class discussions. The unit also contains 10-minute math activities designed to be used outside of the regular math period to review concepts that may have been taught at other times during the year. Homework is designed to build on class investigations and is not given every day. Assessment includes Teacher Checkpoints, which are checklists of concepts that teachers should look for as students work, embedded assessment activities that may involve writing and reflections from the students or brief interactions between students and the teacher, and ongoing assessment that includes observations and portfolio or journal work.

This unit includes an investigation of motions with tetrominoes that is designed to last approximately five hours and an investigation of area also designed to last approximately five hours. Each of the sessions in these areas include suggestions for homework and extensions that continue and expand upon the classwork.

tested using the dynamic figures. Students should then discuss and raise questions with others about what they have discovered.

3. On the overhead projector or chalkboard, display a set of properties of a particular quadrilateral. Reveal the properties one at a time until a student decides a sufficient number of properties have been displayed to identify the shape. That student must then convince the rest of the class that enough characteristics have been given to identify the figure. For example, the following list may be presented.

- It is a closed figure with 4 straight sides.
- It has 2 long sides and 2 short sides.
- The 2 long sides are the same length.
- The 2 short sides are the same length.
- One of the angles is larger than one of the other angles.
- Two angles are the same size.
- The other 2 angles are the same size.
- The 2 long sides are parallel.
- The 2 short sides are parallel.

Next, have the children develop lists, individually or in small groups, that can be used to challenge the others in the class. They may select particular triangles, quadrilaterals other than the parallelogram described above, or various other polygons. Invite discussion of the lists; there should be many questions and observations.

OBJECTIVE: to discover the numerous configurations a polygon may have.

4. Challenge the children to find as many different triangles as possible on the geoboard. By different, we mean noncongruent, that is, not the same size and shape. Because of the variety of such figures, it is helpful to structure this activity using the problem-solving skill of simplifying the problem. For example, ask for as many different triangles as can be made using only two adjacent rows on the geoboard (we count 14 such triangles). Before the children begin, have them estimate how many triangles they can make.

You may wish to simplify the problem even more by asking the students to make triangles on a 2-by-2, 2-by-3, or 2-by-4 arrangement of nails. As the children find the triangles, have them sketch the triangles on a piece of dot paper (see Appendix B) and discuss how they went about finding them. Figure 11–17 shows a few of the possible triangles.

A little later, ask the children to make as many triangles as possible on a 3-by-3 nail arrangement on the geoboard. Put a rubber band on the geoboard surrounding the 3-by-3 area as a guide. Of course, you may use another arrangement as the basis for constructing triangles.

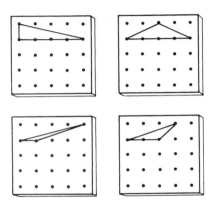

Figure 11–17 Triangles formed on a 2-by-5 arrangement of nails on a geoboard.

Discuss the types of triangles found. There will be **right triangles** (one angle of 90 degrees), **isosceles triangles** (a pair of congruent sides), **acute triangles** (all angles less than 90 degrees), **obtuse triangles** (one angle more than 90 degrees), and **scalene triangles** (no sides of equal length).

Extend this activity by seeing how many quadrilaterals may be made on a certain part of the geoboard. Be sure to have children estimate before they begin. We know that 16 noncongruent quadrilaterals can be formed on a 3-by-3 geoboard. How many squares or rectangles or hexagons may be constructed?

This series of activities for children in pre-kindergarten through middle school plays an important role in children's geometric learning. They help define plane figures and their properties in concrete and abstract terms. We now turn to transformations, symmetry, and dynamic geometry.

Transformations, Symmetry, and Dynamic Geometry

The notions of transformations and symmetry are exemplified by patterns in nature and in the art and architecture of human beings. **Transformations** refer to the movement of shapes by flipping them, rotating them, sliding them, or scaling them. **Symmetry** requires a line or lines about which a figure or design is balanced or a point about which a figure or design is rotated. There is something orderly and pleasant in balance, the characteristic of a figure that suggests an equality of parts. Children often generate symmetrical designs with building materials. Many geometric figures contain fine examples of symmetry, having, in some cases, several lines of symmetry. **Dynamic geometry** refers to an environment in which students may investigate geometric relationships using conjecture and proof. Instruction may be aided using dynamic geometry software that allows students to explore and model the relationships by quickly providing many example and, perhaps, a counterexample. The software helps students whose ability to prove and use mathematical arguments has not been fully developed. A good example of dynamic geometry software is *The Geometer's Sketchpad*. In this application, the user begins with a blank screen and a toolbar. A variety of powerful tools are available that allow the user to complete constructions, transformations, measurements, and graphing. Students are able to discover geometric relationships by visualizing and reflecting and then make conjectures that can be tested. Weblink 11–4 provides resources and examples from *The Geometer's Sketchpad*. The following activities combine transformations, symmetry, and dynamic geometry.

A C T I V I T I E S

Pre-Kindergarten – Grade 2

OBJECTIVE: to develop simple symmetrical patterns with objects.

1. Provide the children with Cuisenaire rods, pattern blocks, or parquetry blocks. Encourage them to make designs. Compliment the students on their efforts and point out the unique characteristics of the designs. For example, point out those made of materials of the same color, those using pieces of the same shape, and those that have line symmetry. Discuss with students what it means for a figure to have balance, using the children's designs as examples. Have the children look around the room, point to shapes that appear to be the same on both sides, and explain the symmetry.

Ask the children to make a design with symmetry. You may structure this activity by designating which pieces to use in making a design; for example, using the pattern blocks, have the children take two red pieces, four green pieces, and two orange pieces for their design. Ask the children to sketch the results or to glue colored paper cut into the shapes being used. Have the children share their designs with others.

2. Provide mirrors with which the children may explore and develop symmetrical patterns. (Inexpensive mirrors are available through school supply catalogs that feature learning aids.) Using Cuisenaire rods, pattern blocks, or parquetry blocks and mirrors, have the children construct symmetrical designs and reaffirm their symmetry.

Ask the children to make a design using three or four blocks or rods. Then have them place a mirror along one edge of the design, note the reflection, and copy the image in the reflection, placing the copy behind the mirror. Thus, the mirror is lying along the line of symmetry.

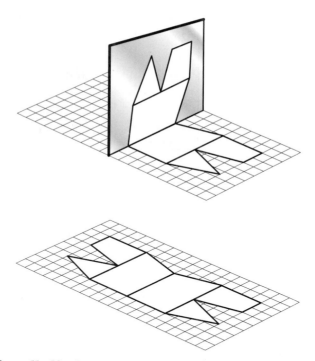

Figure 11–18 A pattern and its mirror image sketched on squared paper.

Then ask the children to remove the mirror and to discuss their symmetrical designs. Say, for example, "What pattern do you see in your design? If your design were a picture, what would it show? See if you can take the reflected design away, mix up the pieces, and then put the design back the way it was before. Where do you think the line of symmetry is? Check it with the mirror. Can you make a new design and its reflection without using the mirror? Try it. Use your mirror to check to see if your design has symmetry."

Finally, have the children sketch and color the pattern and its mirror image on a sheet of squared paper. Figure 11–18 illustrates this process.

3. Stretch a rubber band across a geoboard from edge to edge so there is ample space on each side of the rubber band. In the simplest example, the rubber band would be stretched across the center of the geoboard either horizontally or vertically. Construct a figure on one side of the rubber band and challenge the children to construct the symmetrical image of the figure on the other side. In the beginning, have the children stand a mirror on its edge along the symmetry line and make the image while looking in the mirror. Figure 11–19 provides examples of this activity.

Let the children make up figures and challenge the rest of the class to construct the mirror image of the figure on the geoboard across the line of symmetry, with or without a mirror. Provide dot paper on which the

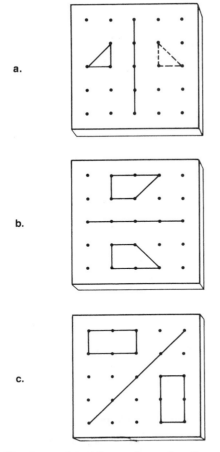

Figure 11–19 Symmetrical figures formed on the geoboard.

students may copy their symmetrical geoboard designs. As the students develop proficiency in recreating images, use diagonal lines as lines of symmetry.

OBJECTIVE: to develop the ability to visualize symmetrical patterns.

4. Ask the children to fold a sheet of paper in half and to cut out some shape from the folded edge. Then have the children open the sheet and observe the symmetrical figure. Provide an opportunity for the children to share their designs.

Next, challenge the class to plan shapes to cut out of folded sheets and to guess what the results will look like. The students may draw what they believe the figures will look like when the paper is unfolded. Then let them cut out the figures and check the results against their estimates.

Another variation of this activity is to punch a hole through the folded sheet with a paper punch. Have the children guess how many holes there will be, then open the sheet to see. Try two holes, then three. Also, try folding the sheet of paper twice and then punching one or more holes through the paper. Add a challenge to this activity by having children guess where the holes will be as well as how many there will be. Display the children's work.

OBJECTIVE: to identify symmetrical figures.

5. Have the children search through magazines for pictures that have symmetry. Have them cut out those pictures. On a bulletin board, put up the heading "These Pictures Have Symmetry" and the heading "These Pictures Don't Have Symmetry." Have the children classify the pictures they have cut out and place each of them under the appropriate heading.

A variation of this activity is to go on a school or neighborhood walk to look for symmetry in the environment. As examples are found, have two or three children sketch the examples on squared paper. When the walk is over, have the students color the sketches and classify them on the bulletin board.

Another variation of this activity is to provide each child with an object you have cut out from a magazine and then cut in half along its line of symmetry. For example, give children one side of a face, half of a flower in a pot, or half of an orange. Ask the children to paste the half-picture onto a piece of drawing paper and to draw the other half of the object using crayons or markers.

Thus far, we have been using line symmetry. "Flipping," or reflecting a shape across a line, produces line symmetry when the shape and its image are viewed. Another type of transformation is produced by **rotational,** or **point, symmetry.** A figure has rotational symmetry if it can be rotated about a point in such a way that the resulting figure coincides with the original figure. Thus, the equilateral triangle in Figure 11–20 may be rotated clockwise about point. In this case, the triangle will coincide with the original triangle three times during one full turn. Each of these positions is shown in Figure 11–20. The first activity that follows presents rotational symmetry.

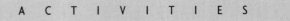

A C T I V I T I E S

Grades 3–5

OBJECTIVE: to introduce the concept of rotational symmetry.

1. Construct a large equilateral triangular shape to serve as a model for rotational symmetry. On the floor, make a masking tape frame in which the triangle fits.

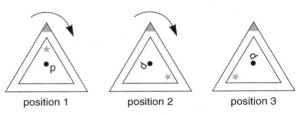

Figure 11–20 Rotations of an equilateral triangle.

Figure 11–21 A reflective tool such as Mira or GeoReflector.

Put a small hole through the model at its point of rotation and insert a pencil or a piece of doweling. Make some sort of mark in one corner of the shape to serve as a reference point when the figure is rotated. Put the shape in its frame, and have the class record its position on their paper.

Invite students to carefully rotate the figure clockwise until it again fits the frame. Have the class record the new position.

Have the students rotate the figure again until it once more fits the frame. Have the class record its new position.

The next rotation will put the figure back in its starting position. Ask, "How many different positions are there when we rotate an equilateral triangle?" There are 3 positions. Continue, "We say this figure has rotational symmetry of order 3. What do you think will be the order for the rotational symmetry of a rectangle, a square, or a regular pentagon? Let's try these figures."

You will need to investigate a variety of plane figures before the students will be entirely comfortable with rotational symmetry. As the students catch on, they will be able to think about and draw figures with a specified order of rotational symmetry.

OBJECTIVE: to introduce reflective tools for exploring transformations and symmetry.

2. Activities involving reflective tools such as Mira and GeoReflector are particularly suited to a study of symmetry. Reflective tools are specially designed tools made of transparent plastic that are used in place of a mirror for exploring line symmetry (see Figure 11–21). Reflective tools are superior to mirrors in several ways. In the first place, you can see through reflective tools, so images are easier to copy. Also, reflective tools stand by themselves and do not need to be held.

As with other new manipulative aids, the initial activity with reflective tools should be a period of free play in which the students look for figures and pictures

to be checked for symmetry. Provide materials such as pattern blocks, tiles, Cuisenaire rods, and magazine pictures. Encourage students to draw patterns on squared paper and to use the reflective tools to investigate the patterns. Interesting discoveries and discussions will result. Additional activities may be found in Giesecke (1996), Gillespie (1994), and Woodward and Woodward (1996).

3. Have students consider the letters of the alphabet as shown in Figure 11–22. Ask the students to identify the letters that have at least one line of symmetry and those with more than one line of symmetry. Have the students visually estimate, then have them write down the letters they believe have line symmetry.

Then, have the students use a mirror or a reflective tool to check each letter for symmetry. It is appropriate at this time to see if the students are able to determine if any of the letters have rotational symmetry. That is, can the letter be rotated about a center point in such a way that the letter appears as it normally does before it has been rotated a full turn? For example, the letter *I* has rotational symmetry of order 2.

An extension of this activity involves finding words that have line or rotational symmetry. For example, both TOOT and CHOICE have line symmetry and NOON has rotational symmetry. Can you find another word that has both?

4. Let the students explore various materials such as pattern blocks using two mirrors or reflective tools. Suggest to the students that they tape the mirrors at right angles and place blocks at the intersection. Increase and decrease the angle of the mirrors to see what images result. Place the mirrors parallel to each other and observe the image of blocks placed between them.

Try using three mirrors, one lying flat and two at right angles on top. Have the students sketch the images they think will result. Examples of two mirror configurations are shown in Figure 11–23.

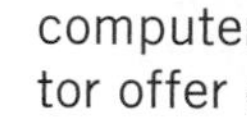

Another application of line symmetry and the images that result from using multiple mirrors can be found in computer software. For example, various applications include word processors, spreadsheets, draw programs, and paint programs. The latter two programs can be used to draw figures and then produce the mirror (flip) image or rotational image of the shape. Other dynamic geometry programs such as *The Geometer's Sketchpad* on a computer or Cabri geometry on a computer or calculator offer even more opportunities for explorations of

ABCDEFGHIJKLMNOPQRSTUVWXYZ

Figure 11–22 Letters of the alphabet used to find symmetry.

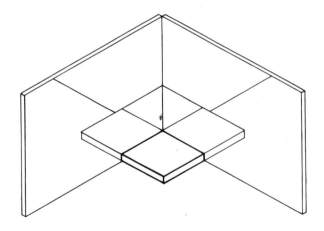

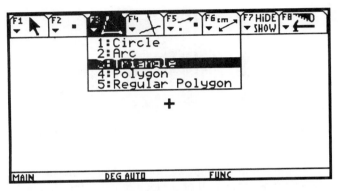

Figure 11–24 Selecting the triangle function on the TI-92 calculator.

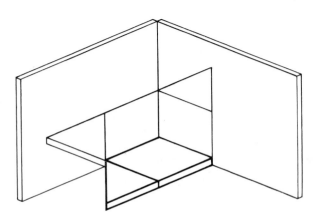

Figure 11–23 Using two mirrors to produce a reflected image.

rotations and symmetry. These exciting graphics features allow students to instantly see the results of using mirrors or rotations.

OBJECTIVE: to construct symmetrical figures.

5. Challenge the children by asking them to construct irregular figures on the geoboard. Provide a line of symmetry; this could be a vertical, horizontal, or diagonal line. Have the children construct the reflection of the figure on the opposite side of the line of symmetry. Then, let the children check their efforts with reflective tools or mirrors.

Let the students experiment with lines of symmetry other than those shown in Figure 11–19. See which, if any, other lines can be used to accurately construct reflected images.

If you have a dynamic geometry software available for computers or calculators, encourage the students to explore concepts of geometry using that technology. For example, with the Cabri geometry capabilities on a TI-92 calculator, students might use the following

strategies to explore lines of symmetry. If you have not used the TI-92, try to find a teacher or student who has experience with the calculator, or use one of the books from the reference list to help you get started.

Grades 6–8

OBJECTIVE: to explore symmetry using dynamic geometry software.

1. On a TI-92, choose F3 and select 3:Triangle (see Figure 11–24). Construct a small triangle on the middle left side of the calculator screen (see Figure 11–25). (This triangle will be reflected across the line of symmetry that you are going to construct next.)

Choose F2 and select 4:Line (see Figure 11–26). Construct a line near the center of your screen by pointing to any point near the center and pushing ENTER. Then use the blue arrow key to move the line where you want it. Push ENTER when the line is in a position that you like (see Figure 11–27). (This line will be used as a line of symmetry. A vertical line might be easiest for students to use, but a diagonal line will make the activity more interesting and will lead to better generalizations.)

Sketch the triangle and the line that are displayed on the calculator screen. Sketch what you think the triangle will look like when it is reflected across the line. Check your prediction with a mirror or other reflecting device.

Choose F5 and select 4:Reflection (see Figure 11–28). Using the pointer and the blue arrow key, move the pointer to the triangle and choose "Reflect this triangle" (ENTER). Then move the pointer to the line you just drew and choose "with respect to this line" (ENTER) (see Figure 11–29). Check to see if the calculator screen looks like your drawing. (If the image goes off the screen of the calculator, try using the grabbing hand to move the triangle or the line until you can see both the line and the image on your screen.)

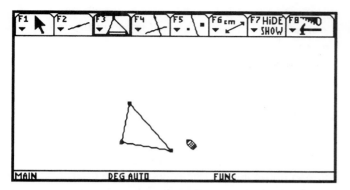

Figure 11–25   Triangle constructed on the TI-92 calculator.

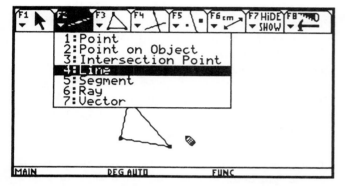

Figure 11–26   Selecting the line function on the TI-92 calculator.

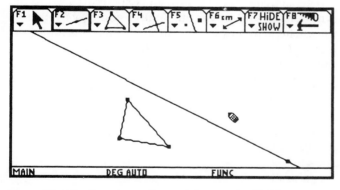

Figure 11–27   Drawing a diagonal line on the TI-92 calculator.

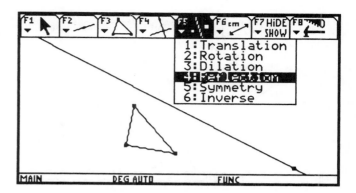

Figure 11–28   Selecting the reflection function on the TI-92 calculator.

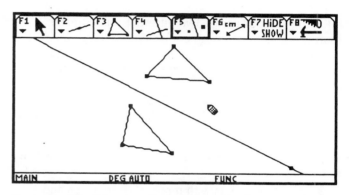

Figure 11–29   Triangle reflected across the line on the TI-92 calculator.

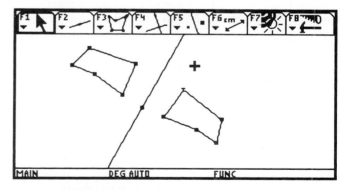

Figure 11–30   Reflecting a pentagon on the TI-92 calculator.

Observe the position of the reflected triangle. How does the position of the reflected triangle relate to the position of the original triangle in relation to the line?

Repeat this activity with other shapes and other lines of symmetry. Be sure to draw a sketch of your prediction each time (see Figure 11–30).

Once you have mastered using a single line of symmetry, try this activity with two or more lines of symmetry (see Figure 11–31).

OBJECTIVE: to investigate congruence, similarity, and symmetry using dynamic geometry software.

2. Understanding congruence, similarity, and symmetry can be facilitated by going to Weblink 11–5, which has four activities. In the first, students choose transformations and apply them to shapes and observe the resulting images. In the second, students try to identify transformations that have already been applied to shapes. In the third, students examine the results of

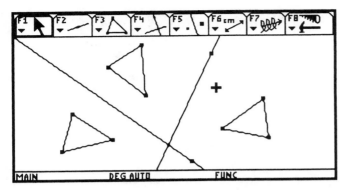

Figure 11–31 Reflecting across two lines of symmetry on the TI-92 calculator.

reflecting shapes across two different lines. In the fourth, students compose equivalent transformations in two different ways. Throughout these activities students make conjectures and engage in discussions with other students about the tasks.

(Thanks to Vlasta Kokol-Voljč of the University of Maribor in Slovenia for her assistance with the following activity.)

OBJECTIVE: to challenge students with problems involving symmetry.

3. Provide students with three green triangles and three blue diamonds from the set of pattern blocks. Have the students make triangles that measure three inches on a side and have (a) one line of symmetry and no rotational symmetry, (b) two lines of symmetry and no rotational symmetry (no solutions), (c) three lines of symmetry and rotational symmetry of order 3, (d) no lines of symmetry and rotational symmetry of order 3, and (e) no lines of symmetry and no rotational symmetry. Encourage the students to make up similar problems, creating other shapes

using four to eight pattern blocks. Be sure discussion about how solutions were reached is part of the activity.

OBJECTIVE: to design tessellations.

4. Tessellations, patterns made by "tiling" a region with shapes, can be produced as simply as placing square tiles or pattern blocks in a region as shown in Figure 11–32a, by combining several shapes in a semi-regular tessellation as in Figure 11–32b, or by creating an Escher-type tessellation in a more artistic arrangement as in Figure 11–32c. In two companion books, Seymour and Britton (1989) and Britton and Britton (1992) have spelled out the nature of tessellations, tessellation art, and the techniques that allow teachers to help students in creating fine examples of tessellations. At the beginning stages, it is suggested that students design their tessellations with paper and pencil.

Colorful and original tessellations result. As the students become more skilled, they may be introduced to *TesselMania! deluxe* (Learning Company, 1999). This clever computer software introduces the creation of tessellations and allows students to rotate and reflect shapes and to tessellate regions at will. Escher-type tessellations are made simply and quickly in *TesselMania! deluxe*. Color enhances these designs and, when printed, the designs help decorate a classroom.

The activities above provide experiences with the symmetry found in various figures and in various settings. The activities focus on transformations and symmetry. These experiences help students not only learn the concept of symmetry but also develop the ability to visualize shapes in the mind's eye. We now turn to space figures.

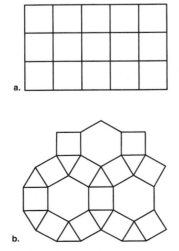

Figure 11–32 Tessellation patterns.

Space Figures and Their Characteristics and Properties

Up to this point, the activities have dealt principally with plane figures—figures of two dimensions. All of us, live in a three-dimensional world. All children's movements, explorations, and constructions have been in space. The exploration of space is the classic example of early mental growth.

As children continue their growth in geometry, activities with three-dimensional space figures are an important part of this learning. Whenever possible, tap children's environments—the classroom, home, and community. The activities that follow are designed to aid in the development of spatial concepts. Again, activities cannot by themselves teach. Augment them with reading, writing, discussion, examples, and thought.

A C T I V I T I E S

Pre-Kindergarten – Grade 2

OBJECTIVE: to identify and draw two- and three-dimensional objects in the environment.

1. Extend the playground or neighborhood walk mentioned earlier to include a search for three-dimensional figures. On a shape walk, ask students to sketch the shapes they observe. The shapes may be two or three dimensional. Students may draw the shapes of windows, doors, faces of bricks, or fences. Or they may draw the shapes of entire houses, individual bricks, garbage cans, or light posts. It is likely that you will need to discuss how to sketch three-dimensional figures. Have the children share with one another their own techniques. Descriptive stories by the class or individuals may help to conclude an investigation of shapes in the community.

2. Ask the children to bring empty containers from home to serve as a collection of commonly found space figures. Expect containers such as cereal boxes, cans with the tops and bottoms removed, plastic soap containers, and tubes from paper towels or toilet paper. Use these materials as a bulletin board or table display. Have the children classify the various figures, using their own categories, by overall shape or the shapes of various faces. Cut the container so it lies flat and the students can examine the pattern of the space figure. In how many different overall shapes are household items packaged?

OBJECTIVE: to copy and build space figures.

3. Encourage children to use a variety of materials to build space figures. Large blocks and cardboard building bricks along with tiles, geoblocks, Unifix cubes, Cuisenaire rods, and pattern blocks are among those commonly found in primary classrooms. Make a construction and ask the children to copy it. Have children make constructions for others to copy.

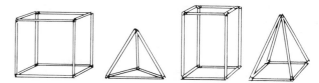

Figure 11–33   Space figures built with straws and pipe cleaners.

A challenging series of work cards accompanies the set of geoblocks. Develop other, similar cards for use with the three-dimensional learning materials.

OBJECTIVE: to discover characteristics of polyhedrons.

4. Straws and pipe cleaners (or straws of two sizes) can be used to construct polyhedrons. Initially, produce two-dimensional figures. As space figures are investigated, it should become apparent that the faces of all polyhedrons are polygons. Thus, when a cube is constructed, an investigation of its faces yields squares. If a tetrahedron is constructed, an investigation of its faces yields triangles. Encourage children to construct various polyhedrons. Several are shown in Figure 11–33.

Have the children compare the space figures, noting the number and shapes of the faces, the number of vertices, and interesting facts about their shapes. Have the children record these findings on a chart and prominently display it.

5. Weblink 11–6 contains an activity entitled "Platonic Solids." With this dynamic geometry software, students interact with the Platonic solids (regular polyhedrons). They are able to rotate the figures, color the faces of the figures, view "wire frame" versions of the figures, and change the size of the figures. The faces, edges, and vertices can be counted.

Encourage the children to construct and manipulate space figures. As they do so, they develop a sense of how figures fit in space. As children begin to analyze space figures, they prepare the way for a more formal study of objects in space.

A C T I V I T I E S

Grades 3 – 5 and Grades 6 – 8

OBJECTIVE: to explore the characteristics of the regular polyhedrons.

1. Among the myriad space figures, there are only five *regular polyhedrons*. A regular polyhedron is one in which all the faces are congruent, all the edges are the same length, and all the angles are the same size. The regular polyhedrons are the tetrahedron (4 faces), hexahedron or cube (6 faces), octahedron (8 faces),

TABLE 11–1 **Characteristics of Space Figures**

Number of	Tetrahedron	Cube	Octahedron	Dodecahedron	Icosahedron
vertices	4				
edges	6				
faces	4				

dodecahedron (12 faces), and icosahedron (20 faces). They are illustrated in Figure 11–1i.

Students explore these shapes most effectively when they can hold them, turn them, and note their characteristics. Provide materials and patterns so the students may construct their own set of regular polyhedrons. (See Appendix B for patterns for the five figures.) The patterns may be copied onto heavy paper or oaktag. Have the students cut out the patterns, crease the fold lines with a paper clip, make the folds, and glue the tabs.

One systematic investigation of the regular polyhedra is discovering the relationship between the number of faces, the number of edges, and the number of vertices. A table, such as the one shown in Table 11–1, can be used as an effective problem-solving tool to display the information gathered. The table provides a way to systematically organize the information as it is collected.

Have the students handle the tetrahedron. Have them count the number of vertices, or corners, of the tetrahedron. There are 4. Record that number in the table. Next, count the number of faces (4) and record that information. Finally, count the number of edges (6) and record that information. Continue counting vertices, edges, and faces for the other figures.

Once the information has been recorded in the table, challenge the students to look for a relationship between the vertices, edges, and faces of a regular polyhedron. Have them look at the numbers for each of the regular polyhedrons. Give the students time and support as they look for this relationship.

A formula named after the Swiss mathematician Leonhard Euler describes the relationship between the faces, edges, and vertices of polyhedra. The formula states that $V + F - E = 2$; that is, the number of vertices plus the number of faces minus the number of edges equals 2. Many students are capable of finding this relationship.

To extend this activity, see if the students can determine if the relationship discovered for a regular polyhedron holds true for any pyramid or any prism.

OBJECTIVE: to explore space figures formed by soap film on wire frames.

2. Provide the students with wire somewhat lighter than coat hanger wire; it should be easy to bend and cut the wire. The object is to construct shapes out of the wire that can be used with soapy water to produce various two- and three-dimensional figures. Figure 11–34 shows four possible wire shapes. Encourage the students to create wire shapes with tightly secured corners.

Have the students dip the two-dimensional shapes in a mixture of liquid soap and water (half and half) and record what happens. Let them trade their wire shapes and experiment some more. Possible explorations include blowing a bubble with a circular frame and then blowing a bubble with a triangular frame. Have students make conjectures about what they believe will happen.

See what happens when the three-dimensional frames are dipped in soap and water. What happens when a diagonal is constructed inside a three-dimensional shape that is then dipped in soap and water? Construct shapes that are not polygons, then dip them and blow bubbles or just dip them.

OBJECTIVE: to combine imagination and knowledge of space figures to create a microworld.

3. Projects using space figures offer motivation for creative learning experiences. One such project was initiated during an introductory class on space figures. As the children and the teacher looked at a set of geoblocks, one child noted that a particular piece looked like an Egyptian pyramid; another student thought that the word *prism* sounded like *prison*. Soon a boy in the class mentioned that it would be exciting to create a city full of shapes. The *geoworld* project was begun. The geoworld was built on a platform of triwall construction board that measured 4 feet by 8 feet. The very first piece of architecture that arose was *tetrahedra terrace*, a series of

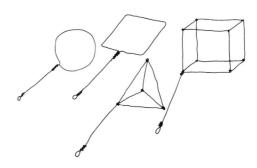

Figure 11–34 Wire figures for soap film shapes.

connected tetrahedrons. Then came the *cuban embassy,* an idea sparked by surveying atlases for possibilities. The cuban embassy was a large cube. It was surrounded by several cubans, who were represented by smaller cubes with personal characteristics. Many other structures were added to geoworld; when the project had been completed, every member of the class felt a deep sense of pride in the creative work of their peers.

OBJECTIVE: to construct a geodesic dome.

4. Another project is the construction of a large space figure. Thus, a cube that measures 1 or $1\frac{1}{2}$ meters on a side may be built and used as a quiet place or reading corner. Zilliox and Lowrey (1997) describe their work with sixth graders who constructed a large rhombicosidodecahedron. The great effort and extreme pride in the task illustrate the positive effects of such construction projects. Among the more interesting of all such figures is the geodesic dome, originally conceived by the late Buckminster Fuller. The following steps result in a rather spectacular geodesic dome, whether it has a radius of 10 or 40 inches.

a. *Make the big decision.* What size dome do you want to build? Decide on the radius desired (half the width at the dome's widest point). Figure 11–35 illustrates what the finished dome will look like.

b. *Construct the dome using two different sizes of triangles.* The size of each triangle is determined by the size of dome desired. One of the triangles, T1, is equilateral, with each side 0.6180 times the length of the dome radius. The other triangle, T2, has one side equal to the length of a T1 side and two shorter sides, each 0.5465 times the length of the dome radius. Thus, for a dome of

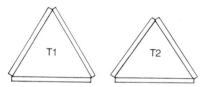

Figure 11–36 Patterns for T1 and T2 triangles for a geodesic dome.

radius 10 inches, the T1 triangle has sides 6.2 inches long, and the T2 triangle has one side 6.2 inches long and two sides 5.5 inches long.

c. *Make a pattern for each triangle.* Figure 11–36 shows one such set of triangles. Note that there is a flap on each side. The flap is used to attach the triangles.

d. *Using the patterns, make 15 T1 triangles and 45 T2 triangles.* For a 10-inch radius dome, oaktag is suitable material; for a 40-inch radius dome, cardboard appliance cartons are best. It is necessary to lightly crease the fold lines on the flaps.

e. *Begin construction.* If you use oaktag, use white school glue to attach the triangles. It will take the cooperative effort of several students to put the final pieces in place and hold them while they dry. If you use cardboard, you can use $\frac{1}{4}$-by-20 hexagonal machine nuts ($\frac{3}{4}$ inches long) and bolts with washers to attach the pieces. Follow these four steps: (1) Make six pentagons and five semipentagons from T2 triangles (see Figure 11–37a). (2) Add T1 triangles to the perimeter of one pentagon (see Figure 11–37b). (3) Fill the gaps between triangles with other pentagons (see Figure 11–37c. (4) Add T1 triangles between and below pentagons. Then, add semipentagons at the bottom (see Figure 11–37d).

As a final touch to the ball-shaped geodesic dome, fill the gaps around the base of the dome and attach the bottom flaps together or to the floor to make the dome more rigid. It is helpful to cut windows and a door into geodesic domes large enough to enter.

During this project, students may wish to send away for a catalog from a company that prefabricates geodesic dome houses or to search for magazine articles about such homes. Some students may investigate some of Buckminster Fuller's other inventions.

Fractal Geometry

Much of the natural world is difficult to describe using common shapes such as triangles, squares, and rectangles. Apart from the human dimension, much

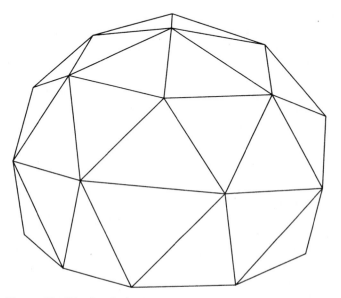

Figure 11–35 Geodesic dome.

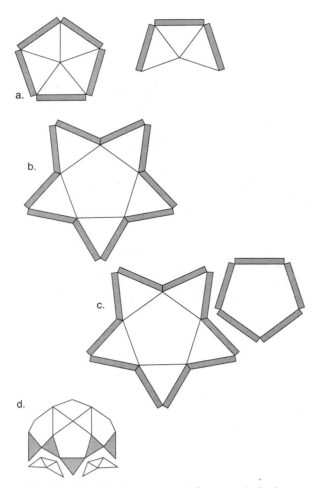

Figure 11–37 Construction sequence for a geodesic dome.

Figure 11–38 Fractal of a Mandelbrot set.

of what occurs in nature appears chaotic. The study of chaos is the study of disorder and irregularity. To describe patterns in nature previously deemed chaotic and, thus, indescribable, Benoit Mandelbrot developed a new geometry, called fractal geometry. The study of fractals is an example of a relatively recent discovery in mathematics. Fractal geometry provides ways for scientists who study things that appear to be chaotic in behavior, such as the way veins or arteries branch, to gain greater understanding of those phenomena.

Fractals are used to design computer models of irregular patterns in nature. Mandelbrot invented the name "fractal" to describe the fractional dimension work that he had completed. Gleick (1987, p. 114) noted, "In the end, the word *fractal* came to stand for a way of describing, calculating, and thinking about shapes that are irregular and fragmented, jagged and broken-up shapes from the crystalline curves of snowflakes to the discontinuous dusts of galaxies." A primary characteristic of fractals is self-similarity. This means that if you were to first look

at a fractal and become familiar with its shape and then magnify or zoom in on a piece of the original you would find smaller, but similar, shapes to that of the original.

Perhaps the most commonly displayed fractal is the image produced by graphing a Mandelbrot set. A Mandelbrot set is a collection of numbers, from the set of complex numbers. By using computers it can be determined if a complex number is a part of the Mandelbrot set. If the complex numbers in the Mandelbrot set are graphed, the result is the image in Figure 11–38 (Dewey, 2002). Dewey has a series of computer-generated images of the Mandelbrot set, illustrating the concept of self-similarity. You are encouraged to go to Weblink 11–7 and view these images.

Let's look at a fractal that is a useful figure in learning about the nature of fractals. It is the Koch curve or "snowflake." Koch snowflakes of level or iteration 1, level 2, and level 3 are shown in Figure 11–39b, c, and d. Notice that the figures are identical in design and different only in detail. This is an example of self-similarity, the characteristic of fractals discussed above. The basic foundation shape for the snowflake, level 0, is an equilateral triangle as in Figure 11–39a.

To construct the first level of the figure, take each side of the triangle and divide it into thirds. Next, using the center third of each side as the base, construct a smaller equilateral triangle projecting from the side of the original triangle. The level 1 snowflake has 12 sides (Figure 11–39b). The level 2 snowflake is constructed by using each of the 12 sides, dividing it into thirds, and constructing smaller equilateral triangles projecting from each side (Figure 11–39c). How many sides does the level 2 snowflake contain?

Besides using fractals to describe patterns in nature such as the shapes of ferns, coastlines,

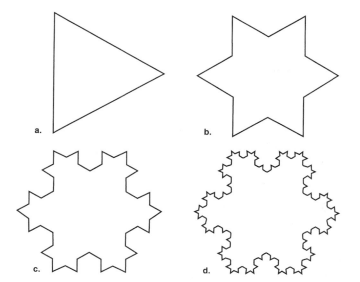

Figure 11–39   Four levels of the Koch snowflake fractal.

Grades 3 – 5 and Grades 6 – 8

OBJECTIVE: to explore the form of the Koch snowflake.

1. Make copies of the triangular grid blackline master (Appendix B) for each student. Begin this activity by having the students color in an equilateral triangle with nine units on a side in the center of the triangular grid as in Figure 11–40a. Challenge the students to locate the three middle units along one side of the triangle and color an equilateral triangle with three units on a side projecting out from the side of the large triangle. Color in the other two three-unit triangles projecting out from the other two sides of the large triangle as in Figure 11–40b. This is the level 1 Koch snowflake. Continue by finding the middle unit along any of the 12 sides of the level 1 snowflake and color the triangle with one unit on a side projecting out from the side. Continue this until there are projections from all 12 sides as in Figure 11–40c. The resulting figure is the level 2 Koch snowflake. Encourage the students to carefully cut around their figure and glue it to a piece of construction paper.

A variation of this activity is to make copies of the triangular grid blackline master on various colors of construction paper and have the students cut out one triangle with 9 units on a side, three triangles with 3 units on a side, and 12 triangles with 1 unit on a side. Next, have the student glue the large triangle on a sheet of construction paper, followed by gluing the 3-unit triangles to the center of each side of the large triangle, and

and the growth of trees, fractals have also become an art form. The work of Musgrave (2002) represents fine examples of using fractals as art. You are encouraged to find the Musgrave images on Weblink 11–8. Another website is that of Lanius (2002) (Weblink 11–9). It contains a unit on fractals for elementary and middle school students. The activities below are based on ones described by Lanius. For additional activities you are encouraged to explore her website.

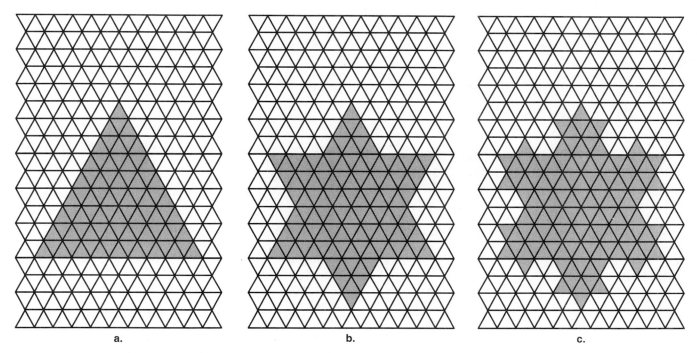

Figure 11–40   Using a triangular grid to color in a Koch snowflake.

completed by gluing the 1-unit triangles to the center of each side of the figure.

2. To extend the investigation of the Koch snowflake, suggest to the students that they see what they can discover about the perimeters of the snowflakes as they move from level to level. You may want to look ahead to Chapter 12 for a discussion of measuring length, including perimeter. Use the snowflakes constructed in Activity 1 and determine the perimeters using the side of the small triangle as the unit. A table like that shown in Table 11–2 might be a useful way to help organize the information about perimeters.

How many levels would it take to have a perimeter of at least 200 units? Make a conjecture and test the conjecture. What do you notice about the size of the figure and its perimeter?

Next, consider the area of the Koch snowflake. You may want to look ahead to Chapter 12 for a discussion of measuring area. See what the students can discover about the areas of the snowflakes as they move from level to level. Use the snowflakes constructed in Activity 1 and determine the areas using the small triangle as the unit. A table like that shown in Table 11–3 might help organize the information about areas.

How many levels would it take to have an area of at least 150 triangular units? What do you notice about the size of the figure and its area?

3. Another procedure for developing the Koch snowflake is to use a combination of ruler and compass to construct the points of the snowflake (see the section on Copying and Constructing Shapes later in this chapter). Distribute to the students large sheets of paper on which is found an equilateral triangle of sides 27 centimeters with the middle third of each side missing as shown in Figure 11–41a. First, have the students construct two sides of an equilateral triangle projecting from the center of each side of the large triangle as in Figure 11–41b. Then have them measure one third of each side of the new figure and construct new triangles in the center of

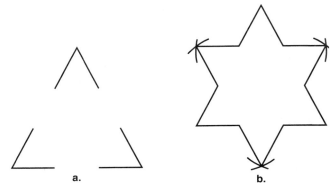

Figure 11–41   Using a ruler and compass to construct a Koch snowflake.

each side, erasing the line in the center third of each side. Continue this procedure for each side of the new figure. The resulting figure is a level 3 Koch snowflake.

4. Students may explore the Koch snowflake using a *Logo* procedure. If you are unfamiliar with *Logo,* you may wish to look ahead to the *Logo* section on Visualization, Spatial Reasoning, and Geometric Modeling later in this chapter. Long and DeTemple (1996, pp. 1000–1001) provide procedures for drawing the snowflake:

```
TO FRACTAL :LEVEL :SIDE
IF :LEVEL < 1[FD :SIDE STOP]
FRACTAL :LEVEL−1 :SIDE/3
LT 60
FRACTAL :LEVEL−1 :SIDE/3
RT 120
FRACTAL :LEVEL−1 :SIDE/3
LT 60
FRACTAL :LEVEL−1 :SIDE/3
END

TO FRAC :LEVEL :SIDE
REPEAT 3 [FRACTAL :LEVEL :SIDE RT 120]
END
```

Students are encouraged to discover the different results when the levels and the lengths of sides are entered as variables in running the procedure FRAC. Thus, how do FRAC 3 200 and FRAC 3 100 vary? What interesting designs will result?

An alternative to constructing a Koch snowflake using *Logo* is using *The Geometer's Sketchpad.* In the *Sketchpad* environment, scripts are written to provide instruction for *The Geometer's Sketchpad* to perform constructions. Chanan, in *The Geometer's Sketchpad Learning Guide* (2000), provides a carefully written description that helps the reader understand how the Koch snowflake is constructed as well as a description of how the script is developed. Students in grades 6–8 could be challenged to use this application.

TABLE 11–2   Perimeters of Koch Snowflakes

Level of Koch snowflake	0	1	2	3	4	5
Perimeter	27	36	?	?	?	?

TABLE 11–3   Areas of Koch Snowflakes

Level of Koch snowflake	0	1	2	3	4	5
Area	81	108	?	?	?	?

This section has focused on how children learn geometric concepts and specific activities to reinforce this learning. The process of learning is developmental; that is, children grow in their abilities to grasp geometric concepts. Children should actively experience geometry. They should be guided in their explorations. They should have time to investigate geometry and discuss their discoveries. Above all, geometry should be an integral part of the mathematics program. It should be extended far beyond the basal textbook and presented throughout the school year.

DEVELOPING GEOMETRIC FLUENCY

Geometric fluency refers to students' abilities to explain geometry concepts and to be able to extend those ideas as they develop skills related to geometry. It means that geometry makes sense to the student, that the student can analyze geometric problems and can make and test conjectures about aspects of geometry. The skills of geometry involve readily identifying and analyzing shapes and relationships, developing mathematical arguments about geometric relationships, copying and constructing shapes, visualizing and spatial reasoning, and using spatial relations and coordinate geometry. Teach the skills in concert with teaching geometric concepts. Developing and practicing skills will, in most cases, follow conceptual development.

Identifying and Analyzing Shapes and Relationships

The collection of shapes easily identified by young children varies with the experience and maturity of the children. The most productive activities for shape identification are those in which the child is actively manipulating and discussing figures. A pre-kindergartner or first grader may call a triangle a rectangle because the names are similar. A second or third grader who has used attribute blocks, pattern blocks, and geoboards and who has discussed the figures will seldom misname the triangle. A second or third grader may, however, misname a rhombus or hexagon. Again, this difficulty can be alleviated through carefully designed experiences.

Primary students should be expected to develop geometric skills at a basic level. Thus, visual skills should include the ability to recognize different figures from a physical model or a picture. Verbal skills should include the ability to associate a name with a given figure. Graphical skills should include the ability to construct a given shape on a geoboard or to sketch the shape. Logical skills should include the ability to recognize similarities and differences among figures and to conserve the shape of a figure in various positions. Applied skills should include the ability to identify geometric shapes in the environment, in the classroom, and outside the classroom.

At the primary level, children develop skills as a result of extending activities used to develop the concepts. It is important that the teacher provide time, materials, and direction. Pay attention to developing visual, verbal, graphical, logical, and applied skills. Refer to the primary activities suggested earlier for developing geometric concepts.

Throughout the study of geometry, students should be encouraged to analyze and reflect on relationships. Using geometry effectively means that students can make sense of what they are observing, touching, and constructing. They can raise questions and can discuss their observations with others. Thinking skills go hand in hand with the physical skills of geometry.

Middle level students should be expected to develop skills at a higher level. Thus, visual skills should include the ability to recognize properties of figures, to identify a figure as a part of a larger figure, to recognize a two-dimensional pattern for a three-dimensional figure, to rotate two- and three-dimensional figures, and to orient oneself relative to various figures. Verbal skills should include the ability to describe various properties of a figure. Graphical skills should include the ability to draw a figure from given information and to use given properties of a figure to draw the figure. Logical skills should include the ability to classify figures into different types and to use properties to distinguish figures. Applied skills should include the ability to recognize geometric properties of physical objects and to draw or construct models representing shapes in the environment. At this level, students should be able to make conjectures, devise informal ways to prove or disprove conjectures, and discuss their observations with other students.

Like children in the primary grades, students in the intermediate and middle grades should learn geometry through activities that use a variety of physical materials that may be complemented with dynamic geometry software. Again, extending the activities intended for conceptual development will provide opportunities to develop skills. As a teacher, you should facilitate activities and discussion throughout the learning process.

Developing Mathematical Arguments about Geometric Relationships

Earlier in this chapter we discussed how young children develop geometric relationships and understandings. As a result of their early experiences, coupled with their developing ability to communicate and their early classroom work, children develop an understanding of geometry. This understanding evolves as new and more refined relationships are developed. Geometry is different from the world of numbers and provides a new and, for many, intriguing subject to investigate. Young students learn to decide that a particular shape may be based on characteristics that they have investigated with their hands and eyes and minds. They establish categories of shapes through experience and discussion. They can "prove" that an equilateral triangle cannot be constructed on a rectangular geoboard but can be constructed on an isometric geoboard. Young children enjoy being challenged to show that the outline of a three-dimensional box will actually become the box if folded in a particular way.

> Geometry offers students an aspect of mathematical thinking that is different from, but connected to, the world of numbers. (NCTM, 2000, p. 97)

Students develop mathematical arguments about geometric relationships through dynamic teaching. Much of Chapter 2 suggests ways for children to construct mathematical ideas and to think about and discuss their work. While not specific to geometry, they are certainly appropriate for helping develop ways to think about geometry.

Particular focus on mathematical arguments should be presented in the middle grades. As students develop a greater understanding of geometric relationships, they are able to make conjectures that they can test by building, drawing, constructing, and employing dynamic geometry software. For example, fourth- or fifth-grade students might engage in this problem: "Consider the four triangles shown on the dot paper [Figure 11–42]. Suppose that the area of the shaded triangle is 4 square units. How would you compare the areas of the other three triangles with the shaded triangle? Construct the triangles on a geoboard or by using *The Geometer's Sketchpad*. Test your conjecture about the areas of the triangles. Explain your conclusions."

Middle school students should begin to lay the foundations for more formal proofs that will come in later grades. Thus, their conjectures and informal proofs should be more challenging. For example, Weblink 11–10 describes two lessons. First, students explore the question "How are the perimeters, areas, and side lengths of similar rectangles related?" Second, they explore the question "How does changing the lengths of the sides of a rectangular prism affect the volume and surface area of the prism?" With dynamic geometry software, the students investigate similar rectangles and prisms, make conjectures, and then test the conjectures. At this point, students can formulate deductive arguments about their conjectures as they work with the software.

Copying and Constructing Shapes

Copying activities were mentioned earlier in connection with parquetry blocks and geoboards. For students at all levels, copying can be challenging and fun. The complexity of the figures to be copied should vary with the age and experience of the children. Inventing shapes is an outgrowth of copying the shapes formed by teachers and classmates. Asking primary children to find as many four-sided figures as possible challenges them to invent shapes.

Intermediate and middle school students can be challenged with the same problem. The results, however, are likely to be different. How many six- or eight-sided figures can be found? The geoboard is a helpful tool for investigating polygons. Rectangular and isometric dot paper are useful for both sketching and recording shapes. Figure 11–43 illustrates both dot patterns. Both rectangular and isometric dot paper can be found in Appendix B.

Another tool children may use to invent shapes is *Logo*. Figures may be designed on the computer and saved for future access. Using *Logo*, the children can discover more than just what shapes are possible. They must consider the sizes of the exterior and interior angles and the length of each side of the figure. Once they invent a shape, have them describe the shape and make a sketch of it to serve as a challenge to other students and to you. A discussion of *Logo* may be found in the next section, Visualization, Spatial Reasoning, and Geometric Modeling.

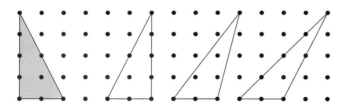

Figure 11 – 42 Comparing the area of four triangles.

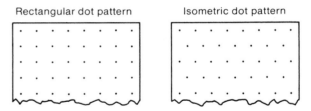

Figure 11 – 43 Rectangular and isometric dot paper.

A skill appropriate at grade 3 through middle school is that of constructing simple geometric shapes using a compass and straightedge. At this level, the goal is to introduce students to techniques of constructing simple figures. The tools used in constructing figures are inexpensive and readily available. A compass that we have found to be reliable and popular with students is the Circle Master Compass, shown in Figure 11–44. Also pictured is a straightedge; a standard school ruler works fine. It should be noted that the compass has a sharp point and care should be taken to assure the safety of students. There are other compass designs such as a GeoTool or Triman compass that avoid sharp points and should be considered if the situation warrants it.

The initial activities should involve copying a given figure. Thus, copying a line segment, an angle, and a circle with a given radius are appropriate. It is expected that the students will have been exposed to terms such as *line, line segment, point, angle, arc, ray, bisector,* and *perpendicular.* Most of these terms will appear in the math book, although words such as *arc* and *bisector* may need to be explained. An **arc** is any part of a circle. A **bisector** is a line that divides an angle or line into two equal parts. **Perpendicular** means to be at a right angle with a line.

Grades 3–5 and Grades 6–8

OBJECTIVE: to use a compass and straightedge to construct simple figures.

1. Copy a line segment, AB, onto a line, m (see Figure 11–45a, b, and c).

   a. Place the compass points on A and B.

   b. Mark the length of segment AB onto line m.

   c. Segment A′B′ is the same length as segment AB.

2. Copy an angle, B, onto a given ray (see Figure 11–46a, b, c, d, and e).

   a. With B as the end point, make an arc crossing the rays at points C and A.

   b. Using the same radius and B′ as the end point, make an arc crossing the given ray at point C′.

   c. Make A′C′ the same length as AC.

   d. Use the straightedge to draw ray B′A′.

   e. Angle A′B′C′ is the same size as angle ABC.

3. Construct a circle with a given radius, r (see Figure 11–47a, b, and c).

   a. Spread the compass points to correspond to the length of the radius, r.

   b. Using the same radius, draw a circle.

   c. The completed circle has a radius equal to r.

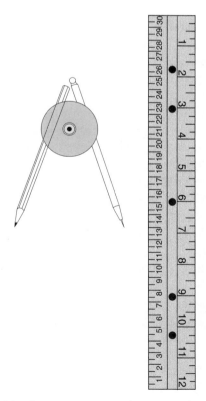

Figure 11–44 Compass and ruler for geometric constructions.

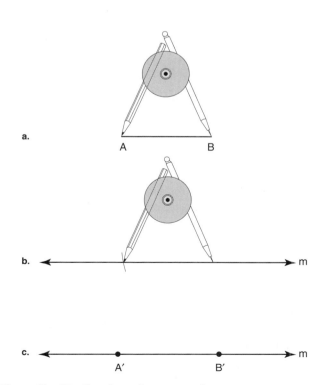

Figure 11–45 Copying a line segment.

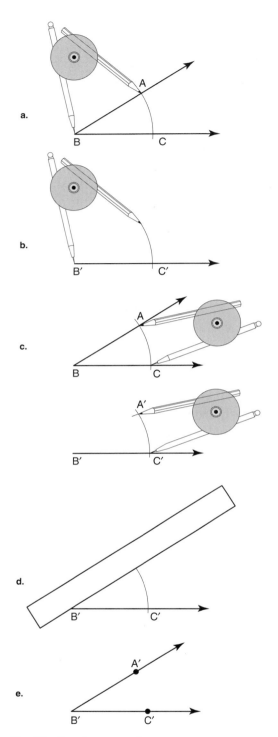

Figure 11–46 Copying an angle.

The next three constructions require a somewhat higher level of skill. Instead of copying a given figure, they involve their own unique set of procedures. The first involves constructing the perpendicular bisector of a segment; the second, constructing a triangle from three given line segments; the third, constructing a hexagon inscribed in a circle.

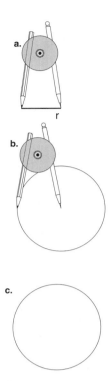

Figure 11–47 Constructing a circle with a given radius.

Grades 3–5 and Grades 6–8

OBJECTIVE: to use a compass and straightedge to construct a perpendicular bisector and a triangle.

1. Construct the perpendicular bisector of a given line segment, AB (see Figure 11–48a, b, c, and d).

 a. Using point A as the center, draw an arc.

 b. Using the same radius and point B as the center, draw another arc.

 c. Place the straightedge at the intersections of the two arcs, points X and Y. Draw segment XY.

 d. Segment XY is perpendicular to segment AB and bisects segment AB at point Z.

2. Construct a triangle with sides equal in length to three given line segments, AB, BC, and CA (see Figure 11–49a, b, c, d, and e).

 a. Draw a line, m. On the line, copy segment AB.

 b. With point B as the center, draw an arc with a radius the same length as segment BC.

 c. With point A as the center, draw an arc with a radius the same length as segment CA.

 d. Use the straightedge to connect points A and B with the intersection of the two arcs at C.

 e. Triangle ABC has sides equal in length to segments AB, BC, and CA.

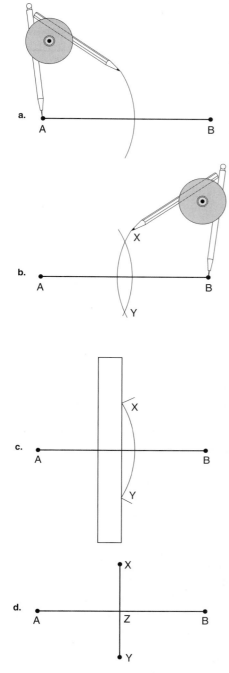

Figure 11–48 Constructing the perpendicular bisector of a given segment.

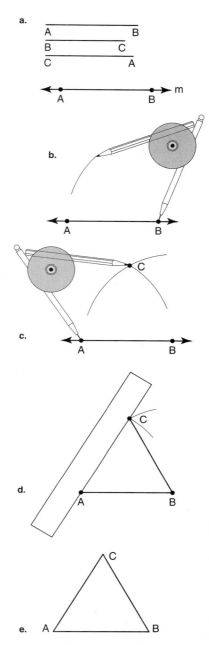

Figure 11–49 Constructing a triangle with sides equal in length to three given line segments.

3. Construct a hexagon inscribed in a circle (see Figure 11–50a, b, c, and d).

a. Construct a circle with a radius of your choice.

b. Using the same radius, place the point of the compass at any location on the circumference of the circle and draw another circle.

c. Place the point of the compass where the circumference of the second circle intersects with

that of the original circle and draw a third circle. Continue around the circumference of the original circle using the points of intersection as centers until a total of seven circles have been drawn.

d. Connect the points of the "star" to form a hexagon inscribed in the original circle. Note that the radius of the circle is also the length of each side of the hexagon. Can you find a simpler way to construct the hexagon?

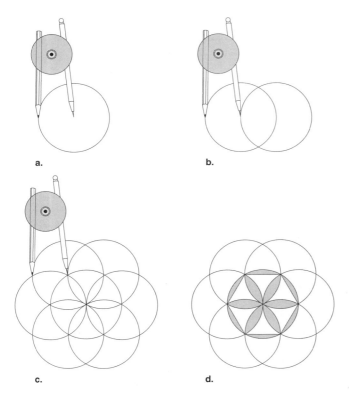

a.   b.

c.   d.

Figure 11–50 Constructing a hexagon inscribed in a circle.

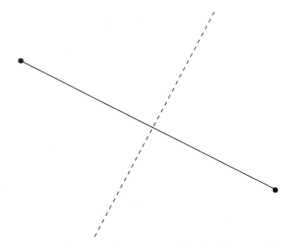

Figure 11–51 Constructing a perpendicular bisector of a line segment by paper folding.

The latter construction shows one of the attractive designs that can result from work with constructions. By coloring parts of the design, students can create attractive patterns that can serve as bulletin board or hallway displays. Do you see a way to connect another set of intersections on the figure to produce a second, larger hexagon?

These are but a small sampling of possible constructions using a compass and straightedge; there are many extensions of construction activities. For example, challenge students to use paper folding or to use a reflective tool to construct a perpendicular bisector of a given line or to explore angle bisectors or medians in triangles. Several such activities are presented below.

A C T I V I T I E S

Grades 3–5 and Grades 6–8

OBJECTIVE: to use paper folding to construct a perpendicular bisector of a line segment and an angle bisector.

1. Provide students with one fourth of an $8\frac{1}{2}$-by-11 inch sheet of paper for ease in folding. Have students draw a line segment about 8 centimeters long using pencil and ruler. Invite them to draw the segment in any configuration on the paper. Challenge the students to fold the paper in such a way that a fold on the paper divides the segment in half and is perpendicular to the segment as in Figure 11–51. Have the students discuss how they made this construction. Perhaps they will suggest that when the two ends of the segment are matched and a crease is made they have found the perpendicular bisector of the segment.

2. On another quarter sheet of paper have the students make an angle using a pencil and a ruler. See if the students can develop a technique to fold the paper so that the fold passes through the vertex of the angle and divides the angle into two equivalent angles. After some practice, it is likely that students will suggest that you must begin at the vertex of the angle and carefully fold so that the rays of the angle coincide with each other in order to produce the angle bisector. It may take several tries for students to perfect this procedure.

OBJECTIVE: to use paper folding to explore the bisectors of each angle of a triangle.

3. When students have gained experience and skill in folding angle bisectors, ask them what they might expect to find about the fold lines if they were to fold bisectors of each angle of a triangle. In small groups, have the recorder write down the conjectures of the group members. Then, have the students try the folds and see what discoveries are made. The recorder should write down the conclusions of the group to use in the follow-up class discussion. Are there conclusions other than the folds will meet at a single point? Will the meeting point always be inside of the triangle? What happens when obtuse or scalene or equilateral or isosceles triangles are used? Would the same thing happen if the medians (the line from a vertex of a triangle through the midpoint of the opposite side) of a triangle were folded instead of the angle bisectors? Encourage conjecture and discussion before and after construction.

OBJECTIVE: to use a reflective tool to construct a perpendicular bisector of a line segment and an angle bisector.

4. Have students draw a line segment about 10–12 centimeters long in any configuration on a sheet of paper. Challenge the students to use the reflective tool and draw a line that divides the segment in half and is perpendicular to the segment. Have the students discuss how they found where to draw their line. The students should soon discover that what they need to do is reflect the endpoints of the segment onto each other and draw the line along the front edge of the reflective tool. This is shown in Figure 11–52. Discuss why reflecting the endpoints on one another in the reflective tool will cause the segment to be bisected and produce a perpendicular to the segment. Compare the process of folding the perpendicular bisector in Activity 1 in this section with the procedure using the reflective tool.

5. On a sheet of paper have students make an angle using a pencil and a ruler. See if the students can develop a technique to draw a line through the vertex of the angle that divides the angle into two equivalent angles. Discuss the suggested techniques. After some practice, it is likely that students will suggest that you must align the front edge of the reflective tool on the vertex and then have one ray of the angle reflect upon the other ray. At this time you can draw the line to produce the angle bisector. Have students write instructions for a student unfamiliar with reflective tools describing how to use them to bisect an angle.

OBJECTIVE: to use a reflective tool to explore the bisectors of each angle of a triangle.

6. When students have gained experience and skill in using a reflective tool to construct angle bisectors, ask them what they might expect to find about the angle bisectors of each angle of a triangle. In small groups have the recorder write down the conjectures of the group members. Then, have the students construct the bisectors and see what discoveries are made. The recorder should write down the conclusions of the group

to use in the follow-up class discussion. Are there conclusions other than the angle bisectors will meet at a single point? Will the meeting point always be inside of the triangle? What happens when obtuse or scalene or equilateral or isosceles triangles are used? Would the same thing happen if the medians of a triangle were constructed instead of the angle bisectors? Encourage conjecture and discussion before and after construction. How does this activity compare with Activity 3 in this section?

In this section several types of tools, particularly the compass and straightedge, were used to explore geometric shapes through construction. The hands-on construction helps students extend their understanding of shapes and relationships among shapes. Many students excel using construction techniques and will continue to experiment with and invent a variety of shapes and designs.

Visualization, Spatial Reasoning, and Geometric Modeling

Several of the activities that have been presented thus far involve students manipulating objects and shapes (geometric modeling) and then conjecturing what they will look like after some change has been made to them. For example, in the previous section we raised the question about what would happen to the angle bisectors of an obtuse triangle. When conjectures are made, visual thinking takes place. The student is invited to use spatial visualization and spatial reasoning, besides construction, to make sense of the problem. That is, the student should be using mental images along with drawings and models. A good example is presented in the Reasoning, Solving, and Posing Geometric Problems section later in this chapter when students working with pentominoes are challenged to estimate which pentominoes can be folded into open-topped boxes before they actually fold the shapes. Visualizing in the mind's eye helps make these conjectures.

> Spatial visualization—building and manipulating mental representations of two- and three-dimensional objects and perceiving an object from different perspectives—is an important aspect of geometric thinking. (NCTM, 2000, PSSM, p. 41)

Representing two- and three-dimensional shapes is an important part of visualization. Some of the representations are made with paper and pencil, some are made using dynamic geometry software, and some are made using software such as *Logo*. Students should be

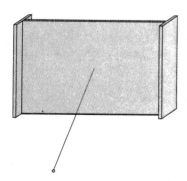

Figure 11–52 Constructing a perpendicular bisector of a line segment using a reflective tool.

encouraged to develop their abilities in spatial visualization through representations and geometric modeling.

ISOMETRIC AND ORTHOGRAPHIC DRAWINGS. The following activities focus on isometric and orthographic representations. These are visual representations used by designers, engineers, and architects. An **isometric drawing** is a drawing that shows a three-dimensional shape drawn in two dimensions. Figure 11–53a shows an isometric drawing. The angles in an isometric drawing are 60° and 120° to represent a perspective view and to reduce distortion; vertical edges remain vertical. An **orthographic projection** is a drawing of three views of an object: a bird's eye view from the top, a view from directly in front, and a view directly from the end (Figure 11–53b). Each of these views correspond to the views shown on the isometric drawing.

A C T I V I T I E S

Grades 3–5

OBJECTIVE: to sketch isometric drawings and orthographic projections from geoblocks.

1. Geoblocks, discussed earlier in this chapter, serve as an excellent aid for developing skill in making isometric and orthographic drawings. Make available to a table group two blocks that have common dimensions and can be combined to make an interesting object (see Figure 11–54a). Then, have the students view the object in such a way that each sees three "sides" of the figure as is shown in Figure 11–54b. Then have each student sketch what the student sees. Drawings may be similar to that shown in Figure 11–54b. Expect some questions about the drawings and some distortion in the drawings as the students begin their work. After the isometric drawings are complete, let the students compare and discuss them. Then have students trade their geoblocks for some from another table and repeat the process to produce another isometric drawing. If there is time, repeat the process, again. Identify the top of the object in the drawing, the front of the object in the drawing, and the end of the object in the drawing. Have the students label their drawings.

2. After the last isometric drawing is completed and labeled from Activity 1, encourage one member of each group to look at one of the objects for which she has an isometric drawing. The view for this observation must be from directly above the object and from the front of the object. Then have the student draw this view. Have the others in the group view and draw the top view. Next, have the students look at the object from directly in front and at eye level and have them sketch the front view. Finally, have the students view the object at eye level directly from the end and sketch the end view. The three

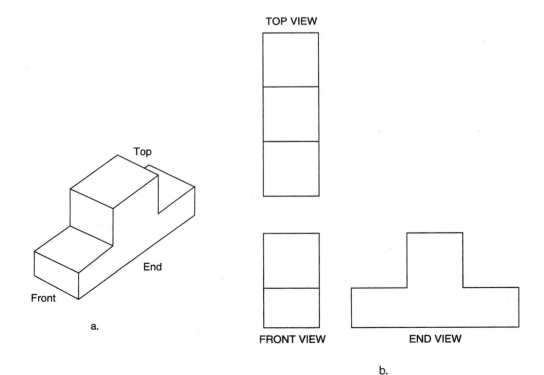

TOP VIEW

Top

End

Front

a.

FRONT VIEW

END VIEW

b.

Figure 11–53 Isometric drawing and orthographic projection.

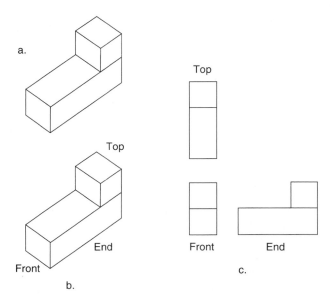

Figure 11–54 Making an orthographic projection from blocks.

views of the object represent the orthographic projection (Figure 11–54c). After students have had some experience sketching isometric drawings and orthographic projections, they will be able to identify figures drawn from orthographic projections, will be able to sketch orthographic projections from isometric drawings, and will be able to make accomplished isometric drawings.

Grades 6 – 8

OBJECTIVE: to explore isometric drawings, orthographic projections, and mat plans.

1. Weblink 11–11 engages students in a variety of activities that focus on isometric drawings, orthographic projections, and mat plans. A mat plan consists of the top views of a solid with the number of cubes in each vertical column displayed on top of the appropriate column. This Illuminations lesson series is interactive and challenging. Students may build shapes, color them, and rotate them. There are problems to solve using spatial visualization and virtual manipulation of the cubes that form the drawings. There is an interesting activity that investigates impossible figures, such as those by Escher.

LOGO. *Logo,* the computer language of turtle graphics, provides a rich environment for children to explore geometric relationships. Children program a turtle to move about the computer monitor. The environment is open-ended, allowing children to discover and invent shapes, angles, complex curves, and the like. *Logo* is a powerful tool for enhancing geometry learning.

> Logo programming can help students construct elaborate knowledge networks (rather than mechanical chains of rules and terms) for geometric topics. (Clements and Battista, 2001, p. 143)

Following are a series of activities that begin by preparing students to use *Logo* and continue by suggesting more challenging activities.

A C T I V I T I E S

Pre-Kindergarten – Grade 2

OBJECTIVE: to explore geometric figures using *Logo* activities.

1. The first *Logo* activities do not use the computer. They are intended to introduce students to sequential order of programming.

a. Find an activity that the children are familiar with. List the individual parts that make up the activity in a series of steps. For example, to put the cat out, we might:

- Call the cat.
- See if the cat comes.
- If not, go find the cat.
- When the cat comes, pick it up.
- Carry the cat to the door.
- Open the door.
- Put the cat outside.
- Shut the door.

Next, write each step on a separate card. Mix up the cards, and challenge the children to put them back in the correct order. Once the children discover how to do this activity, present a series of cards without first showing the appropriate sequence. Have the children order the steps of the procedure by figuring out the sequence. Procedures besides putting the cat out may include making a peanut butter sandwich, preparing for and taking a bath, and getting ready for bed. Allow the children to make up sequences to challenge one another.

b. With masking tape or yarn, construct a large geometric figure on the floor. It may be a square, a triangle, or a rectangle, at first. Later, make a more complex figure, such as those in Figure 11–55. Ask the children to begin by going to any corner and facing an adjacent corner. Have them describe what they are doing as they walk around the boundary of the figure and end up where they started. Limit the descriptions to "step forward," "step back," "turn left," and "turn right." It may be helpful to have direction cards that show what is meant by the four commands. Figure 11–56 illustrates what such cards might look like. Later, have one child

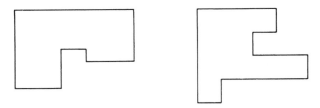

Figure 11–55 Examples of shapes taped on the floor for introducing *Logo.*

forward   back   left   right

Figure 11–56 Direction cards for introducing *Logo.*

give directions to a second child that will guide the second child in walking the boundary of a figure. The second child should follow the directions exactly.

It will soon be necessary to tell a student how many steps forward or backward to take. For example, "Go forward 12 steps." Agree that such steps are taken by putting one foot directly in front of the other.

Next, give a child a drawing of a figure and instruct the child to give another student commands for making the figure. The teacher or a student can lead the entire class in this activity.

c. Put a blindfold on a child and arrange the desks in a simple maze. Have children carefully give commands that will, if followed, lead the blindfolded child around the desks and out of the maze. Use particular caution to avoid any possibility of injury.

2. Weblink 11–12 is a *Logo*-like activity that helps develop skill by inviting students to move a ladybug on the computer monitor. In the first of the three parts in this activity, students are to provide a path that will allow the ladybug to hide under a leaf. In the second part, students have the ladybug draw rectangles of different sizes. In the third part, students plan a series of steps that will allow the ladybug to navigate a maze. Take a few minutes and investigate this Weblink. Consider how you might be able to use it in your classroom.

3. Introduce turtle geometry on the computer by putting a small colored sticker on the computer monitor and challenging the children to see whether they can find the appropriate commands to hide the turtle under the sticker. Encourage the children to estimate the commands before they actually try them. In the beginning, use RIGHT 90 and LEFT 90 to designate the turns but allow the children to experiment with other degrees of turns very soon. The activity with making angles in Plane Figures and

Their Characteristics and Properties should help students understand how to construct various angles. It will take experimentation to determine the size of the turtle steps. Fairly quickly the children will become accomplished at moving the turtle freely around the screen.

To gain practice in moving the turtle about, put an overhead transparency on the screen with several regions drawn on it. A thin transparency will cling tightly to the screen. Have the children move the turtle from one region to another until it has entered all of the regions.

Sketch a simple maze on another transparency and place the transparency on the screen with the turtle in the maze. Challenge the children to get the turtle out of the maze without crossing any boundaries.

From here on, use one or more of several well-written *Logo* manuals, which are carefully sequenced. They contain many challenging figures to test children's abilities to use *Logo.* Resources by Clithero (1987), Cory (1995), Fitch (1993), Kenney and Bezuska (1989), Kilburn and Eckenwiker (1991), and Moore (1984) are found in the references at the end of the chapter.

Grades 3–5 and Grades 6–8

1. More advanced work with *Logo* will help strengthen students' abilities to define geometric figures and to develop procedures for complex designs and patterns. A **procedure** is a set of commands that may produce a simple figure or that may combine other procedures to form a more complex figure.

Ask children, as they work individually or in pairs, to develop a procedure for making a *box* with sides of 50 turtle steps. Next, have them make a *flag* using the box procedure. Then, have them make a *windmill* using the flag procedure. Finally, challenge the children to use the windmill procedure to make a *pinwheel.* The results of these four procedures are shown in Figure 11–57a, b, c, and d. The procedures that may be used to draw these figures are as follows:

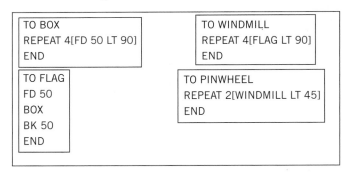

The procedures presented above show how the repeat command can be used to replace a set of commands and streamline the procedures. This is an application that students should be encouraged to use after the repeat command has been introduced.

Ask children to develop procedures for producing a number of polygons of different sizes. This may involve

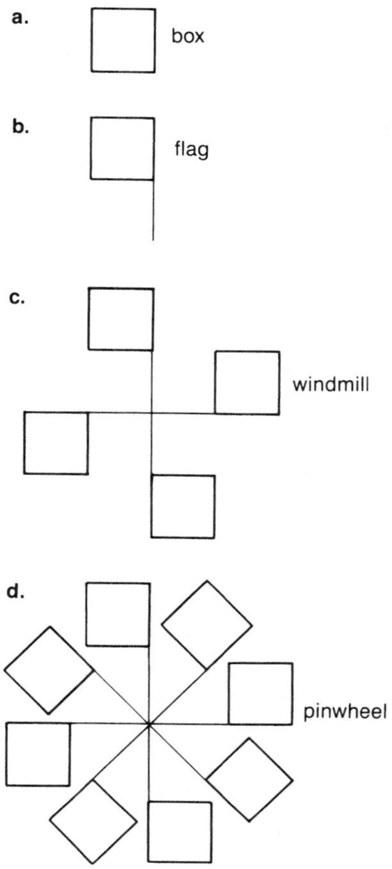
a.
box
b.
flag
c.
windmill
d.
pinwheel

Figure 11–57 Steps in making a *Logo* pinwheel.

using variables within the procedures. Variables present an added dimension to working with *Logo.* Challenge the students to use their skills to reproduce materials like the pattern blocks, the attribute blocks, or a "picture" drawn by students on squared paper. As students develop the ability to design figures, they learn valuable information about plane figures.

Besides using variables as they develop procedures, students will soon be able to use recursion, to employ coordinates to define locations, and to design complex figures.

We believe that *Logo* provides valuable experiences for students that help develop thinking skills, that strengthen spatial visualization, that increase knowledge of geometric relationships, and that motivate creative work.

Location, Coordinate Geometry, and Spatial Relationships

Coordinate geometry provides a rich mechanism for identifying locations and describing spatial relationships. Young children develop language that describes location relationships in their world. Some of those mentioned in Chapter 2 include *over, under, above,* and *below.* This is part of the process of learning about how to describe where an object can be found. As students mature, they become able to tell the direction, the distance, and the position of an object in space. Teachers of young children should guide their students through stories and discussions to describe locations of familiar objects in their environment. For example, children can describe how to go from the library corner of their classroom to the dress-up corner. There are likely several ways to travel between the two locations. Once children have described how far and in what direction to go, a simple model using geoblocks can be built or a map can be sketched on chart paper to act as a visual representation of a preferred route.

Children in grades 3–5 can begin to navigate on a simple coordinate system in the form of a map. Using a coordinate system such as that found on maps is a valuable application of geometry. The map can be an imaginary neighborhood or the neighborhood surrounding the school. One such map activity was presented in Chapter 5 in the Solving and Posing Number Problems section. Direction and distance are used to identify locations and to describe routes on the map.

A C T I V I T I E S

Grades 3–5

OBJECTIVE: to use a rectangular coordinate system.

The sample map shown in Figure 11–58 is the basis for the following activities and questions. Copy it for individual students. Five different yet related activities employ the map. These are briefly described below. Expand each activity to match the needs and abilities of the students.

1. *Where Is It?* Have the students study the map and answer the following questions:

- Laura's Gas Station is at the corner of Second and Walnut. Where is Jack's Market?
- Where is Fire House No. 46?
- Where is Lincoln School?
- Where is Center City Park? (Be careful!)

2. *How Far Is It?* Have the students use the map to follow the instructions and answer the questions below:

- From Tom's Cafe to Fire House No. 32 is 5 blocks by the shortest route. See if you can draw the shortest route.
- How many different 5-block routes can you find?
- How many blocks is the shortest route from Alice's Place to Lincoln School?

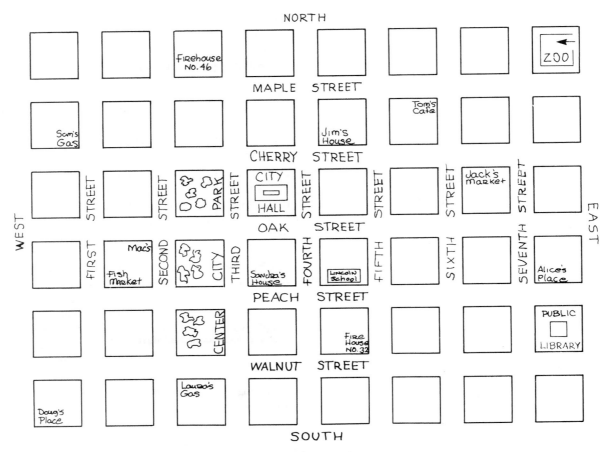

Figure 11–58 Map for introducing a rectangular coordinate system.

- Your bicycle had a flat tire on Sixth Street between Oak and Peach Streets. Give the address of the closest gas station.
- Suppose you are standing at Third and Walnut and someone from out of town asks how to get to Jack's Market. Tell them how to get there.
- You are a jogger and you want to jog around the outside of Center City Park for 2.5 kilometers. Every 10 blocks equals 1 kilometer. Tell where you begin and finish your jog. Are there different ways to do this?

3. *Location Codes.* Have the students use the map to answer the following questions:

- Suppose you are part of a group at Doug's place. All of a sudden, one member of the group says, "I know a new way to tell where places are." He goes on, "Laura's Gas Station is (2,1)," and he writes it down. "Sam's Gas Station is (1,4)." Do you see the code?
- Using the code, where is Jim's house?
- Using the code, where is the zoo entrance?
- What is at (7,1)?
- What is at (3,2)?

4. *Following Directions.* Have the students use the map to follow the directions below:

a. Place an *A* at the corner of Fifth and Cherry Streets. The *A* will represent where you are.

b. Walk two blocks east, three blocks south, two blocks west, and one block north. Place a *B* at the corner where you have stopped.

c. Beginning at *B*, walk one block east, three blocks north, one block east, and place a *C* at the corner where you have stopped.

d. Beginning at *C*, start out walking south and zigzag south and west, alternating one block at a time and walking five blocks in all. Place a *D* at the corner where you have stopped.

e. Beginning at *D*, walk three blocks west, three blocks north, one block east, and place an *E* at your final stopping point (Third and Maple Streets).

5. *A Trip to the Zoo.* Let students play the following game using the map: You and a friend decide to go to the zoo. You both meet at Doug's place and agree to make the trip in an unusual way. You will need a pair of

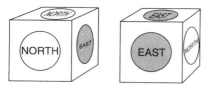

Each die has 3 "East" and 3 "North" Faces.

Figure 11–59 Dice for A Trip to the Zoo activity.

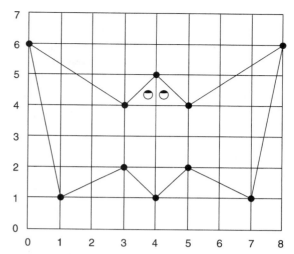

Figure 11–60 Picture resulting from plotting points on a Cartesian coordinate graph.

dice to give directions. You may use dice like those in Figure 11–59 or regular dice.

The faces on the dice give you the directions east and north. East directs you to go one block east, and north directs you to go one block north. (With regular dice, even numbers—2, 4, and 6—direct you to go east and odd numbers—1, 3, and 5—direct you to go north.)

You and your friend want to see who will get to the zoo first by rolling the dice and following the directions. Begin now and see who arrives first at the zoo entrance. If you go directly past City Hall, you get an extra throw.

OBJECTIVE: to reinforce the skill of plotting points on a Cartesian coordinate graph.

6. After children have learned to use ordered pairs of numbers to locate points, they may practice by using points to draw a picture. If you put a dot on each of the following points on a Cartesian coordinate system and connect the dots in order, you will make the picture shown in Figure 11–60: (0,6), (3,4), (4,5), (5,4), (8,6), (7,1), (5,2), (4,1), (3,2), (1,1). Have the children draw their own pictures and then list the points for the other children to use.

Students in grades 4 and 5 who are familiar with negative integers displayed on a number line will be able to transfer that familiarity as they are introduced to the four quadrants of the Cartesian coordinate system. By the time they reach middle school, students should be comfortable working with the coordinate plane. This will allow them to study various relationships, such as those associated with slope, transformations, and shapes. Their work in algebra will involve them in plotting graphs of equations on the coordinate plane. By the time they begin high school, they should be proficient with the Cartesian coordinate system, able to use it solve problems and to support mathematical arguments. A number of websites feature dynamic geometry software for the Cartesian coordinate system. One may be found at Weblink 11–13. At this Maths Online site, the coordinate system applet allows the user to be able to mark points, draw lines, and read the coordinates of the cursor position. The relationship between geometry and algebra can be explored.

ESTIMATING AND MENTAL CALCULATING

Throughout the activities presented in this chapter, we have suggested that you encourage children to estimate, asking, for example, "How many squares do you think can be constructed on a geoboard? How many turtle steps do you believe are necessary to hide the turtle under the shape? Which figures do you think have line symmetry? Can you tessellate with a pentagon?" All of these questions relate to estimating.

For those who actively pursue mathematical thinking, estimating is a valuable skill. As related to geometry, estimation involves the ability to reasonably guess how many, to visualize how figures will look before they are constructed, and to estimate the sizes of one-, two-, and three-dimensional figures.

Constantly challenge children to take a moment and estimate before they complete a project, activity, or exercise. After a while, estimating becomes a part of geometric thinking. The entire mathematics curriculum, then, provides students with practice in estimating. Several activities that reinforce estimation and relate to geometry follow.

A C T I V I T I E S

Pre-Kindergarten – Grade 2

OBJECTIVE: to estimate the sizes and shapes of various figures.

1. On a sheet of paper, draw the outlines of five or six triangles. Use actual cutouts of the shapes to make the outlines. Then put the shapes on one table or counter and the outlines on another. Ask one child to pick up one of the triangles and then move to the edge of the table containing the outlines. Ask another child to look at the triangle being held by the first child and estimate which outline belongs to that shape. Have the child holding the shape put the triangle in the outline to see if it fits. Then ask another child to choose another of the triangular shapes. Continue the activity until all of the shapes have been fitted to outlines. Discuss with the children how they chose a particular triangle.

Extend this activity by using different shapes. Use squares, rectangles, hexagons, and irregular quadrilaterals. To make the estimating more challenging, use 12 or 14 outlines and two or three different shapes at the same time.

OBJECTIVE: to estimate and discover the number of non-congruent triangles that can be made on an isometric geoboard.

2. Figure 11–61 shows an isometric geoboard. Begin by asking children to guess how many different triangles can be made using the first two rows of this geoboard. We find that there are twelve different triangles. (One example is shown on the geoboard in Figure 11–61.) Then have the students construct as many triangles as they can.

Later, have the students guess how many different triangles can be made using three rows of the geoboard. See how many of those triangles the children can construct. It is helpful to provide isometric dot paper for the children to record their findings (see Appendix B). The results make a fine bulletin board display. This activity can eventually be extended to incorporate the entire geoboard.

OBJECTIVE: to imagine and describe various space figures from their patterns.

3. Provide the children with patterns for various space figures. Include patterns for a cube, rectangular box, cylinder, cone, and tetrahedron. Have the children describe the figure they believe will result when the pattern is folded. Use dotted lines to indicate how the pattern will be folded. Encourage the children to sketch or find an example of the resulting space figure. Then have some children cut out

and fold the figure. Compare the estimates with the final product.

A variation of this activity is to show the children several household containers such as a cereal box, a paper towel tube, and a cracker box. Have the children sketch the pattern the container would make if it were cut apart and laid out flat. Cut the containers and compare them with the sketches.

It is helpful for children to have the opportunity to mentally visualize shapes. This allows them to gain experience in using the mind's eye as an aid in working with the visual aspects of geometry. We continue with activities for older students.

A C T I V I T I E S

Grades 3–5 and Grades 6–8

OBJECTIVE: to visualize and construct a figure of a given size and shape.

1. Provide each student with one or more outlines of figures on oaktag or paper. These figures may be triangles, quadrilaterals, squares, rectangles, pentagons, or hexagons. Also provide construction paper.

Have each student observe the outline of a figure. Then, using the construction paper, cut out the shape that will fill the outline. Encourage the students to devise ways to determine the appropriate size for the figure they are cutting out. When the figures have been cut out, have the students place them in the outlines and compare the results. Let the students then exchange outlines and try again.

A variation of this activity is to put one outline on the chalkboard and provide students with construction paper. Have all the students cut out the shape that fits the outline on the board. Again, let students see how well their figures fit the outline.

OBJECTIVE: to determine the results of a set of *Logo* commands.

2. Make a list of several *Logo* commands that will produce a geometric shape or design. Have the children read through the commands and attempt to draw what they believe the results will be. One set of design commands follows:

REPEAT 2 [FD 40 RT 90 FD 60 RT 90]
BACK 60
END

What do you think the results will be? (see Figure 11–62). Have children act out the commands by walking around the room or on the playground.

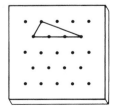

Figure 11–61 Example of one triangle using the first two rows of an isometric geoboard.

Figure 11–62   Result of a set of *Logo* commands.

Invite individual children to suggest sets of commands and let the other children guess what the results will be. Try the commands on the computer. This particular activity helps children visualize geometric figures by mentally or physically acting out a sequential procedure.

OBJECTIVE: to estimate and determine the number of squares that can be constructed on geoboards of varying sizes.

3. Have the students estimate how many squares they will be able to construct on a 5 × 5 rectangular geoboard without using any diagonal lines. After the students have guessed, encourage them to begin to systematically estimate and determine how many squares can be made on 2 × 2, 3 × 3, and 4 × 4 rectangular geoboards without using diagonals. The students should find one, five, and fourteen squares, respectively. See if they can use this information to discover how many squares can be made on the 5 × 5 geoboard.

There is a number pattern involving the square numbers (1, 4, 9, 16,. . .) that will show that thirty squares can be made on the 5 × 5 geoboard without using diagonals. How many squares would you expect on a 6 × 6 geoboard? How many on a 10 × 10 geoboard?

Extend this activity by including squares that involve diagonals. Encourage the students to break the problem into subproblems and then combine the results. Be sure to have the students estimate how many squares can be constructed.

REASONING, SOLVING, AND POSING GEOMETRIC PROBLEMS

Just as estimating is an integral part of geometry, so is solving and creating problems. Once learned and practiced, skills in problem solving continue to serve the learner. Many of the activities discussed earlier were presented in a problem format. Following are other useful activities that provide problem-solving experiences.

A C T I V I T I E S

Pre-Kindergarten-Grade 2 and Grades 3 – 5

OBJECTIVE: to determine patterns for which clues have been given.

1. Make up pattern strips from railroad board, each having approximately 10 squares, 10 by 10 centimeters in size. Place objects on four to six of the squares so that a pattern is suggested. Ask the children to fill in or extend the pattern, depending on which squares have been left blank. For example, in Figure 11–63a the pattern is trapezoid, triangle, triangle, trapezoid, and so on.

The pattern in Figure 11–63b is red triangle, red circle, red square, red diamond, then blue triangle, blue circle, and so on. In Figure 11–63c, the pattern is two rectangles in a horizontal position, two rectangles in a vertical position, circle, two rectangles in a horizontal position, and so on. Finally, let's consider the pattern in Figure 11–63d.

- *Understanding the problem.* What we need to do to solve this problem is to find shapes to put in the empty regions that fit the pattern already started. The figures that we can see are triangles with dots in them.

- *Devising a plan.* We will begin with the group of three triangles and look for likenesses and differences. If we find what we think is a pattern, we

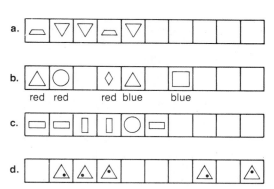

Figure 11–63   Pattern strips.

will move to the right along the row and see if the figures fit the pattern we have in mind (look for a pattern).

- *Carrying out the plan.* Because all of the triangles look alike, we look closely at the dots in the triangles. The first triangle has a dot in the lower-right corner. In the next triangle, the dot is in the lower-left corner. In the next triangle, the dot is in the top corner.

  It seems as though the dot is moving from corner to corner. If that is how the pattern works, the very first square should have a triangle with a dot in the top corner. The next three empty squares should have triangles with dots in the lower-right, lower-left, and top corners. The last empty region will have a triangle with a dot in the lower-left corner.

  We have found the pattern. It looks as if either the dots are moving around to the right inside the triangles or the triangles are rotating to the right.

- *Looking back.* When we put all of the triangles and dots in the empty regions, is the pattern of dots the same from the beginning to the end of the row? Yes, it is. The pattern must be correct.

There are many possibilities for patterns such as these. Invite children to make patterns for their classmates to complete. Children can be skillful problem posers.

OBJECTIVE: to develop spatial visualization using tangram pieces.

2. Tangram pieces were used in Chapter 9 in activities related to fractions. Tangrams offer children the chance to solve puzzles and to engage in creative endeavors, as well. There are seven tangram pieces, as shown in Figure 11–64. All seven may be fitted together to make a square, as in Appendix B.

Initial activities should include providing frames in which the children fit two or more of the tangram shapes. For example, using an *a* piece and a *d* piece, make the shape shown in Figure 11–65a. The children should be able to put the pieces together and achieve success. Later, use a greater number of pieces and make the shapes more difficult to complete. Ask experienced children to make a shape using all but one *e* piece, as in Figure 11–65b.

Another enjoyable tangram activity is to construct pictures of animals, people, objects, and houses using all or some of the tangram shapes. Children may fill in frames, construct their own pictures, or develop figures for other children to complete. The waving man in Figure 11–65c is an example of such a creation.

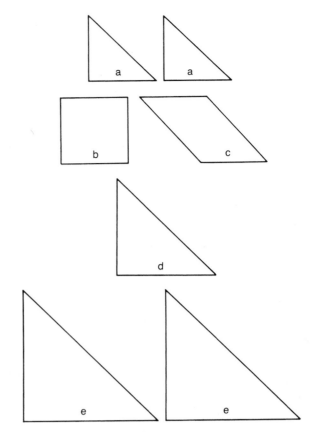

Figure 11–64   A set of Tangram pieces.

A variation of this activity can be found on Weblink 11–14, where students can employ dynamic geometry software to move tangram pieces into frames to make pictures and to make polygons.

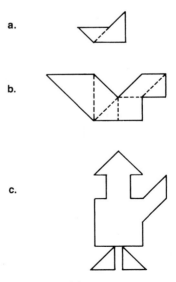

Figure 11–65   Tangram problems.

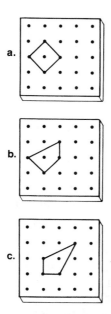

Figure 11−66 Three geoboard shapes from one set of clues.

OBJECTIVE: to use clues to solve mystery shape problems on the geoboard.

3. Provide the children with geoboards. Explain that they will be given clues to the mystery shapes. They should find at least one shape that matches each set of clues. Say, for example, "I am thinking of a shape that has 4 nails on its boundary and 1 nail inside. Can you find it?" Figure 11−66 shows three different shapes that fit the clues; there are others. Once the children have found one solution, encourage them to find others.

Here are additional clues that describe other shapes. "I am thinking of a shape that has. . ."

- 4 nails on its boundary and 0 nails inside
- 5 nails on its boundary and 0 nails inside
- 6 nails on its boundary and 0 nails inside
- 10 nails on its boundary and 2 nails inside

Once children are able to find the mystery shapes, ask them to make up clues for shapes that other members of the class can find. Have them put the solutions on rectangular dot paper. Remind the children that often there is more than one shape that matches a set of clues.

Grades 3−5 and Grades 6−8

OBJECTIVE: to create dodecagons of the same size using a variety of shapes.

1. Provide students with a set of pattern blocks and an example or two of dodecagons constructed using the blocks. Figure 11−67 shows two such figures. The challenge is to see how many different dodecagons of the same size students can make using the pattern blocks.

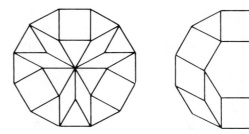

Figure 11−67 Dodecagons constructed using pattern blocks.

There are more than 60 different dodecagons of the same size that can be constructed using the pattern blocks.

Provide outlines of dodecagons on which the students can sketch the pattern blocks used. Let the students color the sketches using the appropriate colors. Then place the figures on a bulletin board as a reference for others who are working on the project.

OBJECTIVE: to develop visual perception.

2. Exploring pentominoes offers students the opportunity to test their perceptual and creative abilities while problem solving. A **pentomino** is a figure produced by combining five square shapes or cubes of the same size. There is one rule: each square must share at least one complete side with another square in the figure or each cube must share a face with another cube in the figure. Three of 12 possible pentominoes appear in Figure 11−68.

Pentominoes are two- or three-dimensional, and two pentominoes are considered the same if one is a flip or a rotation of the other. For instance, the pentominoes in Figure 11−69 are considered the same.

Initially, give students numerous square shapes to explore. Squares of 3 centimeters on a side are ideal.

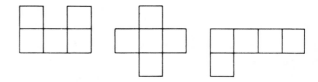

Figure 11−68 Three of the twelve pentominoes.

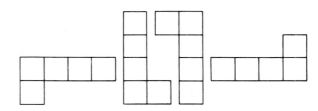

Figure 11−69 Four examples of the same pentomino.

Challenge students to find as many different pentominoes as they can. As they discover the figures, have them shade or color the patterns on a sheet of squared graph paper.

Extend this activity by having students select the pentominoes that they believe can be folded to make a box with an open top. Allow time for students to cut out the pentominoes and to attempt to fold them into boxes. You may continue to extend work with pentominoes by presenting three-dimensional pentominoes with challenging shapes to build. Discovery Toys (1993) has developed a three-dimensional pentomino puzzle set.

3. Another way to investigate pentominoes is to use the small milk containers commonly found in schools. Cut off the top of each container so that the bottom and the four sides are same-sized squares. Then ask the students to see how many of the 12 pentominoes they can make by cutting the cartons along the edges and without cutting any one side completely off. Figure 11–70a shows an example in which a cut was made along each of the four vertical edges and the sides were folded down. Figure 11–70b shows a different pentomino made by cutting along other edges of the milk carton.

4. Once students are comfortable with pentominoes, have them tessellate with various pentominoes. Using only one of the pentomino shapes, is it possible to cover a sheet of paper without leaving gaps? Figure 11–71 illustrates the beginnings of two tessellations.

5. Use pentominoes to further explore symmetry. Have students try to place a mirror or a reflective tool on all or some of the pentominoes so that the reflection is the same as the part of the figure behind the mirror. In other words, do all pentominoes have line symmetry? Identify those that do and those that do not.

6. Have the students consider **hexominoes**, figures constructed using six square shapes. There are considerably more hexominoes than pentominoes. Each of the preceding activities, except the one using the milk container, can easily be done with hexominoes.

OBJECTIVE: to analyze various cubes and determine color patterns.

7. Make available 27 small cubes with dimensions of 2 or 3 centimeters. Have the students construct a large

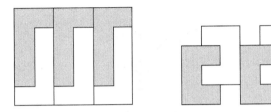

Figure 11–71 Tessellating with pentominoes.

2-by-2-by-2 cube using these smaller cubes (see Figure 11–72a). Then have the students imagine that the large cube has been painted blue. Encourage the students to make a table to record the number of faces of each smaller cube that are painted blue.

Then present the challenge. Have the students construct a large 3-by-3-by-3 cube using the smaller cubes (see Figure 11–72b). Have them imagine that this cube is painted blue. Ask them to make a table to record the number of smaller cubes with (a) no faces painted blue, (b) exactly one face painted blue, (c) exactly two faces painted blue, and (d) exactly three faces painted blue. Extend the problem by asking the students to construct a 4-by-4-by-4 cube and answer the same four questions regarding the faces painted blue. Here, the table will be especially useful. Then have the students try to construct a 5-by-5-by-5 cube and answer the questions.

For a final, more difficult extension, see if anyone can find the various numbers of blue faces on a 10-by-10-by-10 cube. This last problem may be a question of the week.

OBJECTIVE: to combine *Logo* procedures to generate other figures.

8. When students have had an opportunity to work with *Logo* and can design certain simple shapes, such as a square, a triangle, and a circle, encourage them to solve problems using their skills. Have them construct a shape with each side a specified length in each corner of the computer monitor. Have them make the largest visible square or circle. Challenge the

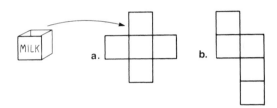

Figure 11–70 Cutting a milk carton to make pentominoes.

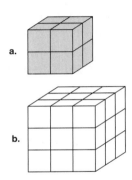

Figure 11–72 Examples of the painted cube problem.

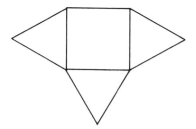

Figure 11–73 Student-posed *Logo* problem.

students to construct a large square with a circle inside it and a triangle inside the circle. See if they can construct three shapes side by side that just barely touch each other.

Here is another opportunity for students to pose problems to present to others in the class. When a design or figure has been posed, ask the inventor to sketch the design on a piece of squared paper and post it near the computer as a class challenge. Figure 11–73 shows one such student-generated problem. In addition, *Logo* resources contain many problems for students.

Children's awareness of geometry in the environment is heightened considerably as you focus attention on various applications of geometry. This awareness also strengthens students' appreciation for and understanding of geometry.

ORGANIZING FOR GEOMETRIC TLC

When students engage in learning geometry, a number of teaching, learning, and curriculum decisions are appropriate. Geometry is a hands-on topic. Thus, a variety of physical objects should be used during the instructional time. Activity should be the basis for learning geometry. The geometry curriculum lends itself well to being interspersed throughout the school year. It offers a change of pace in the mathematics program and is a topic of great interest to some students. How children are grouped for learning geometry should be considered. For example, when younger children are learning concepts such as *near, far, on, in,* and so on, you may wish to have the children all together in a discussion corner or in another area of the room. This allows several children to participate simultaneously, allows the students to carry on a discussion, and allows the teacher to observe the work of the children. Other examples of whole-class activities include introductory work on the geoboard, introductory work with *Logo*, constructions of polyhedra models, and projects such as building toothpick bridges or a geodesic dome.

Cooperative learning groups are appropriate for activities in which materials may be shared and for those in which problems are presented. Examples of learning group activities include geoboard problems, tessellations, pentominoes, mirror symmetry, soap films on wire frames, constructing shapes with a compass and straightedge, pattern block challenges, and projects. Roper (1989, 1990) has developed problem-solving activities using Pattern Blocks that are intended for use in cooperative learning groups. The focus is to construct shapes with the blocks using instructions that are provided for each member of the group.

Individual or pair learning may best take place when students are exploring the *Logo* environment or making line drawings or coloring patterns. Once children have learned how to make objects by paper folding, folding is done individually.

By and large, the types of activities suggested in this chapter tend to be social activities; that is, they are effectively accomplished when children are working together and comparing and discussing their work. Even the skills of geometry are effectively learned as children work side by side informally.

COMMUNICATING LEARNING OF GEOMETRIC CONCEPTS

Description is an important part of communicating in learning geometry. As children observe shapes, discover their properties, develop definitions involving essential characteristics, and draw and construct shapes, their ability to communicate their thoughts is fundamental. For the students, part of the communication process is drawing representations that illustrate their work. Written communication is used to describe their work and to put into words the shapes and forms with which they are working. Oral communication serves a similar purpose. For example, "In your group today, you are to describe the figure that has been provided. The reporter for your group will present the description orally to the rest of you and you will attempt to sketch the figure from the description. Tomorrow, we will do a similar activity but your group's recorder will write a description that you will share with other groups to see if the members of the other groups can sketch the figure that has been described."

Children enjoy writing and illustrating theme books—for example, a book featuring round objects with pictures and written descriptions of round things found at school and at home. Older students may keep journals of shapes with descriptions of the shapes and where they are found. These journals can spark ideas for creative stories about various shapes. The shape descriptions in Norton

Juster's *The Phantom Tollbooth* (1961) will surely inspire writing that includes shapes.

The oral language that children use to describe their movement as they walk around geometric figures made with tape or yarn on the floor becomes the basis for writing *Logo* procedures. The language of the children is translated into the language of *Logo;* likewise, children can read *Logo* procedures and describe them in their own words.

Cooperative and individual writing are appropriate activities for cooperative learning groups. It is a good plan to keep all written material in the individual portfolios for easy access. When a group record has been made, it may be kept in the portfolio of the group record keeper. As group members explore geometric concepts and develop skills, the group recorder provides a chronicle of the thinking process. This chronicle is then shared with other groups during the debriefing time at the end of the activity. Discussion is then invited. Children question one another and seek clarification of the ideas that have been put forth.

CONNECTING AND REPRESENTING GEOMETRIC LEARNING

Mr. Grotting's kindergarten children were puzzled when he held out his clenched fist and said that he had something in his hand and he wanted them to guess what it was. The students made several guesses, including a pencil, a coin, a button, a block, and a cracker. Mr. Grotting said no, it was not any of those items. Then he said he would give a clue: the object is round. Quickly, the children again guessed a coin and a button. No, it was not either of those items. Mr. Grotting asked the students about other items that are small and round. A child asked if was a ball. No. Was it a ring? Yes, that was it. It was one of the rings from the dress-up corner. Mr. Grotting then asked if the children could think of anything else that was round, whether big or small. The children named a bicycle wheel, a skateboard wheel, and a car wheel. A few other items were mentioned before it was time for stations.

In the math station in Mr. Grotting's room this week, the children were asked to find pictures or draw pictures of things that are round. When a picture was found or made, the children dictated a sentence about what the round object was to a parent helper who wrote the sentence beneath the picture. After all of the children had had a chance to find round objects, Mr. Grotting and the class described the variety of round things there are. The pictures were sorted by whether the round objects could be found in the classroom or outside of the classroom. All of the pictures were then put together to form a class book entitled "Things That Are Round." The connection between the geometric idea of circle and how the circle is used in the environment became clearer as a result of the focus on round things. Next, a square will be the focus.

Ms. Perkins had a surprise for her seventh-grade class. This day as the students arrived, many brought pictures, including some photographs, of various geometric shapes that they had seen in their community or in magazines. It had begun just as another assignment, but as the students realized how shapes were used in building construction, in framing and outlining, and in vehicles used in transportation, considerable energy was put forth in documenting the shapes. The category of shapes in nature was discovered by several students, and appropriate examples were brought in. Now, the bulletin board was nearly full of pictures and some objects from this impromptu scavenger hunt. Today, Ms. Perkins's surprise was to show a set of digital photographs she had taken in a teachers' workshop the previous summer. The theme of the photographs, presented from a DVD, was "Geometry in the Environment" and reinforced the findings of the students. After several of the images had been shown, Ms. Perkins challenged the students to work in their cooperative groups to make lists of all the different shapes that they had already seen and were likely to see as additional images were presented. The group discussions were lively. When the group reporters shared with the rest of the class their lists, it became clear that the geometry that the students had been studying surrounded them both in and out of school.

There was not enough time during this day to view all of the photographs, so for the next two days, the photographs and discussions continued. To culminate this mini-unit each of the student groups selected a particular shape and made a collage of two- and three-dimensional representations of that shape from their environment. One group focused on squares and another group focused on rectangles. Other groups chose circles, triangles, polygons with more than four sides, streets and branches, and decorative patterns. By the end of a week, the classroom was beautifully decorated with the group projects. The connection between geometry and the students' world had been clearly made.

ASSESSING GEOMETRIC LEARNING

In assessing geometric learning, consider the objectives. When a school or a district adopts a mathematics textbook series or program, it is, by and large, adopting a collection of objectives. The objectives are found throughout the teacher's guides for each level in the series. The geometry presented in a math program is reviewed and assessed at the end of a chapter or section. Chapter tests help in assessing geometric learning but do not tell the whole story.

Activities provide opportunities for observing the actual performance of the children and making additional assessment. Observations are most helpful when teachers make anecdotal records at the time of or shortly after the observation. With the large number of useful geometry activities, there is ample opportunity for teachers to observe and note children's performance as the children actively engage in learning geometry.

Further, we recommend that you expand on the material presented in the math textbook. Thus, students have a greater opportunity to advance from the first of the van Hiele levels (recognizing shapes) to the second level (establishing relationships between figures and their properties).

1. **Sketch the following on the geoboards below.**

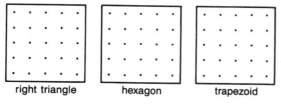

right triangle   hexagon   trapezoid

2. **Circle each pentomino that has exactly <u>one</u> line of reflection.**

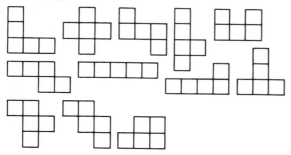

3. **Make the following design with *Logo* commands. Use REPEAT and the procedure SQUARE.**

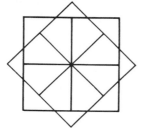

Figure 11–74 Teacher-made assessment activities.

Teacher-made assessments may provide some information regarding content not found in the math textbook. An assessment may require paper and pencil, or it may be a task requested by the teacher. Figure 11–74 shows three sample paper-and-pencil test items.

The same material can be assessed by asking students to construct a particular figure on their geoboards and then to hold the boards up for the teacher to see. Likewise, students can be given pentominoes and asked to use a mirror or a reflective tool to find those figures with exactly one line of symmetry. Another task may be to produce a particular design or figure on the computer using *Logo*. At various times, work completed by the students should be placed in the students' portfolios to use for assessment purposes. Items that might not fit such as a polyhedron model or a geodesic dome could be photographed and the photograph placed in the portfolio or in a computer file.

Problem-based assessment is initiated with a rich learning task. Students work through the problem and record their work. The written record is used for the assessment. Assessment is an ongoing task for the teacher. The more information you gather, the better able you will be to fit instruction to the learning styles of your students. Continually monitoring students as they work is among the most important tasks of the teacher.

SOMETHING FOR EVERYONE

Many of the activities in Chapters 11 and 12 require children to work in visual or in spatial learning modes. Of course, children use other learning modes as they learn the concepts and skills of geometry and measurement. To avoid repetition, the discussion of the learning modes associated with geometry and measurement is presented at the end of Chapter 12.

FOR YOU AS A TEACHER: IDEAS FOR DISCUSSION AND YOUR PROFESSIONAL PORTFOLIO

This section is intended to provide you the opportunity to read, write, and reflect on key elements of this chapter. We list several discussion ideas. We hope that one or more of these ideas will prove interesting to you and that you will choose to investigate and write about the ideas. The results of your work should be considered as part of your professional portfolio. You might consider these two questions as guides for your writing: "What does the material in this chapter mean for you as a teacher?" or "How can what you are reading be translated into a teaching practice for you as a teacher?"

DISCUSSION IDEAS

1. Investigate the geometry of your environment. Select some shops, buildings, or a neighborhood and chronicle all the examples of shape that you can. Discuss your findings and illustrate them with drawings or photographs.

2. Explain how you might teach students who are visually impaired about polygons and space figures. Design and construct several learning aids that would be appropriate.

3. Use dynamic geometry software on either a graphing calculator or on a computer to practice translation, reflection, and rotation transformations. Discuss the value of virtual transformations as part of the geometry curriculum.

4. Construct a geodesic dome with a diameter of 18 inches. Use tagboard for the triangles and white school glue to attach the triangles to each other. Decorate the triangles either before or after you attach them. Discuss the value of constructing a geodesic dome in your classroom.

5. Seek out a website on fractal geometry such as that found at Weblink 11–9 and investigate the site. From that site, link to other sites that feature fractal geometry. Explain to others what you were able to discover from your investigation.

6. Using the discussion about and examples of open-ended problems presented in Chapter 4, design three open-ended problems that focus on geometry, one each for pre-kindergarten–grade 2, grades 3–5, and grades 6–8.

ADDITIONAL RESOURCES

REFERENCES

Arcidiacono, Michael J., David Fielker, and Eugene Maier, *Seeing Symmetry.* Salem, OR: Math Learning Center, 1996.

Bartels, Bobbye Hoffman, "Truss(t)ing Triangles," *Mathematics Teaching in the Middle School,* 3, no. 6 (March–April 1998), 394–396.

Battista, M. T., and D. H. Clements, *Exploring Solids and Boxes: 3-D Geometry.* Palo Alto, CA: Dale Seymour, 1995.

Beaumont, V., R. Curtis, and J. Smart, *How to Teach Perimeter, Area, and Volume.* Reston, VA: National Council of Teachers of Mathematics, 1986.

Bennett, Albert, and Linda Foreman, *Visual Mathematics Course Guide, Vol. I.* Salem, OR: Math Learning Center, 1995.

———,*Visual Mathematics Course Guide, Vol. II.* Salem, OR: Math Learning Center, 1996.

Bennett, Albert, Eugene Maier, and L. Ted Nelson, *Math and the Mind's Eye: V. Looking at Geometry.* Salem, OR: Math Learning Center, 1987.

Britton, Jill, and Walter Britton, *Teaching Tessellating Art.* Palo Alto, CA: Dale Seymour, 1992.

Browning, Christine A., and Dwayne E. Channel, *Explorations: Graphing Calculator Activities for Enriching Middle School Mathematics.* Austin, TX: Texas Instruments, 1997.

Brummett, M. R., and L. H. Charles, *Geoblocks Jobcards.* Sunnyvale, CA: Creative Publications, 1989.

Burger, William F., "Geometry," *Arithmetic Teacher,* 32, no. 6 (February 1985), 52–56.

Burger, William F., and J. Michael Shaughnessy, "Characterizing the van Hiele Levels of Development in Geometry," *Journal for Research in Mathematics Education,* 17, no. 1 (January 1986), 31–48.

Chanan, Steven, *The Geometer's Sketchpad Learning Guide.* Emeryville: CA: Key Curriculum Press, 2000.

Clements, D. H., S. J. Russell, C. Tierney, M. T. Battista, and J. S. Meredith, *Flips, Turns, and Area: 2-D Geometry.* Palo Alto, CA: Dale Seymour, 1995.

Clements, Douglas H., and Michael T. Battista, *Logo and Geometry.* Reston, VA: National Council of Teachers of Mathematics, 2001.

Clithero, Dale, "Learning with Logo 'Instantly'," *Arithmetic Teacher,* 34, no. 5 (January 1987), 12–15.

Copeland, Richard W., *How Children Learn Mathematics.* Englewood Cliffs, NJ: Merrill/Prentice Hall, 1984.

Cory, Sheila. *LOGO Works: Lessons in LOGO.* Portland, ME: Terrapin Software, Inc., 1995.

Cowan, Richard A., "Pentominoes for Fun Learning," *The Arithmetic Teacher,* 24, no. 3 (March 1977), 188–190.

Cruikshank, Douglas E., and John McGovern, "Math Projects Build Skills," *Instructor,* 87, no. 3 (October 1977), 194–198.

Dienes, Z. P., and E. W Golding, *Geometry through Transformations: 1. Geometry of Distortion.* New York: Herder & Herder, 1967.

Discovery Toys, *Pentominoes.* Martinez, CA: Discovery Toys, Inc., 1993.

Findell, Marian Small, Mary Cavanagh, Linda Dacey, Carole E. Greenes, and Linda Jensen Sheffield. *Navigating through Geometry in Prekindergarten–Grade 2.* Reston, VA: National Council of Teachers of Mathematics, 2001.

Fitch, Dorothy M., *101 Ideas for Logo: 101 Projects for all Levels of Logo Fun.* Portland, ME: Terrapin Software, 1993.

Foreman, Linda, and Albert Bennett, Jr., *Visual Mathematics Course I.* Salem, OR: Math Learning Center, 1995.

———, *Visual Mathematics Course II.* Salem, OR: Math Learning Center, 1996.

Foster, T. E., *Tangram Patterns.* Sunnyvale, CA: Creative Publications, Inc., 1977.

Fuys, David, "Van Hiele Levels of Thinking in Geometry," *Education and Urban Society,* 17, no. 4 (August 1985), 447–462.

Fuys, David, Dorothy Geddes, and Rosamond Tischler, *The van Hiele Model of Thinking in Geometry among Adolescents?*

(*Journal for Research in Mathematics Education,* Monograph Number 3). Reston, VA: National Council of Teachers of Mathematics, 1988.

Gavin, M. Katherine, Louise P. Belkin, Ann Marie Spinelli, and Judy St. Marie, *Navigating through Geometry in Grades 3–5.* Reston, VA: National Council of Teachers of Mathematics, 2001.

Giesecke, E. H., *Reflective Geometry Activities with the GeoReflector Mirror: Grades 5–8.* Vernon Hills, IL: Learning Resources, Inc., 1996.

Giganti, Paul, Jr., and Mary Jo Cittadino, "The Art of Tessellation," *Arithmetic Teacher,* 37, no. 7 (March 1990), 6–16.

Gillespie, Norm, *Gateway to Geometry: A School Program for Teachers Using the Mira.* Oakville, Ontario: Mira Math Co., Inc., 1994.

Gleick, James, *Chaos: Making a New Science.* New York: Viking Penguin, 1987.

Juraschek, William, "Getting in Touch with Shape," *Arithmetic Teacher,* 37, no. 8 (April 1990), 14–16.

Kenney, Margaret J., and Stanley J. Bezuska, *Tessellations Using Logo.* Palo Alto, CA: Dale Seymour, 1987.

Kilburn, Dan, and Mark Eckenwiker, *Terrapin Logo for the Macintosh.* Portland, ME: Terrapin Software, 1991.

Long, Calvin T., and Duane W. DeTemple, *Mathematical Reasoning for Elementary Teachers.* Boston: Addison-Wesley, 1996.

Mandebrot, Benoit B., *The Fractal Geometry of Nature.* New York: Freeman, 1983.

Mansfield, Helen, "Projective Geometry in the Elementary School," *Arithmetic Teacher,* 32, no. 7 (March 1985), 15–19.

McKim, Robert H., *Thinking Visually.* Belmont, CA: Lifetime Learning Publications, 1980.

Moore, Margaret L., *LOGO Discoveries.* Palo Alto, CA: Creative Publications, 1984.

———, *Geometry Problems for LOGO Discoveries.* Worth, IL: Creative Publications, 1984.

Morris, Janet P., "Investigating Symmetry in the Primary Grades," *The Arithmetic Teacher,* 24, no. 3 (March 1977), 188–190.

National Council of Teachers of Mathematics, *Principles and Standards for School Mathematics.* Reston, VA: NCTM, 2000.

Onslow, Barry, "Pentominoes Revisited," *Arithmetic Teacher,* 37, no. 9 (May 1990), 5–9.

Piaget, Jean, "How Children Form Mathematical Concepts," *Scientific American,* 189, no. 5 (November 1953), 74–78.

Piaget, Jean, and Barbel Inhelder, *The Child's Conception of Space.* New York: Norton, 1967.

Pugalee, David K., Jeffrey Frykholm, Art Johnson, Hannah Slovin, Carol Malloy, and Ron Preston, *Navigating through Geometry in Grades 6–8.* Reston, VA: National Council of Teachers of Mathematics, 2002.

Rectanus, C., *Math by All Means: Geometry Grade 3.* Sausalito, CA: Math Solutions Publications, 1994.

Roper, Ann, *Cooperative Problem Solving with Pattern Blocks.* Sunnyvale, CA: Creative Publications, 1989.

———, *Cooperative Problem Solving with Pattern Blocks (Primary).* Sunnyvale, CA: Creative Publications, 1990.

Seymour, Dale, and Jill Britton, *Introduction to Tessellations.* Palo Alto, CA: Dale Seymour, 1989.

Stevens, Peter S., *Patterns in Nature.* Boston: Little, Brown, 1974.

Suydam, Marilyn N., "Forming Geometric Concepts," *Arithmetic Teacher,* 33, no. 2 (October 1985), 26.

Teppo, Anne, "van Hiele Levels of Geometric Thought Revisited," *Mathematics Teacher,* 84, no. 3 (March 1991), 210–221.

van Hiele, Pierre M., *Structure and Insight: A Theory of Mathematics Education.* Orlando, FL: Academic Press, 1986.

Wenninger, Magnus J., *Polyhedron Models for the Classroom.* Reston, VA: National Council of Teachers of Mathematics, 1975.

Wilgus, Wendy, and Lisa Pizzuto, *Exploring the Basics of Geometry with Cabri.* Austin, TX: Texas Instruments, 1997.

Wirszup, Izaak, "Breakthrough in the Psychology of Learning and Teaching Geometry," in *Space and Geometry: Papers from a Research Workshop,* ed. J. Larry Martin. Columbus, OH: ERIC Center for Science, Mathematics Environmental Education, 1976.

Woodward, Ernest, and Marilyn Woodward. *Image Reflector Geometry.* White Plains, NY: Cuisenaire, 1996.

Zilliox, Joseph T., and Shannon G. Lowrey, "Many Faces Have I," *Mathematics Teaching in the Middle School,* 3, no. 3 (November–December 1997), 180–183.

CHILDREN'S LITERATURE

Esbensen, Barbara Juster, *Echoes for the Eye: Poems to Celebrate Patterns in Nature.* Illustrated by Helen K. Davie. Scranton, PA: HarperCollins, 1996.

Grifalconi, Ann, *The Village of Round and Square Houses.* Boston: Little, Brown, 1986.

Hoban, Tana, *Shapes, Shapes, Shapes.* New York: Greenwillow, 1986.

Juster, Norton, *The Phantom Tollbooth.* New York: Random House, 1961.

Morris, Ann, *Bread, Bread, Bread.* New York: Lothrop, Lee & Shepard Books, 1989.

Reid, Margarette S., *The Button Box.* New York: Dutton, 1990.

TECHNOLOGY

Battista, Michael T., *Shape Makers: Developing Geometric Reasoning with the Geometer's Sketchpad. Triangle and Quadrilateral Activities for Grades 5–8.* Berkeley, CA: Key Curriculum Press, 1998. (software and book)

Burns, Marilyn, *Mathematics with Manipulatives: Geoboards.* White Plains, NY: Cuisenaire Company of America, Inc., 1988. (video and guide)

Davidson, *Kid Cad.* Torrance, CA: Davidson, 1997. (software)

Dewey, David. Home page. 4 Sept. 2002 <http://www.olympus.net/personal/dewey/mandelbrot.html>

Edmark, *Mighty Math Calculating Crew.* Novato, CA: Riverdeep Interactive Learning, 1996. (software)

———, *Mighty Math Carnival Countdown.* Novato, CA: Riverdeep Interactive Learning, 1996. (software)

———, *Mighty Math Cosmic Geometry Grades 6–8.* Novato, CA: Riverdeep Interactive Learning, 1996. (software)

———, *Mighty Math Number Heroes.* Novato, CA: Riverdeep Interactive Learning, 1996. (software)

———, *Mighty Math Zoo Zillions.* Novato, CA: Riverdeep Interactive Learning, 1996. (software)

Lanius, Cynthia. Home page. 2002 <http://math.rice.edu/~lanius/frac/index.html>

Learning Company. *TesselMania! Deluxe.* Cambridge, MA: Learning Co., 1999. (software)

Musgrave, Ken. Home page. 6 Dec. 2002 <http://www.ken-musgrave.com/>

Sunburst, *Building Perspective Deluxe.* Pleasantville, NY: Sunburst Technology, 2000. (software)

———, *The Factory Deluxe.* Pleasantville, NY: Sunburst Technology, 1998. (software)

WEBLINKS

Weblink 11–1: NCTM Electronic Example: Investigating the Concept of Triangle and Properties of Polygons. http://www.standards.nctm.org/document/eexamples/chap4/4.2/index.htm

Weblink 11–2: NCTM Illuminations activity: Shapes Inside Out. http://Illuminations.nctm.org/swr/review.asp?SWR = 1808

Weblink 11–3: NCTM Electronic Example: Exploring Properties of Rectangles and Parallelograms Using Dynamic Software http://www.standards.nctm.org/document/eexamples/chap5/5.3/index.htm

Weblink 11–4: The Geometer's Sketchpad classroom resources from The Math Forum. http://mathforum.org/sketchpad/sketchpad.html

Weblink 11–5: NCTM Electronic Example: Understanding Congruence, Similarity, and Symmetry Using Transformations and Interactive Figures. http://www.standards.nctm.org/document/eexamples/chap6/6.4/index.htm

Weblink 11–6: Virtual manipulative site featuring Platonic solids. http://matti.usu.edu/nlvm/nav/category_g_1_t_3.html

Weblink 11–7: An easy to understand introduction to the Mandelbrot Set by David Dewey. http://www.olympus.net/personal/dewey/mandelbrot.html

Weblink 11–8: A fractal artist, Musgrave exhibits very impressive fractal landscapes. http://www.kenmusgrave.com

Weblink 11–9: Exceptional site for developing children's understanding of fractals. http://math.rice.edu/~lanius/frac/index.html

Weblink 11–10: NCTM Electronic Example investigating similar rectangles and prisms. http://www.standards.nctm.org/document/eexamples/chap6/6.3/index.htm

Weblink 11–11: NCTM Illuminations site: Spatial Reasoning Using Cubes and Isometric Drawings. http://illuminations.nctm.org/imath/6-8/isometric/index.html

Weblink 11–12: NCTM Electronic Example: Exploring number, measurement, and geometry in a *Logo*-like computer environment. http://www.standards.nctm.org/document/eexamples/chap4/4.3/index.htm

Weblink 11–13: Maths Online website: Drawing plane and coordinate system. http://www.univie.ac.at/future.media/moe/galerie/zeich/zeich.html

Weblink 11–14: NCTM Electronic Example: Developing Geometry Understandings and Spatial Skills through Puzzlelike Problems with Tangrams. http://www.standards.nctm.org/document/eexamples/chap4/4.4/index.htm

Additional Weblinks

Weblink 11–15: Collection of Illumination Web Resources for Geometry for all grade bands. http://Illuminations.nctm.org/swr/list.asp?Ref=2&Std=2

Weblink 11–16: National Library of Virtual Manipulative for Interactive Mathematics. http://matti.usu.edu/nlvm/nav/vlibrary.html

TEACHING AND LEARNING MEASUREMENT

GUIDING QUESTIONS

As your read the following pages, consider these guiding questions:

1. How do the following differ: direct and indirect comparison? arbitrary and standard units? continuous and discrete measurement?

2. What are the concepts related to measurement?

3. What is the nature of activities that help develop measurement skills?

4. How do the activities intended to make sense of area and the skill of measuring area compare?

5. What are the tools of measuring?

6. How does estimating fit into teaching and learning measurement concepts and skills?

NCTM Principles and Standards for School Mathematics

Measurement

Instructional programs from prekindergarten through grade 12 should enable all students to:

Understand measurable attributes of objects and the units, systems, and processes of measurement

Pre-K to 2

- recognize the attributes of length, volume, weight, area, and time;
- compare and order objects according to these attributes;
- understand how to measure using nonstandard and standard units;
- select an appropriate unit and tool for the attribute being measured.

Grades 3–5

- understand such attributes as length, area, weight, volume, and size of angle and select the appropriate type of unit for measuring each attribute;
- understand the need for measuring with standard units and become familiar with standard units in the customary and metric systems;
- carry out simple unit conversions, such as from centimeters to meters, within a system of measurement;
- understand that measurements are approximations and how differences in units affect precision;
- explore what happens to measurements of a two-dimensional shape such as its perimeter and area when the shape is changed in some way.

Grades 6–8

- understand both metric and customary systems of measurement;
- understand relationships among units and convert from one unit to another within the same system;
- understand, select, and use units of appropriate size and type to measure angles, perimeter, area, surface area, and volume.

Apply appropriate techniques, tools, and formulas to determine measurements

Pre-K to 2

- measure with multiple copies of units of the same size, such as paper clips laid end to end;

- use repetition of a single unit to measure something larger than the unit, for instance, measuring the length of a room with a single meterstick;
- use tools to measure;
- develop common referents for measures to make comparisons and estimates.

Grades 3–5

- develop strategies for estimating the perimeters, areas, and volumes of irregular shapes;
- select and apply appropriate standard units and tools to measure length, area, volume, weight, time, temperature, and the size of angles;
- select and use benchmarks to estimate measurements;
- develop, understand, and use formulas to find the area of rectangles and related triangles and parallelograms;
- develop strategies to determine the surface areas and volumes of rectangular solids.

Grades 6–8

- use common benchmarks to select appropriate methods for estimating measurements;
- select and apply techniques and tools to accurately find length, area, volume, and angle measures to appropriate levels of precision;
- develop and use formulas to determine the circumference of circles and the area of triangles, parallelograms, trapezoids, and circles and develop strategies to find the area of more-complex shapes;
- develop strategies to determine the surface area and volume of selected prisms, pyramids, and cylinders;
- solve problems involving scale factors, using ratio and proportion;
- solve simple problems involving rates and derived measurements for such attributes as velocity and density.

NCTM (2000), pp. 102, 170, 240. Reprinted by permission.

Make a copy of the Rectangular Dot Paper in Appendix B. Using rubber bands, construct all of the polygons you can on a geoboard that have an area of two square units. Remember that you may use triangles and irregular figures as well as rectangles. Record all of your solutions on the dot paper.

REFLECTIONS AND REFINEMENT: *After you have completed this task, compare your shapes with those of some of your classmates. How did your solution differ from those of others? As you continue through this term, see if you can find additional shapes to construct. Write what you have found here.*

Measurement provides quantitative information about certain familiar aspects of our environment. These include length, distance, area, volume, capacity, weight, mass, temperature, time, and angle. Of course, this list is not complete. We know that certain specialized occupations require measures not commonly encountered. For example, surveyors, sailors, and pharmacists may use chain, nautical, and apothecaries' fluid measures, respectively.

> Measurement is one of the most widely used applications of mathematics. It bridges two main areas of school mathematics — geometry and number. (NCTM, 2000, p. 103)

In the young child's world, it is enough to find out which is biggest, smallest, longest, shortest, fastest, slowest, warmest, or coolest. Children may ask how much or how long when they want to know about measured quantities. Later, youngsters are intrigued by the entries found in publications such as the *Guinness World Records* (2003). A majority of the records reported include some type of measurement.

A world record has little meaning if the units of length, time, or amount are not understood. The basis for establishing understanding is measuring. From measuring springs a sense of quantity relating to the item being measured. A sense of meters and seconds helps put the world record for the women's 1,500-meter run in perspective.

When, in the course of child development, do these ideas begin to be established? Earlier, we mentioned that children flailing about in their cribs explore space. They explore distance as well. Before children talk, they answer the question "How big are you?" by spreading their arms out, indicating to the pleasure of their parents that they are so big. These are the beginnings of children constructing their own meaning of measurement.

From these early beginnings, children compare objects and judge sizes. They order objects by size, weight, length, and duration. They develop an eye for size. "Her cookie is bigger than mine" expresses this visual comparison. In their early experiences, children develop the ability to measure by perception. By the time they enter first grade, they can begin simple measurement activities. Hiebert (1984, pp. 22–23) noted, "Effective instruction should take advantage of what children already know or are able to learn and then relate this knowledge to new concepts that may be more difficult to learn."

Most measurements require tools. Thus, the materials for teaching measurement include the standard measuring instruments. We recommend using rulers, meter sticks, tape measures, trundle wheels, graduated beakers, measuring cups, measuring spoons, pan balances, bathroom scales, thermometers, timers, and protractors. Other useful materials are geoboards, centimeter cubes, linking cubes, popcicle sticks, Cuisenaire rods, containers of various sizes, string, dynamic geometry software and *Logo*. Teachers should collect objects and materials to help children construct measuring concepts.

Providing the opportunity for students to construct their own meaning of measurement involves more than presenting a series of activities or textbook pages. Not only should measurement be introduced, it should also be practiced throughout the school year whenever measuring is needed. You should be alert to measuring situations and encourage the students to measure when the opportunity arises.

MAKING SENSE OF MEASUREMENT CONCEPTS

The concepts that provide the foundation for measuring skills are those of length and distance, area, weight and mass, time, volume and capacity, temperature, and angle. Angle measure is a concept traditionally developed around age 10, but the utility and popularity of the computer language *Logo* suggests that an earlier introduction to angle measure is appropriate.

By and large, after the concept of measurement has been constructed, children should be provided with a sequence of activities: direct comparison, indirect comparison, arbitrary units, and standard units. Through these activities, children will further refine their understanding of measurement.

Direct comparison means that children take two objects and place them side by side or one on top of the other to discover if they are the same size. This requires that both objects be on surfaces of the same height or in containers of the same diameter.

Using **indirect comparison,** children determine if the sizes of two objects are the same when the objects cannot be directly compared. For example, indirect comparison would be used to find out if a table would fit through a door if the table were not easy to move.

Arbitrary units of measure are used to strengthen a child's understanding of unit. The length of a drinking straw or the area of a floor tile may be used to measure a variety of objects. The transition to **standard units** of measure, those commonly accepted and used throughout the world, follows work with arbitrary units.

The two common standard sets of measuring units are the *metric* and the *conventional systems*. We use the metric system throughout this chapter. Most textbooks for children include sections on both metric and conventional units. The process of measuring is the same regardless of the specific unit being used. You should have little difficulty teaching either metric or conventional units.

> The measurement process is identical, in principle, for measuring any attribute: choose a unit, compare that unit to the object, and report the number of units. (NCTM, 2000, p. 105)

As children move through the sequence just described, they begin by using **continuous measurement.** When a piece of string is stretched along the object being measured and then compared with another object or when two objects are directly compared, continuous measurement is used. The measuring tool (string) does not assign a number to the object; rather, it is used to compare lengths.

Later in their work, children begin to use **discrete measurement.** When a pencil is moved along an object to determine the length of the object or a meterstick is used, the type of measurement is discrete. The measuring tool is used repeatedly, or it shows calibrations of a given unit—for example, centimeters. The transition from continuous to discrete measurement is seen in the activities of this chapter.

> A foundation in measurement concepts that enables students to use measurement systems, tools, and techniques should be established through direct experiences with comparing objects, counting units, and making connections between spatial concepts and number. (NCTM, 2000, p. 103)

When teaching measurement, consider children's stages of readiness. Are children ready to learn measurement concepts and skills when they enter kindergarten or first grade? The work of Piaget (Piaget, Inhelder, and Szemiuska, 1960) suggests that until children have reached certain stages of intellectual development, they will have difficulty measuring successfully. For example, children who are unable to conserve length may believe that a measuring stick changes length as it is moved. Thus, measuring length should be held off until the child is able to conserve length.

More recently, Hiebert found that the absence of conservation did not seem to limit children in learning most measurement concepts. Hiebert (1984, p. 24) noted, ". . . it appears more productive to involve children in a variety of concrete measuring activities than to wait until they develop certain logical reasoning processes."

The teacher can provide experiences in informal measuring to serve as a foundation for later work. It is important during the pre-kindergarten–grade 2 years to provide activities that form the basis for measurement and to introduce measurement skills, thus allowing children to develop their personal understanding of measurement. Prior to involving children in organized activities, time should be provided for children to play with objects, containers, and water, rice, or sand. This play helps children establish the basis for early measurement activities. The activities that follow provide experiences in visual perception and direct comparison for younger students. Indirect comparison, arbitrary units, and standard units are presented in the next section, Developing Fluency with Measurement Tools, Techniques, and Formulas.

Length and Distance

Length refers to the measure of how long a thing is from end to end. **Distance** is the space between points or objects.

In introducing length, allow children to experience long and short distances. Encourage children to directly compare objects in order to determine which object is taller and which is shorter.

A C T I V I T I E S

Pre-Kindergarten – Grade 2

OBJECTIVE: to experience long and short distances.

1. Invite children to name something in the classroom that is long. A brief discussion about the meaning of long may be necessary. Children may suggest that these objects are long: a dry erase board or chalkboard, a worktable, or the bar on the coatrack.

Mention that something that is long has great length and ask which has the greater length, the dry erase board or the worktable. The children will use their visual perception to make this judgement. Next, ask children to name something on the playground that is long and then something that is not found at school that is long. What is the longest thing they can think of, the object with the greatest length?

2. Mark off several long line segments (6 to 8 meters) and several short line segments (2 to 3 meters) on the classroom floor or on the playground with masking tape, yarn, or chalk. Challenge the students to walk along one short line segment, then another short line segment, then a long line segment, and so on, allowing them to find the various long and short line segments. Discuss the meaning of long and short segments as

used here. As a variation, provide long and short curves on which the children may walk.

3. Begin by saying that when the students line up for lunch or playtime, a line with 4 or fewer students is a short line and one with more than 4 is a long line. In the classroom or on the playground, mark 7 or 8 places at which to line up. Have the children get into long lines. This may result in one long line or several lines with at least 5 students in each one. Then have them get into short lines. Challenge them to get into 1 long line and 3 short lines or 2 long lines and 2 short lines. See if they can form the longest line possible or the shortest lines possible.

4. Provide children with 8 or 10 classroom objects. Each object should be able to stand by itself. Objects may include a cottage cheese container, a can, a jar, a book, and a Cuisenaire rod (see Figure 12–1). Spread the objects out on a table.

Discuss which is the tallest object, then the shortest. Are two objects the same height? Find two objects taller than the cottage cheese container. If the children have some difficulty in visually determining the taller and shorter objects, challenge them to devise a way to solve the problem. Putting the objects side by side is an answer you may expect.

A variation of this activity is to provide objects that do not stand on end: pencil, spoon, eraser, stapler, and so on. To be directly compared, the ends of each pair of objects must be lined up. This task is slightly more difficult than the one above. Again, let the students determine how the objects can be compared.

5. In each of two bags, place one Cuisenaire rod. The rods should be about the same length, such as dark green and black or brown. Let students take turns reaching into the bags and telling which rod is longer or shorter merely by touch. Reaching into both bags simultaneously may be the most effective procedure, but let the children experiment.

A variation is to put an entire set of 10 rods in one bag and display another set of 10 rods on a table. Have a child reach into the bag, grab a rod, and then choose a rod from the table that is the same length.

Area

The activities above were intended to show how children can be introduced to perceptual and direct measurement of length. The following activities focus on area. **Area** is a measure of the size of a two-dimensional figure, such as a rectangle or a circle.

A C T I V I T I E S

Pre-Kindergarten – Grade 2
OBJECTIVE: to determine the shape with the largest area.

1. Provide children with a collection of square shapes with sides ranging from 4 to 10 centimeters. Arrange the shapes in a random pattern as in Figure 12–2. Ask the children to tell which shape they believe is the largest or has the largest area. To show which one is largest, compare those selected by holding them up against each other. Order the shapes from smallest to largest by comparing them.

Extend this activity by using several rectangles, circles, triangles, and diamonds. Initially, estimate and compare using the same shape. Later, estimate and compare area using different shapes.

2. Have the students draw around one of their feet on a sheet of paper. Put several of the outlines in a cluster. Ask the children, "Whose foot do you think is the largest or has the largest area?" Then compare those selected by holding them up against each other in front of a window. Find out who has the smallest foot in the same way. Ask, "Are there two children who have the same foot size?"

As a variation, repeat the activity but compare hands instead of feet. Then compare hands with feet and determine the largest area. It will be difficult to make the latter comparison; thus, the activity will help children to see a need for other ways to measure area.

OBJECTIVE: to directly compare areas.

3. Collect several boxlike containers such as a cereal box; half-pint, quart, and half-gallon milk containers; a

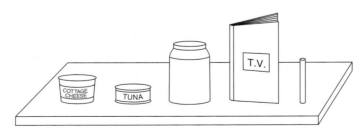

Figure 12–1 Objects used for comparing height.

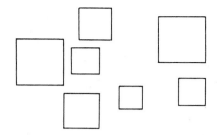

Figure 12–2 Shapes used for comparing area.

raisin box; and a crayon box. Trace the faces of these containers onto tagboard and let the children cut them out, as in Figure 12–3.

Give each child several of the cutout faces. Have the children estimate to determine which of the containers their pieces belong to. Then have them see if the pieces actually fit these containers by holding the pieces against the faces of the boxes.

A variation of this activity is to display the containers and ask the children to cut out a square or rectangular shape the same size as a face of a container. When the shapes have been cut out, have the children compare the cutouts by holding them up against the faces of the containers.

OBJECTIVE: to determine which of various shapes are larger or smaller than a given shape.

4. Cut a piece of cardboard about the size of the top of a student desk. Hold the piece of cardboard up and ask the children, "Who can name a shape in the room that is bigger than this one? Look around and see if you can find one."

After several shapes, such as the door, a window, and the floor, have been named, ask, "Who can see a shape in the room that is smaller than this shape? Let's name them." Suggestions may include a chair seat, a piece of tablet paper, a book, and a compact disc. As items are

mentioned, compare them with the piece of cardboard to reinforce the notion of direct comparison. Periodically, provide a different-sized shape and repeat the process.

Weight and Mass

We turn our attention to activities of direct comparison that involve the weight and mass of objects. **Weight** is a measure of the force of gravity acting on an object. **Mass** is the amount of matter in an object.

A C T I V I T I E S

Pre-Kindergarten – Grade 2

OBJECTIVE: to determine which object is heavier.

1. Have available several classroom objects such as a pencil, scissors, an eraser, crayons, a small box, an orange Cuisenaire rod, a glue stick, and a book. Have children compare the weights of various pairs of these objects and tell which object weighs the most by holding one object in each hand as in Figure 12–4.

Perhaps some items are of equal weight. Have the children compare and recheck pairs until they are able to put the objects in order from lightest to heaviest. Among the objects used should be one or two large objects that are light, such as a paper cup, and small objects that are heavy, such as a rock. This is to help avoid confusing the properties of size and weight.

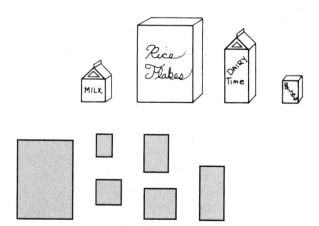

Figure 12–3 Containers and the shapes of their faces.

Figure 12–4 Comparing the weights of objects by holding them in each hand.

To extend this activity, use a pan balance to compare the objects mentioned above to confirm or challenge the order determined by feel. Figure 12–5 illustrates one such balance. Do not be surprised to find discrepancies between the order established by holding objects and that established by using a pan balance. Children enjoy experimenting with the balance and various objects found around the room.

OBJECTIVE: to practice estimating and weighing different materials.

2. Fill several half-pint milk cartons with different materials such as rice, beans, split peas, clay, plaster of paris, and wooden cubes. Seal the cartons and label them by color or letter. Tell the children what the materials are but do not identify the contents of a particular carton. Have the children guess how to order the cartons by weight according to what they contain. Then let the children order the cartons by weight holding them in their hands and using the pan balance to check their estimates.

OBJECTIVE: to determine the amount of one material that weighs as much as a selected object.

3. Collect several common objects such as a dry erase board eraser, a can of soup, a container of cleanser, a stapler, and a tape dispenser. Provide a pan balance and a material such as rice, water, clay, or sand.

Have the children estimate how many small containers of sand it would take to balance the can of soup. Then see how many small containers must be used to balance the soup can, as in Figure 12–6. If the soup

can does not balance, have the children increase or decrease the amount of sand in one of the containers. On the board, record both the estimates and the final results. If the final number of containers is not a whole number, the results should be recorded as, for example, "more than 5 containers but less than 6."

Repeat this activity using other materials and objects. Be sure to have the children estimate each time they begin.

Time

Time is a measure of the period between two events or the period during which something happens. It is also a precise moment determined by a clock. Introduce time to children by having them directly compare the times of events, establishing whether one event takes more time or less time than another. Events may include twenty hand claps, a ball bouncing ten times, ice melting under different conditions, and water emptying out of cans with different-sized holes.

A C T I V I T I E S

Pre-Kindergarten – Grade 2

OBJECTIVE: to determine which event among several events takes the most or the least amount of time.

1. Select several events that require a short period of time to complete. Events that may be used include tapping a foot 20 times; sitting in a chair, standing, and sitting again 10 times; hopping on one foot from one side of the classroom to the other; reciting the words to "Row, Row, Row Your Boat"; moving 20 cubes one at a time from one container to another; bouncing a ball 10 times; and pointing to and naming 10 other students.

Ask the children, "Which of these events can be done the fastest? Let's write on the board those that we think can be done the fastest. Which will be the slowest events? Let's write those down."

Choose two of the events and begin them at the same time. Record the results. Repeat the process for each pair of the events and determine which event takes the least time and which event takes the most time.

OBJECTIVE: to investigate the amount of time it takes ice cubes to melt.

2. Fill two equivalent containers with water, one with warm water and the other with cooler water. Leave a third container empty. Let the children see and feel the cups and the water. Explain, "We are going to put an ice cube in each container. Which ice cube do you think

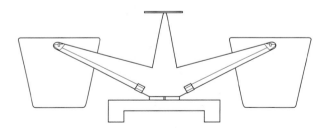

Figure 12–5 Pan balance.

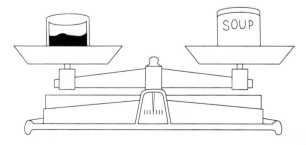

Figure 12–6 Balancing objects with sand.

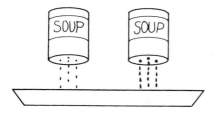

Figure 12–7 Comparing the time it takes to empty each can.

will melt first? Let's write our guesses on the board. How many believe the ice cube in this container will melt first?"

After the guesses are recorded, put the ice cubes in the containers and observe the results. Variations of this activity include using salt water, using very cold and hot water, using varying amounts of water that are the same temperature, and dissolving sugar cubes instead of melting ice.

OBJECTIVE: to estimate and determine which of several containers empties in the least amount of time.

3. Take several soup cans and puncture three holes in the bottom of each one, using a different-sized nail for each can. Have the children inspect the cans and estimate which they think will empty first, second, third, and so on.

Using two cans at a time, pour equal amounts of water in each can and observe them (see Figure 12–7). Repeat this process until the cans have been ordered from fastest to slowest. Similarly, the cans may have different numbers of holes of the same size or different numbers of holes of varying sizes.

Volume and Capacity

The activities above focus on directly comparing events involving the passage of time. The following activities involve volume and capacity. **Volume** is the amount of space contained within a three-dimensional figure. **Capacity** is the amount of space that can be filled.

A C T I V I T I E S

Pre-Kindergarten – Grade 2

OBJECTIVE: to estimate and determine which of several containers holds the greatest amount.

1. Provide the children with several small jars, cans, or plastic containers. For example, you may use a tuna can, a plastic drinking cup, a baby food jar, a soup can, a paper cup, and a peanut butter jar. Have the children estimate which of the containers

temperature. **Temperature** is a measure of the hotness or coldness of a material.

Pre-Kindergarten – Grade 2

OBJECTIVE: to determine relative temperature by feel.

1. Partially fill five plastic containers with water of varying temperature. Use unheated water, warm tap water, cold tap water, water that has one ice cube in it, and water with five or six ice cubes in it. Label the containers with shapes or colors for identification. Have the children put the containers of water in order from warmest to coldest by putting their hands in the water. Have several small groups of children complete the ordering and compare results.

After the containers of water have been in the classroom for an hour or so, have the children repeat the exercise. Discuss the results with the children.

2. Take the children to the playground and let them work in groups of three or four. Have the children search the play area for four things that feel cool to them and four things that feel warm. The children may find the slide and swing supports to be cool; they may find the asphalt and wooden play apparatus to be warm.

Discuss the findings with the whole group. Ask which was the coolest single object and which was the warmest single object. Talk about what the objects are made of.

3. Arbitrarily group children into groups of six or eight. Have the children in each group shake hands and find the individual with the coldest hand. Have those selected form a group and find the child with the warmest hand and the child with the coldest hand. Have those two children circulate among the other children and put their hands against the cheeks of the others.

Ask the children if they know of ways to make their hands warmer. Suggestions may include putting their hands in warm water, rubbing their hands together or rubbing them against their clothing, and clapping their hands. Have the children warm their hands using one of the methods suggested and then have them shake hands again or put their hands against the cheeks of the others.

Angle

The activities above involve children comparing the temperatures of several materials by feeling them. The following activities introduce informally the idea of measuring angles. An **angle** is the space between two rays that share a common end point.

Pre-Kindergarten – Grade 2

OBJECTIVE: to estimate and determine the sizes of angles.

1. In Chapter 11, several activities are described in which children investigate geometry using *Logo*. It is worthwhile for children to experiment with various turns by using commands such as RT 90, RT 30, LT 50, LT 180, and RT 360. At this stage, the children are not measuring angles, but they are developing some initial understanding of angle size. Success with turtle geometry depends on the concept of angle size.

Have children record and label angles of various sizes. Is the angle made with the commands FD 75, BK 75, RT 30, FD 75, and BK 75 the same size as the angle made with FD 75, BK 75, LT 30, FD 75, and BK 75? How are these two angles different?

As children begin to construct simple figures, they will be using exterior angles. An **exterior angle** is the angle between the side of a polygon and the extension of the adjacent side. For example, in order to construct an interior angle of 60° when drawing an equilateral triangle, the procedure makes the turtle turn an exterior angle of 120°, as in Figure 12–9. Children develop skill with exterior angles by designing procedures for drawing a variety of polygons.

2. Trace angles of several sizes on overhead transparencies, putting one angle in the center of each transparency. Place a transparency on the monitor screen so the vertex of the angle is centered on the *Logo* turtle, with one ray in a vertical position as in Figure 12–10. To confirm the alignment of the angle, have the child move the turtle forward and then back to the original position. Realign the angle if necessary.

Have the child estimate the size of the turn necessary to follow the other ray of the angle. Let the child

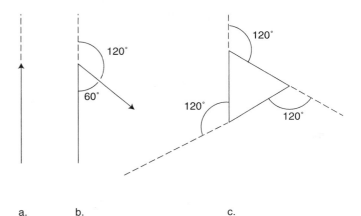

a.   b.   c.

Figure 12–9   Determining angle size by using *Logo*.

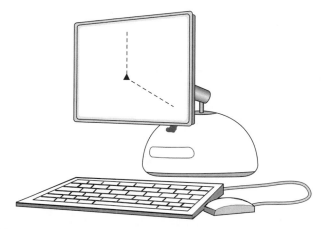

Figure 12–10 Using a transparency for a *Logo* activity on the computer.

test the estimate by turning the turtle in the appropriate direction and moving forward and then back to produce a second ray. Have the child compare the angle on the transparency with the angle made using *Logo*.

Repeat the activity using various angle sizes. Variations include having the turtle turn left for some angles as well as right and having the turtle begin facing in a different direction rather than toward the top of the screen.

The activities in this section were presented to serve as examples to reinforce and supplement textbook activities and to provide a foundation on which to build the skills of measuring. Each activity involved direct comparison. You are encouraged to pay attention to the perceptions and observations of children as they begin these measuring tasks. Some of the perceptions will indicate that further direct comparison measurement activities are needed.

DEVELOPING FLUENCY WITH MEASUREMENT TOOLS, TECHNIQUES, AND FORMULAS

The skills of measurement include using instruments or tools to determine how long, how much, what size, and what temperature. Specifically, the skills of measurement include measuring length, area, weight, time, volume and capacity, temperature, and angle. The skills follow the understanding of early measurement concepts. Then, consistent practice with the tools of measurement is necessary.

The activities presented in the previous section emphasized direct comparison, the first stage in a four-stage teaching sequence. The remaining stages are indirect comparison, using an arbitrary measuring unit, and using a standard measuring unit. The activities in the following section focus on the latter three stages for each type of measurement described.

As children begin measuring, they will find that they will disagree occasionally with others who have measured the same item. Commonly the difference will be slight. What they are experiencing is the approximate nature of measuring. Everyday measurement is approximate. The tools used to measure seldom yield precisely the same results in the hands of children (or adults, for that matter). It is important to let children discover and to discuss the approximate nature of measuring.

> Students in grades 3–5 should encounter the notion that measurements in the real world are approximate, in part because of the instruments used and because of human error in reading the scales of these instruments. (NCTM, 2000, p. 172)

Active experiences with measuring provide children with the chance to construct meaning relative to the measurement process. To build understanding of measurement is the focus of the children's active participation. This understanding leads to skill in measuring. Be cautious about telling children how to measure before they have had a chance to experiment.

Measuring Length

When children in pre-kindergarten–grade 2 have had experience using direct measurement of length for a variety of tasks, they should engage in other types of length measurement. Their experiences will provide a basis for constructing knowledge of length as they work through other classroom measurement activities.

Intermediate-level students should have worked with and used length measurement for some time. They will be engaged in estimating with accuracy and measuring with increased precision. The lengths they measure will be longer. They will easily use a variety of standard units of measure. The common metric units of length include centimeter, meter, and kilometer.

As you introduce various units of metric measurement, discuss the prefixes and their meanings. The mathematics textbook will also introduce and explain them. **Milli** means one-thousandth, **centi** means one-hundredth, **deci** means one-tenth, and **kilo** means one thousand. There are several others, but these are among the most commonly used.

In most instances of measuring with standard units, instruct children to place the ruler or meterstick along the item being measured, with the end of the ruler or

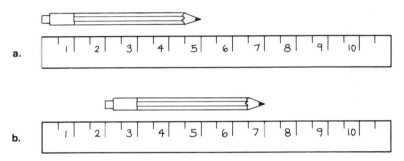

Figure 12−11 Measuring length with standard units.

zero lined up with one end of the item being measured, as in Figure 12−11a. Have children then read the spot on the ruler where the other end of the item being measured falls—in this case, 5 centimeters.

If the starting point is not zero, as in Figure 12−11b, let children discover that the *length* is found by either counting the spaces along the item being measured or subtracting the starting point from the endpoint—in this case, 7 − 2, or 5, centimeters.

A C T I V I T I E S

Pre-Kindergarten − Grade 2

OBJECTIVE: to use indirect measuring to determine length.

1. Cut a strip of paper approximately as long as the average height of a child in your class. Put the name of an imaginary child or a character from a story, such as Garfield, on the strip of paper. Attach the strip to the wall so that one end touches the floor. Have the children estimate whether they are shorter than, taller than, or the same height as Garfield. Record the estimates.

Then have the children cut strips of paper to represent their heights. Ask the children to compare their height with that of Garfield. Finally, have the children order their heights by comparing them and taping their paper strips along a classroom or hallway wall.

Because they will have produced a pictorial representation of class heights, it is useful to describe and discuss their findings and to write down and post these observations beside the paper strips. The observations might include the following:

- We found that 9 of us are taller than Garfield. There are 15 of us who are shorter than Garfield. Mark and Christine are just as tall as Garfield.

- The shortest person in the class is Peter. The tallest person in the class is Dana.

- Five of us thought we were taller than Garfield, but it turned out that 9 of us actually were taller.

A variation of this activity is to have students lie on pieces of newsprint or butcher paper and have others draw their outlines. Comparisons can then be made as before.

2. On one side of the classroom, arrange six to eight objects of varying lengths. Include items such as a piece of yarn, a marking pen, a meterstick, a ruler, a strip of paper, and the edge of a desk or table. Next, mark off a length on the dry erase board or bulletin board. Have the children estimate which of the objects are longer and which are shorter than the mark on the board. Have them check their estimates, but with the condition that they cannot move either the objects or the mark on the board.

A variation of this activity is to provide children with blocks or a similar material and invite one group of children to build a tower on the floor at the front of the room. Invite another group to build a tower on the floor at the back of the room. Challenge the children to estimate which tower is taller. When the estimates have been made, have the children see if they can devise ways to tell which tower is taller without moving the towers.

OBJECTIVE: to use arbitrary units of measure to determine the lengths of objects.

3. Identify five or six lengths to be measured. For example, you might use the sink counter, a student desk, a bookcase, a worktable, a row of books, and a sink. Provide groups of children with sufficient numbers of different measuring units such as toothpicks, paper clips, straws, tongue depressors, and orange Cuisenaire rods. Have each group measure the lengths of the objects indicated using its particular unit; for example, straws, as in Figure 12−12.

Have each group record its results. Because it is unlikely that a measurement will be exactly a whole number of units, have the children record the results as, for example, "longer than 6 straws and shorter than 7 straws."

When the measurements have been made, compare the results. Can any conclusions be drawn regarding the number of units used in measuring and the size of the

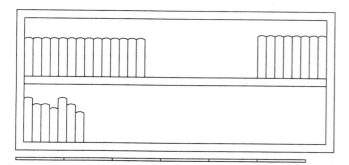

Figure 12–12 Using arbitrary units to measure a bookshelf.

unit? To illustrate the meaning of the above question, have each group put ten of their measuring units end to end and compare the resulting lengths.

4. Announce that a drawing will be held to find three new measuring units. Have all the children write their names on pieces of paper and put the pieces of paper into a container. Draw the name of the child who will provide a *shoe unit*. Draw the name of another child, who will provide a *hand unit*. Draw the name of the third child, who will provide a *thumb unit*.

Have the first child place one foot, with the shoe on, on a piece of tagboard and draw around it. Using this as a pattern, have the children cut out a number of, say, *Margaret's shoes*. Repeat the process for *Sarah's hand* and *Bob's thumb*. Each of these will be a unit of measure.

You may wish to begin this activity by reading *How Big is a Foot?* by Myller (1962). In this story a king commissions a carpenter to construct a bed using the king's foot as a measure. The carpenter constructs the bed using his own foot as a measure and a problem arises. The need for standard units of measure will likely become apparent with some discussion. Welchman-Tischler (1992) richly describes how *How Big is a Foot* may be used in a variety of measurement lessons.

For the next two weeks or so, have the children measure the lengths of many objects using these special units. To extend this activity, have the children use only one of the measuring devices and move it along the object being measured, counting the number of times it is used.

5. Another step in measuring with nonstandard units is to provide students opportunities to measure with a variety of nonstandard measuring tapes. Querin (1998, pp. 16–18) describes such activities. Several different tapes such as those shown in Figure 12–13 are available for children to select and use to estimate and measure the length of various objects in the classroom or hallway.

Invite children to design their own nonstandard measuring tapes using stickers, stamps, or repeated drawings on a strip of paper or several strips glued together.

OBJECTIVE: to measure perimeter.

6. Put several large shapes on the floor. The shapes may be drawn on butcher paper or made with masking tape, string, or yarn. Initially, have children walk around

Figure 12–13 Nonstandard measuring tapes.

the figure and count the number of baby steps or walking steps they take.

Later, have children use other arbitrary units, such as a piece of dowel or an orange Cuisenaire rod. Eventually, have children use a meterstick or a trundle wheel. A **trundle wheel** is a plastic or wooden disk that is attached to a handle. The circumference of the disk is 1 meter. The trundle wheel is pushed along a line or boundary to determine its length.

Challenge the students to look for boundaries to measure. Items that lend themselves to boundary work include the outlines of a desktop, a bulletin board or dry erase board, the classroom, a work area, the gymnasium, and the playground.

7. A direct extension of walking around and measuring large floor figures is to use turtle steps in *Logo*. The side of a figure in *Logo* is defined in terms of a particular distance. By virtue of designing a figure, the length of its boundary is determined. Perimeter, then, comes to be viewed as an integral part of each shape.

8. Continued work on the geoboard helps to establish skill in measuring perimeter. Focus activities on counting the units around various figures. After children have gained experience in using geoboards, they are ready to use the diagonal distance between nails in their calculations. Initially, that distance may be known as a little more than 1 or almost 1.5.

OBJECTIVE: to use standard units to measure various objects.

9. Have available a large collection of centimeter cubes and eight or ten relatively small objects to measure. Objects may include a book, a pencil, a chalkboard eraser, a sheet of tablet paper, a crayon box, a sneaker, a stapler, a workbook, and a desk. Identify these items with letters, colors, or numerals. Have the children connect the interlocking centimeter cubes until they are as long as the item being measured, as in Figure 12–14.

Let the children know they are using a unit called a centimeter. Have them count the number of centimeters

long each item is and record the length on a piece of paper. Because most items are not a whole number of centimeters long, have the children record the length as, for instance, "more than 7 and less than 8 centimeters."

10. Provide groups of three or four children with strips of paper about 35 centimeters long and several centimeter cubes. Have each group carefully mark along an edge of the paper strip using the centimeter cube as the unit and have them number each mark until they have marked off 30 centimeters. Make sure the children are aware that the first mark is labeled *1* and means the distance from the end of the paper strip.

Challenge the children to use their 30-centimeter ruler to find things in the classroom that measure 4, 10, 13, 19, 22, 27, and 30 centimeters in length. To extend this activity, have the children estimate and measure body parts using their ruler: width and length of hands, length of feet, width of a finger, distance around wrists, and length of smile. Have the students record the estimates and measurements.

11. In the gymnasium or on the playground, mark off six to eight lines using yarn, chalk, or masking tape and label each line with a color or letter. These lines should range from 3 to 10 meters in length and should be placed in a variety of directions.

Provide groups of two or three children with record sheets with a space to estimate the length of each line and a space to write in the actual measure. Have the children estimate and then measure each of the lines.

Later, discuss the range of estimates for each line and compare the measured lengths. It may be necessary to go back to the playground and remeasure. To extend this activity, have children find a length between 4 and 6 meters or measure various long objects in the classroom.

These activities have been illustrative of what children in pre-kindergarten–grade 2 can do to strengthen their measuring skills.

> The types of units that students use for measuring and the ways they use them should expand and shift as students move through the prekindergarten through grade 2 curriculum. In preschool through grade 2, students should begin their study of measurement by using nonstandard units. (NCTM, 2000, p. 45)

The following activities for older students begin with arbitrary or nonstandard measurement. By this age, the need to practice measuring with direct and indirect

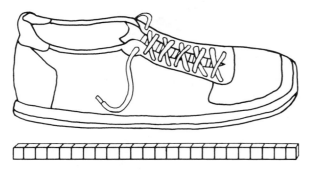

Figure 12–14   Measuring a sneaker with centimeter cubes.

comparison has decreased. The following activities focus on the applications and the precision of linear measurements.

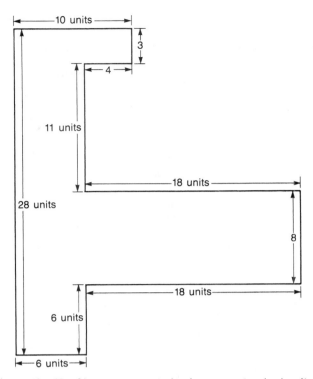

Figure 12–15 Shape constructed using a nonstandard unit.

A C T I V I T I E S

Grades 3–5

OBJECTIVE: to measure lengths using an arbitrary unit.

1. Designate a *measuring unit of the day,* a unit that is easy to provide to students. Possible units might include spaghetti, unsharpened pencils, tongue depressors, and unmarked strips of oaktag. The unit selected may have marks to indicate one-fourth or one-half units.

As a class, agree on a number of common classroom objects to measure, such as length, width, and height of desks; length and width of the room; length and height of the dry erase board or bulletin board; width and height of the door; and so on. In groups, have the students agree to measure certain of these items. Before the measuring begins, have all of the children estimate the sizes of the objects using the selected unit. Then have the children measure the items to the nearest one-fourth unit and record the measures. To extend this activity, have the children draw or write a description of their classroom using, say, spaghetti units.

2. As a class, select an arbitrary unit with which to measure. For example, the width of a sneaker at its widest part may be the unit. Construct a measuring tape or string based on that unit. Then construct a design on butcher paper and carefully measure it using the sneaker-width unit. Sketch the design on a sheet of notebook paper and indicate the measure of each of its lengths in terms of the new unit, as in Figure 12–15.

Send the sketch to another class in the school and tell them the measuring unit, the *widest part of a sneaker.* Ask the class to construct the design on their dry erase board or on butcher paper. Then compare the results by putting the two full-sized designs side by side. Discuss any discrepancy between the two designs.

It is likely that the sizes will differ because of the arbitrary nature of the unit. Let the students discuss why this is the case. Next, create another design using standard units of measure, have another class construct it, and compare the results.

OBJECTIVE: to estimate and measure with standard units.

3. Begin this activity, entitled The Shape of Me, with a worksheet on which are listed several body parts (see Figure 12–16). Ask the children to estimate in centimeters their head width and length; that is, the distance from one side to the other and from top to bottom. Next, have them estimate their shoulder width. Have them continue until they have estimated all parts.

At this point, provide 2-meter lengths of newsprint, kraft paper, or butcher paper to individuals or pairs of children.

Ask the children to construct the body they have estimated using the paper provided. The students should use metersticks, 30-centimeter rulers, or tapes to construct these figures. Have them complete the figures by dressing them using crayons or marking pens and cutting them out. Display the figures around the room. Finally, have the children measure their body parts and compare the results with their estimates. Encourage the students to discuss their results.

4. With the assistance of your class, establish a competition called the Metric Olympics. This series of events will challenge the students to use their estimation and measuring skills. The Metric Olympics consists of six to eight events. These events may include the following:

- *Sponge throw.* Give students an opportunity to throw each of three sponges as far as they can from behind a line. Lightweight sponges can be thrown 3 to 5 meters. Have the officials mark and measure the length of each toss and record the greatest distance for each participant.
- *Length guess.* On a classroom or hallway wall, arrange a piece of yarn or string 12 to 15 meters long, as in Figure 12–17. Have each participant estimate the length of the yarn.

THE SHAPE OF ME

Just for the record let's measure to find out what size we are. But first <u>guess</u> each item below. Then measure using the materials available. You might like to work with a friend.

		My Guess	The Real Me (Measure)
1. HEAD	Width	_____ cm	_____ cm
	Length	_____ cm	_____ cm
2. SMILE WIDTH		_____ cm	_____ cm
3. HEIGHT (top of head to floor)		_____ cm	_____ cm
4. ARMS (length of each arm from shoulder to fingertip)		_____ cm	_____ cm
5. HAND SPAN (width of palm at widest point when fingers are together)		_____ cm	_____ cm
6. SHOULDER WIDTH		_____ cm	_____ cm
7. LEGS (length from hip to ankle)		_____ cm	_____ cm
8. HIP WIDTH		_____ cm	_____ cm
9. FOOT LENGTH		_____ cm	_____ cm
10. WEIGHT		_____ kg	_____ kg

Figure 12–16   Worksheet for The Shape of Me activity.

Figure 12–17   Yarn arrangement for a Metric Olympics event.

• *Cube toss.* Make two lines 3 meters apart. Have the students stand behind one line and estimate how close to the other line they will be able to toss a cube. They must toss the cube at least 1 meter. The winner of this event is the student whose estimate and performance are closest.

• *Paper plate sail.* Have students sail a paper plate as far as they can from behind a line. Measure the distance in meters using a trundle wheel.

• *Standing long step.* Have students predict how far they can step using one giant step. Have them measure from the starting line to where their heel lands. A variation is to estimate the distance covered in three giant steps. Either way, base the scoring on how close students are to their estimates.

• *String feel.* Seat students and ask them to hold their hands behind their backs. Give each one a piece of string, and ask each child to run both hands over the string behind his or her back and estimate the length of the string. Award students within 5, 10, and 15 centimeters of their estimates 3 points, 2 points, and 1 point, respectively.

Measuring Area

Measuring *area* involves determining how much space there is within a plane figure. In pre-kindergarten–grade 2, children count units covering or placed inside a figure. At grades 3–5 and grades 6–8, students can discover the various formulas to calculate area. Both levels require continued manipulation of objects and tools. The common metric units of area include square centimeter, square meter, hectare (equivalent to a square with sides of 100 meters), and square kilometer.

A C T I V I T I E S

Pre-Kindergarten – Grade 2

OBJECTIVE: to indirectly measure and compare the areas of objects.

1. Draw several rectangles of various shapes and sizes on butcher paper or on the dry erase board. The largest dimension of any particular rectangle should be about 50 centimeters. Give each rectangle a letter or color for identification. Ask the children to estimate and then determine which rectangle is largest or smallest. Which rectangles are larger than the red one or larger than the red one and smaller than the yellow one?

Because the children cannot move the rectangles, they must invent a way to compare the sizes of the various shapes. They may cut a piece of paper the size of a given rectangle and compare the paper to other rectangles. To vary this activity, use shapes other than rectangles so children will have the chance to measure squares, triangles, circles, and so on.

Extend this activity by challenging children to determine the relative area of various classroom items. Ask, for example, "Which is larger, the top of your desk or a pane of glass from the window?" or "Which is smaller, the side of the filing cabinet or the top of the worktable?" For each challenge, let the children cut a piece of butcher paper or newsprint the size of one of the items and compare the paper to the other item. The shapes are likely to be different, so additional cutting and rearranging will be necessary.

OBJECTIVE: to use arbitrary units to measure area.

2. Explore length and area on the geoboard by first designating the units of length and area. For example, designate the distance between two nails in any direction except diagonally as one unit. Then use this unit of length to determine the length of the boundary of a particular figure. Figure 12–18 illustrates this type of activity.

Next, ask children to make a figure with a certain number of units in its boundary. Request, for example, "Make a rectangle with a boundary of eight units."

To measure area, have children count the number of square units within a figure. Designate the smallest square on the geoboard as one square unit. Then inquire, "How many square units can we find in this figure?" Let the children count the number of square units contained in a given figure, as shown in Figure 12–19. As they gain experience, the children can construct squares or rectangles with a given number of square units, demonstrating an initial understanding of area.

There are other ways to determine area, beginning with the area of a triangle. At this point, it becomes necessary to identify a half-unit. A half-unit results from constructing the smallest triangle possible on the geoboard, which is one-half of a square unit. Now, the areas of many other geometric figures can be easily determined. Be sure to match the difficulty of the activity with the ability of the children.

3. On the floor of the classroom or gymnasium or on the playground, design several large (2 to 4 square meters) regular and irregular regions. Some may be squares, rectangles, and trapezoids. Others may be irregular curves, including quadrilaterals and shapes that are not polygons. Have the children estimate the areas of the various figures in terms of floor tiles or other square units designated by the students or teacher.

Then place the tiles inside the figure and determine its area. Some judgments will be necessary, as not all figures will hold a whole number of square units. It is helpful to have some half-units available to fit into the figure.

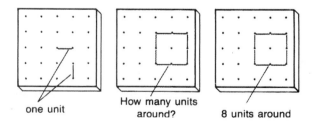

Figure 12–18 Measuring boundaries using arbitrary units.

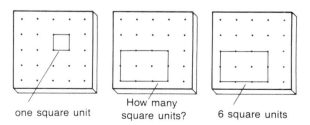

Figure 12–19 Measuring areas using arbitrary square units.

As a variation of this activity, determine how many students can stand within each region. Both of a child's feet must be within the region and all children should be standing comfortably upright. The children can then discover which figures are largest and which are smallest and how all of the figures can be ordered from largest to smallest.

OBJECTIVE: to use standard units to measure area.

4. Provide groups of three or four children with centimeter cubes and various small square and rectangular regions (8 to 24 square centimeters). Have the children estimate the number of cubes that can be placed in each region. Then have the children fill the region with one layer of cubes and count them. Explain that each cube takes up 1 square centimeter of area in the region. The total number of cubes is equivalent to the number of square centimeters in the region. To extend this activity, include regions similar in shape to the region shown in Figure 12–20, irregular polygons, and other closed curves.

5. Have available transparencies of centimeter grids. Also, provide drawings of squares, rectangles, triangles, circles, and hexagons. Later, use drawings of closed curves that are not polygons or circles. Encourage the children to estimate the area of each figure in square centimeters.

Then, lay the centimeter grid over the top of each figure and count the numbers of whole and half square centimeters that fit in the figure. When the figures are less like polygons, it is more difficult to estimate and determine the areas. Introduce the various figures slowly over a period of several days.

Grades 3 – 5 and Grades 6 – 8

OBJECTIVE: to use arbitrary units to measure area.

1. This activity compares the body surface areas of two students to see which student has the greatest body surface area. Ask for two volunteers to serve as patient subjects. Have the class estimate which of the two has the greatest body surface area. Use toilet paper to carefully wrap each of the students, barely overlapping the tissue. Pieces of masking tape will help in this task. Wrap each leg, then the trunk, then each arm. Finally, lightly wrap the head. Then, even more carefully, unwrap each student and compare the amounts of

tissue used. Either count the tissues or place them end to end and compare.

2. Procedures to introduce area using the geoboard continue to be valid for upper elementary and middle school students. And, it is helpful for students to be exposed to additional ways to find the areas of triangles and other polygons. For example, the area of a right triangle whose legs have lengths a and b is one-half the area of a rectangle whose sides have lengths a and b. This is illustrated in Figure 12–21a.

The area of any non-right triangle may be found by subdividing the triangle into right triangles by constructing a segment from the vertex to the base. Then, using the previous technique, find the areas of the right triangles and add them together. This is illustrated in Figure 12–21b.

Finally, if the triangle is similar to the one in Figure 12–21c, it may be stretched into a right triangle. The area of the original triangle is the area of the large right triangle minus the area of the right triangle resulting from the stretch, t.

Another method of finding the area of a triangle or the area of an irregular figure is to surround the figure with the smallest rectangle that contains it. Then, find the area of the rectangle and subtract the areas of the newly formed figures. In Figure 12–22, the irregular figure, f, has been surrounded by a square of 9 square units. The areas of the newly formed figures outside f yet inside the square around f total 6 square units. Thus, f has an area of $9 - 6$, or 3, square units. Challenge the students to form as many different shapes as they can on the geoboard with a total area of, say, 3 square units.

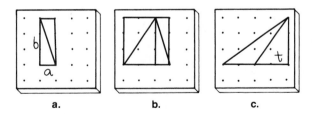

Figure 12–21   Finding the area of triangles on the geoboard.

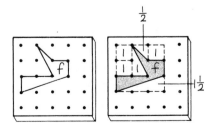

Figure 12–22   Finding the area of irregular figures on the geoboard.

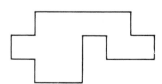

Figure 12–20   Sample shape for measuring with standard units.

The areas of other polygons—parallelograms and trapezoids, for example—may be derived by means similar to those used to find the areas of triangles and irregular figures. This rather brief description is not meant to be complete in terms of the uses of geoboards. References are available; some are listed at the end of this chapter.

3. Prepare sheets on which are drawn square grids measuring approximately 2 centimeters on a side or use the 1-inch graph paper from Appendix B. Encourage the children to take any objects that will fit on the grids and trace their outlines. Have the children count the total number of square regions that are partially inside the outline of the object plus the total number of squares that are completely inside the outline.

The hand outlined in Figure 12–23 completely contains 23 squares, plus it partially contains another 26 squares. We can say, then, that the area of the hand outline is greater than 23 square units but less than 49 square units. We can refine our calculation by finding

the average of the two numbers, 23 and 49. Thus, the area of the hand is approximately 36 square units.

OBJECTIVE: to measure the areas of objects using standard measuring units.

4. The procedure described in Activity 3 above may be repeated using a grid with 1-centimeter squares. The results of measuring should be reported in square centimeters. Similarly, an overhead transparency with a 1-centimeter grid drawn on it may be used. Place the transparency directly on the shape being measured.

The areas of two types of figures can be determined. First are squares and rectangles with dimensions that are whole numbers of centimeters. Second are other polygons with at least two dimensions that are whole numbers of centimeters. These include triangles, quadrilaterals, trapezoids, pentagons, and hexagons. Be sure to have students estimate the area before they find it.

5. This activity utilizes the knowledge students have gained through their use of geoboards. Having made many rectangular regions of varying sizes, students should be able to begin a table that shows the areas of these rectangles (Table 12–1).

Have the students examine the relationships between the lengths, the widths, the products of lengths and widths, and the areas. Once they have discovered that the length times the width equals the area, students are ready to apply that discovery to figures measured with standard measures. Thus, a rectangle with a length of 4 centimeters and a width of 3 centimeters will have an area of 4 by 3, or 12, square centimeters. This finding can be checked using the 1-centimeter transparency grid. Student are now able to measure the dimensions of objects in centimeters or meters and to determine their areas with understanding.

To extend this activity, develop similar tables to show the areas of squares and triangles. From these examples, the formulas for the areas of squares and triangles can be developed.

6. As students develop the facility to determine perimeter and area of a figure, challenge them to use

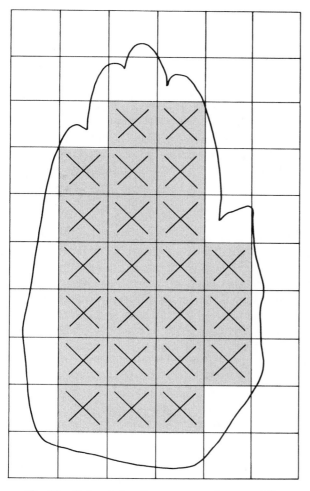

Figure 12–23 Determining the approximate area of the outline of a hand.

TABLE 12–1 Length, Width, and Area of Figures on the Geoboard

Length	Width	Length × Width	Square Units
1	1	1	1
2	1	2	2
3	1	3	3
4	1	4	4
2	2	4	4
3	2	6	6
4	2	8	8

the color tiles to build the shape with the largest area with a perimeter of 20 units. The length of each side of the tile represents one unit and the area of the tile represents one square unit. Encourage the students working in pairs to outline the shapes on grid paper as they construct them with the tiles. When the students have identified the 5-by-5 square as having the greatest area, have them find the figure with the smallest area with a perimeter of 20 units. Let the students draw on the board several possible shapes that have perimeters of 20 units. Perhaps a table would help students "analyze" the relationship between perimeter and area (Table 12–2). You may need to develop an operational definition of what figures can be counted. We would recommend starting with shapes that can be constructed by putting the tiles so that they touch another tile along an entire edge. Touching just at the corners, for example, would not be allowed.

Continue this activity by changing the perimeter to 24, then 28. Have the students write about and then discuss the nature of the shape that contains the greatest area.

Extend this activity by reversing the focus. Now, have the students find the shape with the largest or smallest perimeter given the area. For example, use the area of 24 square units. What is the largest perimeter of a shape with an area of 24 square units? What is the smallest perimeter? Discuss the nature of the shape that has the greatest perimeter. An interesting discussion of the various shapes will ensue.

7. Once students can use various formulas to determine the areas of simple polygons, they are ready to find the areas of large and small regions. Among the large regions are panes of window glass, the tops of tables or desks, the classroom floor or walls, doors, and dry erase boards. Small regions include squares, rectangles, triangles, the faces of cereal boxes or milk containers, and the pages of books. In each case, children should use rulers or meter sticks to measure the dimensions of the region and apply the appropriate formula to determine the area.

TABLE 12–2   Perimeter and Area of Rectangular Shapes

Perimeter	Dimensions	Area
20	1×9	9
20	2×8	16
20	3×7	21
20	4×6	24
20	5×5	25
20	6×4	24
20	7×3	21
20	8×2	16
20	9×1	9

To vary this activity, ask children to draw particular areas on paper, on the board, or on the playground. For example, ask them to draw a rectangle of area 6 square meters or a triangle of area 15 square centimeters.

The area formulas that children should have previously discovered include those for *squares* ($A = s \times s$, where s is the length of a side); *rectangles* ($A = l \times w$, where l is the length and w is the width); *triangles* ($A = \frac{1}{2} \times b \times h$, where b is the length of the base and h is the height); and *circles* ($A = \pi \times r^2$, where r is the radius and $\pi = 3.14$).

8. In the previous activity, pi (π) was used in the formula to determine the area of a circle. Rather than giving the students the approximate value of π (3.14), have the students discover the value of pi. Provide groups with four or five jar lids of various sizes and a cloth measuring tape. Two group members will be responsible for carefully measuring the circumference and the diameter of each circular lid. The recorder writes the measurements in a table that lists the names on the jar lid and has spaces to list the circumference and diameter. Another group member has the job of dividing the circumference of each jar lid by the diameter of that lid. The recorder writes the results to two decimal places in the table. When all of the calculations have been made the "calculator" averages the four or five results. The reporter then goes to the board or overhead projector and records the results of her group's work on a summary chart. The results of each group's work will be very close to each other. A final calculation could be the average of the group results. The final number that represents the ratio between the circumference of a circle and its diameter will be between 3.1 and 3.2. This activity should bring meaning to the value of π. Encourage a curious student to see if she can find some historical information about pi.

9. The dynamic geometry software on Weblink 12–1 introduces the Pythagorean relationship ($a^2 + b^2 = c^2$) visually and provides a basis for an informal, visual proof of the Pythagorean theorem. Students are able to transfer the areas of the squares of the sides of a right triangle to the area of the square on the hypotenuse. The right triangle may be reconfigured by the students, to provide many examples. This electronic activity is a fine example of the Pythagorean relationship.

Measuring Weight and Mass

Remember that *weight* refers to the force of gravity acting on an object, and *mass* is the amount of matter in an object. For any given object on earth, its weight and mass are equal. On a simple balance scale, we simultaneously determine weight and mass when we find that a box balances 124 grams. On the moon or on another body in space, the weight of an object will be different from its weight on earth. The mass, however, remains constant.

We use the term weight in describing the activities in this section. You will see that some activities use the same procedures used to determine mass; namely, the pan balance.

In their work with weight thus far, students have made direct comparisons with objects to determine which are lighter and which are heavier. They have done some work with the pan balance. By the time children have completed grade 2, they should have little difficulty using standard units of weight with either a pan balance or a spring scale. Students in grades 3–5 need activities that provide practice weighing a variety of objects. Common metric units of mass include the gram and the kilogram.

A C T I V I T I E S

Pre-Kindergarten – Grade 2

OBJECTIVE: to determine which of two objects is heavier using indirect measuring.

1. Place an object, perhaps a full can of soup, on one side of the room and another object, perhaps a book, on the other side. Challenge the children to discover which object is heavier without moving either object to the other side of the room. Have available at least one pan balance. For younger children, suggest finding another object or a material such as clay to use to determine the weight of the can of soup. This intermediate object can then be used to check the weight of the book.

This activity may be extended by putting four or five objects on each side of the room and having the children order them by weight. All of the checking must be done with intermediate objects.

OBJECTIVE: to determine the weights of objects using arbitrary measuring units.

2. Use wooden cubes as measuring units. Have available 8 or 10 objects ranging in weight from 10 to 300 grams. The objects may include a board eraser, a marking pen, a pencil, a box of crayons, and a pair of scissors. Ask the students to estimate the weight of each of these objects in terms of the number of wooden cubes it would take to balance the object. Let the children determine how many cubes it actually takes using the pan balance.

Most objects will not balance a whole number of cubes. In these cases, the weight should be reported as, for example, "more than 12 cubes and fewer than 13."

You may vary this activity by using different arbitrary units. Paper clips, washers, beans, and pennies will serve the purpose very well.

Extend this activity by determining the relationships of coin weights. Provide students with one quarter, five dimes, five pennies, and three nickels. The object is to determine the weight of each coin with respect to the other coins. Ask questions such as the following:

- A quarter weighs as much as how many pennies?
- A quarter weighs as much as how many dimes?
- A quarter weighs as much as how many nickels?
- A nickel weighs as much as how many pennies?
- A nickel weighs as much as how many dimes?
- A penny weighs as much as how many dimes?

Discuss how many pennies weigh as much as two or three quarters. Ask how many dimes weigh as much as three or four nickels, and so on.

OBJECTIVE: to use standard units to determine the weights of various items.

3. Find 8 or 10 items with weights that range from 10 to 100 grams. Items may include a small school eraser, a pencil, a pair of scissors, a box of paper clips, a marking pen, and a compact disc. Also provide the children with 100 or so centimeter cubes, each of which weighs 1 gram. Let the children estimate the number of centimeter cubes it will take to balance a particular item. Then have them weigh each item using the cubes. Both the estimate and actual weight should be recorded. If it takes 45 centimeter cubes to balance an item, the children should know that the item weighs 45 grams.

Next, provide 8 to 10 objects that each weigh between 10 and 400 grams. These objects should include items found in the classroom or on the playground. This time, use the set of standard masses that accompany most pan balances. Again, ask the children to estimate the weight of the various objects before the masses are used. A worksheet picturing the objects with space for the estimate and the actual weight may be helpful. Figure 12–24 illustrates part of one such worksheet.

4. Have the children work in groups of three or four. Each group should have access to a pan balance. If there is only one balance, let the groups take turns. Challenge each group to find three objects that each weigh 25 grams or less, three objects that each weigh 50 to 100 grams, three objects that each weigh 150 to 300 grams, and one object that weighs 1 kilogram. Hold the object search in the classroom. Have the students record the objects they find by drawing pictures of them or writing about them. Among the objects students could weigh are containers of water, rice, sand, or beans.

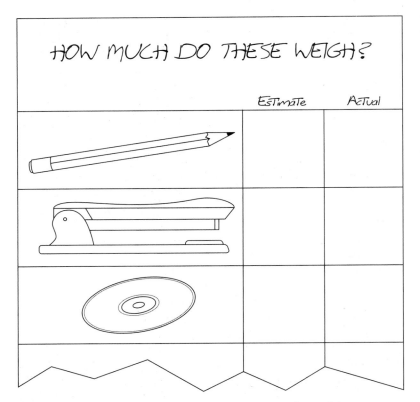

Figure 12–24 Worksheet for estimating and determing weight.

Grades 3–5

OBJECTIVE: to recognize the need for uniformity when using units of measure.

1. Provide a collection of various sizes of washers or stones. Have the students weigh five objects and record the results using the washers, as in Figure 12–25. Objects may include a crayon box, a ruler, a pair of scissors, a textbook, a board eraser—all objects that would be found in another classroom in the school.

The next step is to give another class the measuring units and the pan balance. Ask them to weigh the same

objects that your class weighed and to report back to you on their findings.

Have the students compare the results of the two weighings and discuss why the results were not the same. It is important for students to discover that measuring units must be uniform, particularly if they are arbitrary units.

OBJECTIVE: to use standard units to measure weight.

2. Collect four different materials, such as rice, beans, unpopped popcorn, and centimeter cubes. Put each of these materials in a separate bowl. Separate the class into groups of four. Each group will be a team for a prediction contest. Have each team designate a particular member to be a rice grabber, a bean grabber, and so on. Let the rice grabber estimate the weight of rice that she or he can grab using only one hand. The rice grabber should then grab the rice and put it into a plastic sandwich bag. The rest of the team should weigh and record the results. The other grabbers should do the same thing for their particular materials.

Have the teams calculate the total estimated weight for the four items as well as the actual weight. Have them determine the difference between the estimated weight and the actual weight. The team with the lowest difference is the winner.

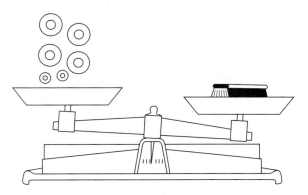

Figure 12–25 Using washers to balance an eraser.

3. Display a one-or-two-liter soft drink container full of rice and an intermediate container such as a tuna can. First, have the students estimate the weight of the rice in the container. Then announce, "We will be trying to find the weight of the rice. But there is a rule: The largest amount of rice that can be weighed is the amount that can be held by the tuna can" (see Figure 12–26).

Have groups of three or four students devise the most efficient plan they can to determine the weight of the rice in the container. Let each group implement its plan and find the weight of the rice. When all groups have finished, discuss the procedures used and compare the various plans. Also compare the weights that each group derived.

To extend this activity, use a container of cubes and weigh to determine the number of cubes in the container. This may involve weighing a sample of the cubes, counting them, and weighing the container of cubes to find how many such samples are in the container. Be sure to subtract the weight of the container from the weight of the jar and the cubes.

4. Provide each group of three or four students with an apple or orange: Have them find the weight of the apple in grams and record it. Have one member of the group take a bite out of the apple. Then weigh the remaining apple and record the weight. Calculate the weight of the bite and record it. Have the group member take another bite, weigh the remaining apple, record the weight, and calculate the weight of the second bite. Continue until the apple has been eaten.

When the children are finished, have them answer questions about the apple: Are all bites the same size? What was the weight of the largest bite? What was the weight of the smallest bite? What was the weight of the average bite? What was the weight of the part of the apple that was eaten? Compare and discuss the results from each group.

Measuring Time

Children develop an understanding of *time* by experiencing events that last varying lengths of time. Younger children who believe that yesterday was a long time ago later come to believe that yesterday was not too long ago when compared with last week. The experiences that these children need include events of various durations. The time it takes the second hand to move from 12 to 12, the time it takes the hour hand to move from 9 to 10, the start of recess to the end, the start of the school day to the end, Monday to Friday, Monday to Monday, the month of February, and the school year are all events that heighten the child's awareness of time.

In pre-kindergarten–grade 2, the skill of telling time depends on experiences children have had at home and at school. When children are in grades 3–5, their abilities to tell time using a clock are more refined.

During the early years in school, students should measure time using various units. These include years, seasons, months, days, hours, minutes, and seconds. The tools used to measure time are the calendar and the clock.

Birthdays and age are important to children and can be used as a starting point for discussing time. Books such as *A Birthday Basket for Tia* by Mora (1992) are also useful in raising awareness of time. In this story, Cecilia prepares a gift basket of objects for her great-aunt's ninetieth birthday. The objects remind her of favorite memories she has shared with her aunt.

Later, students tell time throughout the school day. Children should have practice with instruments such as a digital stop watch that can be used to measure time with greater precision than a sweep second hand.

A C T I V I T I E S

Pre-Kindergarten – Grade 2

OBJECTIVE: to measure various events using arbitrary units.

1. Provide the children with 8 soup cans, each of which has a hole punched in the bottom with a nail. Each hole should be a different size. Mark an "S" on one of the cans and use it as a standard. Have the children fill the standard can and one of the other cans, can A, with water while holding fingers over the holes. Let the cans drain together and compare can A with the standard can, telling whether it takes more time for can A to drain, less time for can A to drain, or the same amount of time for both to drain. Continue these comparisons until all cans have been compared with the standard can and rated.

To extend this activity, compare each can with the others and order the entire collection of cans from those that take the least time to empty to those that take the most time.

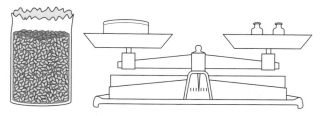

Figure 12–26   Using standard units to measure the weight of rice.

2. Construct a pendulum using string and a 1-or 2-ounce fishing sinker, as in Figure 12–27. As the pendulum swings, have the children practice counting the number of times the sinker crosses a marker at the pendulum's base.

Once children can do this easily, fill one of the cans used as a water clock in the previous activity. As the can empties, have the children count the number of pendulum swings. Record this number. Compare the cans based on the number of pendulum swings and again order the cans.

Extend this activity by timing various events by the number of pendulum swings. Using the pendulum, time events such as how long it takes for the children to take their seats and get ready to begin work after recess, to line up for lunch, to wash their hands before lunch, and to clean the floor before going home.

OBJECTIVE: to use the calendar to measure days, weeks, and months.

3. Have a large, easily displayed calendar with ample regions representing each day. As an introductory activity each morning, discuss that day. Appropriate items for discussion include the date, the weather, important events, what day yesterday was, what date yesterday was, what day tomorrow will be, how many days it has been since the start of the month, how many days are left in the month, how many weeks it has been since the start of the month, and how many weeks are left in the month. Make notations in the region representing that day; a picture or a word or two will suffice. When a month has been completed, display it as the next month is begun.

Counting days and remembering what happened a day ago, counting weeks and remembering what happened a week ago, and counting months and remembering what happened a month ago will help children develop skill in using the calendar to tell time.

OBJECTIVE: to use the clock to tell time.

4. Have a clock with hands that are easy to move. A large wooden or plastic clock with gears that allow the hands to move together is commercially available and can be very useful. It is also advantageous to have a real clock with a second hand to help show the passing of seconds and minutes. Each day on a regular schedule, spend three to five minutes setting the clock and having the children determine the time shown by the hands.

At first, show the time on the hour, such as 10 o'clock, 1 o'clock, and 7 o'clock. Soon, introduce time on the half-hour, then on the quarter-hour, five minutes, and one minute. Let the second hand move around and watch the minute hand move one minute.

Later, use a digital clock set at the same time to show the same time on both types of clocks (see Figure 12–28). It is possible that these youngsters will live in a world that contains only digital clocks and watches.

To extend this activity, challenge the children to play the minute game. Have the children face away from the clock. Then give a command to begin. When they believe a minute has elapsed, they should stand and face the clock. Facing the clock, they can immediately see if they stood before, after, or at the end of one minute. Use this activity for periods of 15, 30, and 45 seconds, as well.

Once the children begin to tell time, they should regularly practice using the clock to time events that take place during school. These events include the periods set aside for reading, mathematics, art, science, and social studies. There are regular times for outside-the-class activities: physical education, lunch, recess, and end of the day. Let children serve as designated timers for a morning or a day, with the responsibility to let the teacher or the class know when certain events are to take place.

Grades 3–5

OBJECTIVE: to develop timing devices with arbitrary and standard units.

1. There are several ways to develop timers. Using a funnel and sand is one way (see Figure 12–29a). Initially, fill the funnel with sand. The amount of time for the sand to empty out of the funnel becomes an arbitrary unit of time, named *funnel time,* or another name that may have meaning.

Develop another timer by using a candle on which several equally spaced marks have been scratched, as in Figure 12–29b. The amount of time for the candle to

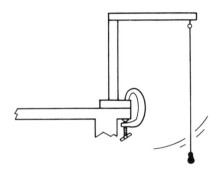

Figure 12–27 Pendulum for measuring the time of an event.

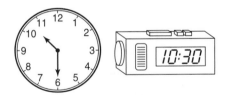

Figure 12–28 Analog and digital clocks.

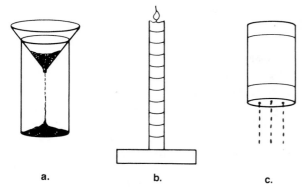

Figure 12–29 Arbitrary timing devices.

burn from one mark to another becomes an arbitrary unit of time.

Construct a third timer by tapping or drilling holes in the bottom of a soup can, as in Figure 12–29c. The amount of time for the water to empty out of the can becomes an arbitrary unit.

Once the timers have been constructed, use them to time various events. Events may include how many blocks can be stacked before the sand timer empties, silently reading while the candle timer burns two intervals, and seeing if the entire class can wash and line up for lunch before the water escapes from the can.

Ask the children how they might make arbitrary units into standard units. Try some of the ideas. Calibrate each timer against a clock with a second hand or a stopwatch. Perhaps the funnel and sand could be made into a one-minute timer. The candle could time intervals of five minutes. The soup can could be used as a three-minute timer. Each timer can be adjusted to measure time in standard units. Once completed, the timers should be used as a clock or watch would be used to time events.

An extension of this activity is for a class to construct one or two sundials. The sundial proved to be a reliable timepiece for centuries before the advent of mechanical clocks. Designing and building a horizontal sundial requires measuring a series of angles and compensating for the school's location on earth. The finished product is very rewarding. Finding a book that describes the steps necessary to construct a sundial is essential. Winthrop Dolan's *A Choice of Sundials* (1975) is such a book.

OBJECTIVE: to use standard units to time events in the classroom.

2. As described earlier, the clock in the classroom should be used to time the events of the day. Some youngsters may have difficulty using the clock at first if they have not had regular experience telling time. Using both traditional and digital clocks on a regular basis will provide the experience needed by students.

When a period is set aside for silent reading, have students record the time they begin and the time they finish. Have a student time a recess and report to you when the time is up. Allow the students to earn minutes of special activity time for certain classroom behaviors.

To extend this activity, have the students survey *Guinness World Records* for some of the many timed events and prepare a collection of the most interesting. Let students collect or draw pictures illustrating these events.

3. Timing events with precision can begin by using the second hand on the clock to determine how much time it takes to clear desks and get ready to go home, or to wash and line up for lunch. To become more precise requires a stopwatch to time these same events to the nearest hundredth of a second. Team relay and individual events in physical education lend themselves to precise timing. Be careful to time events for the interest and motivation afforded by the timing, not to prove that one child is better than another.

A variation of this activity is to have three children, each with a stopwatch, time the same event to the nearest hundredth of a second. Compare the results. Ask, "Why are there differences? What is the best estimate of the event's time?" Perhaps an average of the three times will give the best estimate. Repeat this activity several times.

4. The topic of time often occurs in children's books. For example, in *Max and Me and the Time Machine* by Greer and Ruddick (1983), Steve and Max are transported back in time and begin an adventure that ends when they are transported back to their clubhouse. When reading this story to a class, a discussion of time and some problems related to time would be appropriate. What is the difference in minutes or seconds between the time the boys thought they were spending back in time (3 hours) and the actual time they spent (3 days)? How many years ago was the year 1250? How could you tell time in the year 1250, before the advent of the modern clock? *The Flight of the Doves* by Macken (1992) provides an opportunity for students to discuss distance and time. A boy and his younger sister run away from their evil uncle in England and set out to find their grandmother in Ireland. The adventure begins. The distances they traveled and the time it took can be the focus of discussion. How do these distances and times compare to distance from the school and time it takes to cover them by various means?

Measuring Volume and Capacity

Volume refers to the amount of space contained in a three-dimensional object. Measures of volume include how much material is found in a block of wood or a television. Capacity refers to the amount of space that can be filled. Measures of capacity include how much water or rice will fit into a box or jar. Volume and capacity are closely related. A container's capacity is determined by the volume of the material it will hold. In pre-kindergarten–grade 2, we have a greater emphasis on capacity. At the intermediate level, we emphasize both volume and capacity.

Children in pre-kindergarten–grade 2 expand their knowledge of volume and capacity through a variety of media. They build with blocks, large and small. They fill a space and find how much water, sand, or rice was used. They also find how many cubes it takes to fill a space. The cubes represent cubic units and provide the basis for the measurement of volume.

Children in the middle grades continue to use containers, filling them with a variety of materials. These experiences serve as a basis for developing formulas for calculating volume. The transition to abstract work depends upon the earlier manipulative activities. Common metric volume units include cubic centimeters, cubic decimeters, and cubic meters. Metric capacity units include the milliliter and the liter.

A C T I V I T I E S

Pre-Kindergarten – Grade 2

OBJECTIVE: to determine the capacities of various containers using indirect measurement.

1. Provide the children with one particular container to use as a pouring container and several others to pour water (or sand) into. Ask the children to identify the containers that they believe can be completely filled when they start with the pouring container completely filled. Put those that the children believe can be filled together and those they believe cannot be filled together. Then have the children actually try to fill the containers to discover which ones can be filled.

As an extension, provide six clear containers of various shapes and capacities. Without the children present, pour exactly the same amount of rice into each container, as in Figure 12–30.

Have the children order the containers from those the children believe hold the least to those they believe hold the most. Then, together, pour the rice into a measuring container and let the children discover that all the

containers held the same amount of rice. Discuss with the children the apparent differences in the amounts of rice.

2. This activity requires five containers with volumes that range from 500 milliliters to 2 liters and several infant formula bottles (or tuna fish cans) to use as measuring tools. Ask the children to estimate the number of formula bottles of rice it will take to fill each jar. Then have them find the amount of rice that fills the jars. If the amount is not a whole number, it should be noted as, for example, "more than 8 bottles and less than 9." Encourage the children to record the amount of their estimates and the actual capacities in terms of infant formula bottles. Finally, have the children order the containers by capacity based on the information they have collected.

An extension of this activity can be found in the NCTM electronic example, estimating scoops (Weblink 12–2). The three-part example is a video presentation of a class developing estimating strategies for determining how many scoops of cranberries fit into a container and working in groups to make estimations. The interaction between students and the teacher provide a good model for teaching.

OBJECTIVE: to determine the volumes of several containers using standard measures.

3. Find or construct four or five boxes with metric dimensions. The boxes may be constructed by using a pattern similar to the one shown in Figure 12–31. The dimensions should be whole numbers of centimeters, for example 3 by 4 by 2 centimeters.

Provide the children with centimeter cubes and the boxes. Have them estimate how many cubes they think it will take to fill each box. Then have them carefully stack the cubes in each box to find the actual volume. Explain to the children that the volume of each small cube is 1 cubic centimeter and ask for the volumes of the boxes in cubic centimeters.

Next, find two or three small boxes that do not have metric dimensions and challenge the children

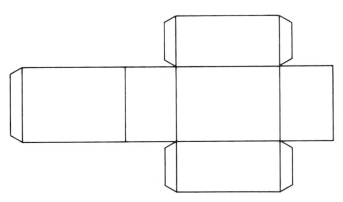

Figure 12–31 Pattern for constructing a box with metric dimensions.

Figure 12–30 Rice poured into variously shaped containers.

to determine the volumes of the boxes using cubic centimeters. Here, the answers may be stated in terms of, for example, "more than 12 cubic centimeters and less than 16."

4. This activity requires centimeter cubes and sets of measuring cups and spoons. The cups and spoons should be intended for use in the kitchen and should be calibrated in metric units. Provide the children with 8 to 10 common containers, the capacities of which must be determined using the materials at hand. The containers may include containers for shampoo, milk, syrup, peanut butter, ice cubes, sour cream, detergent, margarine, film, and greeting cards.

Ask the children which units, those that are stacked or those that are poured, are most appropriate for measuring the capacities of the containers. Have the children estimate the capacity of each container and then use the units to find the actual capacity.

Grades 3–5 and Grades 6–8

OBJECTIVE: to use water displacement as a way to determine which of several objects has the greatest volume.

1. Construct six balls of clay of varying sizes. Also, find a glass jar with straight sides that will easily hold each ball of clay. A peanut butter jar or a quart canning jar should suffice. Put into the jar enough water to completely cover the largest ball of clay without flowing out of the jar.

Engage in a discussion about how the volume of a ball of clay can be determined. Accept and discuss suggestions. Try reasonable suggestions.

If displacement is not suggested, have the children attach each ball of clay to the end of a piece of wire. Submerge the balls, one at a time, in the water while the students observe the water level. Discuss how the water level changes depending on the size of the clay. Have the students determine which ball of clay has the greatest volume.

Extend this activity by using three or four irregular rocks that will fit into a graduated cylinder. Have the students pour water into the cylinder to a level that is clearly marked. Then have them carefully immerse a rock in the water and note the new level of the water. Have them record the difference between the new level and the original level in cubic centimeters; this is the volume of the rock.

OBJECTIVE: to use arbitrary units to determine the capacity of different containers.

2. For this activity, collect an eye dropper, a spoon of arbitrary size, and three containers of moderate size. The containers may be an infant formula jar, a peanut butter jar, and a mayonnaise jar (see Figure 12–32).

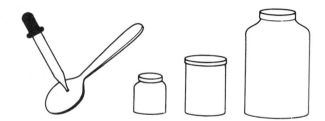

Figure 12–32   Using arbitrary units to determine the capacity of containers.

Ask the students how to determine how many eye droppers of water it takes to fill the large jar. They may suggest using the eye dropper to fill the large jar one drop at a time. Encourage the students to find a method that will take less time and effort. One suggestion may be to discover how many drops of water it takes to fill the spoon. Next, find how many spoons it takes to fill the formula jar. Then, find how many formula jars it takes to fill the peanut butter jar and how many peanut butter jars it takes to fill the mayonnaise jar. Finally, the capacity of the mayonnaise jar can be stated in terms of drops of water.

3. Collect enough milk jug caps to fill a medium-sized paper bag. Asking for help from the children will speed up this collection. Provide students with various containers: a soup can; a tuna can; half-pint, pint, and quart milk containers; a shoe box; a cereal box; and a drinking cup. Have the children estimate and then determine the capacity of each container in terms of the number of milk jug caps. Have them order the collection of containers based on their findings.

An extension of this activity is to select a second unit, such as small shell-shaped macaroni, and replicate the procedure. The results should prove to be the same. Do all students agree that the results will be the same before the second measure is made? Discuss the reasoning for the students' responses.

OBJECTIVE: to calculate the volumes and capacities of various containers using standard measurement.

4. This is similar to Activity 2 above. Ask the students to use an eye dropper to find how many drops of water are in one milliliter. Next, have them determine the number of milliliters of water in a teaspoon and how many teaspoons fill a tablespoon. Then, encourage the students to find how many tablespoons fill a paper cup. With the information they have collected, they should be able to calculate the number of drops of water it takes to fill a teaspoon, a tablespoon, and a paper cup.

Finally, challenge the students to find the number of liters of water contained in 1 million drops of water. A calculator will be very handy in this activity.

TABLE 12–3 Finding the Number of Cubes in a Container

Box	Length	Width	Height	Length × Width × Height	Total No. of Cubes
a	2	2	2	8	8
b	2	2	3	12	12
c	2	3	3	18	18
d	3	3	3	27	27

5. Begin by providing the students with small boxes constructed from oaktag. Make three or four boxes with measurements of (a) 2 by 2 by 2 centimeters, (b) 2 by 2 by 3 centimeters, (c) 2 by 3 by 3 centimeters, and (d) 3 by 3 by 3 centimeters. Also provide a large number of centimeter cubes. Have the children find how many cubes can be carefully stacked in each of the containers and record the number of cubes. Have them use a table like the one in Table 12–3.

Encourage the students to build "boxes" by stacking centimeter cubes using other dimensions and record their results in the table they have already started. After six or eight examples have been recorded, have the students examine the table for patterns.

Expect a variety of responses, but lead the students to notice the relationship between the product of length, width, and height and the number of cubes counted. The students will be discovering the formula for the volume of a box. The common formula for determining the volume of a rectangular container is $V = l \times w \times h$, where l is the length of the base, w is the width of the base, and h is the height.

6. A **prism** is a figure whose ends are congruent polygons and parallel with each other, and whose sides are parallelograms. The congruent polygons are the bases of the prism. Figure 12–33a shows a triangular prism, whereas Figure 12–33b shows a rectangular prism. Notice how the name of the prism is determined by the shape of its bases. The formula for the volume of any prism may be discovered by

first determining the volume of common prisms and using that information to generalize a formula for all prisms. Have students working in groups develop a table that shows the measurements of a square prism, a rectangular prism, and a right triangular prism and challenge them to determine the volume of each figure. The volume of the first two figures may be determined by using the volume formula discussed in Activity 5 above. The volume of the third figure, the right triangular prism, may be determined if the students make the figure into a rectangular or square prism, determine its volume, and then divide the result by 2 (see Figure 12–34). Once the volumes have been found encourage the students to find a common relationship among the dimensions of the prisms and the volumes of the prisms. Have each group discuss its findings and conclusions. Soon, it should be apparent that the area of the base of the prism multiplied by the height of the prism will result in the volume. Be receptive to alternative formulas that result in the correct volumes.

7. Weblink 12–3 provides an interactive environment in which students can explore several types of relationships. In the first part of this activity, students in grades 6–8 examine how side lengths, perimeters, and areas of two rectangles are related. In the second part, students examine three-dimensional figures to discover the relationships among edge lengths, surface areas, and volumes. To help teachers guide students through these activities, Weblink 12–4 provides a sequence of 5 Illumination lessons designed to help students understand topics such as ratio and proportion, scale factor, and similarity that appear in the Weblink 12–3.

Measuring Temperature

Much of what children learn and know about *temperature* comes from their interaction with their environments. When the air is cold, they bundle up. When it

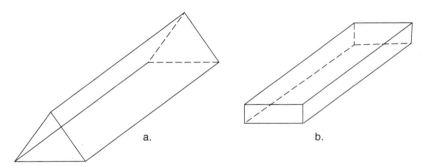

Figure 12–33 Triangular and rectangular prisms.

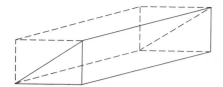

Figure 12–34 Determining the volume of a right triangular prism.

Figure 12–35 Using a thermometer with an arbitrary unit to measure temperature.

is hot, they wear fewer and lighter clothes. In the snow, they shiver. When they are ill, they may feel very warm or they may feel warm yet shiver.

Children's measures of temperature are generally from two sources, the weather and their bodies. Children hear the measure of the outside temperature daily as they watch television or listen to the radio. When they are ill, their body temperatures are recorded, but weather is by far the more common source of measures of temperature.

Children in the primary grades begin to become aware of temperature as they report the daily weather. Expressions like "It is warm today," "It will be cooler tomorrow," and "It is frosty this morning" serve as indicators of temperature. Later, a daily temperature reading may be made and recorded as practice in reading a thermometer.

Students in the middle grades continue to read temperatures and to record and graph the results. There will be work in science that requires reading temperatures, in weather units and in other areas of study. The common metric temperature unit is degrees Celsius. As children are alerted to temperature, they should develop the ability to recognize if various temperatures, such as 20°C, are hot or cold. And, if last night's low temperature was 4°C and today's high was 15°C, children should be able to determine that the difference in temperature from the low to the high temperature was 15°C − 4°C, or 11°C.

A C T I V I T I E S

Pre-Kindergarten – Grade 2

OBJECTIVE: to use indirect measurement to determine temperature.

1. Provide students with thermometer bulbs and tubes from four inexpensive nonmercury thermometers by removing their backings. About halfway up each thermometer tube, mark a spot with fingernail polish. This mark is a reference point with which to judge the movement of the alcohol (see Figure 12–35).

Ask the children to place the four thermometers in four different locations: (1) in a glass of cold tap water,

(2) on a table in the classroom, (3) in a glass of warm tap water, and (4) outside the classroom window. Have the children guess which locations will be the warmest and coolest. Then, using their observations, let the children determine which locations are actually the warmest and coolest.

OBJECTIVE: to use arbitrary units of temperature to measure various materials.

2. Use thermometer bulbs and tubes as in the preceding activity. On each tube, make five equally spaced marks. This may be done by laying the tubes on a piece of lined writing or notebook paper with the bottom of the bulb exactly on one of the lines and then making the five marks.

Next, indicate six locations in which to check the temperature using the "new" thermometers. These locations may be on a countertop, grasped in the hand of a particular student, in a glass of water, in a sunny spot in the classroom or school, near a light source, and outside the window.

Have the students record the temperatures they find as they test the various locations. The thermometers should be kept in a location for about five minutes to allow the alcohol to stop moving. Because it is unlikely that the temperatures will correspond to one of the marks, the record should show the temperature in a location as, for example, "greater than 3 but less than 4."

To extend this activity, have the children record the temperature inside the classroom and outside for each hour during a school day. Then let them construct a graph or table to show how the temperatures varied.

OBJECTIVE: to use standard units to measure temperature.

3. Have the children observe a Celsius thermometer that has been placed in a container of boiling water. *Note: this activity requires you to take special precautions to avoid possible burns from spilled or splashed water.* Ask the children to read the temperature. Next, have the children read the temperature from a thermometer that has been placed in a glass containing chopped ice. (The thermometer should be at room temperature or cooler when it is placed in the ice, not still hot from the boiling water.) Then have the children read the thermometer at room temperature. Finally, check the temperature of the air outside. In each case, have the children write down the temperature they have read from the thermometer.

It may be necessary to spend a little time explaining how the scale of a thermometer is constructed and how it is read. At first, the temperature may be read as, for example, "more than 95 and less than 100." As the students become more proficient at reading the scales, they will be able to be more precise.

Grades 3–5

OBJECTIVE: to use standard units to determine temperature.

1. Mount a Celsius thermometer outside the classroom window so that it may be read from inside the room. If this is impossible, find a location outside where the thermometer may be placed. Mount another thermometer in the room. Have students record the temperature daily at a given time for two weeks. Keep a record on a table labeled for inside and outside temperature or graph the temperatures as in Figure 12–36.

An extension of this activity is Weblink 12–5. In the first part of this lesson, students collect and examine weather data. A table is provided in which to record data. In the second part, students graph and interpret the data that they have gathered. Two different representations of the data are provided by the applet on the website. This electronic example fits nicely in the study of temperature.

2. Collect five different containers such as a paper cup, a heavy coffee mug, an aluminium cup, a glass measuring cup, and a thermos soup container. Into each one (or one at a time) pour the same amount of boiling water and insert a Celsius thermometer. After one minute, record the temperatures in the containers. Then, at 5-minute intervals, record the temperatures in the containers. After 30 minutes, stop. To complete the activity, graph the results. Then, order the containers from the one that holds the temperature for the longest period of time to the one that holds it for the shortest amount of time.

3. This activity requires using a Celsius thermometer. Ask for three volunteers. Have the volunteers, in turn, place the thermometer in their mouths and keep them there for the prescribed amount of time (normally 3 to 5 minutes). Then have them read and record their temperatures.

Discuss why the temperatures range from 36.5 to 37.5 degrees Celsius and when the children may expect the temperatures to be higher or lower. You may wish to check the temperatures of other students to collect more data. Be sure to thoroughly clean the thermometer before reusing it.

Measuring Angles

Experiences with *Logo* provide young children with the opportunity to use angle measure. With a little practice, children can direct the turtle to turn right or left a specified number. The number represents the degrees of a circle; thus, a complete rotation is 360 degrees. The more children work with turns, the greater their understanding of angle measure. As well, children will experience exterior angles as they write procedures for simple polygons. Apart from this exposure that children in primary grades have to angle measure, most angle measurement is introduced in the middle grades.

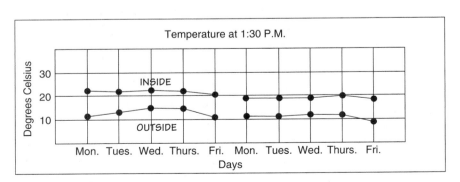

Figure 12–36 Graph of inside and outside temperatures.

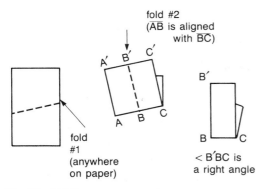

Figure 12–37   Folding paper to make a right angle.

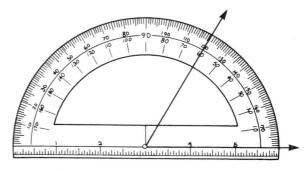

Figure 12–38   Using a protractor to measure an angle.

The protractor is used to measure angles. Once learned, the skill of measuring angles is fairly easy to maintain. Learning to use a protractor, however, requires careful teaching. Skill in measuring angles should begin with establishing an easily identifiable angle measure, 90 degrees.

Grades 3–5 and Grades 6–8

OBJECTIVE: to use a model of 90 degrees to find right angles.

1. The square corner or right angle is easily recognized by children and can be quickly constructed by folding a sheet of paper twice, as in Figure 12–37. Have the students use these models of 90 degrees to check the corners of books, the corners of desks, angles placed on a bulletin board, the corners of a classroom door, and the corners of the dry erase board.

Next, have students determine if various angles are less than, equal to, or greater than a right angle. Provide the students with 10 angles ranging in size from 70 to 110 degrees. Challenge students to estimate whether each angle is less than a right angle (**acute**), equal to a right angle (90 degrees), or greater than a right angle (**obtuse**). After the students estimate, have them use the folded right angle to check their estimates.

OBJECTIVE: to use a protractor to measure angle size.

2. As you introduce the protractor, show students how to place it on the angle so that the vertex of the angle is aligned with the origin of the protractor and one side of the angle, called a **ray,** corresponds to the **referent,** or the 0/180-degrees line of the protractor. Figure 12–38 illustrates a properly placed protractor.

Determining the angle measure requires the student to read the degrees scale, which begins at zero along one of the rays of the angle. In the case of the angle in Figure 12–38, the measure is 60 degrees.

Providing students with explanations and assistance as they begin working with protractors is essential. Provide students with angles to measure. The angles should have rays long enough to accommodate the size of the particular protractor being used. Otherwise, the measuring experience will be frustrating. Angles to measure may be provided on a worksheet or displayed on a bulletin board. If *Logo* is available, it is interesting to measure the angles generated by the turtle to check the accuracy of those angles.

3. In this activity, be sure students have protractors and paper available. Provide the students with five predrawn angles. First, have the students estimate the measure of each angle. Then, to provide an opportunity to construct angles using models, have the students measure the angles and construct copies of them adjacent to the originals.

Next, challenge the children to construct angles of given measures without using models. Have them construct the angles in any configuration on the paper to show that they know how to use both the left and the right scales on their protractors.

OBJECTIVE: to determine the sum of the angle measures of a polygon.

4. This activity begins by challenging the students to see if they can determine the sum of the angle measures of any triangle. Students should use rulers to draw a large triangle on a sheet of paper. The triangles should vary in shape. Let the students see if they can figure how to determine the sum of the angles of their triangles. Students may choose to use a protractor to measure the angles and then to add the angle measures together. To confirm this sum, students may cut out the triangle and then tear the verticies off of the triangle and position them side by side to verify that 180 degrees is the angle sum of any triangle (see Figure 12–39).

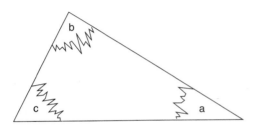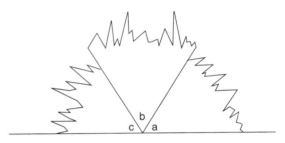

Figure 12—39 A technique to determine the angle sum of a triangle.

5. Have the students sketch any quadrilateral, any pentagon, any hexagon, any heptagon (7 sides), and any octagon. Ask the students to work with their learning groups to determine the number of degrees in the angle measures of the various polygons that they have sketched and to put the information that they have discovered in a table such as Table 12—4. Let this be a problem of discovery, encouraging the students to devise a way to complete the table. What if you had a polygon of 11 sides, how many degrees would there be in the angle sum? What about a polygon of 18 sides? Some students may attempt to tear off the verticies of the polygons like they did for the triangle. Some students may use information that they have gained from working with *Logo*. Others may carefully draw the figures and use a protractor to measure the angles. Some may use the information that they gained from determining the angle sum of a triangle. If line segments are drawn from a single vertex to each of the other verticies of a polygon, triangles will be formed. There will be two fewer triangles than there are number of sides in the polygon; thus, a pentagon will have $5 - 2$, or 3, triangles formed in its interior. With each triangle having 180 degrees, the angle sum of the pentagon will be 3×180, or 540 degrees. A polygon of n sides will have $(n - 2)$ 180 degrees for its angle sum. Be sure to give students the opportunity to make this discovery.

OBJECTIVE: to determine if a particular regular polygon will tessellate.

6. Tessellating was introduced in Chapter 11. You may review this concept by having the students discover what angle measurement is important for a regular figure to be able to tessellate. Let the

students work with pattern blocks to make tessellations using shapes that are the same. Each group will be able to tessellate with equilateral triangles, squares and hexagons. Are there other pattern blocks that will tessellate? The verticies fit together around a common point in a tessellation. What is the angle measure around that point? (360 degrees) How can we use our information about the angle measures of various polygons to determine if certain regular polygons will tessellate? What would happen if we used two or three or more different regular polygons to tessellate (semiregular tessellation)? For example, with the pattern blocks, two squares, a hexagon, and a triangle will tessellate about a common point (see Figure 12—40). Can this be predicted by what we know about the angle measure needed for a tessellation and the angle measures of those figures?

If you have dynamic geometry software available on either a computer or calculator, try the pattern block activity using the drawing, reflection, and angle measurement capabilities. In this way, students can explore a wide range of regular and irregular figures to determine which ones tessellate and to test their conjectures about why only a few regular figures will work.

The activities presented in the Developing Fluency section of this chapter give you some idea how extensive measurement is. There are many types and

TABLE 12—4 Angle Sum of Polygons

Number of Sides	3	4	5	6	7	8	n
Angle Sum	180°						

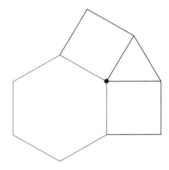

Figure 12—40 Showing that two squares, a hexagon, and a triangle will tessellate.

topics of measurement. Types of measurement include direct, indirect, arbitrary, and standard. Topics of measurement include length, area, weight, time, volume, temperature, and angle. Be prepared to use measurement whenever the opportunity arises in the classroom.

ESTIMATING AND USING BENCHMARKS

In no other area of mathematics is estimating more prevalent than in measurement. Once children get in the habit of estimating before they measure, they are better able to determine if their measuring is accurate. Notice that nearly every activity in this chapter has suggested that students estimate before they measure; therefore, no further activities are presented.

As children gain experience in measurement, encourage them to develop a sense of the various units they are using in their measuring tasks and use these as benchmarks. For example, when children are measuring length, they should know that a centimeter is about the width of a thumb, that a meter is about two average steps, and that a kilometer is about a 5- to 10-minute bicycle ride. When children are measuring volume or capacity, they should know that a cubic centimeter is about the size of a bean, that a cubic meter is a space in which they could put their desk and chair, and that a liter is an amount that would fill three or four drinking glasses. Having this sense of benchmark measuring units gives the children an important foundation for estimation and measurement.

> Elementary school and middle-grades students should have many opportunities to estimate measures by comparing them against some benchmark. (NCTM, 2000, p. 47)

REASONING, SOLVING, AND POSING PROBLEMS

Many of the activities presented in this chapter have been presented in a problem-solving format. That is, students have been challenged to use the skills of problem solving in seeking solutions. We hope you will encourage students to launch into solving a problem without fear of failure or frustration. This requires well-stated problems and considerable teacher support and encouragement. Following are a few examples of activities that provide problem-solving experiences.

A C T I V I T I E S

Pre-Kindergarten – Grade 2

OBJECTIVE: to use estimation and standard measures to solve problems.

1. Present children with five events that require them to use the measurement skills they are learning. Some examples of such events follow:

- Find how much rice it takes to balance a soup can. Tell how much the rice weighs.
- Here is a piece of string. Find an object that is as far from the doorknob as this string is long.
- Here is a sheet of paper. Find a book in the room that is the same size as this piece of paper.
- Find how many centimeter cubes it will take to fill a tuna can. Tell how much all of the cubes weigh in total.
- Use the *Logo* turtle to make a square that has sides of 55 turtle steps. Make two such squares on the screen.

These events are intended for students working in groups of three or four or for the entire class working with the teacher. The size of the class, the amount of help available, and the age and abilities of the youngsters play a role in the organization for this activity. An extension of this activity is presented below as an activity for students in the middle grades.

OBJECTIVE: to use the pan balance to solve a problem.

2. Provide the children with 8 balls of clay or play dough. They should weigh 5, 10, 15, 20, 25, 30, 35, and 40 grams. Challenge the children to divide the balls of clay among 4 children so that each child will have the same weight of clay. Have the children weigh various combinations of clay balls until they have found pairs that weigh 45 grams. They should match the 5- and 40-gram balls, the 10- and 35-gram balls, and so on. A pair of clay balls on one side of the scales should balance another pair on the other side. As an extension, ask the children to create 4 or 6 clay balls to give to other students to solve. Have the children create the balls without using the standard gram masses; let them use only the pan balance.

Grades 3 – 5

OBJECTIVE: to estimate area and volume based on configurations of squares and cubes.

1. On a table or shelf, make arrangements with various numbers of cubes. Challenge the students to find the number of cubes in a pattern without counting. Figure 12–41 on page 420 shows two such patterns. Allow students to create patterns for the others, including you, to estimate the number of cubes.

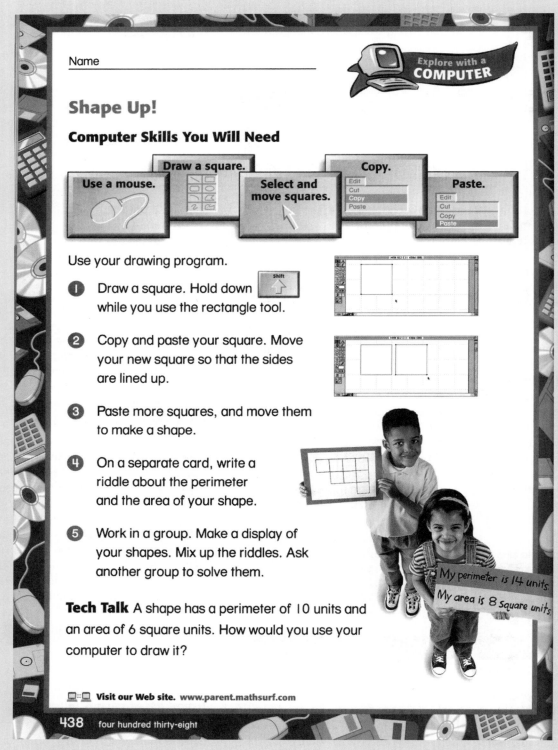

Figure 12–42 From Charles Randall, *Scott Foresman—Addison Wesley Math* [Grade 2]. Glenview, IL: Scott Foresman-Addison Wesley, 2002, p. 438. Reprinted by permission of Pearson Education, Inc.

MATH PROGRAM

The activity shown in Figure 12–42 is from the second-grade Scott Foresman–Addison Wesley Math program. In this activity, students are using the computer to draw squares and design shapes with varying perimeters and areas. Once children have designed their figures, they are instructed to make up riddles about the area and perimeter of the shape. Riddles and shapes are mixed up and then traded, and students are challenged to solve each other's puzzles. As they work on the riddles, students are encouraged to discuss whether it is possible to have more than one shape with a given area and perimeter (it is). They also explore finding shapes with different perimeters for a given area and different areas for a given perimeter.

In addition to the lessons in this chapter about area and perimeter, this chapter also includes measurement of temperature, length, volume, and weight. Students are encouraged to estimate and compare measures (longer, shorter, heavier, lighter, colder, warmer) as well as use a variety of measurement tools. The teacher's manual has suggestions for a variety of learners and learning styles, including ESL students as well as gifted and talented, kinesthetic, and logical learners.

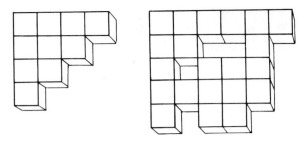

Figure 12–41 Finding the number of cubes in shapes.

Then, move to estimating larger numbers using patterns shaded on squared paper. Perhaps the first estimates should determine if the pattern has more or less than 25 squares. Next, have the students estimate more precisely how many squares are shown. Figure 12–43 illustrates two such square patterns.

- *Understanding the problem.* I need to decide how many squares I believe are shaded in the figure on the left. I cannot count every square. I need to figure out a way to do this so I can do other problems like it.
- *Devising a plan.* I am going to count some of the shaded regions. Then I'll try to fit the regions together in my mind to make a rectangular shape. I'll multiply the length and width to find the answer (make and use a drawing or model and look for a pattern).
- *Carrying out the plan.* In the upper part of the shaded region on the left in Figure 12–43, I see a 3-by-7 rectangle (21 shaded squares). In the bottom part of that shape, I see what is more than another row but not two more rows. I believe there must be a little more than 4-by-7 shaded squares. Thus, I will say there are about 30 shaded squares in the shape. I am interested in knowing how close I am.
- *Looking back.* When I counted the shaded regions, I found 29. My approach for finding the number of shaded regions in that shape was pretty good. I wonder if it will work for the next shape?

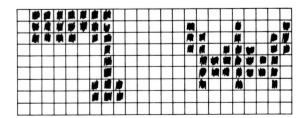

Figure 12–43 Finding the number of shaded squares in shapes on grid paper.

An extension of this activity is to use stacks of cubes with the understanding that there are no holes within a figure. These stacks may actually be constructed or they may be pictured. See Figure 12–44a for a picture. As a variation, a top view of the stack may be shown with the number of cubes in each stack indicated, as in Figure 12–44b. Again, encourage the children to estimate how many cubes are contained in the figure.

OBJECTIVE: to determine when certain vegetables will be ready to harvest.

2. Information for this activity may be easily gathered from garden or seed catalogs or from seed packets. Select two vegetables, such as radishes and beans. Explain to the children that three different kinds of radishes are ready to eat in 22, 25, and 28 days and that three different kinds of beans are ready to be picked in 50, 56, and 68 days.

If the seeds for the radishes are planted on April 20, when could you expect to have ripe radishes? If the bean seeds are planted on June 1, when could you expect to have ripe beans? If you wanted 56-day beans to be ripe on August 20, when should you plan to plant them? If you wanted 25-day radishes to be ripe on May 18, when should you plan to plant them?

This activity may be extended easily by selecting several kinds of vegetables for a garden that should all ripen on a particular day. When should each vegetable be planted? It is necessary to have calendars available for the children to use in seeking solutions to these problems.

OBJECTIVE: to use estimation and standard measurement on a scavenger hunt.

3. Divide the class into teams of three or four students. Give each team a set of scavenger hunt challenges. Here are a sample of such challenges:

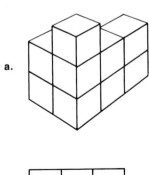

Figure 12–44 Finding the number of cubes in stacks.

- Find how many square meters of floor space each person in our classroom has.
- If there are 100 students in the gym, how many cubic meters does each student have?
- How many square meters does the school playground have?
- Find the number of meters you must walk from our classroom to the principal's office and back.
- Find two pairs of students whose combined weights in kilograms are the same.
- How many turtle steps (*Logo*) would it take to be 1 meter long?
- Find the temperature of the oven in degrees Celsius needed to bake a cake.
- Write a problem similar to these for other students to solve.

It is helpful to have a metric tape measure, a trundle wheel, a metric bathroom scale, a computer with *Logo*, and a metric oven thermometer to assist in the above tasks. Give each team three tasks to complete. The winning team is the first to successfully complete its assigned tasks.

Grades 6 – 8

OBJECTIVE: to solve problems related to amounts of liquid.

1. This is a virtual activity that may be found on Weblink 12–6. Two glasslike containers are shown, each with a designated capacity. The containers are unmarked. The problem is to pour liquids between the containers until a given target amount is reached. You may fill a container to the top, you may empty a container, and you may pour from one container to the other. There are many problems presented, and some impossible target amounts are given. This activity presents challenging problems that should raise questions and spark lively discussions.

ORGANIZING FOR MEASUREMENT TLC

Learning measurement is an active process. Practice should continue regularly throughout the school year. From the time children first experiment with measurement until they are fluent with measuring, their work should be active. Thus, much of the work will be done in individual and cooperative learning group settings. Young children will play individually or with a friend or two at the rice (or sand) table, pouring rice from container to container. At this stage, the experience is individual. Later, when a group of four children are given a particular task, such as ordering five containers

at the rice table from smallest to largest, cooperative learning will be the focus.

Several types of instruction, such as introductory activities, developing skills in telling time, using the geoboard to find perimeter, and debriefing after a cooperative learning activity, may be best presented in the whole-class setting. These are times when it is either most efficient or most appropriate to use the whole-class setting for sharing and discussion to take place. By and large, the whole-class setting is not used by teachers to tell children how to measure, except to summarize procedures that have come from the students' experiences.

Activities in which children work in small groups provide an opportunity for the children to experiment with measuring and, later, to use standard measuring tools. These small-group settings allow children to discuss with one another their findings, to compare their procedures, and to get feedback from one another regarding the various techniques that they used. As the teacher, you will be busy moving from group to group, monitoring the progress of the students, offering occasional suggestions, and answering questions that all members of the group may have. It is important for the teacher to be a presence without interfering with the interaction of the children. An exception would be when you interrupt a group to encourage the children to return to the task at hand or to modify the behavior of disruptive students. As you read the activities presented in this chapter, think about ways in which they can be successfully used in the small-group setting.

COMMUNICATING LEARNING OF MEASUREMENT CONCEPTS

As was the case in learning geometry, description in learning measurement is a focus that should be encouraged. Children should be invited to describe what they discovered and to see if others made the same discovery. They should compare and contrast procedures that they used during their activities. They should design instructions for other students to follow. These experiences may involve oral exchanges in which children can question one another and seek clarification. For example, the spokesperson for a small group may report how her group used a strip of paper to make a measuring tape and how they found objects in the room that were 10, 20, and 30 centimeters in length. Did other groups use the same procedures? Did they find the same or different objects? What made this task easy or hard?

Another type of important communication is describing specifically how a skill is performed. For example, a child may be asked to describe what he would expect a clock to look like if it showed that it is 10:30 in the morning. This may be a writing task or an oral task. A picture may help the student formulate how he might describe the clock face. Many of the skills involved in measuring include specific procedures that can be the focus of descriptive communication.

A learning-group journal can be used to record the work group members have done in measuring. Headings in such a journal might include "How We Made a Centimeter Ruler," "How to Measure Length," "Comparing Our Estimates with Our Actual Measures," "How to Tell Time," and "How We Solved the Volume Problem." The group recorder would be responsible for writing the ideas and descriptions of the group members. There should be an opportunity to share these entries with other class members. Individual group members may wish to write their own summaries of a particularly good description that could be included in the student's portfolio.

CONNECTING AND REPRESENTING LEARNING OF MEASUREMENT

Mr. Roberts was excited about the book and activities that he had discovered at a workshop (Weblink 12–7). The book, *Eat Your Math* (Harris and Jones, 1994), described nine food menus to be used on a monthly basis that integrate mathematics with language arts, music, and arts and crafts. Each menu was accompanied with complete instructions for setting up five stations requiring about 20 minutes each to finish. Each station is identified by an activity focused on a particular food and includes a listing of the mathematics objectives that are being met by the activity, the materials needed, the directions, and pages for a record book for the entire project.

The Pizza Menu was the project that Mr. Roberts decided to start with. His second/third grade blended classroom would enjoy this project. At the first station, students constructed a "favorite toppings" graph by decorating construction paper triangles and putting them on a large butcher paper graph. At the second station, students estimated the weight of a large store-bought pizza that Mr. Roberts had brought in. Then they recorded their estimates and the actual weight they found by using a scale. Next, the students each cut a piece of string that they thought would go around the pizza and then compared their estimates with the pizza. And, they constructed a graph using the strings to show if their estimates were shorter than, longer than, or almost the same as the circumference of the pizza. At the third station, students used individual-sized cardboard pizzas and traced their

circumferences on sheets of one-inch grid paper. Then, the students counted the number of square inches to determine the area of the individual pizzas. At the fourth station, students made individual pizzas using English muffin halves and assorted toppings. The pizzas were cooked in a toaster oven. Each student wrote his or her recipe and drew a picture of the pizza. At the fifth station, the students were given paper circles of various sizes and scissors. Their job was to first estimate and then determine by cutting how many pieces of pizza would result if they cut their circular pizza one, two, three, or four times.

After all of the students finished with the stations, Mr. Roberts had the students look at the graphs that were made and discuss what the graphs showed when all of the students' work was considered together. Both the students and Mr. Roberts were excited about how well the pizza project went and they were all eager to work on the Monster Sandwich Menu next month. The connection between mathematics and food was clear as well as the connections between math and language arts and math and arts and crafts.

Ms. Stahl had challenged her sixth- and seventh-grade students to look around their community over the weekend for bridges. She wanted her students to take pictures of the bridges or sketch the sides and tops of any bridges that they found. She knew that there were not many bridges in town but one of the best was a railroad bridge that could be found on the east side of town. She wanted to raise the awareness of the students about the kinds of shapes that were used in bridge building. When the students returned from the weekend, several had sketches of bridges and one student had a photograph of two bridges that she had found. Ms. Stahl provided magazines for the students to look through for pictures of bridges. As the students worked in groups they were asked to find the most common shape in their bridge pictures. In the ensuring discussion, the students noted that triangles were the most common and even if there were rectangles there were diagonal beams that make triangles out of the rectangles.

This investigation was the initiating activity for a 10-day project to culminate in the construction of toothpick bridges. Ms. Stahl was guided in the bridge project by a small publication, *Building Toothpick Bridges* (Pollard, 1985). On the first day of the project, there was a general introduction to bridge building, including some history of bridge development and a description of various types of bridges. On the second day, construction companies of five students were formed with specific roles to play. During the next few days, the bridges were designed and constructed. Finally, at the end of the project, all of the materials used by each group were judged and the bridges were tested to determine their strength. Besides building the bridges, an economy was established and all materials used in the bridge building had to be ordered and purchased and paid for by checks written by the accountant for the group. On the final day, photographs were taken of the bridges and awards were given to bridge companies for a variety of achievements. Then the strength of the bridges in Ms. Stahl's class was tested. The bridge that held the greatest weight held 2,500 grams.

The bridge project provided students the opportunity to connect ideas and skills of math, science, social studies, and art. The project helped the students view their world a bit differently and certainly raised the awareness of the students about bridges in their environment.

ASSESSING MEASUREMENT LEARNING

Assessing measurement concepts and skills requires clearly stated objectives. Most likely, the objectives will come from the section or chapter of the math textbook currently being used or from the mathematics program being used. The school district, school, or teacher may be responsible for determining whether the textbook or program objectives adequately represent measurement.

Throughout math textbooks, the teacher is provided with assessment procedures. There are pre-tests for chapters about measurement. There are mid-chapter check-ups to see if the students are understanding the measurement skills presented. There is a review of the measurement chapter content, and there is a chapter test. These assessments provide data regarding student proficiency in measurement. Both content and skills are assessed.

It will be crucial to provide additional assessment techniques for material not presented by the textbook. Measurement is best assessed by observing children measuring. Many of the activities suggested in this chapter are nearly impossible to include in a basal math textbook. To assess the activities, observe how the children perform various tasks and jot notes about the children's performances. Anecdotal records are an important part of the assessment process.

Assess measurement skills by asking children to make careful measurements. For example, have them cut a piece of string 17 centimeters long, make a rectangle with sides of 6 and 9 centimeters, respectively, or construct a hexagon on the geoboard with an area of 7 square units. Ask children to make a clay ball weighing 35 grams. Have them put 250 milliliters in a container. Ask them to measure an angle of 55 degrees. Have them find how much time elapses between lunch and dismissal time. Ask the children to report the temperature inside and outside the classroom. Your first-hand observations as children perform these tasks will provide you with valuable information regarding the children's measurement abilities. Projects such as recording weather information and using maps to plan a trip involve active and practical uses of measurement and should be part of the assessment of children's ability to measure.

SOMETHING FOR EVERYONE

Geometry and measurement are good areas for children who may not excel in abstract numerical work in mathematics. These areas are perfect for students who have strengths in the visual and spatial areas. Such children often excel when they are asked to show something on a geoboard or with pattern blocks or to estimate a measurement. They may not be able to give a verbal explanation of what they did, but they can often perform even better than the teacher or the children who are the best students in computation.

Verbal/linguistic learners may have difficulty in geometry and measurement. They will probably be good at defining geometric terms and stating metric conversions, but they may not be as good at spatial activities unless given a verbal explanation of what to do. They may have difficulty actually drawing figures or finding where to start measuring a given figure. They may be able to talk themselves through some spatial activities by reasoning aloud why two tangrams fit together in a certain way or how the faces of a polyhedron are shaped.

Bodily/kinesthetic learners excel when manipulating the geometry materials and the measuring tools. Most measuring requires some initial investigation with a ruler, a meterstick, a measuring cup, a clock, a thermometer, a protractor, or some other measuring tool. Geometry and measurement are topics that lend themselves to active learning and they are popular with students who perform well in active settings.

Promising students in geometry and measurement may not be the same students who excel in other areas of math. This may be disconcerting for students who are used to being star math students. They may be embarrassed to realize that they have no idea how tangrams fit together or where the line of symmetry is.

Students with different learning styles may learn from one another when they work in small groups. Try to develop a classroom atmosphere in which students feel free to ask each other for help. Encourage all types of learners to learn from one another. No one learns in strictly one mode, and everyone can improve skills in different areas.

Encourage promising students in geometry and measurement to go further in these areas. Let them combine geometry skills with skills in other subjects (such as art, mechanical drawing, wood-working, metal shop, or home economics) to create new applications for their learning. Students who are adept at tessellating, for example, may wish to study the artwork of Escher and create their own Escher-type drawings. One place to start is Weblink 12–8. The computer program *Shape Up!* (Sunburst) may motivate student interest in geometry. Students who are good at making scale drawings and at creating three-dimensional models from two-dimensional drawings may wish to make a scale drawing of the classroom and to create a model from a drawing of an ideal classroom.

Another good area for promising students in geometry is that of hypothesizing about geometric relationships. The computer program *The Geometric superSupposer* (Sunburst), is a good program for such capable students. It helps children explore geometric constructions and hypothesize about such things as the comparative lengths of diagonals of various quadrilaterals or the comparative areas of different types of triangles. In this way, students are encouraged to think like mathematicians—making hypotheses and trying to prove or disprove them. Children may do the same with a compass and straightedge as they learn to make their own constructions.

Another good computer program for promising students is *The Factory Deluxe* (Sunburst). It helps students develop inductive thinking in a visual mode as they design geometric products on a simulated machine assembly line. Programming in *Logo* and exploring using dynamic geometry with such programs as *The Geometer's Sketchpad* (Key Curriculum Press) on a computer or *Cabri Geometry II* (Texas Instruments) on a T1-92 are also excellent for students displaying talents in geometric areas.

Students who have difficulty in geometry and measurement may need to be encouraged not to give up. Students may make comments such as, "Tangrams are stupid. I can never do one of those puzzles. Why do we need to do them anyway?" Let these students start with simple tangrams using only two or three pieces or with some of the outlines drawn in and then gradually move on to more difficult puzzles. Be sure to give them tasks at which they can succeed, and let them note their progress.

Discuss with the whole class individuals who must have spatial abilities, such as architects, artists, astronauts, construction workers, electricians, engineers, mapmakers, mechanics, plumbers, and surgeons. Above all, make geometry and measurement enjoyable. Create experiences to help students move to the second van Hiele level in order to prepare them for later, more formal work in geometry.

FOR YOU AS A TEACHER: IDEAS FOR DISCUSSION AND YOUR PROFESSIONAL PORTFOLIO

This section is intended to provide you the opportunity to read, write, and reflect on key elements of this chapter. We list several discussion ideas. We hope that one or more of these ideas will prove interesting to you and that you will choose to investigate and write about the ideas. The results of your work should be considered as part of your professional portfolio. You might consider these two questions as guides for your writing: "What does the material in this chapter mean for you as a teacher?" or "How can what you are reading be translated into a teaching practice for you as a teacher?"

DISCUSSION IDEAS

1. A variety of measurement concepts have been introduced. After becoming familiar with them—for example, length and distance, weight and mass, time, and so on—discuss how you would describe the broader concept of measurement and how you could help students grasp the concept of measurement.

2. Using a geoboard, complete the activities described in the Measuring Area section. Then design five activities of your own that extend those presented. Share the activities with fellow students and help them understand what you have done.

3. Discuss the overriding theme of all of the activities that develop measurement fluency. The common elements of the activities represent the underlying message of teaching measurement.

4. Select a measurement skill such as measuring length, measuring time, or measuring temperature. Write a lesson plan for introducing or reintroducing that skill at grade 3 and at grade 6.

5. Read Billstein's (1998) article "You are Cleared to Land." Answer the questions that Billstein raises on page 454 of the article. Discuss how this article may be used in a middle-level classroom to interest the students in angle measurement and direction.

ADDITIONAL RESOURCES

REFERENCES

Barson, Alan, *Geoboard Activity Cards (Intermediate)*. Fort Collins, CO: Scott Resources, 1971.

———, *Geoboard Activity Cards (Primary)*. Fort Collins, CO: Scott Resources, 1972.

Billstein, Rick, "You Are Cleared to Land," *Mathematics Teaching in the Middle School*, 3, no. 7 (May 1998), 452–456.

Browning, Christine A., and Dwayne E. Channell, *Explorations: Graphing Calculator Activities for Enriching Middle School Mathematics*. Austin, TX: Texas Instruments, 1997.

Dolan, Winthrop W., *A Choice of Sundials*. Brattleboro, VT: S. Greene Press, 1975.

Guinness World Records, *Guinness World Records 2003*. London: Guinness World Records Ltd., 2003.

Harris, Holly, and Sharon Rose Jones, *Eat Your Math*. Corvallis, OR: Callan & Brooks, 1994.

Hiebert, James, "Why Do Some Children Have Trouble Learning Measurement Concepts?" *Arithmetic Teacher*, 31, no. 7 (March 1984), 19–24.

Kaster, Bernice, "The Role of Measurement Applications," *Arithmetic Teacher*, 36, no. 6 (February 1989), 40–46.

Learning Resources. *Intermediate Geoboard Activity Book: Grades 4–6*. Deerfield, IL: Learning Resources, 1990.

Learning Resources. *Primary Geoboard Activity Book: Grades K–3*. Deerfield, IL: Learning Resources, 1990.

National Council of Teachers of Mathematics, *Principles and Standards for School Mathematics*. Reston, VA: NCTM, 2000.

Piaget, Jean, Barbel Inhelder, and Alina Szemiuska, *The Child's Conception of Geometry*. New York: Basic Books, 1960.

Pollard, Jeanne, *Building Toothpick Bridges*. Palo Alto, CA: Dale Seymour, 1985.

Querin, Tari, "Picture Measuring Tapes," *The Oregon Mathematics Teacher* (May/June 1998), 16–19.

Shaw, Jean, "Mathematical Scavenger Hunts," *Arithmetic Teacher*, 31, no. 7 (March 1984), 9–12.

Sime, Mary, *A Child's Eye View*. New York: Harper & Row, 1973.

Thompson, Charles S., and John Van deWalle, "Learning about Rules and Measuring," *Arithmetic Teacher*, 32, no. 8 (April 1985), 8–12.

Varma, Ved P., and Phillip Williams, eds., *Piaget, Psychology and Education*. Itasca, IL: Peacock, 1976.

Welchman-Tischler, Rosamond, *How to Use Children's Literature to Teach Mathematics*. Reston, VA: National Council of Teachers of Mathematics, 1992.

Wilgus, Wendy, and Lisa Pizzuto, *Exploring the Basics of Geometry with Cabri*. Austin, TX: Texas Instruments, 1997.

CHILDREN'S LITERATURE

Greer, Gery, and Bob Ruddick, *Max and Me and the Time Machine*. New York: HarperCollins Children's Books, 1983.

Macken, Walter, *The Flight of the Doves*. New York: Simon & Schuster Books for Young Readers, 1992.

Mora, Pat, *A Birthday Basket for Tia*. New York: MacMillan, 1992.

Myller, Rolf, *How Big Is a Foot?* New York: Atheneum, 1962.

TECHNOLOGY

Key Curriculum Press, *The Geometer's Sketchpad*. Emeryville, CA: Key Curriculum Press, 2001. (software)

Sunburst, *The Factory Deluxe*. Pleasantville, NY: Sunburst Technology, 1998. (software)

Sunburst, *The Geometric superSupposer*. Pleasantville, NY: Sunburst Technology, 1993. (software)

Sunburst, *Shape Up!* Pleasantville, NY: Sunburst Technology, 1997. (software)

Texas Instruments, Cabri Geometry II. Temple, TX: Texas Instruments, 1994. (software)

WEBLINKS

Weblink 12–1: NCTM Electronic Example: Understanding the Pythagorean Relationship Using Interactive Figures. http://www.standards.nctm.org/document/eexamples/chap6/6.5/index.htm

Weblink 12–2: NCTM Electronic Example: Developing Estimation Strategies by Making Connections among Number, Geometry, Measurement, and Data Concepts: Estimating Scoops. http://www.standards.nctm.org/document/eexamples/chap4/4.6/index.htm

Weblink 12–3: NCTM Electronic Example: Learning about Length, Perimeter, Area, and Volume of Similar Objects. http://www.standards.nctm.org/document/eexamples/chap6/6.3/index.htm

Weblink 12–4: NCTM Illumination lessons linking length, perimeter, area, and volume. http://illuminations.nctm.org/lessonplans/6–8/linking/index.html

Weblink 12–5: NCTM electronic example featuring Collecting and Examining Weather Data. http://www.standards.nctm.org/document/eexamples/chap5/5.5/index.htm

Weblink 12–6: Fill and Pour activity from the National Library of Virtual Manipulative for Interactive Mathematics. http://matti.usu.edu/nlvm/nav/category_g_3_t_4.html

Weblink 12–7: Science and Mathematics Consortium for Northwest Schools, Potlatch Project, Eat Your Math. http://www.col-ed.org/smcnws/potlatch/or3.html

Weblink 12–8: A gallery of the work of M. C. Escher. http://www.cs.unc.edu/~davemc/Pic/Escher/

TEACHING AND LEARNING DATA ANALYSIS AND PROBABILITY

GUIDING QUESTIONS

As you read the following pages, consider these guiding questions:

1. What is the place of data analysis and probability in the elementary and middle grades mathematics curriculum?

2. Why is it important for children to be able to sort and classify objects according to their attributes? What are some activities that you might do and materials that you might use to help them develop these skills? How might tree, Venn, and Carroll diagrams be used in this development?

3. What types of charts, tables, and graphs might be used to display data, and how do you decide which is most appropriate?

4. How might you use technology, including computers and graphing calculators, as students learn to organize, display, and analyze data?

5. What are some common misconceptions students might have as they learn data analysis, probability, statistics, and graphing concepts, and how might you help them construct the correct concepts?

6. What are some of the ways in which we use data analysis and probability in our everyday lives and in other subject areas, and how might you use these in your mathematics lessons on these concepts?

NCTM Principles and Standards for School Mathematics

Data Analysis and Probability

Instructional programs from prekindergarten through grade 12 should enable all students to:

Formulate questions that can be addressed with data and collect, organize, and display relevant data to answer them

Pre-K to 2

• pose questions and gather data about themselves and their surroundings;
• sort and classify objects according to their attributes and organize data about the objects;
• represent data using concrete objects, pictures, and graphs.

Grades 3–5

• design investigations to address a question and consider how data-collection methods affect the nature of the data set;
• collect data using observations, surveys, and experiments;
• represent data using tables and graphs such as line plots, bar graphs, and line graphs;
• recognize the differences in representing categorical and numerical data.

Grades 6–8

• formulate questions, design studies, and collect data about a characteristic shared by two populations or different characteristics within one population;
• select, create, and use appropriate graphical representations of data, including histograms, box plots, and scatterplots.

Select and use appropriate statistical methods to analyze data

Pre-K to 2

• describe parts of the data and the set of data as a whole to determine what the data show.

NCTM (2000), pp. 108, 176, 248. Reprinted by permission.

Grades 3–5

• describe the shape and important features of a set of data and compare related data sets, with an emphasis on how the data are distributed;
• use measures of center, focusing on the median, and understand what each does and does not indicate about the data set;
• compare different representations of the same data and evaluate how well each representation shows important aspects of the data.

Grades 6–8

• find, use, and interpret measures of center and spread, including mean and interquartile range;
• discuss and understand the correspondence between data sets and their graphical representations, especially histograms, stem-and-leaf plots, box plots, and scatterplots.

Develop and evaluate inferences and predictions that are based on data

Pre-K to 2

• discuss events related to students' experiences as likely or unlikely.

Grades 3–5

• propose and justify conclusions and predictions that are based on data and design studies to further investigate the conclusions or predictions.

Grades 6–8

• use observations about differences between two or more samples to make conjectures about the populations from which the samples were taken;
• make conjectures about possible relationships between two characteristics of a sample on the basis of scatterplots of the data and approximate lines of fit;
• use conjectures to formulate new questions and plan new studies to answer them.

My Math Journal

Find a partner and a pair of dice and play the following game. Roll both dice and add the two amounts shown together. If the total is odd, you get one point and tally it in the box below. If the total is even, your partner gets a point. The first player to get 10 points is the winner. Keep score below.

GAME ONE

Odd Total	
Even Total	

GAME TWO

Odd Total	
Even Total	

GAME THREE

Odd Total	
Even Total	

REFLECTIONS AND REFINEMENT: *After you have completed this task, compare your work with that of some of your classmates. Did their game results match yours? What does this indicate about the fairness of the game? How does this experimental probability match the theoretical or mathematical probability? Write your hypotheses and discoveries here.*

It is impossible to pick up a newspaper, listen to the radio or television, or browse the Internet without noticing the extensive use of numerical and graphic information. Computers have made it easier than ever before to handle and report large amounts of data. It is therefore critical that all students be able to analyze and understand data and the many ways that it is reported using statistics, tables, charts, and graphs.

Even very young children can begin to make sense of the world as they collect, organize, and interpret data. They might begin with simple diagrams (Venn, Carroll, and tree), charts, tables, graphs (object, picture, and bar), and line plots. As students get older, they should learn to organize and interpret data by constructing and reading more complex diagrams, charts, tables, graphs (circle and line), and plots (box and stem). They should also learn to plot and interpret points, lines, and curves on a Cartesian coordinate system. The emphasis throughout should be on making sense of the data and using that information to make informed decisions.

Children should be on the lookout for uses of probability, statistics, and graphs in their everyday lives. We are all familiar with probability from listening to the weather report each day. If there is a 90-percent chance of rain, we do not want to forget to take our umbrellas. If we buy a lottery ticket, we want to know our chances of winning a million dollars. Any type of scientific experiment depends upon the laws of probability. Drugs are tested to determine if the recovery rate improves when the drug is used and to determine if there are any harmful side effects. Businesses use probability for everything from determining the optimum number of checkout lines to quality control on an assembly line. Insurance company officials use probability to set their rates. Wildlife experts tag wild animals and then use probability to determine the number of animals in an area by looking at the ratio of the number of tagged animals spotted to the number of untagged animals spotted.

In many cases, statistics and graphs are used in conjunction with probability. The statistics for a sports player are analyzed to help determine the probability of having a winning team if that player is hired. Statistics are compiled from the results of polls taken to help businesses plan for the future, and probabilities are determined for the success of the business if certain changes are made. Politicians hire experts in the area of statistics to help them decide the best strategies for winning an election.

An intelligent consumer in today's world must be able to decipher sometimes conflicting sources of information. It is important for children to know some of the fundamental concepts of probability and data analysis as well as how to interpret the charts and graphs used to describe those ideas.

Like other topics, data analysis, probability, statistics, and graphing should be taught using manipulative materials. Children should have numerous chances to perform experiments and collect data to give them practical experience with these topics. Some of the materials include dice, coins, cards, colored cubes, chips, spinners, graph paper, squares, and objects for making concrete graphs.

Children also should make full use of calculators and computers when exploring these topics. Calculators and computers give children the ability to handle more data than they could handle with paper-and-pencil calculations alone. Graphing calculators allow students to graph various types of information and to explore the effects of changing different variables. Computer programs include those for teaching probability, statistics, and graphing, as well as simulations that give children the opportunity to experiment and make predictions.

MAKING SENSE OF DATA ANALYSIS AND PROBABILITY

With the proliferation of computers and the increased availability of all types of numerical information, data analysis and probability concepts have received growing emphasis in the elementary and middle grades mathematics curriculum. The development of these concepts should begin before any formal schooling with sorting and classifying information and build throughout the students' school careers with increasing sophistication.

The NCTM *Curriculum and Evaluation Standards* noted the importance of data analysis and probability topics in 1989, and in 2000, this emphasis was increased in the NCTM *Principles and Standards for School Mathematics*. "The Data Analysis and Probability Standard" in *Principles and Standards for School Mathematics* (NCTM, 2000) is an affirmation of a fundamental goal of the mathematics curriculum: to develop critical thinking and sound judgment based on data. These skills are essential not only for a select few but for every informed citizen and consumer. Staggering amounts of information confront us in almost every aspect of contemporary life, and being able to ask good questions, use data wisely, evaluate claims that are based on data, and formulate defensible conclusions in the face of uncertainty have become basic skills in our information age (Sheffield et al., 2002).

Observing, Inferring, Comparing, and Classifying

Many early mathematical concepts build on preschool children's abilities to make observations and inferences about the world around them. Young children should be encouraged to describe objects both orally and pictorially and to make comparisons, noting similarities and differences between objects, using all five of their senses. As children gather information about the world, they should describe what is being observed and inferred. Language is a powerful tool for gathering and disseminating information, so children should be encouraged to talk to each other and to the teacher while they are engaged in these activities. The activities presented here are generally sequenced from simplest to most complex. Grade levels are listed as a general guide. Choose activities that best meet the needs of your students and adapt them as you see fit.

A C T I V I T I E S

Pre-Kindergarten – Grade 2

OBJECTIVE: to develop the ability to observe and describe using the five senses.

1. Choose several objects that are safe to touch, smell, and taste, such as sugar, fruit, crackers, and cookies. Put one object in a clean bag and ask one child to feel the object without looking inside. Have the child describe what he feels. Then let him sniff the object without peeking and describe what he smells. Encourage the child to take a small bite and to describe the taste. Shake the bag and ask the child to describe what he hears. Finally, let the child look at the object and describe what he sees. Allow the children to bring in objects to place in the bag.

OBJECTIVE: to develop inference skills based on the sense of hearing.

2. Have the children close their eyes and listen to familiar sounds, such as a door closing, someone writing on the board with chalk, and a chair that squeaks. Let the children describe what they hear and make a guess as to what it is. Have them make noises for the other children to guess.

OBJECTIVE: to develop inference skills based on the sense of touch.

3. Let the children feel several geometric figures placed in a "feely box" and guess what they are. See if they can fit a figure into a frame of the same size and shape without looking. Children may be able to match the shape to the frame without knowing the name of the shape.

OBJECTIVE: to develop inference skills based on the senses of sight and touch.

4. Outline several familiar objects. Have the children guess which object matches each outline. Give the children the objects to fit onto the outlines to see if their guesses are correct. Let the children make outlines of their own to exchange with each other.

OBJECTIVE: to distinguish between observations and inferences.

5. Repeat the activity for developing the ability to observe, but let the children guess what the object is at each step. Discuss the difference between observing using the senses and guessing based on observations.

For all of the activities, be sure to discuss with the children the strategies they used to make their guesses. They can learn from each other better ways to make inferences.

Once children learn to observe and describe objects, they should begin to compare two or more objects. Often, children begin to compare objects even before they know the names of the objects. They may say that they want more or fewer even if they do not know the name of what they have. They may be able to tell you what is the same or different about two objects whether or not they know the names of the objects. Children might enjoy reading or listening to the book *Angus Thought He Was Big* (Graham, 1991). This gives you a chance to talk about whether children understand that comparisons do not always remain constant. Children themselves may be small when compared to adults but large when compared to a favorite doll. A child may describe a set as having more when it really has fewer but larger objects. Teachers should assist children in developing difficult comparison concepts. Being able to compare individual objects, and later sets of objects, will help children when they are deciding whether 3 is more or less than 5.

A C T I V I T I E S

Pre-Kindergarten – Grade 2

OBJECTIVE: to compare two or more objects using all of the senses.

1. Discuss the terms *alike* and *different* with the children. Then collect a group of objects from the children. Select two objects at random and ask the children to list all of the ways that the objects are alike or different. List their responses on the chalkboard or on a large sheet of paper. Encourage the children to use all of their senses.

2. Play line-up with the children. One child is the leader. The next child in line must name one way in which he or she is like the leader and one way in which he or she is different. Each subsequent child then names one likeness and one difference between himself or herself and the child directly before him or her. After playing the game, ask the children to tell you what *alike* and *different* mean. Encourage them to suggest other objects that they might use to play the same game.

After children learn to compare objects, they should begin to categorize, or classify, them. **Classifying** is the process of grouping or sorting objects into classes or categories according to some systematic scheme or principle. The children must use specific properties of the objects to be classified and must make comparisons between objects in order to decide on their proper categories. Students should be encouraged to construct their own categories and not just match objects to labels or categories about which the teacher has decided.

The groups into which objects are sorted are called sets. A **well-defined set** is a collection of objects defined so that given any object, it is possible to determine without question whether or not that object is in the collection. Classification systems also serve as a means to describe an object that is not given. By observing the position in a classification scheme the object would occupy, children can give the properties of the object.

As in other types of mathematical problems, children must find the missing part. This requires that they analyze the structure of the problem much as they will later analyze the structure of a numerical equation. Carpenter (1985) has noted that children naturally attend to the structure of a problem and that expert problem solvers put more emphasis on structure than less capable problem solvers. The activities in this section are designed to help children focus on essential structures or relationships.

Young children should begin by sorting objects that differ in only one way, such as shape or color. Use structured materials such as attribute blocks or People Pieces or use collections of materials found around the home or classroom such as buttons, shells, or baseball cards. **Attribute blocks** are usually made from either wood or plastic and vary in attributes such as color, size, shape, and thickness. Each set of blocks like the one in Figure 13–1 contains only one block with each possible combination of attributes. For example, a set of blocks with two sizes (large and small), three colors (red, blue, and green), and three shapes (circle, square, and triangle) would have the following 18 pieces:

large, red circle	small, red circle
large, red square	small, red square
large, red triangle	small, red triangle
large, blue circle	small, blue circle
large, blue square	small, blue square
large, blue triangle	small, blue triangle
large, green circle	small, green circle
large, green square	small, green square
large, green triangle	small, green triangle

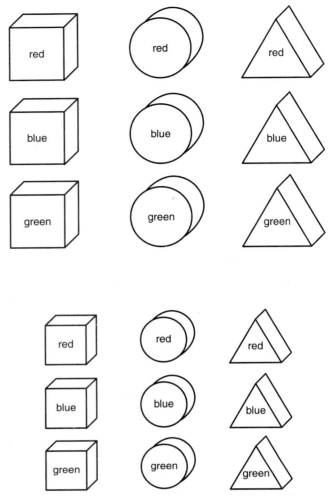

Figure 13–1 Set of Attribute blocks.

Notice the pattern in the listing of pieces. Other sets may have more or fewer shapes, colors, or sizes and may add other variables, such as thickness. You may make a set of attribute shapes of your own by copying the set in Appendix B onto colored construction paper or posterboard or by using the attribute shapes die to punch out pieces of railroad board with a machine such as the Ellison letter machine. These attribute shapes are used for several of the activities in this chapter.

People Pieces is a set of attribute materials consisting of sixteen wooden or plastic tiles with a different person stamped onto each one. The people are of two heights (tall and short), two weights (stout and thin), two colors (red and blue), and two sexes (male and female). List the 16 possible combinations for yourself. Other structured sets you might use include the Animal Tiles from Creative Publications and Zogs from the Addison-Wesley *Explorations 2* book.

The following activities do not require the purchase of any commercial materials.

A C T I V I T I E S

Pre-Kindergarten – Grade 2

OBJECTIVE: to sort materials according to one property.

1. Read *The Button Box* by Margarette Reid (1990) and then give the children a set of buttons that are similar except that some are black and some are white. Ask them to sort the buttons into two piles. Encourage them to create their own classification schemes. How many different ways can they sort the buttons?

2. Give the children a large magnet and a group of materials, some of which are made of iron and some of which are not. Ask the children to use the magnet to classify the materials according to whether or not they are attracted by the magnet.

3. Give the children a basin of water and a variety of materials that will not be harmed when they are placed in the water. Ask the children to sort the materials. Put everything that will float in one pile and everything that will not float in another.

Let children collect their own sets of materials and create their own classification schemes. Children may trade materials with each other to see if they all define the sets in the same ways. Encourage them to classify in many different ways and to discuss their methods of classifying with you and with each other.

After the children are proficient at classifying objects into two categories, the activities should be made more difficult. You may increase the number of materials to be classified, increase the number of categories into which the materials are grouped, or increase the abstraction of the categories, such as classifying pictures of people as happy or sad rather than as male or female. All of these activities should involve categories that are mutually exclusive.

As children become more mature in their reasoning abilities, they can begin to categorize materials into overlapping categories. For instance, children may group a set of toy vehicles by placing all of the trucks in one group and all of the red vehicles in another. For some children, it will be difficult to decide what to do with the red trucks. The teacher should provide opportunities for the children to construct the concept such that they can overlap the circles as shown in Figure 13–2 and then place the red trucks in the intersection of the two circles. The teacher may need to ask a few leading questions to create disequilibrium in the children. For example, if the children are content placing all of the red trucks in the circle for the trucks, the teacher might ask why they are not in the red circle. The following activities

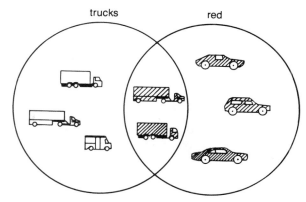

Figure 13 – 2 Venn diagram for organizing intersecting sets of objects.

encourage children to use slightly more complicated classification schemes and to create problems as well as solve them.

A C T I V I T I E S

Pre-Kindergarten – Grade 2

OBJECTIVE: to classify using multiple parallel categories.

1. Ask the children to cut out pictures of animals from magazines or newspapers or to draw different animals. Then have them classify the animals in different ways. They might classify them by type of animal, type of food they eat, or according to their natural habitats, such as grassland, forest, and desert.

2. Give the children a set of buttons or toys with a number of properties or attributes. Ask the children to sort the materials into three categories. See if they can sort the materials into four or more categories. Ask them to tell you the property or properties of each category and how they made their decisions to classify the properties.

Grades 3 – 5

OBJECTIVE: to develop the skills of making comparisons in other subject areas

1. In a social studies class when studying different regions of the United States, ask students to make a list comparing and contrasting two regions of the country. One column of the list should contain everything students can think of that is alike about the two regions and the other column, everything that is different between the two. A similar activity could be done when comparing such things as the Revolutionary War and the Civil War, or democracy and theocracy, or President Lincoln and President Washington.

2. Use the book, *The Magic School Bus inside the Earth* by Cole (1987) to introduce students to different types of rocks. Ask students to collect rocks in the schoolyard or at home, and bring them into the classroom to make comparisons. Using a list of characteristics of various kinds of rocks, ask students to classify the rocks in various ways.

After the children have set up classification systems, they should be able to abstract properties that a group of objects have in common. **Abstracting** may be thought of as the reverse of classification. Children should be able to look at a set of objects that have been classified and discover the similarity among the elements of the set. They should be able to summarize this similarity in a single statement or rule. Some examples of this type of activity follow.

A C T I V I T I E S

Pre-Kindergarten – Grade 2

OBJECTIVE: to abstract a property of a set.

1. Select a small group of children who are alike in some way; for example, all are wearing tennis shoes, have blonde hair, or are wearing glasses. Do not tell the class how the children are alike. A child who thinks he or she knows the attribute chosen may name a child who has not yet been chosen but who also has the given attribute. When all of the children with the given attribute have been named, the children may guess the attribute. Select one of the children to name a new group of children with a new secret attribute.

2. From a set of the attribute shapes from Appendix B, secretly choose an attribute such as small objects. Pick three or four shapes that have the attribute. Let the children guess which of the other shapes belong in the set. After all of the shapes have been chosen, ask the children to identify the attribute they all have in common. Let the children take turns choosing their own sets. Allow the children to make the game more complex by choosing the union or intersection of two or more attributes such as large and red, or small and triangular.

OBJECTIVE: to identify the attributes of two sets and their intersection.

3. Secretly choose two intersecting attributes from a set of People Pieces, such as male and tall. Set up two overlapping circles, and place one piece of each type in the correct section as shown in Figure 13–3.

Let the children take turns picking up a piece and guessing in which section the piece belongs. If the child guesses the correct section, leave the piece in that section. If the guess is incorrect, another child may guess. Don't forget that some pieces will not fit into any section. For example, in Figure 13–3, the label for the

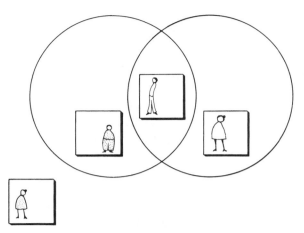

Figure 13–3 Venn diagram puzzle with People Pieces.

left circle might be male and the lable for the right circle might be tall; short females would not go inside either circle. Continue until all of the pieces are placed correctly. Ask the children to identify the proper labels of each section. Have the children describe the pieces in the intersection. Ask the children how they knew where to place each piece and why some pieces are outside the sets. Discuss and check for understanding.

If the activity is too difficult, let the children play with nonintersecting circles. If the children are doing well with two intersecting circles, try the activity with three circles. After the children understand the concept of abstracting attributes of intersecting sets, let them develop their own problems with other attribute materials.

Understanding Probability Concepts

> Ideas from probability serve as a foundation to the collection, description, and interpretation of data. (NCTM, 2002, p. 51)

Many concepts of probability can build on the students' abilities to organize and make sense of data and other information from the world around them.

Probability can be defined as the measure of likeliness of a particular event occurring. Many of the concepts of probability involve terms the children may hear frequently. These include *impossible, certain, uncertain, likely, equally likely, unlikely, random, sample space, independent, biased, unbiased,* and *random sample*. Children should be given opportunities to become familiar with these terms and their meanings. The following activities may be used to introduce young children to the terminology and to give them a chance to apply the terms to daily events.

	trials										
	1	2	3	4	5	6	7	8	9	10	total
H											
T											

Figure 13–4 Tally chart to record flips of head and tails.

ACTIVITIES

Grades Pre-K–2

OBJECTIVE: to define and apply the following terms: certain, impossible, uncertain, likely, and unlikely.

1. Discuss with the children events with which they are familiar and ask whether they can be certain that the events will happen. Are there some things you are positive will happen and some you are positive will not happen? Events that we are positive will happen are called **certain,** and events that cannot happen are called **impossible.** At other times, we are **uncertain** whether or not something will happen.

Give the children a list of statements and ask them to sort them into three piles labeled "Certain," "Uncertain," and "Impossible." Use statements such as the following:

- Tomorrow, it will rain.
- Jane will be here every day next week.
- I will get 100% on my next spelling test.
- The teacher is older than every child in the room.
- Tomorrow, we shall all go to the moon.
- Tonight, the sun will shine brightly at midnight.
- If I flip a coin, it will land either heads or tails.

As the children classify the statements, discuss with them the reasons for the classifications. When they have finished, ask them to classify the uncertain statements further as either **likely** or **unlikely.** Will all children agree on whether or not an event is likely? Is it possible for two children to have different answers and for both to be correct? As children discuss these questions, you will get an insight into their conceptions and misconceptions about early probability concepts. When misconceptions appear, lead the children to activities and experiments to help them correct those ideas. Encourage the students to brainstorm a list of synonyms for the terms *certain, impossible, likely,* and *unlikely.* Ask them to make their own list of statements to classify into these categories.

After children have discussed the probability of weather-related events occurring, they may enjoy reading *Cloudy with a Chance of Meatballs* by Barrett (1978) or *It's Raining Cats and Dogs* by Branley (1987). They might wish to write their own stories with impossible events and discuss the humor in commonly heard phrases.

OBJECTIVE: to develop the concepts of sample space, independent, equally likely, fair, random, unbiased, and biased through use of an experiment and tallies.

2. The **sample space** for a problem consists of all the possible outcomes. The sample space for flipping a coin is heads and tails. Ask the children to predict whether the coin will land with the head or the tail showing if you flip it. Flip the coin and show the children the result. Ask the children to predict the outcomes of several flips of the coin.

Discuss with the children whether one flip seems to have any influence on the next flip. Events are called **independent** if one event has no effect on another. Give each child a penny and ask the children to make a tally of the heads and the tails out of 10 flips, using the chart in Figure 13–4.

Tell the children to record the total number of heads and the total number of tails out of the 10 trials. Use calculators to find the total number of heads and the total number of tails for the whole class. Are the totals close to each other? Can you say that heads or tails are more likely?

If two events have the same probability, then we say that they are **equally likely.** We can say that the coin is a **fair** one if it does not favor either heads or tails. We can also say that heads and tails come up **randomly.** This means that heads and tails have an equal chance of coming up. We may also say that the coin is **unbiased.** It does not favor heads more than tails or vice versa. Use these terms frequently with the children as you perform experiments. Ask the children to define the terms in their own words after they have had a chance to experiment.

Ask the children if the coin would be **biased** if they dropped it flat on the table instead of flipping it. Would the coin be biased if they flipped a quarter instead of a penny? Would the coin be biased if you flipped a play coin with two heads instead of a head and a tail?

Children may wish to explore other questions, such as how many times a certain number of heads came up out of 10 flips of a fair coin. Which number of heads was most likely? Which was least likely? What about tails? Let children propose other questions and experiments of their own and help them tally the results.

Many calculators make it possible to simulate coin flips or other experimental data with equally likely outcomes, and students enjoy using these to quickly carry out a large number of trials. If you have calculators with this capability available, encourage students to compare the results of actually flipping a coin to the results obtained using a calculator. How close are each of these results to the students' predictions?

As children get older, they should begin to explore other areas of probability. They may look at events with more than two possible outcomes, and they may begin to use rational numbers to describe probability. The **probability** of an event is

the number of favorable outcomes
_____
the total number of outcomes

If an event is certain, the probability is 1 because all possible outcomes are favorable. If an event is impossible, the probability is 0 because there are no favorable outcomes. All uncertain events have a probability some where between 0 and 1. An event with a larger probability is more likely than an event with a smaller probability. The following activities give a few ideas for teaching these concepts to students in the intermediate and middle grades and for expanding on other concepts introduced earlier in the primary grades.

A C T I V I T I E S

Grades 3–5 and Grades 6–8

OBJECTIVE: to develop the concept of assigning a numerical probability to equally likely events.

1. Show the children a spinner with three colors as in Figure 13–5.

The sample space in this experiment is red, blue, and yellow. Ask the children whether landing on one color is more likely than landing on another color. Spin the spinner a few times to demonstrate that it is a fair spinner; that is, that it does not get stuck on any of the colors. Tell the children that if the spinner is fair, and if each color is equally likely, they can write the probability of landing on any one color as

the number of favorable outcomes
_____
the total number of outcomes

If you wish to know the probability of getting yellow, the number of favorable outcomes is 1 because there is only one yellow section. The total number of outcomes is 3 because there are three congruent sections altogether. Therefore, the probability of getting yellow is $\frac{1}{3}$.

Ask the children to predict the number of times they could expect to get yellow if they spin the spinner 30 times. Spin the spinner 30 times and record the resulting color each time. How many yellows did you get? Was the actual number close to the prediction?

Ask the children to find the probability of landing on the blue section. What is the probability of landing on the red section? What should you get if you add the probability of the yellow section to the probability of the red section and the probability of the blue section?

Try the experiment using different colors and different numbers of spins. Can you find a formula for predicting the number of times a color will come up? Multiply the probability of the color by the number of spins. Will this always give you the exact number of times the color will come up in the actual experiment? What happens if you add together the probabilities of all the possible outcomes? Will you ever get an answer larger than 1? Ask the children if the spinner would be biased if each child were allowed to turn the spinner so it pointed at her or his favorite color.

Explore the many virtual manipulatives at Weblink 13–1. There are several lesson plans and virtual manipulatives here for exploring probability concepts, including some interesting games and activities using spinners with changeable colored sections. Using this site, students can quickly simulate a large number of spins and compare their experimental probability to their hypotheses about the number of times a spinner should land on a particular color.

2. After the children feel comfortable making predictions with the spinner, try a different material, such as a deck of playing cards. Ask the children to predict the number of times they would draw a black card, a diamond, or a king out of 20 draws. What is the sample space each time? Which is more likely: a black card, a diamond, or a king? Let the children suggest other questions. Discuss with them their strategies and reasoning as they make predictions and perform experiments.

OBJECTIVE: to distinguish between probable and certain events and between independent and dependent events.

3. Put the name of each child in the class on a 3-by-5 card and put all the names in a box. Predict the number of times a girl's name will be drawn out of a given number of draws when you put the name back in the box after each draw. Can you be certain that your own name will be drawn in 10 draws if the name is replaced after each draw? Can you be certain that a girl's name will be drawn in 10 draws? Can you be certain that a girl's name will be drawn in 100 draws?

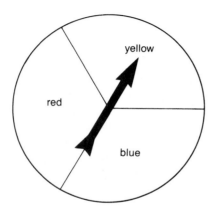

Figure 13–5   A spinner with three equally likely colors.

Even though it is very likely that a girl's name will be drawn, you cannot be certain. It is possible to draw only boys' names if the name is replaced after every draw.

Does it make a difference if the name is not replaced after each draw? Some children may wish to research the difference between dependent and independent events.

As mentioned earlier, if events are independent, the outcome of one event has no effect on the outcome of another event. If the first event does affect the next one, the events are said to be **dependent.** Drawing cards with no replacement involves dependent events, while drawing cards with replacement involves independent events. Ask the children to explain why this is true. If you were drawing names of the class members without replacing the name each time, can you be certain that you will eventually draw a girl's name?

OBJECTIVE: to develop the concept of a random sample.

4. A **random sample** is a sample drawn in such a way that every member of the sample space has an equal chance of being chosen. Random sampling is often used in taking surveys when it is not feasible to survey every possible person or in designing experiments when it is not possible to use every person or event of interest.

Discuss with the children how they might take a random sample of marbles from an opaque bag. Would the sample be random if they were allowed to look into the bag while choosing a marble of a particular color? Would it be random if each child was allowed to choose a marble of his or her favorite color? Would it be random if all of the red marbles were on the top and the blue ones were on the bottom? How could the ideas of random sampling be extended to the activity of taking a random sample of students in the school for a survey?

Put 5 red marbles and 45 blue marbles in an opaque bag. Tell the children you are going to take a random sample of 10 marbles from the bag and use the sample to try to predict the total numbers of red and blue marbles. Let them know that there are a total of 50 marbles and that there are only red and blue marbles. Draw 10 marbles from the bag and record the results. Ensure randomness by replacing the marble each time, blindfolding the person drawing, and shaking up the marbles in the bag.

If you drew 3 red marbles and 7 blue marbles, what would be your prediction for the total numbers of red and blue marbles in the bag? Would you trust your prediction based on the results of only 10 draws? What if you repeated the 10 draws several times?

You and the children can create or find as many interesting probability activities as time permits. Some print and electronic sources of activity ideas for the topics in this chapter are listed in the references at the end of the chapter.

Understanding Statistics Concepts

Statistics are very often reported using rational numbers. Some of the concepts from statistics are quite abstract and should be reserved for higher grades, but children should be introduced to the basic concepts in the primary grades.

Statistics is the collecting and reporting of data. With all the information collected and reported in the world today, we need to have a way of organizing and describing it so that it is understandable. This collection, tabulation, organization, presentation, and interpretation of data is called **descriptive statistics.** This is the type of statistics most suited for study by elementary students.

The study of statistics and probability is a means of making predictions. The ability to draw inferences and make predictions based on the data collected is studied in **inferential statistics.** Inferential statistics is often not presented until college, but with the proliferation of data and computers in the information age, we are now more likely to see inferential statistics presented in middle and high school. Our focus here, however, is descriptive statistics and ways of presenting the subject to elementary and middle school students.

Tables and graphs are often used to describe the data collected (graphs are discussed in the next section). In addition, there are at least two ideas from the area of statistics you should present to elementary and middle school students; these are the concepts of measures of central tendency and measures of dispersion.

Measures of central tendency are ways of reporting data in the middle. Perhaps the most familiar of these measures is the arithmetic average, or the **mean.** The mean is frequently referred to simply as the **average,** the number found by adding together all the values of interest and dividing by the total number of addends.

Friel (1998) discusses two strategies for helping students visualize the mean: using the "fair-share" model and using the balance model. In the fair-share model, for a problem such as finding the mean number of pets in the class, all the pets are combined and then redistributed so that each student has the same number of pets. In the balance model, the mean is the value about which all the data balances by looking at how far from the mean each student's number of pets is and balancing the sum of the differences.

Another measure of central tendency is the median. The **median** is the value found by listing the values of interest in order from the highest to the lowest and taking the one in the middle if there is an odd number or averaging the two middle scores if there is an even number. The **mode,** another measure of central tendency, is the most frequently reported value.

The game Plop It! on Weblink 13–2 allows students to graph their information using a simple bar graph and investigate mean, median, and mode. Students are fascinated as they watch the changes in mean, median, and mode as information is added and subtracted from a bar graph. Students are encouraged to analyze what happens to the measures of central tendency as they change data in the bar graph and to construct graphs that will give them the measures that they want.

Measures of dispersion tell you how spread out scores are. The simplest measure of dispersion is the **range,** which is the difference between the highest score and the lowest score. Statisticians use several other measures of dispersion such as standard deviation, but they are generally too complex for children in elementary or middle grades.

A few suggestions for teaching some elementary statistics concepts follow. You may find that your younger students can understand the concepts when they are presented on a concrete level.

A C T I V I T I E S

Grades 3–5

OBJECTIVE: to develop the concepts of mode, median, and mean on a concrete level.

1. Tell children the following story and ask them to illustrate it using blocks on a grid as shown in Figure 13–6. Sam practiced his spelling words every day. On Monday he missed 5 words, on Tuesday he missed 1, on Wednesday he missed 3, on Thursday he missed 1, and on Friday he got a perfect score.

Ask the children if any score showed up more than once. It did; on Tuesday and on Thursday, Sam missed 1 word. Since that is the only score that shows up more than once, that is the mode.

List the scores from the highest to the lowest: 5, 3, 1, 1, 0. The score in the middle is the median. There-

fore, 1 is the median as well as the mode. Are the median and the mode always the same? The children can make up other scores to check their predictions.

Will the mean be the same? Use the blocks on the grid and the original scores to find the mean number of words Sam missed each day. Given the total number of missed words, figure out how many words would be missed each day if the same number were missed each day. Encourage the children to rearrange the blocks until there are the same number of blocks on each day. The children should be able to rearrange the blocks so that there are 2 blocks on each day.

Ask the children what would happen if Sam missed 3 words on Thursday instead of 1 word. Now, can they rearrange the blocks so that there are the same number on each day? What should they do with the extra blocks? Can they use rational numbers to answer the question? Could Sam miss an average of 2.4 words per day? Did Sam actually miss 2.4 words on any day? If you read an article that says the average family has 2.2 children, does that mean that any family actually has 2.2 children?

Let the children keep records of their own test scores or other data of interest and find the mean, median, or mode. They might wish to survey the class to determine the mean, median, and mode for the number of children in each family or the number of pets in each household. After surveys are taken, encourage the children to ask their own questions about the data and to work in groups to come up with answers. Weblink 13–2 has a number of lesson plans and interactive applets that you might want to use with children as they develop surveys and explore ideas of mean, median and mode.

2. Ask each child to draw around one hand on a sheet of paper and to cut out the drawing. Split the class into groups of six to eight, and ask each group to order the hand drawings from the smallest to the largest. The children may need to decide what is meant by the "smallest" hand drawing. Is it the shortest drawing or the one with the least area? Does the hand begin at the wrist and end at the tip of the longest finger?

Once an ordering scheme is decided upon, ask the children to find the median hand. What is the median if an even number of students are in the group? It should be the average of the two middle hands. To find the average length of two middle hands without measuring, have the students tape the two hands together end to end and then fold the strip in half.

Are there any hands that seem to be the same size? Is there a mode?

Suggest that children find the mean hand length by taping the hands together end to end and then folding the strip. For example, if there are 8 children in the group, tape the 8 hands together and then fold the strip of hands in half 3 times to make 8 equal sections. The

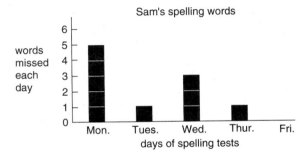

Figure 13–6 Graph of spelling words missed.

length of one of those sections should be the mean of the lengths of the children's hands.

Notice that the mean, median, and mode are found here without measuring. After the children have found these values concretely, ask them to measure the length of each of the hands and to find the mean, median, and mode of the measures. How do these methods compare to the concrete work? Encourage the children to discuss their methods with each other as they are working. Let the children suggest other measures for which they would like to find averages. They might find the average height, shoe size, neck size, and hat size of their group. Is anyone in the group "average"? Does that person have the average size for all the measures?

Are mean, median, and mode always equally useful? If you have to stock dresses for a department store, would you be more interested in the mean, median or mode? Which does the government use in a census report? (See Weblink 13–4 for census information.)

Grades 3 – 5 and Grades 6 – 8

OBJECTIVE: to explore differences in reporting data using the mean, the median, and the mode.

3. The following are the salaries of five semiprofessional basketball players: $80,000, $80,000, $100,000, $120,000, and $620,000. The players are complaining about their salaries. They say that the mode of the salaries is $80,000 and that they deserve more money for all the games and practices. The owners claim that the mean salary is $200,000 and that this is plenty for any team. Which side is correct? Is anyone lying? How can you explain the differences in the reports?

Ask the children to look in newspapers, magazines, and on the Internet for reported averages. Are there any discrepancies in the reports? Are the statistics ever deceiving? Bring in reports for discussion in class. Encourage the children to read any reported statistics critically.

OBJECTIVE: to use a line plot as a quick way to organize numerical data.

4. A *line plot* is a quick way to organize data to show the range and central tendencies, especially if the range is fairly small. It is not a formal graph, but rather is a working graph that can be used in initial data analysis. A line plot is simply a sketch along the horizontal axis in which Xs are used to show the frequency of certain values.

Ask your students to collect data on some information with a limited number of expected values, such as the number of pets in each household. These data can easily be recorded as students are polled in the classroom. The line plot in Figure 13–7 shows how students might record the results.

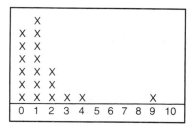

Figure 13–7   A line plot showing numbers of pets in each household.

From this line plot, students can quickly see that most of their classmates have no pets or only one pet, while one student has nine pets. This information can then be analyzed further or graphed more formally, if the children wish.

OBJECTIVE: to use a stem-and-leaf plot as a quick way to organize numerical data.

5. A *stem-and-leaf plot* (also called a stem plot) is another quick way to represent the shape of a data set. Unlike the line plot, the stem-and-leaf plot works best for data that span several decades rather than just a few numbers. This plot is most frequently organized by tens and can also be made quickly as data are reported orally. To make this plot, divide each value into tens and units. The tens are the stems of the plot and the units are the leaves. Ask the children to collect data on information that may have values that span several decades. The plot in Figure 13–8 shows the ages of the people at a family reunion.

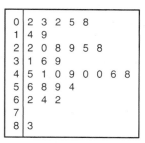

Figure 13–8   A stem-and-leaf (stem) plot showing ages of people at a family reunion.

From this plot, students can quickly see that there are 5 children under 10, 2 teenagers, and no one in their seventies. As you can see, these data are too spread out to put on a line plot, but they can be neatly organized and analyzed using the stem-and-leaf plot.

OBJECTIVE: to use a box-and-whiskers plot to aid in the analysis of data.

6. A *box-and-whiskers plot* (also called a box plot) is another means of looking at data. In this type of graph, you must find the median, as well as the data at the

GRADE 4

Chapter 27

WHAT WE ARE LEARNING

Outcomes

....

VOCABULARY

Here are the vocabulary words we use in class:

Outcomes Outcomes are the results of an experiment.

Event An event is one outcome or a combination of outcomes.

Tree diagram A tree diagram shows all the possible outcomes or choices.

Predict When you predict, you tell what might happen.

Unlikely, likely, equally likely Depending on what information you have, you can tell whether an outcome is *unlikely*, *likely*, or *equally likely* to occur.

Name

Date

Dear Family,

Your child is learning how to predict outcomes and record results of simple experiments with spinners, coins, and tables. Here are some examples:

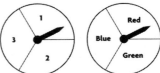

If you use two spinners to play a game, to find the possible outcomes you can list them in a table, make a tree diagram, or multiply.

Table

1-red	1-blue	1-green
2-red	2-blue	2-green
3-red	3-blue	3-green

Tree diagram:

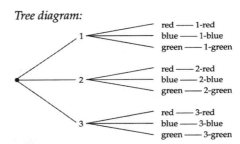

Multiply

3 colors × 3 numbers = 9 possible choices.

The Home Activity provides an opportunity for you and your child to set up an experiment and predict outcomes. As you work together on that and the other pages, remember that doing math with you is one way your child gains confidence and understanding.

Sincerely,

Family Involvement Activities   FA105

Figure 13–9   Excerpts from Harcourt Math, Family Involvement Activities, 2002 National Edition, Grade 4, copyright © by Harcourt, Inc., reprinted by permission of the publisher.

The letter to the family shown in Figure 13–9 is from the Family Involvement activities in the fourth-grade Harcourt Math series. In this activity, the family is encouraged to play a spinner and coin-toss game with the student in order to analyze results of a simple experiment. Activities following these in this introductory letter include predicting the outcome of spinning a homemade spinner and flipping a coin, testing this experimentally, and then comparing the results to the theoretical probability that is found with a table and tree diagram. Families are then encouraged to create, play, and analyze their own game that includes likely and unlikely events and outcomes. This is later extended to include fractions to express the probability of various outcomes.

This home activity accompanies hands-on lessons where students spin spinners and toss number cubes, record results in a chart, and compare these to tree diagrams and organized lists. The teacher's manual includes suggestions for reteaching and challenging students as needed and links to children's literature. Assessment includes multiple-choice questions as preparation for standardized tests as well as traditional homework and tests.

twenty-fifth and seventy-fifth percentiles. If we use the data from the family reunion shown above, we can first find the median by noting that there are 32 people at the reunion and the average of the ages for person #16 and person #17 (when the ages are listed in chronological order) is the median age. In this instance, person #16 is 39 years old, and person #17 is 40. Therefore, the median age is $39\frac{1}{2}$ years old. The median is also the fiftieth percentile. To find the age at the twenty-fifth percentile, we need to find the median age of the first 16 people. This is the average age of person #8 who is 20, and person #9, who is 22. Therefore, the age at the twenty-fifth percentile, the first quartile, is 21. The person at the seventy-fifth percentile is the median of the last 16 people, the average age of person #24 who is 54, and person #25, who is 56 years old. Therefore, the age at the seventy-fifth percentile, the third quartile, is 55.

You are now ready to make a box-and-whiskers plot like the one in Figure 13–10. The right and left sides of the box are the twenty-fifth and seventy-fifth percentiles, and the line in the middle of the box is the median. The two ends of the two whiskers are the ages of the oldest and the youngest person at the reunion, respectively. Can you tell by looking at the plot whether people seem to be bunched in any one age group? Is either of the two extreme ages separated a great deal from the rest of the ages? Encourage students to ask other questions that can be answered by looking at the box-and-whiskers plot.

You may find several other suggestions for handling data in the *Used Numbers* and *Connected Math* series, which are listed in the reference section.

OBJECTIVE: to explore box-and-whiskers plots using the list and plot capabilities of a graphing calculator.

7. If your graphing calculator has the capability of creating box-and-whiskers plots, encourage your students to explore this. This might be a good time to join with the science or health teacher in the development of a project that uses some of the statistics and graphing concepts that students are learning. Ask students to collect data such as heart rate from their classmates in a variety of settings such as at rest, after walking for two minutes, and after running for two minutes, and to store these data in three lists on the calculator. After the data are stored, instruct the students to use the calculator to create a box-and-whiskers plot for each of the three sets of data and compare the results. If the calculator has linking capabilities to the computer, this information can be downloaded into the computer for further analysis and for illustrating the reports that are written on the project.

Look at the three box-and-whiskers plots in Figure 13–11. Which one do you think shows students heart rates at rest, which one shows students' rates after walking for two minutes, and which shows rates after running? How do you know? Which has the largest range of data? The smallest range? What other information do these graphs show? Look at Weblinks 13–1 and 13–3 for a variety of lesson plans and activities for exploring box plots.

OBJECTIVE: to explore scatter plots using the list and plot capabilities of a graphing calculator.

8. The same data that were used to develop box-and-whisker plots can be used to display scatter plots. The scatter plot in Figure 13–12 shows the student heart rates at rest plotted on the *x*-axis and the heart rates after running for two minutes plotted on the *y*-axis.

What relationships do you notice between the rate at rest and the rate after running? What other information can you learn from this graph?

You will find several other suggestions for handling data in the books and technology listed in the reference section of this chapter. You may want to attend a workshop on using various types of graphing calculators and computer graphing programs to feel comfortable using some of the new technology.

Formulating Questions and Displaying Data to Answer Them

> Students should learn through multiple experiences that how data are gathered and organized depends on the questions they are trying to answer. (NCTM, 2000, p. 110)

Before gathering and displaying data, students should think about questions they want to answer. The information that they collect and display should then be related to these questions. In this section, we look at posing questions and designing investigations and studies to answer them.

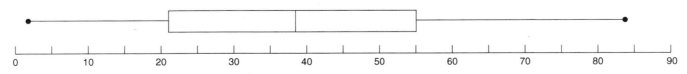

Figure 13–10 A box-and-whiskers (box) plot showing ages of people at a family reunion.

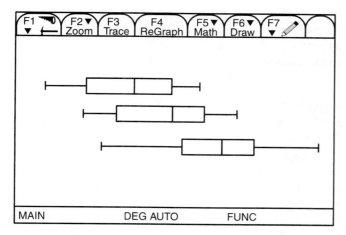

Figure 13–11   Graphing calculator display of three box-and-whiskers plots.

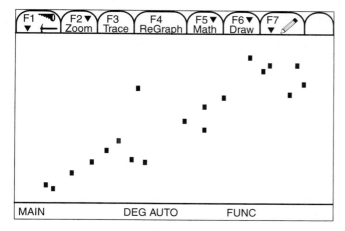

Figure 13–12   Graphing calculator display of a scatter plot.

Graphs, tables, and charts are often used to display the data collected to answer questions of interest to students. Children need to learn to read, interpret, and create these displays in order to become intelligent, discriminating consumers. We have already discussed the importance of making a table or chart when solving problems. In this section, we present ideas for teaching graphing using concrete objects, pictures, and bar graphs in the primary grades and extending to line, circle, and Cartesian graphs in the intermediate and middle grades.

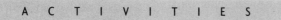

A   C   T   I   V   I   T   I   E   S

Pre-Kindergarten – Grade 2

OBJECTIVE: to develop the concepts of graphs on a concrete and on a semiconcrete level.

1. You can begin teaching the concept of graphing as early as pre-kindergarten. When graphs are made con-

cretely, it is important to use a system to ensure that each object occupies the same amount of space, so that children are not misled by the differences in the sizes of the objects. The focus should be on the number of objects and not their volume. You might mark off congruent squares upon which to place objects. This keeps the objects lined up, gives each object the same amount of space, and forms a good foundation for later work with bar graphs. Try the following with your class.

Set up a two-column grid system on the floor (see Figure 13–13). Bring in a large bowl of apples and oranges for the children's snacks. Let each child choose one piece of fruit, but ask the children not to eat the fruit yet.

While the children are holding the fruit, ask if more children have chosen apples or if more have chosen oranges. Let the children discuss ways to find the answer. They may want to walk around the room to count the children with each kind of fruit or they may want the children to sort themselves into two groups before counting.

After some discussion, ask the children to sort themselves into two groups, one with apples and one with

Children's Snacks

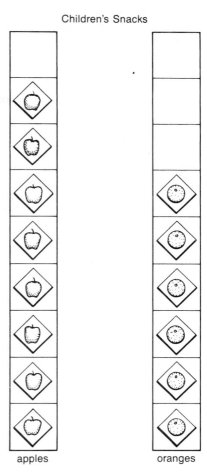

apples   oranges

Figure 13–13 Object graph showing student choices of apples and oranges.

oranges, and then ask the children if they can tell which group is larger without counting. If the sizes of the two groups are similar, they may not be able to tell.

One of the children may suggest that they line up instead of standing in a group and then look to see which line is longer. This is a good introduction to the squares on the floor. When the children line up, they may not all stand the same distance apart, and therefore, the longer line may not have more children.

Have the children stand on the squares on the floor. In this way, they are all the same distance apart. Ask the children again if they can tell which group is larger.

After the children have decided that the longer line represents the most popular fruit, tell them to put the fruit on a napkin on the square on which they are standing and to move away. Now ask the children which is the most popular fruit. Discuss whether it matters if they are standing on the squares or if the fruit alone can represent them. Ask if pictures of the fruit could represent them as well.

Give the children congruent sheets of square paper and ask them to draw a picture of the fruit they chose. (Square self-adhesive notes are good for this because they can easily be stuck to the board or wall and moved around to answer your questions.) Tape the pictures of the fruit in two horizontal rows, with one row directly beneath the other. Again, discuss which fruit was chosen more often.

To go one step further, tell the children that you want to use just a red square to represent a child who chose an apple and an orange square to represent a child who chose an orange. Give each child a piece of inch or two-centimeter graph paper (you may copy the master in Appendix B) while you demonstrate on large graph paper on the board or on graph paper on the overhead projector. Label the graph and the rows as shown in Figure 13–14, and lead the children to color in the appropriate squares.

Ask the children whether all the graphs they made now give the same information. Which type of graph would be easiest to use if you wanted to print the information in the school paper?

The children can follow up this lesson by suggesting other things to graph, such as eye or hair color or favorite books or pets. Children will be much more involved in lessons on graphing if they are graphing information in which they have a personal interest. Use

the information students collect in their graphs as a springboard for more questions. Graphs frequently raise as many questions as they answer. You also might want to explore using a graphing calculator that will make a pictograph or bar graph.

OBJECTIVE: to pose questions, develop surveys to collect data to answer them, and use graphs to display the answers.

2. Discuss with the students questions of interest that they might be able to answer by collecting data from friends and family. After a discussion of what might be an interesting question, tell the students to each develop one question with a limited number of answers that they might ask their classmates or families. They may have questions such as "What is your favorite subject in school?" or "How many hours a night do you watch TV?" for the students and "Do you think seven-year-olds should get an allowance?" or "Should teachers get higher salaries?" for the adults. Or a student might ask the question of both students and adults and compare the responses. Discuss with the children the importance of selecting a random sample and ask how they would choose one.

Before the students survey anyone, ask them to make a hypothesis about the results. For example, if students are surveying whether people think that seven-year-olds should get an allowance, they might hypothesize that parents will generally say no and that students will generally say yes.

After students have decided on a question and hypothesized about the results, help them determine a way to collect and represent the results. They might decide to record the results on a tally sheet. Decide how many people should be surveyed for useful results. Students with similar questions may wish to team up so they can question more people.

Once results have been tallied, discuss the best way to display them. Children asking about favorite pets may make a graph using plastic animals, children asking about favorite sports may draw a picture of each sport for a picture graph, and children asking about allowances may use grid paper to make a bar graph.

After students have displayed the data to answer their questions, ask them to take off any identifying titles and labels and exchange their displays with each other without telling the others what question was asked. Challenge the students to make up questions or stories to go with the data displays that they have been given and to share these with the student who made the display. How many of these questions and stories matched the original questions? Did they match the data displays? Discuss with the students the importance of a title and legends on all pertinent parts of the graph.

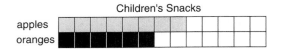

Figure 13–14 Bar graph showing student choices of apples and oranges.

Even though concrete, picture, and bar graphs should be introduced in the primary grades, children in the intermediate grades should review these types of graphs before moving on to other types. For older children, each picture on a picture graph or each square on a bar graph may represent more than one object. Children in the intermediate and middle grades should have experience with these graphs as well as line, circle, and Cartesian coordinate graphs and stem-and-leaf plots. Here are several ideas for teaching graphing concepts in the intermediate and middle grades.

A C T I V I T I E S

Grades 3–5 and Grades 6–8

OBJECTIVE: to create and read picture and bar graphs in which a picture or a bar represents more than one object.

1. Use the results from one of the children's probability experiments as data to be graphed. The children may use their tallies from flipping a coin 100 times. Use a *picture* or *bar graph* to show the results, but let each picture or bar represent 5 flips. Graphs showing 45 heads and 55 tails would look like those in Figure 13–15 a and b.

Ask the children how they would graph the same information if each bar or picture represented 10 flips. Discuss how to use a bar or picture. Tell the children to bring to school bar or picture graphs from newspapers or magazines and then discuss what each bar or picture represents in the graph.

OBJECTIVE: to create and read line graphs (frequency polygons).

2. When there is a continued trend from one point to the next, a *line graph* is useful. Line graphs should not be used unless both axes of the graph represent continuous data, such as time and temperature. It is not appropriate to use a line graph to show the numbers of people with different eye colors, for example, because the line between blue and green eyes would have no meaning.

Line graphs can be used in conjunction with subjects other than mathematics. The following activity may be used with a science lesson on plants. You and the children should find several occasions during the day to use their graphing skills.

Plant a fast-growing seed such as a bean seed and graph the plant's height each day after it has sprouted. If the plant is measured in centimeters, it is convenient to use centimeter graph paper to make the line graph.

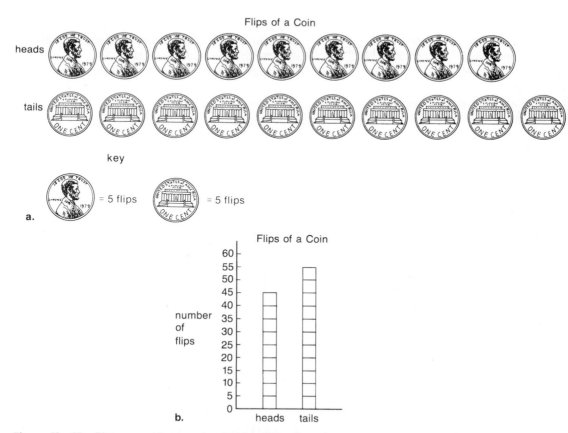

Figure 13–15   Picture and bar graphs showing flips of a coin.

Children may grow the bean plants under several different conditions, such as in a dark closet, on the window sill, with no water, with water every day, and with water once a week. Graph the growth under each condition and discuss the results.

Find examples of line graphs in newspapers and magazines and discuss whether they are used properly. Encourage children to make up questions for each other that can be answered by looking at graphs. Leave these questions in the learning center or copy them for the class to answer.

OBJECTIVE: to create and read circle graphs.

3. A *circle graph* is used to show information dealing with parts of a whole. The circle represents a whole, and the information being graphed is some fractional part of that whole. When children construct their own graphs, it is helpful if they can use a compass to make circles and a protractor to measure angles. This activity can be used before the children have acquired these skills if you cut out sections of a circle ahead of time.

Tell the children that you are going to make a circle graph to represent their pets. If you have 12 children with pets, cut several circular regions out of different colors of construction paper. Cut each circular region into 12 congruent sections (for a different number of children, adjust the size of the regions accordingly). Select a different color of paper to represent each type of pet (dogs, cats, etc.). Let each child select a colored region that represents her or his pet and place the region into the circle. Figure 13–16 shows a circle graph for one group of 12 children.

Encourage the children to ask questions about the completed graph. Fractions and percents can be used to describe the sections of the graph if children have studied these topics.

After children have learned to use a compass and protractor, discuss with them the fact that every circle has 360 degrees. Ask how many degrees would show the number of children in the class who have brown eyes. How would they show the number of children that have blue eyes? Let the children find and graph other data. Discuss circle graphs in newspapers and magazines.

If your graphing calculator has the capability of making circle graphs, show the students how to store the information they have collected on their pets in a list, and then use the calculator to graph the data.

Several computer programs give you this same capability (see the references for a listing of some). Choose a graphing program on the computer that the students are familiar with, and repeat the same project. Ask students to compare the results of creating a graph by hand, using the graphing calculator, and using a computer program. What are the benefits and the drawbacks of each method?

OBJECTIVE: to create and read Cartesian graphs.

4. *Cartesian graphs* are used for locating positions in two-dimensional space. Children may be introduced to Cartesian coordinates in social studies when they look up a point on a map. Maps generally use a letter and a number to give a location. Ask children to study the map in Figure 13–17 and then tell you where the school, the hospital, and the library are, giving the letter for the horizontal location first and then the number for the vertical location.

Encourage the children to make up other maps of their own. They may make up treasure maps and ask other children to find the secret location of the treasure by moving around on the map using horizontal and vertical locations.

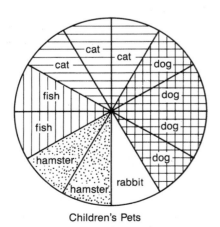

Children's Pets

Figure 13–16 Circle graph illustrating children's pets.

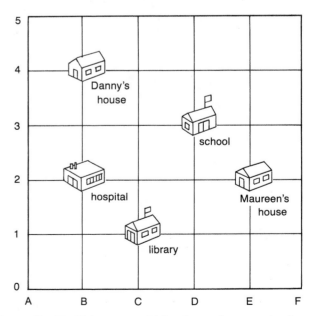

Figure 13–17 Using a map to develop early concepts of Cartesian coordinates.

The game Battleship is a good follow-up to this activity. Children must guess the coordinates of their opponents' hidden ships in order to sink them.

After students are comfortable using letters and numbers to locate points, introduce them to ordered pairs of numbers, in which the first number gives the x-coordinate and the second number gives the y-coordinate. When older students understand the concept of negative integers, let them use all four quadrants of the Cartesian plane.

The Maze Game on Weblink 13–5 is a fun activity where students can practice their point-plotting skills by having them move a robot through a minefield to a target location using all four quadrants of the Cartesian plane.

DEVELOPING FLUENCY WITH DATA ANALYSIS AND PROBABILITY

One function of the mathematics curriculum in the elementary and middle grades is to give children a solid foundation in the basic concepts of data analysis and probability, but much of the fluency and practice of these skills will occur in high school and beyond. However, there are several things that can be done in the elementary and middle grades to help students solidify these concepts.

After children have had sufficient experience with the processes of observing, comparing, classifying, and sequencing and have had experience with relationships and their properties, they are ready for more formal activities involving these concepts. Activities in this section require children to use these early concepts to further develop thinking skills. Children are given the opportunity to practice earlier skills and to both solve and create problems. Even though most of the problems do not require the use of numbers, they do require some fairly sophisticated reasoning abilities. In most instances, children are encouraged to use concrete materials to explore teacher-posed problems and to use these materials or to develop new ones to create their own problems. Computers can be used to simulate some of the same types of problems that children may solve with concrete, physical models.

Carroll Diagrams

After children can classify materials easily according to one or two attributes, they may begin to use **Carroll diagrams,** or charts, to classify materials according to two or more attributes. Carroll diagrams are named after the mathematician-author Lewis Carroll. Used to classify materials according to more than one attribute, Carroll diagrams are a good introduction to later work with data tables and multiplication. An example of a Carroll diagram is given in Figure 13–18, which may be used with the attribute shapes.

A   C   T   I   V   I   T   I   E   S

Pre-Kindergarten – Grade 2

OBJECTIVE: to abstract properties using a Carroll diagram.

1. Place about half of the shapes in a Carroll diagram for which the labels are not given, as shown in Figure 13–19. Let the children try to detect your pattern and

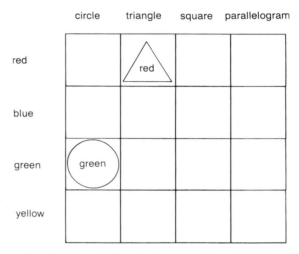

Figure 13–18 Carroll diagram for organizing attribute shapes.

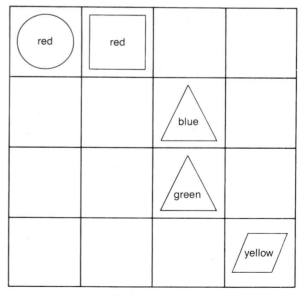

Figure 13–19 Carroll diagram for puzzle with attribute shapes.

place the rest of the pieces in the correct places. After all of the pieces have been correctly positioned, ask the children to tell you what the labels should be. Let them discuss the strategies they used to solve the problem.

2. Divide small groups of children into two teams each. Give each group a set of four People Pieces, such as the tall males. Ask one team to draw a 2-by-2 Carroll diagram for the People Pieces and to label it but not to show the diagram to the other team. (The diagram must be labeled according to the differences in the pieces, in this case the color and weight.) One possible diagram for these pieces is shown in Figure 13−20.

The group with the labeled diagram should then place one piece in the correct place on an unlabeled diagram. The other group must decide where to place the other three pieces and then correctly name the labels for the diagram. Keep track of the number of incorrect guesses as the team places the pieces in the diagram. After one team has correctly placed the pieces and determined the labels, it is that team's turn to make a secret Carroll diagram with another set of four People Pieces.

After students become proficient at solving Carroll diagrams involving two sets of attributes, they should begin to work with diagrams involving three or more sets of properties. Figure 13−21 shows a Carroll diagram for the shape, color, and size of attribute blocks; Figure 13−22 shows a Carroll diagram for the height, weight, sex, and color of People Pieces.

Let the children place the pieces in Carroll diagrams that are already labeled, such as those in Figures 13−21 and 13−22. Explain to the children that they must use all of the labels for each piece.

Let the children make up their own Carroll diagrams and have other students place the pieces in the diagrams. Discuss the construction of the diagrams and the fact that you must use parallel labels, such as male and female, in the same type of position. For instance, male could not label a column if female labeled a row, because you would not be able to find a piece that was both male and female to place in the intersection of that row and column.

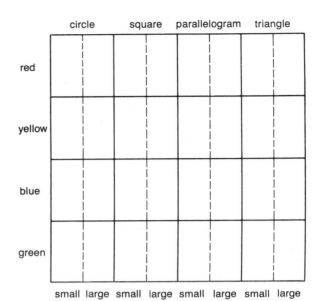
Figure 13−21 Carroll diagram for organizing attribute pieces.

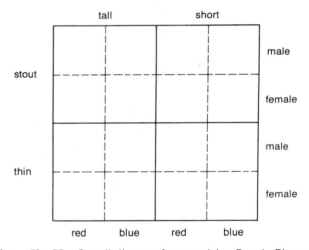
Figure 13−22 Carroll diagram for organizing People Pieces.

The following activities are designed for children who are proficient at filling in and creating Carroll diagrams with three or more sets of labels.

Grades 3−5 and Grades 6−8

OBJECTIVE: to set up Carroll diagrams involving four sets of characteristics and to abstract properties of sets from their placement in a Carroll diagram.

1. Divide the class into groups of four or five and give each group a set of People Pieces. Ask each group to sketch a Carroll diagram using the People Pieces and

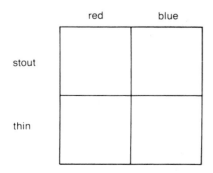
Figure 13−20 Carroll diagram for People Pieces.

showing the color, height, weight, and sex of the characters. Each group should then place the pieces on the table in the order shown on the Carroll diagram.

After the teacher has checked all the Carroll diagrams to determine if the pieces are in the correct places, each team should turn all but three of the pieces over while leaving them in the same positions. The teams should then trade places with each other and guess what the hidden pieces look like in each other's diagrams. Students should take turns pointing at a hidden piece and giving the color, weight, height, and sex. When a student guesses correctly, the piece should be turned face up and left in that position. If the guess is incorrect, the piece should be left face down. Once all of the pieces have been correctly identified, the team that has been guessing should draw a Carroll diagram of the set and compare it to the Carroll diagram drawn by the team that created the problem.

2. The same teams used for the activity just described may be used again for this one. Give each team a set of attribute blocks, and ask the teams to devise a Carroll diagram using the shape, size and color of the blocks, such as in Figure 13–23. Each team should draw the Carroll diagram and place the pieces on the table in the correct places.

After all of the pieces have been positioned and checked by the teacher, the students should exchange the positions of three of the pieces. Teams may then trade places and attempt to discover which pieces are in the incorrect positions. Each team should draw the Carroll diagram for the set at which they are looking and tell where the pieces should go. The team should then check with the original team to see if the diagram is correct.

3. Students may work individually, in pairs, or in small groups to create their own sets of attribute materials. Students should first decide on a theme for the materials to be made. Themes may arise from special days or seasons, such as valentines, snowmen, pumpkins, or spring flowers. After a theme is chosen, the children should decide on three or four characteristics to vary on their attribute materials. Remind the children that all other attributes must stay the same. For example, a group of children may decide to make hearts for Valentine's Day that differ in size, color, and arrows. They might have three sizes (small, medium, and large), two colors (pink and red), and with or without arrows. This set of materials would have $3 \times 2 \times 2$, or 12, pieces in order to have one piece of each type. After the children have decided upon the pertinent attributes for the set, they should draw a Carroll diagram to illustrate all the pieces. The diagram in Figure 13–24 is one possibility.

After the diagram is drawn, the children may make the pieces necessary for the set. The pieces may be drawn on index cards or be cut from poster board. After the set is made, the children may use this set for activities described in this chapter or may develop new activities of their own. Children may exchange sets with each other and draw Carroll diagrams for the other sets.

Tree Diagrams

After the children are comfortable with activities involving Carroll diagrams, they may use other types of diagrams for classifying sets of attribute materials. A **tree diagram** is another useful way of classifying

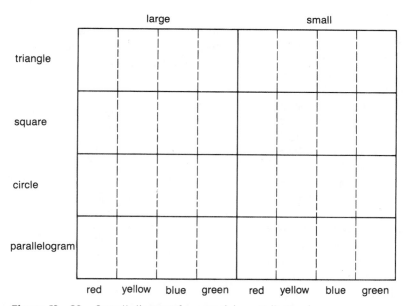

Figure 13–23   Carroll diagram for organizing attribute pieces.

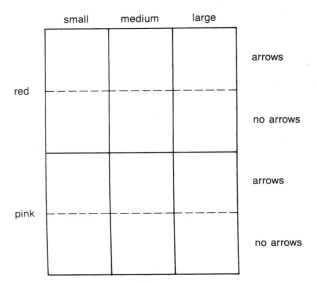

Figure 13–24 Carroll diagram for organizing Valentine hearts.

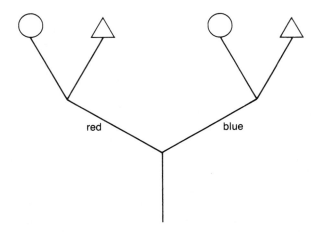

Figure 13–25 Tree diagram for organizing attribute shapes.

materials. In tree diagrams, the branches at each level indicate the characteristics of a different attribute. For example, to show attribute shapes with two colors and two shapes, you could use the diagram in Figure 13–25. Tree diagrams can be used for sequencing as well as for classifying, and the activities described below involve both concepts.

A C T I V I T I E S

Pre-Kindergarten – Grade 2
OBJECTIVE: to classify objects using a tree diagram.

1. Draw a tree diagram such as the one in Figure 13–25 and give the children a set of attribute shapes to place on the tree. The children should begin by placing one block at the foot of the tree. Then they should move it to the first branching of tree limbs. The children should decide which branch to take according to the attributes of the piece. They should continue moving the piece upwards, deciding on the proper branch at each intersection. After the first piece is in place, continue by letting other children decide the proper position for the next block. Continue until all of the blocks are in their proper locations or until all of the children have had an opportunity to place a block.

When children are first learning to use tree diagrams, you should begin with a simple diagram, such as the one in Figure 13–25, and gradually increase the complexity of the task. Ask the children to compare the tree diagram to the Carroll diagram. Use the same set of attribute materials on both diagrams. Encourage the

children to create other diagrams for the same or different sets of materials. Discuss the strategies they use to place the materials on the tree.

2. Draw a tree diagram on the floor and make label cards for the branches. The positions of the cards may be changed at the discretion of the children. Use labels such as those shown in Figure 13–26. Ask each child to start at the bottom of the tree and to walk until he or she comes to an intersection. At each intersection, let the child decide which way to go. The child should continue until the end of the last branch. Ask the children how they decided which way to go at the intersections.

3. Use the tree diagram you have drawn on the floor or one drawn on a large piece of poster board on a table. Collect small trucks and cars to use with this activity (the children may bring in vehicles for this activity). Using attributes of the vehicles you have, label the intersections on the tree. Try using attributes and their negations, such as red and not red, cars and not cars, and with decals and without decals. Let the children

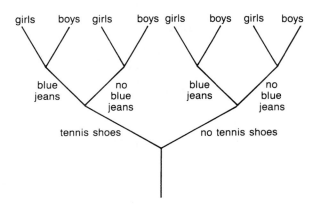

Figure 13–26 Tree diagram for organizing students.

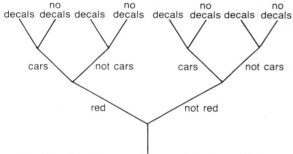

Figure 13–27 Tree diagram for organizing toy vehicles.

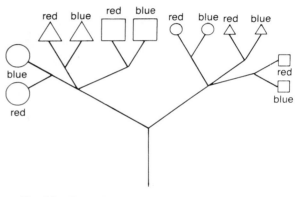

Figure 13–28 Tree diagram for organizing attribute shapes.

take turns driving the vehicles up the tree, deciding the proper turn to take at each intersection. One such tree diagram is shown in Figure 13–27.

After the children become familiar with the activity, let them decide on other labels and sets of materials to classify using tree diagrams. They may develop their own sets of materials or suggest other activities to use with familiar sets such as People Pieces and attribute blocks.

Older children who have had experience classifying materials on a tree diagram may wish to carry the concepts even further. The following activities are designed to further develop concepts using tree diagrams. If older students have not worked with tree diagrams before, they should first try some of the activities described above.

A C T I V I T I E S

Grades 3–5 and Grades 6–8

OBJECTIVE: to use a tree diagram to classify objects.

1. Show the children an unlabeled tree diagram on which the pieces have already been placed on the correct limbs, such as in Figure 13–28. Ask the children to tell you what the labels must be.

After the children have decided on the proper labels, have them label the tree and remove the pieces. Then have them start the pieces at the bottom of the tree and follow them to their correct branches. Discuss with the children the differences between deciding on the labels after the pieces are in place and placing the pieces when the labels are in place.

2. Have the children use a tree diagram to create a set of attribute materials in the same way that they used a Carroll diagram. Ask the children to decide on a theme for a new set of attribute materials and to name three or four categories of properties for these materials. For example, children may decide to create a set of

flowers using roses or daisies with three, four, or five leaves and yellow or white petals. This will give them a set of $2 \times 3 \times 2$, or 12, pieces. Ask the children to sketch a tree diagram that would show all the possible pieces, such as the one in Figure 13–29.

After the tree diagram is drawn, have the children sketch the proper flower at the end of each branch. These sketches may then be transferred to index cards or poster board so that each piece can be individually manipulated. After the sets are made, children may use them for activities in this section or may make up new activities of their own.

3. Tree diagrams may be used for sequencing if a value is assigned to each branch. The branch on the far left is assigned the highest value and the values decrease as you go to the right. Elements are first sequenced according to the branches on the bottom, and the importance of the branches decreases as you move up. This may be illustrated by alphabetizing a set of nonsense words. Put each of the following words on a separate index card:

cat	cab	cot	cob	cut	cub
lat	lab	lot	lob	lut	lub
mat	mab	mot	mob	mut	mub

Sketch a tree diagram in which the bottom branches are labeled with the first letters of the words in alphabetical order from left to right, the middle branches are labeled with the second letters in alphabetical order, and the top branches are labeled with the last letters, again in alphabetical order, as shown in Figure 13–30.

Ask the children to take the words and hang them from the proper branches. Then ask the children to tell you what they observe about the order of the words. This activity is helpful for children who have difficulty alphabetizing words when the first few letters of two or more words are the same.

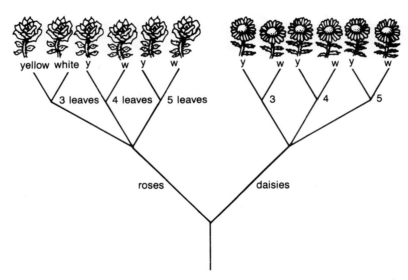

Figure 13–29 Tree diagram for creating a set of attribute materials.

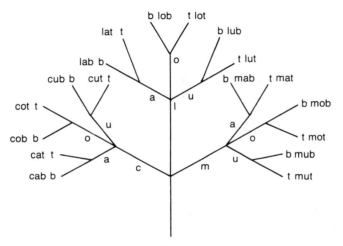

Figure 13–30 Tree diagram for alphabetizing words.

4. When studying binomial nomenclature in science, use a tree diagram to separate kingdoms, phyla, classes, orders, families, genera, and species. Let the students locate the proper position on the tree for a variety of plants and animals. This is a good activity for a bulletin board, as students can draw or find pictures of objects to place on the diagram.

5. Children may use tree diagrams to sequence any set of materials from the greatest to the least. Children may decide to set up an imaginary kingdom with the People Pieces. They may decide that all females are more powerful than males, that the stout ones are more powerful than the thin ones, that the short are more powerful than the tall, and finally that the red are more powerful than the blue. The children should set up a tree diagram such as the one in Figure 13–31

and line up all the People Pieces from the most powerful to the least powerful.

This activity may be done in groups of four or five. Each group may line up the pieces and then show the line-up to another group. The other group should not be shown the original criteria for the line-up or the tree diagram. This other group must then decide on the criteria selected and draw the tree diagram. After the diagram is drawn, ask the original group to determine the accuracy of the drawing. Discuss with the students whether individuals are ever ranked in real life and what types of criteria are used.

As you can see from these activities, skills learned in math class often carry over into other subject areas. Carryover should be encouraged whenever possible. Certainly, in real life, people do not do math for the first 50 minutes of the day, then spelling, and then social studies. These skills must be used together. Encourage the children to find applications for new skills regardless of the subject area.

Venn Diagrams

Another diagram used to classify materials with more than one variable attribute is a **Venn diagram.** Unlike tree or Carroll diagrams, Venn diagrams are not used to give a unique position to each element of a set, but they are useful for classifying by both attributes and the negations of attributes. Young children should begin by using only one or two attributes, while older children may classify using three or even more intersecting categories. Simple intersecting Venn diagrams

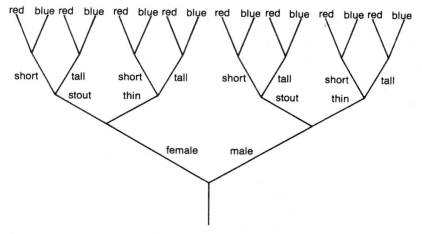

Figure 13–31 Tree diagram for sequencing People Pieces.

were introduced earlier in this chapter. A few more examples of Venn diagrams are introduced here for additional practice.

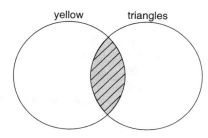

Figure 13–32 Venn diagram for sorting attribute shapes.

Pre-Kindergarten – Grade 2

OBJECTIVE: to classify using Venn diagrams and parallel categories.

1. When you first introduce children to Venn diagrams, use circles with parallel categories, such as colors. Give the children a set of attribute shapes and several large (150-centimeter circumference) loops of yarn or heavy cord. Make three separate circles with the cord and ask the children to put all the red blocks in one circle, all the blue ones in another, and all the yellow ones in another. Do any pieces belong in none of the circles? Ask the children to create other ways to classify the blocks. Discuss their methods of deciding where to place the pieces.

OBJECTIVE: to form Venn diagrams using two intersecting sets.

2. Ask the children to form two circles of yarn and to put all of the yellow pieces in one loop and all the triangles in another. Let the children discuss what to do with the yellow triangles. Lead them to discover that they can overlap the two loops of yarn and put the yellow triangles inside the section where the loops overlap. This is called the **intersection** of the two sets. Note the intersection of the sets in Figure 13–32.

Let the children suggest other labels for the two circles. Discuss how they know whether or not there will be pieces in the intersection. Will there be any pieces in the intersection if the loops are labeled triangles and squares? If the loops are labeled small and triangles, where would a small green square go?

3. Using attribute materials such as People Pieces, ask one group of students to draw, secretly, a Venn diagram with two intersecting loops and to add labels to them such as red and male. Form two intersecting loops with the yarn and put one correct piece in each section. Ask children who did not see the Venn diagram to guess where the other pieces should go. After all of the pieces have been placed in the correct sections, ask the children to identify the labels on the secret Venn diagram.

Let a new group of children decide on another diagram. Discuss with the children such things as whether or not all of the pieces go inside the loops. If any pieces do not belong in the loops, do they help you decide on the proper labels for the loops?

OBJECTIVE: to use the terms *and* and *or* properly when referring to the intersection or union of two sets.

4. Set up two intersecting loops as in the first activity in this group and place the attribute blocks in the proper sections. Using the loops labeled yellow and triangles, ask the children where to find the pieces that are yellow *and* triangles. Note that these pieces are all

found in the intersection. Some children may be confused by the word *intersection* and by ending up with a set smaller than either the set of yellow pieces or the set of triangles.

Later, for addition, the children may read "3 + 4" as "3 and 4." These are not the same concepts, even though they use the same familiar word, *and.* Addition is actually based on the concept of union (or), not the concept of intersection (and). **Addition** may be defined as the number of items in the union of two disjoint sets.

Let the children make up several intersecting sets and describe the pieces in the intersection using the word *and.* Be sure to use mutually exclusive attributes such as color and shape or size and thickness. After the children are comfortable using the word *and,* ask them to find the pieces that are yellow or triangles. Note that these are all of the pieces in the union of the two sets. The mathematical use of the word *or* includes those pieces that are yellow *and* triangles.

Give the children several chances to explore the uses of these words with the attribute shapes and in everyday life. Use statements such as "Today we will take attendance *and* say the Pledge of Allegiance before math class" and "Tomorrow we will go to gym *or* music class." Children may wish to discuss whether the promise in your second statement will be broken if you go to gym *and* music tomorrow.

Later, the use of the terms *and* and *or* with Venn diagrams can lead to a more formal study of logic. A **conjunction** (denoted by $p \wedge q$) consists of any two statements joined by *and.* A **disjunction** (denoted by $p \vee q$) consists of any two statements joined by *or.* A **negation** (denoted by $\sim p$) is the statement "it is not true that *p.*" These very basic concepts of formal logic have their beginning in the study of sets.

OBJECTIVE: to use symbols for union and intersection.

5. After the children are comfortable with the terms *and* and *or* for union and intersection, introduce the symbols for these operations. The symbol ∪ is the symbol for **union.** The union of sets *A* and *B* is the set consisting of all the elements in *A or B,* including those in both *A* and *B.* The symbol ∩ is the symbol for **intersection.** The intersection of sets *A* and *B* is the set consisting of all elements common to both *A and B.*

Using the same materials used in the previous two activities or attribute materials that the children have created for themselves, let the children begin to work problems such as "Shade the sections in your Venn diagram for yellow objects ∪ triangular objects" or "Point to the section for yellow objects ∩ triangular objects." Remember that the concepts of union and intersection are more important than the symbols. Don't overemphasize the symbols with young children.

OBJECTIVE: to form Venn diagrams using negations of attributes.

6. After children can form Venn diagrams with two intersecting loops, try forming Venn diagrams using the negations of the attributes. Put all the pieces that are not male in one section and the pieces that are not red in the other. Ask the children to describe the intersection. Is it the same thing to say "the pieces are not male and not red" as it is to say "the pieces are not male and red"? Where do you find the pieces that are not male or red? Try this activity for yourself. You will find that it is not easy to use the familiar terms *and, or,* and *not* properly in combinations. Note that when you are using the negation of a statement, it is important to identify the universal set. This is the original set of objects under consideration. For example, if your universal set is the set of People Pieces, the red females are not blue and not male, but you do not need to consider red triangles.

After children are familiar with Venn diagrams and the terms and symbols for union and intersection, use Venn diagrams with more than two loops. These diagrams will be difficult for children in the Piagetian preoperational stage, so they are better used with older children. If older children have not had previous experience with Venn diagrams, let them first experience the activities described earlier.

A C T I V I T I E S

Grades 3–5

OBJECTIVE: to classify attribute materials according to three intersecting characteristics.

1. Set up a three-loop Venn diagram for the attribute shapes, such as the one shown in Figure 13–33. Ask the children to place the pieces in the proper locations. Are all of the pieces inside the loops? Does each section have more than one piece?

Completely describe the characteristics of all the pieces in each section. Note that you can tell the color, shape, and size of the pieces in each section if you use the negations of some of the attributes. For example, the pieces in section (a) in Figure 13–33 are red, not squares, and not small. Ask the children to describe the pieces in each section in a similar fashion.

Encourage the children to create other Venn diagrams using attribute materials they have created. Describe the pieces in each section of the Venn diagrams.

2. Ask a group of children to secretly draw a three-loop Venn diagram. Arrange the yarn into three intersecting loops and ask the children with the secret

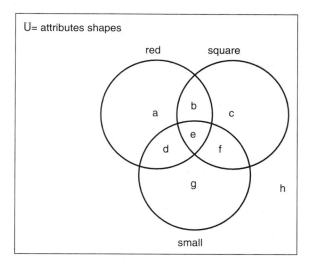

Figure 13–33 Three-loop Venn diagram for sorting attribute shapes.

diagram to place four or five pieces in the correct sections. The children who have not seen the diagram should attempt to place each of the other pieces in a loop by asking the children with the diagram if they have chosen the correct section. After all of the pieces are correctly positioned, the children who placed the pieces should identify the proper labels for the three loops.

In the beginning, use only positive attributes for all three loops and choose attributes so that all sections contain elements of the set. For children who understand the concepts well and really want a challenge, use negations and nonintersecting sets.

Grades 6–8

OBJECTIVE: to use intersection of sets to solve everyday problems.

1. Give the students a problem such as the following involving numbers from your classroom. Give students the following three-question survey and use the results to make a Venn diagram puzzle such as this one.

Do you like math?_____
Do you like to play soccer?_____
Do you like to read?_____

The results of the survey showed that 20 people like math, 15 like to play soccer, and 24 like to read. Ten people like to play soccer and also like to read, 12 people like both math and reading, and 8 people like math and like to play soccer. Five people said that they liked all three activities, and 2 people said that they did not like any of the activities. How many

people were in the total survey? (Note that the people who liked all three activities were also included in the groups that liked two activities, and these people were included in the groups that liked each individual activity.) Use a Venn diagram such as the one in Figure 13–34 to show your results.

After solving this problem, students should conduct their own surveys and make their own Venn diagram puzzles.

OBJECTIVE: to understand the meaning of the complement of a set and to use the symbol for complement.

2. A **complement of a set** consists of all the elements in the universal set that are not elements of the set under consideration. For example, the complement of the triangles in the set of attribute blocks are all the attribute blocks that are not triangles. The children should be familiar with this concept through the use of negations. Two different symbols may be used to denote the complement. The complement of set A may be shown as A' or as $\overline{A}$. This notation is usually read as "the complement of A."

The following activity uses the A' notation. Set up a Venn diagram for the attribute blocks such as the one in Figure 13–35 and label each section as shown.

Ask the children to list the letters designating the sections for various sets and their complements. For example, give the sections for each of the following:

red pieces	red pieces ∩ triangles
(red pieces)'	(red pieces ∩ triangles)'
red pieces ∪ triangles	red pieces' ∪ triangles'
(red pieces ∪ triangles)'	red pieces' ∩ triangles'

Which of the above are the same sections? State the characteristics of each of the above sections in words

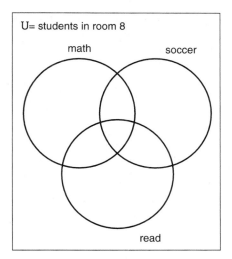

Figure 13–34 Three-loop Venn diagram for solving logic puzzles.

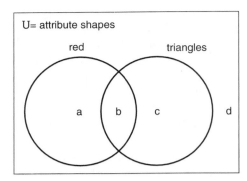

Figure 13–35   Venn diagram for illustrating de Morgan's laws.

rather than symbols, such as "not red and triangles" is the same as "not red or not triangles." This may be stated formally as "the union of the complements is equal to the complement of the intersections" and "the intersection of the complements is equal to the complement of the union." These are known as **de Morgan's laws.** These concepts are fairly complicated and students will need a great deal of experience working with concrete materials before being able to state the properties abstractly.

The activities using either People Pieces or attribute shapes may also be performed using any set of structured attribute materials, such as those made for the seasons or holidays. Encourage children to use their own sets of materials whenever possible.

Another embodiment of these concepts exists in some computer programs. Three programs that reinforce several of the concepts in this section are *Logical Journey of the Zoombinis* (Hancock and Osterweil, 1996), *Tabletop Jr.* (Broderbund, 1995), and *Escape from the Logic Spider* (Critical Thinking Press, 1992). Skills that these develop include identifying, sorting and ordering by attributes (*Logical Journey of the Zoombinis* and *Tabletop Jr.*) and applying logical deductive and conditional reasoning (*Escape from the Logic Spiders*).

Tabletop, Jr. gives primary students an opportunity to develop mathematical concepts of attributes, sorting, statistics, and graphing as they manipulate on-screen materials such as attribute blocks, pizzas, and party hats. The program has 50 challenges with games and puzzles involving such things as putting attribute blocks in Venn diagrams and party hats in Carroll diagrams.

Developing Probability Applications

Probability is a good topic with which to reinforce a student's ability to think systematically. In the previous section, we discussed using tree diagrams to find various combinations for attribute materials. Tree

diagrams are also quite useful in probability for finding combinations and permutations. The concepts of combinations and permutations are important ones in the area of discrete mathematics and should be explored by elementary and middle school students. The following activities suggest ways to reinforce these skills.

A   C   T   I   V   I   T   I   E   S

Grades 3–5 and Grades 6–8

OBJECTIVE: to use a tree diagram to find combinations and permutations.

1. The topics of combinations and permutations are fundamental to the subject of probability. When we want to know how many ways we can select one number of objects from another number of objects, we are finding the number of **combinations.** The order of the selection does not matter when finding the number of combinations. When we are interested in the order, we are finding the number of **permutations.**

If we flip 2 coins, we may be interested in all the possible combinations of heads and tails we could get. We can list the combinations as 2 heads, 1 head and 1 tail, and 2 tails. Are these combinations equally likely?

A tree diagram is useful for determining the sample space. Make a tree like the one in Figure 13–36 in which the tree gives us the Cartesian product of (H, T) × (H, T) or HH, HT, TH, and TT.

Do you think that the chance of getting 2 heads is the same as the chance of getting 2 tails? Is it the same as the chance of getting 1 head and 1 tail? Remind the students that the probability of getting 1 head and 1 tail is

$$\frac{\text{the number of favorable outcomes}}{\text{the total number of outcomes}}$$

Here, you have 2 favorable outcomes, HT and TH, out of the 4 possible outcomes.

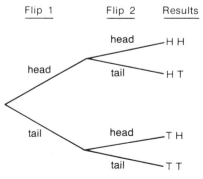

Figure 13–36   Tree diagram illustrating flips of a coin.

Give the children a penny and a nickel to flip and tell them to record the results of flipping the coins together 20 times. Compile the results from the whole class. Did 2 heads come up as often as 1 head and 1 tail? Does this result match your expectations?

Notice that you are reinforcing the skill of making a table as students record the data from the experiment. You may also ask the children to make a bar graph to show the results of flipping the coins. Does the information on the graph coincide with your expectations based on the tree diagram?

After the children can make a tree diagram to show the possible outcomes from 2 flips of a coin, ask them to expand it to show the outcomes from 3 or more flips. Encourage the children to make up other experiments and to use a tree diagram to find all the possible permutations to predict the outcome before performing the experiment. Can they show other results on a tree, such as the suit of two cards drawn or the numbers shown on the roll of 2 dice? How does this relate to earlier work with tree diagrams and attribute materials? How can probability be used to discuss the chance of randomly choosing a given attribute piece?

OBJECTIVE: to extend skills with combinations and permutations.

2. If we want to know the number of different committees of 3 we can form from a group of 5 students, we are looking for the number of combinations. It does not matter who is selected first for the committee. On the other hand, if we are going to pick a chairperson, a secretary, and a treasurer for the committee, we are looking for the number of permutations, because the position of each of the three selections does matter.

Suppose we have 3 children in the group—Danny (D), Maureen (M), and Amy (A)—and wish to select 2 of them. We could select Danny and Maureen; this would be considered the same as selecting Maureen and Danny. Listing all the possibilities, we have: DM, DA, and MA.

Are there any other choices? If we were looking for permutations rather than combinations, then the selection of Maureen and then Danny is considered different from Danny and then Maureen. We must add the following to our list to include all the possible permutations: MD, AD, and AM.

What happens if you are choosing a committee of 3 people out of 5? How many combinations do you have now? Use a tree diagram to help find all the possible permutations. (Remember that for permutations, the order is significant.) Simply list the terms in order from the tree to find all the possible permutations. How can you use a tree diagram to find all the combinations? After you have found the permutations, remove any combinations from your list that have the same elements only in a different order as another combination in the list.

Draw a tree diagram to show all the possible 3-dip ice-cream cones if the choices for each dip are vanilla, strawberry, chocolate chip, and rocky road. Assume that it makes a difference which dip is on the top, which is in the middle, and which is on the bottom. What if the order does not make a difference? Will it affect your tree if you do not want any 2 dips that are the same flavor? If you have calculators with probability functions, explore the use of the keys for finding combinations (nCr) and permutations (nPr). For example, to find the number of combinations possible when you select 3 people for a committee from a total of 5 people, you would push 5 then nCr and then 3 to tell the calculator that the n (total number) is 5 and you wish to select 3 (r). (Different calculators put these numbers in differently, so be sure to check the one you have.) If the order matters and you are finding permutations, you would choose nPr instead of nCr. Compare the results you find on the calculator in Figure 13–37 with those from the tree diagram.

OBJECTIVE: to distinguish between odds and probability.

3. Children (and adults) are often confused about the difference between odds and probability. As mentioned earlier, the *probability* of an event is

$$\frac{\text{the number of favorable outcomes}}{\text{the total number of outcomes}}$$

The **odds** of an event are

$$\frac{\text{the number of favorable outcomes}}{\text{the number of unfavorable outcomes}}$$

Note that the probability of an event shows the number of favorable outcomes out of the total, similar to the part-whole concept of a fraction discussed in Chapter 8, while the odds compare one part (favorable outcomes) to the other part (unfavorable outcomes) as in the ratio concept of fractions.

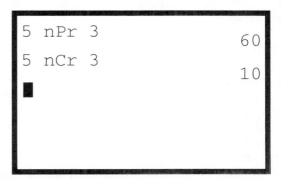

```
5 nPr 3
                        60
5 nCr 3
                        10
■
```

Figure 13–37 Calculator display showing combinations and permutations.

For example, with a fair coin, the probability of getting a head is $\frac{1}{2}$, but the odds of getting a head are $\frac{1}{1}$. The total number of outcomes in the sample space is 2 (head or tail), and the total number of unfavorable outcomes is 1 (the tail). If you randomly draw a marble from a bag containing 5 green marbles and 3 red marbles, the probability of getting a green marble is $\frac{5}{8}$, but the odds of getting a green marble are $\frac{5}{3}$. Because the odds of getting a green marble are greater than 1, does that mean you will always choose a green marble?

Ask the children to return to some of the earlier activities for probability and determine the odds as well as the probability of an event. How could you determine the odds if you knew only the probability? Could you determine the probability if you knew only the odds?

Computer programs can list all the possible outcomes of an experiment as well as simulate events such as coin flips thousands of times. Such listings and simulations can be useful as children practice probability skills. Children may also enjoy writing computer programs for simple probability concepts using the random-number generator. Even some calculators contain random-number generators.

DEVELOPING FLUENCY WITH GRAPHING SKILLS

After children have mastered the basic concepts of graphing and are able to decide on the appropriate graphs to use to display different types of data, they should use graphs in all subject areas whenever they have collected or need to interpret data. Much graphing practice may therefore take place in subject areas other than mathematics. As children construct their own graphs, be sure they clearly label the entire graph as well as all of its pertinent parts, such as the two axes on a line graph or every bar on a bar graph.

Children should practice reading as well as constructing graphs. Children should learn not only to read the data on a graph but also to use the data to solve problems.

After the children have had concrete experiences with a wide variety of graphs, use other computer programs to reinforce graphing concepts. This might be done with the spreadsheet and graphing sections of a program such as Appleworks or Excel, or programs written specifically for graphing such as *Graph Links* and *Data ToolKit* from Harcourt Brace; *Graphers* and *Data Explorer* from Sunburst; or *Tabletop, Jr.* and *Tabletop, Sr.* from Broderbund.

Computer programs allow the children to quickly see the relationships between tables and graphs and to see the effects of editing data and changing variables. This would also be a good time to introduce the program *The Cruncher*, published by Davidson, to elementary students. This program is a good introduction to the use of spreadsheets and can be used to collect, organize, and graph data for student projects such as portfolio entries that are based on the collection and analysis of data on a topic of interest to the students.

In addition to working with computers, children might enjoy the video *Math Vantage: Unit III: Data Analysis* available from GPN. In this series of four 10- to 15-minute programs, middle grade students collect, show, and analyze data and make decisions based upon the data analysis and knowledge of probability. The *Teacher's Guide* and *Student Lessons* add support for teachers who wish to use these lessons.

Teachers might wish to view the *Communication* video from the Annenberg *K-4 Video Library* to see several groups of students during their lessons on data, probability, and statistics. These include a primary class estimating the number of seeds in a pumpkin, a third-grade class working in teams to collect data for a bubble gum contest, and a bilingual first-grade class analyzing information about ladybugs. In all of these classroom excerpts, students are using a variety of means of representing data in their discussions and writing about mathematical concepts.

ESTIMATING AND EVALUATING INFERENCES AND PREDICTIONS BASED ON DATA

Once students have learned to organize data into Carroll and tree diagrams, you might challenge them to predict the number of attribute materials in a set using information about the structure of the sets. The following activities give a few examples of ways in which you might do this.

A C T I V I T I E S

Pre-Kindergarten – Grade 2

OBJECTIVE: to predict the total set of attribute materials when shown a few.

1. Choose a set of attribute materials the children have not seen before. Put the pieces in a paper bag and take them out one at a time. Ask the children to observe the properties of each piece. After the children have seen three or four pieces, ask them to describe a piece they believe is still in the bag. Remind the children that in this set of attribute pieces, no two pieces are identical but there is one piece for each possible combination of crucial attributes. For example, you may have a set of shapes that are red, blue, and green; large, medium,

and small; and circles, triangles, and squares. After the children have seen a large blue square, a medium red triangle, and a small green circle, they may predict that there is still a small green square in the bag. Continue the activity until the children have predicted all the pieces in the set. Ask them how they knew what pieces were still in the bag.

OBJECTIVE: to predict what the distinguishing characteristics will be in a set of attribute materials.

2. Again, choose a set of attribute materials the children have not seen. Choose attributes that can be distinguished by feel, such as shape, texture, and size. You may wish to make your set from scraps of material. Cut three different shapes using four different types of material, such as silk, felt, cotton, and wool. Paste the materials onto a sheet of cardboard in a Carroll diagram such as the one shown in Figure 13–38.

Have the children feel three or four of the pieces without looking and predict what pieces will be in the other positions. After they have predicted one other piece, let them feel that piece if they were correct and then predict another piece. The children may look at the Carroll diagram only after all the pieces have been predicted. Let them discuss their strategies and determine whether or not they could have used any better ones.

Grades 3–5

OBJECTIVE: to predict the total number of objects in a set.

1. Even though the emphasis in this chapter is on activities that do not require the use of numbers, work with sets and Carroll diagrams is a good introduction to the Cartesian product concept of multiplication. Older children who have worked with attribute materials should not only be able to describe the pieces that should be in an attribute set, but should also be able to predict the total number of pieces in a set after they are aware of all the distinguishing attributes. Again, choose a set of attribute materials the children have not seen.

Put the pieces in a paper bag and take them out to show the children one at a time. Ask the children to observe the attributes and to guess how many pieces are still in the bag. Encourage the children to draw Carroll or tree diagrams to aid in their predictions.

After the children have tried predicting a few times, they may be able to give you a formula for determining the total number of pieces in a set of attribute materials. To do so, they must find the number of attributes in each pertinent category and multiply those numbers together. This is the **Cartesian product** concept of multiplication. To find the cardinality of the Cartesian product of two sets, match each element of the first set with each element of the second set. For instance, if a set has four shapes and three sizes, the total number of pieces in the set would be 4 × 3, or 12, pieces.

OBJECTIVE: to estimate and use the cardinality of the Cartesian product to find the total number of combinations.

2. Children may wish to find the total number of different combinations for several familiar circumstances. Tell the children stories about events in everyday life that involve Cartesian products, and ask the children to estimate the number of possible combinations. Let the children figure out the exact number using their formula, a tree, or a Carroll diagram after they have estimated. Some ideas for stories follow:

- Amy received 3 new pairs of pants and 4 new blouses for Christmas. She can wear each of her pants with each blouse. She plans to wear one pair of the pants to school each day with one of the blouses. How many days can Amy go to school wearing a new combination each day? How many different combinations would Amy have if she also received 2 new sweaters, and each sweater goes with each outfit?

- José got a job working in an ice cream parlor. His favorite task is making ice cream sundaes. He likes to make up new combinations. The store has 12 kinds of ice cream, 4 kinds of toppings, and 3 kinds of nuts. How many different sundaes can José make if he puts one dip of ice cream, one topping, and one kind of nut on each sundae?

- Suzanna is in charge of making up names for a new kind of doll. She has decided on 20 good first names, 15 middle names, and 25 last names. How many different names can she make up if each doll gets a first, a middle, and a last name?

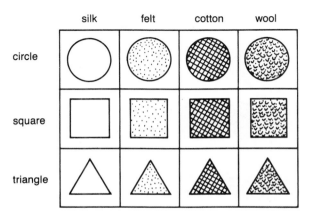

Figure 13–38   Carroll diagram for predicting attributes using the sense of touch.

Be sure the children estimate before they actually figure out the number of combinations. Many of the children will be surprised at the large number of possibilities. Let the children make up their own stories involving combinations for each other.

One of the main uses of probability is to predict future events. In fact, the study of probability began in European gambling halls about 300 years ago in analyzing games of chance to better predict their outcomes. These predictions are based on past events and/or mathematical models and are not just random guesses. The field of probability has grown since then, however, and probability is now used to predict everything from next year's corn crop to population growth in the twenty-first century.

Statistics go hand in hand with probability in predicting future events. Statistics are used to analyze the results of polls and experiments. The results of such an analysis affect, for example, what shows are on television next season, who will be the next president of the United States, and which drugs are approved for fighting cancer. Graphs are often used to display and search for trends in these data.

As part of the activities already mentioned in this chapter, you should frequently ask the children to predict outcomes before performing an experiment. The

following are a few other suggestions for reinforcing estimation skills.

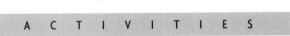

Grades 3–5 and Grades 6–8

OBJECTIVE: to use experimental probability to predict future events.

1. For some events, such as flipping a coin or drawing a card from a standard deck, we can find a mathematical probability without ever touching a coin or a card. For other events, such as tossing a tack or a paper cup, we must actually perform the experiment before we can accurately predict what will happen. Give each child a paper cup and ask him or her to mark a spot 12 inches above a table from which to drop the cup. The cup should be dropped bottom down, as in Figure 13–39.

Ask the children to describe the possible outcomes in the sample space. Let each child drop the cup 20 times and record the numbers of times the cup lands bottom down, top down, and on its side. Let the children predict

Figure 13–39   Using experimental probability to predict events.

the number of times it will land in each of those positions for the next 20 tries, for 50 tries, and for 100 tries.

Combine the results from the whole class and make predictions. Do the predictions become more accurate as students collect more data? How close are the predictions?

How do scientists use their experiments to make predictions? You may be able to get a parent or another adult in the community whose career involves using experimental data to make predictions to talk to the children.

OBJECTIVE: to use opinion polls to make predictions.

2. Before the next class election, take an opinion poll to try to predict the results. Do you have to poll everyone in the school to make a prediction? What is an unbiased sample? If everyone in the school votes, will your sample be biased if you poll only sixth graders? What if you poll only girls? Do some research to learn about the prediction of the winner in the 1948 presidential race between Dewey and Truman.

OBJECTIVE: to use commercial materials to make predictions.

3. Children enjoy using materials that they see every day to make predictions. It is interesting to determine whether common materials such as bags of pretzels or chips or boxes of raisins always contain the same number of objects. Give each pair of children a small bag of pretzels and ask them to predict the number of pretzels in the bag before opening it. After the predictions are recorded, ask the children to open the bag and count the number of pretzels. Make a graph to show the number of pretzels in each bag. Predict the mean, the median, and the mode. Are these the same? Compute to determine each one. Which would best describe the "average" number of pretzels in a bag? Does the size of the pretzel make a difference? Repeat the activity with another material, for example, raisins or small candies of different colors. With the small candies, you can also predict and determine the most common color. Is the most common or least common color the same for every bag? Make a graph to show your findings and make a list of questions that the class would like to explore further. This activity may take place over a month or so and may include writing to the manufacturer for information on how the product is marketed. How do they use statistics and probability to ensure that every bag has at least some minimum amount of food in it?

REASONING, SOLVING, AND POSING DATA ANALYSIS AND PROBABILITY PROBLEMS

Data analysis, probability, statistics, and graphing offer students a number of excellent opportunities to design

and investigate their own problems and experiments. Throughout this chapter, we have discussed the importance of having students make up their own problems and questions. A few additional suggestions for teaching students to create and solve problems in these areas follow.

Pre-Kindergarten–Grade 2

OBJECTIVE: to sequence attribute materials according to likenesses and differences.

1. Give the students a set of People Pieces and tell them that the pieces are going to have a parade. The people have strict rules for their parades. They must march in single file. Anyone may lead the parade, but the next person in line must have one attribute the same as the first person and three attributes different. Each person in line must have one attribute the same and three attributes different when compared with the person directly in front of him or her. The only attributes they may use are sex, height, weight, and color.

- *Understanding the problem.* Each person in the parade matches the person that follows in only one of the four attributes. If only one attribute is the same, the other three will be different. For example, the tall, skinny, blue male could follow the tall, stout, red female because both are tall.
- *Devising a plan.* Try to use all the tall people first, then change to short people (guess and check).
- *Carrying out the plan.* Look for a tall, stout, red female. There are no more, so change the attributes that will be the same for each new piece. Experiment by putting a short, stout, red male next. That works! Continue to add pieces by changing the attributes that are the same.
- *Looking back.* Check to make sure that all of the People Pieces have been used and that each piece is the same in one way and different in three.

To make the activity even more difficult, have the paraders march in a circle so that the first and last people in line also match according to the rules. After the children have tried the parade with the People Pieces, ask them to line up sets they have made using their own rules. They may challenge other students to discover the rules they used and to find one or two pieces out of order.

OBJECTIVE: to place attribute materials on a network according to a given number of differences among various pieces.

2. Give the children a set of attribute blocks and a network similar to the one in Figure 13–40. The children

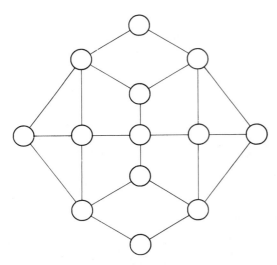

Figure 13-40 Network for attribute game.

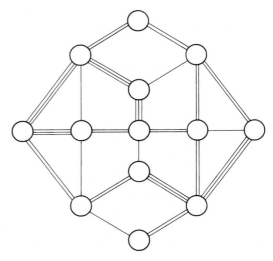

Figure 13-41 Network for attribute solitaire game.

should play this game in two teams. The play starts with one attribute block placed in the center of the diagram. The first team then places an attribute block adjacent to the first one and scores one point for each difference from the first block in color, shape, or size. Teams alternate placing blocks on the diagram and add the number of different attributes on each turn. If a block has lines connecting it to two or more blocks already in place, that team's score is the total number of differences from all the adjoining blocks. Play continues until all of the spaces on the board are filled. The team with the most differences wins.

Students may vary the game by using their own sets of attribute materials. After students have played the game a few times, discuss with them strategies for winning, which should include offensive as well as defensive moves.

3. Network solitaire may be played using a network board similar to the one shown in Figure 13-41. In this diagram, the number of lines between two positions indicates the number of differences there must be between the two connecting attribute blocks. Students may work on this activity alone or in small groups.

The students begin by placing an attribute block anywhere on the diagram and then trying to place other blocks, moving away from the first one according to the number of differences. The activity is complete when all of the spaces on the diagram have been correctly filled with blocks.

Students may check each other or the teacher may check them. As with many problem-solving activities, there are several correct answers. Students may make up networks for each other to solve. Some networks may be impossible, and students should discuss why certain combinations do not work.

Children who have worked with the activities just described and wish for a greater challenge may try some of the following activities. Children who have not tried the previous activities should work through the easier activities before attempting the more difficult ones.

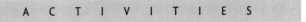

A C T I V I T I E S

Grades 3-5 and Grades 6-8

OBJECTIVE: to place attribute materials in an array according to the number of likenesses and differences between adjoining pieces.

1. This activity is similar to the parade described above. In this case, the People Pieces all wish to move into a 4-by-4 apartment house such as the one in Figure 13-42. The People Pieces are very particular

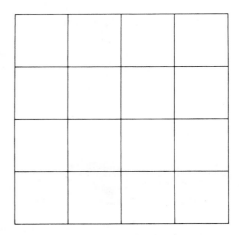

Figure 13-42 Apartment house for People Pieces puzzle.

about their neighbors. Each piece can differ in only one attribute from anyone living to the right, to the left, above, or below; its other three attributes must be the same as those of each of its neighbors. As the children work on placing the People Pieces in the array, they may realize that simply using trial and error can become quite frustrating. Remind them that there are other effective problem-solving strategies, such as looking for a pattern.

This activity is also effective with the attribute blocks or other attribute materials. The students may vary the rules so the pieces have two or three differences. Be aware that not all rules are possible, especially with the People Pieces, which only have two choices for each category of differences.

OBJECTIVE: to choose the correct attribute block with the use of deductive reasoning and questioning.

2. Using a set of attribute blocks, the leader secretly chooses one of the blocks and the rest of the class tries to guess which block it is by questioning the leader. The class may ask only questions of the form, "Does it have any of the attributes of?" (describing the size, color, and shape of one block).

Suppose the block is a small red triangle. If someone asks whether the block chosen is small, red, or a triangle, the leader will answer, "Yes, it has at least one of those characteristics." The leader does not tell the class if they guess the secret block. If the block has none of the characteristics guessed, the leader will answer, "No, it does not have any of those characteristics." Play continues until the class is sure which one is the secret block. One person in the class must announce, "I know which block it is." If the rest of the

class agrees, then that person may describe the block. If the person is correct, he or she may become the next leader.

After the children have played one or two games, let them discuss the strategies they use. Would they prefer to get a no or a yes answer? How do they eliminate a size, shape, or color?

OBJECTIVE: to use the properties of isomorphic sets to solve problems involving patterns.

3. Two systems are **isomorphic** if they have the same structure and the same internal set of relationships. Isomorphic sets must be equivalent and the patterns in two isomorphic sets must be the same. The sets shown in Figure 13–43 are isomorphic. The pieces may be put in one-to-one correspondence and they relate to each other in the same way. After the children have worked with simple isomorphic sets, they may work with more detailed sets. Construct a set of attribute materials that are isomorphic to the People Pieces. This means that the pieces must have four sets of distinguishing characteristics with two choices for each. Make a set of sailboats with purple or green sails, with small or large sails, with a sailor or without, with an anchor or without. After the sailboats are constructed, place the sailboats in a 4-by-4 Carroll diagram next to the People Pieces, which are also in a 4-by-4 Carroll diagram. The diagrams may be similar to the ones shown in Figure 13–44.

Do not put labels on the diagrams. Ask the children to decide on the labels for the Carroll diagram for the People Pieces. Tell the children that the sailboats are isomorphic to the People Pieces and you want them to discover the matching labels for the set of sailboats.

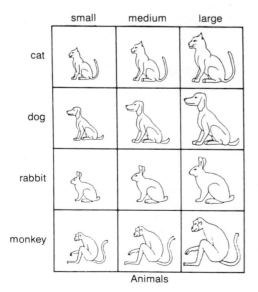

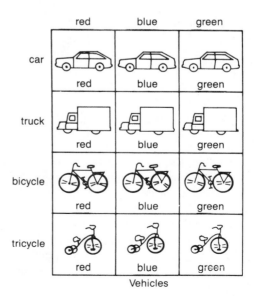

Figure 13–43 Isomorphic sets of attribute materials.

 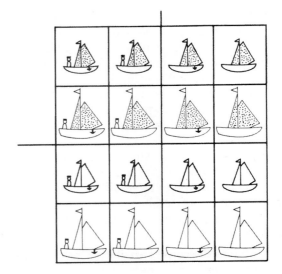

Figure 13 – 44 Additional isomorphic sets of attribute materials.

For instance, the positions that have males in the diagram for the People Pieces all have purple sails in the diagram for the sailboats. Ask the children to finish the following chart, which asks them to match all the characteristics:

males	purple sails
females	_____
red	_____
blue	_____
tall	_____
short	_____
skinny	_____
stout	_____

After the children have matched the characteristics, ask them to develop their own sets of materials that are isomorphic to either the People Pieces or the attribute blocks. A group of students making up a new set should write down the corresponding characteristics and then turn over each piece of the newly created set so that the characteristics of the set are not visible but the set remains in the same Carroll diagram. A group of students who have not seen the new set should then turn the pieces over one at a time and attempt to predict the matching characteristics. Keep track of how many pieces have been turned over before all the characteristics have been identified and matched. The fewer pieces used, the better.

This section gives only a brief idea of the many problems that may be developed using mathematical concepts that often do not involve numbers. Children should be encouraged to develop problems of their own for each other to solve. The classroom should always have a special table or bulletin board that contains problems for the children and a place for the children to suggest new ideas.

A C T I V I T I E S

Grades 3 – 5 and Grades 6 – 8

OBJECTIVE: to use probability to determine the most likely sum of two dice.

1. Make a chart like the one in Figure 13 – 45a and ask the children to keep a tally of the number of times each total comes up when they roll two dice. Combine the tallies from the whole class. Which total came up the most often? The least often? How would you explain these results?

Challenge the students to make a chart or diagram to help them predict the most common total. Some students might choose to make a tree diagram, as in

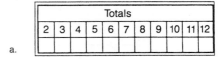

a.

					Totals						
2	3	4	5	6	7	8	9	10	11	12

Which Total Came Up Most Often?

	2	3	4	5	6	7	8	9	10	11	12
Dice	4%	6%	12%	10%	6%	23%	15%	8%	2%	13%	2%
Tree	3%	6%	8%	11%	14%	17%	14%	11%	8%	6%	3%

b.

Figure 13 – 45 Tally chart for sum of two dice.

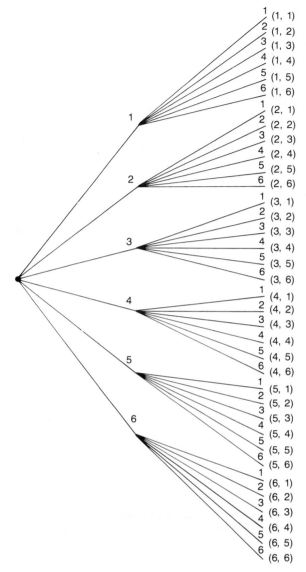

Figure 13 – 46 Tree diagram showing outcomes from rolling two dice.

Figure 13–46, to find all the possible outcomes from rolling two dice. Others might decide to make a Carroll diagram to show the same information, such as the one in Figure 13–47.

List the ordered pairs at the ends of the branches and find the totals. Make a table, like the one in Figure 13–45b, to show the number of times each total came up. How does this table compare to the actual totals found in your experiment?

- *Understanding the problem.* Each member of the class has already rolled a pair of dice 2 times, so we have 52 rolls altogether. And, the chart based on our tree diagram shows what would come up most often if everything were perfect. We need to compare the charts to see what is alike and what is different.

   When we rolled the dice, we got 52 answers. Will that make a difference when we compare? We can tell which numbers come up most often and then next-most often. Or we can change the numbers to fractions or percents and then compare them.

- *Devising a plan.* To compare the different numbers that came up most often, we'll make a small table with two rows. In one row, we'll put the percent of times each number came up when we threw the dice. In the next row, we'll put the percent of times the number appeared on the tree. Then we can compare the percents (make a systematic list).

- *Carrying out the plan.* We count how many times each number was rolled by the class, and Darlene and Ben use their calculators to find the percent each number represents. We put that information in the table. Then Candy and Jackie calculate the percents from the tree or Carroll diagram. We put the results in the table, as shown in Figure 13–45b.

   Now we can compare the results. The first thing we observe is that the number 7 was rolled most often (23 percent) and also appears on the tree diagram most often (17 percent). Now we can make several other important observations.

	Number on First Die					
Number on Second Die	1	2	3	4	5	6
1	(1, 1)	(2, 1)	(3, 1)	(4, 1)	(5, 1)	(6,1)
2	(1, 2)	(2, 2)	(3, 2)	(4, 2)	(5, 2)	(6,2)
3	(1, 3)	(2, 3)	(3, 3)	(4, 3)	(5, 3)	(6,3)
4	(1, 4)	(2, 4)	(3, 4)	(4, 4)	(5, 4)	(6,4)
5	(1, 5)	(2, 5)	(3, 5)	(4, 5)	(5, 5)	(6,5)
6	(1, 6)	(2, 6)	(3, 6)	(4, 6)	(5, 6)	(6,6)

Figure 13 – 47 Carroll diagram showing outcomes from rolling two dice.

- *Looking back.* We were able to find that 7 was the most likely sum of two dice. We found even more information because the table was systematic.

Have the children discuss the other findings from the table. What were the least frequent totals? How many times would you expect to get a total of 7 out of 100 rolls? Would you expect to get a total of 2 very often? Why?

Encourage the children to devise other experiments. Use two spinners, each numbered 1, 2, and 3, or keep track of cards drawn out of two hands that each have cards numbered 1, 2, 3, and 4. Tell children to draw tree diagrams to show all the possible permutations and to use these permutations to predict results for their experiments. How close are the predictions? Encourage students to discuss their strategies as they carry out the experiments.

If you have calculators with a random-number generator, experiment with using that to simulate rolling dice, or spinning a spinner, as in Figure 13–48. How do the simulations on the calculator compare with those using actual dice or spinners? Which gave you results closest to those predicted mathematically?

OBJECTIVE: to use statistics to persuade an audience.

2. Have the children select a problem that directly affects them or the school. This may be a hazardous street in front of the school, lack of appealing food in the cafeteria, or a need for supervised activities after school.

Help the children develop an instrument to collect data to support their case, such as a method of clocking and counting the traffic passing the school, surveys to determine the need for some change in the cafeteria menu, or a method of counting children's after-school activities. Discuss finding a random sampling of times for the traffic count or a random sampling of students and adults to participate in the survey. Discuss the best ways to organize and display the data collected. Help the children present their data to those responsible for making changes, such as members of the traffic bureau or the head cook in the cafeteria.

Claus (1989) reported on a statistics project undertaken by her fourth-grade class. They polled the entire school on cafeteria preferences such as fruit bars versus ice cream and hot versus cold lunches. They presented results to the principal, the PTA, and the school nurse, who used the information to make changes. The use of data collection and statistical interpretation gives students a powerful tool for change.

OBJECTIVE: to create questions for other children to answer by looking at graphs.

3. Graphs are often presented along with a ready-made list of questions to be answered. Turn the tables by asking the children to write the questions. Tell them that the only rule is that it must be possible to answer the questions using the information found on the graph. Encourage children to think of questions that no one else in the room will think of.

Structure some questions by specifying an operation or operations that must be used in the solution. Play a game like the television show "Jeopardy," in which you give an answer and ask the children to come up with the question. Keep the questions in the learning center for the children to work on later.

ORGANIZING FOR DATA ANALYSIS AND PROBABILITY TLC

The topics of probability, statistics, and graphing offer a natural opportunity for cooperative learning groups to explore real phenomena in their environments. Russell and Friel (1989) point out that leading elementary textbook series generally present work in data analysis as exercises requiring students to find information on a table or graph that has already been constructed for them. The textbooks rarely ask students to interpret or collect data. They note that the use of real data requires that students select the problems and questions they wish to explore, collect the data, work with a range of different data representations, including those that make use of technology, and learn to analyze data that is frequently "messy," with either too much or too little information that may or may not answer the questions that the students have asked. After the data have been collected and analyzed, students learn to use data not only to answer previous questions, but also to generate new ones. In their *Used Numbers*, Russell and Stone (1989) developed a num-

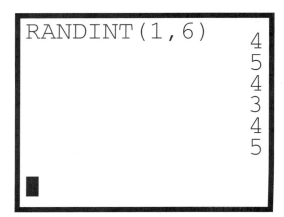

Figure 13–48   Calculator display showing random-number generator.

ber of curriculum modules to help K–6 students learn how numbers can be used to describe, interpret, and make predictions about real phenomena. A typical activity begins with the teacher or a student presenting some information to the whole class about an area of interest, such as the average family size in the community. Students then discuss questions that they are interested in exploring and break into small groups to come up with ways to investigate the topic. The teacher circulates to give help as needed, and students can move from whole-group, to small-group, to individual work in the exploration of the problem. Many of the activities presented in this chapter can be done in this same manner.

COMMUNICATING LEARNING OF DATA ANALYSIS AND PROBABILITY

By the very nature of the topics, this is an excellent area for students to use concrete or visual models to demonstrate findings. Students who have taken a survey to find the answer to a question of interest to the class can use concrete or visual graphs, tables, or charts to display the information they have found. This is an excellent example of information that should be communicated to a larger audience, not just to classmates. Surveys of interest to the children often pertain to the policy decisions of others, such as the principal, the mayor or the city council, the PTA, your congressperson, or the cafeteria manager. Students should be encouraged to write reports of their findings and conclusions and to illustrate their reports liberally with charts and graphs. They may then present the reports to the appropriate parties. Local newspapers or local cable television companies may be willing to publish or broadcast the results if they are approached by a committee of the students. This is an excellent way to integrate mathematics with other areas of the curriculum such as social studies and language arts and to empower the students at the same time.

When writing reports that make use of charts and graphs, students should learn to make use of graphing programs on the computer and the graphing calculator to illustrate the reports. Reports might be in written form or might be more interactive, using a program such as Microsoft PowerPoint on the computer. Using the graphing capabilities of the calculators and computers not only gives the students a deeper understanding of the data they have collected, but also gives them very practical skills in presenting data that they will use throughout their lives.

CONNECTING AND REPRESENTING LEARNING OF DATA ANALYSIS AND PROBABILITY

Mr. Calebreto's second-grade class is studying the weather and discussing how meteorologists make their predictions each day. Mr. Calebreto says that he heard that there is a 50 percent chance of rain tomorrow and asks whether anyone knows what that means. After much discussion, he takes out a coin and says that there is a 50 percent chance of the coin coming up heads. The students have had some experience flipping coins, so they are able to discuss how often heads and tails generally come up for a coin. Mr. Calebreto then flips the coin and announces that it has come up heads. He then asks the students what the chances are of that happening again. Some students think that another head is more likely since the first one and others think it is now time for it to come up tails. Another group of students think that the first flip makes no difference. After a discussion of the coin flip, Mr. Calebreto returns the discussion to the weather and the meaning of a 50 percent chance of rain. The students decide that they should keep track of the predictions each day and keep a chart to see how accurate the predictions are. They will return to the probability discussion each day as they chart both predictions and actual weather conditions.

Mr. Greco's sixth-grade class is studying several double bar graphs that show the percent of males and females in age categories from 0–4 to 80–84. They have noticed that one of the graphs shows a very high percent of people over age 55, another graph shows a much higher percent of males than females, and yet another shows a very large number of both males and females between the ages of 15–19 and 20–24. Mr. Greco has told them that one of the graphs is from a college town, one is from a town with a large retirement community, and one is from a town with a large army base. Students are discussing how they can determine which town is which by looking at the ages and genders shown on the graphs. They decide that it would be interesting to collect data on their own town, make a double bar graph, and compare it to the graphs they are studying. Brittany offers to call City Hall to get the needed information.

ASSESSING DATA ANALYSIS AND PROBABILITY LEARNING

Most of the assessment in the areas of probability and statistics should be informal. Standardized tests for elementary students may include reading graphs and finding measures of central tendency, but they may not include questions on probability and statistics. This does not mean that probability and statistics are unimportant, however. A good foundation in the basic concepts of these topics will greatly help the students as they progress in school.

Piaget and Inhelder (1975) studied the development of the idea of chance in children and found that children's thinking in this area can be divided into three stages. In the first stage (up until about age 7 or 8), children do not understand the concept of randomness. They look for some hidden order and make predictions based on their own preferences or on the misconception that an outcome should "catch up" to the others. Very unlikely events do not surprise them.

In the second stage (from about age 7 or 8 until about age 11 or 12), a broad understanding of randomness is achieved, but children do not understand the effects of large numbers. Very unlikely events do surprise them and cause them to look for a reason. In the third stage, that of formal reasoning, children understand the effect of large numbers and can assign numerical probabilities.

In a review of a number of studies conducted after the Piaget and Inhelder research, Shulte (1987, p. 32) concluded that "the research indicates that students have some understanding of probability and related topics, that this understanding increases with age and instruction, and that probability can successfully be taught in the elementary school in carefully selected experiments." He recommends that probability be included among the topics presented in elementary school.

Teachers should be aware of some of the misconceptions that students may have about probability as well as about graphing and statistics. The following list gives some of these misconceptions:

1. Students may believe that a mathematical probability should give the exact outcome of an experiment. They may believe that if the probability of getting a head is $\frac{1}{2}$, then they should always get 10 heads out of 20 flips of a coin. Be sure the students have many opportunities to perform experiments to see the differences between mathematical and experimental probabilities.

2. Students may believe that the instrument used in a probability experiment has a memory. They may believe that if they have gotten 5 heads in a row with a coin, then it is more likely that a tail will come up on the next flip. Discuss whether the coin has any memory of what came up on the previous flips. The probability of getting a tail remains the same, no matter what came up previously.

3. Students may hold a bias against or in favor of a particular outcome in an experiment. They may feel that 3 should come up most often on a die because

it is their favorite number or that 6 should not come up very often because they do not like it. The activities suggested in this chapter in which the students are asked to tally a large number of experimental results should be discussed with the students to see if the results match their expectations.

4. Students may expect all outcomes to be equally likely, even if they are not. They may think that a total of 2 on two dice should be just as likely as a total of 7. Students should discuss the activity relating the roll of two dice to the tree diagram described in the problem-solving section of this chapter.

5. Students may wish to overgeneralize from their own experiments or surveys. If they take a poll of all the fifth graders in their school, they may wish to say that the results would be the same all over the country. Discuss with them what is wrong with such thinking. Making correct inferences from data is a skill that takes time and experience to develop.

6. Students may confuse the different measures of central tendency. They should be given a number of chances to find the mean, the median, and the mode and to discuss which measure is used in the articles they read and which is most appropriate for a given situation.

7. Students may try to use an inappropriate graph to display data. Discuss with them why a line graph is not good for showing favorite colors. Does the line from blue to green have any meaning? What is a more appropriate type of graph?

8. Students may forget to completely label a graph. How can they interpret a graph if some of the labels are missing?

9. Students may use pictures of different sizes on a picture graph, bars of different widths on a bar graph, or spaces of different sizes between numbers on a line graph. How does this affect the interpretation?

When testing students' understanding of these topics, be sure to observe their work during experiments and while they are developing surveys. Do not rely on paper-and-pencil instruments. You may wish to use an instrument such as "How Many Questions?" (Jensen, 1973), which tests a student's ability to ask questions involving graphs rather than his or her ability to answer such questions. This will give you an idea of how well the students understand what graphs may be used for and how creative the students can be in posing questions.

Encourage students to keep records of their work and to write down any questions they have as they progress. Students often are excellent judges of how well they understand the lesson.

SOMETHING FOR EVERYONE

Many of the topics discussed in this chapter are particularly appropriate for mathematically promising students. Some mathematically promising students may seem to prefer working on abstract problems and may not use concrete materials, even though using these materials may be of benefit to them. Data analysis and probability give children an opportunity to be involved with concrete models and simulations that have direct applications in many fields of interest to them, such as future careers in business and the professions.

Students who need additional challenges can explore topics in probability and statistics, such as the counting processes for finding the number of possible outcomes and methods for finding the probability of a statement involving *and* and *or*. Use counting processes to find the number of five-digit zip codes or seven-digit phone numbers. Encourage the students to develop their own rules for finding the number of possible combinations, with or without repetition. How can you determine the number of ways Event A *and* Event B can happen? Is this the same as determining the number of ways Event A *or* Event B can happen?

Pascal's triangle (which was introduced in Chapter 5) also has interesting applications for finding the number of possible combinations of anything with two possibilities for each move. Encourage children to make connections to earlier learning whenever possible.

Introduce the story, *Socrates and the Three Little Pigs*, by Anno (1986), where Socrates, the philosopher wolf, uses ideas of combinations and permutations to determine the best way to find one pig by itself in one of the five houses in which the pigs live. If your calculators have the capability of finding combinations and permutations, encourage students to explore these functions and to compare them to the mathematics that Socrates uses. Let them investigate problems of their own that use combinations, permutations, or both. Interested students might want to take this further to investigate the uses of combinatorial analysis in computer programming and other everyday problem solving.

Another challenging resource for learning about combinations and permutations is the video kit, *Making Money with Major Munchy: Explorations in Probability.* (Human Relations Media, 1994). This program starts with a video of four teens trying to win a contest by collecting the six letters in the word Munchy from the Major Munchy cereal company. The kit includes worksheets, transparencies, dice for simulations, and a CD-ROM with further explorations including making frequency distributions, creating histograms, and conducting simulations.

The topic of graphing offers opportunities for learning to suit many varied learning styles. Bodily/kinesthetic children learn well when they have the opportunity to make graphs out of the objects themselves. Visual children can learn well using any type of graph. Graphs suit their style of forming a mental image to fit the data collected. Auditory children enjoy the discussions that accompany collecting data and analyzing the graphs.

Use graphing in conjunction with other subjects, such as science, reading, and social studies, to help children learn those subjects as well. Many of the concepts from this chapter do not need to be a separate unit in mathematics. Use opportunities throughout the school day to help children learn the concepts and their uses in the world surrounding them.

FOR YOU AS A TEACHER: IDEAS FOR DISCUSSION AND YOUR PROFESSIONAL PORTFOLIO

This section is intended to provide you the opportunity to read, write, and reflect on key elements of this chapter. We list several discussion ideas. We hope that one or more of these ideas will prove interesting to you and that you will choose to investigate and write about the ideas. The results of your work should be considered as part of your professional portfolio. You might consider these two questions as guides for your writing: "What does the material in this chapter mean for you as a teacher?" or "How can what you are reading be translated into a teaching practice for you as a teacher?"

DISCUSSION IDEAS

1. Work with a group of middle grades students to design an experiment that involves collecting data to answer a question of local interest. You might want to collect data similar to that collected in a census survey and compare it to the national census (Weblink 13–3). Use computer software or a graphing calculator to assist in analysis of your data. Present your findings to the class using a computer application such as Microsoft PowerPoint.

2. Ask two or three six- or seven-year-olds and two or three middle grades students to make predictions about the flip of a coin or the roll of a die. Compare their responses. Are the errors in the two groups similar? How would you design a probability lesson for each group of students based upon the results of your questioning?

3. Use one of the Internet sites, activity books, videos, or one of the children's books on probability such as *Do You Wanna Bet?* (Cushman, 1991) and design a probability lesson for intermediate students that uses some of the ideas in the book. If possible, use the lesson with children and report on the results. What was the main objective of the lesson, and how did you determine whether most of the students had mastered it? What would you change if you taught the lesson again? What would you be sure to keep?

ADDITIONAL RESOURCES

REFERENCES

Barrett, Gloria, and John Goebel, "The Impact of Graphing Calculators on the Teaching and Learning of Mathematics," in *Teaching and Learning Mathematics in the 1990s*, ed. Thomas J. Cooney and Christian R. Hirsch. Reston, VA: National Council of Teachers of Mathematics, 1990.

Bereska, Carolyn, L. Carey Bolster, Cyrilla H. Bolster, and Richard Scheaffer, *Exploring Statistics in the Elementary Grades*. White Plains, NY: Dale Seymour, 1998.

Bestgen, Barbara J., "Making and Interpreting Graphs and Tables: Results and Implications from National Assessment," *Arithmetic Teacher*, 28, no. 4 (December 1980), 26–29.

Bright, George W., Wallece Brewer, Kay McClain, and Edward S. Mooney, *Navigating through Data Analysis and Probability in Grades 6–8*. Reston, VA: NCTM, 2002.

Browning, Christine A., and Dwayne E. Channell, *Explorations: Graphing Calculator Activities for Enriching Middle School Mathematics*. Austin, TX: Texas Instruments, 1997.

Bruni, James V., and Helene J. Silverman, "Developing Concepts in Probability and Statistics—and Much More," *Arithmetic Teacher*, 33, no. 6 (February 1986), pp. 34–37.

Burns, Marilyn, *Math By All Means*. New Rochelle, NY: Cuisenaire Company of America, Inc., 1991.

Burrill, Gail F., Miriam Clifford, and Richard Scheaffer, *Data-Driven Mathematics* White Plains, NY: Dale Seymour 1998. (a series of 11 modules on algebra, geometry, and advanced mathematics)

Carpenter Thomas P., "Research on the Role of Structure in Thinking," *Arithmetic Teacher*, 32, no. 6 (February 1985), 58–60.

Chapin, Suzanne, Alice Koziol, Jennifer MacPherson, and Carol Rezba, *Navigating through Data Analysis and Probability in Grades 3–5*. Reston, VA: NCTM, 2002.

Claus, Allison, "Making Mathematics Come Alive through a Statistics Project," in *New Directions for Elementary School Mathematics*, ed. Paul R. Trafton and Albert P. Shulte. Reston, VA: National Council of Teachers of Mathematics, 1989.

Conference Board of the Mathematical Sciences, *The Mathematical Sciences Curriculum K–12: What Is Still Fundamental and What Is Not?* Washington, DC: CBMS, 1983.

Coombs, Betty, and Lalie Harcourt, *Explorations I & II*. Don Mills, OH: Addison-Wesley, 1986.

Corwin, Rebecca B., and Susan N. Friel, *Used Numbers: Statistics: Predicting and Sampling*. Palo Alto, CA: Dale Seymour, 1990.

Corwin, Rebecca B., and Susan Jo Russell, *Used Numbers: Measuring: From Paces to Feet*. Palo Alto, CA: Dale Seymour, 1990.

Dickinson, J. Craig, "Gather, Organize, Display: Mathematics for the Information Society," *Arithmetic Teacher*, 34, no. 4 (December 1986), 12–15.

DiFazio, Martha Hunt, "Graphics Software Side by Side," *Mathematics Teacher*, 83, no. 6 (September 1990), 436–446.

Dossey, John A., Ina V. S. Mullis, Mary M. Lindquist, and Donald L. Chambers, *The Mathematics Report Card: Are We Measuring Up? Trends and Achievement Based on the 1986 National Assessment*. Princeton, NJ: Educational Testing Service, 1988.

Edwards, Nancy Tanner, and Gary G. Bitter, "Teaching Mathematics with Technology: Changing Variables Using Spreadsheet Templates," *Arithmetic Teacher*, 37, no. 2 (October 1989), 40–44.

Edwards, Nancy Tanner, Gary G. Bitter, and Mary M. Hatfield, "Teaching Mathematics with Technology: Data Base and Spreadsheet Templates with Public Domain Software," *Arithmetic Teacher*, 37, no. 8 (April 1990), 52–55.

Friel, Susan N., "Teaching Statistics: What's Average?" in *The Teaching and Learning of Algorithms in School Mathematics, 1998 Yearbook*, ed. Lorna J. Morrow. Reston, VA: NCTM, 1998.

Friel, Susan N., Janice R. Mokros, and Susan Jo Russell, *Used Numbers: Statistics: Middles, Means-and In-Betweens*. Palo Alto, CA: Dale Seymour, 1992.

Goodnow, Judy, *Cooperative Problem Solving with Attribute Blocks*. Sunnyvale, CA: Creative Publications, 1989.

Holden, Linda, *Thinker Tasks: Critical Thinking Activities*. Mountain View, CA: Creative Publications, 1986.

Holden, Linda, and Ann Roper, *Thinker Games*. Mountain View, CA: Creative Publications, 1987.

Hoogeboom, Shirley, *Animal Attribute Tiles: Activities for Classifying and Sorting*. Mountain View, CA: Creative Publications, 1990.

Hoogeboom, Shirley, and Judy Goodnow, *Reasoning with Teddy Bear Counters*. Sunnyvale, CA: Creative Publications, 1989.

———, *Intermediate Probability Jobcards*. Sunnyvale, CA: Creative Publications, 1991.

Jensen, Linda, *The Relationships among Mathematical Creativity, Numerical Aptitude and Mathematical Achievement*. Unpublished doctoral dissertation, University of Texas at Austin, 1973.

Jones, Graham A., and Roger Day, *Algebra, Data, and Probability Explorations for Middle School: A Graphics Calculator Approach*. Menlo Park, CA: Dale Seymour, 1998.

Lappan, Glenda, James T. Fey, William M. Fitzgerald, Susan N. Friel, and Elizabeth D. Phillips, *Clever Counting: Combinatorics*. Menlo Park, CA: Dale Seymour, 1998.

———, *Samples and Populations: Data and Statistics*. Menlo Park, CA: Dale Seymour, 1998.

———, *Data about Us: Statistics*. Palo Alto, CA: Dale Seymour, 1996.

———, *How Likely Is It?: Probability.* Palo Alto, CA: Dale Seymour, 1996.

Lovitt, Charles, and Ian Lowe, *Chance and Data Investigations* (Vol. I, II). Carlton, Victoria, Australia: Curriculum Corporation, 1994.

MacDonell, Alan, ed., *The Super Source: Probability and Statistics Grades 7–8.* White Plains, NY: Cuisenaire Company of America, Inc., 1998.

Murphy, Elaine C., *Developing Skills with Tables and Graphs.* Palo Alto, CA: Dale Seymour, 1981.

National Council of Teachers of Mathematics, *Principles and Standards for School Mathematics.* Reston, VA: NCTM, 2000.

Nuffield Foundation, *Pictorial Representation.* New York: Wiley, 1967.

———, *Probability and Statistics.* New York: Wiley, 1969.

Piaget, Jean, and Barbel Inhelder, *The Origin of the Idea of Chance in Children.* New York: W. W. Norton, 1975.

Quinn, Robert J., "Developing Conceptual Understanding of Relations and Functions with Attribute Blocks," *Mathematics Teaching in the Middle School,* 3, no. 3 (November–December 1997), 186–190.

Russell, Susan J., and Rebecca B. Corwin, *Statistics: The Shape of the Data.* Palo Alto, CA: Dale Seymour, 1989.

Russell, Susan Jo, and Susan N. Friel, "Collecting and Analyzing Real Data in the Elementary School Classroom," in *New Directions for Elementary School Mathematics,* ed. Paul R. Trafton and Albert P. Shulte. Reston, VA: National Council of Teachers of Mathematics, 1989.

Russell, Susan Jo, and Antonia Stone, *Used Numbers: Counting: Ourselves and Our Families.* Palo Alto, CA: Dale Seymour, 1990.

Sandefur, James T., Jr., "Discrete Mathematics: A Unified Approach," in *The Secondary School Mathematics Curriculum,* National Council of Teachers of Mathematics, 1985 Yearbook. Reston, VA: NCTM, 1985.

School Mathematics Study Group, *Probability for the Intermediate Grades.* Stanford, CA: SMSG, Stanford University, 1966.

———, *Probability for the Primary Grades.* Stanford, CA: SMSG, Stanford University, 1966.

Sheffield, Linda Jensen, Mary Cavanagh, Linda Dacey, Carol R. Findell, Carole E. Greenes, and Marian Small, *Navigating through Data Analysis and Probability in Prekindergarten–Grade 2.* Reston, VA: NCTM, 2002.

Shielack, Jane F., "Teaching Mathematics with Technology: A Graphing Tool for the Primary Grades," *Arithmetic Teacher,* 38, no. 2 (October 1990), 40–43.

Shulte, Albert P., ed., *Teaching Statistics and Probability,* National Council of Teachers of Mathematics, 1981 Yearbook. Reston, VA: NCTM, 1981.

Shulte, Albert P., "Learning Probability Concepts in Elementary School Mathematics," *Arithmetic Teacher,* 34, no. 5 (January 1987), 32–33.

Shulte, Albert, and Stuart Choate, *What Are My Chances? Books A and B.* Palo Alto, CA: Creative Publications, 1977.

Stofac, Valerie J., and Anne Wesely, *Logic Problems for Primary People.* Sunnyvale, CA: Creative Publications, 1987.

Willcutt, Bob, *Critical and Creative Thinking with Attribute Blocks.* Pacific Grove, CA: Critical Thinking Books and Software, 1998.

CHILDREN'S LITERATURE

Anno, Mitsumasa, *Anno's Math Games.* New York: Philomel, 1982.

———, *Anno's Hat Trick.* New York: Philomel, 1985.

———, *Socrates and the Three Little Pigs.* New York: Philomel, 1986.

———, *Anno's Faces.* New York: Philomel, 1989.

Barrett, Judi, *Cloudy with a Chance of Meatballs.* New York: Atheneum, 1978.

Branley, Franklyn M., *It's Raining Cats and Dogs.* Boston: Houghton Mifflin, 1987.

Cole, Joanna, *The Magic School Bus inside the Earth.* NY, NY: Scholastic, 1987.

Cushman, Jean, *Do You Wanna Bet?* New York: Clarion Books, 1991.

Ganeri, Anita, *The Biggest and Smallest.* Hauppauge, NY: Barron's, 1992.

———, *The Fastest and Slowest.* Hauppauge, NY: Barron's, 1992.

———, *The Longest and Tallest.* Hauppauge, NY: Barron's, 1992.

Giganti, Paul, Jr., *How Many Snails? A Counting Book.* New York: Greenwillow, 1988.

Graham, Amanda, *Angus Thought He Was Big.* Hicksville, NY: Newbridge Communications, 1991.

Guarino, Deborah, *Is Your Mama a Llama?* New York: Scholastic, 1989.

Lobel, Arnold, *Frog and Toad Are Friends.* New York: HarperCollins, 1970.

Reid, Margarette S., *The Button Box.* New York: Dutton, 1990.

Srivastava, Jane Jonas, *Statistics.* New York: Crowell, 1973.

———, *Averages.* New York: Crowell, 1975.

TECHNOLOGY

Abrams, Richard (Publisher). *Graph Master.* Watertown, MA: Tom Snyder Productions, 2001.

Baker, Michael O., and Tracy Valleau. *Escape from the Logic Spiders.* Pacific Grove, CA: Critical Thinking Press & Software, 1992. (software)

Broderbund, *Tabletop. Jr.* Novato, CA: Broderbund, 1995. (software)

Broderbund, *Tabletop, Sr.* Novato, CA: Broderbund, 1995. (software)

Davidson, *The Cruncher.* Torrance, CA: Davidson, 1997. (software)

———, *Math Blaster Jr.* Torrance, CA: Davidson, 1997. (software)

———, *Math Blaster Mystery: The Great Brain Robbery.* Torrance, CA: Davidson, 1997. (software)

Edmark, *Mighty Math Carnival Countdown.* Orlando, FL: Harcourt Brace, 1996. (software)

———, *Mighty Math Number Heroes.* Orlando, FL: Harcourt Brace, 1996. (software)

———, *Millie's Math House.* Orlando, FL: Harcourt Brace, 1995. (software)

———, *Sammy's Science House.* Orlando, FL: Harcourt Brace, 1995. (software)

GPN, *Math Vantage: Unit III: Data Analysis.* Lincoln, NE: GPN, 1997. (video and print materials)

Hancock, Chris, and Scot Osterweil, *Logical Journey of the Zoombinis.* Novato, CA: Broderbund, 1996. (software)

Harcourt Brace, *Data ToolKit.* Orlando, FL: Harcourt Brace, 1996. (software)

Harcourt Brace, *Graph Links Grades 1–6.* Orlando, FL: Harcourt Brace, 1996. (software)

Human Relations Media, *Making Money with Major Munchy: Explorations in Probability.* Pleasantville, NY: Human Relations Media, 1994. (video and transparencies)

Roman, John (Exec. Producer), *Calculator-Based Laboratory Video Workshop.* Dallas, TX: Wholesale Electronic Supply, Inc. Education Division, 1995. (video and book)

Sunburst, *Data Explorer.* Pleasantville, NY: Sunburst Communications, 1998. (software)

Sunburst, *Graphers.* Pleasantville, NY: Sunburst Communications, 1998. (software)

WEBLINKS

Weblink 13–1: Statistics and Probability activities from Project Interactivate from the Shodor Education Foundation, Inc. http://www.shodor.org/interactivate/activities/index.html#pro

Weblink 13–2: Plop It! Game from Project Interactivate from the Shodor Education Foundation, Inc. http://shodor.org/interactivate/activities/plop/index.html

Weblink 13–3: NCTM Illuminations activities for data collection and statistics work, grades 3–5. http//illuminations.nctm.org/lessonplans/index.html#35

Weblink 13–4: United States Census Bureau website. http://www.census.gov/

Weblink 13–5: Maze Game from Project Interactivate from the Shodor Education Foundation, Inc. http://shodor.org/interactivate/activities/coords/index.html

SUPPLIERS OF MANIPULATIVE MATERIALS, BOOKS, CALCULATORS, AND COMPUTER SOFTWARE

Activity Resources Company, Inc.
20655 Hathaway Ave.
Hayward, CA 94541
http://www.activityresources.com/

AIMS Education Foundation
P.O. Box 8120
Fresno, CA 93747-8120
http://www.aimsedu.org/

Annenberg/CPB
401 9th St NW
Washington, DC 20004
http://www.learner.org/

Apple Computer, Inc.
1 Infinite Loop
Cupertino, CA 95014
http://www.apple.com/

Classroom Connect
8000 Marina Blvd.
Suite 400
Brisbane, CA 94005
http://www.classroom.com/

Corwin Press
2455 Teller Road
Thousand Oaks, CA 91320
www.corwinpress.com/

Creative Publications
Wright Group/McGraw-Hill
P.O. Box 182604
Columbus, Ohio 43272
http://www.wrightgroup.com/

The Critical Thinking Company
P.O. Box 448
Pacific Grove, CA 93950
http://www.criticalthinking.com/

Dale Seymour/Pearson Learning Group
135 South Mount Zion Road
P.O. Box 2500, Lebanon, IL 46052
http://www.pearsonlearning.com/

Delta Education
P.O. Box 3000
Nashua, NH 03061-3000
http://www.delta-ed.com/

Didax Educational Resources, Inc.
395 Main Street
Rowley, MA 01969-3785
http://www.didaxinc.com/

Don Cohen—The Mathman
809 Stratford Dr.
Champaign, IL 61821-4140
http://www.shout.net/~mathman

EAI Education
Eric Armin, Inc.
P.O. Box 644
Franklin Lakes
NJ 07417-0644
http://www.eaieducation.com/

Educational Resources
1550 Executive Drive
Elgin, IL 60123
http://www.edresources.com/

ETA Cuisenaire
500 Greenview Court
Vernon Hills, IL 60061-1838
http://www.etacuisenaire.com/

FASE Productions
4801 Wilshire Blvd.
Suite 215
Los Angeles, CA 90010
http://www.fasenet.com/

GPN Educational Media
University of Nebraska-Lincoln
P.O. Box 80669
Lincoln, NE 68501-0669
http://gpn.unl.edu/

Hartley Courseware
3451 Dunckel Rd., Suite 200
Lansing, MI 48711
http://www.nol.net/~athel/org/har.html

Heinemann
P.O. Box 6926
Portsmouth, NH 03802-6926
http://www.heinemann.com/

Human Relations Media (HRM)
41 Kensico Dr.
Mount Kisco, NY 10519
http://www.hrmvideo.com/

Key Curriculum Press
1150 65th St.
Emeryville, CA 94608
http://www.keycurriculumpress.com/

Kluwer Academic Publishers
101 Philip Drive
Norwell, MA 02061
http://www.wkap.nl/

Lawrence Erlbaum Associates, Inc.
10 Industrial Avenue
Mahwah, NJ 07430-2262
http://www.erlbaum.com/

Lawrence Hall of Science
University of California, Berkeley
Lawrence Hall of Science #5200
Berkeley, CA 94720-5200
http://www.lhs.berkeley.edu/

MATHCOUNTS
1420 King St.
Alexandria, VA 22314
http://www.mathcounts.org/

The Math Learning Center
P.O. Box 3226
Salem, OR 97302
http://www.mlc.pdx.edu/

Math Solutions Publications
Marilyn Burns Education Associates
150 Gate 5 Road, Suite 101
Sausalito, CA 94965
http://www.mathsolutions.com/

Mathematics Pentathlon Institute
1412 Sadlier Circle East Dr.
Indianapolis, IN 46239
http://www.mathpentath.org/

Mindplay
440 S. Williams Blvd.
Suite 206
Tucson, AZ 85711
http://www.mindplay.com/

NASCO
901 Janesville Ave.
P.O. Box 901,
Fort Atkinson, WI 53538–0901
http://www.enasco.com/

National Academies Press
500 Fifth St., NW
Lock box 285
Washington, DC 20055
http://www.nap.edu/

National Council of Teachers of Mathematics
1906 Association Drive
Reston, VA 22091
http://www.nctm.org/

National Middle School Association
4151 Executive Parkway
Suite 300
Westerville, OH 43081
http://www.nmsa.org/

Optimum Resource, Inc.
18 Hunter Road
Hilton Head, SC 29926
http://www.stickybear.com/

Riverdeep, Inc.
500 Redwood Blvd
Novato, CA 94947
http://www.riverdeep.net

Scholastic
557 Broadway
NY, NY 10012
http://www.scholastic.com/

Summit Learning
755 Rockwell Ave.
P.O. Box 755
Fort Atkinson, WI 53538-0755
www.summitlearning.com/

Sunburst Technology
1550 Executive Dr.
Elgin, IL 60123
http://www.sunburst.com/

Texas Instruments, Inc.
7800 Banner Drive
Dallas, TX 75251
http://education.ti.com/

Trends in International Mathematics and Science Study
National Center for Education Statistics
1990 K St, NW
Room 9045
Washington, DC 20006
http://nces.ed.gov/TIMSS/

Tom Snyder Productions
80 Coolidge Hill Road
Watertown, MA 02172-2817
http://www.tomsnyder.com/

Tricon Publishing
6400 S. Crawford Rd
Mt. Pleasant, MI 48858
http://www.triconpub.com/

John Wiley & Sons, Inc.
605 Third Ave.
New York, Ny 10158
http://www.wiley.com/

BLACKLINE MASTERS

Permission is granted by the publisher to reproduce the forms on pages 476–517.

Pattern Blocks

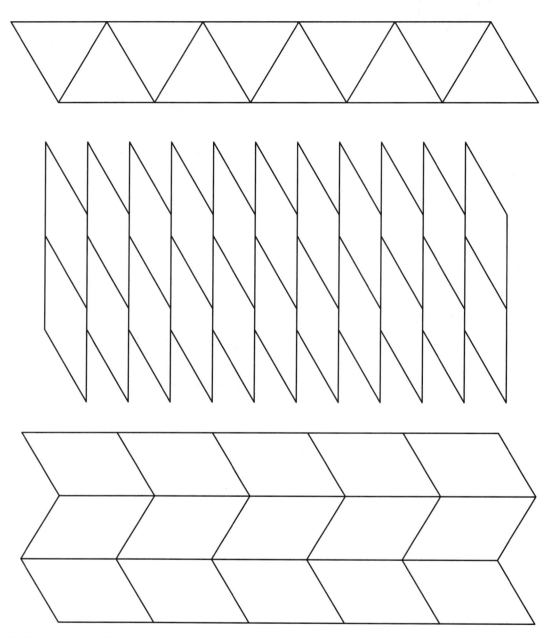

Sheffield and Cruikshank, *Teaching and Learning Mathematics: Pre-Kindergarten Through Middle School*, 5th ed. Copyright © 2005. John Wiley & Sons, Inc.

Pattern Blocks

Sheffield and Cruikshank, *Teaching and Learning Mathematics: Pre-Kindergarten Through Middle School,* 5th ed. Copyright © 2005. John Wiley & Sons, Inc.

Pattern Blocks

Attribute Shapes

Sheffield and Cruikshank, *Teaching and Learning Mathematics: Pre-Kindergarten Through Middle School,* 5th ed. Copyright © 2005. John Wiley & Sons, Inc.

Dot Cards

Sheffield and Cruikshank, *Teaching and Learning Mathematics: Pre-Kindergarten Through Middle School,* 5th ed. Copyright © 2005. John Wiley & Sons, Inc.

Five Frames

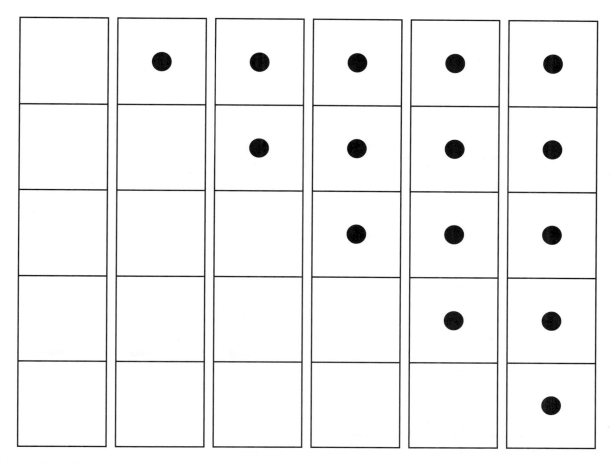

Sheffield and Cruikshank, *Teaching and Learning Mathematics: Pre-Kindergarten Through Middle School,* 5th ed. Copyright © 2005. John Wiley & Sons, Inc.

Ten Frame

Sheffield and Cruikshank, *Teaching and Learning Mathematics: Pre-Kindergarten Through Middle School,* 5th ed. Copyright © 2005. John Wiley & Sons, Inc.

Ten Frames

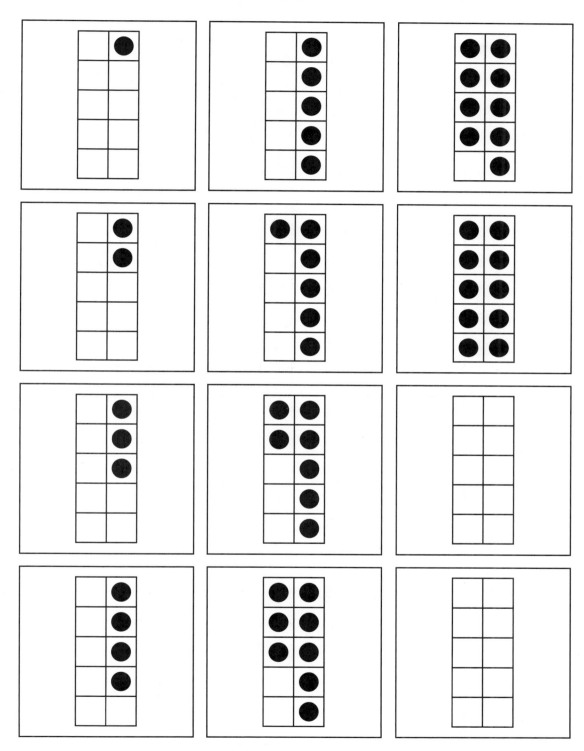

Sheffield and Cruikshank, *Teaching and Learning Mathematics: Pre-Kindergarten Through Middle School,* 5th ed. Copyright © 2005. John Wiley & Sons, Inc.

Base Five Patterns

Base Five Patterns

Sheffield and Cruikshank, *Teaching and Learning Mathematics: Pre-Kindergarten Through Middle School,* 5th ed. Copyright © 2005. John Wiley & Sons, Inc.

Base Five Patterns

Sheffield and Cruikshank, *Teaching and Learning Mathematics: Pre-Kindergarten Through Middle School,* 5th ed. Copyright © 2005. John Wiley & Sons, Inc.

Base Ten Patterns (Decimal Patterns)

Base Ten Patterns (Decimal Patterns)

Base Ten Patterns (Decimal Patterns)

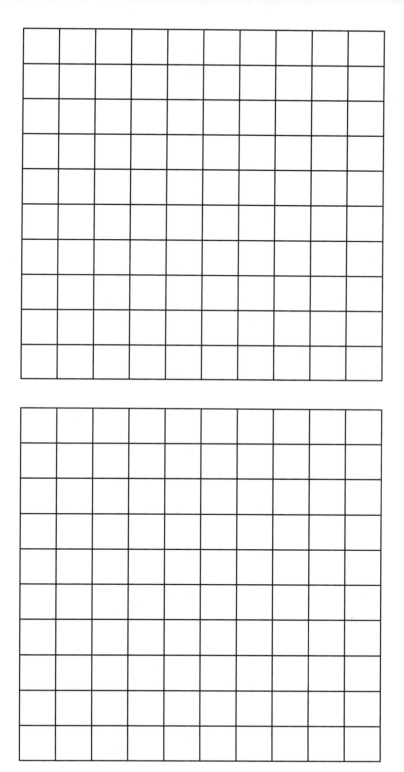

Sheffield and Cruikshank, *Teaching and Learning Mathematics: Pre-Kindergarten Through Middle School,* 5th ed. Copyright © 2005. John Wiley & Sons, Inc.

Base Ten Patterns (Decimal Patterns)

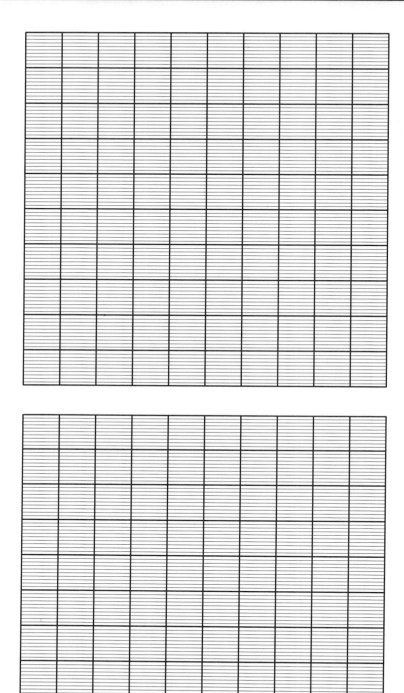

Sheffield and Cruikshank, *Teaching and Learning Mathematics: Pre-Kindergarten Through Middle School*, 5th ed. Copyright © 2005. John Wiley & Sons, Inc.

Hundreds Chart

1	2	3	4	5	6	7	8	9	10
11	12	13	14	15	16	17	18	19	20
21	22	23	24	25	26	27	28	29	30
31	32	33	34	35	36	37	38	39	40
41	42	43	44	45	46	47	48	49	50
51	52	53	54	55	56	57	58	59	60
61	62	63	64	65	66	67	68	69	70
71	72	73	74	75	76	77	78	79	80
81	82	83	84	85	86	87	88	89	90
91	92	93	94	95	96	97	98	99	100

Blank Hundreds Chart

Table for Addition or Multiplication

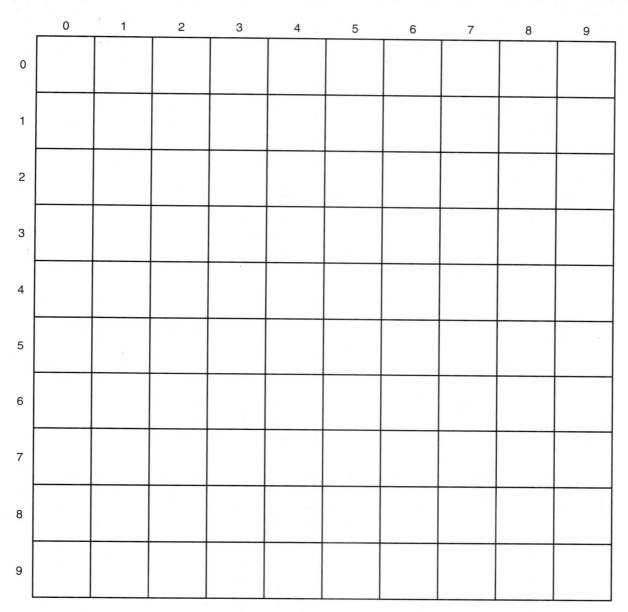

Sheffield and Cruikshank, *Teaching and Learning Mathematics: Pre-Kindergarten Through Middle School*, 5th ed. Copyright © 2005. John Wiley & Sons, Inc.

Centimeter Grid Paper

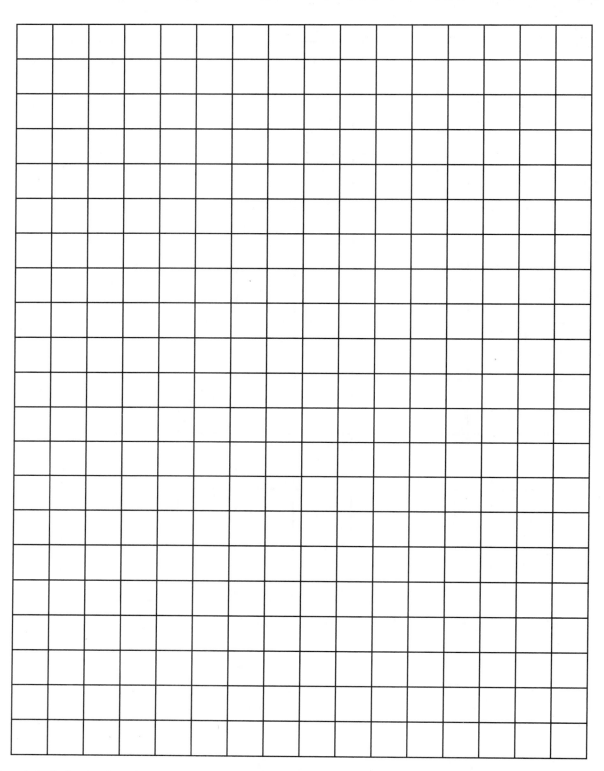

Sheffield and Cruikshank, *Teaching and Learning Mathematics: Pre-Kindergarten Through Middle School,* 5th ed. Copyright © 2005. John Wiley & Sons, Inc.

Inch Grid Paper

Circular Fraction Patterns

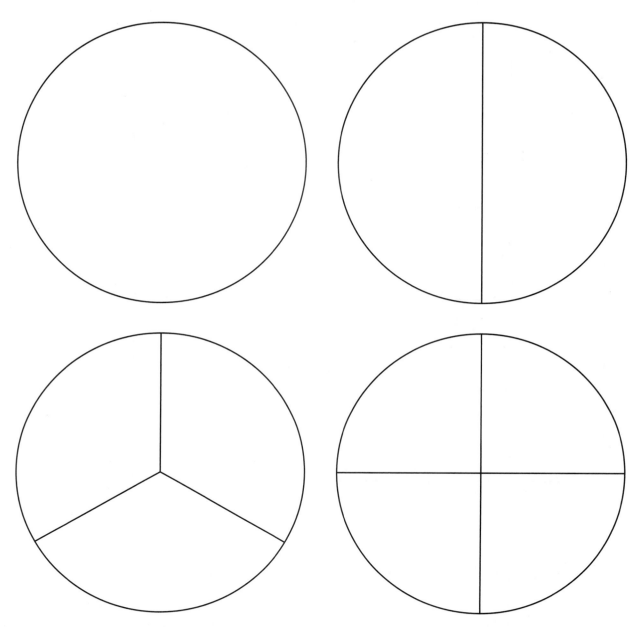

Sheffield and Cruikshank, *Teaching and Learning Mathematics: Pre-Kindergarten Through Middle School*, 5th ed. Copyright © 2005. John Wiley & Sons, Inc.

Circular Fraction Patterns

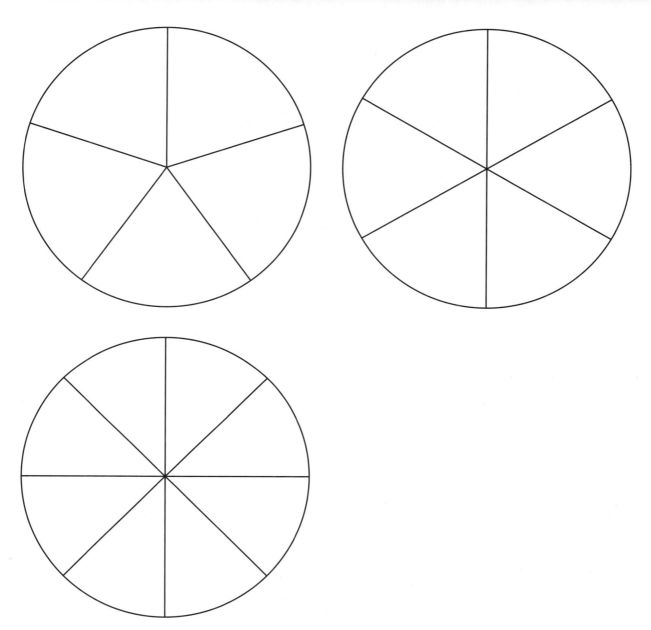

Sheffield and Cruikshank, *Teaching and Learning Mathematics: Pre-Kindergarten Through Middle School,* 5th ed. Copyright © 2005. John Wiley & Sons, Inc.

Circular Fraction Patterns

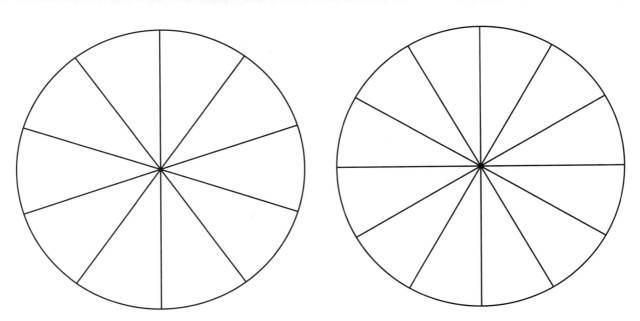

Sheffield and Cruikshank, *Teaching and Learning Mathematics: Pre-Kindergarten Through Middle School,* 5th ed. Copyright © 2005. John Wiley & Sons, Inc.

Rectangular Fraction Patterns

one unit

Rectangular Fraction Patterns

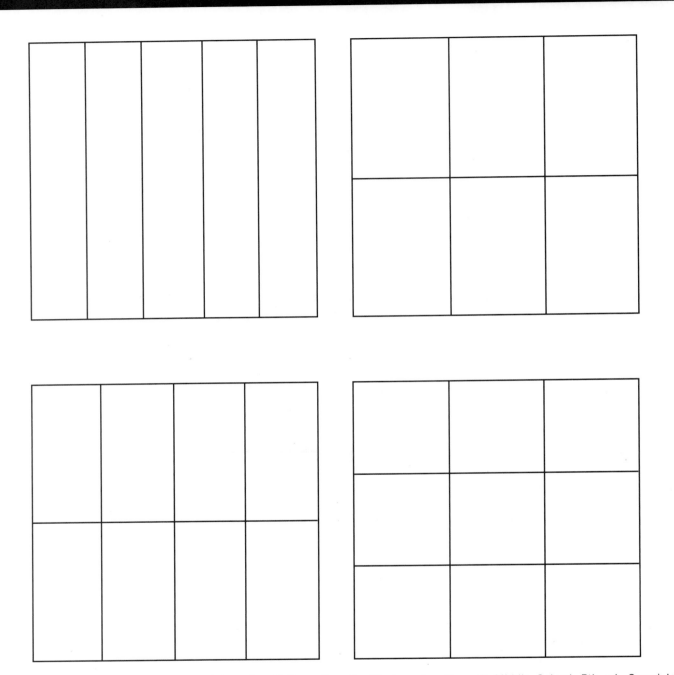

Sheffield and Cruikshank, *Teaching and Learning Mathematics: Pre-Kindergarten Through Middle School,* 5th ed. Copyright © 2005. John Wiley & Sons, Inc.

Rectangular Fraction Patterns

Sheffield and Cruikshank, *Teaching and Learning Mathematics: Pre-Kindergarten Through Middle School*, 5th ed. Copyright © 2005. John Wiley & Sons, Inc.

Rectangular Fraction Patterns

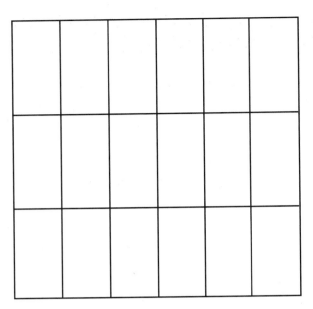

Sheffield and Cruikshank, *Teaching and Learning Mathematics: Pre-Kindergarten Through Middle School,* 5th ed. Copyright © 2005. John Wiley & Sons, Inc.

Fraction Strips

1

$\frac{1}{2}$	$\frac{1}{2}$

$\frac{1}{3}$	$\frac{1}{3}$	$\frac{1}{3}$

$\frac{1}{4}$	$\frac{1}{4}$	$\frac{1}{4}$	$\frac{1}{4}$

$\frac{1}{6}$	$\frac{1}{6}$	$\frac{1}{6}$	$\frac{1}{6}$	$\frac{1}{6}$	$\frac{1}{6}$

$\frac{1}{8}$	$\frac{1}{8}$	$\frac{1}{8}$	$\frac{1}{8}$	$\frac{1}{8}$	$\frac{1}{8}$	$\frac{1}{8}$	$\frac{1}{8}$

$\frac{1}{12}$	$\frac{1}{12}$	$\frac{1}{12}$	$\frac{1}{12}$	$\frac{1}{12}$	$\frac{1}{12}$	$\frac{1}{12}$	$\frac{1}{12}$	$\frac{1}{12}$	$\frac{1}{12}$	$\frac{1}{12}$	$\frac{1}{12}$

$\frac{1}{24}$	$\frac{1}{24}$	$\frac{1}{24}$	$\frac{1}{24}$	$\frac{1}{24}$	$\frac{1}{24}$	$\frac{1}{24}$	$\frac{1}{24}$	$\frac{1}{24}$	$\frac{1}{24}$	$\frac{1}{24}$	$\frac{1}{24}$	$\frac{1}{24}$	$\frac{1}{24}$	$\frac{1}{24}$	$\frac{1}{24}$	$\frac{1}{24}$	$\frac{1}{24}$	$\frac{1}{24}$	$\frac{1}{24}$	$\frac{1}{24}$	$\frac{1}{24}$	$\frac{1}{24}$	$\frac{1}{24}$

Dominoes

Sheffield and Cruikshank, *Teaching and Learning Mathematics: Pre-Kindergarten Through Middle School,* 5th ed. Copyright © 2005. John Wiley & Sons, Inc.

Geoboard Dot Paper

Name:

Rectangular Dot Paper

Isometric Dot Paper

Triangular Dot Paper

Triangular Grid Paper

Sheffield and Cruikshank, *Teaching and Learning Mathematics: Pre-Kindergarten Through Middle School,* 5th ed. Copyright © 2005. John Wiley & Sons, Inc.

Tangram Pattern

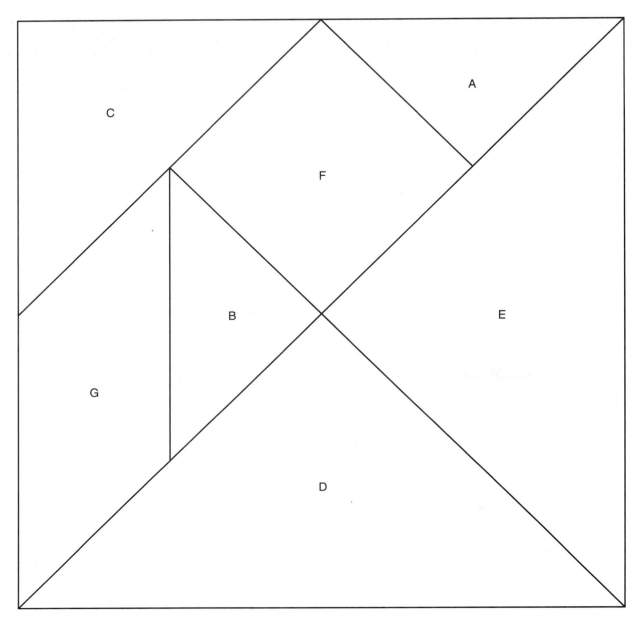

Sheffield and Cruikshank, *Teaching and Learning Mathematics: Pre-Kindergarten Through Middle School*, 5th ed. Copyright © 2005. John Wiley & Sons, Inc.

Regular Polyhedrons

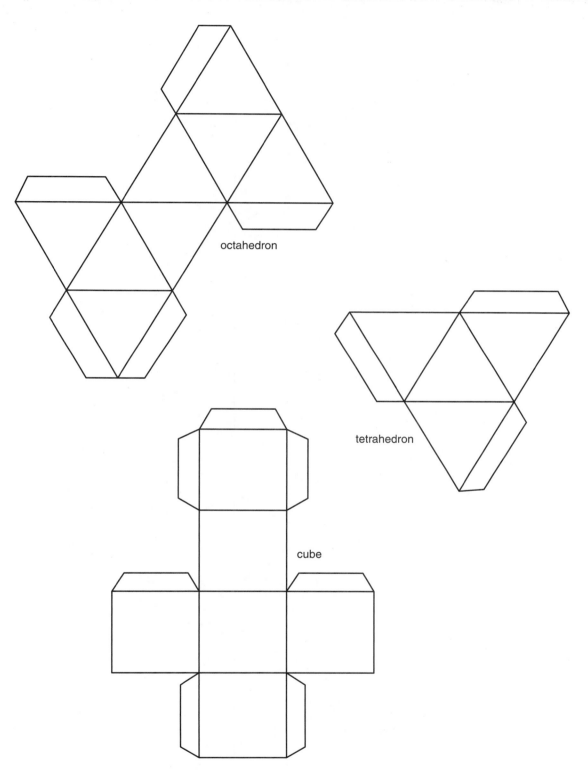

octahedron

tetrahedron

cube

Sheffield and Cruikshank, *Teaching and Learning Mathematics: Pre-Kindergarten Through Middle School,* 5th ed. Copyright © 2005. John Wiley & Sons, Inc.

° Regular Polyhedrons

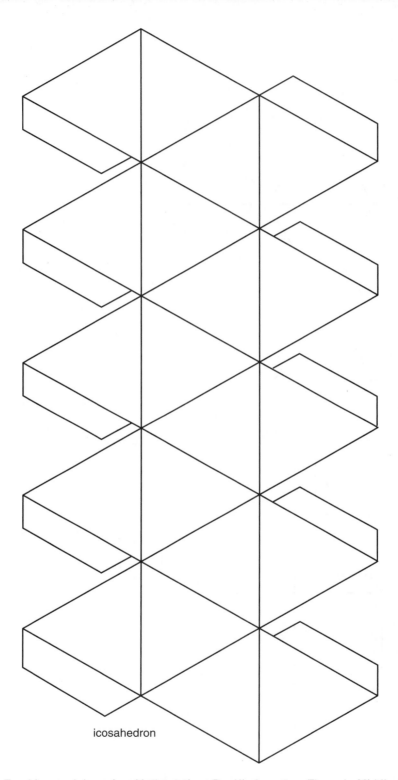

icosahedron

Regular Polyhedrons

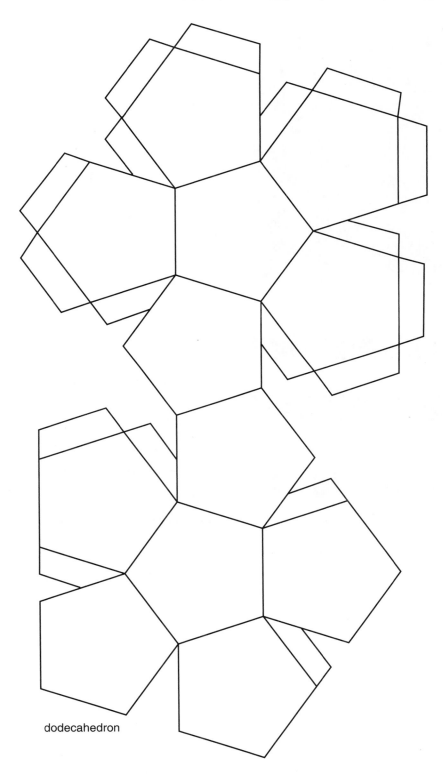

dodecahedron

Sheffield and Cruikshank, *Teaching and Learning Mathematics: Pre-Kindergarten Through Middle School,* 5th ed. Copyright © 2005. John Wiley & Sons, Inc.

Algebra Blocks

Large Coordinate Grid

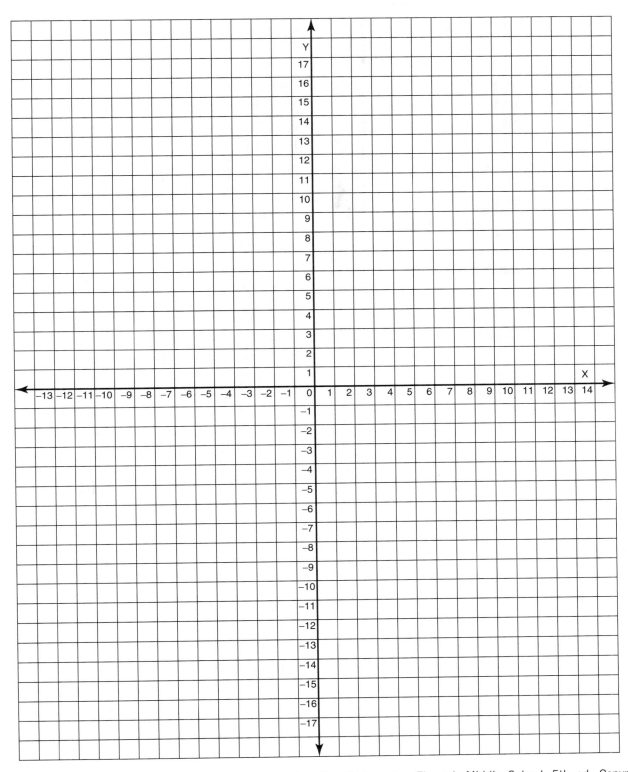

Sheffield and Cruikshank, *Teaching and Learning Mathematics: Pre-Kindergarten Through Middle School*, 5th ed. Copyright © 2005. John Wiley & Sons, Inc.

Small Coordinate Grids

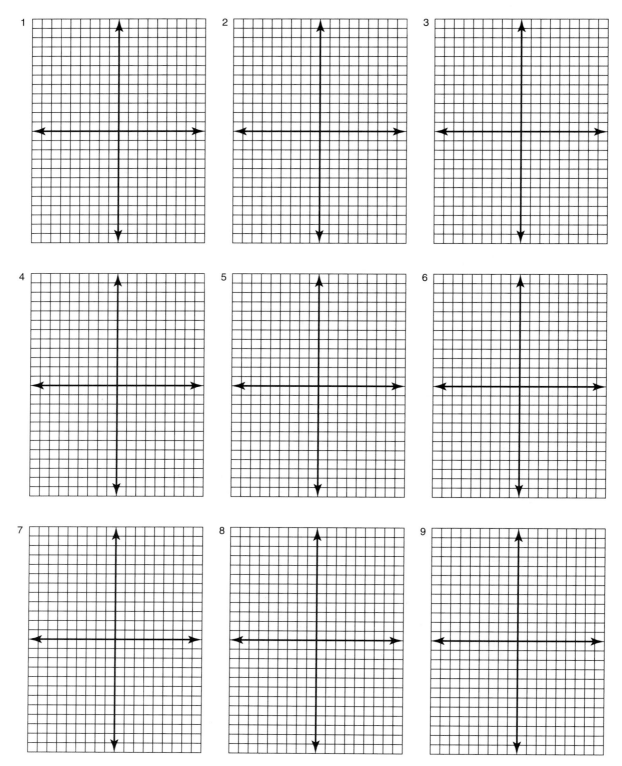

Sheffield and Cruikshank, *Teaching and Learning Mathematics: Pre-Kindergarten Through Middle School,* 5th ed. Copyright © 2005. John Wiley & Sons, Inc.

Lesson Plan Outline

Name _____   Date _____

Grade Level _____   Subject/Topic _____   Time _____

Instructional Objectives: (What are the big ideas in the NCTM Content and Process Standards or your state standards that this lesson addresses?)

Context or Prior Knowledge Needed: (How does this relate to your broad goals for this unit? What prior knowledge do students have and what would they need before this lesson?)

Terms, Symbols, or Vocabulary:

Learning Materials, Physical Models, or Other Aids:

Teaching Strategy
    Relate: (Describe the introductory activity that will engage the students by relating the new knowledge to be learned to previous learning and that will set the stage for the investigation or problem)

    Investigate: (Challenge the students with an investigation or problem that will help them make sense of the mathematical concepts to be learned.)

    Evaluate: (How will you and the students determine if they have mastered your instructional objectives?)

    Communicate: (How will the students communicate their learning with others—journal entries, projects, presentations, etc.?)

    Create: (What new questions might the students create to build on these ideas?)

Reflection and Refinement: (After you have taught the lesson, reflect on what you did well and what you might need to improve. Describe your ideas for improvement.)

INDEX